Financial Services Marketing

T0295805

This fourth edition of *Financial Services Marketing* firmly reinforces the book's role as a leading global educational resource, combining appropriate conceptual principles with practical insights on how financial products and services are marketed in the real world. The authors draw upon their extensive international experience marketing some of the world's best known financial brands including Lloyds TSB and Barclays. Readers will gain a firm understanding of how financial products and services work within the commercial, social, economic, governmental, regulatory and environmental context in which they operate.

This fully updated and revised edition features:

- A brand-new chapter devoted to environmental, social and corporate governance
- Revised coverage of the impact of digital advances in all aspects of business models and marketing practice, including how artificial intelligence (AI) and social marketing are changing financial services and customer experience
- The latest regulatory developments for safeguarding the fair treatment of customers
- New and improved case studies that showcase best practice from around the world
- Upgraded Support Material including new teaching aids and references

Financial Services Marketing is essential reading for advanced undergraduate and postgraduate students studying Marketing for Financial Services, Marketing Strategy and Consumer Ethics in Finance. It is also suitable for executive students studying for professional qualifications and executive MBAs.

Christine Ennew OBE is Emeritus Professor of Marketing at Warwick Business School and was, until recently, Provost at the University of Warwick. She has been actively involved in financial services research for most of her academic career. She has completed a range of funded projects domestically and internationally, most notably in relation to the development of the Trust Index. She has published some 100 articles in refereed journals, presented over 60 refereed conference papers and produced four books.

Nigel Waite cut his marketing teeth in the healthcare and packaged goods markets working with Glaxo Smith Kline and Mars before joining the financial services industry in his early thirties. There he was responsible for marketing a wide range of banking, insurance, investment, savings and loan products for the Lloyds Banking Group and Barclays. The eight years he spent as a board member uniquely qualifies him to appreciate the importance of helicopter vision when it comes to marketing financial products and services. Since the year 2000 he has been an Honorary Professor of Marketing at Nottingham University Business School.

Róisín Waite is Director of Group Digital at Barclays. With almost 20 years working in Financial Services Digital, across insurance, asset management and retail banking, she has extensive experience in both digital marketing strategy and implementation, as well as operational management of banking technology. Róisín was one of the first to graduate from the UK's first MSc in Digital Marketing Communications.

"The definitive resource for Banking and Finance students covering customer decision-making, regulation and marketing of financial services and products."

Dr Sam Beatson, *Module Convenor, Department of Finance,*
Risk and Banking, Nottingham University Business School

Financial Services Marketing

A Guide to Principles and Practice

Fourth Edition

**Christine Ennew, Nigel Waite
and Róisín Waite**

Routledge
Taylor & Francis Group

LONDON AND NEW YORK

Designed cover image: Maxiphoto / Getty Images

Fourth edition published 2025
by Routledge
4 Park Square, Milton Park, Abingdon, Oxon, OX14 4RN

and by Routledge
605 Third Avenue, New York, NY 10158

Routledge is an imprint of the Taylor & Francis Group, an informa business

First edition published by Routledge 2007
Third edition published by Routledge 2017

British Library Cataloguing-in-Publication Data
A catalogue record for this book is available from the British Library

ISBN: 9781032504636 (hbk)
ISBN: 9781032504643 (pbk)
ISBN: 9781003398615 (ebk)

DOI: 10.4324/9781003398615

Typeset in Times New Roman
by Newgen Publishing UK

Access the Support Material: www.routledge.com/9781032504636

For Caryl
For Gerardine, Cara, Marianne, Jonathan and my grandchildren
For Graeme, Imogen and Verity

Contents

List of figures   *xvii*
List of tables   *xxi*
Acknowledgements   *xxii*

Introduction   1

PART I
Context and strategy   7

1 **The role, contribution and context of financial services**   9
   1.1 Introduction 9
   1.2 Economic development 10
   1.3 Government welfare context 11
   1.4 Lifetime income smoothing 14
   1.5 The management of risk 18
   1.6 Poverty and financial exclusion 18
   1.7 Mutual and proprietary supply 21
   1.8 Regulation of financial services 27
      1.8.1 On the role of financial markets 27
      1.8.2 Three major regulatory challenges 27
      1.8.3 UK regulatory architecture, approach and philosophy 28
      1.8.4 Regulatory philosophy 31
      1.8.5 European regulatory reforms 31
      1.8.6 Potential impact of Brexit and future challenges 32
   1.9 Summary and conclusion 34
   Learning outcomes 34
   Review questions 36

2 **The financial services marketplace: structures, products and participants**   37
   2.1 Introduction 37
   2.2 The geography of supply 37

2.3   *Financial advice 40*

2.4   *An outline of product variants 41*

2.5   *Banking and money transmission 42*

2.6   *Lending and credit 47*

2.7   *Saving and investing 49*

    2.7.1 Investing 49

    2.7.2 Saving 53

    2.7.3 Pensions 54

    2.7.4 Savings endowments 55

2.8   *Life insurance products 55*

    2.8.1 Life insurance 56

    2.8.2 Health insurance 57

    2.8.3 Annuities 59

2.9   *General insurance 60*

2.10   *Cryptocurrency 62*

2.11   *Islamic financial services 64*

2.12   *Summary and conclusions 66*

Learning outcomes 67

Review questions 67

3   Marketing financial services: an overview   69

3.1   *Introduction 69*

3.2   *Defining financial services 70*

3.3   *The differences between goods and services 70*

3.4   *The distinctive characteristics of financial service 73*

    3.4.1 Intangibility 74

    3.4.2 Inseparability 77

    3.4.3 Perishability 78

    3.4.4 Heterogeneity 81

    3.4.5 Fiduciary responsibility 83

    3.4.6 Contingent consumption 85

    3.4.7 Duration of consumption 86

3.5   *The marketing challenge 87*

3.6   *Classifying services 87*

3.7   *Summary and conclusion 88*

Learning outcomes 90

Review questions 90

4   Strategic development and marketing planning   93

4.1   *Introduction 93*

4.2   *Strategic marketing 95*

4.3   *Developing a strategic marketing plan 100*

    4.3.1 Company vision and mission 101

4.3.2 *Situation analysis 103*

4.3.3 *Marketing objectives 104*

4.3.4 *Marketing strategy 105*

4.3.5 *Market specific strategy 107*

4.3.6 *Implementation 107*

4.4 *Tools for strategy development 108*

4.4.1 *Growth strategies 108*

4.4.2 *Selecting the product portfolio 111*

4.4.3 *Competitive advantage 116*

4.5 *Summary and conclusion 119*

Learning outcomes 119

Review questions 120

5   Analysing the marketing environment   122

5.1 *Introduction 122*

5.2 *The marketing environment 123*

5.3 *The macro-environment 125*

5.3.1 *The political environment 126*

5.3.2 *The economic environment 129*

5.3.3 *The social environment 132*

5.3.4 *The technological environment 136*

5.4 *The market environment 143*

5.5 *The internal environment 146*

5.5.1 *Resources 146*

5.5.2 *Competences/capabilities 147*

5.5.3 *Auditing the internal environment 148*

5.6 *Evaluating developments in the marketing environment 148*

5.7 *Conclusion 150*

Learning outcomes 152

Review questions 153

6   Understanding the financial services consumer   155

6.1 *Introduction 155*

6.2 *Consumer choice and financial services 156*

6.2.1 *Need recognition 159*

6.2.2 *Information search 162*

6.2.3 *Evaluation of alternatives 163*

6.2.4 *Purchase decision 164*

6.2.5 *Post-purchase behaviour 165*

6.2.6 *Summary 167*

6.3 *Behavioural Economics 167*

6.4 *Marketing responses 168*

6.4.1 *Responding to intangibility 172*

  6.4.2 Responding to inseparability and perishability 175

  6.4.3 Responding to heterogeneity 176

  6.4.4 Responding to fiduciary responsibility 176

  6.4.5 Responding to duration and uncertainty 177

 6.5 Researching financial services customers 178

  6.5.1 The market research process 178

  6.5.2 The purpose of market research 179

  6.5.3 Principal research methods 188

  6.5.4 Ethical issues 192

 6.6 Summary and conclusion 193

 Learning outcomes 194

 Review questions 195

7 Segmentation targeting and positioning   197

 7.1 Introduction 197

 7.2 The benefits of segmentation and targeting 198

 7.3 Successful segmentation 201

 7.4 Approaches to segmenting consumer markets 204

  7.4.1 Customer characteristics: customer-oriented segmentation 204

  7.4.2 Customer needs and behaviours: product-oriented segmentation 208

 7.5 Approaches to segmenting business-to-business markets 210

 7.6 Segmentation in a digital world 212

 7.7 Targeting strategies 215

  7.7.1 Undifferentiated targeting 216

  7.7.2 Differentiated targeting 216

  7.7.3 Focused segmentation 217

  7.7.4 Customised targeting 220

 7.8 Positioning products and organisations 221

  7.8.1 Perceptual mapping 224

 7.9 Repositioning 225

 7.10 Brand Positioning and strategy in practice: perspectives from Interbrand 227

 7.11 Summary and conclusion 229

 Learning outcomes 231

 Review questions 233

8 Internationalisation strategies for financial services   234

 8.1 Introduction 234

 8.2 Internationalisation and the characteristics of financial services 236

 8.3 The drivers of internationalisation 239

  8.3.1 Firm-specific drivers of internationalisation 239

  8.3.2 Macro level drivers of internationalisation 243

8.3.3 The extent of internationalisation in financial services sector 250

8.4 Globalisation strategies 252

8.4.1 International strategies 252

8.4.2 Global strategies 253

8.4.3 Multidomestic strategies 254

8.4.4 Transnational strategies 254

8.5 Strategy selection and implementation 255

8.5.1 Which markets to enter? 255

8.5.2 Method of market entry 256

8.5.3 How to market in international markets 258

8.6 Summary and conclusion 259

Learning outcomes 259

Review questions 260

PART I
Case studies
263

Case study CS1: Microinsurance 265

Case study CS2: China Merchants Bank: *We are here just for you.* 268

Case study CS3: Liiv 273

Case study CS4: Prudential: international marketing strategy 275

PART II
Customer acquisition
279

9 Customer acquisition and the marketing mix 281

9.1 Introduction 281

9.2 The marketing mix 281

9.3 Short-term marketing planning 285

9.4 The role of the financial services marketing mix 287

9.5 The financial services marketing mix: key issues 289

9.5.1 Process 290

9.5.2 Physical evidence 291

9.5.3 People 292

9.6 Customer acquisition and the financial services marketing mix 292

9.7 Digital marketing and customer acquisition 296

9.7.1 Context and convenience 297

9.7.2 Segmentation and targeting 299

9.7.3 Managing the process 300

9.7.4 Migrants, natives and social media 302

9.7.5 Integrating on- and offline 303
9.7.6 Digital organisational structure 304
9.8 Customer acquisition and ethical behaviour 306
9.9 Summary and conclusion 308
Learning outcomes 308
Review questions 310

10 Product and consumer needs   312
10.1 Introduction 312
10.2 The concept of the service product 313
    10.2.1 What customers want 313
    10.2.2 What organisations can provide 316
10.3 Influences on product management 317
10.4 Managing existing product lines 324
    10.4.1 Product attributes 324
    10.4.2 Product modification/product development 327
10.5 New product development 329
    10.5.1 Major innovations 330
    10.5.2 New service lines 335
    10.5.3 The new product development process 336
10.6 Conclusion 338
Learning outcomes 338
Review questions 339

11 Communication and promotion   341
11.1 Introduction 341
11.2 Financial services communications: the essentials 342
11.3 Planning a promotional campaign 348
    11.3.1 Stages in communications planning 351
    11.3.2 Integrated marketing communications 356
11.4 Forms of communication 356
    11.4.1 Advertising 357
    11.4.2 Personal selling 359
    11.4.3 Publicity/public relations 360
    11.4.4 Sales promotion 361
    11.4.5 Direct marketing 362
11.5 The digital effect 363
11.6 Summary and conclusion 370
Learning outcomes 370
Review questions 372

12 Price and cost to the consumer   374
12.1 Introduction 374
12.2 The role and characteristics of price 375

12.3 The challenges of pricing for providers of financial services 376
12.4 Methods used for determining price 380
*   12.4.1 Cost-based pricing 381*
*   12.4.2 Competition-based pricing 383*
*   12.4.3 Marketing-oriented pricing 383*
12.5 Price differentiation and preferred lives 393
12.6 Price determination 395
12.7 Pricing strategy and promotional pricing 397
12.8 Impact of digital marketing on charges and pricing 399
12.9 Summary and conclusion 400
Learning outcomes 401
Review questions 402

13 Customer convenience and distribution   403
13.1 Introduction 403
13.2 Channels of distribution: distinguishing features 404
13.3 Distribution methods and models 406
*   13.3.1 Direct versus indirect distribution 406*
*   13.3.2 Whether products are bought or sold 408*
13.4 Distribution channels 409
13.5 Summary and conclusion 433
Learning outcomes 435
Review questions 436

PART II
Case studies   439

Case study CS5: Aktif Bank – N Kolay Kredi   441
Case study CS6: Customer acquisition at HDFC bank   445
Case study CS7: HUK24: Managing the customer experience for online
**   insurance**   450
Case study CS8: NatWest Accelerator programme   454

PART III
Managing customer relationships and the future of marketing   457

14 Customer relationship management principles and practice   459
14.1 Introduction 459
14.2 Drivers of change 460
14.3 Customer persistency – acquire the right customers 467
14.4 Retaining the right customers 468
14.5 Customer retention strategies 470
14.6 The customer-relationship chain 472

14.7   Lifetime customer value 473

14.8   Digital marketing and its impact on CRM 475

    14.8.1 Context 475

    14.8.2 Customer data management and analytics 478

    14.8.3 Integrating on- and offline for effective CRM 480

    14.8.4 Personalisation 480

    14.8.5 Social CRM 481

    14.8.6 Digital tools – CRM systems 484

    14.8.7 Data privacy and cookies 485

14.9   Relationship marketing in specific contexts 487

    14.9.1 Relationship marketing and the role of intermediaries 487

    14.9.2 Relationship marketing: some international perspectives 488

14.10 Summary and conclusions 490

Learning outcomes 491

Review questions 492

15   Service delivery and service quality   494

15.1   Introduction 494

15.2   The service profit chain 495

15.3   Defining service quality 498

15.4   Models of service quality 498

    15.4.1 The Nordic perspective on service quality 500

    15.4.2 The North American perspective on service quality 501

    15.4.3 Integrating the Nordic and the North American
        perspectives 507

15.5   The gap model of service quality 509

15.6   The outcomes of service quality 512

15.7   Service failure and recovery 515

15.8   Summary and conclusion 519

Learning outcomes 519

Review questions 521

16   Satisfaction, value, trust and fairness in customer relationships   523

16.1   Introduction 523

16.2   Consumer evaluations: value and satisfaction 524

    16.2.1 Customer value 524

    16.2.2 Customer satisfaction 526

16.3   Managing customer expectations 527

16.4   The measurement of satisfaction 530

    16.4.1 Customer satisfaction 530

    16.4.2 Employee satisfaction 533

16.5   Trust 535

    16.5.1 The meaning of trust 536

    16.5.2 Measuring trust: the Trust Index 537

16.5.3 Trustworthiness 539

16.5.4 How trust is won, retained and lost 541

16.5.5 Trust in a digital world 543

16.6 Treating customers fairly 546

16.7 Summary and conclusion 554

Learning outcomes 554

Review questions 556

17 Corporate social responsibility (CSR) and environmental, social and governance (ESG)   558

17.1 Introduction 558

17.2 The origins of CSR 558

17.3 The evolution of CSR 559

17.4 Towards a sustainable future 563

17.5 The evolution of sustainability: navigating ESG in contemporary marketing practices 566

17.6 The relationship between CSR and ESG and key drivers for ESG adoption 568

    17.6.1 Influential organisations in promoting ESG 570

17.7 Global reach of ESG 571

17.8 Practical implications for companies 575

17.9 ESG in practice: examples from financial services and consumer goods 576

    17.9.1 The benefits of embracing ESG 577

17.10 The pursuit of barrier-free brand experience 578

17.11 ESG and inclusive growth 581

17.12 Summary and conclusion 583

Learning outcomes 584

Review questions 585

18 Marketing culture, challenges and evaluation   587

18.1 Introduction 587

18.2 Some observations on culture 589

18.3 People and culture 590

18.4 Product considerations 592

18.5 Pricing, value and a single-customer view 593

18.6 Advertising and promotion 594

18.7 Distribution and access 595

18.8 Processes 599

18.9 Evaluating marketing performance 600

18.10 Summary and conclusions 607

Learning outcomes 608

Review questions 609

PART III
Case studies   611

Case study CS9: The American Express international loyalty programme   613
Case study CS10: Five Talents UK – savings-led microfinance   617
Case study CS11: Safeguarding the financial fortress: cyber detection and
     prevention in financial services marketing – One Brightly Cyber   621
Case study CS12: Starling Bank, UK changing – banking for good,
     and the planet   624

     Index   *628*

Figures

0.1   Marketing as a facilitator of balance   5
1.1   Trend in reduction in global poverty 1981–2017   11
1.2   The growth in the number of older people still in work   15
1.3   French protestors against the increase in the minimum qualifying
      pension age to 64   16
1.4   Age dependency ratio (% of working age population)   17
1.5   Lifetime financial assets profile   17
1.6   The largest European insurance markets in terms of mutual/cooperative
      market share in 2020   22
1.7   Awareness of mutuals by age   23
1.8   Staff views on traits by company type   24
2.1   The geography of supply (general activity and specific forms)   38
2.2   Adults with a bank account globally   43
2.3   Trends in usage of cheques in UK (millions)   44
2.4   Trends in payments methods   44
2.5   Percentage of registered mobile payment users in each age bracket   45
2.6   Santander and the Edge account   47
2.7   Total UK retail funds under management 2006–2021   51
2.8   Types of protection product   56
2.9   Diagrammatic representation of the 3As   58
2.10 The inclusion radar for Turkey's Life and Health Market   59
2.11 Bitcoin – probably the best know cryptocurrency   63
3.1   Deutsche Bank uses archive photographs to emphasise its longevity
      and solidity.   76
3.2   Respondents using mobile banking (%)   78
3.3   Service heterogeneity   81
3.4   The services marketing triangle   87
3.5   Categorising services   89
4.1   How strategic marketing enhances organisational performance   96
4.2   Components of customer value   98
4.3   An illustrative marketing plan   101
4.4   The essential components of marketing strategy   106
4.5   Ansoff's product market matrix   108
4.6   Monzo's digital-only bank has experienced significant market growth   109
4.7   Illustrative BCG matrix   112
4.8   Offensive and defensive strategies   113

4.9	The product life cycle	114
5.1	The marketing environment	124
5.2	Analysing the macro-environment	126
5.3	Household savings rates	131
5.4	First National Bank in South Africa provides ATM facilities at the summit of Table Mountain in Cape Town	137
5.5	An M-Pesa Kiosk in Nairobi	139
5.6	Porter's Five force analysis	143
5.7	Examples of tangible resources	146
5.8	Examples of intangible resources	147
5.9	SWOT Analysis, as prepared by Aseguradora Tajy Propiedad Cooperativa S.A. in relation to the market for insurance in Paraguay	151
6.1	Roles associated with a purchase decision	157
6.2	Stages in consumer decision-making	158
6.3	Examples of customer needs and examples of products that can satisfy those needs	159
6.4	Challenges for consumers when undertaking information search for financial services	162
6.5	Number of customers changing bank current accounts in the UK	166
6.6	Using different types of evidence in marketing	172
6.7	Dealing with complexity and lack of interest	173
6.8	Aviva helps to solve insurance puzzles	174
6.9	Nationwide's Service Quality information	175
6.10	The market research process	179
6.11	Market research functions	180
6.12	Stages in the communications effectiveness research process	183
6.13	Key brand metrics	185
6.14	Opinium's approach to communication evaluation	186
6.15	The benefits of using online communities for market research	190
7.1	Distribution of UK Households by basic Mosaic Group	206
7.2	Life stage: product-need schematic	208
7.3	Characteristics of Nomads, Hunters, and Quality Seekers	214
7.4	Perceptual map for investment fund management companies	225
7.5	Repositioning strategies	226
7.6	Top Ten global brands by value 2022	227
7.7	Interbrand model of brand trajectory	229
8.1	HSBC advertising at Charles De Gaulle Airport in France	235
8.2	Budapest – a new location for Blackrock	247
8.3	Different forms of Internationalisation	253
8.4	Options for market entry	256
CS1.1	Microinsurance covered lives	267
CS2.1	Number of banking institutions in China	269
CS2.2	Numbers of mobile banking app users (millions)	271
CS3.1	Liiv brand appearance.	273
9.1	Translating the 4Ps into the 4Cs	282
9.2	ChatGPT revolutionising AI	284
9.3	Annual marketing plan	286
9.4	Customer needs and the marketing mix	287

9.5	Brank branches give tangibility to an intangible product	290
9.6	PayPal digital payment platform	301
10.1	Customer needs and associated products	314
10.2	The different layers of a product.	317
10.3	Sample product range at KB Kookmin Bank, South Korea.	318
10.4	Vitality insurance app with health focused giveaways	327
10.5	Evaluating blockchain's benefits	331
10.6	The new product development process	336
11.1	Nationwide Building Society's commitment to its branch network	343
11.2	The purposes of marketing communications	349
11.3	Comparethemarket.com	350
11.4	Planning a promotional campaign	351
11.5	Approaches to assessing the effectiveness of promotional campaigns	356
11.6	Maybank's use of colour in advertising	357
12.1	The demand curve	380
12.2	Marketing-oriented pricing	384
12.3	Consumer-reported premium increases, graphed against propensity to switch	390
12.4	Price determination process	395
13.1	The advantages and disadvantages of branch-based distribution	411
13.2	The advantages and disadvantages of internet-based distribution	416
13.3	The advantages and disadvantages of robo-advice	420
13.4	The advantages and disadvantages of NFSRs	422
13.5	The advantages and disadvantages of QFSOs	423
13.6	The prospecting funnel	424
13.7	Passive model of bancassurance	428
13.8	The advantages and disadvantages of bancassurance	429
13.9	The advantages and disadvantages of telephone-based distribution channels	430
13.10	The advantages and disadvantages of direct mail-based distribution	432
13.11	Multi-channel approach for banks	433
13.12	Multi-channel approach for life insurance	434
CS5.1	Aktif Bank Logo	442
CS6.1	HDFC's strategic approach to marketing	447
CS6.2	HDFC's Branches remain important	448
CS7.1	HUK24	451
CS8.1	NatWest	455
14.1	GDP Growth 1990–2024	461
14.2	Per Capita Growth in GDP 1990–2024	461
14.3	Social media engagement ring"social media engagement ring" by pro1pr licensed under CC BY 2.0	464
14.4	The customer-relationship chain	472
14.5	The variables affecting lifetime customer value	474
14.6	Traditional banks face legacy challenges	477
14.7	Top level structure of the customer database	479
14.8	Neobank brands	485
15.1	The service profit chain	495
15.2	Perspectives on quality	499
15.3	The Nordic perspective on service quality	500

15.4	The dimensions of service quality	501
15.5	Service quality perceptions and expectations	502
15.6	Zones of tolerance	503
15.7	Integrating perspectives on service quality	508
15.8	The Gap Model of service delivery	510
15.9	Attitudinal and behavioural loyalty	514
15.10	Dimensions of perceived justice	518
16.1	What does value mean?	525
16.2	Nationwide Building Society branch	533
16.3	Trust in all financial services institutions 2009–2015	538
16.4	Trust and institution type over time	539
16.5	Drivers of trust	540
16.6	Drivers of trustworthiness	540
16.7	Visa – a highly trusted brand	542
16.8	FSA (now FCA) principles regarding fair treatment of customers	547
16.9	Fairness Index for all financial services institutions	550
16.10	Trust in the UK regulatory system	550
17.1	A contingent framework for integrating CSR	561
17.2	Key dimensions of ESG	568
17.3	The reporting landscape	572
17.4	The drivers of financial exclusion	582
18.1	What do you like least?	602
18.2	What advice would consumers give	603
18.3	The components of the Conduct Risk Gap	606
CS9.1	American Express moves into travel services	613
CS10.1	Trust Group meeting in Burundi	618
CS10.2	The impact of Five Talents	618
CS11.1	The Importance of Cyber detection and prevention	622
CS11.2	Market statistics	623
CS12.1	Startling Bank – changing banking for good	625

Tables

2.1	Customer needs and product solutions	42
2.2	UK Personal Debt as at January 2023 adapted from The Money Charity	48
2.3	Types of loan	50
2.4	Global Retail Development Index top ten	50
2.5	Investment vehicles and asset classes	51
2.6	Top 10 Life Insurance Markets 2021	56
2.7	Indicative annual income for life from £100,000	60
3.1	First Reliance Bank's service guarantee	76
4.1	Examples of marketing objectives	105
5.1	Selected birth rates for 2006 and 2011 (births/1000 people)	133
6.1	Insights from behavioural economics/finance	169
6.2	Quantitative analysis techniques	192
7.1	Family Median Net Worth in USA 2020	208
7.2	Basic Targeting strategies	216
7.3	Financial Services Brands in Global Top 100	228
8.1	Insurance penetration in selected OECD and non-OECD markets in 2016–22	242
11.1	Marcoms responses to the characteristic of financial services	345
11.2	Digital communications tools	366
12.1	Hallmark's LTA price positioning in preferred sectors of business	385
12.2	Everyman Insurance's LTA price positioning in preferred sectors	386
12.3	New product-pricing strategies	398
13.1	Examples of typical NFSRs	421
17.1	Integrating CSR, ESG and sustainability	568
18.1	Care about quality of service	601
18.2	Confidence that CEOs and directors intend to put customer interests first	601
18.3	Confidence that CEOs and directors intend to treat customers fairly	602

Acknowledgements

We'd like to express our thanks and appreciation to the many people from around the world who have made this fourth edition possible through the provision of editorial material, case studies, examples of marketing in practice, data and illustrations and encouragement. We include in this list those who contributed to the fourth edition and whose contributions are appearing in full or in modified form in this fourth edition.

Mike Ashurst	International Cooperative and Mutual Insurers Federation
Jake Attfield	Fair4All Finance
Helen Ayres	The Investment Association
Carlos Benitez	Tajy, Paraguay
Alex Bennett	Nationwide Building Society
Sabrina Bianchi	BPER, Italy
Alex Brammer	Nationwide Building Society
Sarah Buckley	EMC Insurance Companies, USA
Liliana Cano	Tajy, Paraguay
Liam Carter	ICMIF
Swee Hoon Chuah	University of Tasmania
Jim Devlin	Nottingham Trent University
Steve Diacon	Nottingham University Business School
James Endersby	Opinium
Mark Evans	Direct Line
Tom Ewart	The Co-operators, Canada
Detlef Frank	HUK 24, Germany
Alex Frean	Starling Bank
Nicole Frost	World Bank, USA
Denis Garand	Independent, Canada
Tom Gitogo	CIC, Kenya
Geoff Henderson	Unimutual, Australia
Sophie Hemne De Robien	Folksam, Sweden
Ian Hughes	Consumer Intelligence
Uzin Hwang	Interbrand, South Korea
Tugce Iskenderoglu	Aktif Bank, Turkey
Scott Jean	EMC Insurance Companies, USA
Mike Johnston	NatWest Group
James Jones	Experian

Susan Kalamchi	The And Partnership
Lucy Kitcher	NatWest
Emily Knight	Consumer Intelligence
Paul Knox-Johnston	Haven Knox Johnston
Stephen Mann	Police Mutual
Mick McAteer	3R Insights
Eunice Min	Interbrand
Owain Mulligan	Bain and Co
Alexia Nightingale	Opinium
Janice Nyokaby	CIC, Kenya
Nigel Oxer	Aviva
Robert Paterson	One Brightly Cyber
The People Experience Team	Nationwide Building Society
Ian Peters	Institute of Business Ethics
Sallie Pilot	Independent
Chris Pond	Financial Inclusion Commission
Natalie Ribeiro	UK Finance
Manfredi Ricca	Interbrand
Sarah Robertson	Experian
Andy Rowlands	Accenture
Canan Sayin	Aktif Bank, Turkey
Martin Shaw	Association of Financial Mutuals
Uwe Stuhldreier	HUK24, Germany
Donna Swiderck	Independent, Canada
Eme Udoma-Herman	American Express, USA
Justin Urquhart Stewart	7IM
Karel Van Hulle	KU Leuven and Goethe University, Germany
Marianne Waite	Interbrand
Emilie Westholm	Folksam, Sweden
Hannah Wichmann	5 Talents
Grace Wilson	Starling Bank
John Wipf	Independent, Canada

Introduction

We are delighted to introduce you to the fourth edition of *Financial Services Marketing*. We hope it will inform and inspire students, practitioners, policymakers, and others who care about the future of the financial services industry and its impact on consumer financial well-being. The first edition was published in 2007 and it is extraordinary to consider the nature and magnitude of changes that have occurred since that time. The world had yet to experience the credit crunch and subsequent financial and economic crisis; digital marketing was in its infancy and now we can hardly imagine a world without its game-changing impact on business models. Editions two and three enabled us to take account of those and, indeed, other drivers of change in the market and consumer behaviour. Since the third edition was published in 2017, the UK has left the European Union (EU), the world has experienced the coronavirus pandemic, Europe is experiencing a full-scale war within its borders, environmental, social and governance considerations (ESG) have become a core part of business activities, and artificial intelligence (AI) is becoming ubiquitous. The fourth edition will enable us to reflect these and other developments to ensure that its worldwide audience can benefit from the most up-to-date body of knowledge.

One thing that hasn't changed since the first edition was published in 2007 is our working definition of marketing; quite simply, we remain firmly of the view that marketing remains all about getting and keeping customers. If we consider some great companies and brands that are widely respected and admired (Unilever, Mars, Virgin, and Apple for example) they all have one thing in common – everything they do revolves around the customer. It is the ways in which they get and keep customers which mark them out. Great and enduring brands and businesses get customers through providing products and services that deliver genuine customer utility and value, and they keep their customers by showing they care, by being professional and competent, and by maintaining their commitment to delivering value-for-money products and services over time. In short, they are trusted. By this we mean they can be relied upon to consistently perform as expected and to operate in ways that show they have a genuine care and concern for their customers. Great companies prosper and earn profits as an outcome of delivering good customer outcomes: profit is a natural consequence of delivering customer value, backed-up by rigorous professional business practices and processes. Great companies understand that the high levels of consumer trust they enjoy are an outcome of their trustworthiness.

From the outset, we want to make clear that an efficient financial services industry is an essential prerequisite for a fully functioning economy and for economic growth. However, and as pointed out previously, the events associated with the various financial crises of this first part of the twenty-first century have placed in stark relief how dysfunctional the

DOI: 10.4324/9781003398615-1

sector can be when it fails to operate properly. In the authors' view, the pre-requisites for a successful financial services sector comprise:

- putting the consumer interest at the centre of all business strategies;
- provision of products that deliver good customer outcomes at a fair price;
- service that suits the lifestyles and preferences of customers;
- sensitivity to customers in vulnerable circumstances;
- alignment of stakeholder interests;
- wise and effective regulation;
- good knowledge of how financial services products are designed and operate;
- an appreciation of the links and inter-dependencies between the various domains that comprise the financial services sector as a whole;
- corporate cultures that facilitate the above;
- having a thirst for innovation that improves the customer experience.

This book has been conceived and written with the express intention of addressing these requirements. We endeavour to bring together the best of the conceptual principles underpinning marketing with the very best of practice from the real world of financial services. For this reason, we continue to make extensive use of case studies and examples from the practitioner community, and we are extremely grateful to them all.

We are also grateful to our publishers, Taylor and Francis, for allowing us to expand this fourth edition to enable us to give greater prominence to issues concerning digital aspects of marketing and the increasing adoption of technology by consumers. This is a trend that has gathered pace because of Covid-19 and we have been able to identify ways in which this has impacted on the customer journey. For this reason, we are delighted to have retained the involvement of Róisín Waite in the author team. Róisín is Director of Digital Communication for Barclays internationally and was a member of the first cohort of students to be awarded an MSc in Digital Marketing in 2011. Thus, she contributes first class academic and practical experience throughout the text to ensure its relevance to those studying for academic and professional qualifications. This has enabled us to expand our coverage of developments in fields such as disruptive technology, fintech and cryptocurrencies to mention but three examples.

Another aspect of commercial life that has gained greater prominence in recent years concerns the interaction of business with the interests of the wider stakeholder community. Of note in this regard is the way in which business in general, and financial services in particular, is responding to the challenges posed by ESG. Indeed, such has the interest in this subject that we have devoted an entire chapter to it. We have been fortunate in securing contributions from leading international authorities on ESG including Sophie Hemne de Robien from Sweden, international ESG guru Sallie Pilot, Liam Carter who is sustainability lead for the International Cooperative and Mutual Insurance Federation, Marianne Waite Director of inclusive design at Interbrand, and Chris Pond, Chair of the Financial Inclusion Commission. See what they have to say in Chapter 17.

Also new in this edition are additional study aids to enable students to keep track of their progress as each chapter unfolds using progress check boxes which summarise key learning points. Another useful aid for instructors and students alike is the inclusion of stop and think boxes. These are aimed at stimulating reflection on what has been learned by the students and include questions that instructors can use during lectures or for discussion during seminars and small groups. A further innovation is the clustering of case studies at the end of each of the three parts of which the book is comprised. These lend themselves to reflection on how the themes presented in each part are made tangible by way of real-world examples. Useful study questions are given for each case that can be used as the basis for coursework assignments, exam questions or group discussion.

A formal approach to the marketing of financial services is a relatively recent phenomenon, even within the developed nations of the world. The marketing of packaged goods, such as confectionary, food, soft drinks and toiletries has been subject to an enormous investment in classical marketing skills and capabilities since the early part of the twentieth century. A continuity of investment in marketing has enabled names such as Coca Cola, Wrigleys, Gillette, Campbells, and Cadbury to become, and remain, leading brands in their respective sectors from the nineteen-twenties and on into the twenty-first century. Competitive pressures have played a major role in sharpening the marketing appetites of the packaged goods sector. Additionally, the relative simplicity of the products and the transparency associated with them have served as catalysts for the development of a "marketing edge". Cost proximity and the need for economies of scale have added further impetus to the development of the marketing skills in this product area.

The financial services sector, on the other hand, has not been subject to the same market pressures to survive and prosper. Until comparatively recently, the financial services industry in a wide range of developed countries has operated within a comparatively benign market environment. In contrast to the packaged good arena, rivalry amongst financial services providers has tended to be more collegiate than competitive. Diversity of supply and relatively low individual company market shares have been a particular feature of many sectors of financial services. However, technological innovation has resulted in widespread disruption of old business models and cost pressures have become acute in many aspects of financial services. You only have to look at the continuing decline of the branch banking model to appreciate the impact of cost pressures on traditional business models. Somewhat analogous is the way in which the rising costs of compliance with regulations regarding the selling practices associated with life insurance and investments have virtually eradicated the direct sales business model in countries such as the United Kingdom (UK). This and other exciting developments will be addressed in Chapter 13.

Financial services products, in general, are far more complex than their packaged goods counterparts. It is fair to say that in retail markets, consumers often have low levels of interest, knowledge and self-confidence when it comes to comparing the range of products on offer. The issues associated with product transparency serve to further weaken consumer power, resulting in a less vigorous form of competition. The drive to improve standards of retail consumer financial literacy in a range of countries since the start of the century has had only limited impact. The interacting challenges presented by complexity in product design and taxation, poor levels of consumer numeracy, and the rules regarding how a country's benefit system works act to limit the ability of consumers to make good quality financial decisions. And, all of this is reinforced by widespread lack of interest in financial services and low levels of consumer engagement. Many retail consumers may have the ability to understand financial services but often lack the motivation to do so.

Two further factors to note that have had an impact on the marketing of financial services are the influence of government, and consumers' attitudes towards financial products.

In many respects, governments have played a crucial role in the development of new products and the associated promotion of those products. This is in marked contrast to the packaged goods industry. The introduction of products such as personal pensions and tax-advantaged savings schemes have presented the industry with major new business opportunities. It is salutary to note how, in the case of personal pensions in the UK, this government-initiated product resulted in wholesale abuse and long-term damage to the reputation of the industry. Arguably, this arose because the industry was far too sales-oriented and insufficiently customer-oriented. It certainly highlights the marketing shortcomings of the sector. Similarly, the government-induced withdrawal of products and the lessening in tax favourability have acted as highly potent sales promotions.

Turning to consumer attitudes, it is in the nature of financial services products that consumers do not gain overt enjoyment from their consumption. On the contrary, a great many financial services products involve the reduction in current consumption pleasure because money is diverted from such consumption as a contingency for some future event. The absence of consumption-associated pleasure, and general level of consumer disinterest have, therefore, served to reduce the importance of marketing within the financial services industry.

All too often one senses that, at least for some financial services organisations, marketing is a term that applies to a department that produces promotional material. As will be seen in Chapter 3, marketing is a broad cultural and philosophical approach to overall organisational behaviour and not some narrow field of functional competence. This book sets out to present financial services marketing as an overarching set of processes that aims to achieve a balance between the key components of the wider environment. As an author team we believe strongly in the importance of students being able to see the big picture. This book has been expressly designed with that in mind. We want students to not only have a solid grasp of the gamut of disciplines that comprise the domain of marketing, but also to appreciate the wider commercial, social, environmental and governmental contexts within which financial services marketing operates. As can be seen in Figure 0.1 it is a matter of balance:

Thus, this book comprises three core parts.

Part I is devoted to strategy and planning. Here we examine the complex inter-relationships that exist between the financial services industry, the State, and the citizen. A theme that runs through this text is the proposition that all three parties should be mutually advantaged through their interactions. Across the globe we see evidence of financial services industries that appear to be engaged in a perpetual struggle for the trust of consumers and the confidence of government and regulators. The authors argue in favour of a marketing approach that is consumer-centric and founded upon the core values of: customer utility, value-for-money, integrity, trust, security and transparency. In our view, the adoption of such values is axiomatic of good marketing practice and is therefore, a prerequisite for the development of a successful financial services industry. In Part I we also address regulation and how new approaches can be expected to impact upon the policies and practices of product providers.

Part I also describes the participants that comprise the financial services marketplace. This gives the context necessary for a full understanding of how the marketplace operates in serving the needs of customers. An aspect of financial services that is often neglected concerns the role played by mutual and co-operative companies. In many parts of the world such companies are playing an important role in addressing the need for financial inclusion. Therefore, we have included many examples of "marketing in practice" that reflect good practice amongst such providers on a global basis. Also included are details of the product ranges that comprise the financial services domain and the different organisational types that comprise the industry. This part of the book also addresses the strategic aspects of marketing and includes, of course, a discussion of consumers who are central to the marketing process.

Figure 0.1 Marketing as a facilitator of balance

Brand strategy has become an even more important aspect of financial services marketing as drivers of change such as the Covid-19 pandemic and digital innovation alter business models and the ways in which customers interact with product providers and brands. And so, we have been fortunate to involve the world leading branding agency, Interbrand, in our coverage of brand strategy. Interbrand is part of the global media giant Omnicom, and this has enabled us to benefit from its experience of branding across cultures and jurisdictions. We are grateful to Manfredi Ricci, Global Chief Strategy Officer at Interbrand for his contribution to the book.

Part II focuses upon the principles and practices that are associated with becoming a customer of a financial services provider. In this new edition we seek to reinforce the 2P2C marketing model that was introduced to readers in the previous edition. This is functionally equivalent to the traditional marketing mix, but we believe that this presentation may be better suited to the contemporary world of financial services than the traditional 4P or 7P models. Emphasis is placed on the idea of managing these marketing tools to deliver a clear strategic position that will drive the process of customer acquisition. Textbooks tend to focus upon the domestic consumer, to the detriment of organisational customers. It is fair to say that business-to-business, or organisational customers, account for the order of forty to fifty per cent of the profits of major clearing banks. Therefore, it is only right that due regard be given to this aspect of customer acquisition. An important addition to Part II is a major augmentation in the attention devoted to state-of-the-art thinking and practice regarding the impact of digital and AI on marketing practice. This is particularly important given the inexorable trend towards remote distribution of products.

Part III is dedicated to the principles and practices that concern the development of customer relationships over time. This is of particular importance in the context of financial services. A focus on short-term organisational gain, to the long-term detriment of the consumer, has been far too prevalent in the industry in the past. Insufficient attention has been given to how to manage existing customer relationships in favour of new customer acquisition, and this book hopes to help redress the balance. In addition, we address the growing importance attached to Environmental, Social, and Governance considerations (ESG) and their role in marketing and business strategy.

The interdependence between the financial services sector and public wellbeing is a theme that emerges throughout the book. It also means that many aspects of marketing practice – and many marketing challenges – are determined by the national context. While the principles of marketing can be expected to have universal relevance, many examples of marketing practice will be nationally specific – especially when they are impacted by Government policy and/or regulation. While it is perhaps inevitable that we will draw heavily on the experience of the UK, given its role as a global leader in financial services, in this edition we have taken account of feedback from our loyal base of advocates by increasing our inclusion of examples from a wider range of countries around the world to make the concepts and principles more concrete.

In conclusion, this is a book that will help students, practitioners, policymakers, and others to develop a firm grounding in the fundamentals of: financial services strategy, customer acquisition and customer development. It draws upon relevant conceptual and theoretical models supported by appropriate practical applications. We have designed the scope and content of this book to help its users to adopt a more complete and rounded approach to marketing and to develop their capacity to see the big picture. We believe this book is unique in this regard and hope it will make a material contribution to improving standards of marketing practice in the financial services industry across the globe and, thereby, advance the cause of consumer financial well-being and economic development.

Finally, we would like to express our thanks to the many academic and other institutional users of previous editions of this textbook. We are grateful for your endorsement of our work and for the feedback you have given us, and which we have endeavoured to respond to in this fourth edition.

Best wishes
Christine Ennew
Nigel Waite
Róisín Waite
January 2024

Part I
Context and strategy

1 The role, contribution and context of financial services

Learning objectives

At the end of this chapter, you should be able to:

1. Understand the economic and social significance of the financial services sector,
2. Recognise the diverse ways in which financial services can impact on key aspects of everyday life,
3. Appreciate the risks to the economy of failures in the regulation of financial services,
4. Appreciate the need to market financial products and services in accordance with the spirit as well as the letter of regulation,
5. Have an appreciation of the ways in which regulation is responding to the various financial challenges that have occurred since 2007.

1.1 Introduction

Product and market context exert a significant influence on the nature and practice of marketing. Marketing activities that are effective for fast moving consumer goods may be wholly inappropriate when marketing, say, aircraft engines. What works in Canada may be inappropriate in China. Accordingly, an understanding of context is essential to understand the practice of marketing. Nowhere is this more evident than in the financial services sector where social, political, economic and institutional factors create a complex context in which financial services organisations (FSOs) and their customers interact. In recent years a development that has had profound implications for the marketing of financial services, and the environment in which they operate, is that of the digital revolution. The nature and impact of these various drivers of change vary from country to country and so it is vital that marketing practitioners have a sound appreciation of how they interact to create the marketing environment in their specific territory. All too often, discussions of marketing practice fail to recognise the importance of explaining and understanding these contextual influences. The purpose of this current chapter is to provide an overview of the context in which financial services are marketed and to explain the economic significance of the sector.

The following sections outline aspects of social and economic activity where the financial services sector has a key role to play and where its activities have significant implications for economic and social well-being. We begin with a discussion of the contribution the sector makes to economic development in general. Subsequent sections go on to explore the role of the financial

DOI: 10.4324/9781003398615-3

services sector in welfare provision, income smoothing and the management of risk. Section 1.6 explores the significance of financial exclusion and its potential impact on the welfare of the poorer groups in society. Section 1.7 reviews key distinctive features of the financial services industry (FSI) – namely the co-existence of mutual and joint stock companies. Section 1.8 addresses the regulation of financial services and given the international scope of this text, there is discussion of how regulation has been unfolding in jurisdictions across the world.

Arguably, the United Kingdom (UK) and European Union (EU) have been in the vanguard of regulatory developments and due weight will be devoted accordingly. There has been a well-established trend regarding the convergence of a range of regulatory developments across jurisdictions as many of the underlying principles and challenges are relevant to countries throughout the world. For example, the six principles that underpin the UK's regulatory theme of Treating Customers Fairly have been adopted in various countries, indeed, they were adopted in their entirety by the Financial Services Board of South Africa.

1.2 Economic development

Economic and political theorists and practitioners sometimes have widely differing views on the nature and value of economic development. These differences have, if anything, become even more apparent in recent years as concerns about the environmental impact of commercial activities have assumed ever greater importance. However, there is a widely accepted view that controlled, managed economic development is, overall, a desirable means of furthering the well-being of humankind. Moreover, economic development that combines the positive aspects of the market economy (particularly innovation and resource efficiency) with the collectivist instincts and community focus of State legislatures is, arguably, most likely to serve the common good. Despite the prolonged economic difficulties experienced globally since 2008, this combination continues to be the dominant framework for managing economic and social well-being. Nevertheless, there does seem to be growing concern regarding some of the unintended consequences of the phenomenon known as globalisation. Whilst this has been hugely beneficial in alleviating poverty in many developing nations, it has, in part, come at the cost of lost jobs and chronic economic stagnation in communities in developed nations. Moreover, the international tensions that have increased as a consequence of Russia's invasion of Ukraine in February 2022 and conflict in the Middle East in 2023 have caused countries to reconsider the security risks associated with offshoring crucial aspects of manufacturing to countries with potentially hostile intentions.

Nevertheless, economic development is being pursued by governments throughout the world. Access to investment capital facilitates economic development, and a vibrant banking sector has a pivotal role to play in this regard. The liberalisation of financial services in the former communist countries of Eastern Europe has enabled inward investment to occur that has helped most of them to be successful in joining the EU. Similarly, many of the rapidly developing economies of Asia are focusing attention on liberalisation of their financial sectors as an aid to economic growth and development. This is particularly evident in China where, according to The World Bank, some 800 million fewer people were living in extreme poverty in 2022 than 40 years previously. According to Manuela Ferro of the World Bank:[1]

China's poverty reduction story is a story of persistent growth through economic transformation.

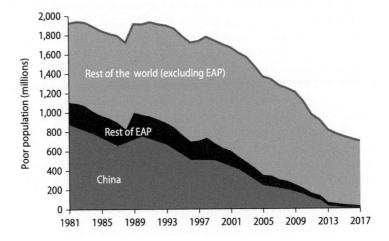

Figure 1.1 Trend in reduction in global poverty 1981–2017[2]

Sources: Lugo, Niu, and Yemtsov 2021, based on PovcalNet adapted from World Bank 2018. Note: EAP = East Asia and Pacific

It is argued that this success is based upon two pillars, namely, a broad-based economic transformation to open new economic opportunities and raise average incomes and, secondly, the provision of targeted support to alleviate persistent poverty, especially to areas disadvantaged by geography and lack of opportunities. Figure 1.1 shows diagrammatically how much that two-pillar approach has contributed to the reduction of global poverty. NB: EAP refers to East Asia and Pacific.

Thus, economic development has the capacity to be truly transformative in lifting people out of poverty. A well-developed financial services system has a crucial role to play in facilitating economic development and widening participation by citizens in its benefits. Commercial banks can provide access to the capital necessary to fund any given development whilst insurance allows entrepreneurs and other actors in the development process to undertake the risks associated with commercial activity. Retail banks provide people with the means to store money, receive and make payments, and provide access to loans. Consumer-focused insurance companies enable people to protect the assets they have been able to accumulate. It should be appreciated that financial services are not the sole prerogative of huge corporations, important though they are, but can also operate at the more local level through what is termed micro-finance and micro-insurance. These latter two entities are playing a pivotal role in encouraging economic activity in many of the poorer parts of the world, as well as among communities in developed countries that may be under-served by larger financial services providers. The set of case studies that completes Part I includes one specifically on micro-insurance and this topic reappears in Chapter 9 with the example of CIC in Kenya.

In addition to its significance at the macro level in facilitating the process of economic development, the financial services sector also plays an important role in delivering social well-being through its impact on the provision of welfare as the next section explains.

1.3 Government welfare context

The well-being of humankind, at least for the vast majority of the world's inhabitants, is significantly influenced by financial well-being. At a macro level, nation states, organisations, and individuals all require access to the financial resources necessary to safeguard their rights of self-determination. Ever since the time of the Bretton Woods Conference in 1944, at which the International Monetary Fund (IMF) was established, countries that have sought support from global financial institutions have had to cede an element of, at least, economic autonomy to such institutions. Indeed, the elected heads of government of Greece and Italy were replaced in late 2011 because of the pressures exerted by the EU, its central bank and the IMF working in concert to stabilise the euro. Similarly, companies that fail to safeguard their solvency and capital adequacy find themselves subjected to the constraints imposed by the financial institutions from which they seek assistance.

However, it is at the level of the individual citizen that we see the relationship between financial assets and autonomy most acutely. As individuals progress through the various stages of life, the balance between income, financial assets and expenditure will vary. In childhood we require money to fund education and health requirements in addition to the expenses necessary to support everyday life. At the other end of the lifetime continuum, in old age, we require relatively high levels of healthcare provision in addition to the money needed to support the necessities of life. Both extremes of the human life cycle are typically associated with the individual not being engaged in paid employment, at least, not in the developed countries of the world.

Throughout history, the family has acted as the primary mechanism for addressing the challenges posed by income and expenditure discontinuities. A feature of the developed countries of the world is that the family has lessened in the importance attached to this role. Family size, structures and role definitions have undergone rapid change since the Second World War in developed countries across the globe. Live births for the 28 countries that comprise the EU fell from 7.5 million in 1960 to a low of just over 4 million by 2021. In addition to falling birth rates there has been a reduction in the incidence of marriage across the EU where the crude marriage rate fell by more than 50% from 8.0 per 1,000 people in 1964 to 3.2 in 2020. This has contributed to the diminution of the significance and role of the family as the primary form of welfare support to individuals as they progress through life. As observed by Eurostat:

> The diminution in the relative importance of the family as a self-sustaining welfare system has evolved in parallel with the expansion of welfare systems organised, provided, and funded by the State in much of the developed world. Quite how causality and correlation are at play in this development is a source of much deliberation and debate. What is not open to debate is that the role of the State in matters concerning welfare advanced significantly during the twentieth century in many parts of the world.

Progress check

- Context is crucial to the marketing of financial services.
- Financial services are a major enabler of economic development.
- Financial services can be a force for good in combatting global poverty.
- Inappropriate financial behaviours can be hugely damaging at the international, national, and individual levels.

Individual requirements such as the need for income during periods of unemployment or retirement, healthcare and education, were progressively transferred from the private and voluntary domains to the public sector. Thus, across the world, governments have, to a greater or lesser extent, assumed a significant role in safeguarding the welfare needs of their citizens. During the period of communist rule in Eastern European and some Asian countries, the State was all-pervasive regarding the provision of welfare services and while the transition process undoubtedly reduced the role of the State, it certainly did not eliminate its responsibility for aspects of individual welfare. However, in many developing countries, the State remains more at the periphery of welfare provision primarily because of limited resources. In such places, the family, and especially the extended family unit, continues to perform the primary welfare role to its members. It is interesting to note that the respective contributions made by the State and citizens are not static but are dynamic. For example, although the public sector continues to play a significant role, recent decades have seen notable reduction in State welfare provision in many developed economies and a tendency to redistribute responsibility back to the private sector and specifically to individuals. This has significant implications for the financial services sector and particularly for products designed to provide individual consumers with benefits such as income protection or payment for medical expenses.

A range of factors have exerted their influence in the relationship between public and private sectors in terms of welfare provision but one of particular note is what might be termed consumerism. This is allied to the growth of consumer cultures throughout the world, which has been driven by a growth in real earnings, increased competition, product innovation, greater sophistication in marketing practice and changes in culture and value systems. The practical consequence of the growth of consumer cultures is that citizens have become increasingly accustomed to receiving choice, quality, convenience and value from their experiences as consumers in the marketplace. Thus, consumer expectations have been fueled predominantly by private sector suppliers of consumer goods and services.

For the State, this has presented two particular challenges. Firstly, the citizen is increasingly coming to expect the same standards of consumption experiences from state-provided services that they obtain from the private sector. It is proving to be increasingly costly and difficult for state bureaucracies to live up to such expectations. There is the ever-present concern of two-tier delivery of welfare services such as education and healthcare. It is acknowledged that great disparities exist in respect of the differentials between state and privately funded provision. For example, the health services provided by, say, France and Germany through their socially funded systems, are the envy of many other parts of the world. Nevertheless, those with money can, as a rule, enjoy the freedom to source a much wider array of health and education facilities than those without. Secondly, the State has the challenge of maintaining standards of living that are increasingly defined by a culture of consumption. This places growing strains on the ability of governments to use their social welfare budgets to fund appropriate lifestyles for claimants such as those of retirement age.

In summary, welfare provision underpins the economic well-being of society. Its provision is increasingly based around a complementary mix of public and private sector activity. Private sector welfare provision is predominantly dependent on the financial services sector and thus the efficiency and effectiveness of this sector has important implications for the economic and social health of an individual country. This is a theme to which we will refer at various points. For the moment, it is perhaps most pertinent to note that one essential element of welfare provision is the concept of income smoothing and the role of the financial services sector in this process is explored more fully in the next section.

1.4 Lifetime income smoothing

Both the State and the financial services industry work in a complementary manner to facilitate the smoothing of income flows throughout an individual's lifetime. Typically, during childhood the individual is acquiring the knowledge and skills upon which his or her future employment will be based. This is a period in life which is all about cost in the absence of any income. Although the family is the principal source of money during childhood and adolescence, the State plays a significant role in financing the costs associated with this life stage. The intergenerational transfer of funds from adulthood (as parents) to one's children forms part of the income smoothing process.

Towards the later stages of life people, at least in the developed nations of the world, typically cease participating in the labour force. As with childhood, this is a period characterised by considerable cost and little or no income from employment. This concept of retirement is a generalisation that is becoming challenged to an increasing extent in countries from the USA to Australia. The stereotypical model of retirement holds that money is transferred to the pensioner in one of two principal ways. First, there is a generational transfer of funds via the taxation system whereby today's workers pay taxes that, in part, contribute to the pensions of those in retirement. Secondly, and to an increasing extent, income in retirement is funded out of the money that the individual has saved during his working life in the form of a pension. Importantly, employer-sponsored occupational pension schemes began to make a growing contribution to an individual's pension entitlements during the second half of the twentieth century. In simple terms, a funded pension scheme involves the transfer of income from one's years in paid employment to the post-employment years. Thus, it is a form of income smoothing that comprises elements of State and privately organised money management.

 Stop and think?

In what ways do you believe financial services further the well-being of citizens in your country?

What would be the consequences of people not having access to insurance?

Compare and contrast the merits of State and private sector welfare provision

In many parts of the world life is more challenging and old age can be simply a continuation of the toil of one's earlier working life. Again, the family is often the only significant vehicle for supporting the elderly in many developing countries. However, there is growing evidence that participation in the workforce by older citizens is rising in many developed countries. Data provided by Eurostat for the years 2004 to 2019 for the EU shows a significant uptick in the percentage of people in the age cohort 55 to 64 years participating in the workforce as

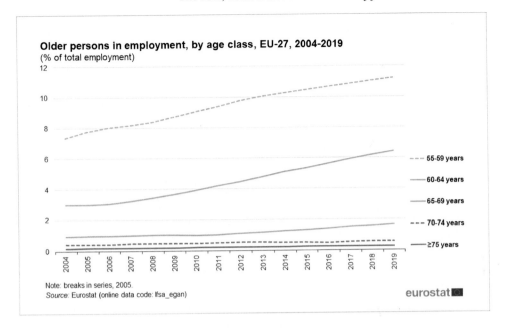

Older persons in employment, by age class, EU-27, 2004-2019
(% of total employment)

Note: breaks in series, 2005.
Source: Eurostat (online data code: lfsa_egan)

Figure 1.2 The growth in the number of older people still in work

shown in Figure 1.2. Indeed, a clear increase in the percentage of people aged 65 to 69 is also in evidence in Figure 1.2. As the Eurostat report observes:

>...the number of persons employed and aged 55-64 years increased by 89.8 %, with a similar expansion in the number of persons employed who were aged 65 years or more (up 82.1 %).

The need to provide an appropriate level of income in retirement is increasing in the agendas of virtually every country. Several factors have contributed to this phenomenon, the most significant of which are demographic. In essence, the proportion of the world's population that is older than 65 years is growing. The principal drivers of this ageing effect are the extension in life expectancy and lower birth rates. In China, demographic forecasts suggest that as many as 25% of the population will be at retirement age or older by 2050. The costs of funding State pension entitlements is placing strains on many countries and a number have responded by gradually increasing the age at which individuals become eligible for their pension. The UK has made a concerted effort to raise pension qualifying ages since 2010 without undue civil unrest. In January 2023 the French government announced that it would be raising the legal minimum qualifying age, which will increase from 62 to 64 years by 2030. This has been met by a wave of strikes as trade unions seek to thwart the government's plans. Meanwhile, Denmark is projected to have the highest retirement age, at 74 years for both men and women. China's retirement age has remained unchanged for more than four decades at 60 for men and 55 for female white-collar workers, even as life-expectancy has risen. Female blue-collar workers retire even earlier at 50.

Figure 1.3 French protestors against the increase in the minimum qualifying pension age to 64

The reduction in birth rate appears to be a consistent feature of most countries as they become more economically developed. This is a consequence of a range of social, economic, and cultural factors and the changing nature of lifestyle choices that are in evidence. A notable explanation for the declining birthrate in many countries is the improvement in the standards of education and education outcomes for girls. Put bluntly, as women become better educated their employment prospects improve and they choose to have fewer children. In contrast, many, but not all, developing economies have much higher birth rates and relatively young populations, although as levels of development increase, the number of children per family does tend to fall.

A major consequence of the ageing effect in developed economies is that the dependency ratio is growing in countries across the globe. This refers to the ratio of dependants (i.e. individuals who have ceased work) to people in the labour force. According to World Bank estimates, having peaked in the late 1960s at about 77%, the global dependency rate had fallen to 55% by 2021. The age dependency ratio shown in Figure 1.4 is the ratio of dependents--people younger than 15 or older than 64--to the working-age population--those aged 15-64. Data are shown as the proportion of dependents per 100 working-age population.

A range of possible solutions are in prospect to address what has been called the retirement savings gap. However, they boil down to some basic options, namely people will have to work for an additional number of years or save more money or, more likely, a combination of the two. In either event, the government and private sector must work together to address this feature of income smoothing.

Thus, it can be appreciated that a range of factors result in income and expenditure discontinuities as well as fluctuations in personal assets throughout an individual's lifetime. Figure 1.5 illustrates a typical asset profile and shows how substantial net assets only

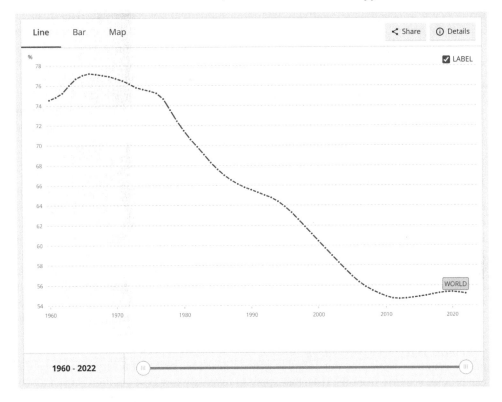

Figure 1.4 Age dependency ratio (% of working age population)
Source: World Bank, https://data.worldbank.org/indicator/SP.POP.DPND

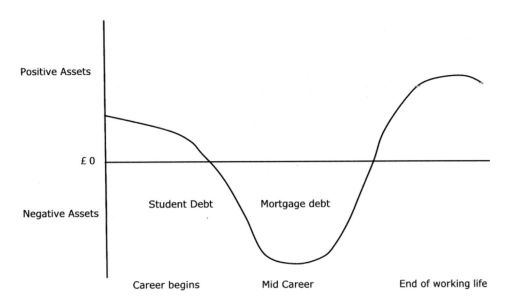

Figure 1.5 Lifetime financial assets profile

really begin to accumulate relatively late in an individual's working life. The financial services industry has an increasing role to play in providing the wide range of products and services that are necessary to smooth income and expenditure flows throughout one's working life.

Alongside the important issues that arise in relation to the variability of assets, income and expenditure over a lifetime, consumers also face a variety of short-term risks and the ability to protect or insure against the adverse consequences of those risks has important implications for social and economic well-being. The next section explores the role of the financial services sector in managing risk.

1.5 The management of risk

An important aspect of how financial services organisations further the cause of economic development is through the provision of the means to manage risk. In simple terms, this is the role played by insurance. General insurance (e.g. insuring risks to property and possessions), health insurance and life insurance[3] are effective means of enabling individuals and organisations alike to take on risks associated with economic advancement. For example, a bank will be unwilling to lend money to a small business owner who wants to invest in additional manufacturing capacity without some form of security. A common type of security is some form of life insurance that will enable the bank loan to be repaid in the event of the death of the borrower.

In many parts of the developing world we are seeing the development of what is called micro-insurance. Typically, this refers to general insurance cover of a very basic level that can provide security from the risks that apply to relatively low-cost yet high-impact assets. Micro-insurance and micro-finance are making important contributions to alleviating the problems of financial exclusion, perhaps the most high-profile exponent of the latter being the founder of Bangladesh's Grameen Bank, Nobel Laureate Professor Muhammad Yunus. In common with micro-finance, micro-insurance addresses the needs and circumstances of those sections of society that the mainstream providers consider insufficiently profitable to serve.

Finally, it is worth pointing out that governments make extensive use of financial services instruments as a means of managing public finances. Virtually all countries use government bonds as a means of raising money. In the UK, National Savings & Investments is a government-owned organisation that promotes a wide range of retail financial services products (FSPs) that play a role in the government's fiscal strategy.

1.6 Poverty and financial exclusion

A key tenet of the United Nations is that the citizens of the world be relieved from the scourge of poverty. Indeed, the relief of poverty has been of fundamental concern to communities for centuries. In Britain the nineteenth century saw the rapid acceleration of poverty up the agenda of all political parties. It was also a period during which many new charitable and philanthropic bodies were established to address the poverty so graphically commented upon in the UK by Marx and Engels and depicted in the works of Charles Dickens. While Europe may have emerged from the worst of the poverty associated with industrialisation in the nineteenth century, the problem of poverty persists throughout the globe and remains a daunting challenge to national and international policymakers.

Progress check

- As countries develop, the State takes over from the family as primary source of welfare and economic support.
- State and private sector complement each other in assisting financial well-being.
- Range of factors exerting pressure on states' abilities to satisfy growing citizen demands and expectations for welfare provision.
- Financial services are crucial to lifetime income smoothing

---

As will be discussed in Chapter 2, easing poverty depends not just on the creation of an income stream, but also on the creation of assets. Exploring the development of the financial services sector in the UK during the nineteenth century provides an illustration of the positive impacts associated with the provision of financial services. Nineteenth-century Britain was witness to the development and growth of building societies and friendly societies. The former aimed at helping ordinary people to build and own their own homes, whilst the latter were often initially formed to ensure that working people could afford a dignified burial.

In the context of financial services, there are also very real concerns at the incidence of financial exclusion. By financial exclusion, we mean the lack of access to and usage of mainstream financial services products and services in an appropriate form (Panigyrakis, Theodoridis and Veloutsou, 2003). No textbook on financial services marketing would be complete without paying due regard to this phenomenon. As commented upon already, financial services perform a key enabling role in advancing economic development and well-being.

Account ownership is the fundamental measure of financial inclusion and the gateway to using financial services in a way that facilitates development. Owners of formal accounts—whether those accounts are with a bank or regulated institution such as a credit union, microfinance institution, or a mobile money service provider —are able to store, send, and receive money, enabling the owners to invest in health, education, and businesses. Given the positive benefits enabled by account ownership, the growth captured in the Global Findex 2021 is cause for celebration. The following points are the headline findings on ownership[1]

Worldwide, the period, spanning 2011 to 2021, saw account ownership increased by 50% to reach 76% of the global adult population. Indeed, between 2017 to 2021, the average rate of account ownership in developing economies increased from 63% to 71%. Recent growth in account ownership has been widespread across dozens of developing economies which is in stark contrast to that from 2011 to 2017, when most of the newly banked adults lived in China or India. Technology has been a key enabler of access to banking services in many developing countries where the traditional branch-based business models of the Old World are impracticable. Discussions later in this book will highlight the role that mobile payments have played in reaching unbanked customers particularly in rural areas and will show how M-Pesa has provided improved access to payment services in East Africa.

Between the last decade or so of the twentieth century and 2010 the UK experienced the inexorably withdrawal of bank and building society branches from poor neighbourhoods and rural communities as such customers became increasingly unprofitable to serve. The trend in branch closures has continued to this day with widespread withdrawal of branch banking throughout Britain's towns and cities. These more recent closures have been driven in particular by changes in customer behaviour as banking via smartphone apps increasingly becomes the norm. An additional factor has been the continued fall in the use of cheques and cash, the latter's reduction having accelerated as a consequence of the lock downs brought in by the government in response to the Covid 19 epidemic. During that period of time half of London's branches were closed or scheduled to be closed according to data analysed by Which?. At the same time, new challenger banks have been launched, such as Atom Bank and Starling Bank in the UK, which benefit from the absence of unresponsive and expensive-to-run legacy systems and without the expense of a branch network. The reduction in bank branches has become a global phenomenon, from Australia, through to Europe and on to North America.

 Stop and think?

What is meant by the term "lifetime income smoothing", and how is this addressed by the financial services industry in your country?

What are the kind of risks that face businesses in your country and what financial services products help to mitigate those risks?

How inclusive do you think banking is in your country and in what ways is fintech helping to address this problem?

These and other developments have resulted in financially excluded individuals falling prey to non-mainstream organisations that exploit the vulnerability of such consumers. This is particularly in evidence with regard to credit and loans where there have long been concerns about excessively high interest charges associated with payday loans and some buy now, pay later (BNPL) schemes. Credit unions offer a viable alternative to many such consumers. Unfortunately all too often they do not have the resources required to provide the necessary infrastructure, nor do they have sufficient promotional muscle. Ideally, financial services should be viewed as providing an inclusive means for improving the financial well-being of all. That is not to say that companies should be expected to become unreasonably philanthropic to the detriment of key stakeholders. Indeed, it is perfectly legitimate for a provider to operate on a niche or "preferred lives" basis. However, the means exist to adopt an inclusive approach to financial services that obviates the need for exploitation of the vulnerable. Policymakers and regulators must focus on the need for inclusiveness and avoidance of exploitation within their goals for the development of the financial services industry.

An important contribution to the debate about financial exclusion and vulnerability was made by the Financial Conduct Authority (FCA) in the UK with its report entitled '*Consumer Vulnerability in Financial Services (Occasional Paper No 8)*' published in February 2015. Discourse on the subject of financial vulnerability frequently appears to revolve around a fairly predictable set of demographics such as the elderly, the disabled and infirm. Occasional Paper No8[5] brought something quite new to the debate by abandoning the concept of the vulnerable consumer and, instead, introducing the notion of consumers in vulnerable circumstances. To quote from the paper:

> Vulnerability can come in a range of guises, and can be temporary, sporadic or permanent. . . . It is a fluid state that needs a flexible, tailored response from firms. Many people in vulnerable situations would not describe themselves as "vulnerable". The clear message is that we can all become vulnerable. (Page 8)

This much wider definition is helpful in a number of ways. First, it moves the thinking of marketing executives on from the dangers of ghetto-ising certain broad brush demographic groups, with all the dangers such an approach can create. Second, it should lead to a much more effective and sensitive approach to setting policy, developing processes and procedures and the associated training to address the service needs of customers who find themselves in circumstances of vulnerability. This should result in better outcomes for customers and reduce the incidence of customer detriment.

In the 2021 the FCA built upon that earlier work by introducing FG21 entitled *Guidance for Firms on the Fair Treatment of Vulnerable Customers*. This included the following definition[6]:

> A vulnerable customer is someone who, due to their personal circumstances, is especially susceptible to harm, particularly when a firm is not acting with appropriate levels of care.

The document included a valuable model of the actions that firms should take to ensure they treat vulnerable consumers fairly which is given in detail in the Support Material and the major headings summarised as follows:

- Understanding customer needs
- Skills and Capability
- Monitoring and Evaluation
- Product and Service Design
- Customer Service
- Communications

1.7 Mutual and proprietary supply

Financial services organisations present themselves in two forms as far as ownership is concerned, namely: mutual and proprietary. In simple terms proprietary companies are owned by shareholders; mutual suppliers are owned by their customers who are known as members and are run for their benefit. So, unlike most financial services organisations, which are run as PLCs (Public Limited Companies), mutuals have no shareholders to pay. Mutuals serve the interests of their members but nevertheless still operate as profit-making entities.

A substantive body of literature exists which sets out to compare the operations of, and outcomes associated with, proprietary and mutual forms of supply. A particular area of focus has been the relative expenses and payouts associated with life insurance firms. Of particular note are the studies carried out by Armitage and Kirk (1994), Draper and McKenzie (1996),

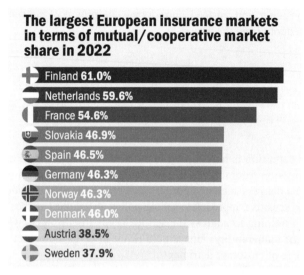

The largest European insurance markets in terms of mutual/cooperative market share in 2022

- Finland **61.0%**
- Netherlands **59.6%**
- France **54.6%**
- Slovakia **46.9%**
- Spain **46.5%**
- Germany **46.3%**
- Norway **46.3%**
- Denmark **46.0%**
- Austria **38.5%**
- Sweden **37.9%**

Figure 1.6 The largest European insurance markets in terms of mutual/cooperative market share in 2020[7]

Genetay (1999), Hardwick and Letza (2000) and Ward (2002). These and other studies concern the merits and demerits of mutual and proprietary forms. Underlying many of these studies is the presumption that the form of ownership is independently implicated in corporate performance. This is based upon a view that there is an inherent conflict of interest between the interests of shareholders and consumers. Therefore, mutuals may be at liberty to concentrate more effectively on meeting the needs of consumers.

Mutuality remains a significant part of the financial services industry in many parts of the world not least in Europe where out of 6,000 insurers it is estimated that some 3,300 are mutual, albeit typically smaller in size than their proprietary counterparts. According to the latest research from the International Cooperative and Mutual Insurance Federation (ICMIF),[8] published in 2022 the European mutual and cooperative insurance sector accounted for 33.4% of the total regional market in 2021, representing a 38% increase from the first available market share figure (24.2%) recorded in 2007 (see Figure 1.6).

More than 150 million EU citizens have an insurance policy with a mutual provider and the sector employs more than 300,000 people. The sector has been subject to consolidation over a considerable period and this trend seems set to continue.

At the global level, the latest research published by ICMIF highlights that in the 10-year period since the onset of the financial crisis (2007 to 2017), premium income of the global mutual and cooperative insurance sector grew by a total of 30% compared to 17% growth of the total global insurance industry. As a result, the global market share of mutual and cooperative insurers rose from 24.0% in 2007 to 26.7% in 2017. The report also highlights that 922 million members/policyholders were served by mutual/cooperative insurance companies in 2017, a 13% growth since 2012. The growing positive socio-economic impact of the mutual and cooperative industry was also evident in the increase in the number of people employed by the sector, which reached 1.16 million in 2017 – a 24% growth since 2007.

Marketing in practice 1.1: ownership and insurance – why mutuals matter

The insurance industry in the UK is made up of 100s of organisations, pursuing individual business plans and prioritises, but all bound- by regulation and competition at the very least- to treat their customers fairly. For some, fairness and customer-orientation is a marketing exercise, but for others it's the reason they exist. Whereas shareholder-owned insurers are predominantly in business to grow the share price and to make profits to pay dividends, the purpose of mutual insurers and friendly societies- who are owned by their customers- is to work to pursue the long-term viability of the business as well as the best interests of its customers. Mutuals do seek to make a profit, but their goal is not to maximise it, and any surplus is shared with the members or ploughed back into the business.

But in an industry where all organisations stress their commitment to serving customers well, how can mutuals differentiate themselves? This is a constant challenge for the sector; big mutuals, such as Royal London, and the building society Nationwide, have spent many £ million promoting the benefits of mutuality. Research from the Association of Financial Mutuals (AFM) shows some success: however, awareness of mutuals is relatively high amongst older audiences, but much less so amongst the young.

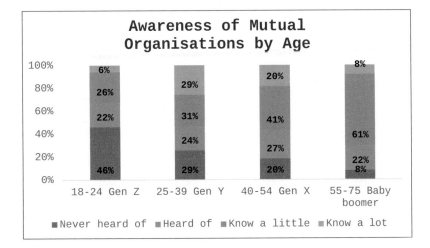

Figure 1.7 Awareness of mutuals by age

The relatively low awareness of mutuals with younger audiences coincides with their preferences to shop for financial products online, and specifically via price comparison sites[2]. Most mutuals however are reluctant to use price comparison sites because they charge high levels of commission, and mainly prioritise price above whether the features of the product match the needs of the customer, or whether the insurer pays claims. As a result, mutual products tend to be sold via brokers, or direct to the customer, and some friendly societies continue to generate sales by member-get-member schemes.

And mutuality does matter, particularly to members of a mutual and to its employees. You need only consider the plans for one of the oldest and largest mutuals, LV=, to demutualise and sell the business to private equity in 2021. The proposal was overturned by members of LV=, who were not convinced that the sale was in their best interests, or that the pay out offered was reasonable[3].

Employees know ownership matters as well. When employees were asked to consider certain traits of their employer, the differences were starkly superior for the workforce of mutuals, compared with their counterparts in non-mutual organisations[4].

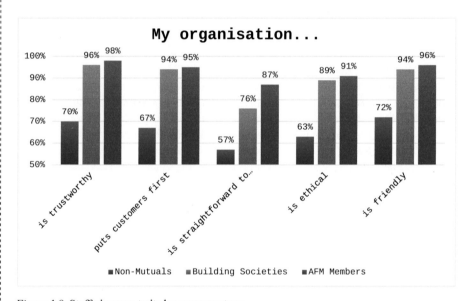

Figure 1.8 Staff views on traits by company type

Some of the factors that employees in a mutual take into account in assessing these traits include:

- Serving the underserved: many mutuals focus on serving people who traditionally find it hard to access insurance cover. This will include operating in markets that others consider unprofitable[5], keeping the minimum premium low (often less than £10), marketing to the self-employed and others that might have difficulty obtaining cover, and providing a range of channels for contact, including speaking directly to the staff in person or on the phone.

- Paying claims whenever possible: data published by the FCA shows the typical health cash plan customer makes an average of nearly 2.5 claims a year[6], whilst friendly societies with an income protection product pay around 95% of claims – much higher than the sector as a whole[7].
- Mutuals tend to be small businesses and work collaboratively with other parts of the local community. The policies they provide help keep people in work, or support them when they're unable to; the payments the sector makes helps support the work of the National Health Service (NHS) and reduce costs to the welfare state, and deliver benefits to local employers: in 2017, an AFM-commissioned report estimated the sector generated savings of over £400 million a year[8].

In recent times in the UK we've seen the growth of B2B mutuals: mutual organisations set up by members of a sector to source their own insurance solutions (for example, Education Mutual, whose strategy is simply described as "by schools for schools"). The trend to developing B2B mutuals is usually because insurance is hard to source, or expensive, or claims are not often paid. NACFB Mutual was established by a trade association to solve the problems its members have with the notoriously-difficult-to-source professional indemnity cover, and its website indicates they can save members up to 30% on price, and secure better cover[9].

Despite all those positive indicators, the sector still has a long way to go to become the major player in UK insurance it once was: in 2021, mutual insurers managed over 32 million policies, and held assets of over £200 billion[10]. That equates to a modest market share of 7.9%, a figure that is much lower than most other major insurance markets in the world (in North America mutual insurers hold 38% market share, and in Europe nearly 33%[11]), where mutuals are protected by legislation and regulation facilitates their growth.

Mutuals have a good story to tell: they need the tools and imagination to tell it better.

Martin Shaw, Association of Financial Mutuals

References

1 Source: Teamspirit research for AFM, May 2021
2 ibid
3 www.bbc.co.uk/news/business-59607693
4 Source: YouGov research for AFM and BSA, December 2019, supplemented by staff surveys of mutual members.
5 Ibid
6 For example, members of AFM hold over half of all Child Trust Funds, and the long-term profit horizon of the product has been seen as an attraction to mutuals, compared to a reason to overlook the market by PLC insurers.
7 www.fca.org.uk/data/general-insurance-value-measures-jul-dec-2021
8 https://financialmutuals.org/resource/as-more-uk-workers-live-with-long-term-illness-income-protection-from-a-mutual-provider-has-never-been-more-relevant/
9 https://financialmutuals.org/wp-content/uploads/2022/11/OAC-Report-The-benefits-to-the-welfare-state-of-mutuality-2.pdf
10 https://nacfb.org/mutual/
11 Source: ICMIF/ AFM analysis, October 2022: https://financialmutuals.org/wp-content/uploads/2022/10/UK-Market-Insights-2022.pdfSupporters

Supporters of the proprietary form point to the powerful influence of shareholders, especially institutional shareholders with their substantial voting power, in exerting pressure on boards of directors to perform. The argument runs that the members of mutual organisations lack the power required to bring due influence to bear on boards of directors and that this results in the potential for under-performance and, possibly, the abuse of power. At worst, the CEO could run the firm like some form of personal fiefdom. Indeed, critics of mutuality will often cite the difficulties of Edinburgh-based Equitable Life as an example of how the governance shortcomings of mutuals can have a devastating impact upon consumer interests. Moreover, proprietary companies are more able to gain access to additional capital should the need arise than their mutual counterparts, and this is a source of competitive advantage for the sector.

There is also a view that proprietaries enjoy high levels of consumer trust. Research conducted by the Citigate Group has shown that mutuals featured only once in the top 20 of trusted investment brands, with Royal London at number 20. Critics of this piece of research argue that it confuses familiarity with trust. Undoubtedly there is reason to believe that consumers do tend to view a well-known household name as implying trustworthiness. Research carried out by the Financial Services Consumer Panel in the UK appears to bear out the point that consumers use brand presence as a proxy for trustworthiness. Thus, because proprietaries are large organisations with substantial marketing communications budgets, they appear to enjoy a greater degree of consumer trust than do mutuals which, because of their size, are unable to invest in brand building to the same degree. There is no doubt that branding is becoming increasingly important in financial services and the creation of global power brands is likely only to be achieved by major proprietary concerns.

Arguably, there is a role for both proprietary and mutual providers of financial services; both forms provide for the diversity necessary to solve the requirements of the marketplace as it continually evolves. The evidence does seem to support the view that de-mutualisation has not necessarily been in the long-term interests of consumers as a totality. There have been short-term gains to directors in the form of share options and windfall payouts to those with membership rights.

Progress check

- Financial services are critical to the management of risk.
- Financial services are necessary for reducing poverty and the accumulation and protection of tangible and intangible assets.
- The digital revolution is a major factor of global financial inclusion.
- There is a great diversity of supply in financial services globally.

In practice, the crucial issue is that of the fitness for purpose of any given corporate form. Fitness for purpose should be determined in terms of how well an organisation satisfies the requirements of its stakeholders. No corporate form should serve the interests of one stakeholder group if it is at the expense of the interests of others.

Mutual companies are often to be found based upon serving the needs of a distinct affinity group. Frequently this relates to a particular employment group such as teachers, doctors, farmers and clergymen to name but a few.

1.8 Regulation of financial services

The need to safeguard the interests of key stakeholders in the financial services domain has been an important force driving new approaches to regulation around the world. Governments, trading blocs and various inter-governmental and non-governmental organisations have been pursuing economic growth and trade liberalisation for at least the past four decades. There has been a desire to encourage the efficient operation of the financial services marketplace through the removal of traditional sector boundaries and the encouragement of competition. Whilst this section discusses aspects of regulation in financial services, drawing on developments in the UK, the direction of travel in the development of regulation globally shows a considerable degree of convergence. We revisit this issue in the discussion of internationalisation in Chapter 8.

Students wishing to learn more about how regulation is organized in a range of significant countries are referred to the Support Material where Faye Lageu provides some international perspectives on the regulation of banking and insurance and gives several examples of how the regulation of insurance business is approached in a range of jurisdictions across the globe. The remainder of section 1.8 was contributed by Mick McAteer of the Financial Inclusion Centre[9].

1.8.1 On the role of financial markets

When discussing financial stability, policymakers and regulators often speak about systemically important financial institutions. However, the nature of the goods and services provided by financial services industry means they are also socially important financial institutions.

Core financial products and services are not discretionary consumer lifestyle goods – they are now in effect necessities in a modern economy. In the UK (and many other parts of the world), these core financial needs are met by a mixed economy of provision to varying degrees. Retirement incomes and social or welfare insurance tend to be met by a combination of State and private provision (with the balance between State and private provision varying between states). In other areas, provision is predominantly provided by the private sector financial services industry with the state regulating the behaviours of the industry. In some cases, access to financial services is regulated. For example, as a result of EU legislation (specifically, the Payment Accounts Directive), UK citizens now have a legal right of access to a basic bank account. Moreover, insurers can no longer use gender as a factor in pricing and benefits, as a result of a ruling by the European Court of Justice.

When determining the role financial markets should play in the lives of citizens, it is not just a question of consumer protection and financial regulation. There is a core set of rights, and the protection of which transcends the rhetoric of economic efficiency.

1.8.2 Three major regulatory challenges

Post the 2008 financial crisis, three major regulatory challenges were identified:

- **Financial stability and systemic risk**: there has been a large body of regulation introduced to restore and maintain financial stability and manage systemic risks. We won't know for sure if this is successful unless, and until, we encounter a new financial crisis. Let's hope this doesn't happen but there are clear risks building up in the financial system as a result of investors "searching for yield" in the sustained low interest rate, low-growth world. Moreover, there are concerns that risk has shifted to the less well-regulated shadow banking system.

- **Prudential regulation**: regulators have also introduced major reforms to improve the soundness of major financial institutions to ensure they can withstand another crisis increasing the amount of capital held on balance sheets and in some cases restructuring.
- **Making markets work for citizens:** the wider economy and society: financial markets need to be reformed so that they are more efficient from the perspective of financial users and more accountable to society. Making the financial services "supply chain" more efficient will deliver benefits for the real economy as well as the ordinary financial users at the end of the supply chain.

Huge intellectual effort and regulatory resources have been devoted to the first two challenges – financial stability and improved prudential regulation. Policymakers and regulators continue to develop sophisticated models to allow them to analyse whether financial markets are working and regulation is effective in prudential terms – for example, capital requirements, liquidity ratios, solvency ratios and so on.

The ongoing financial crisis has kept macro- and micro- prudential regulation reforms to the fore but so far there has not been the same imperative for structural reform of markets – i.e. improving the efficiency and social utility of markets. The appetite for reform may weaken and consumer representatives and reformers are in danger of "winning the war but losing the peace".

More recently, regulatory reforms are being introduced to "encourage" the financial sector to play a bigger role in greening the economy and supporting economic growth. Some of these reforms are very contentious. For example, in the UK the government is using the opportunities provided post Brexit to relax the provisions in the critical Solvency II legislation. The government claims that this will encourage pension funds and insurers to invest in the green transition and in "levelling up"*. But, civil society advocates argue that these arguments are being used as a Trojan Horse for deregulation to allow insurers to generate windfalls for shareholders. The reforms contain nothing that will require financial institutions to fund net zero as a *quid pro quo* for the deregulation.

Policymakers and regulators have also been developing sustainable investment taxonomies, disclosure and labelling schemes aimed at tackling greenwashing and helping investors navigate the expanding market for sustainable investment products. The intent behind these initiatives is welcome. However, again civil society advocates are concerned that these measures are not robust enough and allow financial institutions too much leeway to "mark their own homework" on compliance with green standards.

A perennial problem is the significant imbalance between the resources available to industry trade bodies and consumer advocates to influence regulatory reform at international EU and UK levels.

1.8.3 UK regulatory architecture, approach and philosophy

In 2013 the UK regulatory system was overhauled with an establishment of a "twin-peaks" structure. It is important to recognise that not only was the regulatory system architecture overhauled, the intention was to radically change the philosophy and culture of, and approach to, regulation.

The key elements of the UK regulatory architecture are: The Financial Policy Committee (FPC) and The Prudential Regulation Authority (PRA) within the Bank of England, and The Financial Conduct Authority (FCA).

The soundness and solvency of financial institutions and their conduct towards and treatment of consumers (known as prudential and conduct regulation) was previously regulated in a unified system by the Financial Services Authority (FSA). This has been replaced by the "twin-peaks" approach with the FPC managing systemic risks, the PRA responsible for the prudential regulation of banks, insurers and other major important financial institutions, and the FCA responsible for consumer protection, market integrity and efficiency.

The Financial Policy Committee (FPC) and role of the Bank of England

The 2007–08 financial crisis – unprecedented in scale, severity and surprise – presented an unarguable case for major reform to the way financial stability and systemic risk is managed at UK, EU and international levels. The UK government concluded that the design of the old "tripartite" system – where responsibility for the stability of the UK financial system was split between the Bank of England, the Financial Services Authority (FSA) and the Treasury – allowed systemic risks to financial stability fall between the gaps.

One of the major flaws identified was that too much focus was placed on the soundness and solvency of individual financial institutions and managing risks within those institutions (this is known as micro-prudential regulation). Micro-prudential regulation is of course very important as the financial system is made up of individual financial institutions and people. But the Bank of England has been placed at the heart of the financial system with responsibility for all elements of financial stability, systemic risk management, and crisis resolution concentrated within the Bank. The new PRA is also a subsidiary of the Bank – although operationally independent.

A key element of the government's reforms was to establish the Financial Policy Committee (FPC). The FPC was created in 2011 before the major reforms of 2013. The FPC is a committee of the Court of the Bank of England and under the new system has lead responsibility for ensuring the stability of the UK financial system. Its job is to manage systemic risk through the use of macro-prudential regulatory tools. The Bank is responsible for crisis management including the resolution of failed banks. In addition, the Bank regulates the key parts of the financial infrastructure including payment and settlement systems and central counterparties (CCPs). The FPC is also responsible for liaising with international financial stability regulators.

The Prudential Regulation Authority (PRA)

The PRA is responsible for the oversight of the safety and soundness of banks, insurers and other prudentially significant firms. The PRA is expected to make a significant contribution to the financial stability objectives by ensuring that the behaviour or failure of regulated financial institutions does not have adverse effects on the stability of the financial system.

In terms of supervision, the key difference is the approach to capital and liquidity requirements. Closer attention is paid to the quantity and quality of capital to assess the financial strength of firms, and quantity and quality of liquidity to ensure the firm has a strong chance of maintaining its operations in the event of a crisis. A much more robust approach to risk assessment and stress testing has been adopted.

The Financial Conduct Authority (FCA)

Although the success or failure of the FPC and PRA will have a huge impact on society and the financial security and welfare of households and consumers (after all, if the system fails or individual firms go under, the other consumer outcomes and principles such as access, fairness, choice, effective competition, social utility and so on are rather abstract) perhaps the regulatory authority that makes the most difference to financial users is the FCA.

The FCA regulates the conduct of around 50,000 firms in the UK and, although the PRA is the main prudential regulator for larger firms, the FCA is still the prudential regulator for 48,000 firms.

The FCA's strategic objective is defined as: ensuring that the relevant markets function well. The FCA has a number of operational objectives to support its strategic objective:

- The consumer protection objective: securing an appropriate degree of protection for consumers;
- The integrity objective: protecting and enhancing the integrity of the UK financial system;
- The competition objective: promoting effective competition in the interests of consumers.

The FCA is also subject to various *must* have regards and *may* have regards that determine how it interprets and applies its objectives and responsibilities.

At the time of writing, the Financial Services and Markets Bill is currently going through the UK Houses of Parliament. The Bill sets out to allow the UK financial regulators to take over the functions that were once determined at EU level. It also includes some additional objectives and principles for the regulators. The regulators will have a new principle defined as the "the need to contribute towards achieving compliance with section 1 of the Climate Change Act 2008 (UK net zero emissions target)". Civil society advocates had been hoping that the regulators would be given a clear net zero mandate that would give protecting the environment equal status with other statutory objectives rather than relying on a much weaker regulatory principle.

The regulators will also be given a secondary "growth and competitiveness" objective. The competitiveness and growth objective is defined as: "facilitating, subject to aligning with relevant international standards, the international competitiveness of the economy of the United Kingdom (including in particular the financial services sector), and its growth in the medium to long term." This has proved contentious. Civil society advocates are concerned that this will allow the regulators to be put under undue pressure to deregulate to stimulate economic growth or to help the financial sector attract global business.

The Payment Systems Regulator (PSR)

The other key part of the UK regulatory architecture is the PSR. This was set up under the Financial Services (Banking Reform) Act 2013. The PSR is a fully independent subsidiary of the FCA with its own statutory objectives and is accountable to the UK Parliament in its own right. The PSR is the economic regulator of the critical payments systems designated by HM Treasury and has three main objectives – the competition objective, innovation objective and service user objective.

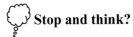 **Stop and think?**

What do you think are the advantages and disadvantages of proprietary and mutual providers of financial services?

What do you believe to be the purpose of financial regulation in your country?

To what extent do you believe that your regulator/s is successful in safeguarding the fair treatment of customers by providers of financial services?

1.8.4 Regulatory philosophy

Not only was the financial regulatory architecture overhauled in the UK, the philosophy and approach to regulation also changed.

Regulators cannot prevent all detriment and remove all risk from the financial system. Realistically a zero-failure regime is not feasible. But from the perspective of consumer protection, the FCA is more consumer focused and interventionist than the FSA and has tougher powers to make financial markets work for consumers including powers on product regulation.

Moreover, a new regime called the Senior Managers and Certification Regime (SMCR) was introduced to ensure that individuals in important positions in financial institutions can be identified and held personally accountable in the event of regulations being breached. The SMCR was phased in from 2016 and consists of three main parts, the Senior Managers Regime (SMR), the Certification Regime, and the Conduct Rules. With the SMR, the most senior people in regulated firms who perform key roles, called Senior Management Functions (SMFs) need to be approved by the FCA or PRA before starting a role. The Certification Regime covers functions that are not SMFs but can still have a major impact on consumers or firms. Underpinning this are the Conduct Rules which set out minimum standards of behaviour expected in regulated firms.

Central to the FCA's approach to regulating retail financial services are the business principles the regulator expects regulated firms to comply with. With regards to consumer protection, two key principles have been Principle 6: A firm must pay due regard to the interests of its customers and treat them fairly (known as Treating Customers Fairly), and Principle 7: A firm must pay due regard to the information needs of its clients, and communicate information to them in a way which is clear, fair, and not misleading.

The FCA is in the process of introducing a new Consumer Duty for regulated firms. The aim of the new Consumer Duty is to set higher and clearer standards of consumer protection and it requires firms to put their customers' needs first and is addressed more fully when considering the issue of fairness in Chapter 16.

1.8.5 European regulatory reforms

A new system of financial regulation and supervision has also been established at the EU level. The EU level equivalent of the Financial Policy Committee (FPC) is the European Systemic Risk Board (ESRB) based in Frankfurt. The ESRB is responsible for macroprudential oversight within the EU. However, in contrast to the UK's system which now operates under to the "twin-peaks" model, the EU has opted to continue to use the sectoral approach to micro-prudential regulation and consumer protection.

The European Banking Authority (EBA), prior to Brexit based in London and now in Paris, replaced the Committee of European Banking Supervisors (CEBS). The European Securities and Markets Authority (ESMA), also based in Paris, replaced the Committee of European Securities Regulators (CESR). The European Insurance and Occupational Pensions Authority (EIOPA), based in Frankfurt, replaced the Committee of European Insurance and Occupational Supervisors (CEIOPS).

The EU regulators have a major reform programme underway covering financial stability, prudential regulation, developing financial market infrastructures, a package of retail investment reforms, tackling money laundering and financing terrorism, developing a capital markets union, and promoting sustainable finance.

1.8.6 Potential impact of Brexit and future challenges

The future of post Brexit regulation in the UK is still to be determined (see also Chapter 8). EU financial markets still matter to the UK and, given the sheer size of the UK financial sector, vice versa. The UK government is determined to deliver a "Brexit regulatory dividend". We are yet to see whether the government will use the opportunity to make UK financial regulation more agile and responsive to emerging market failures. Moreover, the government sees the financial sector as critical to UK economic recovery. It wants the UK financial sector to be more competitive and attract more global business to the UK, including for the UK to become a global centre of green finance.

It remains to be seen whether the government intends the financial sector to become more competitive by reducing regulatory standards or by becoming a beacon of high standards. Signs are not good. Civil society advocates are concerned that the UK government is opting for deregulation to make the financial sector appear more competitive. The present government has announced a package of changes in respect of the so-called the "Edinburgh Reforms" aimed at reducing the regulatory"burden" facing the financial sector. This includes measures such as changing the Ring-Fencing Regime for banks. As mentioned, there are also concerns that the reform of the Solvency II legislation may lessen consumer protection. Moreover, the imposition of a growth and competitiveness objective on financial regulators could weaken regulatory defences and compromise regulatory independence. This could not only affect UK consumers as it risks regulatory arbitrage and a race to the bottom on regulation between the UK and EU.

More generally, there are concerns that placing so much emphasis on growing the financial sector creates wider risks. A successful financial sector is obviously in the national interest of any economy. But, it all depends on how success is defined, and how that growth and success is achieved. The UK government is currently consulting on how success in the financial sector should be defined and measured, and how regulators should be judged against this competitiveness and growth objective described above. Will the government listen to industry groups and define success in narrow commercial terms such as how much the financial sector grows, how much business it attracts from global markets, or how quickly the regulators authorise new firms and products to operate in the UK? Or will it use a more balanced framework and ask: how well does the financial sector support or undermine the needs of the environment, real economy and society?

It is important not to forget the lessons from the 2008 financial crisis. Allowing the UK financial sector to become so big increased the risk of a financial crisis happening and also made the UK economy particularly vulnerable to the impact of that crisis.

Financial market failures come with huge externality costs. The 2008 financial crisis played out in three phrases – financial, economic and social. What started as a crisis in the arcane financial markets was quickly transmitted to the real economy causing a prolonged recession which then created a social crisis as public finances were hit. According to estimates, 10 years on from the crisis, the UK economy was 16 percent (or £300bn) smaller than it would have been if post-crisis growth had followed pre-crisis trends. GDP per capita was £5,900 lower than it would have been if the economy had followed pre-crisis trends.[10]

"Financialisation" can also undermine economic productivity as financial resources are diverted from financing businesses in the real economy to speculative activities, and exacerbate wealth inequality if growth in certain regions outstrip growth in poorer regions.

And now serious questions are being asked about how well the financial sector supports or undermines environmental goals. So far, little has been done through regulation to protect the financial system from climate change or indeed to protect the environment from finance. Arguably, financial institutions continue to finance economic activities on a scale that damages the environment. Can, or will, policymakers and regulators seriously address the causes and consequences of climate change?

Progress check

- Regulation aims to safeguard the resilience of national and global financial systems.
- Fair treatment of customers and financial inclusion are key goals of regulation.
- Regulation involves a wide range of international agreements and arrangements to help safeguard financial stability and fight cross-border crime.
- Regulation should be seen as an enabler of good marketing policies and practices and not an impediment to innovation and commercial success.
- IT innovations such as fintech and generative AI present new regulatory challenges at national and international levels.

So, we do not appear to have the appropriate institutional framework or detailed financial regulations to align financial market behaviours with the needs of the environment, real economy, or society. Understanding the environmental, economic and social utility of finance and how to enhance its utility should be one of the most challenging questions for policymakers, civil society advocates and academics.

One final issue that will become more important going forward concerns fintech and how such firms are regulated. This aspect of financial services represents a complex ecosystem with new possibilities for customer detriment and disconnects between what main boards think is happening at the customer interface and what is the actual customer experience. In essence, at least as far as the UK is concerned, the FCA expects product providers in the digital sphere to confirm to the same rules as traditional firms.

1.9 Summary and conclusions

In this introductory chapter we have been exposed to the vital role that the financial services industry plays in a wide range of aspects of contemporary life in countries across the globe. This includes macro-issues such as safeguarding the prospects for economic development and poverty reduction and underpinning the overall well-being of individuals at the micro level. We have also begun to develop an appreciation of the risks to the financial and economic systems of the entire world from failures to ensure order within the global financial services domain. The risks associated with poor conduct and ill-advised practices on the part of providers of financial services have been emphasised as has the importance attached to marketers of behaving in a prudent and responsible manner. Particular attention has been devoted to how regulation of the financial services sector has been impacted upon by the various financial crises that have been a feature of the period since 2007 and what this can be expected to mean for those engaged in marketing financial products and services in the future. Finally, financial services ought to be provided for the benefit of all, not just the affluent few.

The challenge is for standards of marketing within the financial services domain to reflect the necessary degree of market and consumer orientation. An appreciation of the potential offered by financial services marketing requires it to be placed within the context of government-sponsored welfare systems on a country-by-country basis. The State and private sector of financial services must work in a complementary manner if aggregate stakeholder interests are to be optimised.

Learning outcomes

Having completed this chapter, you should now be able to:

1. **Understand the economic and social significance of the financial services sector.**
    There is a widely accepted view that controlled, managed economic development is, overall, a desirable means of furthering the well-being of humankind. A well-developed financial services system has a crucial role to play in facilitating economic development and widening participation by citizens in its benefits. Commercial banks can provide access to the capital necessary to fund any given development. Insurance allows entrepreneurs, and other actors in the development process, to undertake the risks associated with commercial activity. Retail banks provide people with the means to store money, receive and make payments, and provide access to loans. Consumer focused insurance companies enable people to protect the assets they have been able to accumulate.

2. **Recognise the diverse ways in which financial services (FS) can impact on key aspects of everyday life.**
    Financial services facilitate personal well-being and complement the role of the State in enabling lifetime income smoothing to occur. It enables individuals and organisations to manage risk and, thus, allow for risks to be taken which enhance the quality of life.

The FS industry is a key enabler of economic development and, thereby, has the capacity to be truly transformative in lifting people out of poverty. A well-developed financial services system has a crucial role to play in facilitating economic development and widening participation by citizens in its benefits. Commercial banks can provide access to the capital necessary to fund any given development whilst insurance allows entrepreneurs and other actors in the development process to undertake the risks associated with commercial activity. Retail banks provide people with the means to store money, receive and make payments, and provide access to loans. Consumer-focused insurance companies enable people to protect the assets they have been able to accumulate.

3. **Appreciate the risks to the economy of failures in the regulation of financial services.**

Financial services companies are socially important financial institutions with the capacity to destabilise individual economies and, indeed, global financial systems. There has been a large body of regulation introduced to restore and maintain financial stability and manage systemic risks. Regulators have also introduced major reforms to Prudential Regulation to improve the soundness of major financial institutions and ensure they can withstand another crisis.

4. **Appreciate the need to market financial products and services in accordance with the spirit as well as the letter of regulation.**

The FS industry has a history of being more concerned with acting in accordance with the letter of regulations than with their spirit. In the UK, the FCA has recently introduced new rules aimed at ensuring that firms deliver outcomes that ensure they live up to the spirit of regulation. The aim of the new Consumer Duty is to set higher and clearer standards of consumer protection and it requires firms to put their customers' needs first. In this way, a firm must act to deliver good outcomes for retail customers. The FCA is implementing supporting rules that would require firms to "consider the needs, characteristics and objectives of their customers – including those with characteristics of vulnerability – and how they behave, at every stage of the customer journey." The regulator intends to hold boards and senior managers accountable for meeting the Consumer Duty outcomes. It builds on the six principles of Treating Customers Fairly but is far more interventionist and prescriptive in terms of the obligations on firms to deliver fair treatment to customers.

5. **Have an appreciation of the ways in which regulation is responding to the various financial challenges that have occurred since 2007.**

Regulation also aims to make markets work for citizens, the wider economy, and society. Financial markets need to be reformed so that they are more efficient from the perspective of financial users and more accountable to society. Making the financial services "supply chain" more efficient will deliver benefits for the real economy as well as the ordinary financial users at the end of the supply chain.

Review questions

1. Identify and critically evaluate the respective roles of the State and private sector in the provision of healthcare, education and welfare in your country. To what extent do you consider that the two sectors complement or compete with each other?
2. What forms of mutual financial services provision take place in your country? Compare and contrast the ways in which mutuals and proprietary providers serve the needs of your country's citizens?
3. How are the provision of financial advice and sale of financial services products regulated in your country? To what extent do you think those regulations safeguard the interests of private consumers and business customers?
4. Critically appraise the contribution that financial services make to improving the well-being of citizens in your country?
5. If you had the power and authority, what changes would you make to improve the social purpose of financial services providers in your country?

Notes

1 www.worldbank.org/en/news/press-release/2022/04/01/lifting-800-million-people-out-of-poverty-new-report-looks-at-lessons-from-china-s-experience (accessed September 2023)
2 https://openknowledge.worldbank.org/bitstream/handle/10986/37727/9781464818776.pdf?sequence=4&isAllowed=y (accessed September 2023)
3 It is an industry convention to use the term Assurance but for simplicity let's use "life insurance")
4 www.worldbank.org/en/publication/globalfindex/brief/the-global-findex-database-2021-chapter-1-ownership-of-accounts (accessed January 2024)
5 Occasional Paper No.8 Consumer vulnerability in financial services. *Financial Conduct Authority*, February 2015, page 8.
6 Guidance for Firms on the Fair Treatment of Vulnerable Customers. *Financial Conduct Authority publication FG21 (For Guidance)* (accessed August 2017)
7 www.icmif.org/wp-content/uploads/2020/11/MMS-ENG-1.pdf (accessed January 2024)
8 ICMIF: www.icmif.org/wp-content/uploads/2023/12/European-Mutual-Market-Share-2023.pdf (accessed January 2024)
9 Mick is uniquely qualified to discuss the role of regulation in the marketing of financial services as the CEO of the Financial Inclusion Centre and former Chair of the Risk Committee of the Financial Conduct Authority.
10 10 years on - have we recovered from the financial crisis? | Institute for Fiscal Studies (ifs.org.uk) (accessed September 2023)

References

Armitage, S. and Kirk, P. (1994). The performance of proprietary compared with mutual life offices. *Service Industries Journal*, 14(2), pp. 238–61.

Draper, P and Mackenzie, E (1996) 'The returns to policyholders from alternative organisational structures: Evidence from the UK Life Assurance industry', Working Paper 98.6, Centre for Financial Markets Research, Management School, University of Edinburgh.

Genetay, N. (1999). Ownership structure and performance in UK life offices. *European Management Journal*, 17(1), pp. 107–15.

Hardwick, P. and Letza, S. (2000). The relative performance of mutual and proprietary life insurance companies in the UK. *Insurance Research and Practice*, 15(2), pp. 40–46.

Panigyrakis, G. G., Theodoridis, P. K. and Veloutsou, C. A. (2003). All customers are not treated equally: Financial exclusion in isolated Greek islands. *Journal of Financial Services Marketing*, 7(1), pp. 54–66.

Ward, D. (2002). The costs of distribution in the UK life insurance market. *Applied Economics*, 34(15), pp. 1959–68.

2 The financial services marketplace

Structures, products and participants

Learning objectives

At the end of this chapter, you should be able to

1. Identify the different types of organisations engaged in the provision of financial services,
2. Understand the range and diversity of financial services and how they relate to customer needs,
3. Be aware of the complexity of the industry and the challenges this presents,
4. Begin to appreciate how fintech is changing business models, especially in banking.

2.1 Introduction

This chapter aims to provide an overview of the financial services sector from two perspectives. First, it will set out to describe the geography of supply. These early sections will seek to identify the major groupings of organisations that make up the significant forms of product/service supply. Second, the chapter will seek to provide a solid grounding in the products that comprise financial services. It does not set out to discuss every possible product type and variant that may be encountered in all parts of the world. Rather, it seeks to identify the major product variants that are commonly encountered. In this chapter we will also provide a brief introduction to the types of financial services that are offered according to islamic principles – a sector of the market that has grown significantly at a global level in the past 20 years. Prior to exploring the marketplace in detail, the chapter begins by providing some historical context for the industry.

2.2 The geography of supply

The structure of financial services marketplaces around the world varies according to local environmental characteristics. Factors such as the stage of economic development, government policy on competition, and regulation all exert an influence on local market structures. Physical geography, logistics and infrastructural features such as telecommunications and internet access have also played a part in determining the local evolution of financial services, as do social, religious and cultural factors.

DOI: 10.4324/9781003398615-4

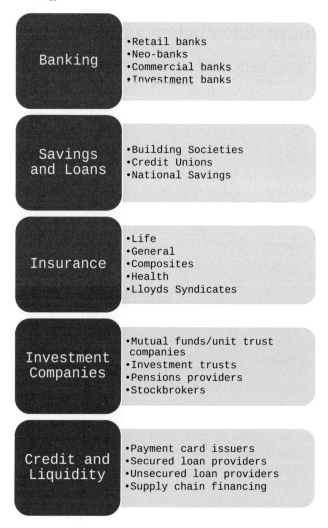

Figure 2.1 The geography of supply (general activity and specific forms)

In simple terms the geography of product providers is based upon the core elements outlined in Figure 2.1. You may notice that there is no specific reference to fintech in this list, largely because it focuses on the fundamental types or product provider and fintech is not so much about fundamental additions to core products as to changes in the way products are supplied and distributed.

The marketplace is far more complex than it has been historically with large, diversified financial services groups spanning many of the above core product domains. Nonetheless, many companies can be found that are specialists with a narrow product focus. Sometimes these are specialist arms of larger organisations such as the Zurich Financial Services subsidiary Navigators and General that specialises in insuring small boats.

A further feature of the geography of supply is the advent of new players to the marketplace. Since the early 1990s these new players have typically been one of two variants, namely what have been termed "new entrants" and, more recently, "disrupters". The former, "new entrants", are no longer quite so new. This term refers to providers with no historical pedigree as suppliers of financial services. For these companies, the move into financial services is part of an overarching strategy of brand stretch as a means of diversification. Examples of such "new entrants" in the United Kingdom (UK) include Virgin, Marks and Spencer Financial Services (now part of HSBC) and leading supermarkets such as Asda, Tesco and Sainsbury (although a number of these are now looking to withdraw from financial services having had limited success). The "new entrants" have tended to be based upon simple products that are, typically, bought rather than sold. Examples include general insurance products such as motor, travel and home contents insurance that are commonly found in display racks at checkouts in supermarkets.

The disrupters, on the other hand, represent something of far greater significance in terms of their potential to redefine markets based upon genuinely novel business models. The facilitator for this new category of product provider is the rapid advance seen in digital technology in recent years. Indeed, the words financial and technology have been conflated to create what is now termed fintech. In its infancy, fintech was viewed as a discreet, additional layer to banking services, however, it is now accepted – if not expected – as a standard financial service offering. For the purposes of this text, the term fintech (and the related term, insurtech) is used to define technologies used to support and enable consumer access to, and management of, their finances through digital means.

Fintech (and Insurtech) concerns the use of digital technologies to create new business models aimed at disrupting markets previously dominated by traditional providers of financial services. Brendan McManus writing in *Wharton Fintech* in the USA on 16 February 2016 explained that fintech as a category ranged from crowdfunding (Kickstarter) and peer-to-peer lending (Lending Club) to algorithmic asset management (WealthFront) and thematic investing (Motif Investing). He went on to explain that fintech also encompasses payments (Xoom), data collection (2iQ Research), credit scoring (ZestFinance), education lending (CommonBond), digital currency (Coinbase), exchanges (SecondMarket), working capital management (Tesorio), cyber security (iDGate) and quantum computing (QxBranch). He noted that:

> Despite operating in such a diverse set of domains, these companies share a common attribute: they build and implement technology which is used to make financial markets and systems more efficient.[1]

There is huge pressure on financial services to innovate, and not only catch up and meet customers' current expectations, but also predict and be able to deliver on future banking expectations with agility and speed. Barriers-to-entry into banking are now significantly lower with Atom, the UK's first app-based bank, receiving a UK banking license in 2016. As an indicator of the apparent speed of customer uptake, the app-based bank, Revolut (which operates across Europe) reported that it had reached 1.5m customers in Feb 2018; by November 2022 they claimed 25m and the following year they claimed 35m. N26 – the German app-based bank claimed a customer base of 8m[2].

Progress check

- Knowledge of and understanding about financial services are generally poor and can result in consumer detriment.
- The ecology of financial services is complex and comprises 5 core industry sectors.
- Fintech has resulted in new business models which pose major challenges to traditional product providers.

Digital banks can operate at a far lower cost, without the infrastructure costs associated with a branch network and complexities of heavy legacy systems. However, bearing in mind 77% of UK customers bank with the big four (HSBC, RBS/NatWest, Barclays and Lloyds), new entrants do still have their work cut out to convince customers to switch to them without any physical presence, to provide reassurance they will adequately protect their data as well as overcoming the traditional apathy to bank switching. Whilst the original wave of "new entrants", such as supermarket banks, have largely failed to dent the dominance of the major high street banks in the UK the more recent wave of digital-only banks, such as Starling, are proving to be far more of a threat. In part this can be explained by the big banks' steady reduction in branches which serves to lessen their differentiation relative to digital-only providers.

Another factor that is threatening the dominance of traditional banks is the reduction in the importance of cash as shoppers increasingly make use of digital payment methods such as Apple Pay and Google Pay. In the UK card payments overtook cash as the main form of payment in the retail sector in 2016 and by 2021, 85% of payments were made by card or bank transfers. It remains the case that cash remains the dominant form of payment by the less affluent members of society, and they are the least profitable customers to serve. Thus, the direction of travel is clearly towards digital payment methods by the more affluent. There is also a generational factor at play with younger consumers failing to see the relevance of traditional branch-based banks compared to older people. Because of their lower cost bases and lack of legacy problems the new digital-only banks can give better returns to depositors and this has become even more apparent in the higher interest rate environment of the early twenties.

2.3 Financial advice

Financial services providers are in possession of far more information and knowledge regarding the products they supply than are their customers; we call this asymmetry of information and knowledge. Consequently, there is the distinct possibility of consumers suffering detriment through the purchase of products that are inappropriate for their needs. Allied to the issue of knowledge asymmetry is the fact that financial products are, typically, infrequent purchases. This lack of familiarity, inexperience and knowledge imbalance heightens the potential for mis-buying and so for many years consumers have made recourse to financial advice. Indeed, the use of financial advisers has been a feature of markets throughout the world for many decades.

Chapter 13 will discuss the detailed workings of financial sales and advice; however, at this point it is important to establish the vital role played by financial advice and sales. In the ideal world financial advice would represent an important means of mitigating consumer mis-buying as the adviser assists the consumer in her decision-making by making up for the asymmetry problem. Such a council of perfection assumes:

- A high level of competence and knowledge on the part of the adviser.
- Independence of advice, given unbiased by special remuneration arrangement between product providers and the adviser.
- Complete transparency regarding any costs incurred for the provision of advice, and a representation of costs that is easily comprehensible to the ordinary consumer.

In practice, the above somewhat idealised features of advice have not emerged on a voluntary basis or in response to competitive forces. In the UK, regulation of financial advice has been necessary to safeguard the consumer interest and improve value-for-money. Indeed, the shortcomings of the ways in which financial advice has operated in practice rank as amongst the principal reasons why the financial services sector suffers from such a poor reputation. Further detail on this issue is available via the Support Material.

 Stop and think?

What is the trend in bank branch numbers in your country and what are the implications for access to banking services?

How is fintech benefitting consumers in your country; can you foresee any disadvantages?

2.4 An outline of product variants

The purpose of this section is to provide a solid grounding of the key product variants that comprise the domain of retail financial services. Readers wishing to learn about aspects of the wholesale market are referred to Pilbeam (2005).

It is arguable whether one should address this issue from the perspective of specific products or the needs such products seek to satisfy. The adoption of a pure product focus is problematic on both philosophical and practical grounds. From a philosophical viewpoint it places undue focus upon products provided rather than the needs of consumers. In so doing, it offends the sensibilities of those who place consumer needs, as opposed to products supplied, as the fulcrum of a marketing orientation. For such individuals any intimation of "product orientation" is to be avoided wherever possible. At the practical level, it is just not feasible to identify every possible product variant from around the globe in a text of this nature. Therefore, a pragmatic approach has been adopted whereby significant mainstream consumer needs are presented together with typical product solutions that are widely encountered. This approach is summarised in Table 2.1.

The needs and product solutions given in Table 2.1 are representative of the needs and product solutions that are typically encountered throughout the world. It does not set out to be exhaustive but gives a sound overview of generally expressed needs and the means of addressing them. The following sections of this chapter set out to tie together consumer needs with product solutions and the means of supply to enable the reader to develop some sense of the real world of financial services.

Table 2.1 Customer needs and product solutions

Customer Need	Product Solution
A means of managing receipts of funds and payment of expenses (money transmission)	Current account, PayPal, Apple Pay, use of cryptocurrencies, microfinance
A secure depository for readily accessible cash	Current account, microfinance
A secure depository for cash that pays interest	Current account, savings account, credit union deposit
A simple means of accumulating a fund of cash on which interest is paid	High interest current account, savings account
Tax-advantaged savings for the medium term	In the UK – individual savings accounts (ISAs), national savings
A means of accumulating a lump sum in the medium to long term	Regular savings endowments, regular savings mutual funds (OEICs, unit trusts, investment trusts)
Long-term capital growth from a lump sum	Mutual accumulation funds, investment bonds, investment trusts, corporate bonds, government bonds
A means of investing a lump sum to generate income	Mutual income funds, corporate bonds, annuities
A means of saving for retirement	Occupational pension schemes, personal pensions, 401k savings schemes, Central Provident Fund
A means of deriving income from a pension fund	Annuities, income drawdown
A means of financing current consumption and the finance of major purchases and projects from future earnings or income	Credit cards, unsecured loans, secured loans, hire purchase, pay day loans, crowdfunding, peer-to-peer lending
A means of financing home purchase	Residential mortgages
A means of releasing liquid funds from one's residential property	Equity release schemes
A means of protecting outstanding loans	Payment protection insurance, mortgage indemnity guarantees
A means of protecting tangible assets from fire, theft, accidental damage and perils of nature	General insurance, microinsurance
A means of protecting people and organisations from claims for pecuniary loss arising from negligence, oversight or non-performance of duties	Liability insurance
A means of protecting human assets from risks associated with death, illness and medical conditions	Life assurance, critical illness insurance, health insurance, permanent health insurance, microinsurance

2.5 Banking and money transmission

The ability to store, send and receive money is fundamental to human financial well-being and according to the World Bank[3]:

> Account ownership is the fundamental measure of financial inclusion and the gateway to using financial services in a way that facilitates development.

Historically, the extent of current account penetration in each country typically reflected the proportion of the population paid by salary. Thus, in the UK some 95% of the population have bank accounts; indeed, a quarter of the population has a current account with more than one bank. Prior to the advent of digital banking models, the cost of providing banking services was high owing to the investment needed in physical branches and all the associated

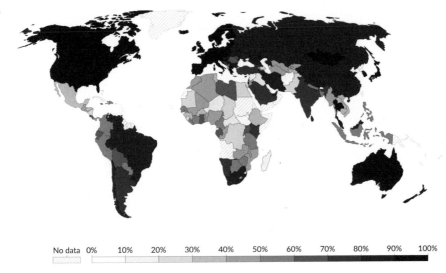

Figure 2.2 Share of adults with an account at a financial institution, 2021

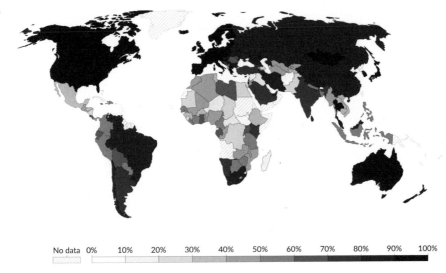

Figure 2.2 Adults with a bank account globally

infrastructure. However, that has all changed as technology has enabled access to banking to be readily available in most parts of the world without the need for costly branches. Thus, between 2011 and 2021 worldwide, bank account ownership increased by 50%, to reach 76% of the global adult population according to the World Bank 2021 Findex Report. Figure 2.2 shows global bank account ownership for 2021[4].

According to The Global Economy.com, Denmark and Iceland can claim to have 100% of their adult population with a bank account while at the other end of the spectrum is Afghanistan where fewer than 10% have access to such a facility.

Technology and changing consumer tastes have also facilitated greater diversity regarding money transmission and payments, as well as reducing the costs of current accounts. The usage of cheques has been in sharp decline for many years initially owing to factors such as the growing use of debit and credit cards and increasingly owing to the growth of digital banking, as can be seen in Figure 2.3.

Indeed, since 2019 the number of cheques has continued to fall to just 185million by 2021. According to UK Finance, the trade body of banking in the UK, 50% of adults were using mobile banking in 2019 and this trend has continued. There is clear evidence of the way in which age impacts upon the propensity of consumers to engage in digital banking as can be seen from Figure 2.4.

Digital payments have yet to win over all adults and there are serious concerns regarding the degree to which they can be trusted owing to their vulnerability to fraud, cyber-attack and power failures. Cheques are a more reliable form of making payments by certain groups of vulnerable consumers and the elderly; there are no pin numbers to remember, and no IT skills are required.

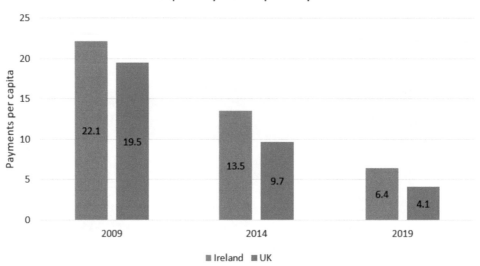

Figure 2.3 Trends in usage of cheques in UK (millions)
Source: *BPFI, UK Finance, CSO, ONS*[5]

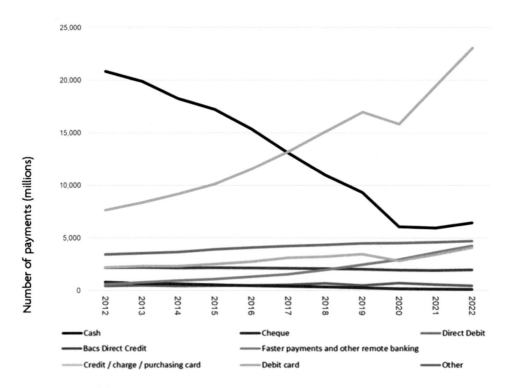

Figure 2.4 Trends in payments methods
Source: UK Payments Market 2020, UK Finance

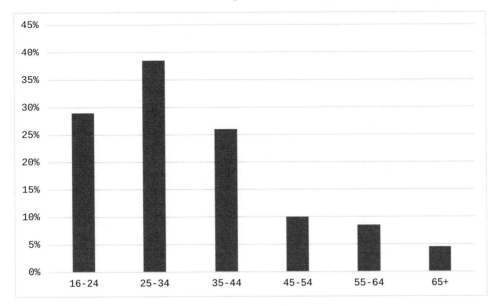

Figure 2.5 Percentage of registered mobile payment users in each age bracket
Source: UK Payments Market 2020, UK Finance

In its 2021 report, UK Finance market research found that younger people are more likely than older people to use either Apple Pay, Google Pay or Samsung Pay as can be seen in figure 2.5 below.

In 2022 UK Finance produced a stand-alone report into digital banking based upon a study carried out by polling firm YouGov on behalf of MagiClick Digital. YouGov surveyed 2,087 UK adults to explore how their attitudes and behaviour in digital banking have changed since March 2020. Some of the key findings from this research are below[6]:

- 81% of adults say the quality of online experience determines who they bank with.
- Use of online web banking overall rose significantly, with half (50%) of those who have used digital banking services more since the pandemic began stating that they have used online web banking more often.
- The highest rise in usage for online web banking was amongst the 55+ age group (60% used this service more often).
- Among those who have used digital banking services more since the pandemic began, 35% of 18–24-year-olds increased their usage, followed by 32% of 25–34-year-olds and 31% of 35–44-year-olds.
- The 55+ age group remain more reluctant to embrace making payments via smartphones and smartwatches, with only 16% of this age group increasing their usage.
- The importance of online experience between different age groups was illuminating, with 46% of those in the 55+ age group stating that it was very important compared to only 26% of 18–24- year-olds.
- Use of all digital banking services has grown since the start of the pandemic, with the largest increases being for use of mobile banking apps, with two-thirds (66%) of those who have used digital banking services more since the pandemic have begun stating they have used mobile banking apps more often.

- This growth in the use of mobile banking apps is led by the under 35s, with 85% of 18–24-year-olds and 79% of 25–34- year-olds using mobile banking apps more often. Use of mobile banking apps within the 55+ age group has also seen a significant increase (52%).
- The use of both website chat facilities and automated chatbots only saw overall rises of 14% and ten per cent respectively.

The introduction of interest-bearing current accounts has served to drive margin out of these aspects of banking. It could be argued that it has also acted as a catalyst for suppliers to become increasingly stealthy in terms of how they levy charges. UK banks and others have come in for growing criticism for what are often considered to be opaque charging practices. Charges for services such as unauthorised overdrafts and the presentation of cheques on accounts with insufficient funds have added to a popularly held sense of mistrust in the banks. The counterargument is that financial institutions must find a means of covering the costs of providing current accounts, given that they are now provided free of transactions charges, and many are interest-bearing. Admittedly, providers of current accounts do advise their customers of their menu of charges from time to time; indeed, they are obliged to by law. However, the overall approach to charging acts to favour the financially astute and well-off, whilst penalising those who are less affluent and less financially aware.

Progress check

- Digital is a major source of disruption to traditional banking models.
- Fintech has resulted in new business models that have been a key facilitator of access to banking in developing countries.
- Microfinance and microinsurance have an important role to play in in developing economies.

Thus, a big challenge for the banks has been how to introduce charges for the provision of a current account in a straightforward and transparent manner without losing significant numbers of customers. In the UK Santander has been highly successful in attracting customers to its 123 Account, an account that levied a monthly account fee currently of £4 per month. In June 2023 the account was closed to new customers and replaced with a suite of accounts under the umbrella name of Edge. The features of the new Edge account comprise:

1% cashback on selected household bills paid by Direct Debit, capped at £15 each month
1% cashback on supermarket and travel spend on your debit card, capped at £15 each month
Monthly interest of 3.5% AER/ 3.45% gross (variable) on balances up to £25,000
You'll need to pay in £1,500 each month and set up two Direct Debits
£5 monthly fee to maintain the account
No fees for using your debit card outside the UK, and when making international CHAPS payments

Figure 2.6 Santander and the Edge account

Indeed, for many banks the current account is seen as a loss-leader that acts as a gateway for the sale of other products that offer better returns. Indeed, it has been suggested that most current accounts held by the typical clearing bank are loss-making. This has resulted in the need to cross-sell other products and services via what are termed customer-relationship management (or marketing) programmes or CRM for short. This marketing phenomenon, which underpins the bancassurance model will be addressed in full in Part III of this book.

2.6 Lending and credit

The provision of loans is one of the oldest financial services dating back thousands of years. In a sense, it performs a key role as a facilitator of income smoothing by enabling consumers to enjoy current consumption from future earnings. As discussed in Chapter 1, domestic indebtedness has grown enormously across developed economies since the mid-1990s. According to the UK-based The Money Charity, people in the UK owed £1,839.3 billion at the end of February 2023. This is up by £66.4 billion from £1,772.9 billion at the end of February 2022, an extra £1,248.60 per UK adult over the year. It must be borne in mind that a significant proportion of this sum is represented by mortgage interest which would seem to be a highly desirable form of borrowing behaviour given its long-term nature and the social desirability of having people buy their own homes. Table 2.2 gives a breakdown of UK personal indebtedness by major type of debt as at January 2023.

There is a somewhat philosophical concern regarding the relationship between the time-scale of the consumption experience and the repayment of any accompanying form of loan or credit. The traditional view was that short-term loans and credit should apply to short-term forms of consumption. Examples of this are, say, loans of up to 12 months' duration to pay for a holiday or short-term credit to fund clothing purchases. The corollary to these are long-term loans, such as 25-year mortgages to fund home purchases. In between lie intermediate loans for purchases of cars and consumer durables such as furniture. The traditional practice has been to have consistency between purpose of loan (in terms of timescale of the

Table 2.2 UK Personal Debt as at January 2023 adapted from The Money Charity[7]

Types of Personal Debt	Total Personal Debt (£bn)	Debt per Household (£)	Debt per Adult (£)
Secured (Mortgages)	1,627.8	57,969	30,605
Unsecured Consumer Debt	210.9	7,510	3,965
Of which, Credit Card Debt	63.9	2,277	1,202
Grand Total (January 2023)	1,839.3	65,510	34,582

consumption experience) and duration of the repayment period. In recent years there has been a weakening in this relationship principally by individuals obtaining long-term loans for short-term consumption.

Consumers face an enormous array of loan and credit arrangements and the advent of the digital economy has served to broaden that array further with the addition of peer-to-peer lending through providers such as Zopa and Buy Now, Pay Later (BNPL) services delivered by providers such as Klarna. In simple terms a loan represents the granting of a specific sum of money to an individual or organisation for them to spend personally in respect of some specific previously agreed item. Credit, on the other hand, refers to a means of financing specific expenditure whereby the funds are transferred to the product provider directly by the credit provider. In this way, the consumer who makes a purchase financed by credit undertakes to reimburse the credit provider for the principal sum plus any interest that may be due.

The principal types of loans encountered are shown in Table 2.3.

Business loans are also to be found in both secured and unsecured forms. In contrast to personal loans, business secured loans will consider a much wider range of assets as potential sources of security.

Principal forms of personal unsecured credit are follows:

- Credit cards
- Store cards
- Unsecured loans
- Credit vouchers and cheques
- Pawnbroking
- Home credit
- Overdrafts
- Hire purchase

The scale of the growth in credit in many developed countries in recent years has been dramatic. India has seen rapid expansion in the demand for credit as observed by Experian[8]:

> With India's financial industry evolving at an unprecedented rate, demand for credit in the country has also seen consistent growth over the years. The rise in the 'affluent middle class' and growth in the rural economy is changing consumer spending patterns and driving the bulk of India's consumption growth. India's domestic credit growth has averaged 15.1 per cent from March 2000 to March 2021, primarily driven by retail loans and increasing penetration of credit cards. The Indian consumer credit market continues to expand at a rate higher than most other major economies globally with 22 million Indian consumers applying for new credits every month.

2.7 Saving and investing

Saving and investing represents the reciprocal of lending and credit. Whereas the latter concerns the allocation of elements of future income to finance current consumption; the former concerns sacrificing present consumption in order to provide for some future consumption event or requirement. It is interesting to note that disagreements exist between various groups of practitioners regarding the exact definition of these terms. One approach, typically found in the life assurance sector, regards saving as referring to a process whereby sums of money are contributed to some form of saving scheme on a regular basis to accumulate a large capital sum at a future point in time. This process of accumulation could see the contributions credited to any of the array of asset classes that are available. The asset classes could include cash-based deposit accounts, such as bank or building society accounts, or pure equity-based vehicles such as a mutual fund saving product. In other words, it is the process of making a regular contribution that is deemed to be saving rather than the characteristics of the asset class into which the contributions are made.

Whereas *saving* concerns the process of the accumulation of funds, investment is the process by which lump sums, which have already been accumulated, are deployed to achieve one of two goals, namely: generation of income or further capital growth. Again, the nature of the underlying asset class is not the issue as it could be anything from cash to equities.

 Stop and think?

What is meant by the term gateway product and what are its implications for FS business models?

What are the linkages between lending and credit and economic development?

What do you believe is the relationship between the adoption of digital forms of FS and the different demographic groups in your country?

However, the banking community typically uses saving not as a verb to describe a process, but rather, to describe a certain class of asset, namely, those that are cash-based. Thus, they regard investment as the accumulation and deployment of funds into non-cash asset classes such as bonds, equities and property. There is no correct answer, but when talking about actions, it common to think of saving as a regular process and investment as a one-off. In the context of products (or asset classes), savings are usually cash based and investments are usually equity/bond based.

2.7.1 Investing

The investment market globally has expanded enormously in the past 25 years. A particular feature of the market during the current millennium has been the expansion that has occurred in developing countries. Whereas the population of the developing world has grown by 21% since 2,000 to reach over 6.2 billion people, retail investment sales in those markets have increased more than 350% and now represent more than half of total global retail sales. Leading global management consultancy firm A.T. Kearney has developed the Global Retail Development Index that ranks the top 30 developing countries for retail investment. The index is based upon a rich and robust evaluation of key indicators of market attractiveness both now and for the foreseeable future. Its metrics include factors such as political stability,

Table 2.3 Types of loan

Loan Type	Key Characteristics
Unsecured loans	Relatively high interest rates to compensate lender for lack of security.
Secured loans	Usually secured on the borrower's residential property equity via a second (or subsequent) charge. These are known as second mortgages. Relatively low interest rates charged owing to presence of security.
Mortgages	A loan made for the purpose of purchasing one's home. Typically a long-term loan which is at a relatively low rate of interest and secured upon the property. In the UK most mortgages are variable whereby the rate of interest charged fluctuates as base rates vary. Many other countries favour the certainty of fixed-rate mortgages.
Re-mortgage	This too applies to situations in which a homeowner wishes to replace an existing mortgage with one from another lender. This normally occurs because the borrower can obtain a home loan at a lower rate from an alternative lender.
Equity release	These are loans that are secured upon residential property for older people. There are two principal variants, one by which the lender secures an interest in the property and the other which does not.

Table 2.4 Global Retail Development Index top ten[9]

Rank	Country	GRDI Score	Population Million	GDP per Capita PPP*
1	China	72.5	1,372	14,190
2	India	71.0	1,314	6,209
3	Malaysia	59.6	31	26,141
4	Kazakhstan	56.5	18	24,346
5	Indonesia	55.6	256	11,112
6	Turkey	54.3	78	20,277
7	UAR	53.6	10	66,997
8	Saudi Arabia	52.2	32	53,565
9	Peru	51.9	31	12,077
10	Azerbaijan	51.2	10	18,512

*PPP – Purchasing Power Parity
NB Brazil 20th, Russia 22nd

debt indicators, incidence of terrorism, business risks, business efficiency and estimated market potential to name but a few. The top ten markets are shown in Table 2.4 from which the importance of Asia is clear to see as four of the top ten places taken by Asian countries. Brazil and Russia were twentieth and twenty-second respectively, reflecting the economic challenges that each of them is likely to be exposed to for some time to come.

The retail investment market in the developed world has also grown enormously over the past 25 years. In the USA, according to Statista the total value of mutual funds under management has grown from $6.97 trillion in 2000 to $22.1 trillion by 2022. According to data supplied by the UK-based The Investment Association (IA), total UK funds under management had risen to £1.59 trillion by the end of 2021. The trend over the last ten years can be seen in Figure 2.7 from which it can be seen that the fallout from the financial crises of 2007/8 seems to have been fairly short lived. This is explained to a large degree by the sustained low level of interest rates paid on deposits and the impact of the Bank of England's policy regarding quantitative easing. This reveals an interesting aspect of how consumers respond to significant changes in the marketplace.

CHART 1: **TOTAL ASSETS UNDER MANAGEMENT IN THE UK AND IN UK FUNDS (2007-2022)**

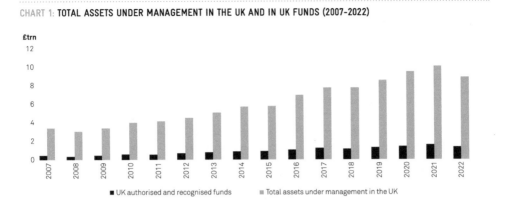

Sources: The Bank of England, The Investment Association, The Office of National Statistics

Figure 2.7 Total UK retail funds under management 2006–2021

Source: Bank of England, The Investment Association, The ONS

Table 2.5 Investment vehicles and asset classes

Investment Vehicles	Underlying Asset Classes
Deposit accounts	Cash deposits that pay interest
Direct shareholding	Shares from which income is derived in the form of the dividend and rising share values provide for capital growth.
Unit trusts/mutual	Funds a collective investment medium whereby risk is spread through the investment of the lump sum in the shares of a range of stock markets and companies. Assets may also comprise property and cash.
Investment trusts	A collective investment whereby the bundle of assets is used to create a closed company.
Insurance bonds	Typically, a form of packaged investment comprising equities, usually presented as income bonds or equity growth bonds.
Corporate bonds	These are loans that the bondholder makes to the bond issuer. Interest is paid periodically at a given rate, known as the coupon. The principal is repaid at a specified time.
Government bonds	These are loans made to the government (and sometimes to municipalities). Like corporate bonds, interest and principal are paid/repaid according to agreed rates and time.
Premium bonds	An open-ended non-interest-bearing loan to the government whereby cash prizes are paid in lieu of interest.

It is interesting to note that ONS data on household wealth comprises four components, namely:

- net property (value of residences minus mortgage debt)
- physical (household contents, vehicles)
- private pension
- net financial (savings or investments minus financial liabilities)

Net property and net financial assets together accounted for more than 75% of total wealth. The typical investment vehicles and their underlying assets are specified in Table 2.5.

No discussion of investment would be complete without reference to investment in property. In many countries, residential property equity represents a substantial proportion of domestic assets. In Australia, for example, a relatively high proportion of people live in owner-occupied households and home ownership rates have been stable at around 70% for many decades. According to the Australian Bureau of Statistics, residential land and dwellings are also the single largest component of household net worth (65%), comprising more than twice the value of the next most significant component – superannuation (27%).

Investment funds in which the underlying assets are shares, or stock, in commercial organisations are structured typically in one of two ways, namely, actively or passively managed. In the case of the former, a fund manager personally selects the companies whose stock will comprise the fund for which he is responsible. He uses his market knowledge and ability to analyse the performance and evaluate the strategies of the companies that are appropriate for his fund. For example, the manager of a fund that specialises in large American companies will research the sectors that comprise the US market – tech companies, pharmaceuticals or automobiles for example – and evaluate the performance and prospects of large companies that operate in those sectors. Passive fund management, on the other hand, involves the use of computer-based models to track the market and construct a portfolio of shares that reflects the companies that comprise the given stock market and weights their share of the market. Because these passive funds track a market, they are often referred to as index tracker funds.

As one might imagine, tracker funds are considerably cheaper to run as they do not incur the expense associated with the running of a department of active fund managers with all the associated costs and this is reflected in much lower charges to customers. According to internet investment business Motley Fool,[10] charges for managed funds tend to be a lot higher than index trackers. A typical managed fund charge has charged around 1.5% a year, whereas the average index tracker charges around 0.25%, and some charge even less than that. The argument that active fund managers advance to justify their much higher charges is that trackers do just that, they track a stock market index, and this means that investors can never outperform the market.

Numerous studies over many years have pointed to the benefits that accrue to individuals from having recourse to some form of financial assets, however modest. In the USA, Page-Adams and Sherraden (1996) reviewed the finding of 25 studies that addressed the personal and social effects of asset holding, including:

- personal well-being,
- economic security,
- civic behaviour and community involvement,
- women's status and,
- the well-being of children.

The studies that were analysed indicated the positive effects that assets have on life satisfaction, reduced rates of depression and alcohol misuse. It is often observed that assets appear to be associated with an individual's sense of self-direction and being oriented towards the future.

A report published by Kerris Cooper and Kitty Stewart for the Joseph Rowntree Foundation in 2013 examined in detail 34 studies regarding the relationship between financial well-being and children's well-being and prospects and observed that:

There is strong evidence that households' financial resources are important for children's outcomes, and that this relationship is one of cause and effect. The review found strong evidence that income effects are non-linear: an additional dollar or pound makes most difference to children in households on lower incomes than for those in better-off households. (p71)

Research in the UK by Brynner and Despotidou (2000) has corroborated evidence from the USA regarding the impact of financial assets on life outcomes.

2.7.2 Saving

The accumulation of a larger sum from small contributions can be accomplished in a wide variety of ways. The simplest vehicle for savings is through some form of cash-based deposit account such as those offered by a wide range of providers in countries across the world including post offices, banks, building societies and credit unions. It is worth pointing out that product innovation has somewhat blurred the boundaries between current and deposit accounts in recent years. Indeed, many high interest current accounts offer significantly higher rates of interest to depositors than those offered by traditional deposit accounts.

Progress check

- Saving concerns the accumulation of a sum of money.
- Investing concerns the utilization of a lump sum to either generate an income or achieve capital growth.
- Asset class plays a key role in investment strategies, over the long-term stocks outperform cash.
- The life outcomes of individuals are greatly enhanced if they have access to some kind of fund of money, and governments often incentivize people to save.

Many people like to build up a cash fund to have a financial cushion as a contingency against some future financial uncertainty. This is known in the financial advice community of rainy-day money and, as a rule of thumb, is recommended to equate to six months' worth of likely spending. This purpose of saving came to the fore during the Covid pandemic when in countries across the globe people ran down their cash deposits as incomes took a hit. In September 2021 households in the USA had accumulated savings of $2.1 US trillion. By May 2023 this had fallen to just $0.6 US trillion as households used their savings to cover income shortfalls.

The inherent risk aversion associated with keeping one's savings in deposit accounts carries with it the very real risk of the erosion of the value due to inflation and the lack of investment upside that, over the long-term, accrues to funds invested in the stock market. According to Officialdata.org, since 1900 US stocks have returned an average of 9.81% per annum, this compares with just 0.8% for cash. Hence there is an enormous long-term opportunity cost of using an investment strategy based upon cash deposit accounts as opposed to one based upon investing in stock.

2.7.3 Pensions

Saving cash sums in a deposit account on an ad hoc basis represents the simplest form of saving whereas pensions represent arguably the most complex form. Indeed, a pension is nothing more than a form of saving for a future event, ie: the time at which an individual ceases full-time paid employment.

It is normal for pensions to enjoy some form of incentive from the government to engage in this form of saving. The rationale is simple: the greater the extent to which individuals provide for their own retirement needs, the less will be the burden placed on state finances and the taxpayer. It is customary to conceptualise pensions as being either personal or occupational. Whereas the former is a scheme which is entered into on behalf of the individual, typically by that individual, the latter are group schemes run on behalf of an employer.

Occupational pension schemes (OPSs) are principally of two types: defined benefit (also known as final salary) and defined contribution (also known as money purchase). Defined benefit schemes enable the employee to accumulate a pension entitlement that is based, typically, upon a proportion of their salary in the 12 months leading up to her date of retirement, hence the term "final salary'". In the typical scheme, each year of pensionable service will entitle the employee to a pension equivalent to, say, one-sixtieth of her final salary. Such a scheme would be termed a "sixtieth" scheme. Less generous employers may offer an "eightieth" scheme whereas more generous firms may offer a "fortieth" scheme, with executive pensions being even more generous.

A crucial feature of the defined benefits scheme is that the risk for meeting future pension liabilities rest with the employer. The drop in share prices between 2000 and 2003, and again since 2008 has resulted in many OPSs experiencing severe funding difficulties. For these, and other reasons, there has been a marked shift away from defined benefit and towards defined contribution schemes. The latter variant has much in common with personal pensions in that contributions from the employee and employer are credited to the employees' individual pension account. Upon retirement, the employee will receive a pension which is based upon the value of her personal fund as at the date of her retirement. Thus, the fund will reflect the value of contributions made and the performance of the assets into which the contributions have been allocated. Accordingly, the risk is shifted from the employer and onto the employee. This benefits the employer by introducing control and certainty as its pension liabilities are discharged fully based on any contributions that it makes on behalf of its staff.

Typically, the governments of developed countries are anxious to encourage long-term saving into a pension scheme of one form or another and they can often be quite complex for citizens to understand. Arguably, it is the government-influenced nature of pension schemes and their associated tax treatment in the UK that results in the on-costs relating to the provision of financial advice. As with the UK, the USA has experienced dramatic changes in the retirement planning landscape in recent decades. In the early 1980s some 60% of workers were members of defined benefit schemes; however, this figure is now nearer to 15% as companies have acted to lessen their pension liabilities and achieve cost savings. And to make matters worse, fewer Americans are saving enough for retirement as, according to a data released by the Schwartz Center for Economic Policy Analysis, fewer employees are being offered the opportunity to participate in a 401(k) scheme. Indeed, in 2011, almost half of working Americans were not offered a retirement account by their employer whereas in 1999 some 61% of workers were offered such plans.

In common with the UK, defined benefit pensions in the USA are far more prevalent among state and local government workers than those in the private sector. Indeed, according to the US Bureau of Labor Statistics just 15% of private sector workers had access to a defined benefit scheme as of March 2022, compared with 86% of state and local government workers.

Personal pensions operate in a similar way to defined contribution OPS schemes. The individual selects a pension provider and then makes contributions to a fund of their choice made available by that provider. At the date of retirement the funds accumulated are used to purchase an annuity, and this becomes the source of income in retirement. Thus, the individual will not be certain of the value of her ultimate pension until she reaches retirement date as it will be a function of investment performance and prevailing annuity rates. This is a simplification of the variants to be found in the field of pensions. No reference has been made to features such as income drawdown and withdrawal of tax-free lump sums. Details vary enormously from country to country depending upon local tax regimes and prevailing legislation and rules.

2.7.4 Savings endowments

The savings endowment is a form of regular saving that in the UK is offered by companies authorised to offer life assurance contracts. Indeed, a defining characteristic of the savings endowment is that lump sum is payable to the beneficiary in the event of the death of the customer before the targeted maturity date of the contract. Most countries have an endowment type of product, although often described under another name. Germany is very heavily based upon endowment-type vehicles for mortgages and life plans.

A variant on the savings endowment has been the "mortgage endowment", a product which has been widely sold in the UK. This has a structure which is virtually identical to the savings endowment. However, as the name implies, this form of saving performs the dual roles of building-up a fund, the value of which is intended to be equivalent to the mortgage sum provided by the mortgage lender, and acting as a means of repaying the mortgage in full should the customer die prior to the contractual maturity date of the loan. Sales of mortgage endowments in the UK have virtually disappeared in response to high charges (again to pay for commission) and a sharp worsening in investment returns. Additionally, there have been many cases of mortgage endowments termed the "endowment mis-selling scandal". The consumers' organisation, Which? has been especially vocal on this matter and has set up a website that consumers can use to register their concerns and seek guidance regarding how to investigate claims for compensation. Well over half a million hits were registered by the website, an indication of the extent of consumer concern.

2.8 Life insurance products

The term "life insurance" is somewhat ambiguous in that it is often used to denote the range of product groups that are supplied by the life insurance industry. As such it comprises life and health protection and savings products, pensions and collective investment schemes.

The global life insurance market is dominated by the continents of North America, Asia and Europe. The dominance of the USA as a life insurance market can be clearly seen in Table 2.6.

Table 2.6 Top 10 Life Insurance Markets 2021

Rank	Country	Turnover $US Million 2020	Turnover 2021
1	United States	567,292	609,642
2	China	347,544	365,456
3	Japan	300,698	295,850
4	United Kingdom	238,922	284,284
5	France	137,464	185,445
6	Italy	129,342	146,001
7	Germany	106,709	109,961
8	South Korea	103,054	101,866
9	India	84,690	96,679
10	Taiwan	91,155	89,059
	Total top 10	2,106,870	2,284,243
	Rest of the market	630,306	713,326
	Total life	2,727,176	2,997,569

Source: Adapted from Atlas Magazine, 8 August 2022

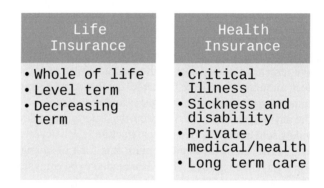

Figure 2.8 Types of protection product

It is customary for the life insurance market to be segmented according to whether products are provided on an individual or group basis. Quite simply, the former is related to policies priced, provided and paid for at the individual consumer level. The latter refers to pooled arrangements, typically schemes that are provided to an employer that provides a given level of cover to all members of staff such as a death-in-service benefit of, say, three-and-a-half times salary.

The major categories of protection products are shown in Figure 2.8:

2.8.1 Life insurance

As the name implies, a whole-of-life policy provides for the payment of an agreed sum-assured upon death on an open-ended basis. On the other hand, a term life policy provides for the payment of a given sum-assured upon the death of the life-assured within a specified number of years, for example within a ten-year period in the case of a ten-year term policy. Compared with whole-of-life, term insurance is normally considerably cheaper, and thus provides relatively high levels of cover for comparatively low premiums.

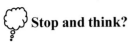 **Stop and think?**

Do you think people should be encouraged to take out life insurance, if so, why?

What sources of income do people have access to in your country when they retire?

What are the respective roles of the state and private sector in the provision of healthcare?

A variant of term insurance is decreasing term insurance. This provides for a sum-assured to be paid upon death that gradually reduces as the term progresses. Most commonly, it is used as a form of mortgage protection where the customer is gradually paying off the debt through what is called a capital repayment mortgage.

2.8.2 Health insurance

Critical illness insurance was first devised in South Africa in the 1970s and pays out an agreed sum – assured upon the diagnosis of a life endangering illness such as cancer or coronary heart disease. It can be bought as a stand-alone policy or as an added feature to, say, a term insurance policy as a means of guarding against a range of health-related risks.

Permanent Health Insurance (PHI) is a form of policy that provides for the replacement of lost income should be policyholder be unable to work because of an acute illness or chronic disability. This is particularly important for individuals who are self-employed or do not enjoy generous sickness benefits from their employers. This is an important market opportunity for both mainstream and micro-insurance providers.

Private health insurance provides the policyholder with cover in respect of medical costs. The insurer either reimburses the policyholder for costs incurred or makes direct payment to the medical services provider up to an agreed limit. The nature and extent of private health insurance is closely linked to the State-provided health services of any given country. For example, the scope of private health insurance in the UK is comparatively limited given the role played by the National Health Service (NHS). In the USA, on the other hand, there is an enormous private medical health insurance sector whereby more than half of all healthcare funding is provided by the private insurance sector, compared with 15% in the UK. France sits somewhere between the two with about 28% of healthcare being funded by private insurance sector.

Long-term care is a form of insurance that pays toward the costs associated with long-term nursing care for the elderly. As with private medical insurance, the extent of demand for this type of insurance is heavily dependent upon the scope and extent of provision made by individual countries' welfare systems. Even within the UK, long-term care costs are state financed in Scotland and Wales but not in England.

In Chapter 1 we saw how financial services play a key role in furthering social good in areas such as poverty reduction. Other areas of concern include health and life expectancy inequalities. In March 2023 the SwissRe Institute published a report called *The Life and Health Insurance Inclusion Radar*. This is based upon an innovative way of measuring insurance inequalities and their sources in both advanced and emerging markets. Below there is an abridged version of the methodology that gives guidance of where individual markets need to devote effort to reduce insurance inequalities.

Research insight 2.1: SwissRe-The Life and Health Insurance Inclusion Radar

We consider "inclusive insurance" to be the provision of appropriate risk protection cover to all people in society. The underlying assumption of this study is that when Life and Health (L&H) insurance is more inclusive, the industry will be better positioned to help narrow mortality and health protection gaps. In this study, in an attempt to assess how inclusive the private L&H markets in different countries are, we develop a framework based on three drivers or inclusivity. Our premise is that protection gaps will shrink if private sector L&H insurance is made more available, accessible, and affordable to society at large, including hitherto underserved communities (typically low-income households).

*   Availability = the existence of protection products/plans that adequately meet the range of mortality and morbidity protection needs of society.
*   Accessibility = the places, people and processes deployed to connect available insurance products with the potential buyers.
*   Affordability = whether insurance product premium price-points are reasonable within the financial resources of intended buyers and convey fair value.

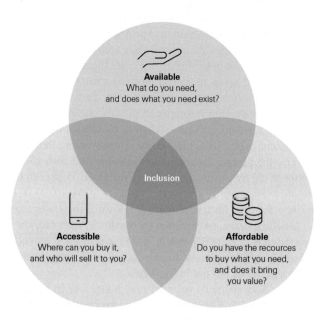

Source: Swiss Re Institute

Figure 2.9 Diagrammatic representation of the 3As

Research insight 2.1: Swiss Re – the Life and Health Insurance Inclusion Radar

The Inclusion Radar framework

We have developed a framework we call the L&H Insurance Inclusion Radar based on the 3As above to measure the degree of inclusivity of different markets. For each of the three dimensions, we have selected several sub-indicators that we seek to quantify using primary and secondary-sourced data and analysed these for a sample of 16 countries (five advanced and 11 emerging markets). The scores for the respective sub-indicators are aggregated using weighted averages to reflect the quality of data and, in terms of influence, our assessment of each sub-indicator's contribution to inclusion. We thereby derive an Inclusion Radar score (also referred to as "Radar score") of each dimension as a representation of its contribution to making the respective L&H insurance market inclusive. The separate dimension Radar scores are further aggregated using an arithmetic mean to determine an overall Inclusion Radar score for each market. These overall scores are also aggregated using the population of each country as weights. Below in Figure 2.10 we see the results of this analysis for Turkey.

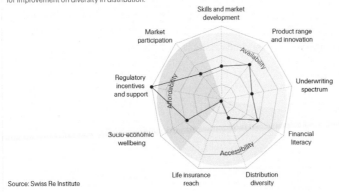

Emerging markets example: Turkey

Turkey's strength is how its market characteristics support better L&H insurance Affordability, especially its large middle class, relatively low poverty rate, a regulatory environment that supports microinsurance growth, and favourable tax rules. Conversely, Turkey's challenges are in the Accessibility dimension, with an insurance penetration rate that is disproportionately low, and room for improvement on diversity in distribution.

Source: Swiss Re Institute

Figure 2.10 The inclusion radar for Turkey's Life and Health Market

Source: The Life and Health Insurance Inclusion Radar, Swiss Re Institute, March 2023

2.8.3 Annuities

An annuity is how a lump sum, typically a maturing pension fund, is converted into regular income. Following a successful claim, it pays a regular monthly income until

Table 2.7 Indicative annual income for life from £100,000

Annuity type	Age 60	Age 65	Age 70
Single life, level	£6,760.08	£7,511.04	£8,311.56
Single life, escalating at 3%	£4,660.68	£5,407.20	£6,278.88
Single life, escalating at RPI*	£3,997.44	£4,704.48	£5,654.64
Joint life 50%	£6,251.28	£6,917.16	£7,655.28
Joint life 100%	£5,970.96	£6,426.96	£7,133.52

*RPI: Retail Price Index
Adapted from www.retirementline.co.uk

death. This is an open-ended arrangement which involves the pooling of thousands of customers' funds to arrive at a given level of income. Therefore, the consumer bears the risk of losing the bulk of their pension fund if she were to die soon after retiring as her surplus fund remains part of the general pool. As might be imagined, this is becoming an increasingly contentious matter as people choose to avoid taking such a risk with their long-term savings.

The level of annuity payable is determined by actuarial calculations and is a function of variables such as the age at which the annuity commences, gender and health status. Additionally, there are variations such as whether the annuity is level, escalating or indexed or has any other form of guarantee. Table 2.7 gives an idea of the actual amounts of pension income that are generated by annuities as of December 2023:

2.9 General insurance

In simple terms, whereas life insurance provides benefits in the event of death or illness during a prolonged contract period (possibly for the whole of one's life), general insurance provides for the payment of benefits in respect of risks to tangible and intangible non-human assets. The typical array of general insurance risks is as follows:

- Motor vehicles
- Property
- Personal possessions
- Liability
- Financial loss
- Creditor
- Product warranty
- Marine, aviation and transport
- Accident and health
- Pets

General insurance is normally based upon annual contracts whereby the premium is paid in respect of a 12-month period of cover. Thus, the cover expires at the end of 12 months and the customer must either renew the policy for the next 12-month period or seek cover from another supplier.

General insurance tends to be more price-led than life insurance and the introduction of the telephone and internet as means of transacting business have only served to heighten the intensity of competition. In the UK it remains a highly diverse sector with some 904 companies authorised to transact general insurance according to the Association of British Insurers.

 Marketing in practice 2.1: ICMIF, reinsurance – what is it and how does it work?

Introduction

In simple terms, reinsurance is insurance for the insurance providers. The obvious question is why should an insurer, whose business is to underwrite risk, wish to insure some of the risks that it has accepted? The answer is – when it is pricing the risks that it insures, the insurer will rely on historic claims data and trends in the claims data to derive its best estimate of the future claims experience. It will rely on its underwriters to ensure that the premiums charged for insurance are in line with the risks presented. However, even if the pricing and underwriting processes are properly carried out, this will not guarantee that a portfolio of insurance business will be profitable.

By its very nature, insurance business is unpredictable, and random variations from the pricing basis in either the number of claims or the average claim size (or both) can have a very significant effect on the profitability of the portfolio.

Reinsurance can protect an insurer's portfolio from these sources of variability and hence provide a more stable claims experience.

How does reinsurance work?

A portfolio of insurance business is made up of many policies covering broadly similar risks (in terms of the events covered). If the insured event occurs, the insurer is liable to make a payment to the policyholder and reinsurance does not affect this liability. Reinsurance works by reimbursing part of each claim to the insurer under a reinsurance arrangement (often referred to as a reinsurance treaty). The agreement will specify:

- The group of policies to which the treaty applies,
- The rights and obligations of each party under the treaty,
- What proportion of each claim is payable by the reinsurer,
- How the reinsurance premium is calculated.

Where a treaty is in place and policy falls within the group of policies covered by a treaty, then the insurer must reinsure the business and the reinsurer is obliged to accept the business.

Marketing in practice 2.2: ICMIF, reinsurance – what is it and how does it work? (Continued)

The reinsurance market

With climate change intensifying the frequency and severity of natural disasters, the reinsurance market has been profoundly affected by the unprecedented insured losses arising from such events. This has strained the financial reserves of reinsurers and necessitated a fundamental rethinking of risk assessment and pricing strategies within the industry. This has been further complicated by rising inflation post-Covid, leading to reduced capacity and higher reinsurance costs following many years of excess capacity and depressed rates. The reinsurance sector's resilience is paramount in the face of these mounting challenges, enabling it to support insurers and policyholders in times of crisis.

The top five global players are Munich Re, Swiss Re, Hannover Re, Berkshire Hathaway and SCOR.

Source: Mike Ashurst, Vice President, Reinsurance & Professional Development, ICMIF.

Marketing in practice 2.1 outlines one form of insurance which is less well known but of considerable importance – namely, reinsurance. This is relevant to all forms of insurance, both life and general.

Readers wishing to learn more about reinsurance are referred to Mike Ashurst's paper on the Support Material.

2.10 Cryptocurrency

Cryptocurrency is a virtual currency which exists solely digitally and not in any physical form. Unlike traditional banking, whereby transactions are managed on a centralised ledger, cryptocurrency is verified using a distributed ledger, known as blockchain (blockchain is explained in greater detail in Chapter 10). There are a variety of cryptocurrencies currently traded, the best-known include Bitcoin, Etherium and Tether. They are generally traded via crypto exchanges and these have come under a great deal of scrutiny, most notably with the largest one, FTX, going bust in 2022, along with several competitors.

Mainstream investment into cryptocurrency has been restrained for several reasons: its intangibility, lack of regulation, and market volatility make the majority of regular investors feel nervous. The UK regulatory body, the Financial Conduct Authority (FCA), has issued stark warnings to anyone investing in them:

Investing in cryptoassets, or investments and lending linked to them, generally involves taking very high risks with investors' money…If consumers invest in these types of product, they should be prepared to lose all their money.[11]

Figure 2.11 Bitcoin – probably the best know cryptocurrency

Source: "Nobody gets me Bitcoins!" by zcopley licensed under CC BY-SA 2.0

Echoing this, Bank of England Governor Andrew Bailey said in 2021 of cryptocurrencies (a stance he reiterated in January 2024):

> I'm going to say this very bluntly again…They have no intrinsic value…Buy them only if you're prepared to lose all your money.[12]

Interestingly, while China was one of the first and largest adopters of cryptocurrency, accepting it as a payment mechanism from 2013, it banned its use in 2023, ostensibly due to its use in financial crime. There is speculation over whether "backed-crypto", known as "stablecoins", where digital currently is linked to government backed currency will have greater success but, as yet, there is insufficient evidence as to their long-term stability.

Cryptocurrency is largely unregulated. In the UK, unlike regulated finance whereby eligible consumers are protected up to a point under the Financial Services Compensation Scheme, there is no protection for losses incurred from crypto investments. The FCA has increased scrutiny on companies that facilitate cryptocurrency trading and in 2021 they banned Binance, the current largest cryptocurrency exchange, from operating any regulated activity in the UK. The increased scrutiny of crypto exchanges is unsurprising given the demise of FTX, which lost £1bn in client money and resulted in its founder, Sam Bankman-Fried being extradited to the US where he was found guilty of 7 federal charges and faces up to 110 years in prison. The FCA also introduced regulation of the marketing of cryptocurrency in October 2023 meaning all materials must carry prominent warnings about the risk of losing money. The US has taken a similar stance to the UK, focusing its regulation on platforms that trade in crypto as opposed to the currencies themselves.

Advertising of cryptocurrency has been controversial. In 2021 the Advertising Standards Authority (ASA) banned an advertising campaign in London for the cryptocurrency exchange, Luno, that declared:

> "If you're seeing Bitcoin on the Underground, it's time to buy."[13]

The ban came into place a week after Bitcoin lost 30% of its value. Similarly, in 2021 the US the actor Matt Damon came under fire for his *"fortune favors the brave"* advert that saw him compare those willing to invest in crypto to pioneers such as the Wright brothers and astronauts when he said:

> "History is filled with almosts — those who almost adventured … who almost achieved … but ultimately, for them it proved to be too much. Then there are others: The ones who embrace the moment and commit. And in these moments of truth, these men and women, these mere mortals, just like you and me … as they peer over the edge, they calm their minds and steel their nerves with four simple words that have been whispered by the intrepid since the time of the Romans: "Fortune favors the brave"".[14]

The ad played to huge NFL audiences and attracted a great deal of negative press for encouraging ordinary people to invest in a volatile currency, that lost two-thirds of its value within months. Damon subsequently issued a statement apologising for his participation in the advert and promotion of cryptocurrency. This brings into sharp relief the risks that are associated with the inappropriate promotion of financial services. Throughout this book we emphasise the responsibilities placed on those engaged in the marketing of financial services to behave according to the highest ethical and moral standards.

Crypto is not currently widely accepted as a payment method by high street retailers. There are several travel and tech companies, such as Microsoft, that allow payment using cryptocurrency and there are also payment service providers such as BitPay who offer a digital wallet allowing customers to buy, store and spend crypto anywhere that Mastercard is accepted. Across banks, there are variances in how "crypto-friendly" they are, i.e. whether allow and place restrictions on interactions with crypto exchanges. In the UK, the challengers Revolut and Monzo take a positive stance, allowing deposits and withdrawals, and crypto debit card purchases. Of the traditional banks, Barclays allows deposits and withdrawals to certain exchanges on a case-by-case basis but doesn't allow crypto debit or credit card purchases. Lloyds, NatWest & Royal Bank of Scotland have a similar stance to Barclays, with varying daily limits on payments to crypto exchanges, however they do allow crypto debit card purchases. Santander, HSBC and The Co-Operative Bank amongst others, currently do not allow the direct transfer of funds to a crypto exchange. The inconsistency and hesitancy in how established banks are approaching cryptocurrencies speaks to the lack of widespread faith in its long-term viability, stability and trustworthiness. The house view of this publication is that cryptocurrency has not yet established itself as a viable financial services product that can be ethically mass marketed as a stable and credible investment to consumers.

2.11 Islamic financial services

In Chapter 2, the range of conventional financial services was discussed in some detail. Such products are widely available across many different markets worldwide and have been so for some time. In addition, over the last 30 years a new range of financial services have emerged structured around Islamic principles. Islamic financial services in themselves are not new but their widespread development owes much to the pioneering work of the central bank of Malaysia, Bank Negara. The core product for an Islamic financial service is the same as the core product for a conventional financial service. Murabaha and a mortgage will both fulfil the consumer's need to purchase an asset and pay for it in the future but operate in rather different ways. In particular since paying or receiving interest is against the teaching of Islam and thus *haram* (unlawful), financial institutions use alternative, non-interest-based approaches to providing Islamic financial services (see for example Mills and Presley, 1999). The following are examples of some of the main approaches to the provision Islamic financial services.

- **Murabaha**
  This is an alternative to conventional loans and is sometimes referred to as cost-plus financing. Under *Murabaha*, the bank purchases the goods which the customer requires from a third party. The bank then sells the goods to the customer for a pre-agreed (higher) price with deferred payments. Customers wishing to deposit money with a bank may make deposits into a Murabaha fund and then will share in the returns from such transactions. In Malaysia, Bay Bithamin Ajil (BBA) is the most common form of murabaha with payments being made in instalments sometime after the delivery of the specified goods. Arab Malaysian Banks' al-taslif Visa card is a product based on BBA financing while Bank Muamalat offers both house purchase and fixed-asset purchase on BBA principles. In the UK, the Islamic Bank of Britain provides unsecured personal lending based on Murabaha while Al Baraka Islamic Bank in Bahrain provides financing for commercial clients to purchase finished goods, raw materials, machines or equipment on the same basis.

- **Musharakah**
  This is a form of equity funding (partnership finance) in which both a business and a bank would invest in a particular venture. The profits would be shared between both parties and both parties would bear any losses. This is probably the purest form of Islamic financing with return being uncertain and both parties sharing the profit and the loss. Jordan Islamic Bank offers Musharakah-based financing to commercial clients as does Emirates Islamic Bank.

- **Mudarabah**
  This is a contract between provider of capital and an entrepreneur. The provider (referred to as the *rabb al-mal* or the sleeping partner), entrusts money to the entrepreneur (referred to as the *mudarib* or the working partner) in connection with an agreed project. When the project is complete the *mudarib* returns the principal and a pre-agreed share of the profit to the *rabb al-mal*. Any losses are borne by the *rabb al-mal*. The operation of mudarabah with the bank as the provider of capital is a basis for making loans. Where the depositor is the provider of capital and the bank is the entrepreneur, then mudarabah serves as a basis for taking deposits, as for example with Arab Malaysian Finance's GIA Quantum deposit service or Affin Bank's Tiny Tycoon Savings account.

- **Al-Ijara**
  This is a form of leasing finance. The bank will purchase the asset required by the customer and then leases the asset to that customer at a pre-arranged rate with the asset to be used productively and in ways that do not conflict with Shari'ah law. Emirates Islamic Bank is one of many banks that provides leasing for equipment, vehicles, etc., on the principles of Al-Ijara.

- **Qard Hasan**
  This is a beneficial (interest free) loan in which the borrower is obliged to repay the principal to the lender, but any additional payment is entirely optional. Qard Hasan loans are offered by most Islamic banks although are often restricted to particularly needy customers. Qard Hasan loans are usually funded through some bank capital and also through *zakat* donations.

- **Amanah and Al Wadi'ah**
  These approaches are both concerned with guaranteeing and securing a sum of money. In practical terms products based around Amanah (in trust) and Al Wadi'ah (safe keeping) are similar. They all guarantee the return of the principal (whether an individual takes

a loan or makes a deposit) but there is no additional payment. Affin Bank bases their current account on Al Wadi'ah while HSBC base their Mastercard on Amanah.

- **Al Kafalah**
  These are effectively documentary credits but with a non-interest based commission. Most commercial banks will offer these letters of credit for a variety of business activities.
- **Takaful**
  This is a form of Islamic insurance based on the Koranic principle of *Ta'awon* or mutual assistance. It provides mutual protection of assets and property and offers joint risk sharing in the event of a loss by one of its members. In Takaful the equivalent of insurance premiums (donations) are divided between two funds. A small part of the donation is paid to the mutual fund and this fund is used to make payouts should the insured event happen. The larger part of the donation is paid into an investment fund and the surpluses from the investment fund are subsequently equitably distributed between the participants and the insurer according to the principles of *al- mudarabah*. The size of individual donations is dependent upon both risk factors (such as health and lifestyle) and the desired compensation (amount payable on death).

It should be clear that these financial instruments can meet the same set of financial needs as conventional products. What makes these financial instruments distinct is the avoidance of interest payment and a reliance on an approach which is much closer to equity-based finance, such that both parties effectively share the risk element. For many Muslim customers, this approach to providing financial services is very attractive because it is consistent with religious beliefs (see for example Newaz, Fam and Sharmal, 2016). Increasingly, products provided on Islamic principles are also proving attractive to non-Muslim customers. In Malaysia, for example it was estimated that the penetration of Islamic retail banking sits around 40% (Thambiah, Ramanathan and Mazumder, 2012) with non-Muslims constituting a significant part of the customer base (Hume, 2004). A quick glance at the savings options offered by online platform, Raisin, will show a number of products that are offered using islamic principles but to a market dominated by non-muslims. At the same time, some customers are concerned about the apparent risk associated with many Islamic financial services. While these risks are very small in practice, their existence does mean that the marketing of Islamic financial services must emphasise safety and security and try to reduce consumers' perceptions of risk, particularly so if the bank or insurance company wishes to extend its target market beyond Muslim customers.

2.12 Summary and conclusions

This chapter has outlined the diverse range of organisations involved in the provision of financial services and introduced different types of products that these organisations offer. As such it provides the background against which the marketing of financial services takes place. Financial services are provided by many different organisations and, traditionally, specific organisations such as banks specialised in the provision of specific services (i.e. banking services). Increasingly, across the world these institutional boundaries have begun to break down and while organisations continue to be defined by their type (bank, insurance company), they increasingly offer a much broader range of financial services. Moreover, the advent of fintech is revolutionising some of the business models which have dominated a number of sectors of the financial services industry up until the present.

The products described as "financial services" are many and varied and while this chapter has only provided a brief introduction to how these products work, it should be apparent that they are designed to meet a range of very different financial needs and that many are highly complex. It is, perhaps, unsurprising then that many actual and prospective customers find such products difficult to understand. As will be explained further in the next chapter, the complexity of the product creates important marketing challenges.

Learning outcomes

Having completed this chapter, you should now be able to:

1. **Identify the different types of organisations engaged in the provision of financial services.**
   Proprietary, mutual, and cooperative forms of governance dominate ownership models. The principal FS industry sectors comprise: Banking, savings and loans, insurance, investment, credit, and liquidity. The marketplace is far more complex than it has been historically with large, diversified financial services groups spanning many of the above core product domains. A further feature of the geography of supply is the advent of new players to the marketplace.

2. **Understand the range and diversity of financial services and how they relate to customer needs.**
   Having examined the principal sectors that comprise the FS landscape, each customer need was discussed and the individual products aimed at satisfying those needs were presented. We also saw how a range of environmental factors are driving changes in the supply side such as the global reduction in physical branch outlets.

3. **Be aware of the complexity of the industry and the challenges this presents.**
   The varied core industry sectors, vast number of competitors, and wide array of products present FS consumers with many challenges when attempting to address their needs in an optimal manner.

4. **Begin to appreciate how fintech is changing business models, especially in banking.**
   New disruptive technologies are of far greater significance in terms of their potential to redefine markets based upon genuinely novel business models. The facilitator for this new category of product provider is the rapid advance seen in digital technology in recent years. The words financial and technology have been conflated to create what is now termed fintech. In its infancy, fintech was viewed as a discreet, additional layer to banking services, however, it is now accepted – if not expected – as a standard financial service offering. For the purposes of this text, the term fintech is used to define technologies used to support and enable consumer access to, and management of, their finances through digital means.

Review questions

1. In what ways has the business customer sector benefited from new forms of competition in the fields of banking and insurance?
2. What does asymmetry of knowledge mean and what are its consequences for FS consumers?
3. How has technological innovation impacted upon product supply and services delivery in your country?

4. What do you consider to be the characteristics of a responsible approach to lending and borrowing money? What options do citizens have in your country for finding help and advice when they get into debt that they feel they can no longer service properly?
5. What are the respective advantages and disadvantages of the mutual and shareholder forms of governance for being a successful affinity-based provider of financial services?

Notes

1   www.whartonfintech.org/blog-archive/2016/2/16/what-is-fintech (accessed January 2024)
2   www.statista.com/statistics/941342/europe-largest-online-banks/ (accessed January 2024)
3   www.worldbank.org/en/publication/globalfindex/brief/the-global-findex-database-2021-chapter-1-ownership-of-accounts (accessed January 2024)
4   Demirgüç-Kunt, Asli, Leora Klapper, Dorothe Singer, and Saniya Ansar. 2022. *The Global Findex Database 2021: Financial Inclusion, Digital Payments, and Resilience in the Age of COVID-19.* Washington, DC: World Bank. doi:10.1596/978-1-4648-1897-4. License: Creative Commons Attribution CC BY 3.0 IGO (accessed Janua12ry 2024)
5   https://bpfi.ie/sharp-decline-in-cheque-usage-with-45-falloff-since-2016-as-consumers-adopt-electronic-payments/ (accessed February 2024)
6   Mark Lusted, CEO MagiClick (accessed August 2023)
7   //themoneycharity.org.uk/media/April-2023-Money-Statistics.pdf (accessed September 2023)
8   Source: Experian www.experianplc.com/newsroom/press-releases/2021/india-s-consumer-credit-market-projected-to-grow-at-a-higher-rate-than-most-major-economies-worldwide-according-to-latest-experian-invest-india-credit-ecosystem-review-repor (accessed September 2023)
9   A. T. Kearney, Global Retail Development Index 2016. (accessed October 2017)
10   www.fool.co.uk/investing-basics/isas-and-investment-funds/index-trackers-vs-managed-funds/, (accessed February 2017)
11   www.cnbc.com/2021/01/11/crypto-investors-risk-losing-all-their-money-uks-fca-warns.html (accessed September 2023)
12   www.cnbc.com/2021/05/07/bank-of-englands-bailey-crypto-investors-risk-losing-all-their-money.html (accessed September 2023)
13   www.cnbc.com/2021/05/26/bitcoin-time-to-buy-ad-banned-by-the-uk-for-being-irresponsible.html (accessed September 2023)
14   https://youtu.be/QafuF1qH--M (accessed September 2023)

References

Brynner, A. J. and Despotidou, S. (2000). *Effect of Assets on Life Chances*. Centre for Longitudinal Studies, Institute of Education, London.

Devlin, J. F. (2003). Brand architecture in services: The example of retail financial services. *Journal of Marketing Management*, 19(9–10), pp. 1043–65.

Hume, J. (2004). Islamic finance: Provenance and prospects. *International Financial Law Review*, 23(5), pp. 48–50.

Mills, P. S. and Presley, J. R. (1999). *Islamic Finance: Theory and Practice*. Basingstoke: Palgrave Macmillan.

Newaz, F. T., Fam, K.-S. and Sharma, R. R. (2016). Muslim religiosity and purchase intention of different categories of Islamic financial products. *Journal of Financial Services Marketing*, 21(2). pp. 141–92.

Page-Adams, D. and Sherraden, M. (1996). What We Know About Effects of Asset Holding: Implications for Research of Asset-Based Anti-Poverty Initiatives. St. Louis, MO: Centre for Social Development. (No 96[1]).

Pilbeam, K. (2005). *Finance and Financial Markets*. Basingstoke: Palgrave Macmillan.

Thambiah, S., Ramanathan, S. and Mazumder, M.N H. (2012). The determinants of Islamic retail banking adoption in Malaysia. *International Business & Economics Research Journal,* 11(4), pp. 437–42.

Waite, N. (2001). Welfare and the Consumer Society: New Opportunities for the Third Way. The Canford Centre for Customer Development, on behalf of The Association of Friendly Societies.

3 Marketing financial services

An overview

Learning objectives

At the end of this chapter, you should be able to:

1. Identify the extent to which services in general and financial services in particular are different from goods,
2. Understand the implications of these differences for marketing practice,
3. Understand the way in which services can be classified and the position of different types of financial services within this classification.

3.1 Introduction

Marketing is an approach to business which focuses on improving organisational performance by satisfying customer needs. As such, it is naturally externally focused. But marketing cannot just focus on consumers; good marketers must also be aware of and understand the activities of their competitors. And to deliver what the customer wants and to do so more effectively than the competition requires an understanding of what the organisation itself is good at, the resources and capabilities it possesses and the way in which they can be deployed to satisfy customers. While in very general terms, marketing processes and activities are relevant to all organisations, we will also argue that there are some distinctive features of services in general and financial services in particular that can affect the way in which marketing principles are implemented. Put simply, the kind of advertising that works for Coca Cola is probably not right for Prudential and the selling strategy used for Ford cars would not work for a Baillie Gifford unit trust.

The purpose of this chapter is to outline how both services in general and financial services in particular may differ from physical goods and to explore the implications of these differences for the practice of marketing. The chapter begins by defining financial services; it then examines, from a marketing perspective, the differences between goods and services. The next section explains the distinctive characteristics of financial services and their marketing implications. As part of the discussion, a number of generic principles are identified which may be used to guide financial services marketing. The chapter concludes with an examination of service typologies and considers their relevance to financial services.

DOI: 10.4324/9781003398615-5

3.2 Defining financial services

As discussed in Chapter 2, financial services are concerned with individuals, organisations and their finances, that is to say, they are services which are directed specifically at people's (or organisation's) intangible assets (i.e. their money/wealth). The term is often used broadly to cover a whole range of banking services, insurance (both life and general), stock trading, asset management, credit cards, foreign exchange, trade finance, venture capital and so on.

These different services are designed to meet a range of disparate needs and take many varied forms. They usually require a formal (contractual) relationship between provider and consumer and they typically require a degree of customisation (quite limited in the case of a basic bank account but quite extensive in the case of venture capital).

The marketing issues that arise with such a variety of products are considerable.

- Some financial services may involve very short-term transactions (e.g. stock trading) while others are very long term (mortgages, pensions).
- Products vary in terms of complexity; a basic savings account for a personal consumer may appear to be a relatively simple product whereas the structuring of finance for a leveraged buy-out may be highly complex.
- Customers will vary both in terms of their needs and also their levels of understanding; corporate customers may have considerable expertise and knowledge in relation to the types of financial services they wish to purchase while many personal customers may find even the simplest products complex and sometimes confusing.

With so much variety and so many different types of financial service, it may appear to be difficult to make general statements about marketing financial services. Indeed, not all marketing challenges are relevant to all types of financial services and not all solutions will work in every situation. The art of marketing is to be able to understand the challenges that financial services present and to identify creative and sensible approaches which fit to the circumstances of any given organisation, a particular service and a specific customer type.

3.3 The differences between goods and services

Financial services are, first and foremost, services and have long been seen as different from physical goods. Like many things, services are often easy to identify but difficult to define. In one of the earliest marketing discussions of services, Rathmell (1966) makes a simple and rather memorable distinction between goods and services. He suggests that we should recognise that "a good" is a noun – while "service" is a verb – goods are things while services are acts.

However, perhaps the easiest definition to remember is that proposed by Gummesson:

> "Services are something that can be bought and sold but which you cannot drop on your foot." (Gummesson, 1987), p22.

Fundamentally, services are processes or experiences[1] – you cannot own a bank account, a holiday or a trip to the theatre in the same way as you may own a car, a computer or a bag of groceries. Of course, we can all talk about services in a possessive sense (my bank account, my holiday, or my theatre ticket), but we do not actually possess the services concerned; the bank account represents our right to have various financial transactions undertaken on our behalf by the account provider while the holiday ticket gives us the right to experience some mixture of transportation, accommodation and leisure activities. Thus, despite these apparent signs of ownership, financial services themselves are not possessions in any conventional sense.[2] The bank account details and the holiday ticket are, in effect, merely our "certificates of entitlement" to a particular experience or process.

Since the start of the current century, long-standing beliefs about the distinctive nature of services have been challenged. The "service-dominant logic" in marketing thought has argued that in most cases physical goods are simply there to provide a service and that the entertainment provided by a TV or the cleaning provided by washing powder is as much of a service as is using a bank account or going to the theatre (see for example Vargo and Lusch, 2004). Subsequently, the "service-dominant logic" has had a major impact on marketing thinking with the nature of value and the role of consumers in value creation becoming a major focus of research. Given the importance of being customer centric and delivering value to customers, this is a welcome development. The "service-dominant logic" challenges marketers to genuinely think differently – to recognise that marketing is about so much more than getting consumers to buy again or buy more. Bettencourt, Vargo and Lusch (2014) stress the importance of marketers thinking about marketing as being concerned with how the firm can help customers accomplish a particular goal or find solutions to a particular problem. Customers, they argue, acquire a product "to get a job done". Getting that job done requires resources from both consumer and supplier, it requires input from both and it creates value. Theirs is a very powerful argument that marketing is about engaging and working with consumers to provide them with value to enable them to "get the job done".

 Stop and think?

Think about the financial services that you have? How do they provide value – ie how do they help you to accomplish a particular goal? What contribution do you have to make to realise that value?

This argument in itself is something that few would disagree with. However, it does not automatically discount the case for treating goods and services as distinct. Although we can recognise the service element in many, if not all, physical goods, the ownership distinction remains and the process or experience element is much greater in the case of true services than it is in the case of services provided by physical goods. Accordingly, in line with many of the major texts on services marketing, this chapter will explore some of the major differences between services and physical goods and consider the marketing implications.[3]

It is the fact that services are predominantly experiences that leads to their most commonly identified characteristics:

•   ***Intangibility.*** Services lack physical form and cannot be seen or touched or displayed in advance of purchase. As a consequence, customers only become aware of the true nature of the service once they have made a decision to purchase.

- ***Inseparability.*** A service does not really exist until a customer wishes to consume that service. Financial advice only comes into existence when someone wants it. In effect, services are produced and consumed simultaneously, and often (but not always) in the presence of the consumer.
- ***Perishability***. Services cannot be inventoried. They come into existence when a customer uses them and typically cannot be stocked up for future use in the same way as physical goods can.
- ***Heterogenity***. The fact that customers service needs are different and that service consumption involves interaction between customers and producers also tends to lead to a much greater potential for variability in quality (*heterogeneity*) than would be the case with physical goods.

This approach to categorising the distinctive characteristics of services is sometimes referred to by the acronym IHIP:

Intangibility,
Heterogeneity,
Inseparability,
Perishability.

Although widely used in services marketing, it has attracted criticism in recent years. As well as the critiques associated with the "service-dominant logic", others, including Lovelock and Gummesson (2004), have argued that the framework has serious weaknesses. Intangibility, they argue, is ambiguous. Many services involve significant tangible elements and significant tangible outcomes. Heterogeneity (variability) is seen to be less effective at distinguishing goods from services because variability persists in many physical goods and is being reduced in many services as a consequence of greater standardisation in systems and processes. Inseparability, though important, is not thought to be able to differentiate goods from services as an increasing number of services can be produced remotely and thus can be seen as separable. Similarly, it is argued that some services are not perishable and some goods are. Thus, Lovelock and Gummesson suggest that the IHIP simply does not adequately distinguish between goods and services. They argue instead for a focus on ownership (or lack of it) and the idea that services involve different forms of rental (rental of physical goods, of place and space, of expertise, of facilities or of networks).

While recognising that the IHIP framework is open to criticism, it is probably the dominant paradigm in services marketing and provided that it is used sensibly, it remains a useful framework for understanding the differences between goods and services. Each of the IHIP characteristics will be explored in the following sections in relation to financial services but at this point it is important to emphasise that it could be misleading simply to view services and physical goods as complete opposites. While seeking to maintain a distinction between the two types of product, many services marketers recognise the existence of a goods-services continuum with highly intangible services (such as financial advice, education or consultancy services) at one extreme and highly tangible goods (such as coffee, sports shoes or kitchen utensils) at the other extreme.[4] Then, towards the centre of this continuum there are many goods which are similar to services (such as cars) and many services which are similar to goods (such as fast food). As Research insight 3.1 shows, this idea has been recognised for almost as long as we have acknowledged the existence of services marketing.

Research insight 3.1: G. Lynn Shostack – "Breaking free from product marketing"

Lynn Shostack's paper in the *Journal of Marketing* in 1977 is one of the formative articles in the development of services marketing. Shostack starts by noting the problems experienced by practising marketers who have switched from product to services marketing. Academic marketing appeared to have no readily available frameworks which could guide marketing practice in these environments. Shostack's response is to emphasise the importance of intangibility, not just as a modifier but as a fundamental characteristic of services – she notes that no amount of physical evidence (however provided) can make something as fundamentally intangible as entertainment or advice into something tangible. A service is an experience rather than a possession.

Of course, physical goods do provide a service but the distinction between the two is illustrated with the example of cars and airlines. Both provide a transport service but the former is fundamentally tangible but with an intangible dimension, while the latter is intangible but with tangible dimensions. The car provides transport but is also something that the customer can own – the airline also provides transport but without any ownership element.

Thus, Shostack argues that we should view goods and services as existing on a continuum from intangible dominant to tangible dominant. She supports this framework with a molecular model of products which comprises a core or nucleus and several external layers. The nucleus represents the core benefits provided to the consumer while the layers deal with the way in which the product is made available to the consumer including price, distribution and market positioning via marketing communications. The nucleus for air travel is predominantly intangible while that for the car is predominantly tangible.

Finally, Shostack considers the marketing implications of her analysis. She suggests that the abstract nature of services requires the marketing processes to emphasise concrete, non-abstract images or representations of the service to provide consumers with a tangible representation of the service which will make sense to them. By contrast, because consumers can see, picture and feel physical goods, such tangible images are far less important and marketing programmes can, therefore, concentrate much more on abstract ideas and images to attract consumers' attention.

Source: Shostack, G. L. (1977). Breaking free from product marketing. *Journal of Marketing*, 47(Summer), pp. 73–80.

3.4 The distinctive characteristics of financial service

The discussion above briefly outlined some of the areas in which services are different from physical goods and introduced some of the basic features of financial services. In this section we explore the characteristics of services in more depth and consider specifically their implications in the context of financial services. In what follows, intangibility is considered as the dominant service characteristic; intangibility then leads to inseparability and this in turn results in perishability and variability (heterogeneity). Finally, three further characteristics are introduced which relate specifically to financial services – fiduciary responsibility, duration of consumption and contingent consumption – and their marketing implications are discussed.

Progress check

- Financial services are services which are directed specifically at intangible assets (i.e. money/wealth).
- Fundamentally, services are processes or experiences – and cannot be owned in the same way as a physical product can be owned.
- It is common to think of differences between services and goods as being defined by intangibility, heterogeneity inseparability and perishability (IHIP).
- The service-dominant logic argues that everything is about service and even physical goods are providing value through service. This reminds us of the importance of ensuring that marketing focuses on delivering benefits/solutions to consumers, but despite this argument, the IHIP distinctions can continue to provide useful insights.

3.4.1 Intangibility

Since services are processes or experiences, intangibility is generally cited as the key feature which distinguishes services from goods. In practice, this means that services are impalpable – they lack a substantive physical form and so cannot be seen, touched, displayed, felt or tried in advance of purchase. A customer may purchase a particular service, such as a savings account, but typically has nothing physical to display as a result of the purchase. In some cases, services may also be characterised by what Bateson (1977) and others have described as mental intangibility – i.e. they are complex and difficult to understand and for many customers, they may not be of particular interest.

From the customer perspective, these characteristics have important implications. Physical intangibility (impalpability) and mental intangibility (complexity) mean that services are characterised by a predominance of experience and credence qualities, phrases used to describe attributes which can either only be evaluated once they have been experienced or even when experienced cannot be evaluated. Physical goods, by contrast, are characterised by a predominance of search qualities which are attributes that are rather more easily evaluated in advance of purchase.

Thus, the potential purchaser of a car may take a test drive, the buyer of a TV can examine the quality of the picture, and a clothes shopper can check fit and style before buying. In comparison, the service offered by a financial adviser can only really be evaluated once the advice has been experienced, leaving customers with the problem that they do not really know what they are going to get when they make the purchase decision. Even more difficult from the consumer's perspective is not being able to evaluate the quality of the service that has been purchased. The technical complexity of many services may hinder consumer evaluation of what has been received; a lack of specialist knowledge means that many consumers cannot evaluate the quality of the financial advice they have received and only the most dedicated investment enthusiast would really be able to determine whether a fund manager has made the best investment decisions in a particular market.

Of course, it is possible to argue that, ultimately, a consumer can evaluate financial advisers or investment managers based on the performance of a portfolio or a particular product. However, inadequacies in either service may take time to come to light and even when a particular outcome occurs – for example, the value of a portfolio of assets falls – how certain can the consumer be that this failure was genuinely due to poor advice or was in fact the product of unforeseeable market problems? In contrast, even with relatively complex products such as a smartphone or a TV, there are a number of immediately visible manifestations of the quality of the product (responsiveness and connectivity of a smartphone, the sound and picture quality of a TV) giving the consumer something tangible to evaluate and potentially a clearer idea of the relationship between cause and effect – a poor quality picture is most likely to represent a problem with the performance of the TV set.

Overall, the predominance of experience and credence qualities means that the financial services consumer is much less sure of what she or he is likely to receive and consequently rather more likely to experience a significant degree of perceived risk when making a purchase decision. Thus, financial services marketing must pay particular attention to ways in which the buying process can be facilitated. The following issues may be particularly important:

- Provide physical evidence or some physical representation of the product. Physical evidence may take the form of items directly associated with a service (e.g. the policy documentation that accompanies an insurance policy) or the environment in which the service is delivered (e.g. the rather grand premises in prime locations occupied by banks). An alternative (or even a complement) to actual physical evidence is to create a tangible image or even to offer physical gifts to prospective consumers when they purchase a financial service. For example, Kansas-based Equity Bank experienced an increased take-up of its digital account when it offered a smart, hi-tech toaster as a physical gift to accompany account opening[5].
- Place particular emphasis on the benefits of the service (as the service-dominant logic would remind us). Barclays Bank has used the strapline "Making money work for you", to reinforce the point that they are trying to focus on meeting customer needs. Marketers must recognise that customers do not want a mortgage as such but they do want to own a house; they do not want a savings account but they do want to be able to pay for their child's education. Thus, for example, the Malaysian bank Maybank promoted its insurance products by offering customers options including "I want to protect my car" and "I want to save for my child's education". In New Zealand, InsuranceBASE promoted a range of insurance products with the headline "Protect you Family. Keep those close to you safe, no matter your situation". One United Kingdom (UK) based company goes so far as to trade under the name "Protectyourfamily".
- Reduce perceived risk and make consumers feel less worried about the outcome of their purchase, perhaps by encouraging other customers to act as advocates for the service or by seeking appropriate endorsements from 3rd parties. The investment fund "Fundsmith Equity" emphasises that it is "Morningstar Gold rated", so you can invest with confidence". Wealth managers, Northern Trust emphasise their 2022 awards of "Custodian of the Year" in the European Pension Awards and "Best Private Bank in the US" from the Financial Times Group. Some financial services providers even go so far as to offer service guarantees. In the US, First Reliance Bank offers a very detailed guarantee as outlined in Table 3.1.

Table 3.1 First Reliance Bank's service guarantee

Service Guarantee	Mortgage Guarantee
• You will be immediately greeted with a smile and warm welcome. • You will be greeted and waited on in less than 5 minutes. • We will complete your transaction correctly the first time. • Your phone call will be returned within 24 hours. • Your service issue will be resolved within 24 hours. Or, we will pay you $5! No Strings Attached!	• Give you a decision before the end of the next business day. • Return all calls the same day and contact you at least once a week until the closing. • If you ask, we will be happy to accompany you to your closing. • We will meet our closing date.

Source: www.firstreliance.com/personal/better-banking/service-guarantees/ (accessed 10/01/2024)

•   Build trust and confidence to reassure consumers that what they receive will be of the appropriate quality. Many financial services organisations make particular efforts to emphasise their longevity – the fact that they have been in business for, in some cases, hundreds of years serves as a mechanism for signalling their reliability and trustworthiness. In the US, Bank of America's private banking arm emphasises its longevity as a means of building confidence – "For more than 150 years, The Private Bank has been the advisor of choice for the affluent". Similarly, the DeutscheBank reassures customers and a broader group of stakeholders by emphasising its long history and global reach (see Figure 3.1). The Bank's historical archive and its commitment to

Figure 3.1 Deutsche Bank uses archive photographs to emphasise its longevity and solidity

Source: Reproduced with permission from Deutsche Bank AG Historical Institute

understanding and explaining its history is a powerful reminder of the bank's stability, durability and reliability.

 Stop and think?

Would the offer of a free gift influence your decision to purchase a financial service? What sort of gifts would work and what sort wouldn't? Do you think guarantees make a difference?

3.4.2 Inseparability

The nature of services as a process or an experience means that services are inseparable – they are produced and consumed simultaneously. A service can only be provided if there is a customer willing to purchase and experience it. Thus, for example, financial advice can only be provided once a specific request has been made; until that request is made, the advice does not exist – there is only the potential for that advice embodied in the mind of the adviser. The provision of a service will typically also require the involvement of the consumer to a greater degree than would be the case with physical goods. As few services are totally standardised, the minimum input from the consumer would be information on needs and wants. For example, an investment adviser would, as a minimum, need to know an individual's attitude to risk and whether they wanted to invest for capital growth or income, before advice could be given.

In many instances, the input from the customer will need to be more extensive and the customer will have a significant role to play in value creation. Because the customer actively engages and interacts with the provider, services are often described as interactive processes. While this interaction has traditionally been face-to-face, developments in information and communications technology mean that an increasing amount of interaction is taking place remotely. This is a process which has been accelerating as more and more banks are able to offer mobile banking via smartphone applications as well as via computers, as Figure 3.2 shows.

As a consequence of the interactive nature of services, the way in which the service is performed may be as significant to customers as the service itself. Where service is delivered face to face, front line staff may be of particular importance in this process. As the group with whom the customer typically has greatest involvement, they can and do play a decisive role in customer evaluations of the service experience.

From a marketing perspective, inseparability then presents some interesting challenges. Given the interactive and inseparable nature of service provision, the following issues may be of particular significance:

*   Ensuring that the processes for service delivery are clearly specified and customer oriented – in effect the service should be designed to suit the customer rather than to suit the organisation. For example, many banks might find it preferable to have product specialists – i.e. staff who focus attention only on specific products, but a customer with multiple services from a particular company will much prefer to deal with a single

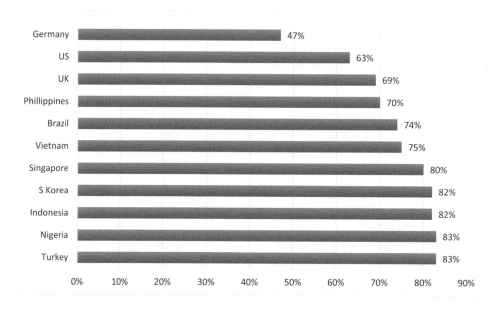

Figure 3.2 Respondents using mobile banking (%)

Source: statista.com[6]

individual. Westpac Banking Corporation in New Zealand stresses to its business customers that it offers "One number for all your banking needs". Similarly, banks worldwide commonly promote their premier banking services by offering the services of a "dedicated" or "single" relationship manager.

• Ensuring that all staff involved in service provision appreciate the importance of a customer-oriented approach and are empowered to be responsive and flexible in customer interactions. Handelsbanken, Sweden's second largest bank, prides itself on a policy of devolving responsibility to individual branches. It claims that over 95% of credit decisions are made locally with only very small numbers being referred to the head office, which largely operates to support the branches rather than control them.

• Identifying methods of facilitating customer involvement is a way which will enhance the quality of the service provided. This may be as simple as making clear exactly what information is required from the customer or may extend to outlining and explaining the responsibilities of the customer. Most financial services providers have terms of use which outline customer responsibilities, although often these are presented in the style of legal documents which may limit the extent to which customers really understand their responsibilities.

3.4.3 Perishability

The fact that services are typically produced and consumed simultaneously also means that they are perishable. Services can usually only be produced when consumers wish to buy them and when there is little or no demand service providers cannot take advantage of the quiet period and "manufacture" surplus services for sale when demand is high. Thus, services are perishable and cannot be inventoried. If an investment adviser's time is not taken up on one particular day, it cannot be saved to provide extra capacity the next day. If the counter staff in a bank have a quiet period with no customers, they cannot "save" that time to use when queues build up.

This characteristic of perishability presents marketing with the task of managing demand and supply in order to make best use of available capacity. Issues that require particular consideration include:

- Are there identifiable peaks and troughs in demand for a particular financial service? Bank branches, for example, may be particularly busy during lunch breaks, while tax advisors may experience a peak in the demand for their services as the end of a tax year approaches.
- Are there mechanisms for reducing demand at peak times and increasing it at off-peak times? Tax advisors, for example, might consider offering discounted fees for customers who use their services well in advance of tax deadlines.
- Is there the opportunity to adjust capacity such that variability in demand can be accommodated (either through changing work patterns or some degree of mechanisation)? Traditionally, many providers would employ part-time staff to boost capacity during periods of heavy customer demands and of course ATMs and mobile/online banking provide many standard banking services quickly as an alternative to queuing for face-to-face service. There are also a growing number of providers who use remote conferencing facilities to make best use of available advisor capacity. One of the earliest examples of this approach came from Spain, where Bankinter used specialist advisor capacity at one branch to provide advice to customers at another branch by using a video link (Economist, 2012a).

However, beyond the very basic transactions, financial services had generally found mechanisation to be challenging – not least because customer circumstances, needs and knowledge are so highly variable. Thus, it is probably not surprising that providers have been heavily dependent on people for the delivery of customer service. But customer expectations about the speed and availability of service have created a major challenge. The development of 24/7 call centres, the growth in outsourcing (and specifically offshoring) were all strategies to reduce the costs of providing customer service whenever it was needed. But even the call centre model is proving costly and waiting times are too long for many customers. Developments in artificial intelligence are creating new models to address the need for cost effective, 24/7 tailored customer service. Research by Personetics, a leading fintech company has highlighted the growth of the use of chatbots to enhance the provision of service and the customer experience in financial services. The increase in bank closures has has necessitated alternative ways to assist with the increased demand for online servicing which chatbots can help fulfil. Covid-19 also accelerated the adoption of chatbots to cope with the increase in telephone and online traffic when people couldn't bank in person. Marketing in practice 3.1 provides further insight into these developments.

Marketing in practice 3.1: chatbot banking

By implementing a chatbot, banking providers can interact with their customers across a range of digital platforms and provide real-time service and advice. The fact that the chatbot is a technology-based solution that uses conversation rather than menu-based interfaces makes it more convenient and accessible for a range of customers. The chatbot market has grown considerably in recent years; its market across financial services was valued at USD $890M in 2022 and is projected to reach around $6B in 2030.

Chatbots provide an always-on service and respond to queries immediately, useful in both customer facing functions and for internal operations such as employee knowledge bases. As well as customer and client servicing, they're extensively used for across FS activities such as processing applications, identity verification, transactions, cross-selling, fraud-detection, and personalised financial advice. As technology evolves, generative AI is extending the capabilities of chatbots, to provide ever more human-like interactions (discussed more in Chapter 10). Cornerstone Advisors reported in 2023 that ratings of mobile banking scored higher with a chatbot; 8.51 out of 10, compared with 7.96 out of 10 without chatbot assistance.

It's now commonplace for banks to offer chatbots across websites and mobile apps. HSBC's chatbot "Amy" offers 24/7, instant answers on banking products and services in English, Traditional and Simplified Chinese on its websites. Nordic bank Nordea promotes a "chat-first" approach, utilizing its chatbots as the first-line response to resolve customer queries, reporting a 91% resolution rate for private bank customers. In the UK RBS's "Cora" chatbot is available across website and app to assist with over 150 banking queries from making payments to questions about mortgages. "Ceba" chatbot for Commonwealth Bank in Australia is unusual in that it also offers human escalation where necessary. US insurer Lemonade, used its chatbot, AI Jim, in its groundbreaking 3 second claim settlement process.

In their global survey, Personetics reported that 46% of respondents are either already using bots (15%) or have an active project in place (31%). Only 13% of financial institutions surveyed said they had no plans to develop chatbots. Globally, 80% of financial institutions see chatbots as an opportunity and anticipate being able to use them to deal with significant volumes of customer service enquires. But it's not just about volume, there is also a clear expectation that chatbots have the potential to improve customer service and enhance a bank's engagement with the "millennials" segment of the market.

Sources:www.nextmsc.com/report/chatbot-market-in-bfsi (accessed 15/01/2024)www.crnrstone.com/whats-going-on-in-banking-2023 (accessed 15/01/2024)www.fintechfutures.com/2022/11/nordea-partners-boost-ai-for-chat-first-virtual-agent-drive/ (accessed 15/01/2024)www.rbs.co.uk/support-centre/cora.html (accessed 15/01/2024)www.lemonade.com/blog/lemonade-sets-new-world-record (accessed 15/01/2024)

Chatbots have developed rapidly over the past decade and yet opinions remain divided. For many, chatbots have the potential to make finance more accessible, efficient and customer centric and to transform the way in which consumers interact with financial services providers. Proponents of AI and its application via chatbots argue that as they become increasingly able to offer human-like and deeply personalised support, they are setting a new standard for how customers expect to be serviced. But evaluations of AI and chatbots are not universally positive. Chatbots have made it easier to shift away from traditional branch banking by providing an alternative to the human interactions many customers value. And while the greater convenience and the cost effectiveness works for many customers, those who are less comfortable with digital technologies may find them exclusionary.

 Stop and think?

What has your experience been of engaging with chatbots. Are you confident that they will give you sensible responses. Why might some customers be resistant to the use of such facilities?

3.4.4 Heterogeneity

The inseparability of production and consumption leads to a fourth distinctive characteristic of services – variability or heterogeneity. Service variability can be interpreted in two ways as Figure 3.3 shows.

The first type of variability is easily understandable as a response to differences in customer needs. The obvious implications for marketing are:

- Service processes need to be flexible enough to adapt to different needs and the more customer needs vary and the higher their expectations, the greater the need for flexibility.

Services required by customers are not standardised

- Different customers will want and will experience a different service. This source of variability essentially arises from the fact that customers are different and have different needs. To varying degrees, services will be tailored to those needs, whether in very simple terms – such as the amount a consumer chooses to invest in a savings plan – or in very complex ways such as the advice provided by accountants, consultants and bankers to a firm undertaking a major acquisition.

Services experienced vary from customer to customer

- Customers with similar needs may have different service experiences and the same customer may have different experiences at different times. In effect, this type of variability arises not because of changing customer needs; it is primarily a consequence of the nature of an interaction between customer and service provider but may be influenced by events outside the control of the service provider.

Figure 3.3 Service heterogeneity

Thus, for example, business banking for small and medium-sized enterprises will need to accommodate the needs of the long-established small, local shop and the fast-growing biotechnology company which primarily sells in international markets. Equally, brokers may need to be able to adapt their service to the person who buys and sells stock infrequently on a small scale and the enthusiast who tracks the market and trades frequently and/or in volume.

• Empowering staff to respond to different needs and situations becomes increasingly important, so that processes can be adapted as and when necessary. Typically, this would imply decentralising service systems and delegating authority such that non-contentious modifications to a service could be dealt with by customer contact staff. Thus, for example, a bank may delegate a range of lending powers to account managers such that every requested change in the normal terms of a loan to a small business does not always require head office approval.

The second form of variability provides more problems as it effectively represents fluctuations in the level of quality that the consumer receives rather than variations in the type of service they require. Essentially, this form of heterogeneity arises as a consequence of inseparability and the importance of personal interaction but may also be influenced by external events. Customers are different and so are service providers; customer contact staff are people rather than machines and will experience the same range of moods and emotions as everyone else (although with the development of chatbots, this is changing). Differences arise between individuals (from one employee to another) and within individuals (from one day to another). The service provided by an account manager who is feeling happy, relaxed and positive at the start of a new week will almost certainly be better than that provided by the same account manager at the end of a long day, suffering from a headache and feeling undervalued.

From the consumer side, quality variability within and between service experiences may also arise if customers are not able to clearly articulate their needs. The greater the willingness of the customer to supply appropriate information about their needs and circumstances, the more likely it is that they will receive the quality they expect. The customer who is able to clearly explain their risk preferences, the purpose of their investment and the characteristics of the rest of their portfolio is likely to get better advice than the customer who simply requests advice on an investment that will give a "decent return".

In addition to the impact of personal factors, we must also recognise that there are many factors which are outside the control of a service provider but which may have a significant effect on the service experience and the quality of the service product. The performance of an investment fund, for example, may be influenced by broad macroeconomic forces which fund managers cannot change. The global financial crisis of 2007–8 had a significant negative impact on the performance of many personal pensions and equity-based investment products with falling property prices, falling bond yields and falling stock markets, eroding the value of investments held by many individuals. While poor product performance on this occasion was largely outside the control of individual providers, many would argue that the industry as a whole bore some responsibility for the outcomes. The Covid-19 pandemic also saw some major disruptions in financial markets; the value of equity investments fell dramatically and low interest rates to stimulate the economy had negative consequences for many savers. Many financial products underperformed, but this reflected broader economic conditions beyond the control of individual providers.

Thus, both personal interactions and uncontrollable external factors can result in consumers feeling that they have experienced considerable variability in the service and in some case, an unsatisfactory experience. To address this aspect of variability, service marketers may need to pay particular attention to the following:

- Concentrate on motivating and rewarding staff for the provision of good service and encouraging consistency in approach. Internal marketing campaigns to emphasise the importance of good customer service may be one aspect of this – equally important may be the way in which staff are treated and rewarded. A reward mechanism based simply on the number of calls taken by a customer service agent for a telephone banking service may create an incentive for the service agent to close calls as quickly as possible (to maximise throughput) rather than properly addressing the customers' needs (which would take longer and mean a lower call throughput).
- Identify ways of trying to persuade customers to articulate their needs as clearly as possible, whether by identifying scripts for use by the service provider or through marketing communications which specifically ask customers to share information. The growth in online provision of services and online quotations (particularly through comparison websites, such as moneysupermarket.com or confused.com in the UK) has helped this process by structuring and clarifying the types of information that customers need to provide, at least for some of the more straightforward financial services such as insurance quotes and standard loans.
- If a service is relatively simple from the consumer perspective, consider mechanisation to limit quality variability. ATMs, chatbots and online/mobile banking are all able to offer a more consistent quality to customers. Even for relatively complex products such as collective investments there are a growing number of online platforms which provide a standardised service for purchase, sale and portfolio monitoring.
- Think carefully about how a service is presented to customers; be explicit about the factors which can affect the performance of a product. Most equity-based products do highlight to customers that the value of investments can go down as well as up, but often such warnings are presented in small print and it is debatable whether customers read or understand these warnings. It is common to see companies relying on past performance figures as a way of signalling the quality of their product despite the fact that these are largely unreliable as indicators of future performance. Furthermore, research has suggested that the way in which such past performance information is presented may have a significant impact on risk perceptions and consumer choice (Diacon and Hasseldine, 2007).

3.4.5 Fiduciary responsibility

Fiduciary responsibility refers to the implicit responsibility which financial services providers have in relation to the management of funds and the financial advice they supply to their customers. Although any business has a responsibility to its consumers in terms of the quality, reliability and safety of the products it supplies, this responsibility is perhaps much greater in the case of a financial service provider. There are probably two explanations for this:

- First, many consumers find financial services difficult to comprehend. Understanding financial services requires a degree of numeracy, conceptual thinking and, perhaps most importantly, interest. Many consumers are either not able or not willing to try to understand financial services. Instead they rely on a professional – whether a bank, an investment company, an insurer or a financial adviser to provide them with appropriate financial services. Others may depend upon the advice they receive from members of their reference group such as family members, friends and work colleagues.

- Second, the "raw materials" used to produce many financial products are consumers' funds; thus, in producing and selling a loan product, the bank has a responsibility to the person taking out a loan but at the same time, it also has a responsibility to the individuals whose deposits have made that loan possible. This particular issue was highly visible during the global financial crisis when customers of some banks lost their savings as a consequence of defaults on the loans that those banks had made. Similarly, insurance is based on pooling risk across policyholders. When taking risks (selling insurance) and paying against claims, an insurer has a responsibility to both the individual concerned and to all other policyholders. Paying claims that are not justified will ultimately increase the insurers' costs and thus increase the premiums paid by other customers.

Thus, rather than just having to consider responsibility to the purchaser, many financial services organisations must also be aware of their responsibility to their suppliers and indeed, it is conceivable that the needs of suppliers may take precedence over the demands of a customer. For example, because of its responsibilities to its existing car insurance customers, an insurer may feel that it cannot respond to demand from customers considered to be high risk. Similarly, a bank may decide not to offer credit to a borrower if it is concerned that the outcome may be an increase in the customer's indebtedness. Indeed, a failure to fully appreciate this responsibility has led to heavy criticism of credit card companies in the UK for providing credit cards to individuals with little prospect of repaying their debt. And there has been similar criticism of banks and other lenders for the reckless mortgage lending to sub-prime customers which resulted in large losses for many buyers of mortgage-backed securities and ultimately precipitated the global financial crisis. The growth of payday lending (short term, high interest loans) and buy now, pay later (BNPL) purchasing options has raised concerns that these arrangements may make it easier for vulnerable customers to accumulate debt.

From a marketing perspective, this presents the rather unusual problem of customers wishing to purchase a particular product (e.g. loan, insurance, credit card, etc.) and the organisation turning them away and refusing to supply that product because the customer is considered too risky.

To recognise the issue of fiduciary responsibility, it is important to:

- Think carefully about the process of segmentation, targeting and positioning to ensure that products are not targeted at customers who are unlikely to be eligible. Careful market targeting can help prospective customers judge whether the product is appropriate for them. If segmentation is more complex, then targeting the right group can be more challenging. However, if market segmentation is clear, this can be a relatively straightforward process – for example, motor insurer "Sheilas' Wheels" emphasises that it is an insurance company targeting female drivers as illustrated by the statement on its web site (relying on the use – typically in Australian English – of Sheila as a generic name for women):

We keep our Sheilas happy by supplying fabulous 5 Star Defaqto rated car and home insurance, and that's helped us to become one of the UK's leading direct insurers. Our call centres are full of friendly staff that go the extra mile to provide great customer service, whatever your query may be." (www.sheilaswheels.com/)

• Ensure that staff involved in selling financial services are clearly aware of their responsibilities not to sell products that are inappropriate to the customers' needs. Probably one of the most damaging experiences for the financial services sector in the UK was the extensive mis-selling of personal pensions to people who could not afford them or did not need them. When the scandal came to light, it cost the industry billions of pounds in compensation and probably more in loss of reputation. And yet in spite of this experience, mis-selling continued, most recently in relation to payment protection insurance, suggesting that the industry had failed to fully appreciate this important point.

3.4.6 Contingent consumption

It is in the nature of many financial services products that money spent on them does not yield a direct consumption benefit. In some cases, it may create consumption opportunities in the future; in other cases it may never result in tangible consumption for the individual who made the purchase. Saving money from current income reduces present consumption by the same amount and for many people present consumption is far more enjoyable than saving. For some individuals, the level of contributions required to build up a reasonable pension fund at retirement requires just too much foregone pleasurable consumption to provide the necessary motivation.

In the case of general insurance, most customers would not wish to consume many aspects of the service – they would hope never to have to make a claim against a given policy. Similarly, in the case of life insurance, the consumer will never be the recipient of the financial benefits of the contract given that their payment will only occur upon her or his death. Of course in both cases, the consumer buys more than just the ability to make a claim against the insured event; they buy peace of mind and protection. However, these latter two benefits are particularly intangible and consumers may still be left questioning the benefits that they receive compared to the prices they pay. Indeed some authors go as far as to suggest that not all customers fully understand insurance and view it more as investment than protection (Kunreuther, Pauly and McMorrow, 2013).

Such contingent consumption presents major challenges to marketing executives as they seek to market an intangible product that reduces current consumption of consumer goods and services for benefits that they may never experience. To address the issue of contingent consumption, the following may be helpful:

• The benefits associated with the product must be clearly communicated and in as tangible a form as possible. Marketing strategies for long-term savings plans (including pensions) might seek to demonstrate the significant benefits and pleasure associated with future consumption while also demonstrating that losses in current consumption are minimal. Similarly, insurance providers seek to convince policyholders that they receive the benefit of peace-of-mind from having been prudent enough to safeguard the financial well-being of their dependents or their assets.
• Consider issues relating to product design which might increase the attractiveness of products designed for the longer term. For example, some flexibility in payments, the ability to temporarily suspend payments or even the ability to make short-term withdrawals may help to reduce consumer concerns about their ability to save on a regular basis.

3.4.7 Duration of consumption

The majority of financial services are (or have the potential to be) long term – either because they entail a continuing relationship with a customer (current accounts, mortgages, credit cards) or because there is a time lag before the benefits are realised (long-term savings and investments). In almost all cases, this relationship is contractual which provides the organisation with information about those customers and can create the opportunity to build bonds with customers that will discourage switching between providers. The long-term relationship between customer and provider creates considerable potential for cross-selling, reinforced by the amount of information that providers have about their customers. However, for such a relationship to be beneficial and for cross-selling opportunities to work, the organisation has to work at the relationship; simply ignoring customers for several years and then expecting them to make further purchases is unlikely to be effective.

From a marketing perspective this suggests that the following areas will require particular attention:

- Manage relationships carefully. If the product is long term, then regular contact between organisation and customer can help maintain a positive relationship. If the product is one that is continuous (e.g. a mortgage), regular communication is probably an integral feature of the product but should still be managed carefully to ensure that forms of customer contact are appropriate. In both cases, there may be opportunities for cross-selling, but bombarding customers with lots of different products may be far less effective than carefully targeting a smaller number of offers.
- Be prepared to reward loyalty, where appropriate. Valued customers that the organisation wishes to retain should be treated as such. One of the great frustrations experienced by loyal customers is the policy of some financial services providers to offer more favourable terms to new customers than they offer to existing customers.
- Respect customer privacy and ensure that data that is collected relating to customers is managed appropriately.

Progress check

- In addition to intangibility, heterogeneity, inseparability, and perishability, financial services marketers also need to take into consideration the impact of fiduciary responsibility, contingent consumption and duration of time over which many financial services are consumed.
- These characteristics give rise to a range of marketing challenges and force marketers to think carefully about how they develop their marketing campaigns.
- Key considerations include thinking about how to make the service and the benefits offered clear and tangible: building trust and confidence and reducing perceived risks: ensuring customers and staff understand their roles and responsibilities: giving consideration to options to automate service: managing capacity and careful and responsible targeting of customers.

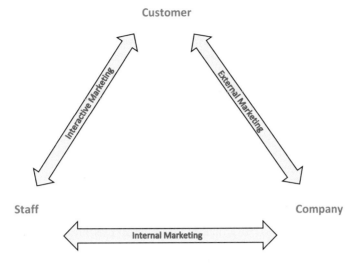

Figure 3.4 The services marketing triangle

Source: Adapted from Kotler, (1994)

3.5 The marketing challenge

In the discussion above, we have identified a range of marketing challenges which confront services marketers. Perhaps one of the most commonly recurring themes in this discussion has been the importance of people and the ways in which the service delivery process is managed. In contrast with a discussion of physical goods, we have placed much less emphasis on the conventional forms of marketing which involve communications (in their broadest sense) from the organisation to the customer. That is not to imply that the more traditional forms of marketing are not relevant; they most certainly are, but there are other dimensions of marketing which are equally important to services marketing. These are neatly summed up by Philip Kotler in his services marketing triangle shown in Figure 3.4.[7] Service marketing requires external marketing (from the organisation to the customer) to present the nature and attributes of the service offer. It also requires internal marketing to ensure that staff are motivated and have the information to deliver the service offered. And of course, interactive marketing between customer and employee takes place during every service interaction; in many respects any service organisation employee who comes into contact with a customer will find himself or herself in a marketing role. The intrinsic quality of the core service is important but so is the way in which a service is delivered, and the nature of the service interaction may have a significant impact on the customer's evaluation of the overall experience.

3.6 Classifying services

From the discussion so far, it should be clear that there are a number of important differences between physical goods and services. But, as was emphasised earlier, these differences appear to exist, not so much as absolute differences but as points on a continuum. Even in that part of the continuum which we would classify as services, there is considerable variety among different types of services. In so far as we have argued that many marketing activities are context specific, it would be misleading not to discuss some aspects of these variations. After all, services with different sets of characteristics will present different types of marketing problems.

Recognising this issue has encouraged many service marketers to search for systematic approaches to classification in order to provide further guidance on the conduct of marketing. Indeed, this process dates back to the early days of services marketing. The resulting classification schemes are many and varied and make distinctions such as

- Professional versus other services.
- Individual versus organisational customers.
- People-based versus equipment-based services.
- High or low customer contact services.
- Public sector or private sector/profit vs. nonprofit.

Probably one of the most comprehensive attempts to categorise and classify services was provided by Lovelock (1983). He produced five different classification schemes:

- The nature of the service act (whether it involves tangible or intangible actions) and the recipient of the service (people versus things).
- The nature of the relationship with the service provider (formal or informal) and whether the service is delivered continuously or on a discrete basis.
- The degree of standardisation or customisation in the core service and the extent to which staff exercise personal judgement in service delivery.
- The capacity to meet demand (with or without difficulty) and the degree to which demand fluctuates.
- The number of outlets and the nature of the interaction between customer and service provider.

The difficulty with Lovelock's initial framework is that it results in five different systems for classification and it may not always be clear which is the best to use for any given situation. More recently, Lovelock and Yip (1996) produced a much simpler classification which is outlined in Figure 3.5.

Financial services are essentially directed towards individuals' assets and so in that sense they may be partly possession-processing services; some financial services may also be directed to people (tax advice, financial advice). Most financial services have the potential to be considered as information based in the sense that they can effectively be represented as information and delivered remotely. For example, an individual can withdraw money from a bank account in Germany using an ATM in Australia because information can be conveyed to the Australian bank that there are sufficient funds available to allow the cash withdrawal to be made via the Australian bank's system which is then credited with the appropriate sum by the German bank. As we shall see in Chapter 8, the idea that many financial services are essentially information-processing services can have important implications for the ways in which services business internationalise.

3.7 Summary and conclusion

Any product, whether it is a physical good, a service or some combination of the two, exists to provide some mix of functional and psychological benefits to

People processing	Possession processing	Information processing
•These are services directed towards people (e.g. healthcare, fitness, transport) and typically require the consumer to be physically present in order for the service to be consumed.	•These are services (such as equipment repair and maintenance, warehousing, dry cleaning) which focus attention on adding value to people's possessions. These require the service provider to be able to access those possessions but there is often rather less reliance on the consumers' physical presence for the full service to be delivered.	•These are services which are concerned with creating value through gathering, managing and transmitting information. Obvious examples include the media industry, telecommunications, consulting and most financial services. Although inseparability may be important in some applications (e.g. consultancy, financial services), there is much great potential for remote delivery because there is a reduced dependence on physical interactions.

Figure 3.5 Categorising services

consumers. Through providing benefits to consumers and delivering long-term satisfaction, such products should enable organisations to achieve their stated goals. In that sense, services and physical goods have much in common. They also display some very important differences and those differences have significant marketing implications. Services are processes, deeds or acts; they are not something that the consumer possesses, rather they are something that the consumer experiences. In essence, services are intangible – they lack any physical form. As a consequence they are also inseparable, being produced and consumed simultaneously, with the customer involved in the production or delivery of the service. Inseparability in turn leads to perishability and quality variability.

Arising from these characteristics, services marketing must pay particular attention to tangibilising the services and reducing consumer perceived risk. Furthermore, the process of service delivery also attracts marketing attention because the involvement of the consumer in the process suggests that the nature of delivery may have a significant impact on consumer evaluations of the service. Finally, within that process, the "people" element may be of considerable significance because it is typically the service provider's staff with whom the customer interacts. The rather different elements of marketing in a service business are neatly summed up by Philip Kotler who stresses a need for not only external marketing but also internal marketing and interactive marketing.

Inevitably, not all services are the same and the degrees of intangibility, inseparability, perishability and heterogeneity will vary considerably. In fact, most service marketers would probably recognise goods and services as existing along a continuum rather than as polar extremes. Many attempts have been made to classify services according to the characteristics they possess and their marketing implications. While such schemes are necessarily crude, they do provide useful insights into both current marketing challenges and areas for new service development.

Learning outcomes

Having completed this chapter you should now be able to:

1. **Understand how services in general and financial services in particular are different from goods.**
    Services are processes, deeds or acts; they are not something that the consumer possesses, rather they are something that the consumer experiences. In essence, services are intangible – they lack any physical form. As a consequence they are also inseparable, being produced and consumed simultaneously, with the customer involved in the production or delivery of the service. Inseparability in turn leads to perishability and quality variability.
2. **Explain how these differences have implications for marketing practice.**
    Services marketing must pay particular attention to tangibilising the services and reducing consumer perceived risk. Furthermore, the process of service delivery also attracts marketing attention because the involvement of the consumer in the process suggests that the nature of delivery may have a significant impact on consumer evaluations of the service. Finally, within that process, the "people" element may be of considerable significance because it is typically the service provider's staff with whom the customer interacts. The rather different elements of marketing in a service business are neatly summed up by Philip Kotler who stresses a need for not only external marketing but also internal marketing and interactive marketing.
3. **Understand how services can be classified in different ways and different types of financial services can be positioned differently within this classification.**
    Inevitably, not all services are the same and the degrees of intangibility, inseparability, perishability and heterogeneity will vary considerably. In fact, most service marketers would probably recognise goods and services as existing along a continuum rather than as polar extremes. Many attempts have been made to classify services according to the characteristics they possess and their marketing implications. While such schemes are necessarily crude, they do provide useful insights into both current marketing challenges and areas for new service development.

Review questions

1. Choose a financial services provider and look at examples of how it markets its services. How does this provider seek to address the issues of intangibility, inseparability, perishability and heterogeneity?
2. What are the differences between external marketing, internal marketing and interactive marketing?
3. Look at the way in which three insurance companies market life insurance products. How effective are these insurers in conveying the benefits of risk reduction and peace of mind?
4. Look at the way in which three pension providers market personal pensions. How effectively do these marketing campaigns deal with the fact that pensions are long-term products characterised by considerable potential uncertainty?

Notes

1 See for example Bateson (1977); Shostack (1982); Parasuraman, Zeithaml and Berry (1985); Bowen and Schneider (1988).
2 According to some writers, this absence of ownership rights with respect to a service is one of the key factors which distinguishes physical goods from services.
3 See for example Wilson, Zeithaml, Bitner and Gremler (2016).
4 However, Grönroos (1978) is rather critical of this notion because it has potential to distract from the idea that fundamental differences do exist between goods and services. He suggests maintaining a much sharper distinction to enable academics and practitioners to recognise the need for rather different marketing approaches.
5 https://thefinancialbrand.com/news/checking-accounts/the-toaster-effect-free-gifts-can-boost-new-account-openings-by-15-or-more-160914/ (accessed January 2024).
6 www.statista.com/chart/27528/share-of-mobile-bankers-by-country/ (accessed January 2024)
7 Adapted from Kotler, P. (1994) *Marketing Management, Analysis, Planning and Control*, Eaglewood Cliffs, NJ: Prentice Hall.

References

Bateson, J. (1977). Do we need service marketing? In P. Eiglier, E. Langeard, C. H. Lovelock, J. E. G. Bateson, & R. F. Young (Eds.), *Marketing Consumer Services: New Insights* (pp. 77–115). Marketing Science Institute.

Bettencourt, L. A,, Lusch, R. F., & Vargo, S. L. (2014). A service lens on value creation: Marketing's role in achieving strategic advantage. *California Management Review*, 57(1), 44–66. https://doi.org/10.1525/cmr.2014.57.1.44

Bowen, D. E. and Schneider, B. (1988). Services marketing & management: Implications for organizational behaviour. *Research in Organizational Behaviour*, 10, pp. 43–80.

Diacon, S. and Hasseldine, J. (2007). Framing effects and risk perception: The effect of prior performance presentation format on investment fund choice. *Journal of Economic Psychology*, 28(1), pp. 31–52.

Grönroos, C. (1998). Marketing services: The case of a missing product. *Journal of Business and Industrial Marketing*, 13(4/5), pp. 322–38.

Gummesson, E. (1987). The new marketing – Developing long-term interactive relationships. *Long Range Planning*, 20(4), pp. 10–20.

Kotler, P. (1994). *Marketing Management: Analysis, Planning, Implementation and Control*. 8th ed. Englewood Cliffs, NJ: Prentice-Hall.

Kunreuther, H. C., Pauly, M. V. and McMorrow, S. (2013). *Insurance and Behavioural Economics: Improving Decisions in the Most Misunderstood Industry*. Cambridge: Cambridge University Press.

Lovelock, C. H. (1983). Classifying services to gain strategic marketing insights. *Journal of Marketing*, 47(3), pp. 9–20.

Lovelock, C. H. and Gummesson, E. (2004). Whither services marketing? In search of a new paradigm and fresh perspectives. *Journal of Service Research*, 7(1), pp. 20–41.

Lovelock, C. H. and Yip, G. S. (1996). Developing global strategies for service businesses. *California Management Review*, 38(2), pp. 64–86.

Parasuraman, A., Zeithaml, V. A. and Berry, L. L. (1985). A conceptual model of service quality and its implications for future research. *Journal of Marketing*, 49(4), pp. 41–50.

Rathmell, J. M. (1966). What is meant by services? *Journal of Marketing*, 30(4), pp. 32–36.

Shostack, G. L. (1977). Breaking free from product marketing. *Journal of Marketing*, 47(Summer), pp. 73–80.

Shostack, G. L. (1982). How to design a service. *European Journal of Marketing*, 16(1), pp. 49–63.

The Economist. (2012a). Spain: Dispatches from the Hothouse. Special Report: International Banking, 19 May, p. 10.

Vargo, S. L. and Lusch, R. F. (2004). The four service marketing myths: Remnants of a goods-based, manufacturing model. *Journal of Service Research*, 6(4), pp. 324–35.

Wilson, A., Zeithaml, V., Bitner, M.J. and Gremler, D. (2016). *Services Marketing: Integrating Customer Focus Across the Firm*. 3rd European edn, UK. McGraw Hill.

Zeithaml, V. A., Parasuraman, A. and Berry, L. L. (1985). Problems and strategies in services marketing. *Journal of Marketing*, 49(2), pp. 33–46.

4   Strategic development and marketing planning

Learning objectives

At the end of this chapter, you should be able to:

1. Explain the importance of planning marketing activities,
2. Understand the value of taking a strategic approach to marketing,
3. Outline stages in the process of planning marketing,
4. Understand some of the tools and techniques that are used in developing marketing strategies.

4.1 Introduction

Planning is an essential element of marketing. Planning will help to ensure that an organisation's marketing activities are consistent with its objectives, with the capabilities of the organisation and with the needs of the marketplace. Effective planning must establish targets, identify how and when those targets are to be achieved and establish who will take responsibility for the relevant marketing tasks. By stating objectives, procedures, processes and personnel requirements prior to undertaking marketing activities, the plan also provides a framework for the monitoring and control of marketing activity.

Planning has always been an important activity. Arguably, it is of particular value in an operating environment that is complex, uncertain and dynamic. Chapter 5 will discuss some of the challenges that the marketing environment presents to financial services organisations; what is clear is that change is inevitable, it happens increasingly quickly and it can often be complex. For example, the increasing sophistication of information and communications technologies (ICT) has given rise to rapid growth in new businesses and business models under the generic term "fintech"; more recently, generative AI offers the capacity to redefine ways of working and marketing practices and growing concerns about the climate crisis are transforming the way many organisations do business. The result is new market opportunities and new services that have the potential to deliver enhanced value to customers and to providers, but also new competition and new threats to established ways of working. While many aspects of these developments may not have been known with certainty five years ago, planning encourages managers to think about the future, about different future possibilities and to adopt a strategic focus so that the organisation can be better placed to

DOI: 10.4324/9781003398615-6

respond effectively to a rapidly changing environment. The growth in concerns about the climate crisis and about social responsibility has moved ESG (Environmental, Social and Governance) issues up the marketing agenda and financial services organisations need to give such factors full consideration in the development of their marketing activities as Chapter 17 explains more fully. Research on the practice of planning and its impact on business performance highlights that the relationship between the two is complex, but there is evidence of genuine benefits from a structured approach to strategy development and planning as Research insight 4.1 shows.

Research insight 4.1: strategic planning and performance in the financial services sector

This study was conducted at a time when both phone banking and internet banking were becoming better established in the United Kingdom (UK) and when the traditional branch networks were under pressure because of their relatively high costs. The theoretical context for the work was the debate about the extent to which formal planning and strategy development had a positive impact on organisational performance. A number of studies are identified which have found evidence of the positive outcomes of planning processes within a variety of organisations. Against this background, the authors established that there was little research that addressed the involvement of middle managers and their associated business units in the planning process. They collected data from 58 branch managers across two major Scottish banks addressing perceptions of the impact of specific management practices on planning, marketing effectiveness and overall performance. Quantitative data was collected via face-to-face interviews and the underlying relationships were analysed using neural networks.

The neural network approach is particularly appropriate for identifying complex and multilayered relationships and the results of the analysis highlight that the links between management practices and their outcomes at branch level are indeed complex. Of particular significance in the findings is the positive impact from planning and budgeting practice on competitiveness (via the latent variable – management effectiveness). Planning, implementation and control is also found to have a positive impact on competitiveness and on marketing effectiveness. But, while noting the importance of formal planning and long-term orientations, the study also highlights the importance of flexibility and the ability to respond to changes in the external environment. Planning processes must not be overly rigid and need to be built on a sound understanding of both the environment and the organization's capabilities.

Source: Moutinho, L. and Phillips, P. A. (2002). The impact of strategic planning on the competitiveness, performance and effectiveness of bank branches: a neural network analysis. *International Journal of Bank Marketing*, 20(3), pp. 102–10.

See also Hoffman, 2007 and Song et al., 2011.

The types of changes that are outlined more fully in the next chapter have created significant competitive threats for established financial services organisations. At the same time, many of these changes have also created new opportunities. Faced with this sort of operating environment, it would be unwise to adopt an unplanned approach to marketing. It would be equally unwise to rely on a simple tactical approach, supplying the same products to the same markets. When faced with a complex, changing and uncertain environment it becomes increasingly important for organisations to adopt a strategic approach to their markets. Such an approach will encourage careful consideration of products offered and markets served and should provide an organisation with the means to allocate its resources effectively and efficiently in the pursuit of specified objectives.

This chapter deals with both strategy and planning in relation to marketing. The chapter will begin by defining strategic marketing. The next section will examine the structure of marketing plan and will briefly review stages in the planning process. Section 4.4 will examine strategy development and will explore the different tools that can be used to guide strategic thinking. The focus throughout will be on the strategic aspects of marketing planning, including strategies for growth, sources of competitive advantage and methods for planning the product portfolio.

4.2 Strategic marketing

It is generally thought that organisations in the financial services sector have been slow to adopt a strategic approach to their marketing activities. For a long time, the marketing of financial services was largely concerned with how best to advertise and sell an existing set of products in a given market; indeed, many people think that this is what marketing is all about. However, there is more to marketing. A strategic approach to marketing in the financial services sector needs to concern itself with understanding consumers and deciding how best to respond to their needs. It must also focus attention on the competition and try to identify how to outperform key competitors.

The adoption and implementation of a strategic approach to marketing should impact positively on organisational performance. The logic for this is as simple as Figure 4.1 shows.

The concept of the service-profit chain which is discussed in Part III of this book stresses the importance of retention in improving performance on the grounds that it costs less to retain a customer than it does to acquire one. More generally, Doyle (2000) has long argued that investment in strategic marketing in order to increase revenues is a far more effective way of improving shareholder value than trying to reduce costs. The degree to which costs can be reduced is limited and while cost control will be important, the best opportunities for enhancing financial performance arise from growing the volume and/or the value of sales. Strategic marketing is essential to revenue growth because it focuses the organisation on customers, competitors and the challenges of a constantly changing marketplace. Central to Doyle's view is the argument that marketing expenditure should be viewed as an investment (rather than an annual cost) and its impact monitored over a longer time period. Investment in activities such as brand building, establishing new distribution networks or moving into new markets are all long-term activities. Their initial impact on sales may actually be quite limited; their longer-term impact could be quite considerable.

Delivering superior value

• Enabled through understanding of customers and competitors

Customer acquisition and retention

• Enabled through the offer of superior value

Enhanced organisational performance

• Profit and cash flow improved by successfully growing new business and keeping existing business

Figure 4.1 How strategic marketing enhances organisational performance

 Stop and think?

Which financial services organisations do their marketing well? Do you think they also deliver better organisational performance?

Thus, a strategic approach to marketing has at its heart organisational performance and the idea that performance can be enhanced if the organisation is market oriented, if it understands the changing market environment and can respond in ways which result in the delivery of a level of value to customers that is superior to that offered by competitors. In that sense, we can think about strategic marketing as being a broad, generic approach to marketing. The specific form that strategic marketing takes will vary across organisations and markets and will be represented by the organisation's marketing strategy.

Within any financial services provider, strategies develop at several levels. A corporate strategy is concerned with the overall development of the business and will include specific strategies for different areas (e.g. an IT strategy, a human resource strategy, a marketing strategy). The marketing strategy focuses specifically on the organisation's activities in relation to its markets. Like any strategy, marketing strategy is concerned with being both efficient and effective.

- **Efficiency** is about doing a particular activity well. An efficient phone banking operation will be one that is highly cost effective and reliable; customer requests will be carried out accurately, quickly and costs will be kept low – typically through high degrees of standardisation and automation.
- **Effectiveness** is concerned with doing the right thing. Thus, an effective phone banking operation is one that offers the right services to the target consumers – the services that consumers need and want.

To be effective, a financial services provider must have the right sort of services and be offering them to the right customers. This in turn means that an understanding of the environment is essential because it is only by understanding the market, and how it might change, that an organisation can be confident that it is doing the right thing. As the case study at the end of Part II shows, when the Indian banking sector liberalised in the mid-1990s, the success of one of the early entrants, HDFC Bank, was largely due to its awareness of changing customer expectations and the identification of a significant group of mid-market customers who were prepared to pay for better service. In focusing on this segment, HDFC provided a valued service to a segment of the market whose needs were not met by other providers of banking services and was able to build a strong competitive position in the Indian retail banking sector.

A good marketing strategy will have the following features:

- It will identify specific objectives that the organisation wishes to achieve;
- It will commit resources (money, time, people) to help achieve these objectives;
- It will involve a thorough evaluation of the marketing environment;
- It will aim to match environmental opportunities and organisational capabilities;
- It will focus on the delivery of superior value.

Delivering superior value to customers and being distinct from the competition (and better) lies at the heart of strategic marketing and the development of a competitive marketing strategy. Delivering superior value starts with the organisation itself and the capabilities that it has. Value is essentially something that is offered to the customer and is considered to be quantified by the price paid (sometimes referred to as value-in-exchange). This perspective thinks of a product or service as a bundle of attributes which together should deliver value by meeting customer needs (and doing so more effectively than the competition). But many marketers might argue that this is a narrow view and in order to determine how best to deliver value to customers, we need to begin by thinking carefully about what exactly is meant by the term "value". The emergence of the "service-dominant logic" in marketing (see Chapter 3) has generated a renewed interest in the role of value in marketing strategy. This school of thought argues for a customer-based perspective on value (see Vargo and Lusch, 2004) and proposes that value arises "in use" rather than in exchange. The idea of value-in-use is not a new one and indeed has been present in marketing thinking for over 50 years. It emphasises the idea that value is something that customers create through their acquisition and use of a product or service.

Figure 4.2 Components of customer value

Source: Adapted from Almquist, Senior and Bloch (2016)

If we think of these two perspectives (value-in-exchange and value-in-use), then as Grönroos (2009) has argued we can separate out the providers' "value proposition" from the consumers' value creation process. Providers will identify features and attributes that they consider to be important and that they believe will offer value to consumers. But ultimately, value creation depends on how the consumer realises benefits from the acquisition and use of a given product or service. One important implication of this distinction is that marketing strategies need to consider not just how to propose value to customers in order to encourage purchase but also how to support and facilitate them in its creation. In effect, good marketing will depend upon an ability to understand and respond to the ways in which consumers seek to create and realise value.

Based on a recent large-scale study in the US, Almquist, Senior and Bloch (2016) identified a range of fundamental building blocks for customer value, grouped into 4 categories, as shown in Figure 4.2:

They grouped components of value into four categories – namely functional, emotional, life changing and social impact and Figure 4.2 gives examples of these components. Their research showed a clear link between the ability to deliver customer-relevant value and subsequent revenue growth, and while they identified 30 elements of value, they noted that companies usually only ever delivered in relation to a subset – the ones that helped their customers realise value. Interestingly, in the case of retail banking, the key components of value were identified as "provides access", "avoids hassle", "reduces anxiety" and "heirloom" (i.e. a good investment for the future). But they also noted that irrespective of sector, perceived quality remained the most important driver of positive word of mouth and thus revenue growth.

In practical terms, the value that consumers receive will be based on the costs associated with a product or service and the benefits that they realise. By implication, superior value depends on reducing costs to the customer or from increasing benefits. On the cost side, an online funds supermarket can formulate a value proposition based around reduced charges for the purchase, management and sale of mutual funds. A current account provider may offer value to current account customers through a guarantee of "no fees for ATM withdrawals internationally". However, it is worth noting that this value can only be realised by customers who use their ATM cards to make such withdrawals – it has no value to customers who do not travel abroad. Marketing in practice 4.1 provides an example of the way in which ANZ is delivering value for customers by enhancing speed and convenience for customers, starting with home loan applications.

Marketing in practice 4.1 ANZ delivers enhanced customer value

In early 2022, Australia and New Zealand Banking Group (ANZ) revealed its new digital platform – ANZ Plus. This platform was developed in partnership with some of the world's leading software companies with a view to building something that used the latest technology, enhanced security and could be developed and adapted as the market environment changed. The customer response was hugely positive with over 100,000 customers signing up in the first year. A key feature of the platform was that even once launched, the bank was able to add new features easily and cost effectively. One of the early initiatives was the inclusion of home lending on the platform, allowing customers to apply online, manage their application via their app and secure a quick decision. Customers also had access to the services of an ANZ Plus Coach should they need it.

A customer seeking a home loan could easily create, via the app, a statement of their financial position based on their income and expenditure. This would ensure that they had a very clear view of what they could afford. The app was able to access real time estimates of property values to support customer decisions and applications. Rapid credit assessments, based on the property value and the consumers financial position allows quick decisions to ensure that customers were in the best position to secure their preferred property.

Source: www.afr.com/companies/financial-services/anz-plus-launches-digital-home-loans-plots-multi-year-expansion-20231113-p5ejfp

https://bluenotes.anz.com/posts/2022/10/anz-news-plus-home-loans-deposits-customers-results22

The benefits side of the value equation is potentially more complex – there are numerous different ways in which customers may realise benefits and thus value as we saw above. In some cases benefits may simply be functional – does the service offer better terms and conditions? A savings provider offering favourable savings rates or easy access; a mortgage lender offering free property valuations; an investment bank offering research insights and timely market information would all be examples of value propositions that focus around functional benefits. But benefits may also be more emotional – perhaps around the reassurance and confidence that providers of life insurance and pensions offer or the sense of 'specialness' that many banks offer to their premium banking customers. In some cases, benefits may be closer to the life changing category, an example being the sense of specialness created by platinum or black cards. Just the possession of such cards may communicate something about individual status and identity. Finally, some financial services providers may be able to deliver value through social impact, such as a very explicit emphasis on environmental, social and governance issues (see Chapter 17 for a more detailed discussion).

Progress check

- Planning is a key part of marketing; the future is uncertain but planning helps us to prepare.
- A strategic approach to marketing should enhance organizational performance.
- Value is at the heart of strategic marketing. A strategic approach to marketing will focus on delivering value to consumers in response to their needs and priorities – and doing so more effectively than the competition.

Again, these propositions only yield benefits if customers make use of them – services that make premium banking customers feel special (e.g. concierge services, access to meeting rooms, preferential hotel rates) may be attractive but will only really deliver genuine value if they are actually used. Some classifications of value go beyond the functional and emotional dimensions of value and consider elements of value such as social value, psychological value, convenience value and security value. The distinction between emotional and functional value is perhaps the simplest categorisation and research suggests that the relevance of other more fine-grained categorisations of value may vary according to specific context.

4.3 Developing a strategic marketing plan

A marketing strategy is essentially a statement of how an organisation plans to compete for business in its particular market and most marketing strategies will be presented in the form of an overall marketing plan. Philip Kotler (1994) defined strategic planning as:

> the managerial process of developing and maintaining a viable fit between the organisation's objectives and resources and its changing market opportunities. The aim of strategic planning is to shape and reshape the company's business and products so that they combine to produce satisfactory profits and growth.

Every organisation has its own approach to preparing marketing plans and there is no single correct approach. However, good plans do have a number of important features:

- The plan should have a logical structure;
- It should contain explicit marketing objectives which link to corporate objectives;
- It should analyse the environment (both internal and external) and the current position of the organisation;
- Based on this analysis, the plan should identify which combinations of products and markets the organisation will serve and how it will compete (segmentation, targeting and positioning);
- It should contain specific decisions relating to key marketing variables such as product, price, promotion and place (the marketing mix);
- It should conclude with an outline of the appropriate methods for implementing the identified strategy, including issues relating to budget, accountability and evaluation.

Although the plan needs to provide clear guidelines as to how marketing activities are to be managed, it should have some flexibility to allow the organisation to adapt and respond to

Figure 4.3 An illustrative marketing plan

unexpected changes. In essence, the marketing plan is about looking to and preparing for an unknown future.

As we have said, there is no single format for a plan, but one possible approach is outlined in Figure 4.3. This presents the key elements of a marketing plan and also highlights the importance of feedback which may lead to adjustments to the plan once it has been put into operation.

4.3.1 Company vision and mission

Vision and mission focus attention on organisational purpose. Vision typically looks to a long-term future, and specifies what the organisation aspires to be. As an example, HSBC in Turkey defined its vision and mission as follows[1]:

Vision: To be the leading international bank in Turkey.
Mission: Throughout our history, we have been where the growth is, connecting customers to opportunities. We enable businesses to thrive and economies to prosper, helping people fulfil their hopes and dreams and realize their ambitions. This is our role and purpose.

The mission statement requires that the organisation defines the area of business in which it operates and defines it in a way which will give focus and direction. In effect, the mission statement spells out the purpose of the organisation – its broad goals and the way in which those will be delivered. Some organisations have replaced the word "mission" with "purpose". Whichever term is used, this element of a strategic marketing plan is to outline the goals of the organisation and identify, in broad terms, the ways in which the organisation will achieve those goals. For example, insurance giant, AXA defines its mission in the following way:

> As one of the largest global insurers, our purpose is to act for human progress by protecting what matters.[2]

The nature of the corporate mission depends on a variety of factors. Corporate history will often influence the markets and customer groups served – for example, CIC in Kenya (see also Chapter 9) highlights the importance of its co-operative heritage[3].

> Our Mission Statement: To enable people to achieve financial security
> We are first and foremost a co-operative. This is our identity and heritage which we are unashamedly proud of. Consequently, we shall consider ourselves successful only when all our stakeholders achieve financial security on account of association with us.

Credit Agricole's rural and mutual tradition influences the way in which it approaches its market. Although it is in no way restricted to serving the agricultural community, Credit Agricole's heritage means that the bank places particular importance on involvement in the local community, being close to the customer and the bank prides itself on having an extensive branch network. Similarly, culture in its broadest sense will also be an important influence, perhaps most notably with Islamic banks as is apparent in the mission statement of BankIslami in Pakistan[4]:

> The Vision of BankIslami is promoting global economic prosperity based on Islamic financial system.
> The Mission of BankIslami is Saving Humanity from Riba by offering Shariah compliant, customer-centric, innovative financial solutions and creating value for our stakeholders while upholding social responsibility and transparency.

There is no formula for creating mission and vision statements, but it is often helpful to think of a mission statement as trying to encompass the following elements:

- the types of customers (is the organisation dealing with a subgroup such as high net worth or Muslim consumers or looking to serve a broad market?),
- the needs being satisfied (e.g. managing wealth, providing financial security),
- the technology used (e.g. Shariah compliance).

This way of defining the mission is helpful from a marketing perspective because it forces managers to think about customers and their needs. Indeed, ideally the mission statement would avoid mentioning a product. For example, an insurance company should perhaps think of its mission as being "meeting consumer needs for risk reduction and financial security" rather than simply "insurance". By focusing specifically on needs and not on the product, the mission statement can help to guide the development of the organisation. It can also help the organisation avoid "marketing myopia" – a problem that arises when organisations focus too much attention on their products and not enough on their customers' needs.

When organisations outline their mission and vision or their purpose they draw attention to the sorts of services that they offer, why and to whom. Increasingly, they include a statement about the way in which they will work – their values – and in many cases these are then linked to both business practice and the nature and development of the brand. Consider again the example of CIC group in Kenya. They are explicitt about both their value proposition to consumers and their values:

Value Proposition
"To offer simple, flexible insurance and financial services built around our customers' needs."

Our Core Values

- Integrity – Be fair and transparent.
- Dynamism – Be passionate and innovative.
- Performance – Be efficient and results driven.
- Co-operation – Live the co-operative spirit.

Our approach to business growth is research driven. We seek to understand our customers and their needs, and innovatively develop appropriate products that address their needs, wants and desires.

4.3.2 Situation analysis

In many senses, marketing strategies and plans are concerned with obtaining a "fit" or "match" between an organisation and its environment. To be effective, an organisation needs to be able to use its resources and capabilities in an environment in which they will have most value. Consequently, any marketing plan will require a thorough analysis of the external environment and internal environment. This analysis will help the organisation to meet customers' needs more effectively than the competition and make the most of its available resources. Details about the process of analysing the marketing environment are outlined in more detail in the next chapter. The results of a PEST (Political, Economic, Social and Technological) analysis, a five-force analysis and SWOT (Strengths, Weaknesses, Opportunities, Threats) analysis all provide essential input to a good marketing plan.

Marketing research and market intelligence provide much of the information used in an analysis of the marketing environment. This information may be gathered in a variety of formal and informal means, ranging from customer surveys, commercial databases, informal contacts, consultancy reports and dedicated competitor analysis. Chapter 6 provides some further background on the market research process.

It must be appreciated that the SWOT plays a key role in producing guidance at both the strategic and tactical levels. A well-founded, intelligently approached SWOT analysis ensures that opportunities are not overlooked and choices are made that play to the company's strengths. The quality of the SWOT is a function of the quantity of the situation review. Superficial, casually conducted situation reviews result in assessments of strengths and weaknesses, and opportunities and threats that have limited value. A degree of detail is required that is commensurate to the market or product area in question.

It is important to grasp the point that when we refer to a strength we should seek to identify aspects of the organisation's assets, capabilities and competencies that represent a relative competitive strength. It is not sufficient simply to identify those aspects of the company's operation that it considers it is good at. The search for competitive advantage calls for the matching of external opportunities with a company's relative strengths. Similarly, the identification of weaknesses should search for areas of relative competitive weakness. Such features render the company particularly vulnerable to external threats and need to be addressed with far more vigour than simply those areas in which the company performs no worse than the rest of the industry.

 Stop and think?

How important do you think values are to customers? Do you take notice of the values of an organisation? If not, why not?

Therefore, SWOTs will often benefit from the degree of focus that can often only be achieved at the product group level. In the case of a life insurance company this might involve a separate plan for protection, pension and investment product groups. Each plan will have to be consistent with the bigger picture and it is the job of senior marketing management to ensure that effective coordination occurs.

4.3.3 Marketing objectives

Once the nature of the marketing environment has been fully analysed, and an appropriate SWOT has been completed, it is then possible to outline specific marketing objectives. These marketing objectives are not ends in themselves – they are intermediate outcomes which will lead to the organisation achieving its corporate objectives. Thus, when specifying marketing objectives, it is essential to ensure that they are derived from and will contribute to corporate objectives. For example, if corporate objectives emphasise expansion, then marketing objectives may be specified in terms of growing market share or sales volume or sales value.

Marketing objectives should be clear, measurable, realistic and time limited. A particular problem in specifying objectives is the potential confusion between intended goals and the means by which those goals should be attained. The former represent objectives whereas the latter concern processes. Sometimes, what are specified as objectives in a marketing planning document are, in fact, simply a representation of planned activities. Some examples of marketing objectives, as shown in Table 4.1 may serve to illustrate the point.

Table 4.1 Examples of marketing objectives

	Specification of Objective	Commentary
Example 1	To achieve a 12.5% increase in volume sales of new personal pensions during the budget year.	A sound objective – it specifies a measurable outcome, i.e. a 12.5% growth in sales, it qualifies that it concerns personal pension sales volumes and specifies timescale for achievement.
Example 2	To increase pension sales by year end.	An objective, but one that is poorly drafted. It gives no target level for the increase to be achieved, nor does it qualify whether it concerns case volumes or premium value. Finally, it does not specify whether it concerns all sources of pension growth or whether it relates to growth from new sales as opposed to securing growth from existing pension customers.
Example 3	To promote personal pensions through the branch network.	Not an objective, at least not at the level of a marketing plan. Instead, it represents but one of the range of actions that in combination should achieve a given objective.
Example 4	To re-price the personal pension product to improve competitive rating.	A process element which outlines a marketing action rather than a valid objective.

To qualify as a valid marketing objective, ideally the following minimum conditions must be satisfied:

- The desired outcome must be specified, e.g. growth in sales, growth in market share, level of consumer awareness, level of customer satisfaction;
- The outcome must be sufficiently well-qualified to eliminate ambiguity and facilitate precise measurement: e.g. growth in number of policies sold to new customers, growth in market share by new business premiums;
- A specific quantum of outcome must be proposed, e.g. a 7.5% growth in new business sales volumes;
- The timescale for achievement of outcome must be specified, e.g. by the end of the second quarter.

Without well-defined objectives it is impossible to properly evaluate outcomes.

4.3.4 Marketing strategy

Once the environment has been analysed and the objectives set, the marketing plan must move on to consider the choice of marketing strategy. Of course, the overall corporate strategy will affect the choice of marketing strategy, but the marketing strategy focuses specifically on the choice of markets and how the organisation plans to compete and create value in those markets.

The main component of a marketing strategy is often described as STP (Segmentation, Targeting and Positioning). These three components are shown in Figure 4.4:

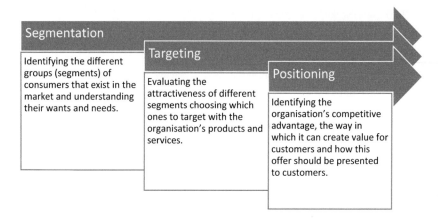

Figure 4.4 The essential components of marketing strategy

The process of segmentation, targeting and positioning is discussed in more detail in Chapter 7. Research insight 4.2 outlines the efforts of a small US bank to build a successful marketing strategy through careful segmentation, targeting and positioning.

Research insight 4.2 Parish National Bank (PNB), New Orleans: segmentation, targeting and positioning in strategic marketing

The financial services sector in the US has experienced a period of deregulation, techno-logical innovation and changing patterns of competition. The Financial Modernization Act of 1999 repealed many of the restrictions that had previously restricted competi-tion in US banking. Barriers to operating across sectors were lifted and, at the same time, restrictions on interstate and international banking were disappearing. Regulatory changes, combined with changing market conditions resulted in increased competition and a trend towards greater consolidation. Small local and regional banks increasingly became "endangered species".

Parish National Bank (PNB) is a small commercial bank operating in four parishes of New Orleans. Faced with this changing environment, the bank needed to develop an appropriate response. Some smaller banks had responded by aggressively looking to grow in consumer markets and thus position themselves as acquisition targets; others sought to identify particular niches where they could continue to compete effect-ively. PNB choose the latter course of action. Among the different market segments available, the bank identified local small businesses and small business employees as an attractive market segment. To deliver value to customers in this segment, PNB positioned itself as "high tech and high touch" and aimed to provide customers with good banking relationships, innovative services and appropriate use of web-based technologies to support delivery.

Source: Henson and Wilson (2002).

Progress check

- A marketing strategy and plan outlines how an organisation plans to compete for business in its particular market.
- There is no single correct format – what is important is a logical structure.
- This structure needs to be clear about the organisation's purpose and the environment in which it operates. It should include clear objectives and be explicit how value will be delivered through careful segmentation, targeting and positioning.

4.3.5 Market specific strategy

The market specific strategy outlines the detailed decisions about how to market specific products and services to particular groups of consumers. This stage will include an indication of the necessary level of marketing expenditure as well as details on the product itself, how it will be promoted, how it will be priced and how it will be distributed (the marketing mix). These decisions must be guided by the choice of market position. Thus, for example, if an organisation has chosen to position itself as serving wealthy consumers with a high-value, personalised product, then the market-specific strategy will need to look for an appropriate (relatively high) price, decide on which product features to customise and choose ways of promoting and distributing the product that will appeal to the chosen consumer groups. These decisions are discussed in more detail in Part II of this book.

4.3.6 Implementation

Implementation is concerned with how the marketing plan is put into practice. It must consider budgets, accountability and evaluation. Timescales should be identified and some consideration may also be given to contingency planning. However well thought out the marketing plan may be, the market is always changing. Consequently, certain planned activities may turn out to be inappropriate or ineffective; it is important to be aware of these and be able to respond – i.e. to modify the strategy as new information becomes available.

Effective financial control is essential for the credibility of a marketing plan; indeed, it is vital for the credibility of a marketing function as a whole. Budgets need to be produced on an accurate and defensible basis. They require a sufficient level of detail to facilitate effective control and the pursuit of efficiency gains. Lack of attention to detail can be a particular problem. For example, it may be relatively easy to identify the total cost of a direct mail campaign, but if cost per individual contacted and cost per sale are ignored, resources may be badly allocated. For example, one direct marketing team in the banking sector established a total budget for a campaign which resulted in them planning to spend more in terms of cost per sale than the total margin of the product being promoted.

The plan should make clear where responsibility and accountability lies for the different activities within the plan. Ownership should be made clear and unambiguous, and sole ownership for a particular task should always be sought. It is common to encounter a plethora of shared accountabilities which result in an unclear sense of ownership. Indeed, well-defined accountability is a necessary prerequisite of an appropriate appraisal system and performance review.

One increasingly important dimension of implementation is internal marketing. Internal marketing deals with the way in which an organisation manages the relationship between itself and its employees at all levels. It plays an important role in creating and maintaining a market-oriented corporate culture. The process of internal marketing is seen as particularly important in the financial services sector, not least because of the importance of people in the marketing process. Internal marketing helps to ensure that staff understand the product itself and believe in what the organisation is trying to do. If an organisation's own employees are not market oriented, if they do not support the overall corporate and marketing strategies, then the chances of successful plan implementation are minimal.

4.4 Tools for strategy development

Later chapters will consider many elements of the marketing plan in more detail. The remainder of this chapter will introduce some of the techniques that organisations can use to help develop marketing strategies within the context of the marketing plan. These tools help managers to think about the best approach to pursue. They can provide useful insights and recommendations. However, good marketing managers will use these tools carefully – they do not provide definite answers and they do not tell you exactly what your organisation should do. What they can do is to help you think about the marketing challenges being faced and about how the organisation might respond to these challenges.

We begin by looking at tools that might help marketing managers think about the different options for growth. Then we move on to look at frameworks that might be helpful in thinking about managing the product portfolio (the mix of products and services to be offered to different target markets). Finally, we will look in a bit more detail at the issue of competitive advantage and how, in broad terms, organisations can think about setting themselves apart from the competition.

4.4.1 Growth strategies

An organisation that is looking at how best to grow and expand can think about this problem by considering whether to look at new products or new markets. The available choices are represented in Ansoff's Product/Market Matrix. This suggests four possible options which are outlined in Figure 4.5 – market penetration, market development, product development and diversification.

	Products	
	Existing	*New*
Markets *Existing*	**Market penetration**	**Product development**
New	**Market development**	**Diversification**

Figure 4.5 Ansoff's product market matrix

- **Market penetration:**

Market penetration means trying to sell more of the existing product to the existing market. To do this, an organisation may try to persuade existing users to use more, persuade non-users to use or attract consumers from competitors. There are many examples of the marketing tactics that would support a market penetration strategy. Promotional offers such as "Air Miles" and "Cashback" are widely used to encourage existing customers to make greater use of their credit cards. For example, Citibank in Malaysia ran its "Travel and Foreign Spend" campaign in 2022 to offer up to RM500 cashback to cardholders for certain levels of travel and overseas spend. In a variant of this approach, American Express tries to attract new customers to its credit cards with an offer of 5% cashback (max £100) for the first three months spend.

Usually, a market penetration strategy is more appropriate when the market still has room to expand. Market penetration works best in those contexts in which there is a marked difference between the current market size and the potential market size. In a mature market where most likely buyers have already bought the product, market penetration is more difficult because the organisation will need to attract customers directly from competitors and this is often more difficult than trying to attract new customers to the market. In the UK, the market for current accounts is largely saturated. Most providers appear to be focusing their efforts on retaining customers and exploiting opportunities to cross-sell. However, newer entrants to banking – many of which are so-called neobanks – have tried to follow a market penetration strategy by encouraging customers of other banks to switch their accounts. Atom Bank which offers mobile banking only has tried to penetrate the UK market by exploiting its lower cost base to offer attractive savings rates and a level of convenience that is associated with app-only delivery.[5] Similarly, Monzo has seen considerable success with a digital-only operating model and an emphasis on product innovation and customer service. While some neobanks have

Figure 4.6 Monzo's digital-only bank has experienced significant market growth

Source: Shutterstock

grown by reaching new customers, many have been able to attract customers from their competitors.

- **Market development:**
Market development involves the organisation trying to identify new markets for its existing products. Most commonly this strategy is associated with expansion into new markets geographically. For example, when American International Group (AIG) became the first foreign insurer to obtain a licence to operate in China it was engaging in market development via geographical expansion. The Raisin savings marketplace (see also Chapter 8) which originated in Germany grew rapidly in its first decade with expansion into a number of European markets and the US, taking the basic business model developed in the German market and using it in a range of other domestic markets. In the US, Morgan Stanley was originally established as an investment bank. The Glass-Steagall Act prevented an expansion into other domestic markets and so Morgan Stanley grew primarily by overseas expansion. However, deregulation has meant that movement into new market segments is also an important approach to market development. For example, following its conversion from Building Society to bank, the UK-based Alliance and Leicester pursued what might be thought of as a market development strategy when it moved to offer its banking services into corporate markets.

- **Product development:**
Growth through product development means developing related products and modifying existing products to appeal to current markets. The diversity of new mortgage products that have become available in the UK market are examples of modifying existing products to make them more attractive to current markets. The history of American Express is dominated by a series of examples of product development. Initially, the company focused on money orders, travellers cheques and foreign exchange. In 1958, American Express issued its first charge card. Subsequently, the company also launched credit cards, targeting both new customers and existing charge card customers. Similarly, China Merchants bank, having established its position in the mainstream retail market, developed its core banking product to specifically target its high-net-worth customers. More recently, Monzo has moved into digital wealth management, offering its customers a new approach to investing. Monzo is best known as a digital bank but has developed a simple set of investment portfolios largely targeting its existing consumers and trying to make it easier for them to invest as well as save. A strategy of this nature relies on good service design, packaging and promotion and often relies on company reputation to attract consumers to the new product.

- **Diversification**
Diversification tends to be the more risky strategy, as it involves an organisation moving into new products and new markets. Pure diversification may be relatively unusual in financial services, but the development of bancassurance represents a form of diversification as established banks move into the provision of insurance-related products. Similarly, the decisions by traditional banks to offer Islamic banking products might also be seen as a form of diversification. It might also be argued that the decision by investment bank Goldman Sachs to move into retail banking through its Marcus brand also constitutes a form of diversification. More radical forms of diversification might include the decision, almost 2 decades ago by UK supermarkets to move into financial services or the possibility that a company such as Amazon might decide to offer a greater variety of financial services having already made commitments to co-branded credit cards.

4.4.2 Selecting the product portfolio

Part of any marketing strategy involves a consideration of how to manage a range of different products. This requires decisions about which products need to be developed, which need to be maintained and which should be dropped. Details of product strategy are discussed in greater depth in Chapter 10, but at a strategic level there are tools available to help marketing managers evaluate the existing range of products and make decisions about what should happen with each product. Two common approaches which are used to determine product portfolios are first, matrix-based approaches which seek to categorise products based on indicators of market attractiveness and the organisation's competitive strength and second, the concept of a product life cycle.

Matrix-based approaches

Two of the most widely recognised of the matrix-based approaches are the Boston Consulting Group (BCG) matrix and the General Electric Business Screen (GE). Both the BCG and the GE matrices require a classification of products/business units according to the attractiveness of a particular market and the strengths of the company in that market. The underlying logic is that the strategy for a product with a strong competitive position in a very attractive market is going to be very different from the strategy for a product with a strong competitive position in a weak market or a weak competitive position in a strong market. The BCG matrix bases its classification scheme purely on market share and market growth, while the GE matrix relies on multivariate measures of market attractiveness and business strengths. Not only is guidance on marketing strategy based on a product's position in the matrix, but organisations are thought to need a spread of products across the matrix because different positions typically have different implications for marketing resources.

 Stop and think?

Would you consider getting a credit card from Amazon? Why or why not? How might you feel about getting a loan from Amazon or getting insurance for your possessions?

A simple example of the BCG matrix is presented in Figure 4.7 for a hypothetical bank; the division on the horizontal axis is usually based on a market share identical to that of the firm's nearest competitor, while the precise location of the division on the vertical axis will depend on the rate of growth in the market with 10% usually seen as a reasonable cut-off point. Products are positioned in the matrix as circles with a diameter proportional to their sales revenue. The BCG matrix relies on the assumption that a larger market share results in lower costs and thus higher margins.

The appropriate strategy for a particular product will depend upon its position within the matrix. The Question Mark (or problem child) has a small market share in a high-growth industry. The basic product is popular, but customer support for the specific company versions is limited. If future market growth is anticipated and the products are viable, then the organisation should consider ways of adding value to their offer and increasing marketing expenditure on this product. Otherwise, the possibility of withdrawing the product should be considered.

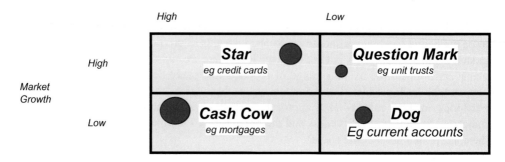

Figure 4.7 An Illustrative BCG matrix

The Star has a high market share in a high-growth industry. By implication, the star has the potential to generate significant earnings currently and in the future. However, at this stage it may still require substantial marketing expenditures to maintain this position, but this would be regarded as a good investment for the future. By contrast, the Cash Cow has a high market share but in a slower growing market. Product development costs for the cash cow are typically low and the marketing campaign is well established, so the cash cow will usually make a reasonable contribution to overall profitability.

Finally, the Dog represents a product with a low market share in a low-growth market. As with the cash cow, the product will typically be well established but may be losing consumer support and may have cost disadvantages. The usual strategy would be to consider withdrawing this product unless cash flow position is strong, in which case the recommended strategy would be to cut back expenditure and maximise net contribution.

The BCG matrix is potentially useful, but its recommendations must be interpreted with care. In particular, it is important to recognise that it focuses only on one aspect of the organisation (market share) and one aspect of the market (sales growth). And understanding context will be key to making sensible recommendations. In the example about, the bank's current accounts have been categorised as "dogs" but withdrawal is unlikely to be a sensible strategy because the current account is a foundational product and the basis on which may other products may be cross-sold.

The GE matrix works on similar principles but concentrates more generally on trying to measure the attractiveness of the market (rather than just measuring market growth) and competitive strength (rather than just market share). This means that the GE matrix gives a broader picture of the strengths and weaknesses of the product portfolio, although it is often more difficult to construct.

Best (2013) suggests using a version of the GE matrix to guide the choice of offensive versus defensive strategies, as shown in Figure 4.8. Comparing market attractiveness and competitive strength results in a series of recommendations about the most appropriate way for the organisation to compete in its market. These strategic options are classified as either offensive or defensive.

Offensive strategies include invest to grow, improve position and new market entry and are very similar to Ansoff's growth strategies. For example, "invest to grow" involves marketing expenditure to grow market share or even to grow the overall market. It is essentially equivalent

	Low	Competitive Advantage	High
High	New market entry Improve market position	Invest to grow Improve position Optimise position	Invest to grow Protect position
Market Attractiveness	Improve position Optimise position Harvest	Improve position Optimise position Harvest	Invest to grow Protect position Optimise position
Low	Harvest Divest	Monetise Harvest or Divest	Monetise Harvest or Divest

Figure 4.8 Offensive and defensive strategies

Source: Adapted from Best (2013) p354

to a market penetration strategy and may involve, for example, aggressive marketing, or value enhancement to gain customers. As part of its growth strategy, BankIslam in Malaysia offered discounts on its standard portfolio of loan products to existing customers and to their families. "Improve position" entails investing resources to enhance the value offered to consumers relative to the value offered by competitors. In the increasingly competitive credit card market in China, China Merchants Bank strengthened its position through a partnership with social network provider RenRen. It now offers its co-branded credit card customers the facility to use RenRen's location-based services, including the ability to "check-in" and receive location-specific promotional information.[6] Such an approach is similar to a product-development strategy as discussed above. Finally in the list of offensive strategies, "new market entry", as the description suggests, is effectively equivalent to market development and diversification strategies.

Defensive strategies are classified as protect position, optimise position, monetise and harvest/divest. A strategy of protecting a position is appropriate where an organisation has a currently strong position in an attractive market and the aim is to discourage new entrants and limit the expansion potential of other competitors. In a market where growth is slowing down, optimising a position involves focusing attention on maximising the return on marketing investment. Typically, such an approach would involve trying to focus attention on the profitable customers and controlling marketing expenditure. Trying to persuade less profitable customers to make more use of low-cost channels such as the phone and internet and less use of high-cost channels such as the branch is one example of an optimising strategy. Monetising is a more aggressive version of optimising and focuses on maximising cash flow without actually preparing to exit from the market. An example may be the decision to introduce fees for small value bank accounts that are relatively high cost to maintain. Finally, a harvest/divest strategy goes a stage further and involves maximising cash flow from a product prior to exiting the market. If there is no opportunity to maximise cash flow, then an early market exit would be preferred. However, given the long-term nature of many financial services, product withdrawal can be complicated as is discussed in Chapter 10.

The product life cycle

The product life cycle (PLC) is widely used as a tool for market planning, in that it can be employed both to guide an organisation in the determination of the appropriate balance of products and in the development of a suitable strategy for the marketing of those products. Its usefulness has been regularly challenged and, clearly, there is a risk that the PLC could oversimplify the evolution of a product. While recognising these limitations, it remains a potentially helpful way of thinking about the strategic management of products.

The product life cycle as shown in Figure 4.9 suggests that a given product or service will pass through four basic stages, from introduction, through growth to maturity and eventually into decline. The role of marketing is generally considered to be one of prolonging the growth and maturity phases, often using strategies of product modification or product improvement which are frequently regarded as less risky than developing completely new products.

Assessing the existing product range according to life cycle position can give some indication of the balance of the existing product portfolio. Furthermore, according to the stage in the life cycle, the organisation can obtain some guidance as to the appropriate marketing strategy.

*   **Introduction**
    A period of slow growth and possibly negative profit, as efforts are being made to obtain widespread acceptance for the service. Cash flows are typically negative and the priority is to raise awareness and appreciation of the product with the result that the marketing mix will place a high degree of emphasis on promotion. Thematic investment (see Marketing in practice 5.3 is one example of a service that might be thought of as being in the introductory stages of its life cycle.
*   **Growth**
    Sales volumes increase steadily and the product begins to make a significant contribution to profitability. Increase in sales can be maintained by improvements in the features,

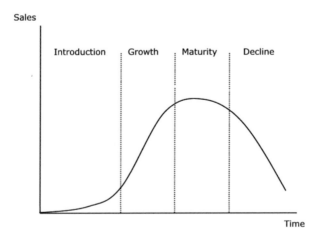

Figure 4.9 The product life cycle

targeting at more segments or increased price competitiveness. It is at this stage that the new service will begin to attract significant competition. Growth services currently include smartphone banking applications, and, in some markets, mobile payment systems. Unit trusts and other related types of investment products are probably also comfortably in the growth stage of the product life cycle in countries such as the UK, have possibly reached maturity in the US but may still be at the introductory stage in countries such as China and India.

- **Maturity**

  Sales growth is relatively slow and the marketing campaign and product are well established. Competition is probably at its most intense at this stage and it may be necessary to consider modification to the service and the addition of new features to prevent future decline. Many bank current accounts are products which can be seen as having reached maturity and in many cases are being modified in attempts to prolong their life cycles. For traditional banks, the innovations around digital and mobile banking might be examples of initiatives to sustain these products. Equally, the addition of service extras to long established products such as car or house insurance are valuable options for keeping mature products competitive without resorting to pure price competition.

- **Decline**

  Sales begin to drop away noticeably, leaving management with the option of withdrawing the product entirely, or at least withdrawing marketing support. In the financial services sector, product withdrawal may be difficult as some products such as life insurance cannot simply be withdrawn from the market because some customers will still be paying premiums. Some products will move to the decline stage of their life cycle because they are no longer fit for purpose – for example, a history of poor performance has pushed endowment policies (life insurance-based savings) into the decline phase of their life cycle in the UK. Others may enter into decline because of changes in either regulation or government policy. Thus for example, in the UK, the government decision to withdraw funding for Child Trust Funds (products to ensure that every child had some savings available to them at age 18) resulted in the product being withdrawn from new sales. Although not always straightforward, it can be important to distinguish between a product that is generically in the decline stage of its life cycle versus a product sector from which a provider chooses to withdraw. Citibank for example has withdrawn from mainstream retail banking in a number of markets in order to focus on private banking and wealth management. This is a strategic choice because mainstream banking is in decline.

The use of the product life cycle in marketing planning can provide some guidelines for the allocation of resources among service products, enabling the organisation to attach high priority to growth products, medium priority to mature products and consider possible withdrawal of declining products. However, as was the case with the BCG matrix, the recommendations should be interpreted with care and not simply followed without question. In particular, it is important to recognise that life cycles will differ very dramatically across product types – they may be very short or very long. Some products may appear never to reach the decline phase; others may never get past the introduction stage. The life cycle for a product class (bank accounts) will typically be much longer than the life cycle for a specific brand. Moreover, the marketing recommendations must be interpreted with care to avoid the potential for the life cycle becoming a self-fulfilling prophecy. For example, if a product looks as though it has reached maturity and possibly started to decline, the reduction of marketing support will tend to ensure that the predicted actually occurs. Finally, it is essential not to think only of a product's position in the life cycle. As Hooley (1995) has shown, strategy and performance may be driven as much by market position (specifically, market share) as by life cycle stage – and of course this partly explains the Citibank decision noted earlier.

Progress check

- Strategy tools can help to develop marketing strategy. It is important to remember that these offer guidance only and must always be used in combination with market research and judgement.
- Ansoff's product-market matrix is useful in thinking through options for growth.
- Matrix-based approaches and the Product Life Cycle help with thinking about the product portfolio taking into account product strength and market conditions

---

4.4.3 Competitive advantage

Identifying the organisation's competitive advantage is an essential part of any marketing strategy. The strategist, Michael Porter suggests that to compete effectively, an organisation must focus either on low costs or on differentiation. A low-cost strategy relies on a relatively standardised product and the organisation offers value through low costs and thus low prices. In essence this is an approach that seeks to offer value primarily by focusing on opportunities to reduce cost to the consumer. The differentiation-based approach means that the organisation offers a product that is distinctive and offers value to the customers because of the range of features it possesses and their ability to deliver functional, emotional or other benefits. For differentiation to be successful, the higher price received by the organisation must outweigh the costs of supplying the differentiated product. At the same time, the customer must feel that it is worth paying extra for the distinctive image of the product and the additional features offered.

Using these two routes to competitive advantage and considering the nature of the target market, Porter (1980, 1985) identifies three broad strategic options as shown below. This is an approach that focuses very explicitly on what providers offer – i.e. the nature of their value proposition, but says rather less about strategies to help consumers realise that value.

- **Cost leadership:**
  A cost leadership strategy involves trying to be the lowest cost producer, usually by concentrating on providing relatively standardised products. Low costs allow the organisation to attract customers by offering lower prices and thus the promise of better value. Such a strategy typically requires up to date and highly efficient service delivery systems. It can be argued that cost leadership had been a traditional strategy in many areas of financial services. As a consequence, many organisations are finding it increasingly difficult to gain significant cost advantages over their competitors and are instead

tending to focus more attention on differentiation. The neobanks have benefited from significantly lower costs than traditional banks, because of their reliance on digital channels and this has given them a cost advantage, although very commonly, they continue to compete by seeking differentiation.

- **Differentiation Leadership:**
  A differentiation-based strategy means trying to offer something that is seen as unique, distinct and able to create value for customers. A perceived uniqueness and the associated customer loyalty protects the firm from its competitors, from the threat of entry and from substitute products. HSBC, Citibank and American Express may all attempt to claim a perceived uniqueness based on their global presence and experience. The Raisin savings platform (see Marketing in practice 8.1) has differentiated itself through the ability of offer easy access to multiple savings accounts, while M-Pesa (see Marketing in practice 5.4) stands out because of the breadth of its network coverage.

  Research in the financial services sector suggests that differentiation may be difficult to attain for many providers – and where differentiation is achieved it may be difficult to protect from copying by competitors. Devlin and Ennew (1997) highlight the difficulties that UK providers of financial services experience in trying to create a clear competitive advantage based around either price or differentiation in a mass market and highlight the greater opportunities associated with either focus- or niche-based strategies.

- **Focus/niching:**
  This approach uses either costs or differentiation but concentrates on specific segments of the market – market niches. The aim of focus/niching is to identify part of the market with distinctive needs which are not adequately supplied by larger organisations. Differentiation focus is the most common form of focus strategy and implies producing highly customised products for very specific consumer groups. Marketing in practice 4.2 provides an example of a company following a very clearly defined niche strategy in relation to a specific market segment – medical professionals in the UK National Health Service. In the US, Golf Savings Bank offers golf-related rewards to PGA members and builds its brand via the sponsorship of significant golf tournaments. Another example of a differentiation-based focus strategy would be the UK's Ecology Building Society which specialises in lending that supports sustainable housing, sustainable communities and sustainable enterprises.

Porter's analysis stresses the importance of avoiding a situation where the organisation is "stuck in the middle" – i.e. trying to be all things to all consumers. He argues that the firm trying to perform well on costs and on differentiation is likely to lose out to firms concentrating on either one strategy or the other. However, this concept of "stuck in the middle" has been criticised for its ambiguity and in any consideration of Porter's framework, it is essential to be aware of the importance of value. As discussed earlier, value is based on the relationship between costs and benefits. Superior value can be offered by either adding benefits or reducing costs in areas of relevance to customers. Porter's cost and differentiation-based approaches to building competitive advantage can, most sensibly, be thought of as approaches to delivering value that concentrate on either reducing costs relative to a given range of benefits (cost leadership) or improving benefits relative to a given cost (differentiation).

Marketing in practice 4.2: Medical Professional

Medical Professional was incorporated in the UK on 14 June 2013 as an independent financial advisory service that provides specialist advice to medical professionals and is a member of the Vision Independent Financial Planning network. Their business proposition focuses on the traditional values of honesty, reliability and trust has been designed to put their clients at the centre of everything they do. Their target market is very specific – it is Hospital Doctors, General Practitioners, Dentists and Nurses. Their specialist knowledge of the career paths of professionals working in the UK's National Health Service (NHS) and the NHS Pension Scheme enables them to provide truly holistic financial advice on an independent and bespoke basis.

Medical Professional aims to provide a truly bespoke service to their customers. They have created and developed innovative NHS Pensions and Benefit Calculators to help them provide personalised advice. These calculators can be tailored to each individual's specific circumstances and enable Medical Professional to offer specialist advice and to select the best products on offer to ensure that clients achieve exactly what they set out to do.

Medical Professional has built detailed and specialist knowledge of a complex set of pension arrangements and the implications for their clients and as a consequence are ideally placed to adapt and innovate in response to changing customer needs and changing regulatory environments.

Alongside the benefits that Medical Professional offers the company has a clear focus on cost control, keeping overheads low and operating with transparent and competitive charging structures. Most companies look at each investment transaction individually when they apply their initial advice charges, as opposed to what a client has invested with them over time. Medical Professional, on the other hand, takes into consideration all the investments they make and discounts its charges accordingly. This enables clients over time, as they build on their investment portfolios, to achieve better value. Moreover, Medical Professional can also link family investments into clients charging structures and so family members can benefit from available discounts.

When a client transfers funds from another provider, either by choice or necessity, their existing provider will sometimes make a charge on exit If this is the case, and a client is making a transfer under advice from Medical Professional, the business takes this into consideration when applying its own charges and discounts the initial advice charge wherever possible. This is to help avoid "double charging" for clients which Medical Professional feel is both unfair and unreasonable.

Feedback from the Vision Network from their "Treating Customers Fairly" questionnaires sent out to clients post sale, showed that Medical Professional's overall service was rated at 100% for satisfaction and 100% would recommend them to family and friends.

Source: Adapted from 3rd Edition material supplied by Ralph Stratton, Managing Director, Medical Professional. Further detail at www.medicalprofessional.com/ (accessed 18/12/2024)

4.5 Summary and conclusion

The market for financial services has become increasingly competitive in recent years. Regulatory changes (current and future), developments in information technology, globalisation and fluctuations in economic performance have resulted in an increasingly competitive market environment. In such an environment, success requires a planned and strategic approach to marketing. Developing a plan to guide marketing is of considerable value because it encourages careful thought and analysis.

The organisation must have a clear mission and objectives, and it must understand its operating environment and be clear about the products and markets it serves. In making choices about products and markets, it is essential that the organisation tries to develop a match between its own particular strengths and the needs of the different segments of the market.

There are many different tools available to help an organisation develop its marketing plan and its marketing strategy. These tools provide a way of analysing information about the organisation and what it is doing. They also provide recommendations about strategic choices, which when combined with the marketing manager's knowledge and understanding of the environment can be a useful aid for strategy development.

Learning outcomes

Having completed this chapter, you should now be able to:

1. **Explain the importance of planning marketing activities.**
    Planning will help to ensure that an organisation's marketing activities are consistent with its objectives, with the capabilities of the organisation and with the needs of the marketplace. Planning provides a systematic analysis of what marketing activities are being undertaken, why and how. It is of particular value in an operating environment that is complex, uncertain and dynamic – as is the case with the financial services sector world-wide. Change is inevitable, it happens increasingly quickly and it can often be complex. Change can create new market opportunities and enable new services that have the potential to deliver enhanced value to customers and to providers. But, change can also bring new competition and new threats to established ways of working. While many aspects of these developments may not be known with certainty, planning encourages managers to think about the future, about different future possibilities and to adopt a strategic focus so that the organisation can be much better placed to respond effectively to a rapidly changing environment.
2. **Understand the value of taking a strategic approach to marketing.**
    The adoption and implementation of a strategic approach to marketing should impact positively on organisational performance. An understanding of customers and competitors will enable an organisation to deliver superior customer value to the market. In turn, superior customer value will facilitate both customer acquisition and customer retention. Successfully growing new business and keeping existing customers will have a positive impact on organisational performance, and particularly on profit and cash flow. Investment in strategic marketing in order to increase revenues is a far more effective way of improving shareholder value than

trying to reduce costs. The degree to which costs can be reduced is limited and while cost control will be important, the best opportunities for enhancing financial performance arise from growing the volume and/or the value of sales. Strategic marketing is essential to revenue growth because it focuses the organisation on customers, competitors and the challenges of a constantly changing marketplace.

3. **Outline the stages in the process of planning marketing.**
    Every organisation has its own approach to preparing marketing plans and there is no single correct approach. However, good plans do have a number of important features:
    *   The plan should have a logical structure;
    *   It should contain explicit marketing objectives which link to corporate objectives;
    *   It should analyse the environment (both internal and external) and the current position of the organisation;
    *   The plan should identify which combinations of products and markets the organisation will serve and how it will compete (segmentation, targeting and positioning);
    *   It should contain specific decisions relating to key marketing variables such as product, price, promotion and place (the marketing mix);
    *   It should consider the appropriate methods for implementing the identified strategy, including issues relating to budget, accountability and evaluation.

4. **Understand some of the tools and techniques that are used in developing marketing strategies.**
    There are a range of tools and techniques that can be used to help marketing managers to think through the way in which they will approach their markets and how they seek to compete effectively and deliver value to customers. Ansoff's Product-Market matrix provides guidance by considering options based around new or existing markets and new or existing products. Thinking about the mix of products and the way in which they may be managed can be helped through matrix-based approaches which compare the attractiveness of a market with the strength of a product's position. The Product Life Cycle can also be used in thinking about managing the product portfolio. Finally, Porter's generic strategies can help with thinking about how to compete. All of these tools are useful, but they bring most value when used in conjunction with broad-based analysis of the organisation and its market and careful managerial judgement. They do not give answers, but they do help managers think through options in a structured way.

Review questions

1. Why is it important to plan marketing activity?
2. What is your organisation's corporate mission – how might this help guide the future development of marketing activity?
3. What are the essential elements of a marketing plan?
4. Explain the differences between market development and product development. Find examples of both from the financial services sector.
5. What is the difference between cost leadership and differentiation leadership? Using Michael Porter's generic strategies, how can organisations try to create a competitive advantage? Identify examples of organisations that you think are using these approaches.

Notes

1 www.hsbc.com.tr/en/about-hsbc/hsbc-turkiye/our-vision-our-purpose-our-values (accessed January 2024)
2 www.axa.com/en/about-us/our-purpose (accessed January 2024)
3 www.cicinsurancegroup.com/wp-content/uploads/2023/05/The-CIC-Insurance-Group-PLC-Int egrated-Report-Financial-Statements-2022.pdf (accessed January 2024)
4 https://bankislami.com.pk/mission-vision-values/#:~:text=The%20Mission%20of%20Ban kIslami%20is,upholding%20social%20responsibility%20and%20transparency.&text=Ban kIslami%20is%20strongly%20committed%20towards,Shariah%20Excellence (accessed January 2024)
5 www.theguardian.com/money/2016/may/14/digital-app-only-banking-smartphone?CMP=share_b tn_link (accessed February 2017)
6 www.prnewswire.com/news-releases/china-merchants-bank-and-renren-to-pioneer-social-credit-card-123737319.html (accessed September 2012)

References

Almquist, E., Senior, J. and Block, B. (2016). The elements of value. *Harvard Business Review*, September (available at https://hbr.org/2016/09/the-elements-of-value)
Best, R. J. (2013). *Market Focused Management*, 6th Edition, London: Pearson.
Devlin, J. F. and Ennew, C. T. (1997). Understanding competitive advantage in retail financial services. *International Journal of Bank Marketing*, 15(3), pp. 77–82.
Doyle, P. (2000). Value-based marketing. *Journal of Strategic Marketing*, 8(4), pp. 299–311.
Grönroos, C. (2009). Marketing as promise management: Regaining customer management for marketing. *Journal of Business and Industrial Marketing*, 24(5), pp. 351–59.
Henson, S. W. and Wilson, J. C. (2002). Case study: Strategic challenges in the financial services industry. *Journal of Business and Industrial Marketing*, 17(5), pp. 407–418.
Hoffman, R. C. (2007). The strategic planning process and performance relationship: Does culture matter? *Journal of Business Strategies*, 24(1), pp. 27–48.
Hooley, G. J. (1995). The lifecycle concept revisited: Aid or albatross? *Journal of Strategic Marketing*, 3(1), pp. 23–39.
Kotler, P. (1994). *Marketing Management: Analysis, Planning Implementation and Control*, 8th Ed. New Jersey: Prentice Hall.
Moutinho, L. and Phillips, P. A. (2002). The impact of strategic planning on the competitiveness, performance and effectiveness of bank branches: A neural network analysis. *International Journal of Bank Marketing*, 20(3), pp. 102–10.
Porter, M. E. (1980). *Competitive Strategy*. New York: Free Press.
Porter, M. E. (1985). *Competitive Advantage*. New York: Free Press.
Song, M., Im, S., Bij, H. v. d. and Song, L. Z. (2011). Does strategic planning enhance or impede innovation and firm performance? *Journal of Product Innovation Management*, 28(4), pp. 503–20.
Vargo, S. L. and Lusch, R. F. (2004). The four service marketing myths: Remnants of a goods-based, manufacturing model. *Journal of Service Research*, 6(4), pp. 324–35.

5   Analysing the marketing environment

Learning objectives

At the end of this chapter, you should be able to:

1. Understand the major components of the overall marketing environment and their role in the development of a marketing strategy,
2. Analyse key features of the macro and market environments and what they may mean for marketing practice,
3. Appreciate ways of thinking about the organisation's internal environment and what this means for strategic decisions,
4. Understand the process of SWOT analysis and its role in making sense of information about the marketing environment.

5.1 Introduction

In Chapter 3, marketing was described as being concerned with satisfying customer needs, trying to do so more effectively than the competition and making appropriate use of the organisation's own resources and capabilities in this process. Accordingly, one of the first stages in any marketing process is to understand the environment in which an organisation operates. Indeed, the concept of being "market-oriented" originally championed by Kohli and Jaworski (1990) and Narver and Slater (1990) has, at its heart, the ideas of gathering, sharing and responding to information relating to both customers and competitors. Like many other organisations, providers of financial services operate in a rapidly changing envir onment. Globalisation and developments in information and communications technology (ICT) combined with changing customer needs and changing government policies create increasing degrees of complexity and uncertainty. In the past decade the issue of climate change has further added to the complexity of the operating environment giving rise to significant shifts in consumer attitudes and behaviours as well as in government policy, and this has had very significant implications for the financial services sector.

Marketing forces organisations to look outside and to develop an awareness and understanding of the environment in which they operate. An organisation that understands and responds to its operating environment should be able to deliver superior performance through its ability to satisfy customers more effectively than the competition and through

DOI: 10.4324/9781003398615-7

its ability to anticipate changes and developments in its key markets. However, an analysis of the external environment must be accompanied by a good understanding of the internal environment to enable an organisation to deploy its resources and capabilities most effectively in meeting the challenges posed by the changing marketplace. Even the best prepared organisations can be challenged by the rare and unexpected – events that those in finance sometimes call "Black Swan" events. The Covid-19 pandemic, the Russian invasion of Ukraine and the escalating conflict in the Middle East are all recent examples and while forward thinking and planning can help organisations manage through such events, their rarity and the scale of their impact usually means that few, if any, individuals have significant direct experience of responding to such challenges.

Historically, the financial services sector had always been thought of as relatively stable. In most countries, providers were heavily regulated and while the marketplace did change, that change tended to be slow and predictable; competition was limited and the types of financial services required by, and offered to, customers were relatively simple. In such an environment, marketing was largely a tactical activity, concerned with determining how best to advertise and sell the existing set of services. Indeed, in many cases, financial services organisations had advertising and sales departments, rather than marketing departments. As the pace of change accelerated and uncertainty increased, the marketing function had to take a more active role in understanding the changing environment and identifying implications for the products and services offered by their particular organisation.

This chapter will introduce the key elements of environmental analysis that are relevant to financial services providers. This is a process that is integral to strategic development and planning, as outlined in Chapter 4. The term 'marketing environment' is used to describe the range of external and internal factors which affect the way in which an organisation interacts with its markets. As such it is very broad and any analysis of the environment will generate a large volume of information. Thus, effective environmental analysis must be able to distinguish the more important factors from the less important ones. That is to say, analysing the environment involves, first of all, identifying and understanding what is happening and then assessing which developments are most important to the organisation concerned.

The chapter will begin by defining the elements that comprise the marketing environment. Subsequent sections will review the process of analysing the external environment (both at a macro and a market level) and then explore the analysis of the internal environment focusing particularly on resources and capabilities. Finally, the nature of SWOT analysis will be explained as a method for summarising information about the marketing environment and identifying options for future strategy. By its very nature, the process of analysing the environment and attempting to anticipate how a market will develop in the future is not a once-off but, rather, a continuous process. The nature of the operating environment and the ways in which it changes is one of the main sources of uncertainty confronting marketing planners. Environmental analysis cannot remove this uncertainty but it can help to reduce it.

5.2 The marketing environment

There are a number of components in the overall marketing environment. At the simplest level, we can distinguish between the internal environment (conditions within the organisation) and the external environment (conditions outside the organisation). The external environment can then be divided into the macro-environment and the market environment. The macro-environment is concerned with broad general trends in the economy and society which can affect all organisations, whatever their line of business. The market environment

Figure 5.1 The marketing environment

describes those factors which are specific to the particular market in which the organisation operates. The external environment may create opportunities for an organisation to exploit or may pose threats to current or planned activities. An outline of the key layers in the marketing environment is presented in Figure 5.1.

Marketing as a strategic activity is concerned with managing the relationship between the organisation and its environment. This may mean adjusting and adapting the organisation's marketing activities to respond to external changes in the environment. It may also mean trying to change the environment to make it better suited to what the organisation wishes to do. That is to say, the environment should not be viewed simply as a constraint – rather it should be viewed as something which can, if necessary, be influenced and changed by an organisation. Lobbying for changes to the regulatory framework is one very obvious example of an attempt to change the external environment. Equally, mergers and acquisitions serve as a means of altering patterns of competition and changing the resources and capabilities available to a particular organisation. Some forms of marketing communications may be employed to influence customer needs and expectations while branding decisions and distribution strategies can sometimes be used to build barriers to market entry by potential competitors. The extent to which aspects of the environment can be managed varies. Typically, macro-environmental factors are seen as being least controllable while market environmental factors are more controllable.

Understanding all aspects of the marketing environment and understanding the potential implications for future strategy lies at the heart of effective marketing. The future is, by definition, unknown, but careful analysis of existing trends and a good understanding of the market and its key players can help financial services gain a better perspective on what the future might look like. In many cases, scenario planning may be used to consider different possible futures. Some scenarios will be more likely than others but understanding them and their implications is invaluable in planning how best to compete. Marketing in practice 5.1 outlines how the Foresight Factory works with financial services brands (and others) to help them understand their future and, particularly, the drivers and the implications of social change.

Marketing in practice 5.1: forecasting the future

In 1964 the Boeing company looked to the future and anticipated that aviation was about to change drastically. Their insight was that substantial numbers of people wanted to travel on intercontinental routes. They believed that the unmet demand for long-haul travel was so large that a radically new type of aircraft was required – one which was much bigger than any existing commercial airliner. They backed their vision of the future by designing and building the 747 "jumbo" jet, an aircraft so successful that Boeing enjoyed 30 years of commercial advantage before their principal rival, Airbus, developed a competitor aircraft.

Anticipating the future is vital to every brand. Failure to anticipate changing behaviours and attitudes can leave brands beached. Similarly, technology can pull the ground from a formerly successful company (as the case of Kodak makes clear).

The Foresight Factory advises brands on social and economic change and what it means for them. They gather rich data across 27 countries from a diversity of sources including consumer surveys, press releases, patents, innovations and other media and commercial signals and make use of AI, machine learning and other analytical techniques to understand changing consumer sentiment. And this is all supported by dedicated field research where emerging new perspectives need to be tested.

Often change can only be properly understood when viewed through the long lens of history. Many changes happen quite slowly – such as rising affluence across the Western world – and yet the impact of these changes only becomes truly apparent when we look backwards. Change can be measured through quantitative means and it's the direction and scale of change that provide a true sense of significance.

Foresight Factory works to a time horizon of three to five years ahead. Public sector strategists tend to look rather further ahead – often a decade or more. In those cases consumer research is of little value and we rely on the creation of scenarios and the involvement of experts to agree on some credible visions of the future.

The Foresight Factory has developed a process that allows them to identify and prioritise the trends that have the greatest impact for any given brand. This analysis is of huge value in helping companies understand the context in which they operate. Often brands will take this further, using their key trends as the stimulus for new product development so that new products address current and future consumer needs.

Source: Adapted from material provided by Barry Clark, Future Foundation for 3rd Edition with further information available at www.foresightfactory.co/strategic-foresight-for-gro wth/ .

5.3 The macro-environment

The macro-environment is concerned with broad general trends within the economy and society. The macro-environment is typically of much greater relevance when considering the development of broad strategies while the market environment will be much more

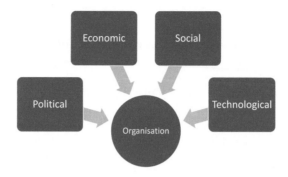

Figure 5.2 Analysing the macro-environment

important when considering the development of specific business/product strategies. Traditionally the analysis of the macro-environment was referred to as PEST or STEP analysis.

- **PEST** = Political, Economic, Social, Technological
- **STEP** = Social, Technological, Economic, Political

More recently, these acronyms have been extended to include, for example:

- **STEEP** = Social, Technological, Economic, Environmental, Political
- **SLEPT** = Social, Legal, Economic, Political, Technological
- **PESTLE** = Political, Economic, Social, Technological, Legal, Environmental

These different names are merely acronyms that serve as an easy way of remembering which factors to cover in an analysis of the macro-environment. What is most important is that any analysis of the macro-environment is comprehensive and includes all the factors likely to affect an organisation. The following discussion is structured around the PEST framework, for simplicity, but it covers all of the factors listed above. This framework is shown in Figure 5.2 and discussed in more detail below.

5.3.1   The political environment

The "political environment" covers a range of issues including party politics, the character of the government itself and also the legal and regulatory system. The financial services sector is, perhaps, one of the more politically sensitive sectors of any economy because of its role in the economic development and well-being of a country as explained in Chapter 1. The risks, complexities and importance associated with financial services also mean that it is one of the most heavily regulated sectors of an economy. Inevitably then, there is considerable interdependence between the sector and the political environment and nowhere is this better illustrated than in the controversy around the United Kingdom (UK)'s decision to leave the European Union (Brexit). The decision itself caused major turmoil within the sector and this was reinforced by uncertainty about its longer-term impact, including for London as a major financial centre.

The political character of a government, and the potential for change, can have important implications for business both nationally and internationally. Consider for example the implications of China's ambitious One Belt, One Road (OBOR) initiative to structure international trade routes and support this with major investments in infrastructure across a series of partner countries. While the direct impact may primarily be in relation to the trade in goods, that growth in trade and its impact on economic activity has major implications for the financial services sector.

At a national level, some political parties may be more favourable to the business community than others and this attitude is often reflected in legislation and regulation. The importance of government macroeconomic policies has already been mentioned, but there are a wide range of government activities which affect the financial sector including sector-specific policy formulation, legislation, decisions on government spending and partial privatisation. For example, the policy of privatising a range of previously state-owned industries in the UK during the 1980s is widely credited with changing public attitudes to share ownership and creating demand for small-scale share-dealing services.

Two aspects of the political environment defined in its broadest sense are of particular relevance to financial services – namely industry regulation and consumer protection. Regulation generally refers to a set of rules and legal requirements that guide the operation of the industry and the conduct of firms within the industry. As such, it is specific to financial services. Financial regulation is typically concerned with licencing providers, guiding the conduct of business, enforcing relevant laws, protecting customers and preventing fraud and misconduct. Consumer protection refers to a regulatory system which focuses specifically on the rights and interests of the consumers in their interactions with businesses and other entities. Typically, consumer protection legislation applies across all sectors of the economy and, consequently, there will be some overlap between industry specific regulation and economy-wide consumer protection systems.

 Stop and think?

Think about key political events and decisions in your country or state. How might those events and decisions affect financial services providers and financial services consumers?

Some aspects of financial services regulation were discussed in Chapters 1 and 2. In the UK, for example, the regulation of financial services went through a major change as a consequence of the global financial crisis which resulted in the replacement of the Financial Services Authority (formerly the highest single financial services regulator) by a number of new bodies. The Financial Conduct Authority (FCA) assumed responsibility for the regulation of the way in which both retail and wholesale providers conduct their business. The Prudential Regulation Authority (PRA) focuses its attention on ensuring the stability of the UK financial system and all other matters are dealt with by the Bank of England's new Financial Policy Committee (FPC).

As was noted in Chapter 1, regulation varies considerably across countries and some examples of this are outlined in Marketing in practice 5.2.

Marketing in practice 5.2: the diversity of approaches to regulating financial services

China

Until recently, China had three specialist financial services regulatory bodies – the China Securities Regulatory Commission (CSRC) was the first to be established in 1992, to regulate the securities sector. The China Insurance Regulatory Commission (CIRC) was set up in 1998 to regulate the insurance sector and the China Banking Regulatory Commission (CBRC) was set up in 2003 to increase the independence of the Central Bank and improve regulatory efficiency. CBRC's main regulatory instrument is the rating system for assessing commercial banks, which is published annually. In 2018 CIRC and CBRC were merged into a single China Banking and Insurance Regulatory Commission (CBIRC). In 2023 the regulatory structure was further consolidated with the creation of the National Administration of Financial Regulation (NAFR) which will cover all sectors except the securities industry and will also assume responsibilities for consumer and investor protection.

US

In the US, the responsibility for regulation is effectively split between the Securities and Exchange Commission (SEC) which regulates all aspects of the securities industry, and both the Federal Reserve System (FRS) and the Federal Deposit Insurance Commission (FDIC), which regulate most of the banking sector. The SEC is concerned with investor protection, fair, orderly, and efficient markets, and facilitating capital formation. It places particular emphasis on informed decision-making and requires all public companies to disclosure any meaningful information so that that all investors have access to the same pool of knowledge on which to base decisions. The Federal Reserve is the US central bank and has, as one of its responsibilities, the supervision and regulation of the banking and financial system. It has particular responsibility for domestic banks that choose to become members of the Federal Reserve and for foreign banks. The FDIC is the primary regulator of banks that are chartered by individual states but which choose not to be members of the Federal Reserve. Its primary function is to promote public confidence in the financial system of the USA and one of its best-known policy instruments is deposit insurance (to a maximum of $100,000)

Australia

The Australian Prudential Regulation Authority (APRA) is responsible for the supervision of banks, insurers, credit unions, building societies, friendly societies and superannuation funds. APRA seeks to establish and enforce appropriate standards to create an efficient, stable and competitive financial system and (as was the case with the FSA in the UK) it relies on an approach which is essentially self-regulation – i.e. senior management in regulated institutions is responsible for compliance with APRA requirements. The Australian Securities and Investments Commission (ASIC) is responsible for regulating financial markets, securities, futures and corporations in order to protect customers, investors and creditors.

These examples focus on specific regulatory arrangements that govern the way in which firms within the sector are required to behave. Additional regulations relating to consumer protection cover a wide range of topics including, but not necessarily limited to, information provision (particularly advertising), product liability, privacy rights, unfair business practices, fraud, misrepresentation and other forms of interaction between businesses and consumers. Regulations for consumer protection vary considerably across countries. In the UK, responsibility for consumer protection rests with the Competition and Markets Authority (CMA) (which replaced the Office of Fair Trading in 2014). Rather than traditional consumer protection, the CMA has a broad-based responsibility to promote competition and to ensure that markets work effectively and for the benefit of consumers, businesses and the economy. However, the CMA does have responsibility for the enforcement of consumer protection legislation and for enhancing the conditions for consumer decision-making.

Similar systems operate in many other countries. For example, in the US, the Federal Trade Commission and the US Department of Justice have responsibility for enforcing federal legislation and there are parallel organisations at state level. In Australia, the Trade Practices Act 1974 and related consumer protection legislation is enforced by the Australian Competition and Consumer Commission (ACCC), and its work is supplemented by equivalent state-level agencies. In China, consumer protection is the responsibility of the State Administration of Industry and Commerce (SAIC). Its particular responsibilities include regulating product safety, preventing unfair competition and protecting consumers' legal rights. The work of SAIC is supplemented by the China Consumer's Administration (CCA) – a nationwide organisation which provides independent information and education to customers, receives consumer complaints and provides support for customers wishing to take legal action. In Singapore, the Consumer Protection (Fair Trading) Act of 2004 is a major component of the consumer protection regime. Its aim is to create a much fairer trading environment by identifying a series of unfair trading practices for which consumers would have recourse to the law.

With growing economic integration, the analysis of the political environment must also consider the role of supra-national organisations such as ASEAN (Association of South East Asian Nations), APEC (Asia Pacific Economic Community), NAFTA (North American Free Trade Area) and the EU (European Union). The moves by ASEAN and the General Agreement on Trade in Service (GATS) to liberalise the financial sectors of South East Asian economies is often cited as one of the factors that contributed to the need for much greater consolidation in the domestic banking and insurance sectors. Specifically in the banking sector, the Basel Committee on Banking Supervision which comprises central bankers from 13 countries has developed international standards for measuring the adequacy of a bank's capital with a view to creating greater consistency in the management of risk across banking systems (see Chapter 2). The resulting standards, enshrined in the Basel III accord, can have important implications for lending decisions.

Of course, when thinking about the political and legal environment, we should also recognise other more general provisions that might affect the operation of financial services organisations including health and safety legislation and employment legislation. Not all aspects of work-related legislation and regulation will directly affect marketing, but good environmental analysis will at least be aware of their existence and their potential impact.

5.3.2 *The economic environment*

The economic environment covers all aspects of economic behaviour at an aggregate level and will include consideration of factors such as growth in income, interest rates, inflation, unemployment, investment and exchange rates. Government economic policy (both actual and intended) is typically a central component because of its impact on economic perform-ance. The nature of consumer demand for financial services will inevitably be affected by eco-nomic performance; higher levels of economic growth will result in higher levels of demand for existing financial services as well as creating demand for new ones. Research insight 5.1

 Research insight 5.1: the impact of economic conditions on purchasing financial services

While it might seem like an obvious topic to study, the impact of economic conditions on customer purchases of financial services is somewhat under researched. This paper seeks to address that gap and looks at the impact of specific economic variables as well as broader socio-demographic factors on the probability of purchasing a number of financial products. The research uses a statistical technique (proportional hazard models) which allows the impact of a range of variables to be estimated. The data on which the analysis is based were provided by a major international insurance company based in the UK. The data set covers around 50,000 customers using the direct sales channel for the period between 1999 and 2003. Variables in the data set include product purchase, payment and termination as well as a broad range of individual consumer characteristics. The products under consideration were collective investments, life insurance and protection products.

As well as individual consumer data, the analysis also considered broader macro-economic factors. Consumer prices and a consumer confidence indicator were used as traditional drivers of demand. The unemployment rate was used as a broader indication of the strength of the economy. The FTSE All Share Index, and Bank of England base interest rate were included as indicators of the attractiveness of other types of products (and in the case of base rate, the impact of mortgage costs).

The research compares two different types of proportional hazard model to assess their effectiveness in addition to its primary focus on understanding the impact of economic factors on purchases. While individual-specific characteristics do influence purchase decisions, the results demonstrate the over-riding importance of economic influences. The impact of individual specific factors varies depending on the economic environment. For example, when the economy is unfavourable, certain groups are much more likely to purchase than others: if unemployment rises, it is the more affluent consumers and older consumers who are more likely to continue to purchase. Rising prices will have a negative impact on purchasing – but the effects are weaker for older consumers and stronger amongst younger ones. Increases in interest rates have little impact on the purchases of younger consumers (who typically do not have mortgages) and rises in the stock market (which may make other products more attractive) tend to have a bigger impact on older consumers. Understanding these impacts is poten-tially of considerable value to marketers – whether in relation to thinking about the lifetime value of customers or in relation to thinking about how to target marketing communications according to economic climate. The research also points to the value of considering both overall economic conditions and individual characteristics.

Source: Tang, Thomas, Thomas, and Bozzetto (2007).

provides some insights into the impact of economic conditions on the purchase of financial services.

The growth in equity investments by private consumers and the increased demand for mutual funds is another aspect of longer-term changes in patterns of demand. In addition to the level of income and rate of growth, the proportion of income that is saved is likely to be another key consideration. Figure 5.3 provides data on household savings rates for a range of countries worldwide since 2000. China is distinguished by very high levels of household savings as a percentage of income and all countries show a marked increase in household savings at the start of the Covid-19 pandemic (although in later years some countries saw a big drop in savings as individuals used their savings to replace lost income as economic conditions deteriorated). As well as affecting overall economic performance, the savings rate provides an indicator of the potential size of the market for savings and investment products.

Equally important macroeconomic influences will be interest rates and inflation. Typically, high real interest rates, (based on the difference between inflation and nominal interest rates) would be expected to encourage savings; low real interest rates would be expected to encourage borrowing. In practice, of course the situation is more complex; Chinese households report high levels of savings, not because real interest rates are high but rather because welfare provision is limited and families are saving in order to provide for key needs such as education, health and retirement income. Conversely, both the UK and the US displayed negative real interest rates since the onset of the global financial crisis and yet savings went up and borrowings went down. Such outcomes reflect the need to be aware of the interactions between a range of economic variables. UK and US customers may have been faced with poor (even negative) returns on their savings, but with uncertainty about future employment and income, they may elect to reduce debt, reduce consumption and increase savings. Similarly, the low cost of borrowing after the financial crisis did not increase demand for loans, partly

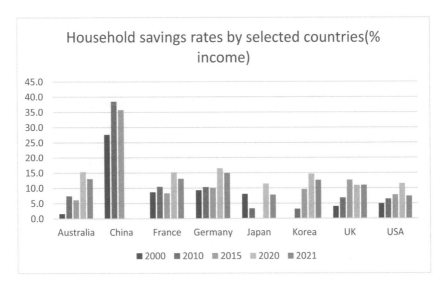

Figure 5.3 Household savings rates

Source: https://data.oecd.org/hha/household-savings.htm, accessed 06/01/2024 because of the unfavourable conditions elsewhere in the economy and partly because of an (over) reaction by the banks to their previously liberal approach to lending. However, after a sustained period of low interest rates, further cuts to the cost of borrowing in 2016 did appear to have a positive impact on savings. This changed once again during the pandemic with savings rates increased dramatically as the graph shows; post pandemic, rapid inflation and rising (though often still negative) interest rates further challenged savings and borrowings and created considerable turmoil in many financial markets.

Progress check

- In order to understand the marketing environment it is essential to consider the macro environment (which encompasses broad high level developments that will impact on business activity): the market environment (issues specific to a particular market) and the internal environment (aspects of the organisation itself and what this means for how that organisation might compete).
- There are many frameworks that can support this type of analysis and what is key is to ensure that any analysis is systematic and comprehensive.
- The political environment deals with a range of factors, including party politics, the political character of the government itself and also the legal and regulatory system.
- The economic environment considers aspects of economic behaviour at an aggregate level – essentially those factors that define the health of the economy overall.

5.3.3 The social environment

The social environment is extremely broad and covers all relevant aspects of a society including demographics, culture, values, attitudes, lifestyles, etc. The following discussion will highlight those aspects which may be of particular significance in relation to the financial services sector.

Demographics

The demographic environment encompasses all factors relating to the size, structure and distribution of the population. The potential market for any product is affected not only by the number of individuals within the population but also by the age structure and regional distribution of that population. Although the world population is growing, the pace of change in many Western economies is slow and in some cases, virtually zero. Population changes depend on both birth and death rates and while death rates have been falling worldwide, the fall in birth rates in many economies has largely counteracted this effect. Table 5.1 provides sample data on birth rates for a range of countries over time.

In 2006, Hong Kong had the lowest birth rate (number of births per 1,000 people) of any country in the world and displayed a similarly low level in 2011. Despite signs of an increase in 2016, the birthrate fell back again in 2022. Many developed economies, the UK included, were also characterised by low birth rates. Such economies typically have ageing populations, a feature which may have important implications for pension products, health insurance and

Table 5.1 Selected birth rates for 2006 and 2011 (births/1000 people)

	2006	2011	2016	2022
Niger	50.7	50.1	44.8	46.9
Nigeria	40.4	39.2	37.3	34.0
Philippines	24.9	25.0	24.0	22.2
India	22.0	20.6	19.3	16.5
United States	14.1	13.7	12.5	12.2
China	13.3	12.3	12.4	9.7
United Kingdom	10.7	12.3	12.1	10.8
Japan	9.4	8.4	7.8	6.9
Germany	8.3	8.3	8.5	9.0
Hong Kong	7.3	7.5	9.1	7.9

Source: Compiled from CIA World Fact Book, available online at www.cia.gov/
the-world-factbook/field/birth-rate/country-comparison/ (accessed 04/01/2024)

long-term care insurance. In contrast, other countries are experiencing rapid growth in population, largely as a consequence of high birth rates and falling death rates. For example, Nigeria has a birth rate of close to 40 and India has a birth rate that is only slightly less than 20 (see Table 5.1). Even allowing for falling death rates, such countries will have a very young population and potentially a very different profile of demand for financial services. The interesting case is that of China, which although still developing rapidly, has an unusually low birth rate – a legacy of the government's "one-child policy" – and as a consequence, faces many of the challenges that characterise developed Western economies, including healthcare provision for the elderly and its own pensions crisis. Indeed, some estimates suggest that by 2050, a quarter of the Chinese population will be over 60.[1] Pressures are increasing for the raising of the retirement age, employee contributions are being increased and the estimated deficit in pension funds across China is currently being reported as being close to $500bn.[2] And most recently, new reports have highlighted that the population of China is now actually falling, despite many political efforts to increase birthrates.

There are a number of other aspects of population structure that might be relevant to financial services. The regional distribution of the population and particularly the balance between urban and rural areas may be important – particularly so in relation to retail banking and the distribution of branches. China has witnessed a significant growth in the number of rural banks as government policy has sought to support local markets and increase productivity by improving access to financial services. In India (as Research insight 5.1 shows) the large rural population with limited access to bank branches has created the conditions for the rapid growth of mobile payments. Household structure is also relevant; in many Western economies such as the UK there has been a tendency towards a declining household size and an increase in the number of single person households as individuals leave home but delay marriage. This trend will have implications for mortgage products and life insurance products – single mortgage holders may feel less need for life insurance cover if they have no dependents to worry about. And, of course, the decline of the extended family in many parts of the world creates greater demand for products that provide financial support in retirement, including pensions, care insurance and equity release products.

Culture

Understanding consumer needs is central to any marketing activity and those needs will often be heavily influenced by cultural factors. Culture is a complex idea and is difficult to define.

As a general rule, it can be thought of as a term that defines "how we do things here" – it relates to how people behave, what they believe, what they value, their customs and traditions and what is considered acceptable and unacceptable. Any type of marketing must recognise the significance of culture, and financial services are no exception. In principle, the biggest challenge that culture presents is in relation to international markets, where an ability to understand the prevailing culture and adjust and adapt to it are essential. However, an understanding of culture and cultural changes is also relevant in domestic markets. The nature of marketing communications, the use of colour and particular symbols can all touch on cultural sensitivities. Some countries may have a relatively homogeneous culture; others can be very diverse. In the US, for example, marketers must be sensitive to the different heritage and cultures of the indigenous, Hispanic, African and European communities. In the UK, there is also considerable diversity with significant proportions of the population being of south Asian or Caribbean heritage. Different cultural backgrounds may reflect themselves in different responses to marketing communications, different decision-making processes and different product preferences.

One of the strongest elements of culture is religion and this provides a very clear example of the way in which culture can affect marketing. Paying or receiving interest (*riba*) is against the teaching of Islam and thus *haram* (unlawful), as highlighted in Chapter 2. Islam forbids all forms of economic activity, which are morally or socially injurious. *Riba* is harmful because it is seen as wealth generated purely by the ownership of money rather than by genuine economic activity. The prohibition of interest in Islamic law (*Shari'ah*) presents a major challenge for traditional banks whose business revolves around interest margins. Equally, it presents a major opportunity for the growing number of specialist Islamic banks (sometimes called participation banks). Estimating growth rates for Islamic financial services is not entirely straightforward but there is widespread consensus that growth has been rapid over the past two decades and future double-digit growth can be expected[3]. Globally, the largest single market for Islamic banking is in the Kingdom of Saudi Arabia and the sector is dominated by GCC countries (Gulf Co-operation Council) although Malaysia – one of the pioneers of Islamic financial services continues to be a very significant player. Further detail about Islamic financial services is provided in Chapter 2.

 Stop and think?

Look at the websites and marketing imagery used by a sample of financial services providers that you are familiar with. How well do you think it reflects the cultural diversity of your country or state?

Other social influences

A range of other issues relating to social structures and social values may also be important for financial services providers including changing patterns of work, changing social structures and changing values. These factors may affect the ways in which people may wish to access financial services – for example, people who are working longer hours may place greater importance on being able to access their bank accounts through mobile and internet banking. Social influences may also affect the types of financial services demanded. Thus, for example, with an increasing value being placed on education, prospective parents may seek financial services that allow them to save for their children's education. With more people travelling internationally, demand for internationally recognised debit and credit cards will continue to increase. And with growing numbers of individuals working outside of their home county, there has been sustained growth in the demand for international money transfer services. With growing numbers of consumers being concerned about environmental or ethical issues there is a demand for financial services that are provided in a way that respond to these concerns and are consistent with these values (see also Chapter 17). This trend has been touched on in reference to the earlier discussion on Islamic finance but its impact may be broader still if consumers seek to invest in stocks or mutual funds which have a "green" (environmentally friendly) or "sustainable" dimension. Marking in Practice 5.3 provides an example of new financial services that are emerging in response to the emergence of this market segment.

Marketing in practice 5.3: robo-advice and thematic investing

Traditional financial advice from a trained financial planner is relatively expensive and often requires that the individual has a minimum amount to invest. As a consequence, many individuals who are new to investing and have relatively small amounts to invest find it difficult to access appropriate advice about the management of their portfolio. This gap in the market was addressed with the emergence of robo-advice – essentially an automated, digital, financial planning and investment service. Robo-advisers offer automated investment advice at a much lower cost and for smaller investment portfolios than was the case for human advisers.

The robo-advice model relies on gathering a standard set of information from customers via a questionnaire. Typically, robo-advisers request information about financial situation, financial goals, attitudes to risk and other relevant considerations. Using this information, an algorithm provides advice and can automatically invest funds on the consumer's behalf.

In recent years, robo-advisers have started to offer "thematic portfolios" to enable individuals to direct their investments towards key priorities for them and/or key trends shaping the future.

- Nutmeg (www.nutmeg.com/) offers three future-focused themes: technological innovation, resource transformation, or evolving consumer. These are not technically ESG funds but they do focus on relevant topics including sustainability, health, energy and water.
- Wealthify (www.wealthify.com/) offers 5 Ethical Plans with all fund providers being signatories to the Principles of Responsible Investing (PRI)
- Moneyfarm (www.moneyfarm.com/uk/) also offers ESG (Environmental, Social and Governance) portfolios and thematic portfolios in the area of technology, society, and sustainability.

Each of these companies has recognised an emerging trend in terms of consumer attitudes and preferences; and developments in the digital business model have enabled them to provide a cost-effective thematic investing service to the smaller investor.

5.3.4 The technological environment

Technology essentially refers to our level of knowledge about "how things are done". That is to say, understanding this aspect of the marketing environment is much more than simply being familiar with the latest hi-tech innovations, although it is fair to say that this has been one of the areas in which there has been particularly rapid and significant change as earlier discussions of fintech have highlighted. Technology affects not only the type of products available but also the ways in which people organise their lives and the ways in which goods and services can be marketed.

In the financial services sector, the single most important aspect of technology has been ICT – information and communications technology. ICT has had a dramatic impact on the delivery of financial services, the types of financial services that can be offered and the ways in which those services are marketed. In particular, developments in mobile technologies over the last ten years are transforming the ways in which providers deliver financial services and the ways in which consumers consume them.

The emergence of open banking (see for example www.nationwide.co.uk/ways-to-bank/open-banking/) has allowed third parties to develop applications and services around financial institutions' existing products. Raisin (see Marketing in practice 8.1) is perhaps one of the best-known examples of a successful start-up based on open banking arrangements. Other innovations include services that allow customers to access all their financial information in a single place via money management apps or web sites or services that draw on a customer's financial information to offer more personalised services. Open banking protocols have also made many aspects of online payments simpler and more convenient for customers. Given that open banking is about sharing personal data between organisations, it is not without risk although strict regulatory controls do seek to minimise these risks.

For a long time, financial services have been delivered via ATMs and by telephones. The last two decades have seen increasing use of the internet as a delivery channel, initially via PC/laptop but increasingly via smartphones and tablet devices. Branch networks and sales networks may still be important but it is hard to imagine them operating without a range of technology-enabled forms of distribution. ATMs were first introduced in the US in the 1970s and at that stage their main function was to dispense cash. As technology developed and consumer acceptance of ATMs increased, machines were developed with a much wider range of functions which allow individuals to undertake an extensive range of banking activities. Customers can usually undertake most standard banking transactions 24 hours per day including withdrawal, deposit, balance updates, balance transfers and bill payment. Increasingly, ATMs also offer value-added services including charitable donations, mobile phone top-ups, account opening and account management. The development of ATMs has certainly provided much greater flexibility for consumers in terms of their access to bank services (see Figure 5.4); they have also served as an additional marketing tool as banks use the ATM transaction to promote other services.

Technology developments are not just about expanding the range of services offered. Developments in biometrics can be used to improve both security and ease of use for consumers. In the 3rd edition of this book, we noted some of the early adopters of biometric ATMs including the Brazilian bank, Bradesco, which combined conventional passwords with biometric sensors to enable it to identify customers based on the vascular pattern in their hands.[4] Japanese bank Japan Seven uses facial recognition for ATM access as does Caixa bank in Spain. Qatar National Bank uses iris recognition and First National bank in South Africa uses fingerprint recognition[5]. Take-up of biometrics has been faster in some emerging markets than

Figure 5.4 First National Bank in South Africa provides ATM facilities at the summit of Table Mountain in Cape Town

Source: Image provided by author

it has been in many developed economies with the ethical and legal implications associated with the storage and use of biometric data often seen as a significant barrier.[6]

The telephone has a long history for the purchase and management of financial services, supporting interpersonal interactions and paper-based transactions (e.g. telephoning to obtain an insurance quote). After ATMs, phone banking was the next major initiative in service delivery with the first systems appearing in the mid 1980s. Most financial services providers now offer phone banking systems using a mixture of automated voice recognition outside of reasonable working hours and personal contact during reasonable working hours.

Most financial services are also available online. The development of the World Wide Web in the early 1990s provided a major impetus for the development of computer-based banking. Until this point in time, and with a few notable exceptions, computer-based banking was largely restricted to corporate markets. In the mid-1990s, the early adopters launched their internet banking services in the US, Europe, Japan and Australia and New Zealand. Regions such as South East Asia, South Asia, the Middle East and South America rapidly followed. Initially, for retail customers, internet banking did not replace the traditional branch – it became essentially an alternative, complementary channel of distribution. In recent years the emergence of purely digital banks has changed the position and a large number of retail banking consumers rely only on digital services. The neobanks are the best examples[7] – NuBank in Brazil, Monzo, Revolut and Starling in the UK; Chime in the US and N26 in Germany are leading examples of new, digital banks and benefit from being able to avoid the costs associated with building a physical presence.

The internet also proved effective for dealing in a range of other financial services including insurance, loans, mortgages, share trading and mutual fund trading. However, as online transactions have become commonplace for standard financial services, consumer willingness to access more complex products through such channels has increased. Already, in the UK, online investment fund platforms such as Fidelity and Hargreaves Lansdown are offering pensions alongside other investment products and similar services are available across a range of markets. The development of robo-advice mentioned earlier is a further example of more complex financial services being provided through digital channels.

Mobile internet has brought about major transformations in the delivery and consumption of financial services. Traditional computer-based access to the internet and the web required consumers to be in a specific location. Smartphones and tablet devices enable customers to engage with financial service providers virtually whenever they wish. Such developments have had a number of important consequences for marketers.

- First, many financial services providers, and particularly banks, have seen an increase in the number of customer interactions and transactions but a reduction in visits to the branch, with important implications for the potential to cross-sell to those customers.
- Second, the availability of a variety of smartphone apps allows many transactions to be automated, including payments. Peer-to-peer payment systems have appeared in a range of countries as well as a range of applications which exploit the potential of technology to engage with customers in increasingly diverse ways.
  - Apple Pay was launched in the USA initially in 2014 allowing individuals to make payments directly through their phone.
  - In 2015 RBS launched touch ID on their mobile banking app and were the first bank to introduce an interactive banking app on the Apple Watch.
  - Western Union developed a mix of both website and mobile payment systems to facilitate transfers around the world.
  - Quicken loans in the US offers applications and approval end-to-end through its mobile app and has grown exponentially through its ability to move and scale quickly with agility.
  - Other more generic forms of contactless payment systems have emerged in a similar timescale with increasing numbers of debit and credit cards able to provide such services. Mobile payments have been of particular significance in the developing world because the traditional branch-based infrastructure is limited but mobile telephony is widespread; one of the earliest mobile peer-to-peer payment systems – Safaricom's M-PESA system is outlined in Marketing in practice 5.4. Two years before Apple Pay, the Dutch-Bangla Bank Limited launched a mobile service which, in addition to services such as peer-to- peer transfers and bill payments, also allowed the phone to be used for cardless ATM withdrawals and to receive regular salary payments.[8]

Marketing in practice 5.4: the M-Pesa mobile payments system

Figure 5.5 An M-Pesa Kiosk in Nairobi

Source: "M-PESA kiosk outside Kibera centre in Nairobi" by wrcomms licensed under CC BY-SA 2.0

In 2007, Safaricom (a commercial affiliate of Vodaphone) launched the M-PESA payment system in Kenya; subsequently M-PESA has been launched in Tanzania, South Africa, Afghanistan India and parts of eastern Europe. Initially developed as a mechanism to allow microfinance borrowers to repay their loans, M-PESA stores value and permits payment via the user's mobile phone. Money can be deposited into a SIM card app (and withdrawn) via a range of authorised retail outlets, and SMS technology can be used to send payments to others, pay bills and purchase airtime. Users engage with agents distributed across a wide range of outlets who operate rather like an ATM – they will take deposits and credit them to a mobile account or provide funds and debit them from an account. And the mobile account can also be used to make payments. Users pay a small fee for withdrawal transactions (but not deposits) and the retail outlets receive payments from Safaricom when they accept deposits or facilitate withdrawals.

In 2010, Safaricom reported over 9.0 million registered customers, close to 17,000 retail outlets, and monthly person-to-person transfers in excess of $300m. By 2012, estimates suggested that the customer base had grown to 14m and by late 2014 it had reached 17m. In 2020, estimates suggested that 72% of Kenyans and 43% of Ugandans had M-PESA mobile accounts. And academic researchers have suggested that economic growth tends to be higher in areas where there is a high level of penetration of mobile money systems such as M-PESA.

The number of M-PESA registered retail outlets is substantially larger than the number of conventional banking outlets giving M-PESA extensive reach into the Kenyan population. One of the challenges in countries such as Kenya where the banking infrastructure is relatively under-developed is that large proportions of the population have no access to banking. A system such as M-PESA builds on the widely available mobile phone network to provide a viable alternative to conventional branch-based banking. Initially much of the M-PESA activity focused on person-to-person transactions – effectively replacing transactions that would have occurred through non-technology mechanisms. But as the level of uptake increased, more and more institutions have engaged with M-PESA and thus in addition to bill payments, companies now pay salaries via M-PESA and there are plans for the system to be used to make purchases at retail outlets.

Source: www.vox.com/future-perfect/21420357/kenya-mobile-banking-unbanked-cellphone-money (accessed 18/12/2023)

- Third, customers' ability to control and manage their financial situation is being substantially improved as personal finance apps allow them to pull together information from all of their online accounts into a single location. For example, Santander's Spendlytics app breaks down user's spending into categories to make tracking and managing their spending habits easier. Enhanced information availability and a growth in self-service transactions have the potential to increase the extent to which consumers feel "in-control" of their finances. According to a recent survey by ING, 48% of respondents feel more in control of their finances as a consequence of using mobile banking.[9]

However, as mobile banking is making online banking redundant, so Artificial Intelligence (AI) may in turn eliminate mobile banking. For example, Alexa (Amazon Echo) allows users to utilise bank voice recognition, and as the Internet of Things (IoT) expands and our devices become ever-more connected, many of our personally initiated financial services needs will be taken care of. For example, a car can now recognise when a service is due or a part is faulty part; the next step may be for that car to order the part to the garage and book an appointment using its own digital wallet. Marketing in practice 5.5 outlines some of the opportunities that another development, the Internet of Things, might offer for financial services. While these opportunities are considerable, there are also real challenges associated with the integrity of personal data and the increased risk of cybercrime as a consequence of vastly increased levels of connectivity (De Cremer, Nguyen and Simkin, 2016).

Marketing in practice 5.5: the Internet of Things

The Internet of Things (IoT) refers to the connection of devices and objects through digital means, allowing them to share data about their state, location and usage. Estimates suggest that there were 6.4bn connected devices in 2016 and it is predicted this will grow to 29.42bn by 2030[10]. It's estimated that transactions from wearables (e.g. smart watches) will hit $75bn by 2025.[11] These devices will need to be linked to digital wallets, offering banks huge opportunities to be the conduit for IoT transactions which rely on a connected supply chain.

As the number of connected devices grows, there is an onus on their manufacturers to ensure their security is robust and mitigate vulnerability to hackers. In 2023, Deloitte identified that 62% of consumers have concerns around the privacy and security of their smart home devices[12], a 10% increase from their 2022 survey[13].

The IoT has sparked a paradigm shift in how financial service products are priced and delivered. The payments space has been revolutionized by cashless payments from smart phones and watches. Apps track spending habits and proactively offer help with budgeting. Banks have improved security by using behavioural data to detect and flag suspect transactions to customers in real-time. Biometrics are being used to authenticate customers and reduce fraud. ATMs can restock cash themselves. The IoT has had a huge impact on pricing, with telematics (GPS data on how people drive) being used to reduce car insurance premiums, insurtech (smart devices, e.g. connected home security systems) used to reduce home insurance premiums, and wearables (e.g. smart watches) to reduce life insurance premiums.

Beyond payments and digital wallets, the IoT is also changing financial services product design and pricing. This is in the form of how products are packaged and sold, and how they're fulfilled. For example, car insurance claims payouts relying on verification that a car alarm was set, and the vehicle was parked off road, as per policy terms.

The data gleaned from connected devices enables financial services to better understand their customers' circumstances and needs, for example, tracking a business's activity could indicate when it may have additional growth financing needs, by revealing when leased machinery is working at full capacity or how well stock is selling.

The use of biometrics and the IoT may help financial inclusion; opening possibilities to offer credit to people with no or low credit history or lacking formal documentation to confirm their identity.

Clearly these technology-enabled services and distribution channels offer many important benefits to an increasingly large number of customers. Internally, they also offer significant cost benefits to organisations – whether by reducing fraud through more effective monitoring of customer activity or through directly reducing the cost of interacting with customers. The cost of internet-based transactions has been estimated to be 10% of the cost of phone transactions and 1% of the cost of in-branch transactions. The ability to automate many routine transactions has increased and self-service is now the norm for so many financial services. But all these developments may present a problem in that they reduce the number of visits to the branch and thus reduce the opportunities to cross-sell additional financial services. A growing challenge for many banks concerns the management of large branch networks at a time when more and more of their customers are looking to alternative forms of delivery. Consequently, greater attention is being paid to the design, layout and function of branches to encourage customer visits. Increasingly, banks are looking to create relaxed welcoming environments that may have more in common with a coffee shop than a traditional bank branch with its austere interiors and its emphasis on security and separation of staff and customers.

There is also significant potential for the IoT to impact the marketing environment. It can aid the streamlining of contractual processes as connected devices will be able to capture data and feed it into digital platforms that govern and verify "smart contracts" in real time. This offers particular benefits for trade finance, enabling the ability to track goods globally. The IoT can provide banks and other financial services providers with real-time access to trade data, eliminating the need for manual checks and paper documentation such as bills of lading. GPS data could automatically alert the issuing bank once a shipment arrives at a port, and sensory technology would provide information on the condition of delivered objects.[14]

As well as the highly visible impacts on service delivery and the implications for costs, developments in ICT also have important implications for marketing practice – both in terms of understanding and targeting customers but also in terms of enabling new segments to be reached. Rapid developments in processing power allow financial services to collect and process huge volumes of customer information. Marketing databases can be developed based on the information provided by customers in, say, an application for a credit card or a mortgage. This data can then be used to understand existing customers more thoroughly and also to identify the types of consumers most likely to buy certain products. This knowledge enables branches and call centres to target customer communications with much a greater degree of accuracy. And with developments in mobile telephony, this information can be used for real-time engagement with consumers. Combining information on past spending habits with knowledge of customer location allows targeted special offers to be provided to customers, via a smartphone, at a time when they might be most likely to respond positively. The opportunities for much enhanced customer targeting are considerable, but this kind of detailed analysis does give rise to concerns about privacy, with growing numbers of customers feeling uncomfortable that their behaviour is apparently so visible to their financial services provider.

With better customer information and better analytics, the potential to target new market segments is much increased. The sub-prime market has always been a challenge to serve because of high default rates. But lenders such as US-based ZestCash have used a much larger variety of customer data than would be the case for traditional lenders and this has allowed them to offer loans to customers who would appear to have poor credit history. Traditional credit scoring systems rely on a small number of variables to provide relatively crude classifications. More complex analytics can be used to provide a much finer-grained classification of individuals and in so doing open up new markets segments. However, there remains an imperative for providers to approach such markets with care, not least because of the potential detriment to so-called sub-prime consumers who are being invited to borrow small amounts at very high interest rates and who may then struggle with repayments. Sub prime and payday lending has attracted considerable interest from regulators because while these companies provide an important service, they are usually working with vulnerable customers.

The nature and importance of customer-relationship management and the importance of effective use of customer information is discussed in greater detail in Part III of this book.

Progress check

- Social and cultural factors are broad ranging and can have significant impact on both the types of services required by consumers and their responses to the marketing approaches developed by providers.

- Aside from the obvious differences between countries there are also significant trends emerging in terms of the composition of domestic populations, and this is in terms of cultures, family structures, age structures and ways of working and living.
- The technological environment has had some dramatic impact on financial services and is likely to lead to further significant changes in the way in which these services are provided. Innovations around digital and mobile delivery have been some of the most visible developments and have dramatically changed the way in which financial services are delivered.

5.4 The market environment

The market environment focuses on the immediate features of the market in which the firm operates. Understanding this aspect of the environment is of particular importance as the market environment will have a very immediate impact on an organisation's activity. There are many different approaches that might be used to understand what is happening in the market environment. One of the most widely used is the idea of analysing the five forces that determine market/industry profitability, an approach that was developed in the 1980s by Michael Porter. This is shown in Figure 5.6.

An effective marketing strategy will need to understand how these forces work together and what they mean for the organisation. If a particular market environment is favourable or attractive then an organisation should find it easier to compete effectively. A market is considered favourable or attractive if the forces working against an organisation are

Figure 5.6 Porter's Five force analysis

Source: Adapted from Porter, M. (1980). Competitive Advantage. Boston: Free Press

relatively weak. Where the forces are strong, they impose constraints upon what an organisation can do and marketing strategies will need to consider how best to neutralise and respond to the problems that the organisation faces. Thus, for example, customers may be in a strong position (high-bargaining power) because it is relatively easy to switch between different providers. In this situation, a bank may consider focusing attention on marketing strategies that build a strong relationship with customers (perhaps via cross-selling a range of products), making them more likely to remain with the bank. If successful, this strategy will make the market more attractive and thus enhance the bank's competitive position.

Porter argues that market or industry attractiveness and profitability depends (as economic theory would suggest) on the structure of the industry and specifically on five key features:

- Bargaining power of suppliers
  Powerful suppliers can force up the prices paid by an organisation for its inputs and thus reduce profitability. Suppliers in financial services include the suppliers of essential business goods and services (computing equipment, training, etc.), and to the extent that these suppliers are in a strong position they can affect the prices paid for relevant goods and thus affect costs. It could also be argued that in some instances, the term "suppliers" could also include customers. Customers making deposits with financial institutions are effectively acting as a supplier of certain essential raw materials and again, if these suppliers are in a relatively strong position they can impact on the cost of providing certain related financial services. As banks have deleveraged following the global financial crisis, their dependence on retail deposits has reduced and this is one factor which explains the very low rates on savings products in many developed economies.

- Bargaining power of consumers
  Powerful consumers can insist on lower prices and/or more favourable terms which may impact negatively on profitability. Clearly, the bargaining power of buyers in financial services varies considerably. In personal markets, it seems that the bargaining power of individual consumers is relatively weak, although consumer pressure groups may partly counterbalance this, particularly through their evaluations of the performance of financial institutions. One factor which may weaken the position of retail consumers is their lack of knowledge about the way in which certain financial products work and regulators have historically focused particular attention on improving consumers' understanding as a way of strengthening their position vis-à-vis providers. In corporate markets, of course, the situation may be rather different with relatively large businesses being in a rather more powerful position.

- Threat of entry
  A profitable industry will generally attract new entrants; if it appears relatively attractive for new organisations to enter a market, profitability will tend to be eroded. While there are certainly barriers to entry to the financial marketplace, not least of which are the many regulatory requirements, the financial sector does attract a variety of new entrants. In some cases, these are new entrants from other sectors of the domestic economy. A growing number of retailers offer consumer credit and store cards to fund consumer purchases. In the US, General Motors offers credit cards, while in the UK, supermarkets such as Tesco and Sainsburys offer a wide range of financial services alongside their

traditional grocery products. Richard Branson's Virgin Group, originally in the music business, now offers a range of financial services from credit cards to personal pensions. And while Amazon has yet to make its mark, there is a common expectation that the internet giant may yet expand into financial services. Perhaps the greatest threat to incumbents in recent years comes from the fintech and Insurtech providers who have moved into a range of traditional retail markets. In many cases these new entrants may still rely on traditional financial services providers which are then offered to consumers using the new entrants' own brand. Even though they may depend upon existing suppliers of financial services, they still constitute a significant new source of competition. The threat of new entry is not restricted to firms in other sectors of the economy; there is increasingly a very real threat from new entrants from overseas as is discussed in greater detail in Chapter 8.

- Competition from substitutes

  The existence of products which are close substitutes enhances customer choice and provides an alternative way of meeting a particular need. Thus in markets where there are close substitutes, the buying power of consumers is effectively enhanced because they have a much greater degree of choice. The extent to which there are real substitutes for financial services is perhaps limited, although certain sections of the market, such as investment services, gold, jewellery, antiques and other collectibles may be regarded as substitutes for investments in mutual funds, equities and other forms of saving. It is interesting to note the extent to which increasing numbers of people view investment in property as a substitute for traditional investment in pensions and as a vehicle to provide income and capital in old age. This, in part, has fuelled a rapid increase in what is termed the buy-to-let market across a range of countries.

- Rivalry between firms

  Clearly, the greater the degree of competition, the more likely it is that the industry will be less profitable and therefore less attractive. While there are few close substitutes for financial services (as indicated above), there is considerable competition within the industry. Most countries have seen some degree of consolidation in their financial services sector and while this has reduced the number of competitors, the remaining players are often strengthened resulting in increased competition. Moreover, as financial markets have liberalised and the barriers between institutional types have been reduced, competition has also increased. Insurers no longer compete just with other insurers — they also compete against banks, savings institutions and investment companies. The development of bancassurance[15] in many financial sectors worldwide is just one example of this type of development. Equally, in the banking sector, current accounts and housing finance may be offered by companies that traditionally specialised in insurance. In Malaysia for example, the insurer AIA now offers housing finance in direct competition with traditional suppliers. In the UK, Scottish Widows, originally a provider of life insurance, is one of a number of such firms which also offers housing finance because of the natural interdependencies between the two products.

These five forces determine the attractiveness of the industry through their impact on either costs incurred or prices received or both. The development of an effective marketing strategy will depend upon a thorough examination of the market in order that the organisation can identify strategic approaches to counterbalance the effects of these five forces.

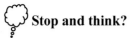 **Stop and think?**

Can organisations influence their market environments through their marketing activities? What approaches might be used to reduce the bargaining power of suppliers or customers? How might an organisation address the threat of entry or competition from substitutes?

5.5 The internal environment

Clearly, the internal environment is the area in which the firm can exercise greatest control. Understanding the internal environment requires analysis of an organisation's resources and capabilities in order to understand how these might be used to create a competitive edge in the delivery of financial services to the organisation's target market.

5.5.1 Resources

The term resource is used to describe any inputs which are used by an organisation to produce its outputs. Resources are normally categorised as either tangible or intangible. Some examples of tangible resources are shown in Figure 5.7.

In contrast, intangible resources typically do not have any physical form and some may not have any obvious monetary value, but for many organisations they can be one of the key resources that help to create competitive advantage. Some examples of intangible resources are shown in Figure 5.8.

Human resources

- This includes number and type of staff, and their particular skills and qualities (attributes such as flexibility, adaptability, commitment, etc. may be of particular significance in many organisations). Fintech startups typically rely on their distinctive skills and knowledge of digital operations.

Financial resources

- This includes a variety of factors including cash holdings, levels of debt and equity, access to funds for future development, relationships with key financial stakeholders, including bankers and shareholders. Leading international banks such as HSBC and Citibank may see their financial strength as a significant resource.

Physical/operational resources

- This may encompass premises, equipment, internal systems (e.g. IT systems) and operating procedures. Capital One, the credit card company might point to its systems for rapid development and product customisation as being a key resource for the company. For a domestic bank, a branch network may still be a key resource, particularly when competing against new international entrants.

Figure 5.7 Examples of tangible resources

Specialist knowledge of experience

- Investment companies might focus on the skills and knowledge of their fund managers in delivering superior returns to customers. Banks such as Standard Chartered emphasise their heritage and knowledge of particular markets.

Brand names and brand equity

- American Express might cite the strength of its brand as a significant intangible resource, Nationwide Building Society in the UK focuses particular attention on its status as a mutual organisation (see Chapter 1) and the fact that this means that it is "on the side of its customers".

Internal Culture

- Corporate culture which is typically defined as the prevailing value system within an organisation is widely recognised as an important intangible resource. This value system may be one that has arisen through time or it may be one that is actively created and managed by senior staff. A corporate culture associated with rapid innovation and risk taking will have different marketing implications to a culture oriented towards high quality and an exclusive image, and this in turn will differ from an organisation with a low-risk culture looking to follow the market with a standard product.

Figure 5.8 Examples of intangible resources

Some commentators also make a distinction between internal resources which actually belong within the organisation, and external resources which are outside the organisation but still are under its control such as formal or informal networks, personal contacts, locations, surroundings, etc. Some financial services providers might look to their relationships with networks of financial advisers as an important external resource.

5.5.2 *Competences/capabilities*

The words "competence" and "capability" are often used interchangeably, although some would suggest that they have slightly different meanings. For our purposes, we will use the two words interchangeably. They refer to certain skills or attributes that are necessary to be able to operate within a particular industry. Competences or capabilities would be present amongst most organisations in an industry: without those competences the organisation would not be able to operate. Operating in the banking industry requires competences in relation to deposit taking, lending, service provision, financial management, treasury, etc. Equally, insurers require competences in relation to premium collection and management, underwriting, customer service and claims management. Key to an analysis of competences is the ability to identify those in which an organisation is noticeably more effective than its competitors. These core competencies or distinctive capabilities provide a basis for delivering superior customer value and thus creating competitive advantage. A core competence will typically arise from a combination of resources and competences which are of value in relation to a particular market. Capital One's success in the credit card business and in consumer credit more generally has been built on its core competence in relation to customer analytics and information-based marketing (and these arise from the combination of capabilities in relation to data analytics and the depth in breadth of data that the organisation has). Deutsche Bank would probably claim its knowledge of investment banking and risk management as a core competence while China Merchants Bank would perhaps argue that its core competences reside in its information systems and the associated capacity to deliver personalised service. Increasingly, the collection and productive utilisation of data from customers is playing a critical role in the development of effective marketing strategies and the skills associated with these activities are at a premium.

The distinguishing features of core competences are that they are only possessed by the successful organisations in an industry; they are important in fulfilling customer needs and they are difficult to copy. Core competences provide an organisation with a genuine competitive edge in the marketplace. When properly exploited, core competences are the basis for delivering superior customer value (Prahalad and Hamel, 1990).

5.5.3 *Auditing the internal environment*

An analysis of the internal environment requires a careful evaluation or audit of the organisation's resources and capabilities. This is more than just assessing the quantity or a resource or capability – it is also about assessing quality. A good audit might consider:

- Specificity – are the resources/capabilities unique to a particular type of industry or are they generic? Resources/capabilities which are unique and important to a specific industry are often more likely to provide a base for developing a core competence.
- Substitutability – can this resource/capability be replaced with another? Substitutability may allow for greater flexibility in the process of delivering value for customers.
- Mobility – could this resource/capability be easily transferred to a competitor (for example, staff may be an important resource but are potentially quite mobile). Where resources are mobile, there is a need to think carefully about how to protect them and retain their value within an organisation.
- Contribution – what is the importance of a particular resource/capability in terms of adding value to the overall offer? Resources/capabilities with a key role to play in delivering superior value to customers may require more protection and investment than resources which are less strategically significant.

An internal analysis may also focus on internal structures (e.g. how does marketing relate to other activities), recruitment and reward systems for staff, the effectiveness of internal communication and the degree of centralisation. Although these may not be directly related to marketing, they may have important implications for what marketing does. Thus for example, a bank that rewards a group of staff based on the number of credit cards they sell or the number of new accounts they open may create an incentive for those staff to deal with every customer as quickly as possible and pressure them in to buying. This may yield short-term benefits but the danger would be that in the longer term the customers recruited in this way will be less satisfied and perhaps less profitable.

5.6 Evaluating developments in the marketing environment

The kind of analysis described in the previous sections will generate a large amount of data. The process of SWOT (Strengths, Weaknesses, Opportunities, Threats) analysis is one of the simplest techniques for summarising information about the marketing environment and guiding the direction of strategy. The information collected in the environmental analysis can be classified as either external (i.e. it relates to the outside environment) or internal (i.e. it relates to the organisation itself). External information may present the organisation with an opportunity, or it may create a threat. Equally internal information may describe either a strength or a weakness. So, any evidence produced by the environmental analysis may be:

- **Strength**
  Any particular resource or competence that will help the organisation to achieve its objectives would be classified as a strength. This may relate to experience in specific types of markets – for example, HSBC may point to its accumulated knowledge of Asian markets. Specific skills or abilities may also constitute a strength as would resources such as a strong brand image, an extensive branch/ATM network or expertise in terms of customer analytics. Many fintech based providers point to the beneficial impact of their specialist digital expertise which enables them to innovate more effectively than traditional suppliers.
- **Weakness**
  A weakness describes any aspect of the organisation which may hinder the achievement of specific objectives. Weaknesses are often the opposite of strengths, so for example a small branch network, poor internal information systems or an unfavourable brand image may all constitute weaknesses. Increasingly the apparently dysfunctional internal cultures of some UK banks which emerged during the scandals surrounding the fixing of LIBOR[16] may be regarded as a weakness and reports have suggested that the revelations prompted a large increase in the number of customers considering switching banks.
- **Opportunity**
  Any feature of the external environment which is advantageous to the organisation, given its objectives, would be classed as an opportunity. Credit card issuers may see the growing demand for foreign travel as an opportunity to increase the sale of credit cards. Insurers looking at the Chinese market might see the current low take-up of life insurance as an opportunity. The growth in the number of migrants has fuelled the market for remittances which has grown significantly over the past decade and while there have been slowdowns in recent years, the World Bank reports that remittances to Latin America and the Caribbean are expected to have grown 8% in 2023 and those to South Asia by 7%[17].
- **Threat**
  A threat is any environmental development which will create problems for an organisation in achieving its specific objectives. Opportunities for one organisation may be a threat for others. The UK's decision to leave the European Union was regarded as a threat by many UK-based providers because of its impact on their ability to operate in Europe. Equally the emergence of peer-to-peer payment systems might be regarded as a threat to traditional providers of banking services.

Once information has been classified in this way it can be presented as a matrix of strengths, weaknesses, opportunities and threats. For SWOT analysis to be of value it is important to ensure that strengths and weaknesses are internal factors, specific to the organisation and that opportunities and threats are factors which are present in the external environment and are independent of the organisation. A common mistake in SWOT analysis is to confuse opportunities and threats with strategies and tactics. For example, the ability to contact customers via direct mail is not an opportunity; it is a marketing tactic. The relevant opportunity would be the existence of a segment in the market that would respond favourably to promotion via direct mail.

Given the volume of information, a SWOT analysis should concentrate only on the most important strengths, weaknesses, opportunities and threats. Whether a strength or weakness is important will depend upon the extent to which it is relevant to the overall competitive strategy and the extent to which it is distinct to the organisation. Whether an opportunity or a threat is important depends upon how likely it is to happen and how significant its effect would be. Thus, for example, a provider of housing finance may consider a major economic downturn to be something that would have a big impact on new and existing business but if the likelihood of this happening is low, then this factor should not be seen as a serious threat. Figure 5.9 provides an illustrative SWOT analysis for Aseguradora Tajy in the context of the insurance market.

Having formulated this matrix, it then becomes feasible to make use of SWOT analysis in guiding strategy formulation. The two major strategic options are:

- **Matching**
  This entails finding, where possible, a match between the strengths of the organisation and the opportunities presented by the market. Strengths which do not match any available opportunity are of limited use while opportunities which do not have any matching strengths are of little immediate value from a strategic perspective. Thus, for example, Tajy may consider a strategy of using its existing client portfolio to cross-sell new agricultural insurance products while using its cooperative heritage to develop new markets with other non-shareholding cooperatives (i.e. cooperatives that are not formally linked to Tajy).
- **Conversion**
  This requires the development of strategies which will convert weaknesses into strengths in order to take advantage of some particular opportunity, or converting threats into opportunities which can then be matched by existing strengths. Tajy, for example, might decide that it is essential to invest to strengthen its information infrastructure, converting a weakness into a strength and allowing it to take advantage of insurance demand from non-shareholding cooperatives.

SWOT analysis is probably one of the most widely used tools in marketing and strategic planning and it is simply a method of structuring information of both a qualitative and a quantitative nature. Its advantages arise from the fact that it is easy to use, does not require formal training and therefore is accessible to all levels of management across a broad field. This simple technique provides a method of organising information and identifying possible problems and future strategic directions.

5.7 Conclusion

The environment within which organisations operate is becoming increasingly complex and turbulent and, as a consequence, increasingly uncertain. Understanding the nature of this environment and its implications for the organisations is a key element in any marketing strategy. The environment must be analysed at a number of different levels, from broad, macro factors, through to market-specific and finally organisation-specific factors. However, although these elements of the environment constrain the activities of the organisation, it is increasingly important to recognise that the organisation itself, through its marketing activities, can influence the environment to produce conditions which are more favourable to the success of its strategies.

Strengths		Weaknesses	
Customer/Associate	Recognised brand, with strong customer base.	Customer/Associate	Has not grown the sales force.
Customer/Associate	Alliance with strategic partners at national and international level.	Internal Processes	Physical appearance outdated.
Financial	Good liquidity.	Growth and learning	Outdated organisational structure.
Growth and learning	Recognised as a socially and environmentally responsible company.	Internal Processes	Limited application of technology.
Customer/Associate	Institutions representative of the sector are our shareholders.	Internal Processes	Processes not well defined or automated.
Growth and Learning	Principals have an open-door policy.	Customer/Associate	Failure to update the business model.
Customer/Associate	Strategic location of the company's retail distribution network.	Customer/Associate	Not recognising the potential for new and updated products.
Growth and Learning	Young and enthusiastic workforce.	Growth and Learning	Not exploiting human talent.
Growth and Learning	Extra benefits that motivate employees to stay.	Growth and learning	Lack of specialised training.
		Internal Processes	Agencies not online.
		Customer/Associate	Weaknesses in marketing campaigns.

Opportunities		Threats	
Customer/Associate	Growth of demand in the non-shareholding cooperative market.	Customer/Associate	Growth in numbers of new insurance companies.
Internal Processes	Access to technological advances.	Customer/Associate	Losses/damage resulting from poor physical infrastructure.
Customer/Associate	Growing linkages with state projects – strategic alliances.	Internal Processes	Growth in reports of cyber attacks.
Customer/Associate	Expected introduction of compulsory insurance for drivers.	Financial	Planned increase in taxation of the cooperative sector.
Customer/Associate	Transparency of public and private procurement processes.	Customer/Associate	Poor insurance culture among consumers.
Growth and Learning	Growing public interest in CSR.	Internal Processes	Outdated regulatory environment.
Customer/Associate	Increasing customer concern about insurance.		
Growth and Learning	Higher market sensitivity for CSR projects.		

Figure 5.9 SWOT Analysis, as prepared by Aseguradora Tajy Propiedad Cooperativa S.A. in relation to the market for insurance in Paraguay

Source: Supplied by Aseguradora Tajy Propiedad Cooperativa S.A

Learning outcomes

Having completed this chapter, you should now be able to:

1. **Understand the major components of the overall marketing environment and their role in the development of a marketing strategy.**

    The environment in which organisations operate comprises an internal and an external environment. And the external environment is often seen to consist of the macro-environment – high level and general trends that have an aggregate impact across a country or region – and a market environment – which focuses more specifically on what is happening in a particular sector of an economy. Marketing as an approach to business forces organisations to look outside and to develop an awareness and understanding of the environment in which they operate. An organisation that understands and responds to its operating environment should be able to deliver superior performance through its ability to satisfy customers more effectively than the competition and through its ability to anticipate changes and developments in its key markets. However, an analysis of the external environment must be accompanied by a good understanding of the internal environment to enable an organisation to deploy its resources and capabilities most effectively in meeting the challenges posed by the changing marketplace.

2. **Analyse key features of the macro and market environments and what they may mean for marketing practice.**

    There are a range of frameworks which outline the components of the macro environment – this chapter is structured around PEST (Political, Economic, Social and Technological). There is no single best model and the requirement is to ensure that any analysis is broad ranging, forward looking and aware of a range of future and long term developments as well as understanding trends and decisions that might affect an organisation immediately. One of the most widely used frameworks for analysing the market environment is the 5-force analysis which focuses attention on understanding the drivers of competition and of market attractiveness. As with the macro environment what is key to a good environmental analysis is a systematic and structured approach with careful assessment of the implications of particular trends for an organosation and its stakeholders.

3. **Appreciate ways of thinking about the organisation's internal environment and what this means for strategic decisions.**

    Understanding the internal environment requires analysis of an organisation's resources and capabilities in order to understand how these might be used to create a competitive edge in the delivery of financial services to the organisation's target market. These resources may be tangible or intangible. Resources work with competences or capabilities – the things that the organisation needs to be able to do to function. Organisations need to be able to identify core competences; these are the things that the organisation does and which may combine with certain resources to give the organisation the ability to do things better than the competition. Core competences are only possessed by the successful organisations in an industry; they are important in fulfilling customer needs and they are difficult to copy. Core competences provide an organisation with a genuine competitive edge in the marketplace.

4. **Understand the process of SWOT analysis and its role in making sense of information about the marketing environment.**

   The process of SWOT (Strengths, Weaknesses, Opportunities, Threats) analysis is one of the simplest techniques for summarising information about the marketing environment and guiding the direction of strategy. The information collected in the environmental analysis can be classified as either external (i.e. it relates to the outside environment) or internal (i.e. it relates to the organisation itself). External information may present the organisation with an opportunity or it may create a threat. Equally internal information may describe either a strength or a weakness. So, any evidence produced by the environmental analysis can be classified as strength or weakness if it is an internal feature of the organisation. And if it's external then it is either an opportunity or threat. In thinking about strategy, marketers may look to focus on ideas that match strengths to opportunities, or which convert weaknesses into strengths or convert threats into opportunities.

Review questions

1. Why is it important to understand the external environment? What role does marketing play?
2. Choose a financial services provider; summarise the opportunities and threats that the macro-environment creates.
3. Choose a market that you know well (e.g. current accounts, mutual funds, credit cards, housing finance) and analyse the five forces. Identify any opportunities and threats.
4. Prepare a SWOT analysis in relation to the market that you analysed in question 3. Include both market-level opportunities and threats and any macro level opportunities and threats that you think may be relevant.
5. In what ways do factors in the physical environment, such as climate-related issues, impact upon financial services?

Notes

1 www.bbc.co.uk/news/business-11288492 (accessed June 2012)
2 www.chinaeconomicreview.com/gambling-with-retirement-china-pension-reform, (accessed February 2017)
3 www.thebanker.com/The-Banker-s-Top-Islamic-Financial-Institutions-2023-1698828332 (accessed January 2024)
4 www.bradescori.com.br/site/conteudo/interna/default.aspx?secaoId=680&idiomaId=2 (accessed August 2012)
5 www.aratek.co/news/biometric-atm-the-future-of-secure-financial-transactions (accessed January 2024)
6 www.theguardian.com/money/2014/may/14/fingerprints-vein-pattern-scan-atm, (accessed January 2017)
7 See for example https://fintechmagazine.com/banking/top-10-neobanks-in-the-world (accessed 23 January 2024)
8 See http://newsroom.dutchbanglabank.com/newsroom/?cat=13 (accessed August 2012)
9 See www.slideshare.net/ING/ing-mobile-banking-2015-report. (accessed February 2017)
10 www.statista.com/statistics/1183457/iot-connected-devices-worldwide/

11 Nekovee, Maziar; Bhata, Jagadeesha; AlQahtanib, Salmam (2022). FinTech enablers, use cases, and role of future internet of things. University of Sussex. Journal contribution. https://hdl.handle. net/10779/uos.23491676.v1

12 www2.deloitte.com/us/en/insights/industry/telecommunications/connectivity-mobile-trends-sur vey.html#explore (accessed January 2024)

13 /www2.deloitte.com/us/en/insights/industry/telecommunications/connectivity-mobile-trends-sur vey.html (accessed January 2024)

14 http://santanderinnoventures.com/fintech2/(accessed January 2024)

15 The term "bancassurance" or "allfinanz" is used to describe a system in which banks broaden their product offerings to include a more extensive range of insurance, savings and investment products which would have traditionally been offered by more specialised companies.

16 London Inter Bank Offer Rate – an interest rate which was used as the basis for pricing many finan-cial products. In 2021 it was replaced by SONIA – the Sterling Overnight Index Average in the UK and the US now uses SOFR – the Secured Overnight Financing Rate.

17 https://knomad.org/publication/migration-and-development-brief-39 (accessed January 2024)

References

Kohli, A. K. and Jaworski, B. J. (1990). Market orientation: The construct, research propositions, and managerial implications. *Journal of Marketing*, 54(2), pp. 1–18.

Prahalad, C. K. and Hamel, G. (1990). The core competence of the corporation. *Harvard Business Review*, 68(3), pp.79–90.

Narver, J. C. and Slater, S. F. (1990). The effect of a market orientation on business profitability. *Journal of Marketing*, 54(4), pp. 20–35.

Tang, L.L., Thomas, L.C., Thomas, S. and Bozzetto, J. (2007) It's the economy stupid: modelling financial product purchases. *International Journal of Bank Marketing*, 25 (1), 22–38. (doi:10.1108/02652320710722597).

6 Understanding the financial services consumer

Learning objectives

At the end of this chapter, you should be able to:

1. Understand the range of factors that influence the consumer decision-making process in financial services,
2. Be aware of the different ways in which financial services providers can influence the buying process,
3. Be aware of some of the differences between final consumers and business consumers in relation to financial services,
4. Understand some of the ways in which behavioural economics can help understand consumer decision-making and policy formulation,
5. Understand key elements of the process of researching financial consumers.

6.1 Introduction

Understanding consumers – their needs, their expectations and their responses to marketing activity is central to effective marketing. Looking through the contents list for academic journals in the area would suggest that there has been a considerable amount of research done to explore and evaluate the factors that influence consumer decision-making, and yet our understanding of how consumers buy financial services is still somewhat imperfect. For many personal consumers, financial services are not seen as particularly interesting or exciting purchases; they are seen as complicated and often it is difficult for consumers to identify differences between a bank account from, say, HSBC and one from Standard Chartered or between an insurance policy from AXA and one from AIA. Consumers find it difficult to evaluate their purchase in advance and consequently experience high levels of perceived risk. Furthermore, as explained in Chapter 3, financial services are often seen as uninteresting and consumption is contingent – i.e. the services in themselves do not generate a current consumption benefit, indeed, they can serve to reduce current consumption pleasure. In some cases, financial services may create consumption opportunities in the future; in other cases, they may never result in tangible consumption for the individual who made the purchase (e.g. life insurance). Many consumers would regard them as "distress purchases" (i.e. things that they have to buy but don't want to), and often have little incentive to learn more about such products. Thus, many personal consumers are often rather uninterested and relatively passive buyers.

DOI: 10.4324/9781003398615-8

The same may not be true of business customers (B2B), many of whom will have detailed knowledge of financial services and of their companies' financial needs. They will have specialised and experienced financial teams with detailed knowledge of financial institutions and the functioning of financial markets. Their purchases of financial services will be seen as important factors contributing to the performance of the business and, consequently, they are likely to be much more active and better informed during the buying process. Of course, this is something of a generalisation and we must be careful not to stereotype consumers too much. Some retail customers may be very knowledgeable; some businesses, particularly small and medium-sized enterprises, may have quite limited understanding of financial services. However, the comparison helps to show that trying to understand financial services buying behaviour can be very complicated.

This chapter aims to provide an explanation of how consumers make decisions when buying financial services. The main focus will be on personal consumers but, where appropriate, the experiences of personal consumers will be contrasted with the experiences of business customers. The chapter begins with a discussion of consumer decision-making based around established information-processing models of consumer choice. It then proceeds to explore some aspects of behavioural economics and finance and shows how insights from this work help us to understand particular aspects of buyers decision-making and why people sometimes appear to make decisions that are not obviously rational. The chapter then proceeds to examine some of the marketing approaches that organisations might use. The chapter closes with a brief overview of the process of researching financial services consumers.

 Stop and think?

Think about your bank account – why did you choose that bank? Who influenced your decision?

6.2 Consumer choice and financial services

It is important to bear in mind that the term "customer" may be multifaceted, and reflect a number of roles which work together to result ultimately in consumption. As Figure 6.1 shows, these roles might include prompting interest in making a purchase (need recognition); influencing choices; making decisions, making the actual purchase and then using whatever has been purchased. In the consumer domain all five roles are frequently performed by the same person, especially with regard to what are termed routine purchases.

However, in the B2B domain, very often these roles are carried out by separate individuals or, possibly, groups of individuals. We call this a decision-making unit (DMU), and its nature can have important implications for the organisation of marketing activities. Where the DMU comprises a number of different individuals, it becomes essential for marketers to understand who is involved, the roles that those individuals play and their different needs and expectations. For example, the DMU selecting a management company for a corporate pension scheme might comprise representatives from finance and from HR; representatives from finance may be particularly concerned about management charges and investment strategies while representatives from HR may be more concerned about the degree of flexibility and the services provided to the organisation's staff. Both factors will be relevant but it will

Figure 6.1 Roles associated with a purchase decision

be of great value to a prospective management company to understand who in the DMU is concerned about what and who will carry the most weight in the decision-making. This sort of detailed knowledge about the DMU can be a major challenge when marketing financial services to corporate clients.

There are many different frameworks for understanding consumer behaviour. Indeed, there is a growing interest in researching consumers from interpretivist perspectives to understand, in-depth, the meaning, nature and significance of consumption of certain types of goods and services to individuals. However, the majority of research on financial services consumers has relied on traditional and largely cognitive-based approaches to understanding consumer behaviour. These approaches to understanding consumers are based on the notion that consumer choice is the result of some form of systematic processing and evaluation of information. The consumer is seen as a problem solver who moves sequentially through a series of stages in a decision-making process prior to making a purchase. One of the best examples of this approach for final consumers is probably the Engel-Kollat-Blackwell model (Engel, Blackwell and Miniard, 1991) which is outlined in very simplified form in Figure 6.2.

The decision process begins with the consumer recognising a "need"; they gather information on how to address that need; they compare the different alternatives, make a decision and then act. There are many variations of this approach in marketing textbooks but a key feature of this general approach is the idea that there is a sequence from the pre-purchase stage, moving onto purchase and then onto post purchase evaluation.

Treating consumer choice as a problem-solving process may have a certain intuitive appeal, but it also has a number of weaknesses. In particular, this approach assumes a high degree of rationality in purchase decisions, it assumes that decision-making is very logical and linear and it assumes a degree of consistency in behaviour. It is important to recognise these limitations and to be aware that consumer choice in financial services is potentially a

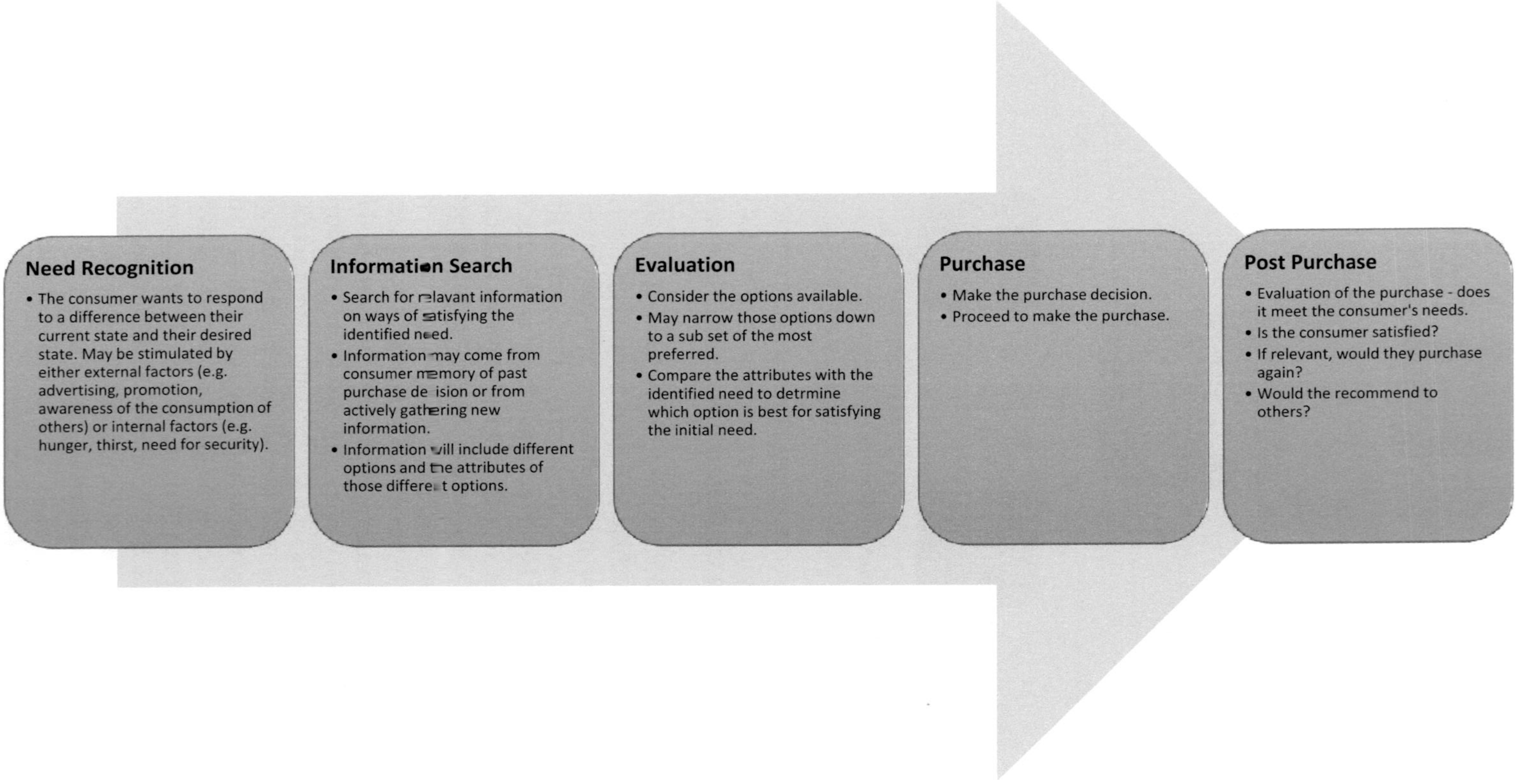

Figure 6.2 Stages in consumer decision-making

Source: Adapted from Engel, Blackwell and Miniard (1991)

Need Recognition
- The consumer wants to respond to a difference between their current state and their desired state. May be stimulated by either external factors (e.g. advertising, promotion, awareness of the consumption of others) or internal factors (e.g. hunger, thirst, need for security).

Information Search
- Search for relevant information on ways of satisfying the identified need.
- Information may come from consumer memory of past purchase decision or from actively gathering new information.
- Information will include different options and the attributes of those different options.

Evaluation
- Consider the options available.
- May narrow those options down to a sub set of the most preferred.
- Compare the attributes with the identified need to detrmine which option is best for satisfying the initial need.

Purchase
- Make the purchase decision.
- Proceed to make the purchase.

Post Purchase
- Evaluation of the purchase - does it meet the consumer's needs.
- Is the consumer satisfied?
- If relevant, would they purchase again?
- Would the recommend to others?

very complex process. However, the simple framework outlined in Figure 6.2 is helpful as a way of structuring the discussion of consumer choice in financial services. In particular, it is useful as a means of understanding some of the different ways in which marketing can influence the choice process. Not all five steps in the decision process need necessarily apply sequentially to all purchase occasions. In some cases, and for frequently purchased and simple products, consumers might proceed directly from problem recognition to purchase because they are familiar with the means of satisfying a given need (e.g. renewing a motor insurance policy). Given that many financial services are complex and infrequently purchased, it might be reasonable to expect that the choice process may be more thorough and considered, although in practice, anecdotal evidence suggests that some consumers may actually make quite impulsive purchases, not least because of a lack of interest in the product.

6.2.1 Need recognition

This is concerned with understanding needs and wants and the extent to which consumers are motivated to satisfy those needs and wants. Needs and wants for personal customers will vary according to personal circumstances, whereas the needs of business customers will depend upon the stage of development and the situation of the business. For personal customers, there are a range of "needs" which may be satisfied through the purchase of financial services as Figure 6.3 shows.

For many personal consumers, "needs" of this nature are intrinsically uninteresting and often there is a preference to ignore certain "needs" which may be associated with unpleasant events such as burglary, illness or death. In many instances, customers may simply be apathetic. Because financial services are products that many people would prefer not to think about, there is a danger that certain financial needs are not recognised. The relatively low take-up of products such as critical illness insurance (which pays out on the diagnosis of a

Figure 6.3 Examples of customer needs and examples of products that can satisfy those needs

life-threatening condition) may in part be due to consumer reluctance to consider the possibility that this will happen to them. Equally, the complexity of many financial services and the lack of transparency in marketing may mean that customers are unable to recognise the ways in which those services might meet their needs.

The difficulties that many retail customers experience is often attributed to a lack of financial literacy or capability. There is scope for digital solutions to simplify financial products and provide means for organisations to communicate to consumers in more simple terms, for example bank accounts that graphically display spending habits to assist customers in managing their money. A growing number of banking apps now offer this facility; many savings apps allow customers to distribute money between different "pots" according to the purpose for which the customer is saving. The development of robo-advice as noted in Chapter 5 has made the process of investing more straightforward for those consumers who may have previously struggled to access investment products. The customer simply has to select their preferred level of risk (high, medium, low) and thematic preferences they may have (e.g. technology, sustainability). Digital innovations such as these provide solutions based around the customers' lifestyle needs, taking the onus off the customer and simplifying the process.

Financial capability or literacy is generally concerned with the extent to which individuals have the knowledge and skills necessary to fully address their financial needs and make appropriate decisions. Financial literacy helps consumers to plan ahead, to ensure that they have appropriate protection, to reduce their dependence on welfare services and to help them manage risk. The significance of financial literacy is such that countries worldwide have put in place initiatives to encourage and support consumers in the acquisition of better knowledge and understanding of financial services. Such approaches range from initiatives to encourage personal financial education in schools through to web-based advisory services targeted towards adults. One such example is shown in Marketing in practice 6.1.

 Marketing in practice 6.1: the UK's Money Helper Service

The United Kingdom (UK) government launched the Money Advice Service in 2011 with a remit to improve money-management skills for members of the public. The specific objectives of the Money Advice Service were laid out in the Financial Services Act 2010. In brief, these were concerned with enhancing knowledge and understanding of financial matters and improving the ability of individuals to manage their financial affairs. In April 2012, the Money Advice Service also assumed responsibility for funding and improving debt advice. Alongside the Money Advice Service, the Government also operated specialist pensions related services.

In 2018 the different advisory services were combined to create the Money and Pensions Service (MaPS) with a remit to provide free and impartial advice on debt, on broader money issues and on pensions to members of the public.

The service is provided through a range of different channels. The website provides information on a broad range of financial services and significant life events (such as marriage, retirement, redundancy) that might impact on financial needs. The site also offers a range of tools to help individuals to manage their finances (such as savings calculators, budgeting tools). For greater interactivity, web chat is available as is telephone advice. Partner organisations can embed Money Helper tools and calculators in their own web sites and there is also a dedicated Money Helper site for employers to help them support their staff.

As well as helping to address information needs and financial difficulties, the Money Helper service aims to improve financial resilience by encouraging better budgeting and increasing the number of individuals who have savings. It also invests significantly in programmes to deliver financial education to young people, working with parents, schools and a range of other agencies.

Source www.moneyhelper.org.uk/ (accessed 20 January2024)

As a consequence of the lack of intrinsic appeal and the complexity of the range of financial services available, it is often argued that consumers do not actively recognise that they have "needs" for various financial products; rather they remain essentially passive participants in a decision process until the point of sale. At this point, the marketing process then starts to focus on the identification and activation (some would even suggest creation) of those needs. This raises a number of issues. Clearly, marketing is much more difficult in those instances in which customers are largely uninterested and unaware of the benefits of the product. It becomes impractical to rely to any degree on "consumer pull" and, instead, many organisations emphasise "sales" push – i.e. actively pushing products to consumers and persuading them of the benefits of purchase. As the discussion about behavioural economics later in this chapter shows, there are reasons why some financial services may need to be "bought and not sold". But, a greater reliance on "sales push" through personal selling, particularly for the more complex products does create potential problems – a situation in which customers have limited knowledge and interest combined with an industry which has to rely heavily on active selling creates considerable potential for mis-selling – i.e. selling products that are clearly inappropriate for the person concerned.

The difficulties that consumers experience in relation to need recognition are often compounded by a lack of transparency in marketing. A common source of complaint in many parts of the world is that key aspects of product design and pricing are not clearly displayed and explained. "Transparency" is the word applied to this form of openness, and regulators around the world have paid particular attention to increasing transparency across all aspects of marketing practice. However, it is particularly difficult to achieve the desired degree of transparency in an area which is often characterised by variable and uncertain outcomes, product complexity and relatively poorly informed consumers. The chapter on pricing, for example, explains the complexity that applies to financial services and the range of different pricing approaches with which consumers need to be familiar in order to make well-judged choices.

For corporate customers, the range of basic needs is likely to be similar to those outlined for personal customers, although many of the products used to satisfy those needs may be more complex, particularly when the customer represents a large business organisation. In addition, business customers, particularly those from larger organisations, will have a much better understanding and awareness of their own needs, suggesting that marketing may need to be less concerned with helping consumers to understand what their needs are and more concerned with deciding how best to meet those needs.

6.2.2 Information search

Information search describes the process by which consumers gather information either from their own memories or from external sources – whether marketing communications, from other consumers or from independent third parties. To the extent that the nature of financial service induces consumer passivity, the degree of information search is likely to be limited. Even when consumers are willing to be more active in the purchase process, information gathering presents problems: many financial services are long term, continuous or both, meaning that customers may have limited direct experience of relevant products and need to rely heavily on other information sources. Examples of the specific challenges are shown in Figure 6.4.

The difficulties associated with information search may be compounded by lack of transparency and/or aggressive marketing. In the UK, for example, Adams and Clunie (2006) highlight the financial losses experienced by consumers of Split Capital Investment Trusts which had been aggressively promoted as being relatively low risk with high potential returns but which in the face of declining stock markets proved to be highly risky and generated significant losses.

While information search is clearly problematic, it is important to recognise that there has been a considerable increase in consumer understanding and knowledge of financial services and there has been a considerable growth in the various sources of independent information. Most daily papers have sections devoted to personal finance and there are a growing number of specialist publications to provide information and advice to customers including Smart Investor (Australia), Outlook Money (India), Investors Chronicle (UK) and Money (US). In addition, organisations such as Which? in the UK and the Consumers Union in the US provide regular advice and product comparisons. In addition, most leading web portals also provide a growing amount of financial information. For example, in the UK, Motley Fool

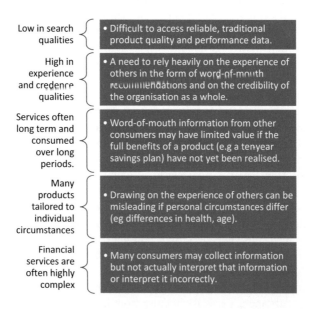

Figure 6.4 Challenges for consumers when undertaking information search for financial services

(www.fool.com) provides advice about investment and other financial services; Money Expert (www.moneyexpert.com) provides product comparisons and uSwitch (www.uswitch.com) provides product comparisons and advice on switching. Indeed there has been a substantial growth in the number of price comparison sites and these are discussed in more detail in Chapter 11. Thus, personal consumers are generally thought to be better informed than they were in the past. However, the simple availability of information does not necessarily mean that it can always be used to good effect. As behavioural economics shows (see later in this chapter and the case study on the instructor web site), simply providing more information does not necessarily result in better decisions.

It is probably easier for corporate customers who have more experience of using financial services and are better able to evaluate competitor offerings. In addition, the key decision makers are likely to have more specialist knowledge (indeed many may be professionals in the area or have significant professional experience) and so information search should be more straightforward, even if the original needs are rather more complex.

Progress check

- Understanding buyer behaviour is central to effective marketing. This can be challenging in financial services because many customers are not particularly interested in financial services, find them complicated and even difficult to differentiate.
- One widely used approach to understanding buyer behaviour focuses on the idea that decisions are based around information processing models, with customers gathering information in response to a need and then making a purchase decision.
- In a typical information processing model, the first stage is the identification of a particular need and this is then followed by a process of gathering information on different ways of responding to this need.

6.2.3 Evaluation of alternatives

If there are difficulties for consumers with respect to the gathering of information, these difficulties are magnified when the consumer attempts to evaluate alternative services. Like many services, financial services are processes rather than physical objects; the predominance of experience qualities makes pre-purchase evaluation difficult and where credence qualities are significant, post-purchase evaluation may also be problematic. Typically, alternatives are evaluated in relation to dimensions specified in the initial problem-recognition stage; if consumers are in some senses inert or inactive in relation to problem recognition then the criteria being used for evaluation are likely to be poorly defined. However, even accepting that consumers can make evaluations, the process of so doing will be complicated by a number of features of financial services. There are a variety of different products which may satisfy a particular need; for example, the consumer who wishes to accumulate wealth may consider a range of products from national savings certificates to mutual funds to simple equity investments. The risk-return characteristics of these services vary considerably, as do the prices and there is rarely any easy way to make direct comparisons across different service types. These problems have been exacerbated by the lack of transparency in the pricing and promotion of many financial services (Diacon and Ennew, 1996). As a consequence, many consumes rely on financial advisers to assist with such evaluations, but even then the position may be complex, particularly if there is the potential for the recommendations of a financial adviser to be influenced by the commission they receive from selling a particular product.

🗯️ **Stop and think?**

Do you trust your current account provider? Do you trust them to do some things and not others? Why or why not?

The presence of credence qualities in many financial services also makes evaluation complex. Products which contain a significant element of advice, or which require "managing" over the course of their life, may be difficult to evaluate even after purchase. In particular, the performance of many long-term investment products is determined partly by the skill of the relevant fund managers but by economic factors which are beyond the control of the supplier. Thus, consumers expose themselves to certain risks (both actual and perceived) in purchasing these products but will subsequently experience difficulties in determining whether poor performance was due to company-specific factors or to external contingencies. A consequence of this situation is a tendency for customers to evaluate service providers (rather than the services themselves) and to rely heavily on trust and confidence as attributes of those providers. Indeed, trust is a concept that lies at the heart of the relationship between a financial services supplier and its customers. The fund of trust that a financial services brand can instil in the public represents a major asset. Those involved in marketing financial services must place priority on engendering the trust of consumers and avoiding policies and practices that serve to undermine trust.

6.2.4 Purchase decision

Purchase is normally expected to follow logically as the result of the evaluation of alternatives unless any unexpected problems materialise. However, earlier discussions have suggested that for many financial services customers, needs are only created or activated at the point of purchase. Accordingly, the actual process of purchase will often be the result of an active selling effort by a supplier. Customer interaction with sales staff is then likely to be of particular significance in the purchase process. Even with developments in relation to digital delivery, the significance of face-to-face interaction is likely to continue in the medium term. However, while sympathetic, unpressured selling may be highly effective, the complexity and riskiness of financial services, combined with their common status as "avoidance" products, means that many customers may be vulnerable to "hard" or "over" selling. There can be little doubt that this has been the case in the past in some parts of the market (Ennew and Sekhon, 2014) and that it has resulted in a significant loss of consumer confidence in those parts of the industry where confidence is so important. Indeed, the UK financial sector has been characterised by a history of mis-selling including personal pensions, endowment policies and most recently payment protection insurance, all of which can be significantly attributed to poor marketing and selling practice.

Furthermore, the purchase process is influenced by the inseparability of production and consumption in financial services. The development of remote channels has reduced the impact of personal interactions in service delivery, but for many financial services front-line employees still play an important "boundary-spanning role" in the production of services, as do the consumers themselves in their capacity as "partial employees" (Bowen and Schneider, 1988). Therefore, an important influence on the purchase process may be the interaction between buyer and supplier. When services depend upon input from both service employees and consumers for their production, the quality of the service output very much depends on the nature of the personal interactions of these parties.

Fiduciary responsibility is often highlighted as an important characteristic which distinguishes financial services from other services and goods; one dimension of fiduciary responsibility is that suppliers need to exercise discretion with respect to the sale of certain products. For example, it would be inappropriate for a bank to lend money to a business which had few prospects for survival and success. However, until a consumer has signalled an intent to purchase it may not be possible to identify whether or not it is appropriate to provide that product to that customer. Thus, the consumer effectively faces the added problem that even if a conscious decision to purchase has been taken, the financial institution concerned may be unwilling to provide the product.

6.2.5 Post-purchase behaviour

The post-purchase evaluation of financial services is difficult for the reasons mentioned earlier. Indeed, it is often suggested that evaluation may place rather more emphasis on functional aspects of the service (how things are done) rather than technical aspects (what is done) because the latter are more difficult to evaluate (Zeithaml, 1981). The difficulties of post-purchase evaluation would tend to suggest that the risk of cognitive dissonance among consumers is high and that this may subsequently reduce brand loyalty. Evidence for this is ambiguous; for continuous products such as bank accounts, a high level of cognitive dissonance might be reflected in high levels of switching. In practice, the number of consumers changing banks, although increasing, is still low. In their 2012 global survey, Ernst and Young[1] reported an increase in the numbers of customers planning to change banks from 7% to 12% worldwide, although they noted considerable variability with 23% of Chinese and 20% of Brazilian consumers indicating plans to switch compared with only 9% in the EU and 5% in the US. A comparatively low level of planned switching may reflect a low level of dissonance; alternatively, given switching costs, consumers may be willing to tolerate high levels of dissonance before being motivated to act. In 2013 in the UK a new Current Account Switching Service (CASS) was launched to ease the process of changing banks by automatically moving incoming and outgoing payments to a new account and closing the old one. Since its launch the CASS has facilitated approximately 10m switches[2] with the annual level of switching in the UK shown in Figure 6.5. From these figures it is not clear whether the CASS has enabled higher levels of switching. It is notable that levels of switching fell during the pandemic but have increased more recently reflecting perhaps higher levels of customer engagement but also increasingly proactive marketing, especially from the neobanks.

While banking switching rates are relatively low, there is still a higher propensity for consumers to switch as a result of poor customer service in financial services than other industries.[3] As banking products are fairly similar in term of their offer, customer service has become a key differentiator within the industry. The quality and provision of a range of channels through which customers can interact with their bank is of considerable importance and the growth in digital banking, although often less personal, has been seen by many to offer a better service.

However, where a high degree of trust is established between buyers and seller, there can be considerable benefits for both parties. The establishment of trust can bring about a degree of inertia in buyer–seller relationships. Since an irreversible amount of time and effort is required by an individual in order to acquire the necessary experience and information on

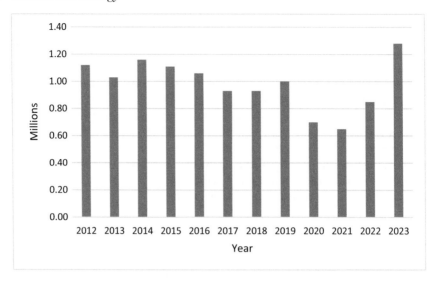

Figure 6.5 Number of customers changing bank current accounts in the UK

Source: Data from https://www.statista.com/statistics/417417/number-of-switching-current-bank-accounts-annua lly-uk/ (Accessed 24/01/2024)

which to assess an institution's reliability, it is usually the case that once satisfied, a consumer is more likely to remain with that institution than incur the costs of searching for and vetting alternative suppliers. This does create a potential problem for marketing in that organisations may fall into the trap of assuming that once acquired, customers will remain with the organisation resulting in insufficient attention to customer retention and an overemphasis on customer acquisition.

As will be discussed in part III of this book, there is a much greater awareness in the financial services sector of the importance of customer retention alongside customer acquisition. In the last two decades, a range of loyalty programmes have emerged associated with financial services (the case of American Express is considered in part III). While some programmes have been quite ambitious offering very tangible rewards such as free coffees, discounted meals, cinema tickets and free entry tourist attractions, there is perhaps an increasing focus on simpler programmes linked to levels of use, providing cashbacks or points. For example, ICDC in China offers points based on spending on their credit card and points are redeemable for cash discounts, air miles and charity donations. Barclays Blue Rewards is a scheme that actually charges a membership fee and requires a minimum monthly payment into the customers account. In return it offers up to 10% cashback from certain retailers, and cashback on other services from Barclays.

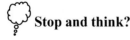 **Stop and think?**

Think about the financial services you have – to what extent does the provider of that service try to reward you for your loyalty? What sort of rewards do you think might have most impact on you?

6.2.6 Summary

From the discussion above, it should be clear that there are good conceptual reasons for expecting consumers to encounter difficulties with respect to the choice of financial services. The severity of these problems will vary across market segments. For example, the problem of complexity may be rather less important for a corporate buyer evaluating different leasing companies than it would be for an individual evaluating pension providers. Furthermore, corporate buyers may well be expected to express needs more actively and accurately than personal customers. Nevertheless within the personal market there are clearly some subgroups of customers who are more actively aware of their needs than others. Allowing for this variation in the degree and type of difficulties consumers may experience, there are a number of themes which seem to be of particular relevance to the choice process; these include the importance of trust and confidence in the supplier, the concern about customer passivity, the relative importance of functional aspects of the service product and the importance of interaction and contact with people.

The Engel et al. model assumes a highly rational approach to decision-making in which an individual seeks to optimise well-defined preferences and mitigate the associated risks through the acquisition of knowledge. Such a rational approach is more likely to be a feature of the B2B environment where purchasing takes place in order to satisfy the financial goals of a company. However, this model of economic rationality may not hold true to such an extent in the consumer domain. Factors such as relative financial illiteracy and the often-observed low level of interest in and engagement with financial services can result in consumer behaviour that seems far less economically rational. Behavioural finance and behavioural economics are fields of knowledge that seek to explain why it is that human beings individually and collectively approach decision-making in what seems like an irrational and illogical manner. Further insight into this perspective on consumer choice is provided in the following section.

Progress check

- Following problem recognition and information search, the information processing approach to buyer behaviour considers the process of evaluating alternatives, making the purchase decision and post-purchase behaviour.
- The evaluation of alternatives is part of the process in which many of the challenges that customers face with financial services are particularly apparent; the ability to build trust and confidence in consumers can play an important role in supporting decision making at this stage.
- Some of these complications around evaluation also affect the final purchase decision and a particular area of concern is the extent to which some financial services providers may actually push the sale of products that may not be suitable.
- Post purchase, buyers will assess and try to evaluate their decisions and there continues to be a role for marketing in both reassuring buyers and encouraging loyalty.

6.3 Behavioural Economics[4]

Behavioural economics (or behavioural finance) is an umbrella term for a range of approaches that seek to understand and explain observed consumer behaviour more accurately than predictions associated with traditional economic theory. Traditional economics is based on the assumption that people act in a completely rational and self-interested manner. People are assumed to take full account of all information available to them and to act according to this information and their preferences. Standard economic models incorporate such assumptions, as by implication do any policies based upon such models. Until relatively recently, approaches to consumer policy were effectively predicated on the notion of the rational consumer. The working hypothesis had been that provided consumers are supplied with as much information as possible and efforts are made to improve financial capability, then consumers should make more informed and better choices in financial services markets.

However, it is increasingly apparent that rational, information-processing models do not accurately explain actual or observed consumer behaviour for a number of reasons. In the case of financial services we are often considering complex decisions that require considerable mental effort on topics that are not always easily understood (or indeed terribly interesting). As a consequence, people often make what might be regarded is non-rational decisions and often fail to respond logically given the available information. This has given rise to a considerable body of research to try to understand the issues that affect consumer decision making in practice and to assess the implications for marketing practice and for policy.

The objective of behavioural economics is to bring psychological insights into economics in a systematic manner, in order to better explain human behaviour. In doing so, the impact of the typical mental short-cuts, or heuristics, that consumers employ in their decision making are taken into account, as are other systematic biases, anomalies and framing effects that impact on consumer choice and behaviour. By paying greater attention to the psychology of decision making, behavioural economics can offer some valuable insights for marketing students and for marketing practitioners.

Table 6.1 outlines some of the key issues within behavioural economics and notes some of the implications for marketing practice.

The insights afforded by behavioural economics are of great interest to policymakers and practitioners in financial services. An understanding of the implications of behavioural economics for elements of consumer behaviour may help in fashioning a choice architecture that is more likely to bring the desired consumer responses. From a commercial perspective, the objective is to use the lessons provided by behavioural perspectives to enable companies to present choices in a manner that maximises take-up of products and services, encourages behavioural loyalty and thereby helps to cement relationships between firms and customers. From the policymakers' perspective, insights from behavioural economics may be used to encourage consumers to engage with financial services to a greater degree and to make increased levels of provision in areas such as pensions and other saving and, whilst doing so, to make investment decisions which are in the consumer's long-term interests.

6.4 Marketing responses

The first part of this chapter highlighted some of the problems which confront consumers when choosing financial services. These difficulties are partly due to the generic characteristics of services and to the unique features of financial services and also partly due to the practices employed within the industry itself. Given the existence of these problems, effective marketing must concern itself with reducing or minimising the difficulties which consumers face in the purchase process. In order to examine the current evidence on industry responses, this section considers the nature of strategies and tactics employed in relation to selected characteristics of financial services – intangibility, inseparability/perishability,

Table 6.1 Insights from behavioural economics/finance

Concept	Explanation	Sample Implications
Loss Aversion, Prospect Theory, the Disposition Effect and the Endowment Effect	A related set of concepts linked by the idea that people are loss averse – we are more sensitive to losses compared to gains of similar magnitude. Investors have a tendency to continue holding assets that have dropped in value and to sell assets that have increased in value (Disposition Effect). Individuals also tend to place a higher price or value on an object if they own it than if they do not (Endowment effect).	Explains consumer anxiety about financial service products involving a risk to their capital; May result in underinvestment in higher risk assets – something that may be significant when individuals are savings for the long term; Many savers and investors continue to use products that are more expensive or less rewarding than alternatives, something that can be partly explained by the endowment effect.
Status Quo Bias and the Default Option	The tendency to stick with current choices/patterns of behaviour, in other words to have an exaggerated preference for the status quo. Sticking with the status quo involves less mental effort than considering more pro-active courses of action.	Makes it attractive (but sometimes questionable) to use "opt-outs" to sell additional product features. For example, a firm may offer a "free subscription" for a fixed period, which then reverts automatically to a full payment contract unless the customer actively cancels the subscription. A positive use of the "status quo bias" is automatic enrolment into personal pension plans. This is not the same as compulsion, as an individual retains the right to opt-out. However, as long as opting-out becomes a conscious choice and requires some effort on the part of the individual, most tend not to.
Framing Effects and Anchoring Effects	Factually equivalent information can provoke a very different response from consumers depending on the way the choice is presented, or "framed". People have a preference for positive rather than negative frames, an effect which follows on from loss aversion. Equally, choices may be influenced by other presentational approaches. For instance, a fee or rate of return expressed as a percentage may provoke a significantly different behavioural response to the same factual information expressed in absolute monetary terms. The anchoring effect is a type of framing effect where the appraisal of options is affected by an original starting value (or anchor).	The framing of pricing, is an example of attribute framing. It is likely that the typical customer would take a very different view of being told that he/she is paying a 3% up-front charge as opposed to £3000 when deciding whether or not to invest £100,000 into an investment product. The presentation of past performance statistics for investment products is another example of attribute framing. Although such information may be of limited value (past performance is no guide to future performance), it is readily available and one of the few search attributes (i.e. available prior to purchase and use) that consumers can use. Research has shown that the timescale used in past performance presentation can influence investment decisions[7], as can whether identical data on past performance is presented in a line graph or as a bar chart representing annual yields.

(continued)

Table 6.1 (Cont.)

Concept	Explanation	Sample Implications
Hyperbolic Discounting and Procrastination	The best way to think about hyperbolic discounting is that we typically prefer short-term gratification over longer term returns – saving for the long term is often much less attractive than current consumption. The effects of hyperbolic discounting may be exacerbated by our tendency to procrastinate. When a consumer is aware that prompt action would be in his/her interests but nevertheless delays taking action then procrastination is said to occur.	This suggests that an investor might be willing to forgo some current expenditure now for the prospect of enjoying a more comfortable retirement in 20 years, however that same individual would be less willing to sacrifice current consumption in the short term and is therefore likely to defer starting to save for a pension until "next year". Of course, next year, like tomorrow, never comes, so many may never start saving of their own volition This corollary of hyperbolic discounting helps explain the need for an automatic enrolment pension scheme which takes advantage of the status quo bias and also gives some backing to the old adage that products such as pensions are not bought, but instead have to be sold.
Mental Accounting	Consumers engage in mental accounting when they treat sums of money differently depending on where they came from and/or where they are kept. Mental accounting violates the standard economic assumption that all money is treated equally regardless of its source or destination and doesn't come with labels on.	The fact that people tend to engage in mental accounting can have both positive and negative consequences for financial services consumers. Often consumers may have different accounts for different types of expenditure. For example, money may be allocated to regular savings and to paying off credit cards – a given customer may then have both credit card debt at a high interest rate and savings attracting a lower interest rate. Investors may take greater risks with returns they have earned from past investments – risks that they might not have taken had they been dealing with the regular income. Mental accounting may also help explain why many investors appear to be willing to pay perhaps thousands of pounds in commission, rather than a few hundred pounds in the form of a fee when taking investment advice. Commission isn't paid explicitly by the investor, but is normally deducted from funds prior to investment. This is in stark contrast to a fee, which has to be paid directly from the investor to the advisor.
Availability Effect and Salience	People judge the likelihood of an outcome occurring by how easily the outcome can be brought to mind. They are said to rely primarily on evidence which is most easily available to them and/or evidence that has particular salience.	Insurance against certain types of events (e.g. flooding) is more likely to be purchased immediately after disasters and tends to decline as memories fade. The "availability effect" may also help explain the tendency for investors to invest too much money in the stock market when it has enjoyed a period of strong growth and too little when it has been falling and prices generally represent a bargain.

Overconfidence	People have a natural tendency to be overconfident. It is a well-documented psychological bias. People's confidence systematically exceeds the accuracy of their choices. For example, in experiments relating to investment decisions, most people believed that their predictions were more accurate than they actually were.	Overconfidence in many facets of their life may well help explain why large numbers of consumers choose not to insure themselves against unforeseen circumstances, as they have a misplaced confidence that such occurrences are less to happen than is actually the case. It may also explain why most investors choose actively managed funds rather than passive index trackers, when evidence suggests that there is a greater chance that their managed fund will underperform the relevant index (and tracker fund) rather than outperform it. The investor in question may be overconfident in his/her ability to pick a fund that is likely to outperform.
Trust	Faced with incomplete information and the potential for the opportunism of others, people rely on trust regarding the behaviour of their trading partners. The more an individual trusts another individual or organisation, the less it is necessary to check information and impose controls. As a result, trust acts as a lubricant with the potential to reduce the cost of transacting significantly. Trust is a heuristic that people use when taking others' word for something without having to check for themselves.	It is sometimes argued that voluntary and community organisations may be better placed to deliver advice and services to the socially and financially excluded than the private or public sector as they are generally more trusted by such segments of the marketplace. However, studies of trust in financial services by the Financial Services Research Forum (see Chapter 16) have repeatedly shown that levels of trust in financial services organisations are higher than is normally assumed and compares favourably with other commercial and public sector organisations.

Source: An abridged version of the case study provided by Devlin and Chuah which is available on the companion web site

heterogeneity, fiduciary responsibility and the long-term nature and uncertainty of many of the products. However, it should be noted that many of these responses can address more than one service characteristic.

6.4.1 Responding to intangibility

Intangibility is probably the dominant characteristic of any service and there are a variety of strategies which can be used to mitigate its effects as Figure 6.6 shows. The simplest approach is to find some means of tangibilising the service. The provision of some physical evidence (whether essential or peripheral) is probably the most common approach to dealing with intangibility as discussed in Chapter 3.

Peripheral evidence is probably becoming less important as online delivery increases, but essential evidence – typically relating to the brand remains powerful and it is perhaps no surprise that many long-established providers of financial services value imposing buildings because of what they symbolise in terms of tangibility, safety and security.

Using physical evidence or imagery to tangibilise a financial service is a key element of most marketing strategies. Nevertheless, there are pitfalls associated with this approach, particularly with respect to the development of a tangible image. The image developed necessarily creates expectations in the consumer's mind and if the organisation cannot match those expectations, then customer satisfaction may decrease.

Tangibilising a service addresses the problem of lack of physical form but is less effective in relation to product complexity and lack of consumer interest. Two key strategies are important in this respect as Figure 6.7 shows.

In the UK, Aviva has operated a campaign on television and in the press that focuses directly on the difficulties that insurance might present in terms of complexity and stresses the role that the company can play in helping customers to make the right choices. By demonstrating its understanding of the challenges facing consumers, Aviva is trying to reduce perceived risk and reassure customers that Aviva will be able to help "solve" your insurance puzzles. Figure 6.8 shows an example of Aviva's award-winning campaign with a creative presentation that focuses very directly on solving a puzzle.

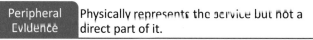

Peripheral Evidence	Physically represents the service but not a direct part of it.

- A free gift that comes with a purchase.
- A cheque book cover or a wallet for insurance documents.
- Note that online delivery limits options for this type of evidence.

Essential Evidence	Tangible and a key part of the service offer.

- The physical premises of a provider - whether branch or head office.
- Organisation names the represent stability and security such as "Prudential", "Anchor Bank". Ping An - the name of one of China's largest financial servcies providers translates as "safe and well".
- Tangible (and sometimes quirky) representations of the brand eg Direct Line's Red Telephone; CIMB's Octopus.

Figure 6.6 Using different types of evidence in marketing

Complex Products Makes choice difficult and risky - marketing needs to reduce perceived risk for the consumer.

- Build trust to ensure customers are confident that their finances are being safely managed.
- An emphasis on the longevity of the institution is often helpful to reassure customers.
- Third party endorsements can be used to signal independent asesssments of quality and reliability.
- Word-of mouth recommendations from other customers are helpful as a reassurance to buyers.

Lack of Consumer Interest Many consumers do not recognise the value of financial services and do not engage with them.

- Consumption of financial services is often "contingent" (see Ch 3) and their intrinsic value is limited.
- Importance of focusing on the ultimate benefits to the consumer of different financial services.
- Loan products often emphasis the benefit from the final purchase that the loan enables.
- Pension providers may focus on security and comfort in retirement.

Figure 6.7 Dealing with complexity and lack of interest

Third party awards such as UniCredit's recognition as "Bank of the Year 2023 Global Winner" in the The Banker Awards or Halifax's position as best overall Mortgage Lender (What Mortgage Awards 2023) may provide independent endorsements for consumers to consider. Increasingly, with the growth of social networking, financial institutions are encouraging individual customers to provide recommendations via services such as Twitter and Facebook. For example, HDFC Bank, like many others has its own Facebook page (www.facebook.com/HDFC.bank) and this provides an opportunity for customers to share by word of mouth and to make recommendations to other potential customers. Of course, as an inspection of the page will show, it also provides an opportunity for negative as well as a positive recommendation.

In the UK the FCA requires providers to publish information about their service quality to ensure consumers have good information. Figure 6.9 provides an example of the information published by Nationwide Building Society.

The lack of consumer interest in many financial services and the fact that consumption is essentially contingent can often be addressed by focusing on the benefits gained from the purchase of the product. Thus, promotional material for personal loans tends to emphasise the purchases which can be made as a result of the loan (whether cars, hi-fi equipment, holidays or houses). Similarly, marketing for life insurance and other related protection products will emphasise the benefit of security for the policyholder's dependents. Because financial services are generally products that consumers would prefer to avoid and because they have no obvious value in themselves, marketing must put extra effort into emphasising the benefits that these services provide. Barclays, for example uses the message "Find your way to new adventures" when encouraging customers to set up savings goals in the Barclays App.

 Stop and think?

As a consumer how useful do you think the information provided by Nationwide – and indeed other banks – is in reassuring you about the service the bank provides?

Figure 6.8 Aviva helps to solve insurance puzzles

Source: Reproduced with the permission of Aviva

Service quality indicators

As part of a regulatory requirement, an independent survey was conducted to ask customers of the 16 largest personal current account providers for Great Britain and 11 largest personal current account providers for Northern Ireland if they would recommend their provider to friends and family.

We have published this information at the request of the Competition and Markets Authority so you can compare the overall quality of service from personal current account providers.

We asked customers how likely they would be to recommend their personal current account provider to friends and family.

Overall service quality – Great Britain

Ranking

1	monzo	80%
2	Starling Bank	79%
3	first direct	78%
4 =	Nationwide	(67%)
4 =	ETRO BANK	67%

There's more information to help you compare providers in the Competition and Markets Authority service quality results:

Service quality results for Great Britain

Overall service quality – Northern Ireland

Ranking

1 =	monzo	81%
1 =	Starling Bank	81%
3	BARCLAYS	72%
4	HALIFAX	71%
5 =	HSBC UK	69%
5 =	Nationwide	(69%)

There's more information to help you compare providers in the Competition and Markets Authority service quality results:

Figure 6.9 Nationwide's Service Quality information

Source: Reproduced from the Nationwide web site with permission of Nationwide Building Society

6.4.2 *Responding to inseparability and perishability*

The fact the services are typically produced and consumed simultaneously means that financial services are perishable and, most significantly for this discussion, that customers have considerable difficulty with respect to pre-purchase evaluation. Although an *ex ante* evaluation of a particular product may be difficult, consumers can evaluate the organisation and can draw on the experience of others. Accordingly, a common theme in the marketing of financial services is to emphasise the performance and quality of the organisation and its people in order that there will be a halo effect from organisation to product. Such approaches are often reinforced by active attempts to secure word-of-mouth recommendations. Third party endorsements and word of mouth were discussed earlier in the context of perceived risk but they are equally relevant in responses to inseparability and perishability. American Express, for example, actively encourages existing customers to recommend new customers and rewards those customers who do introduce new members. Savings platform Raisin does the same by providing rewards both to the person who makes the referral and the person who signs up.

Furthermore, given the importance of the interaction between customers and employees and the potential role of employees in inspiring trust and confidence, many organisations are increasingly looking at human resource policies, training and internal marketing as means of building more effective relationships with customers. These relationships are seen as being of considerable significance both in reducing the level of perceived risk pre-purchase and the levels of dissonance post-purchase. Increasingly, staff need to use their expertise in a diversity of environments as fewer interactions take place face-to-face and more take place through remote channels. First Direct, for example, when recruiting staff for the launch of its telephone banking service placed much greater emphasis on the interpersonal skills of customer contact staff than it did on their detailed knowledge of banking practice. When Lloyds TSB decided to use Twitter (now X) as an alternative mechanism for engaging with customers, it chose to specifically work with staff who already had some experience of using this communication channel.

6.4.3 Responding to heterogeneity

A logical consequence of inseparability and the important role played by people is that the quality of service delivery has the potential to be highly variable. Clearly the potential for such variability will hinder the process of evaluation by consumers. Traditionally, strategies to address the variability of quality have focused on trying to ensure consistency through either mechanisation of service delivery for simple services or through enhanced staff training and development for more complex services. These two approaches remain relevant but with developments in technology there is increasing overlap, particularly with complex services where some elements can be automated, but there is still a need for human interaction whether through face-to-face or electronic channels. At the same time as some customers seek the flexibility and convenience of digital delivery (as provided by the neobanks), others continue to value the branch network as offered by, for example, Nationwide. And of course, in some cases consumers look for both. HDFC Bank in India has worked hard to grow both its physical branch network and its digital channels, while recognising the need for the two to be properly integrated to give customers a seamless service. Automation cannot entirely address the issue of variability, not least because automated solutions can still generate service failures and traditional staff training and development work that has focused on face-to-face interactions needs to develop a broader range of skills associated with the use of different channels.

6.4.4 Responding to fiduciary responsibility

The concept of fiduciary responsibility concerns itself with the implicit and explicit responsibilities of financial institutions with respect to the products they sell. The impact of fiduciary responsibility is arguably at its greatest at the purchase stage when a consumer may find that despite an active marketing campaign which has stimulated a decision to purchase, the institution indicates that it is unable to provide the product. For example, a common complaint from both personal customers and smaller businesses is that banks will actively promote the fact that they offer a variety of loans but will then turn down applications from some customers. Similar issues arise in relation to insurance where many companies are increasingly looking to sell only to good risks. In part this may simply reflect the overall importance of profit and an unwillingness to supply loans or insurance when the risk is too high. However, we should perhaps note that such decisions may also reflect an element of fiduciary responsibility in the sense that financial services suppliers are obliged to recognise that many of their "raw materials" are also the funds provided by other customers.

An extension of the idea of responsibility in relation to the management of funds is evidenced in the case of the Co-operative Bank in the UK. The bank's positioning and promotional campaign revolves around their ethical stance and their commitment to the responsible sourcing and distribution of funds. Similarly, Investment Managers, Baillie Gifford promotes some of its specialist investment funds with the message "We invest in big themes that change the world".

The selling process itself is also an area of concern because of the substantial information asymmetries which exist between supplier and customer. As discussed earlier in the section on behavioural economics, both the status quo bias and procrastination can give rise to a failure on the part of customers to act on certain financial needs and as a consequence some degree of encouragement or persuasion is required through the sales process. To address these problems is difficult. The simplest route is perhaps to emphasise honesty and prudence as themes in promotional campaigns. Consider for example, the HSBC campaign which claimed:

> We believe that the way forward is to offer a range of financial services honestly, simply and with integrity. That is how we have accumulated 23 million customers in 81 countries and territories.

Furthermore there are difficulties for financial service organisations in that fiduciary responsibility means that they may be promoting products to those individuals who are unlikely to be able to purchase because they are considered to be poor risk; while clearly this is something that many suppliers seek to avoid, in practice the identification of who is an appropriate customer is difficult and even with sophisticated marketing information systems, this process will be less than perfect.

Finally, with respect to fiduciary responsibility there is the issue of the purchase (sales) process itself. Given the information asymmetries which exist between supplier and customer, many customers are vulnerable to high pressure selling and bad advice. Indeed this is probably the issue which has done most to undermine the image of the financial services sector in recent years. Nevertheless, there are ways in which these issues can be tackled both internally and externally. One approach which a number of organisations have adopted is to reconsider their reward systems with a view to eliminating or at least reducing the reliance on commission-based selling. In a number of cases the nature of the reward structure (i.e. our salespeople aren't paid just on commission) is often used as a component of advertising in order to reassure consumers of the high standards of the supplying organisation.

6.4.5 Responding to duration and uncertainty

Many financial services are either consumed continuously (current accounts, credit cards) and therefore require a long-term relationship or else they only yield benefits in the longer term and the precise nature of these benefits may be uncertain. As indicated earlier, these features of financial services will tend to increase the perceived risk associated with the purchase and decrease the consumers' ability to evaluate the service both *ex ante* and *ex post*. To address this problem, there is again a tendency to rely heavily on marketing activities which emphasise the longevity of the supplier, trust, confidence and reliability. A good illustration of this approach is the web copy used by Clerical Medical which emphasises the origins of the company during the early part of the nineteenth century and its success at serving particular customer groups since that time.

> Clerical Medical has been providing pensions and investments since 1824. We've always been dedicated to providing consistent, dependable services and products that meet our clients' investment needs. (www.clericalmedical.co.uk/)

Identifying the right sort of approach to address the challenges associated with marketing financial services – particularly to personal consumers – depends upon having a good understanding of target consumers. While the next chapter talks in more detail about segmenting and targeting consumers, the remainder of this chapter will provide a brief overview of the issues that arise in researching the financial services consumer.

Progress check

- Taking into account the ways in which buyers make decisions and the distinctive characteristics of financial services, marketers need to think about how best to develop campaigns that address these characteristics.
- Key considerations will include how to make a service offer more tangible, how to engage customers and signal the way in which financial services can deliver benefits. Third party endorsements can provide reassurance about quality and ensuring that staff are customer service focused helps to reduce some of the concerns that consumers might have about the choices they make.
- Many financial services organisations will try to emphasise their longevity to encourage consumers to feel confident that their finances are in safe hands.

6.5 Researching financial services customers[5]

This section gives a brief overview of how market research can help marketers understand a range of aspects of consumer behaviour in order to build, grow, promote and make strategic business decisions. This includes the research approaches that can help brands deliver better products and services, assess and develop their brand, marketing, and communication strategies, and improve key stakeholder relationships. It covers the various qualitative and quantitative methodologies and techniques that marketers have at their disposal, as well as ethical and data protection issues that need to be considered when conducting financial services research.

A well-executed research programme can provide the insight needed to address a range of commercial challenges, whether that be reducing customer churn, delivering a differentiated proposition or targeting customers more effectively. Some of the outcomes that a client might expect from market research include:

- Better profits through effective customer acquisition and retention.
- A differentiated financial offer within a competitive market context.
- Being able to identify cross-selling opportunities for enhanced profitability.
- Better understanding of the implications of industry regulation and what it means for their brand and business models.
- Heightened customer loyalty to establish long term revenue streams.
- Insightful learning that will deliver competitive advantage.
- More cost-effective marketing plans and strategies.
- Better ROI on specific business initiatives

6.5.1 The market research process

The typical process for conducting a market research project is outlined in Figure 6.10:

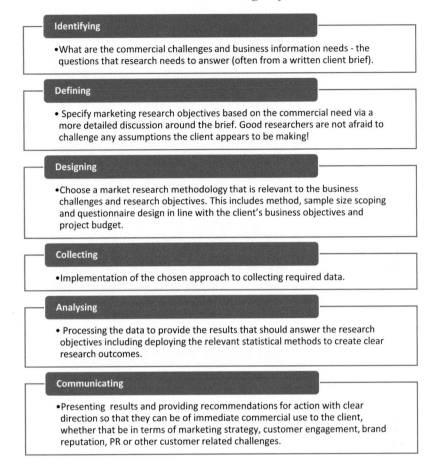

Identifying

•What are the commercial challenges and business information needs - the questions that research needs to answer (often from a written client brief).

Defining

• Specify marketing research objectives based on the commercial need via a more detailed discussion around the brief. Good researchers are not afraid to challenge any assumptions the client appears to be making!

Designing

•Choose a market research methodology that is relevant to the business challenges and research objectives. This includes method, sample size scoping and questionnaire design in line with the client's business objectives and project budget.

Collecting

•Implementation of the chosen approach to collecting required data.

Analysing

• Processing the data to provide the results that should answer the research objectives including deploying the relevant statistical methods to create clear research outcomes.

Communicating

•Presenting results and providing recommendations for action with clear direction so that they can be of immediate commercial use to the client, whether that be in terms of marketing strategy, customer engagement, brand reputation, PR or other customer related challenges.

Figure 6.10 The market research process

6.5.2 The purpose of market research

Market research agencies and consultancies help their clients use insights to build, grow, promote, and make strategic business decisions across a number of issues encompassing the whole marketing lifecycle. These are outlined in Figure 6.11.

Each of these types of research is explored in more detail below.

1 Product and service development

This type of market research plays a key role in the management of product strategy and will inform many of the questions and issues that are discussed in Chapter 10. This type of research typically addresses issues such as:

- Key customer needs?
- The features of the offer that will attract consumers?
- The size of market opportunity?
- The key benefits which need to be communicated in order to drive uptake?

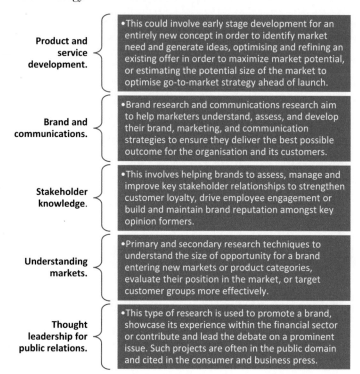

Figure 6.11 Market research functions

Various research approaches will be required at different stages in the lifecycle of new product and service development, including:

a) **Idea creation**
    Usage and Attitudes Studies are often used at an early stage to identify customer needs, understand customer behaviour and perceptions of a given category and identify routes to market. Similarly, Ideation labs bring together key stakeholders within the business to develop new ideas and build new product categories.

b) **Concept testing and optimisation**
    Qualitative research with a small number of consumers can be used to test and refine product and service concepts with customers. Quantitative research works with a larger number of consumers to optimise and define the final product or service features to guide product marketing prior to launch.

c) **Product strategy**
    Typically, quantitative research is used to benchmark the performance of a product or service at launch and measure market share and impact.

Marketing in practice 6.2 shows how USA-based investment company Foresight Investments (the real name has been withheld at the client's request) used consumer market research from Opinium to refine its product proposition and plan its entry to the UK market.

Marketing in practice 6.2: foresight investments – launching a new direct to consumer investment platform

Background

Having successfully developed a direct-to-consumer investment platform in the US, the client identified an opportunity to develop this offer for the UK market, in order to grow their business.

Research objectives

To do this, the client needed research to help develop and shape their product proposition including market viability and communications strategy. The research was used to answer the following questions:

1. What are consumers looking for in an investment platform?
2. What features are required to trigger uptake?
3. What is the size of market opportunity?
4. How should the brand best communicate the offer?

Approach

Qualitative

The first phase of research was designed to explore investors' needs from an investment platform, highlight the key decision criteria, and test a number of communication messages for the new proposition.

Opinium Research conducted two focus groups in London with self-directed investors with a minimum of £50,000 assets. In order to ensure the groups were as homogenous as possible and provide consensus of opinion, they were split by age with one group aged 35-44 and one aged 45-55. Each focus group consisted of 8 respondents and were held in a viewing studio allowing key client stakeholders to observe.

Quantitative

The second phase of the research was designed to help refine the proposition. The key objectives from this stage were to:

1. Understand the relative importance of product elements in driving overall preferences.
2. Understand the importance of fees and the price premium each feature commands.
3. Understand the trade-off between price and service.
4. Understand what the optimal product configuration is in order to drive uptake.
5. Understand how all the above varies by market segment.

Research was conducted using Opinium online consumer panel with 500 self-directed investors with an appropriate fund of investable assets. A choice-based conjoint analysis approach was used to define the optimal product features and charges to maximise customer reach. This approach allowed us to measure the influence of different product features on investors' likelihood to purchase by measuring the derived importance of each feature.

Respondents were presented with several product propositions, each one containing a different assortment of product features including brand profile; investment tools such as investment calculators and access to advice; price, and customer service. Conjoint analysis then determined the relative importance of each feature on consumer choice.

Key outcomes

Our research fed directly to senior management providing clear recommendations on how to optimise the proposition and how best to prepare the business launch communication programme. The launch was a great success and five years on the business continues to perform well.

2 Brand and Communications

This type of research encompasses two categories of research approaches, namely: communications research, and brand evaluation. Their aim is to help marketers understand, assess, and develop their brand, marketing, and communication strategies to ensure they deliver the best possible outcome.

Category 1: Communications research. This involves the whole communications cycle from early-stage ideation, creative development, through to market campaign evaluation. This strand comprises quantitative and qualitative methodologies to answer questions such as:

- How successful is the communication strategy?
- How does the message fit with existing perceptions of the brand?
- What drives positive and negative reactions?
- Are the desired messages being understood?
- Is the communication delivering the desired response?

Four stages are involved in the communications research process and they are presented schematically in Figure 6.12.

The types of research required at the different stages in this process are explored in a bit more detail below.

- **Stages 1 and 2: Identifying the consumer insight and early-stage creative development:** Qualitative approaches are best suited for identifying idea potential, exploring alternative or generating ideas, these might include:
  - **Group discussions** are the ideal forum to generate ideas for communication concepts as participants can build on each other's comments and viewpoints. Groups also generate rich debate and discussion to evaluate different concepts and how they could be developed.

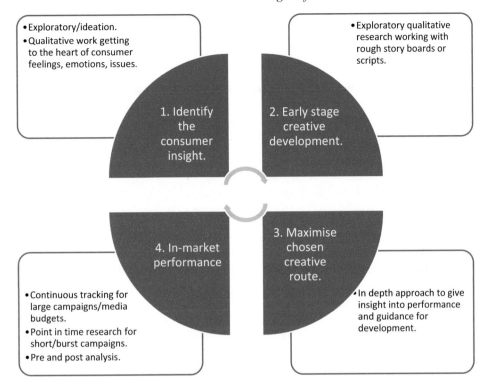

- Exploratory/ideation.
- Qualitative work getting to the heart of consumer feelings, emotions, issues.

- Exploratory qualitative research working with rough story boards or scripts.

1. Identify the consumer insight.

2. Early stage creative development.

4. In-market performance

3. Maximise chosen creative route.

- Continuous tracking for large campaigns/media budgets.
- Point in time research for short/burst campaigns.
- Pre and post analysis.

- In depth approach to give insight into performance and guidance for development.

Figure 6.12 Stages in the communications effectiveness research process

- **Individual in-depth interviews:** Advertising is generally consumed individually, so if concepts are slightly more developed then in-depth personal interviews are a more effective way to gain insight into how the concepts are being processed and understood.
- **Online insight Communities:** Short term online communities can be used to develop communication concepts iteratively. These communities are very flexible allowing coverage of multiple pieces of communications stimuli to be tested. They can also be used for test-measure-learn by changing stimuli and retesting with the same group. This approach is ideal for the fast development of communication stimuli.

- **Stage 3: Maximising the chosen route**
  Quantitative research is best suited to refine the chosen communication route, giving real insight into performance and clear recommendations into future development, as well as evaluating how successful the communication is in making an impact and getting a response.

- **Stage 4: Measuring in-market performance**
  Two possible quantitative approaches can be used to measure in-market performance depending on the type of communication activity.
  - **Continuous tracking:** The best way to way evaluate the impact of large scale / consistent marketing activity is to conduct continuous interviewing over time. This provides a continuous picture of changes in key baseline metrics as different campaigns and spend patterns are used.

- **Point in time:** Pre / Post dip methodology is a point in time evaluation of activity rather than a continuous read, ideally suited for a read on a specific campaign. The pre-dip takes place before activity, attaining a base level for key metrics The post-dip would occur after the activity has taken place. This will show the impact on key metrics.

Category 2. Brand evaluation research: This involves either an iterative or a continuous research programme to understand brand strength in a given category relative to the competition.Research will be used to answer questions such as:

- How strong is my brand?
- What does my brand stand for?
- How can I strengthen my brand positioning?
- How does my brand stack up to the competition?

Brand evaluation can be used in the following ways:

a) **Brand deep dive:** Point in time quantitative research to understand the current brand health, provide market understanding and feed into strategic planning.
b) **KPI monitoring:** Monitoring brand performance on KPIs identified in strategic deep dive or in brand plans.
c) **Real time read of brand performance:** Continuous monitoring of brand and competitive performance highlighting changes in consumer attitudes and effectiveness of marketing activity.

Many research agencies offer their own bespoke approaches to new product development, brand and communication evaluation or stakeholder understanding. Marketing in practice 6.3 and 6.4 provide examples of approaches which Opinium has developed to help clients build, grow, promote, and make strategic business decisions for their brand.

 Marketing in practice 6.3: the Opinium Connected Brand Framework

The Opinium Connected Brand Framework (CBF) benchmarks current brand health within a given category, allowing the intangible asset of brand equity to become tangible.

The Index measures four key metrics as shown in Figure 6.13 (emotion, prominence, distinction and dynamism). Decades of research and experience have shown that these metrics are what make brands successful. Statistical analysis is then used to help clients understand where they are positioned – and how to grow their brand.

The framework is shown to correlate highly with market share of a brand, meaning that clients can have confidence that the insights and recommendations will lead to real-world impacts for their business, and Opinium's database of normative data bears this out. In Opinium's framework, brands with higher CBF scores are more successful in terms of market share.

Opinium's approach enables the ability to drill down into each of the key metrics to understand what factors dictate success across each aspect of a brand. This allows clients to understand the best ways to maintain their strengths and address their weaknesses.

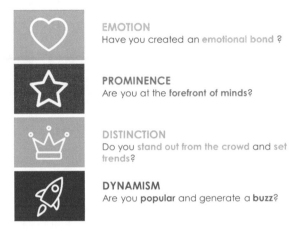

Figure 6.13 Key brand metrics

 Marketing in practice 6.4: the Opinium approach to communication evaluation

Opinium has a consistent philosophy which is used when conducting communications research which is based on the evaluation of 3 key areas.

- **Making an impact**
  A key area for successful communication is to engage and entertain. Brand association to the communication and fit with existing perceptions of the brand are also key factors, enabling an understanding of what drives positive and negative reactions, and also understanding the role of creative elements such as music and humour.
- **Landing the message**
  Once an impactful engaging piece of copy has been created the next area to evaluate is the ability to deliver the desired messages. Are the desired messages being taken out and understood? Consumers can often misconstrue communications and do not actually take out what clients are intending so it is important to delve into this area of communications to ensure the desired strategy is being delivered. Opinium uses a mixture of open and closed questions to attain consumer message take out.
- **Generating a response**
  The final area that is crucial to evaluate when considering communications research is getting the desired response. This of course can differ hugely depending on the media, this could be a call action to drive consumers to the website, to phone the call centre, to make a donation or even to have a more positive opinion of the brand/cause.

These three areas are evaluated in Opinium's creative development and evaluation tool kit based on testing claims, developing communications, developing creative messages and then optimising that message as Figure 6.14 shows.

Figure 6.14 Opinium's approach to communication evaluation

3 Stakeholder knowledge

This involves helping brands to assess, manage and improve key stakeholder relationships to strengthen customer loyalty, drive employee engagement or build and maintain brand reputation amongst key opinion formers.

Research will be used to answer questions such as:

- How strong is the stakeholder relationship with the brand?
- How strong is my brand reputation?
- Which measures will strengthen relationships or reduce churn?
- Which company processes need to be improved from the stakeholder's perspective?
- What are the reasons for inadequate performance?

Both qualitative and quantitative research techniques can be used to measure stakeholder relationships as follows:

a) **Identifying needs**

   Before evaluating stakeholder experiences there may be a need for initial qualitative research to identify the key issues which need to be validated amongst a wider sample in the quantitative stage.

b) **Evaluating experiences**

   Quantitative research may be used to measure stakeholder engagement amongst a wider representative sample to evaluate experiences across the whole customer or employee lifecycle and identify priority areas for action. Mystery shopping can also be used to evaluate and identify weaknesses in customer processes or services. These are often qualitative projects and require researchers or recruited respondents to undertake a series of tasks that could range from applying for a financial product online through to making an enquiry about a product via a call centre or through visiting a financial adviser. They are often frequent or on-going programmes that allow organisations not only to identify areas of weakness but also to see where they are servicing clients well.

c) **Action planning**

   Action planning workshops are used to ensure that results are embedded throughout the business bringing together all key stakeholders from the organisation to communicate and leverage the key findings, understand root causes of weaknesses and assign owners and plans for action.

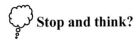 **Stop and think?**

Digital technologies have made it much easier for organisations to approach consumers for feedback whether in relation to purchase or simply in relation to contact. How often are you asked for feedback? How often do you respond and how honestly do you respond? What do you think this means for the reliability of market research?

4 Understanding Markets

This often involves both primary and secondary research techniques to understand the size of opportunity for a brand entering new markets or product category, to evaluate their position in the market, or to target customer groups more effectively. This type of research encompasses:

a) **Market sizing** – understanding the potential market size for existing or new products to feed into business planning or product strategy assessments.
b) **Industry review** – exploring the key challenges and opportunities facing an industry plus the key opinion formers who really matter.
c) **Customer segmentation** – getting under the skin of customers and identifying how different customer groups behave, ultimately allowing for more granular targeting and more relevant and salient marketing messages, products and services to be delivered to each customer segment.
d) **Competitive landscaping** – evaluating a brand's position within the market by understanding key competitor positions and overall market share.
e) **Market forecasting** – projecting anticipated business growth or market trends.

5 Thought leadership and research for public relations purposes

This form of research is used to promote a brand, showcase its experience within the financial sector or contribute and lead the debate on a prominent issue. Such projects are often in the public domain and cited in the consumer and business press. Popular examples in the UK include the Nationwide and Halifax House Price Indices published on a regular basis which typically attract significant press coverage[6].

Various research approaches including secondary desk research, qualitative and quantitative research are used to support and maximise the impact of a PR campaign in the following ways:

- **Headline generation:** Generating coverage and securing buy in from the media to feed into national, regional or trade press releases.
- **Reputation building:** Building or consolidating a brand's association with a topic or area of expertise.
- **Dispelling myths:** Elevating the reputation of a sector or issue by highlighting misconceptions.

The research approaches described above are not exhaustive or set in stone. In most cases, a combination of research approaches is required in order to meet the overall commercial objectives. Best practice dictates that each individual client brief should be treated as bespoke and tailored to suit the specific business challenges in question.

6.5.3 *Principal research methods*

In this section we examine the different forms of qualitative and quantitative research methods that are commonly used to gain insights into consumers, their attitudes and behaviours.

Qualitative research plays a crucial role in analysing business problems. In crude terms, it can answer the where, what, when, why and how type questions that organisations face. It is best used for research that is exploratory and developmental. Qualitative research is designed to talk to a relatively small number of people in a target audience. While it can scrutinise intensely the depth and range of consumer attitudes and beliefs, it can never measure incidence or forecast quantity.

There are a number of qualitative research approaches which can be deployed:

* **Focus groups**
  Group discussions (usually containing 6-8 respondents facilitated by a moderator) are the ideal forum to generate ideas as participants can build on each other's comments and viewpoints. This methodology generates rich debate and discussion, and normally lasts between 1-2 hours. Focus groups are of huge benefit in informing quantitative survey content, as well as generating in-depth standalone insight.
* **In-depth interviews**
  In-depth interviews can be conducted via a telephone, face-to-face, or, increasingly, online. These are interviews conducted on a one-to-one basis, and which seek to explore issues at a deep level, similar to that of a focus group.

  In-depth interviews can be conducted either as standalone research, or more usually as part of a multi-methodology approach, either pre or post a quantitative research phase. Depth interviews are often the most suitable solution where it is deemed too difficult to recruit participants to a physical location at a specific time (i.e. for a focus group); for instance, where the target audience are "C-suite" executives or where the sample is geographically dispersed. They are also often used to research sensitive subjects where respondents would feel less comfortable discussing issues in front of other people such as in a focus group.
* **Ethnographic interviews**
  The aim of ethnography is to provide rich, holistic insights into people's views and actions, as well as the nature of the location they live, through the collection of detailed observations and interviews. With ethnographic interviews, not only can individual behaviours be profiled, but you can observe how everyday life unfolds, using actual behaviour as a stimulus. By being able to see what respondents do / where they go / the facilities they have available to them and to hear them talk about them, in situ, adds an extra dimension and level of analysis which cannot be obtained from traditional focus groups or in- depth interviews.
* **Online Insight Communities**
  Online Insight Communities are a qualitative research methodology used for many types of market research, but particularly for projects requiring participants to use a product or service and where audio and visual data is preferred or required. They are often used for early-stage development, such as new product development or concept testing and for anything requiring "lean" and "agile", test-measure-learn, principles.

  Unlike long-term online communities used to build brand engagement, online insight communities are exclusively research focussed. They are usually short-term, lasting between a couple of days to a few weeks; they use a dedicated online platform to conduct the research; and participants are recruited specifically for the research. For this reason, they are sometimes referred to as "Pop-up Research Communities".

Online insight communities are not dissimilar to focus groups, but have particular benefits in relation to the recruitment of participants, the tasks they can be asked to undertake and the resulting outputs. These are shown in more detail in Figure 6.15 and Marketing in practice 6.5 illustrates how such communities can be used.

Marketing in practice 6.5: Freshcorp – using an on-line community for insights to increase sales

An FMCG company wanted to compare the packaging and design of their home care product compared to competitors, in order to maximise sales in supermarkets.

A week-long insight community was created to get participants to engage with the client's and competitor's products, talk about what they like and dislike and their experience of using the products.

Details:

- Participants: 20 people who use similar home care products and shop at a large supermarket.
- Fieldwork: 5 days (including over a weekend.)
- Expected time per day: 15-20 minutes plus longer over a weekend.

Members of the target audience are recruited into the community and set various tasks with each day building on the previous day.

- Day 1: Introduction and warm-up. Introduce the community and remind people of the requirements. Ask simple questions about current usage of home care products and why they choose them. Get participants to provide photos of these.
- Days 2-4: Instore buying behaviour and product comparison. Get participants to go into their usual supermarket, find the product shelf, photograph it using their smartphone and purchase the product. Understand their perception of the shelf, ease of use and how product packaging appears in context. Participants record 4-5 minute videos comparing the two products purchased based on a set of questions.
- Day 5: Ask participants to provide a final product preference, explain why and provide an opportunity for closure at the end of the community.

Outputs:

The client was provided with a report summarising the findings, with an executive summary and recommendations. A face-to-face presentation was also delivered. At the presentation videos from the community were shown, allowing the clients and their stakeholders to see first-hand the opinions of participants. Clients were impressed with the approach as it gathered a level of insight that they weren't able to get through existing approaches, particularly in terms of how the products worked.

In this way FreshCorp was able to develop its products to better meet customer needs and stand out from the competition on supermarket shelves.

Recruitment of Participants

- Research can be conducted anywhere - Participants are able to login using a computer or smartphone, so can be from across a country or even globally.
- Participants can also take part at a time convenient to them - while fieldwork takes place during set times participants are able to log in whenever they have time, meaning they don't need to attend a particular venue at a particular time.

Tasks

- Various tasks can be set, such as open questions, poll questions, marking-up visuals, ranking items. Exact questions and tasks will depend on the platform used.
- Participants can be set in-home or in-store tasks. Participants can be asked to use a service, such as a website or purchase items from stores, and provide feedback on the service or product following their experience.
- With mobile-enabled platforms participants can take photos and videos as they interact with products or services, at home, at work or in store.
- Participants are familiar with online communication and interaction - Most participants will regularly use online communities such as Facebook. The platforms are intuitive to use and arguably more engaging and less threatening than a focus group which most participants will never have attended.

Outputs

- Visual data - If suitable, participants are able to provide photos and videos of themselves, their homes and where they shop. This provides more data than participants are able to recall or communicate directly, often in an almost ethnographic way - for example, what other products are on a shelf or the type of interior decor a person has in their kitchen.
- Bringing the participant to life - Showing videos and photos to clients can be a powerful way to get the research findings across to clients in debrief meetings and presentations.
- Iterative product and service development - Feedback gathered in a community can be used to iterate a concept, service or product. This iterated version can be put back to the same participants in the research community a couple of days later. This allows for a more efficient development cycle for the client.

Figure 6.15 The benefits of using online communities for market research

Quantitative research asks people for their opinions in a structured way. It involves relatively large numbers of respondents and its aim is to provide statistically robust evidence upon which organisations can make sound business judgements. To get reliable results, large numbers of people need to be interviewed in order that they are representative of the target market under scrutiny.

Quantitative research can be undertaken in a range of ways:

- **Online research** is the most commonly used method of reaching respondents and tends to be conducted through online panels where respondents sign up to receive market research surveys. The advantages of online research are:
  - Can reach specific target audiences or nationally representative samples
  - Reach large volumes of respondents
  - Cost-effective
  - Quick to set up
  - Allows significant complexity
  - Allows complex quota management
  - Allows the display of visual stimuli
- **Mobile surveys**
  Mobile research gives researchers the ability to extract dynamic, real-time insight from consumers who are on the move and "in the moment". It allows real-time, in-location and "in the moment" feedback from consumers.
- **CATI (Computer Assisted Telephone interviewing)**
  This is a methodology comprising structured telephone interviews, which is usually best suited to achieving harder to reach respondents such as B2B customers.
- **Other quantitative methodologies**
  Other less frequently used research methodologies include face-to-face interviews and postal surveys. These are often used either for street interviews or for groups of people where online penetration is lower, such as the elderly or in rural areas or countries where online penetration is still very low.

Statistical analysis is usually required with quantitative research to make sense of data patterns and to illustrate what is driving consumer behaviour, i.e. what is leading them to respond to research in a particular way. Various techniques allow researchers to identify challenges and opportunities and to offer evidence-based solutions. A host of analytical techniques can help marketers understand a variety of business questions such as:

- What are the must-haves of my brand versus the nice-to-have features?
- How much should I spend on advertising?
- How can I communicate marketing messages most effectively?
- What key features or attitudes are associated with my brand?

Common quantitative analysis techniques (by no means exhaustive) used for financial services projects are outline below in Table 6.2:

Table 6.2 Quantitative analysis techniques

Name	Description	Illustrative Applications
Conjoint analysis.	A technique that helps researchers to identify important and unimportant criteria in consumer decisions. Uses a subset of possible attribute features (e.g., branch location convenience, low or no fees, availability of ATMs, customer service hours) to determine the relative importance of each feature in consumers choice.	Often, consumers have difficulty assessing what criteria are most important to them when asked outright. They may say that good interest rates, good customer service and easy account access are equally critical to them when choosing a savings account, but in reality are always making trade-offs, selecting, e.g. a more convenient service over one they believe to offer higher quality, or selecting a service with an excellent reputation over one they believe to be less expensive.
Maximum Difference scaling (Max Diff).	Asks respondents to choose the most important and least important items for a list of 3 -6 items such as features of a car insurance policy or credit card.	Used to understand consumer preferences for multiple items such as brand attributes or service features and can help companies develop and best communicate products and services in order to maximise sales potential. It is often used to differentiate importance scores which can lack differentiation when asked directly through rating questions.
Cluster Analysis.	A statistical process that clusters individuals together based on a statistical analysis of relevant criteria. Essentially, it is a way of classifying people who have similar needs or characteristics and demand similar products and/ or services, so that companies can more easily target different customer typologies with different types of marketing messages.	In segmentation studies, cluster analysis might group consumers together who are most strongly oriented toward (group 1) convenience of branches and ATMs, (group 2) toward exceptional customer service, or (group 3) high interest rates over product flexibility.
Key driver analysis.	This statistical technique (often via regression analysis) is used to understand which factors most influence a given outcome.	It is often used when exploring customer satisfaction or loyalty and brand preferences as it can help researchers understand which brand, product or service components or attributes have the greatest influence on customers' purchase decisions.

6.5.4 Ethical issues

When talking to consumers, both in general, and, more specifically, in the context of discussing potentially sensitive financial matters, professional market research practitioners should always adhere to best practice and industry standards. In the UK, the Market Research Society is the main industry association. Others, such as AIMRI

(Alliance of International Market Research Institutes), ESOMAR (European Society for Opinion and Market Research) and BIG (Business Intelligence Group), are relevant to best practice in financial services. There are a number of rules and guidelines that should be adhered to when conducting financial services research. For further information on best practice, the MRS website contains up-to-date information for UK professionals.[9]

Nearly all UK banks subscribe to the Banking Code and the Business Banking Code. These Codes describe how banks should treat their customers, respond to complaints, and so on. These Codes also contain rules and guidelines for how customer data can and cannot be used. Banks adhering to these Codes sign up to treat all customer personal information as private and confidential (even when they are no longer a customer). Banks must not reveal names, addresses or details about customer accounts to anyone, including other companies in the group, other than in a few exceptional cases, such as when they are asked to give the information by law. This means that banks that adhere to this Code have made a commitment to their customers not to pass their data to anyone else for any other purpose, and that bank records are therefore different from other client databases commonly used for research. As the MRS Code of Conduct notes, "Care must always be taken with regard to data gathered as to who owns it and controls it and the customer must always be clear as to who is controlling the data".[10]

6.6 Summary and conclusion

Although there has been a considerable amount of empirical research examining customer choice, our understanding of the buying process for financial services is still limited. One obvious way to try to understand how buyers make decisions is to think about the different stages in a decision-making process – namely, problem recognition, information search, evaluation of alternatives, purchase and post-purchase reactions. Not every decision will involve all of these stages, but this framework does have a clear logic and can help with thinking about different ways of engaging with customers. It is apparent both conceptually and from existing empirical evidence that certain characteristics of financial services present a number of problems for consumers when they make choices and there are a variety of strategies and tactics which marketers can use to address these problematic aspects of consumer choice. Some of these issues have been explored in greater detail by researchers working in the areas of behavioural economics and finance.

These potential complexities in relation to understanding buyer behaviour in financial services mean that investment in understanding customers is crucial. Over the past decade there have been explicit moves to ensure that market research makes its way further up the business agenda and into both boardrooms and the minds of shareholders. Since the late 2000s in particular, research has necessarily become much more decision and action oriented. Agency market researchers are now expected to provide more than just analytical reporting; increasingly they are expected to support the client company in an advisory and problem-solving role.

Learning outcomes

Having completed this chapter, you should now be able to:

1. **Understand the range of factors that influence the consumer decision-making process in financial services.**
    Financial services are low in search qualities and high in experience and credence qualities. Information is difficult to collect and interpret and there is a tendency to rely heavily on the experience of others rather than on supplier-provided information. Evaluation is even more complex, partly because of the lack of search qualities but also because of the complexity of many of the products and the reluctance of many suppliers to facilitate comparisons across products. Consumer needs often do not become apparent until the actual point of sale and the problems of information search and evaluation mean that the buyer is always likely to be vulnerable to the "hard" sell. Having bought a particular financial service, a customer may still find evaluation difficult and many buyers experience high levels of cognitive dissonance post-purchase.

2. **Understand the different ways in which financial services providers can influence the buying process.**
    There are a variety of strategies and tactics which marketers can use to address these problematic aspects of consumer choice; these include tangibilising the service, emphasising particular dimensions of image and investing in staff training and internal marketing. However, there are also many aspects of the marketing of financial services which have tended to reinforce some of the problems experienced by consumers. In particular, pricing and product benefits are often not clearly presented and the historic reliance on commission-based selling has resulted in a number of well-publicised and damaging cases of over-selling for certain products. Some of these problems are being rectified by a combination of company-specific actions and industry-wide regulation. However, from a marketing perspective it is crucial that financial services organisations recognise that they operate in a high-contact business where the nature of buyer–seller interactions and the establishment of long-term relationships based on confidence and trust have real implications for successful retention of customers and recruitment of prospects.

3. **Recognise some of the differences between final consumers and business consumers in relation to financial services.**
    While there may be many aspects of the decision-making process that are comparable between personal and business consumers, there are also important differences between the two types of buyer. While there will be very knowledgeable retail buyers, and relatively uninformed small business buyers, it is probably fair to say that the key differences between the two groups relate to the numbers of individuals involved in decision making and the higher levels of understanding and engagement among corporate customers.

4. **Recognise some of the ways in which behavioural economics can help understand consumer decision-making and policy formulation.**
   The distinctive characteristics of services highlight a range of challenges for consumer decision making. Behavioural economics/finance tries to understand these in more detail and demonstrates why certain types of behaviour – which might appear to be non-rational can explained with careful consideration of the psychological processes of decision making.

5. **Understand key elements of the process of researching financial consumers.**
   Understanding consumers – both what and why they buy and also how they respond to marketing campaigns – is key to effective marketing. Market research provide a means of systematically understanding consumers and other stakeholders. There is a wide range of techniques and approaches and key to effective research is to ensure that the right approaches are used in relation to the research questions under consideration.

Review questions

1. What are the main differences in buyer behaviour between retail and business consumers for financial services?
2. How might consumers collect information to help them choose between financial services? How can marketing help this process?
3. Why is it important to tangibilise a financial service?
4. How can financial services organisations build trust and confidence?

Notes

1 www.ey.com/GL/en/Industries/Financial-Services/Banking—-Capital-Markets/Global-consumer-banking-survey-2012—Adapt-business-models, (Accessed September 2012)
2 www.currentaccountswitch.co.uk/ (Accessed January 2024)
3 www.cgi.com/sites/default/files/pdf/br_fs_consumersurveyreport_final_july_2014.pdf. (Accessed February 2017)
4 This section draws heavily on the analysis prepared by James Devlin and Swee-Hoon Chuah originally published in previous editions and now available via the instructors' website.
5 This section of the chapter has been provided by Alexa Nightingale of the market research company, Opinium Research.
6 See www.nationwidehousepriceindex.co.uk/reports and www.halifax.co.uk/media-centre/house-price-index.html (Accessed December 2023)
7 Thaler, R., & Benartzi, S. (1999). "Risk aversion or myopia? Choices in repeated gambles and retirement investments". *Management Science, 45*, 364–38.1
8 Pensions Commission (2004) "Pensions: Challenges and Choices: The First Report of the Pensions Commission". London: HMSO.
9 www.mrs.org.uk
10 www.mrs.org.uk/standards/codeconduct.htm

References

Adams, A. and Clunie, J. (2006). The split capital investment trust saga: Lessons for financial services marketing. *Journal of Financial Services Marketing*, 10(3), pp. 218–27.

Bowen, D. E. and Schneider, B. (1988). Services marketing & management: Implications for organizational behaviour. *Research in Organizational Behaviour*, 10, pp. 43–80.

Diacon, S. R. and Ennew, C. T. (1996). Ethical issues in insurance marketing in the UK. *European Journal of Marketing*, 30(5), pp. 67–80. https://doi.org/10.1108/03090569610118786

Engel, J. F., Blackwell, R. D. and Miniard, P. W. (1991). *Consumer Behaviour*. 6th ed. Chicago, IL: Dryden Press.

Ennew, C. T. and Sekhon, H. (2014). Trust and trustworthiness in retail financial services: An analytical framework and empirical evidence. In: T. Harrison and H. Estelami (eds.), *The Routledge Companion to Financial Services Marketing*, 1, pp. 148–65. London: Routledge.

Zeithaml, V. (1981). How consumer evaluation processes differ between goods and services. In: J. H. Donnelly and W. R. George (eds.), *The Marketing of Services*, pp. 186–90. AMA Proceedings.

7 Segmentation targeting and positioning

Learning objectives

At the end of this chapter, you should be able to:

1. Appreciate the benefits that arise from segmentation,
2. Explain different approaches to segmenting a market,
3. Understand the issues involved in selecting a target market,
4. Understand the role of positioning in communicating the value proposition,
5. Appreciate the ways in which digital marketing is impacting upon segmentation.

7.1 Introduction

The process of segmentation, targeting and positioning (STP) is central to effective strategic marketing. Segmentation is concerned with the process of identifying different groups of customers who are similar in ways that are relevant to marketing. To segment a market, it is important to understand who your customers are, why they behave in particular ways, and how they may be grouped together. Targeting decisions can then be made based on the range of identified segments. In order to choose the most appropriate target markets, it is necessary to understand what different segments want and the extent to which the organisation can supply those wants. Finally, having identified target markets, the organisation must then consider how to position itself in those markets. Positioning refers to the way in which an organisation tries to communicate its value proposition to its target market in order to convince customers that it has a distinctive offer. In effect, positioning is about the way in which the organisation tries to build and communicate its competitive advantage, and is, therefore, concerned with how to differentiate a brand or company from its competition.

This chapter will review segmentation, targeting and positioning. It will begin by explaining the benefits of segmentation and targeting for both providers and customers. The requirements for successful segmentation will be examined in general terms and approaches to segmenting final consumer and corporate markets will then be explored in more detail. The chapter continues with a discussion of different approaches to market targeting and the final sections will explain the key elements of positioning and repositioning and will also address how digital marketing is impacting upon segmentation strategies.

DOI: 10.4324/9781003398615-9

7.2 The benefits of segmentation and targeting

Segmentation is essentially a process whereby a provider of goods or services chooses to group prospective customers together based on a set of common characteristics that have significant implications for its marketing activity. In practice this means how best to use the individual components of the marketing mix to achieve marketing goals. Common characteristics that might be used to segment a market include variables such as age, income, personality and life-style. Based on those common characteristics, segments are expected to respond differently to marketing activities – they may want different features, be more or less price sensitive, respond to particular types of marketing communications or use different channels. Targeting is then concerned with the identification of an appropriate set of segments which the organisation will seek to serve. Implicit in any decision to undertake segmentation and targeting is the realisation that no single organisation is capable of being "all things to all people". It is inevitable that certain products will have particular appeal to certain kinds of individuals. At one extreme, each individual customer could be presented as a segment of one because each individual has different needs. In such a case, the marketing mix is bespoke to match the characteristics and needs of a single person or organisation. This practice is perhaps more common than might at first be imagined. In retail markets, financial advisers provide a service encounter that is unique to the individual client as do private bankers. In corporate markets, a customised approach is essential in dealing with large corporate clients. Advances made in the field of information technology and digital marketing have had far-reaching implications for the financial services sector, not least of which through the ways in which it has made marketing to a segment of one, previously only a marketer's dream, not only practically but economically feasible.

At the other extreme, the whole population could be treated as if it was a single homogenous segment. Traditionally, banks would have treated the personal banking market as homogenous and provided a single standard current account to all customers. Increasingly however, there is a recognition that customers do have differing banking needs and that there is the potential to develop specific products for specific segments. Thus, for example, Barclays offers over ten different current accounts in the United Kingdom (UK) market, targeted to a variety of segments including children, students, people with very high incomes and people with very low incomes.

Segmentation and targeting are how several important benefits are secured for both providers and consumers of products and services. These benefits are summarised as follows:

- **Efficient resource utilisation**
  An indiscriminate use of the marketing mix is a wasteful use of precious resources. By identifying and targeting discrete segments of consumers (retail or corporate) a company can limit the scope of individual components of the mix and thus reduce costs. To take a simple example, an advertising programme involving the use of the press media will be less expensive if it involves the use of magazines that are read by a discrete target segment of consumers rather than the entire population. Similarly, products designed for a given segment should have only the features needed by that segment. Thus, segmentation results in greater resource efficiency which benefits consumers through better value, shareholders through reduced waste and lower costs, and the environment through the more efficient use of resources.
- **Effective targeting of new customers**
  The logical next step from segmenting a market is the selection of segments to target for marketing activities. Nowadays, it is unusual for a company to have a completely indiscriminate approach to targeting new customers. As the costs of customer acquisition

have increased and companies become increasingly focused upon customer profitability, they must be selective in respect of which kinds of people or organisations they want to be their customers.

It must be appreciated that different customers display different characteristics and behaviours that impact upon customer value. For example, in the UK, SAGA targets people aged over 50 for its range of leisure and financial services. SAGA can price its motor insurance premiums very keenly as the over-50s represent a low-risk group in terms of propensity to incur motor claims. Thus, SAGA can be very price competitive and deliver superior value to this group of consumers in a way that would not be possible if the company was trying to serve a mass market. To quote from the company's website[1]:

> We are focused on building Saga into the largest and fastest-growing business for older people in the UK and delivering sustainable growth for our investors by creating 'The Superbrand' for this age group.

To achieve this, we will:

- commercialise and grow our database
- build exceptional insights into "Generation Experience",
- deliver a brand re-positioning,
- create a content platform where we reach millions of customers every day, and
- deliver an exceptional colleague experience.

In Australia the insurance company Australian Seniors also specialises in providing a wide range of insurance products to people aged over 50 years. Other examples of companies that target a specific segment include Sheila's Wheels in the UK that focusses on female drivers whilst Haven Knox Johnston is a UK-based company that has carved out a market leading position by specialising in insuring boats and allied risks associated with enjoying water-based activities. In Marketing in practice 7.1 we see how the company has set out to position iteslf as being the approachable, knowledgeable, fun-loving partner that supports those who love life on the water.

Marketing in practice 7.1: Haven Knox Johnston

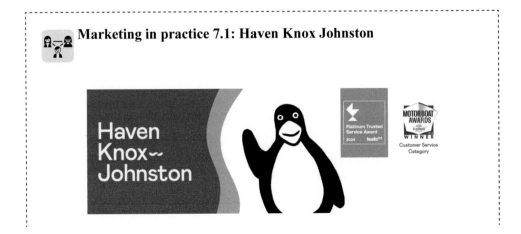

Our mission

Quite simply our mission is to blow traditional boring boat insurance right out of the water.

Gone is the stale imagery of blue sky, teak deck and boat. Our new dynamic brand positions us squarely in the retail insurance sector with our crew, our policies and our services at front and centre.

We aim to provide our customers with consistently excellent boat cover that's "ship-shaped" around them, from a crew that knows boats as well as they do. And with 26 years of experience behind us, and a new look and new horizons ahead, we're excited to be bringing Haven Knox Johston back to an ever-growing, always-changing market.

Our vision

We want every boater on every waterway, from rivers and estuaries to coastal waters and oceans, to know our name, to be delighted with our customer service, and ultimately to insure their pride and joy with Haven Knox Johnston.

It sounds bold, it sounds big, it sounds ambitious – and it is. But we believe in our crew, and we love broad horizons. Who's with us?

Our values

Our crew believes in:

Great customer service

Anyone who goes out boating knows how invaluable it can be to have a solid crew to help with everything from navigation to sailing, and locks to mooring up. Which is why, with the intrinsic knowledge and strength we have in our crew, we've based our rebrand on how we form part of our customers' support crew. Because we're always on hand whenever our customers need us – even if it is just to talk boats.

The power of knowledge

We like to keep things clear and simple. All our policies are in plain English – you won't find much insurance jargon muddifying the waters. And you can't beat a boat insurance crew who are also mad about boats. There's an empathy there that just can't be faked. Whatever problem a customer has, there'll be someone on the crew who knows just how that feels – and just how to help.

Enjoying ourselves on the water – and in the office

Because boats are brilliant. And while no one's pretending boat insurance could possibly be as fun, it doesn't have to be a drag either. Our passion and enthusiasm come through in all we do – whether we're working with our customers to shipshape their cover perfectly, or picking up the phone to answer their calls.

Source: Paul Knox-Johnston

- **Facilitation of competitive advantage**

  The more specific an organisation's approach to segmenting the market, the easier it is to establish and maintain competitive advantage. This arises because competitive advantage is a relative concept that involves differentiating an organisation from its rivals in the eyes of its customers. Self-evidently, the more indiscriminate the approach to targeting, the wider the array of competitors against whom an organisation will have to seek to differentiate itself. In the case of SAGA, it only needs to maintain a competitive advantage over those other organisations that also seek to target the over-50s, such as RIAS. This presents SAGA with a smaller set of key rivals than if it were to target the entire adult population. In turn, this makes it easier to achieve and maintain differentiation.

- **Directing the marketing mix**

  Best practice dictates that each target segment chosen by an organisation should be subject to a specific and relevant marketing campaign. In this way marketing activities are managed to achieve the best fit with the needs and characteristics of each target segment. Some financial services providers are affinity-based and this allows for particularly close targeting of the marketing mix. The Police Mutual Assurance Society (PMAS) in the UK has a mix that makes full use of its affinity relationship with the UK's police service. For example, it makes use of locally based police officers as part of its distribution processes. So-called Authorised Officers act as a conduit for communication between both serving police officers and civilian staff and PMAS. In France, Maif is an insurance company dedicated to serving the needs of teachers. Their marketing mixes take advantage of the close relationships they enjoy with their respective affinity groups to achieve a bespoke approach.

- **Enhances customer satisfaction**

  Segmentation and targeting are an effective means of enhancing customer satisfaction because product offers should achieve a close match with customer needs and wants. Clearly, the more precisely a product and its features reflect the characteristics of a given group of individuals, the greater the degree of satisfaction they should experience from its consumption. The corollary to this is that the absence of well-managed segmentation results in a generalised approach to the market. This results in customers feeling that several product features are irrelevant to them and that communication messages lack real relevance to their personal circumstances and preferences. Therefore, such consumers will always be vulnerable to competitors with a more focused approach to segmentation that enables them to deliver greater customer satisfaction. Alongside these benefits, there are also costs associated with segmentation. Identifying, measuring, and maintaining a system of segmented markets is a cost in itself. Additionally, costs are incurred through the development of different products and different marketing campaigns for these different segments, thus limiting opportunities for economies of scale. Any exercise involving market segmentation must be aware of these costs and look to implement market segmentation only where the benefits outweigh the costs.

7.3 Successful segmentation

There is no best way to segment a market. On the contrary, as will become clear in subsequent sections, there are a variety of approaches that can be used with varying degrees of complexity and sophistication. Ultimately, a commercial judgement must be made to ensure the best fit between the incremental costs that segmentation entails and the incremental value that can be realised. For an organisation to get an approach to segmentation that is "right" for it depends on a good understanding of the market, the right skills and knowledge and careful evaluation of the different options. In terms of skills and knowledge, the following areas are of particular importance:

- **Understanding of the market**
  Managers seeking to segment a market must display a sound understanding of the marketplace in which they operate. This understanding should be based upon the ability to integrate all relevant sources of knowledge to form a cohesive, whole picture of the market. Not only does this involve hard, objective facts such as market values, number of customers, frequency of purchase, competitors and their respective market share, but it also involves more subjective and qualitative-based inputs. Such inputs include an understanding of consumer choice and an awareness of the strategies of competitors. A sense of touch for the market provides the marketing manager with the capacity to identify opportunities for differentiation and competitive advantage.

Progress check

- Segmentation, targeting, and positioning (STP) is central to effective strategic marketing.
- Segmentation and targeting processes enable marketing resources to be used more efficiently.
- Segmentation, targeting, and positioning lead to higher levels of customer satisfaction.

- **Analytical skills and resources**
  Access to appropriate data and the ability to manipulate and interpret it is vital. The more varied the data about a market the greater the number of options for segmentation. Markets vary considerably with regard not only to the variety of data sources that are available but also in respect to recency, frequency, consistency and accuracy of data.
- **Commercial judgement**
  A wide range of "common characteristics" can be used in market segmentation. These vary from basic demographic criteria such as age and gender through to subtle and complex criteria based upon personality traits. A fine judgement must be made regarding the impact that a chosen approach to segmentation is likely to have on the commercial outcome. This entails careful consideration of costs and benefits for any given method of segmentation.
- **Creative insight**
  To be successful, segmentation calls for a combination of elements of marketing as both art and science. Science is required in terms of the gathering of information, its analysis and the use of various modelling and simulation processes. Ultimately a judgement must be made regarding which approach is most likely to facilitate effective differentiation

and competitive advantage. This requires a high degree of creative insight if one is to identify a segment that can be successfully penetrated. It also requires creative intuition regarding how to translate the company's aspirations into a concrete marketing mix that appeals to the segment. In the UK it is understood that the Co-operative Bank chose the ethical consumer segment more based on creative insight than conventional factual analysis. Its positioning based upon an ethical approach to banking was first presented in the 1990s and continues to this day.

Thus, good segmentation combines elements of science and art, namely, issues that are both quantifiably objective and qualitatively judgemental.

In terms of evaluating different options for segmentation, there are several factors that require consideration. Organisation-specific criteria relating to fit with current activity and ability to serve will clearly be important. Equally, it is helpful to evaluate proposed methods of segmentation in terms of their performance in several key areas. One common approach is to focus attention on the following criteria:

- **Measurability**: This is concerned with the extent to which the preferences, size and purchasing power of different segments can be measured. Certain segmentation variables are difficult to measure, making segment size and purchasing power difficult to identify. An investment company may identify small investors who are risk averse as an attractive market segment but may find it difficult to find out exactly how many people fall into this category because of the difficulties of measuring risk aversion without dedicated primary data collection. In contrast, the segment of women over 60 will be much easier to measure as such data is readily available. The growth of big data and sophisticated analytics is increasingly addressing the challenge of measurability, allowing for greater sophistication with measurement.
- **Profitability**: The degree to which segments are large and/or profitable enough. A segment should be the largest possible homogenous group of customers that is economically viable for a tailored marketing programme. Medical students are one very distinctive and homogenous segment of the market, but it probably would not be viable for a bank to develop a distinct current account just for this particular group because the costs of doing so would probably not justify the returns for a low margin product such as current accounts. The situation may, of course, be different for higher margin products.
- **Accessibility:** This refers to the degree to which the segments can be effectively reached and served. Traditionally it had always been the case that simple segments (e.g. retail customers in social class A; professional services firms) were easy to access because they were easy to identify and could be reached through a variety of media that they were known to favour. More complex segments were always more challenging. The segment of internationally oriented, rapid-growth companies could be very attractive as a target market for a range of export financing products but traditionally would have been difficult to reach. Digital technologies are changing this and making more complex segments much easier to reach. For example, increasing volumes of marketing communications can be targeted based on terms used in search engines and associated online activity, allowing companies to access more specific market segments in a way that was not previously possible.

- **Relevance:** The degree to which the common characteristics used to group customers are relevant to customer decisions. A segmentation system which groups individuals in terms of lifestyle and establishes that the type of credit card carried (standard, gold, platinum) depends on an individual's aspirations and self-concept uses a personality-based characteristic to explain preference. This type of characteristic is likely to be a more relevant predictor of consumer decisions on which card to carry than say a characteristic such as age or income. From the discussions so far, it is clear that there are a variety of approaches used to segment markets. What they all have in common is the search for a set of common characteristics, i.e. characteristics that all customers in a group share and which are in some way associated with the manner in which those consumers respond to marketing activities. The next sections explore the common characteristics that are used in segmenting customer and business markets.

 Stop and think?

How does the process of STP result in more efficient use of a firm's resources?

What aspects of STP might be thought of as being objective and empirically based, and which do you think are more subjective?

What types of variables might form part of a process to evaluate a firm's approach to segmentation?

7.4 Approaches to segmenting consumer markets

Earlier in this chapter segmentation was described as the process of grouping customers around a common characteristic that is of relevance to marketing. The choice of *common characteristics* is crucial in determining a successful outcome when segmenting a marketplace as this effectively defines target markets and thus impacts on what the organisation will be expected to deliver to that market. The types of common characteristics then can be used to segment consumer markets and can be divided into two broad categories: customer-oriented segmentation and product-based segmentation.

7.4.1 Customer characteristics: customer-oriented segmentation

This comprises characteristics that define who the customer is, where she lives, the kind of person she is, the kind of lifestyle she leads and views she holds. Thus, it is entirely customer-centric as an approach to segmentation. In specific terms, the sort of characteristics used in segmentation can be broken down as follows:

Demographics

- Age,
- Gender,
- Family relationships,
- Ethnic group,
- Religious affiliations,

- Life stage,
- Education attainment.

Socio-Economic

- Income,
- Financial assets,
- Social class,
- Occupational status,
- Geographic – country of domicile,
- Region or locality,
- Metropolitan,
- Urban vs. rural.

Psychographics

- Attitudes,
- Lifestyle choices,
- Beliefs,
- Motives,
- Personality type.

One widely used approach to consumer-oriented segmentation is based around geodemographics – a combination of demographics, socio-economic and geographical information. The underlying principle of geodemographics is the belief that households within a particular neighbourhood exhibit similar purchasing behaviours, have similar attitudes and expectations, and similar needs. Neighbourhoods can therefore be classified according to the characteristics of the individuals who live there and can then be grouped together, even though they are widely separated. Geodemographics are thus able to target customers in particular areas who exhibit similar patterns of behaviour.

Several commercial systems for this type of segmentation are available. In the UK, leading products include MOSAIC (Experian) and ACORN (CACI), both of whom offer generalised classification and financial services-specific classifications. Experian's MOSAIC is also delivered across a range of markets including the US, France, Germany and Australia. Marketing in practice 7.2 focuses on the UK and describes what MOSAIC is, its applications in the field of financial services, and how it is informing the future direction of consumer segmentation.

It must be appreciated that choice of characteristic to use in segmentation is a contextual matter dependent upon the considerations given at the start of this section. Trade-offs must often be made, especially with regard to practical issues concerning implementation. Demographic variables are usually the simplest to use as they readily lend themselves to requirements of accessibility and measurability, and most marketing media provide customer profiles based on demographic information. However, they are often weak in relation to relevance as demographics alone rarely explain why someone makes a particular purchase.

Life stage is an approach to segmentation that is particularly relevant in the context of financial services. This is because of the long-term nature of many of the products encountered

🗣️ Marketing in practice 7.2: the MOSAIC approach to consumer classifications and customer segmentation

Historically, consumer classifications in the UK were constructed using a significant proportion of Census data along with a range of geo-demographic attributes. Census data, although insightful, was, and still is limited by virtue of its increasing vintage from collection (Census data can be up to 10 years old before it is updated), and with the 2021 Census happening in the midst of Covid, there are further potential bias within the latest Census. Its usefulness is also hampered by the geographical aggregation of data at Output Area Level (Output Areas include, on average, aggregated and anonymised data expressed on the occupants of more than 120 residential dwellings).

Modern classifications are constructed using a range of more versatile inputs including property information including Council Tax Property Valuations as well as market research, lifestyle surveys and other more responsive commercially available data make up the majority of additional feeds. Although Census data is still a component, it is primarily used to calibrate the statistical models. These inputs, of which there can be in excess of 400 in any one classification, are selected on the basis of their volume, quality, consistency and sustainability. To be input into any classification, data must enable the accurate identification of, and the discrimination between, a wide-range of consumer behaviours. It must also be capable of measuring change over time to ensure an accurate assignment of "segments" can be applied to a person, household address or postcode.

Experian's Mosaic classification, for example, segments the UK population into 15 high level Groups before identifying a further 66 distinct "Household" types. At its finest level, Mosaic recognises the differences between occupants, including adult children and elderly parents, who may all be living under the same roof. Figure 7.1 below shows the distribution of UK Households by basic Mosaic Group.

Group	Group Name	One-Line Description	UK Households (%)
A	City Prosperity	High status city dwellers living in central locations and pursuing careers with high rewards	4.20
B	Prestige Positions	Established families in large detached homes living upmarket lifestyles	7.25
C	Country Living	Well-off owners in rural locations enjoying the benefits of country life	6.94
D	Rural Reality	Householders living in less expensive homes in village communities	6.99
E	Senior Security	Elderly people with assets who are enjoying a comfortable retirement	8.41
F	Suburban Stability	Mature suburban owners living settled lives in mid-range housing	6.38
G	Domestic Success	Thriving families who are busy bringing up children and following careers	6.75
H	Aspiring Homemakers	Younger households settling down in housing priced within their means	9.19
I	Family Basics	Families with limited resources who budget to make ends meet	7.13
J	Transient Renters	Single people renting low cost homes for the short term	5.11
K	Municipal Tenants	Urban residents renting high density housing from social landlords	6.73
L	Vintage Value	Elderly people with limited pension income, mostly living alone	6.70
M	Modest Traditions	Mature homeowners of value homes enjoying stable lifestyles	5.14
N	Urban Cohesion	Residents of settled urban communities with a strong sense of identity	4.91
O	Rental Hubs	Educated young people privately renting in urban neighbourhoods	8.17

Figure 7.1 Distribution of UK Households by basic Mosaic Group

Consumer classifications are commonly used by financial organisations to provide a deeper understanding of existing and potential customers including their economic, demographic and lifestyle characteristics.

This insight is used to target, acquire, manage and develop profitable relationships. The application of such segmentation systems is also often applied to geographies to provide actionable insight to ensure that products and services are made available to groups of individuals that are most likely to be attracted by them. For example, identifying areas that would benefit from pop-up or mobile branches.

The use of consumer classifications in digital advertising

Digital advertising is now the norm for many financial organisations and depending on the outcomes that the organisation is driving, consumer classifications can be highly relevant especially high up the marketing funnel. Today, consumer classifications including Mosaic, and are readily available to buy within the digital marketplaces to create digital audiences. If other identifiable characteristics are also required for a digital audience, for example credit risk, these can be easily overlaid to create a bespoke audience for the financial organisations. The use of first party data is now widespread with financial services, consumer classification is used to overlay insights to increase the level of personalisation across digital advertising.

What next?

With the use of consumer classifications in the UK now common in financial service providers, the continued use of consumer classifications, and consumer insight more generally, has been fuelled by the increased availability of good quality data in the UK, and the increased need for financial organisations to work smarter. However, with this increase of the availability of data coupled with higher scrutiny of privacy and regulation, choosing the right consumer classification is key for financial organisation, and this is set to continue in the future. Financial organisations have high levels of due diligence to follow for the use of any consumer classification.

Source: Sarah Robertson, Director of Product, Experian Marketing Services

and the duration over which utility is experienced. The basic principle upon which the life stage approach is based is that people progress through varying stages in their lives, each of which is associated with different product needs. Figure 7.2 shows schematically a set of typical life stages and the associated product needs that are indicated.

From Figure 7.2 the role performed by the current account as a gateway product can be fully appreciated. It also demonstrates the ways in which financial complexity develops as individuals progress from adolescence through to being middle-aged with children. It is interesting to note how the balance between assets and liabilities alters at different life stages.

A student graduating from a four-year course of study at a public institution in the USA in 2021 will, on average, have incurred debt of $26,700, compared to private school borrowers, who graduated with an average debt of $33,600. For post graduate study leading to an advanced degree the debt is considerably greater. For example, over half of people

Lifestage

Single in Fulltime Education → Single working → Married → Young Married with Children → Married Middle Aged with Children → Married Middle-Aged Empty nester → Married Active Retired → Independent Single Retired → Dependent Single Retired

Product Needs

Single in Fulltime Education	Single working	Married	Young Married with Children	Married Middle Aged with Children	Married Middle-Aged Empty nester	Married Active Retired	Independent Single Retired	Dependent Single Retired
Current A/c	Current A/c	Current A/c	Current A/c	Current A/c	Current A/c	Current A/c	Current A/c	Current A/c
Deposit A/c	Credit Card	Credit Card	Credit Card	Credit Card	Credit Card	Credit Card	Credit Card	Credit Card
	Travel Ins	Travel Ins	Travel Ins	Travel Ins	Travel Ins	Content Ins	Content Ins	Content Ins
	Loans	Loans	Loans	Loans	Loans	Building Ins	Building Ins	Building Ins
	Motor Ins	Mortgage	Mortgage	Mortgage	Mortgage	Motor Ins	Motor Ins	Annuities
	Deposit A/c	Life Ins	Life Ins	Life Ins	Life Ins	Deposit A/c	Deposit A/c	Investments
		Content Ins	Content Ins	Content Ins	Content Ins	Pension	Pension	Power of attorney
		Building Ins	Building Ins	Building Ins	Building Ins	Investments	Investments	Long-term care
		Motor Ins	Motor Ins	Motor Ins	Motor Ins	Travel Ins	Travel Ins	
		Deposit A/c	Deposit A/c	Deposit A/c	Deposit A/c	Annuities	Annuities	
			Pension	Pension	Pension			
					Investments			

Figure 7.2 Life stage: product-need schematic

Table 7.1 Family Median Net Worth in USA 2020

	Age years					
	<35	*35-44*	*45-54*	*55-64*	*65-74*	*>75*
$US 000	14	91	169	213	266	255

Source: Adapted from The Average Net Worth by Age and Education Level, Of Dollars and Data, April 16, 2020, Nick Maggiulli based on Federal Reserve data

with law degrees have at least $150,000 in student loan debt according to the American Bar Association.

Adult indebtedness continues to grow as credit card and unsecured loan debts accumulate. A major step increase in indebtedness occurs when the individual takes out a mortgage to fund home-purchases. Gradually, net indebtedness reduces until a point, typically at an age between 50 and 60, when the individual becomes a net asset holder. This is precisely why the over-50s are the primary target for investment product marketing activity. Alternative forms of life stage can be designed to reflect different lifestyles such as people who remain single, those who marry but have no children, those who get divorced and so on. Table 7.1 shows graphically how income varies among American households depending upon the age of the head of the household.

Psychographic variables may offer the greatest potential for differentiation and creativity in executional terms. However, they may present particular challenges in terms of determining measurability, profitability and accessibility. Netherlands-based Triodos Bank has targeted that segment of the population who have a particular preference for socially responsible banking practices, and has branches in Germany, France, Belgium, Spain and the UK in addition to the Netherlands. Thus, the bank has set out to position itself as "the ethical bank". It is an interesting example of a bank using an essentially psychographic variable as the basis of its segmentation strategy in a similar way to the Cooperative Bank in the UK.

7.4.2 Customer needs and behaviours: product-oriented segmentation

This approach to segmentation comprises variables that define the nature of the utility that consumers seek to gain from the consumption of a product or service. It also incorporates the nature of the consumer's interaction with the product. Thus, it is more of a product-centred approach to segmentation than its customer-oriented counterpart. In specific terms it can be broken down as follows:

Core financial needs – banking

- Savings,
- Investing,
- Home ownership,
- Retirement planning,
- Life assurance,
- Health insurance,
- Possessions insurance.

Product/service usage – frequency of purchase

- Frequency of service usage,
- Quantum of purchase,
- Means of accessing service,
- Means of purchase,
- Timing of purchase,
- Timing of accessing service.

Progress check

- STP are crucial to the identification, execution and maintenance of competitive advantage.
- Segmentation is a process of grouping customers around a common characteristic of relevance to marketing.
- Lifestage is an approach to segmentation that is particularly relevant to financial services marketing.

Product attributes – pricing

- Value,
- Ownership status of provider,
- Feature simplicity/complexity.

In practice, many financial service providers use multivariable approaches to segmentation which draw upon characteristics that are both customer and product oriented. For example, an investment company might choose to target a segment defined in the following terms:

Women in the age group 35 to 60 who want to invest for retirement and favour an ethical approach to investment.

In such a case, due attention must be paid to matters concerning measurability and so on, to ensure that the segment is accessible to marketing activities and is commercially viable.

7.5 Approaches to segmenting business-to-business markets

The benefits that accrue from segmentation apply equally within the context of business-to-business marketing. Indeed, the costs of acquiring a new customer in the organisational business arena are usually considerably greater than in the consumer arena and so too are the income flows. This makes effective targeting of marketing resources even more important. As discussed elsewhere, managing B2B and B2C relationships involve points of both comparison and difference. As with the consumer marketplace, there are various approaches to segmenting the organisational domain with the following characteristics being the ones most widely used.

Business demographics

- Industrial sector,
- Organisation size, (e.g. turnover, assets, number of employees),
- Organisational structure (centralised, branch-based),
- Ownership (proprietary, mutual, core-quoted company, subsidiary company).

Business geography

- International (head office domicile, countries represented),
- Single country (national centralised, regions, metropolitan, town).

Business processes

- Decision-making (by tender, by negotiation, individual/committee-based),
- Choice criteria (lowest cost, degree of customisation, service intensity, product/service range, performance criteria),
- Image and positioning,
- R&D and innovation.

Business performance

- Business growth rate,
- Return on capital,
- Market sector growth rate,
- High margin/low margin.

Markets served

- Commercial markets,
- Consumer markets,
- High-net worth individuals,
- Mainstream mass market,
- Lower social-economic groups,
- Niche markets,
- Product specialisms.

As with consumer market segmentation, multivariable segmentation is often encountered in the B2B domain. For example, a general insurance company might choose to target a business segment defined in the following terms:

businesses in the hotel, catering and leisure sectors with a turnover of less than £25m per annum serving high net-worth individuals and with a particular need for liability insurance.

The EMC Insurance Company in the US has used sector-based segmentation in B2B markets and has elected to target its offerings to educational establishments and local government and municipalities in the USA. In the following example of Marketing in practice 7.3 we see how EMC integrates its approach to segmentation with its mission and key business processes.

 Marketing in practice 7.3: EMC insurance companies – Business to Business segmentation

EMC represents a good example of an insurance business that is primarily focused on serving the needs of business customer segments, in its case educational establishments and local government and municipalities in the USA, ie: this is an example of segmentation by sector.

EMC Insurance Companies was formed in 1911 as a mutual company to insure its association members and to provide a better cost alternative to the stock companies of that time. Today, the company operates in 42 states, offering commercial insurance products, workers' compensation, bonds, and personal insurance in select markets. About 90% of the company's business is in commercial lines, with expertise in insuring specialty markets. For example, about 1,600 school districts and over 5,000 municipalities and local governments throughout the Midwest are insured by EMC.

The company's mission is "to grow profitably through partnership with independent insurance agents and to enhance the ability of our partners to deliver quality financial protection to the people and businesses we mutually serve."

Local Service: EMC serves its agents and policyholders through a network of branch and service offices strategically located throughout the country. This enables the company to provide exemplary local service in underwriting, marketing, loss control and claims. Agents and policyholders can communicate directly with a local EMC representative who understands their insurance needs and who has the authority to make decisions. Branch offices can market products and services to meet the needs of their individual marketing territories, taking advantage of differing opportunities for profit. Today, EMC has 21 branch and service offices across the United States and a home office in Des Moines, Iowa.

Long-Term Perspective: To EMC, mutualism is a beneficial structure that allows the company to take a long-term approach to business strategies and decisions, and to emphasize conservative investing and careful risk selection. The company's strategic decisions are based on long-term results rather than short-term profits and the company is focused solely on the insurance industry. EMC's three long-term goals are excellent underwriting results, financial strength, and loyal agents and policyholders.

Independent Agency System: EMC is committed to the independent agency system and believes its partnership with independent agents adds real value to the insurance process. Because the company distributes its products solely through approximately 3,000 independent agencies in 42 states, EMC's success is directly tied to the success of its agents, which creates strong, stable partnerships.

Claims: EMC's claim philosophy is simple and straightforward: investigate every claim, explain what is covered and what is not covered, and pay the claims owed as quickly as possible. The primary goal is to handle every claim as fairly and quickly as possible, regardless of the type or size.

Loss Control: EMC invests more than its competitors on average on loss control to enable the company to provide top-quality services that add value to its commercial insurance products and reduce the risk of insured losses. Highly qualified professionals provide a broad range of exceptional loss control and loss prevention services that address a wide variety of needs—usually at no cost to customers.

EMC Today: EMC recognizes the distinct tradeoff when subscribing to its long-held philosophies and mutual structure. Often additional expenses are incurred by putting these philosophies into action. This conscious tradeoff; however, is fundamental to the company's long-term success and enables EMC to operate as a distinctive service provider and provide long-term value, creating its *Count on EMC®* brand promise. EMC Insurance Companies has maintained its reputation as a strong, financially stable company for 100 years. Today, EMC Insurance Companies is among the top 60 insurance organizations in the United States (based on net written premium) with net worth of over $1.0 billion, assets over $4 billion and more than 2,200 employees.

For more information, visit www.emcins.com.

Source: Scott Jean, EMC President and CEO

7.6 Segmentation in a digital world

At various points in this book reference has been made to the notion of marketing to a segment of one. By their very nature, services lend themselves to such an approach, particularly given the characteristic of inseparability (introduced in Chapter 3) by which we mean that each service encounter is "freshly made" at the moment of consumption. Marketing to a segment of one is now not only technically feasible but economically viable given the advances in systems functionality associated with the digital era. Individual web portals can be created that become the focal point for the client and her relationship with the provider and are based upon a detailed and intimate knowledge of the client, her financial behaviour and consumption and service predilections.

This development has to be seen in the context of other themes in the wider environment of the consumer experience such as the growing desire, and indeed expectation, to be treated as an individual. As people progress up through the various stages of Maslow's hierarchy towards self-actualisation, it is axiomatic that they will want to be treated as an individual, and nowhere more so than in their dealings with banks and related financial institutions. Thus, the confluence on the one hand of the ability to deliver an individualised customer experience together with the consumer's growing expectation to be treated as an individual presents certain challenges and opportunities to the marketer of financial services. Providers of financial services will need to deliver a quality of consumer experience against ever more exacting standards established in the consumer goods and associated commercial domains.

This changing context begs the question of what "segment of one" means to the traditional approach towards the development of segmentation strategies? Does this mean that having broadly based segments are now to be consigned to history? Does it mean that we must have one approach to segmentation when it comes to new customer acquisition and another when it comes to marketing to one's existing customers? Does it mean that all marketing activities now must be re-oriented around the segment of one? And what does this mean for corporate positioning and repositioning in the absence of clearly identifiable macro-segments?

In essence, the answer to these questions is that segment of one complements other more broadly based segmentation; they are not mutually exclusive. So a bank can continue to, say, target student accounts at people in the age group 17 to 23 years, and use the range of media that such a segment can be expected to consume to achieve communication objectives such as awareness, attitude formation, call-to-action, but aim to engage on an individualised basis from the point at which the prospect has made their first contact with the bank. Should the prospect become a client, then they can expect to be treated to a highly personalised service, notwithstanding the fact that the terms and conditions of his account will conform to the core features that apply to the product component of the student segment's marketing mix. Thus, "segment of one" is an enhancement to basic segmentation and not a substitute for it.

Accenture's 2017 "Financial Services Global Distribution & Marketing Consumer Study"[3] identified three consumer segments:

- Nomads are digitally active, open to new banking delivery models (GAFA – Google, Amazon, Facebook, Apple) and not loyal to traditional banks. They value innovation and evolution of banking, embracing new technologies (circa 39% of respondents).
- Hunters are seeking value-for-money. They trust and are loyal traditional banking providers and value human interaction to assist with decision-making (circa 17% of respondents).
- Quality seekers want trust. They expect high-quality customer service and robust data protection. They want financial services providers they can trust to protect their insurance and wealth management.

Figure 7.3 Provides useful insights at a more granular level into those three segments.

A 2019 Accenture study expanded this to span four personas, but the principles remained the same; consumers fall into three or four buckets of tech savviness and digital appetite from low to high. Key takeaways were an increased appetite for closer integrations between physical and digital banking channels, and levels of comfort sharing personal data in order to receive a more personalised service. Financial service providers should understand and harness these risk appetites in order to most effectively build trust with segments by

	NOMADS	HUNTERS	QUALITY SEEKERS
Searching for the best deal on price	32%	83%	11%
Loyalty is driven by trust their personal data will be protected	38%	26%	53%
Say high quality customer service is key in keeping loyal	36%	28%	49%
Consider using alternative banking providers	78%	0%	0%
Want brands with conveniently located branches	36%	35%	45%
Willing to share personal data with bank	78%	58%	61%
Willing to share data with a third party for relevant services	74%	47%	53%
Willing to use automated support on selecting accounts	85%	61%	64%
Would find location-based offers useful	54%	29%	32%
Want blend of physical and digital services	61%	49%	50%
Would like access to personal advice via mobile channel	53%	31%	37%
Would like new communication methods, e.g. wearables or virtual reality	45%	15%	20%

Figure 7.3 Characteristics of Nomads, Hunters, and Quality Seekers[3]

meeting their individual needs. It's important they understand who is willing to share data in order to get a more personalised offering, presenting them with tailored experiences that will reinforce their brand values and increase trust. Brands should also explore how they can create incentives to encourage greater first-party data sharing to fuel their personalised offering.

The tech giants offer a threat not only from the ever-decreasing barriers to entry in banking but also to traditional banks' data ownership. The emergence of digital players offering mobile wallet (Google) integrated payments services (Apple Pay) threatens to poach banks' access to payment insights which is crucial to their segmentation and targeting. Paradoxically the advantage the banks still retain is trust and data privacy; consumers are still more likely to trust their primary bank with their personal data, and as cited above, are increasingly inclined to share their data with a trusted provider in exchange for a tailored offering. Banks will need to leverage this advantage and work to provide a best-in-class digital experience that can rival the offerings of GAFA. Two out of every five millennial respondents said they would consider banking with Google or Amazon and over a third would consider buying insurance from them. If these are realised, the traditional financial services market is seriously under threat from the tech giants. The caveat is that millennials tend to be less affluent and have less surplus cash to invest. Thus, despite gaining new entrants and greater traction with the millennial audience, their ability to truly disrupt may be moderated by their lesser financial viability.

As far as customer propositions are concerned, this does not replace the need for product providers to identify points of differentiation that resonate with either their overall customer universe or individual segments. It compliments core propositions and positioning statements with the added value of a customer experience that is truly personalised.

Data is the key to successful digital segmentation. It enables organisations to understand where, and how, people are likely to consume content. This is particularly relevant for pay per click (PPC) advertising which relies on understanding which search terms particular audiences are most likely to use. The most effective segmentation strategies reflect customer personas based on geographic, demographic, behavioural and psychological data. With the demise of third-party cookies, marketeers are having to work harder to gather data in an ethical way that leaves customers in control of their data and privacy. Zero party data – data customers voluntarily share via quizzes, surveys and polls in order to receive targeted offers – and first-party data – data collected on a specific website to serve you tailored content on solely that site – is key to this. Real-time segmentation enables organisations to tailor website experiences in the live environment using first-party cookie data and customers click patterns, to serve the most relevant and compelling content, layouts and call to actions.

Where "segment of one" has real traction is in its potential to add significant value to the worth of a company's existing customer base. In the following two sections of this book the reader will learn to appreciate the increase that has occurred across the world in the costs associated with acquiring new customers relative to upselling and cross-selling to existing customers. Modern approaches to the management of customer data, the development of a single customer view and use of state-of-the-art communications methods are enabling financial services providers to achieve a step change in their ability to leverage the value of their customer base. Arguably, these developments will result in a shift in the balance of power between sales and marketing functions within individual financial services firms. It will move the centre of gravity inexorably in favour of the marketing function as the returns on investment from what it does will increasingly overshadow those of traditional sales functions.

7.7 Targeting strategies

In addition to choosing the basis upon which to segment a market, choices must be made regarding which segments to target. This is not necessarily a sequential process. Indeed, choice of segmentation criteria and choice of targets (i.e. the targeting strategy) is an interactive and interdependent set of processes which may well require a high degree of iteration before a final strategic position is arrived at. Segments must be evaluated in terms of their attractiveness to the organisation, their profit potential and the organisation's ability to deliver the required service. This information can then be taken into consideration in deciding which segments to target. The basic array of targeting strategies is as follows:

Table 7.2 Basic Targeting strategies

Basic Segmentation	Strategies Features
Undifferentiated	Serves an entire marketplace with a single marketing mix which does not distinguish between subsegments of the market.
Differentiated	An aggregate marketplace, such as banking, is organised into a number of segments, each of which is targeted with a tailored marketing mix.
Focused	A choice is made to target a small subset of the segments of a multi-segment marketplace with a single marketing mix that best suits the needs of that segment.
Customised	Each individual that comprises the target market is the subject of a marketing mix that is tailored in some way to the individual's specific needs.

7.7.1 Undifferentiated targeting

It should not be assumed that an undifferentiated strategy is necessarily an inherently inferior form of strategy. An analysis of customer characteristics may simply reveal the absence of a compelling variable upon which segmentation could be based. Equally, it may be the case that the cost of segmenting the market and producing a set of bespoke marketing mixes is not commercially justifiable.

Life insurance companies using an essentially commission-only sales force have adopted a largely undifferentiated strategy. This is sometimes referred to as "playing the numbers game" whereby the low cost of new customer acquisition and the heavy up-front charges meant that almost any new customer thus acquired was likely to contribute to profits. In several countries, notably the UK, a range of developments, such as the regulation-induced increase in new customer acquisition costs, lower product margins and the pressure to improve persistency rates have all served to make the life insurance industry more discriminating in its approach to gaining new customers. And so there has been a growing tendency to move away from an undifferentiated approach. Admittedly, the attempts to introduce segmentation have sometimes been somewhat elementary, often based simply upon a minimum income threshold. Most of the life insurance companies that operated with an undifferentiated approach are no longer open to new customers.

 Stop and think?

Which customer segments would you target if you were planning to launch a new Fintech bank and why them?

What approach might you take to segmenting the market for motor insurance?

Which segments would you target if you were planning to launch a financial advice business?

7.7.2 Differentiated targeting

This arises when a company has been able to identify a commercially valid basis upon which an aggregate market can be broken down into segments. The fast-moving consumer goods sector has probably been the best exemplar of differentiated marketing. Differentiated segmentation is gaining in popularity within the financial services sector. The major UK clearing banks such as Barclays, Lloyds and HSBC show a growing usage of differentiated marketing. Typical generic segments that are encountered among mainstream clearing banks include:

Business banking marketplace segments

- Business start-ups
- Sole traders and partnership
- Small businesses (typically with 5–50 staff)
- Medium business (typically 50–250 staff)
- Large business (typically 250–1,000 staff)
- Large corporate market (more than 1,000 staff)

Retail banking marketplace segments

- Student banking
- Ordinary current account customers
- High net worth customers (e.g. earning more than £50,000 p.a.)
- Private banking customers (e.g. have investable assets in excess of £500,000)

The illustrative banking segments shown above reveal a basic approach to segmentation. In the case of B2B banking, segmentation is typically based on business demographics. As far as B2C banking is concerned, it is typically based upon demographic or socio-economic characteristics. To a large extent, this comes down to the practicalities of the typical large clearing bank which could have over 50,000 staff of which more than 10,000 are based in some 2,000 or more branches. Segmentation must reflect the practicalities of gaining the engagement of a huge and diverse workforce in implementing a segmentation strategy. In the Natwest case study at the end of Part II we see how the RBS sub-brand NatWest Bank, has set out to differentiate itself in the highly competitive B2B segment of new business start-ups and small businesses. Through its Accelerator programme NatWest is providing a nationwide solution to the needs of this business segment.

7.7.3 Focused segmentation

This approach to segmentation is encountered in circumstances where a company breaks a market down into a set of segments but chooses to target a small subset of available segments and in some cases only a single segment. A focused approach may take several different forms.

Single segment concentration

In this approach, the organisation concentrates only on a single segment in the market and supplies products tailored specifically to the needs of those customer groups. This approach is often described as niche marketing. It is potentially highly profitable because the organisation focuses all its efforts on a particular segment of the market where it has a strong differential advantage. At the same time, there are risks associated with this approach because if the segment was to disappear or a new competitor entered the market, the organisation could be vulnerable to a significant loss of business. The general insurer Hiscox focuses on high-net worth clients, whereas the Ecclesiastical Insurance Company focuses upon providing general insurance to churches and allied organisations. Endsleigh Insurance has carved out a niche for itself by focusing upon the student segment. Also to be found in the educational space is the specialist Australian insurer Unimutual, presented below.

Marketing in practice 7.4: Unimutua – business-to-business segmentation in the Australian insurance market

For many years the words "Protecting Wisdom" have been the slogan of a uniquely focused, discretionary mutual in Australia, Unimutual. The company was created in 1989 by a few public universities to meet risk-cover needs that the insurance market could either not provide, or not provide economically. From a very modest beginning, the mutual is now recognised as the leading provider of property and liability risk protection for Australian universities and associated entities. In 2023 Unimutual provided asset protection for buildings and real property valued at circa AU\$ 60 billion.

Universities are large and complex institutions with very special needs of which commercial insurers have been traditionally wary. They have the operational complexity of small cities with the unique attributes of thousands of people working together to create the future. These institutions are critical to the development of knowledge and innovation not only for the country, but play a global role as well. Today a total of nine Australian institutions hold prominent places on the list of the world's top 100 higher education institutions. Universities present complex risk profiles and this is often a challenge for commercial insurers to understand and support but provides the perfect environment for mutual collaboration and cooperation. For example, Unimutual has, at times, been the only provider of affordable protection for some liability covers, including medical malpractice and clinical trials.

Unimutual's market-leading position has been achieved by understanding and focusing on the particular risks that universities face and tailoring bespoke cover for its members. Operating on a not-for-profit basis has meant taking a long-term view that marries risk exposure with risk retained and pooled amongst the membership with proactive risk management. A good example is the preservation of research materials lost to spoilage. This issue was identified by Unimutual as an emerging risk in 2011 with increasing claims amongst members. An exercise undertaken collaboratively with members determined that there had been rapid increases in both volume and values of research material and that the losses being experienced were largely preventable. Through the mutual's leadership, programmes were put in place which resulted in significant reduction of losses, thereby facilitating the long-term protection of research assets and ensuring research continuity. Here are two examples of how we preserve research material lost to spoilage:

Example 1: We have introduced best practice standards in risk prevention, developed by Unimutual in conjunction with our members. This includes ensuring that all temperature-controlled research has back-up generators and alarms attached to the refrigeration units. This stops the losses occurring in the first place.

Example 2: Where losses do occur, we have an agreed approach to financially valuing the research and how we pay for the research to be reinstated. One recent example is where there was a loss of fish samples from Antarctica when a refrigerator was disconnected by accident. We will pay for a fishing expedition to go to Antarctica to collect new samples and for the cost of the researchers redoing the research.

Unimutual is alive to the changes that digital marketing and technology are bringing to the market, many of which are being embraced, but shows that at the same time old-fashioned standards of personal service, based on face-to-face interaction have a place in the digital age. As a direct consequence of this approach, both staff and customer satisfaction remain high and staff turnover remains low.

Unimutual's unique approach to the relationship with its members is based on four, interdependent foundations:

- First, the close day-to-day working relationships and partnerships built by Unimutual staff with members;
- Second, the Unimutual team's knowledge of the discretionary mutual sector and the education sector;
- Third, a deep understanding of the risk management needs of the sector, and sharing insights and advice with all members, regardless of its origin;
- Fourth, the mutual structure and ethos which allows Members to take an active role in their mutual, including representation on the Unimutual Board and participation in working groups and committees.

These service characteristics have set Unimutual apart from its competitors, giving it a reputation for personnel who value collegiality and are committed to deliver service to members. These elements are now as important as its financial stability and the reliability and quality of its products. The mutual ethos and service difference has served Unimutual well during periods of global financial uncertainty.

Australian universities are both the engine room of the national economy and nursery of its future innovation and leadership. They play a vital role in the present and future of Australia, and must be free to create, explore and innovate. Since 1989, the sector has learned that relying solely on the commercial insurance market to provide protection for the risk profiles of these institutions represents poor risk management. In Unimutual they have created a solution which is aligned to their values and goals and has a common aim – the protection of wisdom.

Source: Geoff Henderson, CEO, Unimutual

Selective specialisation

Selective specialisation is another type of niche marketing. However, rather than concentrating only on one segment, the organisation chooses to operate in several (possibly unrelated) segments. This approach to targeting is less focused than single segment specialisation but probably less risky. NFU Mutual is a good example of a company that exhibits what might be called a selective specialisation strategy. Originally called National Farmers Mutual, the company was set up to provide for the particular needs of the farmers and the farming-related community in the UK. However, such narrow focus limited the opportunities for achieving economies of scale and so in the early part of the 21st century the company gradually widened its market definition to include all those living in rural areas of the country and individuals with an affiliation of some sort with country living.

Product specialisation

Most markets can be seen as comprising a number of different customer groups and a number of different but related products. The organisation that concentrates on supplying a particular product type to a range of customer groups is pursuing a product specialisation strategy. This approach to market targeting may be particularly appropriate to organisations with particular strengths or knowledge in relation to a given technology or product. Thus, Al Baraka Islamic Bank in Bahrain, and the Islamic Bank of Britain can be seen to be pursuing a product specialisation strategy by offering Islamic financial services (a particular product type) to a range of different customer groups (segments) which range from retail customers needing very simple banking products through to businesses requiring very complex financing arrangements. Bank Islam in Malaysia is a good example of an Islamic bank that has broadened its customer offerings into a wide array of financial services.

Market specialization

This is the opposite approach to product specialisation. Rather than concentrating on a particular product, the organisation chooses to specialise in meeting the needs of a particular customer group. This strategy may be most suitable where knowledge of the customer group's particular needs is a particularly important basis for establishing a competitive advantage. Private banks pursue this type of approach in relation to high-net-worth individuals – they seek to provide a range of different financial products to meet the needs of the high-net worth customers (HNWIs). Examples of private banks include Swiss-based Bank Lombard Odier & Co Ltd which has a presence in numerous countries around the globe. In the UK Close Brothers is a private bank which describes its strategic focus in the following way:

> We remain committed to our traditional values of service, expertise and relationships alongside teamwork, integrity and prudence, to help the people and business of Britain thrive over the long term.[2]

7.7.4 Customised targeting

This approach represents the ultimate manifestation of the segmentation concept, based as it is upon a separate, tailored marking mix for each customer. Some markets lend themselves more naturally to a customised approach, especially those that are in service sectors involving a high degree of human interface. In the financial services sector, customised targeting is most in evidence as part of a hybrid strategy in which a distinct set of services such as investment banking is offered to a particular segment such as large corporations and then the service is customised to individuals within that segment. The functionality offered by digital marketing has created new opportunities for customised targeting that would have been impossible only a few years ago.

7.8 Positioning products and organisations

Positioning represents a logical step that follows the processes of segmentation and targeting. Having selected the criteria upon which to segment a market and then made the choice of which segments to target, the company must then decide how best to present itself, either corporately or as a specific product brand, to the individuals that comprise its target segments. Positioning is a piece of marketing jargon that concerns the issue of perception. At the core of positioning lies a brand or company's competitive advantage in terms of how it differentiates itself from the competition and how it delivers value to its customers. Thus, positioning is about how a company or brand wants itself to be perceived in the minds of the individuals who comprise its target segments. The choice of *position* is based upon the agreed form of differentiation. The objective of positioning is to generate and maintain a clear value proposition to customers, thus creating a distinctive place in the market for the brand or organisation. When successful, positioning results in a brand or company being seen as distinctive from its competitors.

To be commercially advantageous, positioning should be based upon product and service characteristics that:

- Are relevant to the target segment,
- Achieve differentiation from the competition,
- Can be communicated clearly to the market,
- Can be sustained.

Positioning is a truly strategic concept that requires a considerable investment over a prolonged period of time. It is the primary manifestation of competitive advantage and represents a considerable source of brand and corporate value. To be successful it requires alignment between how an organisation, or brand, wants itself to be perceived and how it is actually perceived by consumers.

The brand characteristics upon which positioning may be built can relate to demonstrable product and service attributes or image-related factors. McDonald's has historically based its positioning on features concerning fun, food and family which is perceived appropriately through the entirety of the consumer's engagement with the brand. Burger King, on the other hand, has a positioning that is based on more explicit references to product quality communicated in a more serious manner than McDonald's. L'Oreal is an example of a brand whose position is based more on image than specific product features. Its hair and skin care products use the tag line "Because I'm worth it" to convey the notion of products that are about self-indulgence, and they are priced accordingly. Designer label luxury goods are positioned very much on the basis of an image of exclusivity rather than the tangible features of the products themselves.

Positioning is less well-developed as a concept in the field of financial services than in the field of consumer goods. Much current activity operates to an overwhelming extent at the corporate level as opposed to that of the individual product or brand. In this context, organisations have relied on positioning with respect to product/service attributes or image-related factors in much the same ways as is observed in the tangible goods domain. Morgan Stanley's position is based on product/service attributes and emphasises "excellence in financial advice and market execution". Similarly, Standard Bank of South Africa aims to be "Simpler. Faster. Better.". Examples of approaches that are more image based include HSBC which positions itself as "the world's local bank", to create that image of a bank which delivers value on the bases of both local knowledge and global strength. Similarly, in Japan, where banks have traditionally placed most emphasis on serving corporate clients, Shinsei Bank emphasises its orientation towards satisfying retail customers and building strong relationships.

Cooperative Bank is an example of an organisation that positions itself based on an image-related attribute. When it conducted a review of its competitive position in the early 1990s, it anticipated that its future position would be based upon product or service attributes. Such attributes could have included factors like: number of branch outlets, range of services, quality of service delivery, charges, interest rates, investment returns and so on. This is a fairly predictable approach to branch-based financial services and it would have been difficult for the Cooperative Bank to differentiate itself from its larger rivals on such a basis. A spark of intuition and judgement resulted in its choice of "the ethical bank" as the basis for its position. Another financial institution with fine ethical values and the associated positioning is the leading Swedish insurer Folksam. Below we see how Folksam's ethical stance is reflected in its approach to investment fund management.

Marketing in practice 7.5: Folksam – a responsible investment philosophy

Folksam has around SEK 600 billion under management on behalf of around four million customers. All the assets Folksam manages, regardless of whether they are insurance portfolios or personal savings, are covered by exclusion and engagement criteria.

As an investor and an owner, we are able to focus on a number of sustainability-related issues that we know are important to our customers. Our goal is to deliver a competitive return and at the same time to be a leading responsible asset owner. Whether in equities, interest bearing securities, real estate or alternative investments, we apply the same criteria when it comes to investor and owner responsibility. We always work on the basis of the following principles:

- Responsible risk management
- Responsible investments
- Responsible ownership

The Folksam Group's investment criteria apply to all asset classes. We have both engagement criteria and exclusion criteria. The engagement criteria are about how we take responsibility as an owner. Our starting point is always to try to guide our holdings in a more sustainable direction. However, if we find that an asset is not compatible with our view of sustainability after advocacy dialogues, we may choose to sell. Through our investments, we try to influence holdings to take greater responsibility regarding issues relating to climate and the environment, human rights, and anti-corruption.

Folksam is a founder member of the Principles of Responsible Investment (PRI). The Folksam Group is also one of the initiators of the UN-convened Net Zero Asset Owner Alliance, launched during the climate conference in New York in September 2019. Together with some of the world's largest pension and insurance companies, the Folksam Group has committed to our investment portfolios having net-zero greenhouse gas emissions by 2050. At the end of 2022, the Owner Alliance consisted of 83 organisations with a total managed capital of around SEK 110,000 billion. Focus within the alliance is on achieving a real climate transition in the world economy, and using the force of change that exists when many owners join together with a common and clear goal.

The work within the alliance includes the members agreeing on new targets and methods for measuring work towards net-zero greenhouse gas emissions. In addition, the members jointly conduct advocacy dialogues with portfolio companies with the aim of getting more people to change and take greater responsibility in the climate issue.

The Folksam Group believes it is important to exercise our right to vote as a shareholder, and we vote annually at both Swedish and foreign Annual General Meetings. The General Shareholders Meeting is also a good opportunity to ask the companies questions about sustainability, as both the Board of Directors and management are present. The company also has the opportunity to inform its shareholders directly what it is doing in this field. The Folksam Group has been raising sustainability issues with boards and management teams at Swedish General Shareholder Meetings for nearly 15 years. In 2022, physical annual general meetings made long-awaited comebacks after the coronavirus pandemic and the Folksam Group was thereby again able to ask questions on the spot in the meeting rooms. This year's questions were asked on the theme of human rights. In the run-up to the AGM season, the Folksam Group also traditionally sent a letter to the respective holding's board chairman, in which we summarised our basic expectations of our holdings in relation to sustainability issues, at the same time we explained why human rights were specifically identified as the theme of the year. The Folksam Group's conditions for corporate governance in companies outside Sweden differ from those in the Swedish holdings, since we are a minor owner in the foreign companies. In 2022, however, we and several other international investors submitted a sustainability-related proposal to the annual general meeting of the major bank HSBC for the second consecutive year. The proposal built further on the climate impact work we conducted towards the bank in recent years. The proposal was withdrawn before the AGM because the bank met several of our requests. The Folksam Group plans to continue to follow HSBC's transition efforts.

Folksam believes that environmental, social and corporate governance issues can affect the performance of investment portfolios and recognises that applying these principles may better align investors with broader objectives of society. Responsible Investment can contribute to improved corporate performance on environmental, social and governance issues.

Source: Emilie Westholm, Head of Responsible Investment and Corporate Governance, Folksam

A variant on product/service positioning is positioning that is based upon serving the needs of the distinct target segment, i.e. a focused positioning strategy. By means of such a strategy the organisation is trying to create the perception that it has a unique understanding of the needs of the individuals that compromise its target segment. The implication is that the overall value proposition will be seen to be superior to that of competitors in the eye of customers. Police Mutual Assurance in the UK, and Maif in France position themselves as specialising in the needs of employees of the police service and education sector respectively. In Australia, Unimutual specialises in meeting the insurance needs of universities and other higher education establishments.

Although positioning in the field of financial services is overwhelmingly at the corporate rather than product-brand level, there is a growing incidence of portfolios of organisational brands that reside within an overall corporate structure. Smile.co.uk is positioned as a youthful, approachable high-tech brand within the Cooperative Financial Services umbrella organisation that includes the *ethical* Cooperative Bank. Lloyds Banking Group includes (among others) the Bank of Scotland, Halifax, Scottish Widows, Birmingham Midshires, Black Horse and Lloyds Bank brands within its overall brand architecture.

7.8.1 Perceptual mapping

It is important to have some understanding of the type of processes that are used to determine a company or product's position. One commonly used approach is perceptual mapping. This relies primarily on information about consumer perceptions of both the organisation and its competitors. This information may be based upon either quantitative research-based data or more subjective judgements. It is important to remember that it is not simply a product that is being positioned but, rather, the complete product or corporate offer including product and service features, image, quality and pricing. Perceptual mapping requires that an organisation first identifies the main features of a product category available to consumers. The next step is to establish the relative importance of those features to consumers and the relative performance of competing offers. Market research is used to arrive at the relative importance of features and competitive ratings. Qualitative research methods, such as the use of focus groups and individual depth interviewing, are useful means of seeking original and insightful new positions.

Through the research and evaluation process, the organisation typically tries to identify two major dimensions of themselves or their product that could form the basis of competitive advantage. This is partly a matter of judgement but may also be supported by more detailed statistical analysis of consumer perception. Figure 7.4 presents a hypothetical perceptual map that might apply to the investment fund management sector. It assumes that the chosen discriminators upon which Company A wishes to base its position are *personalisation of advice* and *range of funds*. The advice dimension may also signal something about price given that personalised advice will tend to be more expensive.

Company A potentially has a competitive advantage arising from its position as a company that is seen to deliver highly personalised advice and a broad range of funds. Its nearest rival is Company F and it needs to ensure it maintains a close watch on Company F to ensure it continues to maintain a relatively superior position. Company D offers a very limited range of funds but with moderately personalised advice which may appeal to some segments of the market. Company E appears to deliver a reasonable range of funds but with more generic robo-advice. Company B delivers highly personalised advice but with a limited range of funds which tends to look like a weak position when compared with Company A and Company F. Finally, Company C looks to somewhat "stuck in the middle" by being just average on both dimensions.

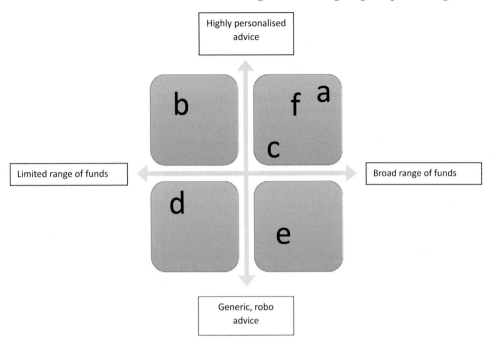

Figure 7.4 Perceptual map for investment fund management companies

Whatever position is decided upon, it must satisfy some basic tests of its likely effectiveness. Jobber (2004) identifies a set of four such tests, namely:

- **Clarity**: is the basis of the position clear and straightforward to grasp?
- **Credibility**: can the position be justified and validated by the evidence available?
- **Consistency**: is the essence of the position communicated consistency over time in all elements of the marketing mix?
- **Competitiveness**: does the position result in benefits to the customer that are demonstrably superior to those provided by its competitors?

The crucial test is whether the company, or brand, is perceived to be distinctive. Positioning presents particular challenges to the financial services industry owing to the intangibility of its products, the absence of patent protection, and the ease with which products and services can be copied by competitors. Arguably, positioning is still developing in many areas of financial services around the world. There often seems to be little that discriminates between the mainstream banks and insurance companies, certainly as far as the perceptions of consumers are concerned. In time we can expect to see more distinctiveness but it will require a degree of sustained consistency that has so often been absent in the past.

7.9 Repositioning

An important aspect of positioning is that it is contextual and impacted upon by forces within the marketplace. By its very nature it requires customers to draw comparisons between the array of competing offers to which they are exposed. As with any aspect of marketing strategy, positioning needs to be reviewed on an appropriate basis at periodic intervals to ensure that it delivers the differentiation it desires. Over time, market forces may exert pressures that threaten the relevance and value of the position. Consumer preferences and priorities change, competitors are continually creating change and new ways of satisfying needs arise from the forces of innovation. Thus, companies must be very vigilant in protecting their competitive advantage.

However, a given position can sometimes be threatened or, indeed, lose credibility and competitive relevance. Examples of problems with long-standing successful positions abound in the consumer goods and retailing areas. For much of its history the Guinness brand's position was based on connotations of health-giving properties. That position became untenable as concerns about alcohol came to the fore. Additionally, the brand was becoming increasingly irrelevant to younger generations of beer drinkers. Many well-known consumer brands as well as Guinness have had to engage in major repositioning activities that have resulted in new positions that have achieved differentiation and renewed competitive advantages. In the case of Guinness, the brand has been repositioned with new product variants and a somewhat quirky modern style of advertising, initially featuring the cult actor Rutger Hauer. Toyota undertook a far more radical approach to repositioning itself in the executive car market with the Lexus brand. In addition to a new brand, a whole new range of vehicles has emerged and is distributed and serviced through distinctive dealerships. Jobber (2004) identifies four basic repositioning strategies which are outlined in Figure 7.5.

The approach illustrated in Figure 7.5 is helpful in enabling managers to conceptualise the nature of repositioning that they could consider should there be concerns regarding the robustness of their current position. In common with similar such 2 × 2 matrices, a degree of caution should be exercised as one often encounters a degree of ambiguity when seeking to apply them in practice. The important issue is to use the model to think through the extent to which repositioning should involve the consideration of product/service development, new market development or a combination of the two. It might also lead to the conclusion that the answer lies in creating new perceptions about the product among existing markets, that is, image repositioning.

Progress check

- Positioning concerns how a company or brand wants itself to be perceived by the marketplace and its customers.
- A company or brand's position must be revalidated over time. This may result in the need for re-positioning.

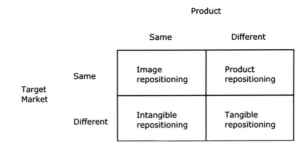

Figure 7.5 Repositioning strategies

7.10 Brand Positioning and strategy in practice: perspectives from Interbrand

With 24 offices in 17 countries Interbrand is a division of the global media giant Omnicom and is a brand consultancy, specialising in areas such as brand strategy, brand analytics, brand valuation, corporate design, digital brand management, packaging design, and naming. Established in 1974 in New York the company has developed a unique approach to brand positioning and repositioning. For many years it has conducted an audit of the world's most valuable brands (see Figure 7.6). This is based upon Interbrand's evaluation of the value of the actual brand and not the market capitalisation of the companies themselves. Its most recent 2022 report shows the top ten global brands as follows:

As Interbrand comments:

> For the first time ever in 2022, the average brand value of a Best Global Brand has reached over US$3 trillion. The overall value of the Top 100 brands has reached US$3,088,930m, a 16% rise from 2021 (US$2,667,524m). That was the fastest rate of brand value growth ever recorded, demonstrating the growing contribution a company's brand has in driving its economic success. While financial markets have shown significant swings over the last few years, the value of the world's strongest brands have steadily increased driving customer choice, loyalty and margins.

Some twelve financial services brands feature in the top 100 and they are shown in table 7.3.

In what follows, Manfredi Ricca, Global Chief Strategy Officer for Interbrand, gives an insight into the company's unique approach to brand strategy.

Interbrand's approach to Brand Strategy

Traditional branding approaches have often looked at strategy as a definition of "what a brand stands for" – typically a vision, a mission, a set of values, and so forth. While these might be helpful exercises in some cases, they often struggle to drive any action, tend to remain abstract and static, and frequently remain confined to the marketing or brand department.

Figure 7.6 Top Ten global brands by value 2022

Source: Interbrand-Best Global Brands 2022

Table 7.3 Financial Services Brands in Global Top 100

Position	Brand	Brand Value $US
24	JP Morgan	24.3
27	Amex	22.1
34	Allianz	18.7
37	Visa	17.3
38	Paypal	17.1
41	Mastercard	16.1
43	Axa	15.7
49	Goldman Sachs	14.5
57	Citi	13.0
65	HSBC	11.2
66	Morgan Stanley	11.0
76	Santander	9.0

Interbrand's approach – named Interbrand Thinking & Making, or Interbrand™ – departs sharply from those conventions, on the basis of two main changes. Because today customer expectations move faster than businesses, brands must be thought of in dynamic terms. We therefore believe strategy is less about defining a *positioning* to own, and more about identifying a *trajectory* to evolve along.

In other terms, a powerful strategy focuses on *where* to go next – and, most importantly, *how* to get there. This reflects a universal – but often forgotten – principle: a strong strategy must deploy a brand's advantages and resources to reach a certain objective.

We therefore like to see the core of brand strategy as being defined by three elements. An Ambition (a set of timebound, measurable objectives); a Trajectory (a credible, different and relevant promise) and a set of Moves (the tactics that bring the promise to life). The result is more powerful than the typical "brand on a page"exercises because it does more than set out a set of definitions ("here's what the brand *is*") – it builds a tangible action roadmap ("here's what the brand *will do*"). Visually, this is best illustrated as a route with a clear "From", "To" and "By" as shown in Figure 7.7.

We start by defining the "From".

We do this through a framework called the Departure Point analysis, which defines the brand's status quo and context through three lenses: people, the business, and their interactions. This should sound logical: after all, if we consider brands as providers of experiences, these three lenses explore their demand, their supply and their currency.

This multidisciplinary approach combines very different skills – from psychology to ethnography, from customer journey mapping to financial analysis. This enables us to gain an equally deep understanding shifting expectations, the brand's advantages, and how the two come together through products, services and experiences.

We then define the "To": what we call the Ambition – a measurable goal or set of goals that people in the organisation know can realistically be achieved within a given timeframe.

We then build the Trajectory: the brand's most effective route towards the ambition.

The Trajectory forms a guiding policy that defines the brand's Moves – the tactics. These can be incremental Moves such as, for instance, rethink a website or launch a campaign; or what we call Iconic Moves™, such as opening a new channel for the category, venturing into entirely new competitive arenas, or introducing new technologies.

In Marketing in practice 7.6 we see how Interbrand used its methodologies to help BPER in Italy to achieve a new, differentiated brand position. An additional example,

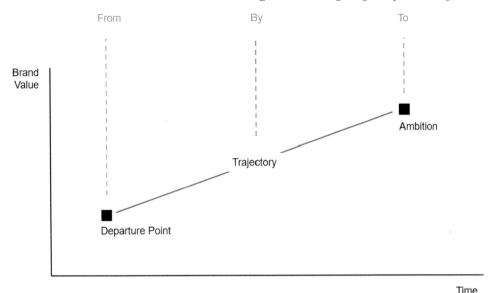

Figure 7.7 Interbrand model of brand trajectory

this time from South Korea, is to be found in the case study section that follows this chapter.

7.11 Summary and conclusion

Segmentation, targeting and positioning are at the heart of the development of any marketing strategy. To compete effectively, an organisation must first identify different groups of consumers or business customers within the marketplace. These groups need to be different from each other but customers within each group must be relatively similar in terms of their needs and wants, i.e. the common characteristic.

Few organisations have the resources to serve every segment within the market and must select a series of market segments to target. These target markets must be chosen according to the nature of customers' wants and the organisation's ability to supply those needs. The decision must also take levels of competition into account.

Once target markets have been identified, the organisation must pay careful attention to how it wishes to present itself. This means that the organisation must have a clear idea of its source of competitive advantage and be able to communicate it effectively to target consumers. Over time, the competitive advantage a company gains from its distinct position may become eroded as competitors adjust their strategies and as consumer tastes change. This may require a company to reposition itself in order to achieve a new source of competitive advantage.

Providers of financial services can now compliment their standard approach to segmentation with a segment-of-one approach. This is particularly relevant in the context of marketing to a company's existing customers and will be discussed in detail in Part III.

Marketing in practice 7.6: the BPER case, Italy

Background

BPER Banca is an Italian banking group offering multichannel banking services to individuals, SMEs, corporate and public entities. The company is based in Modena, in Italy's northern region of Emilia Romagna, with also a strategic headquarter in Milan's financial district. With branches across all of Italy, the group is the country's third by number of branches and the fourth by deposits, and is floated on the Italian stock market. Having grown by acquisitions, by 2013 the bank's brand portfolio was composed of several regional banks with virtually no visible link and no real positioning on the market.

"Our analysis of internal and external brand perceptions across places where our banks were present had revealed a significant opportunity", recalls Sabrina Bianchi, Head of Brand & Marketing Communications. "A single brand would allow us to design a customer journey that would integrate our different cultures into a single vision, thus helping us create synergies, build value and grow our business."

The work

Together, Interbrand and BPER embarked on an ambitious programme that started with an in-depth analysis spanning quantitative and qualitative research, as well as interviews across the group's leadership. "The information basis generated by the audit enabled us to identify the drivers of choice that served as a foundation for our new trajectory," says Bianchi. The strategy built on the group's recognised advantages – its co-operative roots, its unique understanding of local contexts and the ability to create exceptional customer intimacy. Revolving around the notion of *Making choices together to grow together*, the strategy married the empathy of a hyperlocal bank and the consultative power of a national group.

This trajectory served as the guide for the group's subsequent moves over the years. "It has been a basis, a model and a north star," says Bianchi. "It has guided our transition to the group's new brand architecture, centred around BPER Banca as the main brand", says Bianchi. "It has enabled us to reinvent our brand's identity and lead BPER Banca onto path to grow its awareness in a consistent way, with no meandering" It is about strategy, yes, but also tactics. "Every format and touchpoint, and our entire tone of voice must reflect that strategy and that's possible only to the extent that the brand's ecosystem is founded on that trajectory", adds Bianchi.

On the back of a strong strategic foundation, BPER and Interbrand worked together to develop a new identity, which eventually found its anchor point in a simple symbol – or, rather, a punctuation mark. A colon. Why? Again, another step along the trajectory of making choices together to grow together. "The colon represents the beginning of a dialogue", notes Bianchi. "The ability to share thoughts and projects, eventually reaching desirable goals together. All our communication is based on providing helpful, transparent and open message."

Inasmuch as many rebranding programmes are initially met with diffidence, things went differently when the new brand was unveiled in 2015. "On the morning of the launch, before every single employee found on their desk a kit sharing the strategy and the new design, and tuned in to a video from our CEO. This sparked countless manifestations of pride and belonging to a new brand combining diverse cultures. That was the beginning of a growth path that has led us to become the third national bank".

Impact

Brands are not created; they are built over time through moves that should be coherent and accumulative, weaving a narrative that combines newness in experience with consistency in strategy. The initial goal of unifying the regional banks under a single, new brand was to focus investments on building a powerful asset. "We have achieved our ambition in terms of sheer awareness, which was essential. We're now at a level that is in synch with being Italy's third banking group".

The journey continues, however. "Our focus has now shifted towards strategically creating equity. Since 2015 we have been on a journey punctuated by many moves and constant measuring", points out Bianchi. "We have worked with employees and clients to reinforce our narrative. We have become storytellers across digital and social channels. Growth and new acquisitions bring new challenges, and we have therefore constantly adjusted our strategy to navigate change – but the solidity of the original trajectory means we've never had to reinvent it".

Source: Manfredi Ricca, Global Chief Strategy Officer, Interbrand

---

Learning outcomes

Having completed this chapter, you should be able to:

1. **Appreciate the benefits that arise from segmentation.**
   Segmentation is essentially a process whereby a provider of goods or services chooses to group prospective customers together based on a set of common characteristics that have significant implications for its marketing activity. Segmentation and targeting result in several important benefits both for providers and consumers of products and services, they include: efficient resource utilisation,

effective targeting of new customers, facilitation of competitive advantage, directing the marketing mix, enhancing customer satisfaction.

2. **Explain different approaches to segmenting a market.**

   Several approaches were examined for the segmentation of consumer markets, amongst which are: Consumer characteristics such: as demographics (e.g.: age, gender, life stage); socio-economic situation (e.g.: income, social class, location); and psychographics (e.g.: attitudes, beliefs, personality type). Also examined were customer needs such as if the need is for saving, home ownership and retirement, as well as behaviour-related factors such as frequency of service usage, quantum of purchase, and means of accessing service. We also considered product-related factors such as product attributes, for example, pricing, value, and simplicity of features.

   Due consideration was given to the ways in which organisational customers can be segmented. That included: business demographics, processes, geography, performance and markets served.

3. **Understand the issues involved in selecting a target market.**

   We saw that there is no best way to segment a market and that ultimately a commercial judgement must be made to ensure the best fit between the incremental costs that segmentation entails and the incremental value that can be realised. For an organisation to get an approach to segmentation that is "right" for it depends on a good understanding of the market, the right skills and knowledge and careful evaluation of the different options. In terms of skills and knowledge, the following areas are of particular importance: understanding the market, analytical skills and resources, commercial judgement, and creative insight. Additionally, the chosen segments must pass tests of, measurability, profitability, accessibility and relevance.

4. **Understand the role of positioning in communicating the value proposition.**

   At the core of positioning lies a brand or company's competitive advantage in terms of how it differentiates itself from the competition and how it delivers value to its customers. Thus, positioning is about how a company or brand wants itself to be perceived in the minds of the individuals who comprise its target segments. The choice of *position* is based upon the agreed form of differentiation. The objective of positioning is to generate and maintain a clear value proposition to customers, thus creating a distinctive place in the market for the brand or organisation. When successful, positioning results in a brand or company being seen as distinctive from its competitors. To be commercially advantageous, positioning should be based upon product and service characteristics that:
   - Are relevant to the target segment.
   - Achieve differentiation from the competition.
   - Can be communicated clearly to the market.
   - Can be sustained.
   - Appreciate the ways in which digital marketing is impacting upon segmentation.

5. **Appreciate the ways in which digital marketing is impacting upon segmentation.**

   Data is the key to successful digital segmentation. It enables organisations to understand where, and how, people are likely to consume content. This is particularly relevant for pay-per-click (PPC) advertising which relies on understanding which search terms particular audiences are most likely to use. The most effective segmentation strategies reflect customer personas based on geographic, demographic, behavioural and psychological data. Real-time segmentation enables organisations to tailor website experiences in the live environment using first-party cookie data and customers click patterns, to serve the most relevant and compelling content, layouts and call to actions. Where "segment of one" has real traction is in its potential to add significant value to the worth of a company's existing customer base.

Review questions

1. What are the criteria for effective segmentation?
2. What variables do you think are most suitable for segmenting the market for credit cards?
3. What are the advantages of a differentiated approach to market targeting?
4. When will focused market targeting be most appropriate?
5. What factors should be considered when trying to develop a competitive position?
6. Suggest the type of ways in which the concept of segment-of-one can be applied when marketing to existing customers.

Notes

1 corporate.saga.co.uk/about-us/strategy (Accessed October 2023)
2 www.closebrothers.com/our-purpose (Accessed October 2023)
3 Source: Accenture Financial Services. (2017). Global Distribution & Marketing Report

Reference

Jobber, D. (2004). *Principles & Practice of Marketing*. 4th ed. Maidenhead: McGraw-Hill.

8   Internationalisation strategies for financial services

Learning objectives

At the end of this chapter, you should be able to:

1. Identify the key drivers of internationalisation in the financial services sector,
2. Understand the factors influencing the choice of internationalisation strategy,
3. Explain the marketing implications associated with internationalisation.

8.1 Introduction

Internationalisation is a broad term. It extends beyond basic notions of trade and exporting to encompass all aspects of business activity that take place across national borders. Exporting is often thought of as simply the first stage in a process which may extend to the establishment of a fully-fledged business presence in an overseas market. Most discussions of service marketing, including those relating to financial services tend to focus heavily on marketing in a domestic context. Equally, many textbooks on international strategy and marketing tend to focus predominantly on the activities and issues associated with companies providing physical goods. And yet services account for an increasingly large share of world trade and there is a long tradition of international activity within the financial services sector. World Trade Organisation (WTO) figures suggest that the value of world trade in commercial services almost doubled in the ten-year period after 2005 and was around 25% of the value of the trade in merchandise (World Trade Organisation, 2016) although this does not include the business undertaken by foreign affiliates. Financial services were the second fastest-growing sector after computer and information systems and the total value of trade in financial services in 2014 was $349 billion.

Data from the UN Conference on Trade and Development (UNCTAD, 2023) shows that the Covid-19 pandemic significantly disrupted trade patterns and this was particularly in evidence in 2020 when the value of service exports globally declined by 17%. In 2021 and 2022, trade in services and goods bounced back. In 2022, the value of trade in services increased by almost 15% and estimates suggest a growth rate of 7% in 2023. In 2022, global services exports represented around 7% of World GDP and 23% of global trade and were valued at $7.1 trillion. Financial services trade grew by around 16% between

DOI: 10.4324/9781003398615-10

Figure 8.1 HSBC advertising at Charles De Gaulle Airport in France

2019 and 2022, although services trade was dominated by travel and transport and by IT services.

Particularly in corporate markets, there is a long tradition of international activity in financial services. The US-based Citibank has been operating in France since 1906, Argentina since 1914 and Brazil since 1915. The UK Bank, Barclays, formed its international division in 1925 through the merger of the Colonial Bank, the Anglo Egyptian Bank and the National Bank of South Africa. HSBC may be a household name in many parts of Europe (see Figure 8.1) but its name reflects the initials of the Hongkong and Shanghai Banking Corporation Limited, which was founded by a Scot, Thomas Sutherland in 1865. Offices initially opened in Hong Kong and then in Shanghai with the banks focus being financial support for the growth in trade between Europe, India and China. In the insurance sector, Prudential established its first overseas agencies for the sale of general insurance products in the 1920s and for the sale of life products in the 1930s. And yet, despite this long tradition of international activity, most discussions of financial services marketing pay relatively little attention to the activities of firms in overseas markets.

The purpose of this chapter is to provide an overview of the marketing dimensions relevant in the internationalisation of financial services. The first section explores the implications of the characteristics of financial services for the process of internationalisation, drawing on frameworks developed in earlier chapters. Thereafter, a brief review of the drivers of internationalisation in financial services is presented. The chapter then proceeds to outline different strategies for internationalisation and considers their relevance to financial services. Finally, there is a brief discussion of the broader marketing challenges associated with operating in international environments.

8.2 Internationalisation and the characteristics of financial services

The distinctive characteristics of financial services and their marketing implications were discussed in Chapter 3. These characteristics also have implications for internationalisation. The intangibility of financial services means that there is nothing physical to move from producer to consumer. In principle, this intangibility may make it relatively easy to export some financial services, particularly in corporate markets. For example, if investment bank UBS handles an equity trade in New York for a client in Japan it is effectively exporting its services; nothing physical is transported but a service is provided remotely. In retail markets, exporting is often more difficult: consumer reactions to intangibility often make it difficult to supply financial services without a physical presence in the domestic market. Inseparability implies a need to focus particular attention on how to manage interactions with customers in different locations while heterogeneity reminds us of the additional challenges associated with providing a consistent service across different countries. And of course, concerns about fiduciary responsibility mean that financial services providers face the challenge of operating in potentially diverse regulatory environments if and when they internationalise.

The difficulties associated with internationalising in retail markets are increasingly mitigated by the impact of digital delivery. In particular, the emergence of the neobanks with digital-only models has enabled greater cross-border provision of retail services. For example, neobank Revolut which was launched in 2015 claims some 30m customers worldwide[1], including nearly 7m in the United Kingdom (UK), nearly 3m in Romania, 2.5m in Poland, over 2m in France and close to 2m in Spain. This is a significant geographic spread in less than a decade of operation. And while Revolut will have faced the challenges of securing regulatory approvals and getting digital and business infrastructure in place it has been able to access international markets without the challenge of needing to develop a physical high street presence. Marketing in practice 8.1 explains how savings platform Raisin has grown internationally in a similar time frame.

 Marketing in practice 8.1: Raisin's international expansion

Raisin GmbH is an innovative digital savings marketplace which connects customers with an extensive range of savings account. Originating in Germany in 2013 (a country known for its high savings rates); it subsequently expanded into the European Union (EU) more broadly (including moves into Austria, France, Spain and Ireland in 2016) and then in 2017, launched a UK offer based in sterling. In effect, Raisin makes use of open banking protocols to operate a series of savings marketplaces. They trade under a range of brand names including Weltsparen, Raisin, Savedo, and Zinspilot. What makes Raisin distinct is that it provides customers with a single account from which they can easily allocate funds across a range of partner banks and credit unions. In effect what Raisin does is hold custodial accounts with partner banks and can then move customers funds into and out of that account based on the savings allocations that customers make when they deposit funds into their Raisin account.

Deposits are typically covered by standard deposit guarantee schemes and so the risk to consumers is low while the interest rates are often very attractive and consumers benefit from easy access to an extensive range of savings opportunities. Deposit takers benefit from reaching an extensive consumer base at a lower cost than they would expect if operating in isolation.

Building on its success in Europe, Raisin sought further international growth and the US was identified as an attractive market – not just because of the overall size of the market but because of the large number of small regional banks and credit unions wishing to attract deposits. In such a market, an intermediary could be hugely effective for banks who wished to reach a large consumer-base and for consumers looking for the best savings rates.

Market entry required the creation of a US subsidiary – under the brand name of "SaveBetter", (although this subsequently reverted to the Raisin brand); a CEO was hired in 2019 and the company's tech solutions were adapted and relevant regulatory approvals secured. In 2021, SaveBetter was launched. If anything, growth has been faster in the US than in Germany and this may reflect the generally larger volumes of individual savings and the market leading rates offered by bank and credit union partners.

As a group, Raisin boasts over 1m customer worldwide and works with over 400 banks worldwide in 30 markets.

Source: https://fintechmagazine.com/venture-capital/raisin-uk-experience-driven-digital-savings-marketplace; https://thefinancialbrand.com/news/bank-marketing/digital-marketing-banking/raisin-deposit-marketplace-savebetter-gains-banks-customers-161462/; www.raisin.com/en-us/about-us (all accessed 02 February2024)

In terms of service classifications, financial services are typically heavily information-based and, therefore are easily digitised. It is this feature that makes export relatively straightforward in principle. However, the complexity of many financial services suggests that significant interpersonal interaction is often required in their delivery. This has important implications. First, there is often a strong pressure for a financial services organisation to have a physical presence in the market which it is delivering its services. Many buyers (particularly those in retail markets) feel a need to be able to access their service provider, are reassured by a physical presence (even if they may deal with a provider remotely) and regulators commonly require such a presence. Thus, in comparison with suppliers of manufactured goods, financial services providers will often be less reliant on exports and much more likely to internationalise by establishing overseas operations as the case of Raisin's entry to the US market demonstrates. The tendency to prefer or need to establish an overseas entity will, in turn, raise important issues in relation to the nature and management of service delivery.

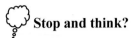 **Stop and think?**

Think of cultural characteristics (broadly defined) of a market you know well. What features would you highlight to a potential international entrant as being relevant to the development of a marketing campaign?

One of the major challenges that organisations face when operating internationally relates to cultural differences, and the greater the difference in cultures, the greater the challenges. Cultural differences impact on financial services internationalisation in two ways. First, there are issues related to familiarity and use of financial products. In many Islamic countries, the prohibition on interest means that credit card holders will seek to pay off accounts at the end of each month rather than accumulating interest charges. Variable rate mortgages have traditionally been more common in the UK, whereas many countries in continental Europe have a long-standing tradition of fixed-rate mortgages. Second, culture can impact significantly on interactions where the two parties have different heritages. Cultural differences can affect the development of long-term relationships where the creation of trust plays a central role. For example, the rather direct negotiating styles of the British and Americans may appear quite threatening and even rude in Japan, thus inhibiting the development of mutual trust. In addition, cultural differences are often a source of misunderstandings in communications with all sorts of negative consequences for service provision. For example, Egg, the UK-based internet bank invested £280m expanding in France but withdrew after two years; a poorly thought through and culturally insensitive advertising campaign was one of a number of factors that contributed to the failure of this venture. In contrast, UK banks relying on offshore outsourcing to deliver customer service to domestic customers from bases in India have invested considerably in ensuring that local staff are familiar with key aspects of British culture and can engage more effectively with British consumers.

Given the significance of cultural differences, it is perhaps not too surprising that many examples of the internationalisation process in financial services have started with moves into environments which are in some respects culturally similar. For example, many Spanish banks have tended to concentrate their international activity in South America or that many UK financial services providers initially established overseas operation in countries which were then colonies and in which there were substantial anglophile market segments. 'Cultural proximity' is a useful piece of shorthand to describe this phenomenon.

Although the nature of financial services presents important challenges to internationalisation, it is apparent that there are clear attractions to international operations and these are encouraging many financial services to expand beyond their domestic market. The next section explores the conditions that influence financial services providers to operate globally.

Progress check

- There is a long history of international activity in financial services, but probably more so in corporate than retail markets.
- The distinctive characteristics of financial services have implications for internationalisation. The fact that financial services lack physical form and are information-based might suggest that it is reasonably straightforward to operate

across borders. In reality there are many challenges to address, including customer expectations and regulatory requirements.

- International expansion is attractive and there are a growing number of oganisations now operating beyond their national borders.

8.3 The drivers of internationalisation

When considering the drivers to internationalisation, it is useful to distinguish between firm-specific and macro-environmental factors. Firm-specific factors are those factors which create incentives for individual firms to move into international markets. Macro-environment factors are those features of the overall environment which create conditions which favour internationalisation for all firms. Naturally, the two are related and interdependent.

8.3.1 Firm-specific drivers of internationalisation

At the level of the individual firm, the motives for expanding beyond the domestic market by a given provider may be divided into push and pull factors. Push factors are essentially domestic market conditions which will tend to encourage a firm to look outside its national markets. Pull factors are features of non-domestic markets which encourage a firm to consider expanding operations overseas. Each of these will be considered in turn.

Push factors focus essentially on conditions in the domestic market which may in some way inhibit a firm from achieving its strategic goals. The simplest example of a push factor might be slow growth, high costs or high levels of competition in the domestic market. Cost considerations, for example, have been a major driver of the decisions of many financial services providers to establish call centres in countries such as India. Another "push" factor might well be domestic regulation. For example, in the US, the Glass-Steagall Act of 1933 which, until its repeal in 1999, prevented banks from engaging in both commercial and investment banking has been identified as one factor encouraging US banks to expand overseas where they could engage in activities which were not permitted domestically. In Spain, domestic competition and pressures on profit margins were identified as one reason why a number of banks looked to expand internationally.

More commonly, overseas expansion is thought to be influenced by pull factors which make overseas markets attractive as places to do business. For example, Cardone-Riportella and Cazorla-Papis, (2001) noted that a low level of competition, limited penetration of banking services and increasing deregulation in many Latin American countries made them attractive target markets for Spanish banks looking to move overseas. Marketing in practice 8.2 highlights the evolving potential of insurance market in Latin America.

 Marketing in practice 8.2: insurance in Latin America – challenges for co-operative insurers?

The Latin American insurance market may be relatively young, but it has experienced significant growth over the past decade and is generally thought to be relatively resilient in the face of challenging economic conditions. The cooperative/mutual insurance sector in many of the region's markets has been a significant contributor to that growth.

The total insurance industry in Latin America grew by 11.3% compound annual growth rate (CAGR) from 2007 to 2014, making it the fastest-growing region in the world. (At the other end of the spectrum, during the same period, the European market shrank by 0.3% CAGR and the North American market grew by just 0.7% CAGR.) Since then, the Latin American market has sustained average real growth rates in excess of 3% with the exception of 2020 when the Covid-19 pandemic resulted in a 3% fall in premiums written.

In its market review, insurance company, Swiss Re forecasts growth of 3.4% in real terms for Latin America for 2024 with Life and Health expected to grow by 3.3% and non-life growth to be in the region of 4.5%. There is considerable variation in the composition of demand for insurance across markets. Argentina, Brazil, Chile and Mexico are generally the larger markets and while Life Insurance accounts for a significant share of the market in Brazil, Chile and Mexico, Casualty Insurance has the largest share of the Argentinian market.

In the period between 2007 and 2014, the cooperative sector in Latin America grew by 14.4% CAGR, according to the International Cooperative and Mutual Insurance Federation (ICMIF), which annually measures and reports on the size of the cooperative/mutual sector across the globe. In the middle of the last decade, it noted that Latin America was home to some of the world's fastest-growing cooperative/mutual insurers. Altogether, the Latin American cooperative/mutual insurance sector (hereafter referred to simply as "cooperative" because this is the dominant business model) represented 12.1% of the total regional market in 2014. There were strong indications based on consistent performance and trend data for the previous seven years that this market share would continue to grow.

The Latin American markets are mostly well adapted for the expansion of the cooperative concept within the insurance context. The cooperative business model is widely used in agriculture and industry, while cooperative education is commonplace in many Latin American schools. This contrasts with other regions in which the term "cooperative" is less common and/or less well understood.

Since 2014 the Latin American market has remained strong although the cooperative sector has not grown in the way that was expected. Since 2011, total assets held by Latin American co-operative insurers grew from $31billion to $37.7 billion – an increase of 21.7%, but over the same period, the market share of these insurers fell slightly from 10.9% to 10.5% having peaked at 12.5% in 2014. In effect the traditional joint-stock insurers were able to grow faster than co-operative ones. In the life sector of the Latin American market, co-operative insurers had a market penetration of 6.7% in 2021 whereas in the non-life sector, penetration stood at 12.9%.

ICMIF highlights the important social role that co-operative and mutual insurers play in markets worldwide and how this may give such insurers a competitive edge in their engagement with customers, who are structurally at the heart of the business. One such example is Argentinian insurer, La Segunda which, during the recent pandemic, supported a range of preventative actions to limit the spread of the virus and also supported the health system to provide aid to vulnerable people. La Segunda's biotech company, DetXMol S.A. also contributed with the development of testing kits for the virus.

Source: Updated from 3rd Edition version prepared by Faye Lageu, Senior Vice President, ICMIF (International Cooperative and Mutual Insurance Federation).www.swissre.com/dam/jcr:72b875cb-03d9-4e25-b325-b3e715e1a0eb/20023-10-03-sri-latin-america-report-2023.pdf (accessed 24 January2024)

Probably the commonest pull factor is the size and growth potential of markets in other countries. The liberalisation of the economies of India and China have contributed to rapid growth in both countries and this, combined with their size, has made both markets highly attractive and encouraged a large number of financial services providers to seek to establish a presence in these countries. In India, HSBC, DBS (Singapore), JP Morgan Chase and Deutsche Bank are among some of the well-known names with a significant presence, although foreign banks account for a relatively small share of the market with less than 5% market share for deposits and loans. DBS Bank India Ltd is one of the largest with close to 600 branches and over 1,000 ATMS. In contrast, the 12 public sector banks have 85,000 branches and over 1m ATMs between them. However, while small, there is evidence to suggest that their activities are highly profitable[2], although a number of foreign entrants have found operations in India and competition from domestic banks to be challenging and a number have either exited or scaled by their operations. Citibank for one withdrew from retail banking in India (as it did in a number of its international markets).

The dramatic growth in its economy in the early part of the 21st century mean that China was especially attractive to banks with large numbers entering the market, despite some significant regulatory challenges. And while some of these challenges have eased in the past decade, the geo-political environment has become rather more difficult and the growth of the Chinese economy has slowed. As with India, there are a significant number of well-known banks operating in China but their market share remains small compared to that of the domestic banks. In contrast with India, there are concerns about weakening profitability in core business areas. However, commentators suggest that the Chinese market will continue to be attractive in the longer term, despite short term pressure on margins. In particular S&P have highlighted the areas of wealth management and cross-border financing as being particularly attractive because they are much less dependent on net interest margins and are areas where many foreign banks have particular capabilities[3].

 Stop and think?

What do you think makes a market attractive for retail banking? How might you want to balance the potential that a market offers relative to the costs and difficulties of entering that market?

A number of international markets may be attractive to insurers because of the combination of growing incomes and the relatively low levels of expenditure on insurance products. Table 8.1 provides data on insurance penetration worldwide and highlights the potential attractiveness of international expansion for insurers from the mature markets of Korea, France, Hong Kong, the US and the UK.

Although many emerging economies such as the BRICS, the CIVETS and the Next-11[4] offer the attractions of both scale and growth potential, there may still be attractive opportunities in more mature markets. For example, ICICI Bank identified an attractive niche opportunity in Canada providing retail banking services to new Canadian immigrants of South Asian origin (see Neilson and Chandha, 2008).

Table 8.1 Insurance penetration in selected OECD and non-OECD markets in 2016–22

Year	2016	2017	2018	2019	2020	2021	2022
OECD							
Australia	5.1	4.6	4.2	3.7	3.5	3.3	3.2
Canada	4.5	4.4	4.5	..	..	..	..
France	10.7	10.6	10.6	10.6	10.0	10.6	10.3
Germany	6.2	6.4	6.4	6.6	6.9	6.7	6.2
Japan	7.6	7.3	7.7	7.3	7.1	7.1	7.8
Korea	11.7	11.0	10.5	11.1	11.4	10.9	11.7
Mexico	2.2	2.3	2.3	2.4	2.5	2.5	2.4
Netherlands	9.8	9.5	9.3	9.2	9.6	9.0	8.3
New Zealand	2.5	2.4	..	3.4	3.5	3.4	..
Poland	2.9	3.0	2.8	2.7	2.6	2.5	2.2
Spain	5.5	5.2	5.1	4.9	5.0	4.9	4.6
Türkiye	1.5	1.4	1.3	1.4	1.5	1.4	1.5
United Kingdom	9.6	12.6	13.1	11.8	11.4	11.5	11.4
United States	11.2	11.2	11.3	11.5	12.4	12.2	12.1
Non-OECD							
Argentina	2.6	2.6	2.3	2.1	2.5	2.2	2.1
Brazil	3.3	3.2	3.2	3.4	3.3	3.2	3.3
Egypt	..	0.7	0.6	0.6	0.6	0.7	0.7
Hong Kong	17.6	18.0	18.2	..	22.1	20.5	19.0
India	3.6	3.6	..	3.8	4.2	..	..
Indonesia	1.8	1.9	1.8	1.7	1.6	1.6	..
Malaysia	4.6	4.4	4.3	4.5	5.0	4.8	4.5
Singapore	8.1	8.8	..	8.7	10.7	10.7	9.6
South Africa	12.7	..	..	..	12.4	12.5	7.0

Data extracted on 28 Jan 2024 from OECD.Stat (measuring premiums as a % of GDP)

International markets may also be attractive because they provide an opportunity to leverage a particular competitive strength. For example, Kuwait Finance House expanded into international markets in order to build on its expertise in the design and delivery of Islamic financial services. Expansion internationally may also provide a means of adding value to the company's service. For example, many financial services providers moved overseas to follow their international customers and thus be in a position to offer them an integrated service. This has been of particular relevance to the international expansion of banks. Deutsche Bank was established in 1870 with a specific mandate to support the international trade activity of German companies; it established its first overseas offices in Yokohama, Shanghai in 1872 and while both were short-lived, Deutsche Bank re-established a presence on the ground in Asia through the Deutsch-Asiatische Bank and grew a very significant footprint in China over the next two decades. After the Second World War, Deutsche Bank's presence in China came to an end until 1981 when the bank opened a representative office in Beijing. This and subsequent developments placed considerable emphasis of the need to provide direct support to customers operating in those areas.[5]

While the factors that affect individual firms and create incentives for expansion overseas are clearly important and need to be fully understood, there are also broader, macro level factors which mean that some industries or some sectors may be more suited to globalisation than others. These factors are discussed in the next section.

8.3.2 *Macro level drivers of internationalisation*

At the macro level, there are a series of developments in the business environment which make internationalisation an increasingly attractive activity. The different forms that such internationalisation can take are discussed in greater detail in the next section where specific distinctions are drawn between global, international and transnational strategies.

Yip (1994) originally identified five drivers of globalisation, namely

- Market;
- Cost;
- Technology;
- Government;
- Competition.

Lovelock and Yip (1996) subsequently explored the applicability of these factors in the service sector. The rest of this section explores the drivers for globalisation in financial services based around Yip's framework.

Market drivers

This category refers to those features of the marketplace that encourage globalisation. Of particular significance are:

- Common customer needs: in markets where customer needs are essentially the same across the world, globalisation is thought to be an attractive strategy because a business can offer a relatively standardised product across a series of markets. In the global securities business, the needs and expectations of investment houses are generally very similar across countries and consequently, the securities houses who serve those customers are increasingly operating in a global market.
- Global customers: If customers themselves operate globally, then, there is an incentive for the companies that supply them to operate on a similar scale. One of the important drivers in the internationalisation of banking has been the internationalisation of the businesses that those banks serve. Equally, in the personal market, a company such as American Express needs to operate globally because the customers it serves are effectively global, not just in terms of where they live but also the extent to which they travel. HSBC's Expat Explorer initiative (Marketing in practice 8.3) also reflects the increasingly global nature of a segment of its customers.
- Global distribution channels: If channels of distribution are themselves global, then it is much easier for companies that sell through those channels to operate globally. Although we tend to think of financial services as being characterised by relatively short distribution channels, it is important to remember that financial services are typically information intensive and developments in electronic distribution systems have, in some senses, created global distribution systems. Networks such as Cirrus, for example, which allow customers to withdraw funds from ATMs worldwide provide a means by which banks can make some aspects of their service available to customers globally.
- Transferable marketing: If marketing campaigns developed in one country are easily transferred to other countries, then global operations are much easier to implement.

Marketing in practice 8.3: HSBC Expat – reaching a global audience with content that informs, educates and entertains

HSBC Expat is a specialist division of HSBC which provides financial services to expats. When this service was launched the main business challenges were: low awareness of specialist services among expats, and that reviewing/reorganising finances is a low priority for people moving or settling abroad.

HSBC researched the expat life cycle in focus groups and interviews and explored expat information needs. We learned that to move abroad is to step into the unknown – and expats are looking for content to help. The research also highlighted that that people moving and living abroad seek factual, "formal" information from companies, but also insider, "informal" information from peers. Moving abroad is an emotional, as well as a rational decision. Respondents said that information about life abroad was generally poor and fragmented – with a lack of authoritative sources – an opportunity for HSBC Expat to help educate them about this and in the process about our financial services for expats.

HSBC decided that it needed to engage with expats at all stages of their journey, establishing HSBC Expat as a trusted source of information to help expats make the most of their time abroad with three main priorities:

- Reach a global audience on a relatively small budget,
- Generate positive media coverage,
- Strengthen our positioning as an expert in expat life.

In 2007, HSBC established the HSBC Expat Explorer Survey. The survey has grown to become the one of the largest survey of expats, with some 20,000 respondents in 2021. Each year the survey reveals a number of key insights which focus on experience, economics and family, along with trends in key markets. (See for example www.expat.hsbc.com/expat-explorer/)

The HSBC approach was inspired by the content mission and values of the BBC, and aimed to:

- Inform
  Help customers make decisions about where to move based on their priorities and our survey data.
- Educate
  Share practical advice on how to make their move abroad a reality.
- Entertain
  Explore the emotional side of moving abroad, and share the personal experiences of those who have already moved.

To develop inspiring and useful content, HSBC sourced the views of customers (the Expat Explorer survey), industry experts (such as broadsheet journalists for advice articles) and its own employees (interviews with international secondees).

The survey provides a platform from which HSBC have leveraged the insights from expats worldwide to create a suite of interactive tools at *expatexplorer.hsbc.com*:

- Interactive data visualisation to bring the survey data to life, allowing expats to see and compare country rankings from the latest survey based on a choice of 27 criteria.
- Expat Careers (expatexplorer.hsbc.com/survey/careers)
- A tool to help users find the country most suited to their career priorities such as work/life balance or career progression. Users can learn about the local business culture, and the local job market or read articles on securing and making the most of a job abroad.
- Expat Country Guides (expatexplorer.hsbc.com/country-guides)
- Guides to 45 countries with information on moving, living, working and money. They include country rankings for each topic and local tips from expats, as well as key phrases, and advice on accommodation, money, tax, cost of living and business culture.
- Expat Hints & Tips (expatexplorer.hsbc.com/hintsandtips)
- Expats provide their "top tips" for other expats, which can be filtered by country and a choice of 18 themes, from accommodation to shopping.

HSBC combined the best tips with comments on social media to create a crowd-sourced video about expat life: www.youtube.com/watch?v=DhH7Ln79Liw

Results

The content is a true partnership between HSBC and expats: designed specifically to meet their information needs identified through research, and provided largely by other expats themselves. The campaign has delivered as follows:

- Reach a global audience on a relatively small budget
  More than 1.5 million expats in 214 countries have used the online educational resources for expats. The Expat Life video is the most viewed expat video on YouTube. Paid and organic social media have achieved KPI's above-industry average, and campaign emails achieved twice their average click-through – enabling HSBC to reach a wider audience more cost effectively. The content has also driven a steady increase in organic search traffic and leads to the website.
- Generate positive media coverage
  The survey results have been reported in thousands of articles worldwide, including Wall Street Journal, Huffington Post, Bloomberg, CNBC and Lonely Planet.
- Strengthen HSBC positioning as an expert in expat life

Feedback from expats on social media was extremely positive:

- "What a wonderful service. Country comparisons on so many levels. Just insightful and helpful in today's global world."
- "Amazing! I'm sharing the video with expat friends all over the world!"
- "It made me emotional. This could be us."
  One in ten people using these educational tools and content for expats went on to research financial products on the HSBC Expat website, showing the marketing value of an educational approach.

Source: Adapted from copy provided by Richard Fray, Digital Marketing Manager, HSBC Expat for 3rd edition.

Marketing activities which are specific to a particular environment and not easily transferred increase the costs associated with operating overseas. Indeed, many companies operating or looking to operate globally pay particular attention to ensuring that their campaigns are designed to be transferable. In the early part of the current millenium, HSBC developed a powerful branding campaign based on its understanding of cultural differences worldwide, supported by the claim to be "The World's Local Bank". And while it subsequently decided to cease using that particular message, its branding and advertising continued to stress the banks' awareness of the importance of local knowledge. Although the bank aims to localise its services to individual countries, it gains significant economies from a globally transferable marketing campaign and a global brand.

Cost drivers

Cost drivers are concerned with the extent to which expansion globally can enable a firm to reduce its costs. Most commonly, cost drivers are associated with the economies of scale – the cost savings that are associated with expanding the scale of operations. Such cost savings are often thought to be relatively unimportant in the service sector, including financial services. However, cost savings may arise in other ways, most obviously through access to lower cost resources. In financial services, developments in IT have facilitated the separation of front- and back-office processing and consequently, one form of expansion overseas has been in the form of outsourcing business processes to lower-cost countries. This has more recently been augmented by the outsourcing of certain front office functions, including outbound telemarketing and customer service. In the UK, a range of financial services providers including Lloyds TSB, Barclays, Zurich Financial Services, Prudential and Capital One have all outsourced a range of activities to India to benefit from lower costs in that market.

Technology drivers

Technology drivers are, in many respects, closely related to cost drivers – at least in a financial services context and are seen as another factor that can enable international activity. Developments in information and communications technology have been of particular significance in relation to internationalisation because they have facilitated global distribution and have supported outsourcing for a range of business processes. Outsourcing and offshoring (moving activity to lower-cost locations internationally) have been of particular significance in the financial services sector over the past ten years or so. Indeed, in order to support digital platforms that run on a 24/7/365 basis, it has become necessary to outsource development support in order to ensure immediate failover response and support is available at all times. Moreover, as businesses move their digital operational support away from physical infrastructure to cloud-based solutions, outsourced support models become even easier to manage on a global basis.

Traditionally discussions of outsourcing (and offshoring) have focused on cost drivers and specifically on the potential to reduce the transactions costs associated with the production and delivery of a service through the use of external providers. While clearly cost considerations are important, the strategic management literature argues that outsourcing decisions should not only be based on cost alone. For example, a strategic need to enter foreign markets may lead to an outsourcing partnership with a domestic firm, irrespective of the scale of cost savings. More generally, outsourcing decisions may need to consider issues related to the management of organisational competences and capabilities. Thus, for example, it may be more cost effective to outsource the acquisition of certain specific capabilities that are required for a limited period of time rather than develop them internally.

As an illustration, in January 2017, Blackrock announced the establishment of a centre of technology and innovation in Budapest (see Figure 8.2). The enterprise was developed in conjunction with the Hungarian government and Hungarian Investment Promotion Agency, who provided significant funding to support the recruitment and training of new 500 staff at the site. The project is one that was mutually beneficial; the government was able to retain local talent and offer home-grown job opportunities to skilled technology graduates (as opposed to losing them to other countries). In turn, Blackrock were able to tap into a wealth of skilled technologists at competitive rates whilst contributing to Budapest's economic and technological growth by creating jobs and bringing "financial and business processes, technologies and products, as well as the development of new management methods and its creative marketing function to Budapest" (Hungarian Minister of Foreign Affairs and Trade Péter Szijjártó).[6]

Research on the outsourcing practices of UK financial services providers (Odindo, Diacon and Ennew, 2004) suggests that many outsourcers have experienced positive impacts on an organisation's cost bases and quality and that these cost-based benefits dominated thinking about outsourcing. Some organisations have reported that technology-based outsourcing has facilitated a more active focus on the management of core competences and thereby strengthened competitive position. Nevertheless, there is evidence that outsourcing can present problems, the most obvious of which is that an outsourced service provider may turn into a competitor as a consequence of having had access to key information about the outsourcer's

Figure 8.2 Budapest – a new location for Blackrock

processes. In the longer term, there is also a concern that over-reliance on outsourcing may discourage the development of core skills and capabilities. It is also worth noting that outsourcing and particularly offshoring have been regarded as controversial practices – in part because of the consequence for employment in the outsourcer's home market and partly because of customer concerns about the experiences associated with outsourced customer service.

 Stop and think?

What do you think about outsourcing customer service to an offshore provider? How might consumers react to engaging with someone from a different culture when discussing financial issues? How important is it that customer service agents engage informally with customers during calls?

Government drivers

Government drivers to globalisation refer to any aspect of government or public policy that make it easy (or difficult) for foreign firms to operate in a domestic market. Most commonly, government drivers are the presence or absence of restrictions on market entry or the presence of regulatory systems which restrict what foreign entrants may do. Marketing in practice 8.4 looks at the implications for financial services of the UK's decision to leave the European Union (EU). It is worth noting that the immediate impacts post Brexit were less than had been expected but the biggest disruption arguably came from uncertainty about what Brexit might look like rather than Brexit itself.

 Marketing in practice 8.4: BREXIT and the UK financial services sector

At the time of the vote to leave the European Union in 2016, London, and the UK in general, was arguably the world's leading financial centre – somewhat ahead of New York and a long way ahead of its EU competitors. The UK was a market leader in many cross-border financial services at the time (16% of cross-border lending, 29% of international insurance premium income, 37% of foreign-exchange trading). And the City of London was of huge importance to the UK economy. Financial services accounted for around 7% of the UK's GDP. Banking was probably the UK's single largest export; the sector directly employed 1.1m people and contributed around 12% of UK tax revenue. Unsurprisingly, then, the UK's decision to leave the European Union (Brexit) caused turmoil in the country's financial services sector.

The strength of the City of London as a financial centre was seen by many as dependent on the EU's "passporting" arrangements which meant that financial services providers did not need separate regulatory or capital requirements to operate across the EU. For international providers, London could serve as a base from which the whole EU market could easily be reached. Following the vote, the most immediate anxiety was that providers currently based in London would start considering options to relocate to other European capitals (Frankfurt, Paris, Dublin).

There was no precedent for Brexit and little consensus on the economic consequences for the UK. Many in the industry expressed considerable anxiety about the consequences for the City of London, while proponents of Brexit argued that in such a global industry, the loss of passporting may have little substantive impact and the strength of the City, particularly its related and supporting industries, was such that Brexit would not threaten its global position.

As is so often the case, the situation was complex and variable. The significance of passporting differed considerably across sectors. For investment banking, it played a key role – the loss of passporting would require that a bank sets up in another jurisdiction within the EU; for hedge funds and general investment it was much less relevant. Of course, there was an alternative which might allow the UK to continue its EU operations under the principles of equivalence (i.e. on the basis that the UK's regulatory framework would be EU compliant).

When the UK left the EU in January 2021, Government was able to bring in reforms to domestic regulation and some extensions to the regulator's powers. There was widespread discussion of a so-called "Big Bang 2.0" – another round of deregulation in financial services that would support UK growth and competitiveness. Detail of planned reform was released in late 2022 – the "Edinburgh Reforms", although the proposals were widely thought to be modest and variable in the extent to which there was divergence with the prevailing EU regulatory environment.

The medium and longer term impact of Brexit on UK financial services remains to be seen and there continues to be a degree of uncertainty for both domestic and international providers. In a review in 2023, the House of Lords noted that there had been some movement of jobs from the UK to the EU but rather less than expected. It warned against complacency, but observed that current estimates suggested that 7,000 jobs had been lost (much less than some of the most pessimistic estimates that suggested 75,000 job might go).

Accounting Firm EY ran its Brexit Tracker[7] from 2016 to 2022. In 2022 it noted that the number of firms that had moved or were planning to move had stabilised. They also noted that the worst fears of commentators had not materialised, although they suggested that some relocations were likely to continue. Their data also suggested that 44% of financial services firms had moved at least some activity from the UK as a consequence of the Brexit decision (97/222). Their data also suggests that some of the biggest changes occurred in the years after the vote when there was considerable uncertainty and that the announcements of change declined as the future regulatory position become clearer.

Sources: House of Commons Library, (2016).
The *Economist,* (2016).
James and Qualglia, (2023)
Tobin, (2023)

Competition drivers

Competition drivers relate to a range of factors associated with the nature and level of competition in different markets. A move into an international market might be prompted by the entry of a competitor into the home market. Equally, the entry of a competitor into a new market might create an incentive for a company to follow suit in order to maintain some degree of competitive parity. Financial centres such as the City of London, New York, Tokyo and Hong Kong are typically targets for overseas expansion – competitive reasons dictate that it is sensible to be based alongside key competitors in these strategically important markets. In examining Chinese companies' penetration into major financial centres, Wang (2004) has observed that the choice of overseas location by Chinese banks encouraged others to copy their strategies. The followers tended to set up an overseas presence in cities which pioneers had previously entered.

Progress check

- Firm-specific drivers of internationalisation are those factors which create incentives for individual firms to move into international markets.
- Macro-environment factors are those features of the overall environment which create conditions which favour internationalisation for all firms.
- Naturally, the two are related and interdependent, although not every organisation is able to take advantage of all the opportunities offered by the marketing environment.

8.3.3 The extent of internationalisation in financial services sector

Clearly there are many examples of financial services providers operating internationally, and in many sectors of the industry, the macro-environment favours international operations. In particular, financial services targeted towards large corporates lend themselves to international operations because of the similarity in customer needs and the fact that many customers themselves are global. In contrast, personal financial advice is more suited to domestic provision because needs do vary, distribution is essentially personal and regulations are very different. Retail banking is predominantly domestic but there are a growing number of banks (this might include HSBC and Santander, among the traditional banks as well as many of the digital-only neobanks) offering their services in a range of markets worldwide; some of the target market may be expatriate staff (see Marketing in practice 8.2), but the rest will be domestic nationals and the service provided is usually broadly similar to that offered in other countries. Many insurers are following a similar strategy and establishing networks of operations worldwide. Marketing in Practce 8.5 outlines the experience of the EU in trying to encourage greater international activity in financial services among member countries.

As well as there being variety in the extent to which financial services providers operate globally, there are variations in the approaches that they adopt. The next section explores in some detail the different ways in which organisations may choose to operate in non-domestic markets.

Marketing in practice 8.5: internationalising financial services in the European Union (EU)

In 1985 the European Commission published a White Paper "Completing the Internal Market" which proposed a series of measures to create a single internal market among the countries of the then European Community. This was codified in the Single Europe Act of 1986, the first major amendment to the Treaty of Rome (which had initially established the EU in 1957). This Act required that the measures outlined in the 1985 White Paper should be implemented by the end of 1992 and included provision for mutual recognition of national product standards and a range of other measures to eliminate barriers to trade within the Union. The Single European Market formally came into being in 1993 underpinned by the "four freedoms" – free movement of goods, services, labour and capital.

In the case of financial services, the single European market aimed to eliminate restrictions on cross-border activity, thus encouraging greater competition, greater efficiency, lower prices and better service for customers. Given the high level of regulation in financial services and considerable differences in industry tradition, the single market relied on the principle of mutual recognition – if a financial services provider was licenced to operate in its home market then it was effectively free to provide services to consumers throughout the EU.

Recognising some of the particular difficulties with financial services, the European Commission developed a Financial Services Action Plan (FSAP) in 1998 which focused on eliminating barriers to cross-border trade. The Action Plan focused on developing a genuine single market for wholesale financial services, creating open and secure retail markets, ensuring the continued stability of EU financial markets and eliminating tax obstacles to financial market integration.

Subsequently, in December 2005, the Commission published a White Paper, "Financial Services Policy 2005–2010", to outline its policies for the rest of the decade. The White Paper focused its attention on ensuring that existing policy changes were implemented and consolidated, improving regulation, enhancing supervisory convergence, increasing competition between service providers and expanding the EU's influence in global markets.

The period prior to the global financial crisis (2007-8), saw an increase in levels of integration and interdependence, although changes were arguably much greater in the business to business market than in retail markets. This process was significantly disrupted by the financial crisis which then sparked a regulatory approach in the EU that focused on greater centralisation and a transfer of some powers from national to EU levels.

Although formal legal restrictions on cross-border activity in financial services were largely removed by the Single European Act, progress towards a genuine single market in retail financial services was initially slow. Genuine cross-border trade in financial services failed to grow substantially and most providers serving non-domestic markets did so by establishing a physical rather than an export presence, with that physical presence typically being via mergers and acquisition rather than greenfield developments.

In retail markets, non-domestic providers initially found it difficult to gain signifi-cant market share without a substantial physical presence. Customers often lacked awareness of or trust in non-domestic providers; legal differences could complicate asset-backed lending and differences in tax arrangements and consumer protection legislation could be a barrier in certain retail markets. Santander, for example moved into the UK market, initially via an alliance with RBS and then through the acquisition of Abbey National, Brandford and Bingley and Alliance and Leicester. The position has changed dramatically with the emergence of digital providers: as Marketing in practice 8.1 showed, Raisin quickly moved into other EU markets, the same is true of N26 and Revolut.

In business markets, progress has been rather faster and the degree of integration is much greater, although considerable effort has been required to address areas such as capital adequacy requirements and accounting standards.

Source: European Commission (2006), EU (2023)

8.4 Globalisation strategies

Thus far, the words "internationalisation" and "globalisation" have, to some extent, been used interchangeably. However, researchers in international business would distinguish between the two and see them as potentially quite different approaches to operating out-side of domestic borders. In particular, Ghoshal and Bartlett (1998) suggested that the right approach to internationalisation would depend on the extent to which there were:

- Pressures to integrate activities across markets – i.e. pressures to exploit economies of scale and offer a relatively standardised product which leverages around particular assets or competences;
- Pressures to be locally responsive, adjusting and adapting a service offer to local (country specific or regional) needs.

This led to the identification of four basic options for internationalisation as outlined in Figure 8.3.

8.4.1 International strategies

An international strategy is, in many senses, a weak or unstable position. Such a strategy involves doing broadly the same thing in a series of different markets, but without any attempt to integrate to get costs down or to tailor the service to the specific market. While pressures for integration or responsiveness may not be strong, firms following an international strategy will always be vulnerable to competitors who are able to integrate and outperform them in terms of costs or competitors who are able to customise and outperform them in terms of benefits offered to the consumer. Historically, this is probably the strategy that many financial services organisations operated in the early stages of internationalisation. HSBC, for example, traditionally operated across a range of markets, offering relatively standard banking services but under a different brand and name in each country. In the UK, HSBC

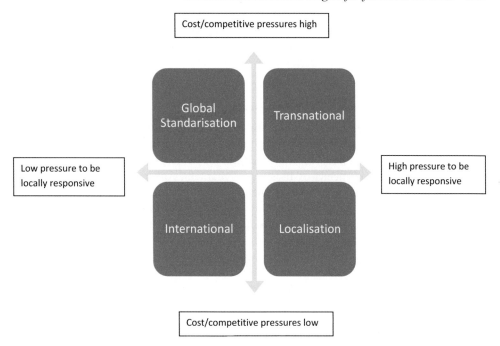

Figure 8.3 Different forms of Internationalisation

Source: Adapted from Ghoshal and Bartlett, (1998)

traded as Midland Bank, in Australia as Hong Kong Bank of Australia, in the Middle East as British Bank of the Middle East and in the USA as Marine Midland Bank. In 1998, the bank announced a move to create a unified brand for all its operations worldwide in order to be able to integrate marketing activities, improve marketing effectiveness and increase share-holder value. In effect, HSBC was moving away from an international strategy and towards a global strategy by more fully integrating its marketing activities worldwide.

8.4.2 Global strategies

A global strategy essentially focuses on integrating business activities across markets in order to ensure greater efficiency in operations; differences between markets tend to be discounted and the pressure to be locally responsive is considered to be weak. Rather than focusing on possible differences in customer needs, a global strategy focuses on similarities and sees different international markets as essentially homogenous. Typically, such a strategy is associated with manufacturers of highly standardised physical goods and emphasises econ-omies of scale in production and marketing. Matsushita is the example cited by Ghoshal and Bartlett (1998), with 90% of its production concentrated in highly efficient plants in Japan and yet 40% of its revenue coming from sales overseas.

In many senses, it is difficult for any financial services provider to be truly global because regulatory regimes vary across countries and limit the extent of true standardisa-tion. However, in retail markets, banks such as HSBC and Citibank are arguably following something close to a global strategy with recognised global brands and strong presence worldwide. The same may be said of American Express, Visa and Mastercard. In corporate markets, Bank of Tokyo Mitsubishi, with its diversified global network and ability to provide a full range of services to customers worldwide, is probably also following something close to a global strategy.

8.4.3 Multidomestic strategies

A multidomestic strategy arises when the pressures for integration are low and the pressure for local responsiveness are high. Such a strategy is characterised by operations across multiple markets, but with a high degree of decentralisation to ensure that services are tailored to the needs of those local markets. Any pressures on costs which might encourage integration are outweighed by the importance of local responsiveness; if a head office exists, its control is relatively weak and the organisation is perhaps best thought of as a federation of semi-autonomous companies. Multidomestic strategies are probably most closely associated with manufacturers of products which are in some way culturally sensitive (e.g. food, personal care) and where adaptation is essential. Multidomestic strategies are relatively unusual, but are more common in the financial services sector, not least because of the presence of country specific regulatory regimes. Multidomestic strategies may be particularly appropriate for relatively information-intensive and people-focused services such as financial advice where local responsiveness is essential. For example, De Vere and Partners – one of the largest chains of independent financial advisors – operates in 30 different countries worldwide. Differences in regulation and differences among consumers mean that scope for integration is limited and that their advice must be tailored to customer and country context. Life insurer Legal and General has also adopted elements of a multidomestic strategy; while it seeks to retain a common and consistent brand, it tailors what it offers and the companies it establishes to its chosen markets.

8.4.4 Transnational strategies

According to Ghoshal and Bartlett (1998), transnational strategies are a relatively recent phenomenon and have emerged in markets where there are significant pressures to keep costs low through global integration and also a need for a high degree of local responsiveness. This approach requires a high degree of global coordination and careful management of operations to fully exploit opportunities for increased efficiency, while retaining the flexibility to tailor the service to a given market. In principle, a transnational strategy creates a strong competitive position, being more locally responsive than a global strategy and lower cost than a multidomestic strategy. There are probably relatively few examples of genuinely transnational strategies in services, not least because of the difficulty of delivering both integration and responsiveness. In the service sector more generally, McDonald's is sometimes cited as an example of a service-based company moving towards a transnational strategy, using supply chain management systems and global branding to ensure a high degree of integration, and within this framework, adjusting the products offered in each country to accommodate the tastes and expectations of domestic consumers. In financial services, given that IT enables a greater degree of remote delivery and facilitates the separation of front- and back-office activities, there may be the potential for providers who are developing global strategies to become increasingly transnational. Neilson and Chandha

(2008) argue that ICICI Bank is developing a transnational approach in a niche banking segment – Indian expatriates; the corporate brand is managed from the bank's headquarters in India and the back-office dimensions of customer service are also managed through India. Local subsidiaries, whether in Canada, UK or Russia are responsible for monitoring local market conditions, identifying local opportunities and developing a responsive approach to marketing.

Progress check

- The way in which an organisation decides to approach international markets depends upon balancing the pressures to keep costs low with the pressures to offer services that are more customised to a particular market.
- An international strategy assumes that both costs pressures and the need for differentiation is low. It is increasingly seen as a difficult approach to sustain.
- A global strategy works when it is possible to offer a relatively standardised service and focus on low costs and operational efficiency;
- A multidomestic strategy arises when the cost pressures are low and the pressure for local responsiveness are high.
- A transnational approach tries to ensure that the offer is responsive to local needs while keeping costs low.

8.5 Strategy selection and implementation

From the discussion of different strategic approaches to international markets in the previous section, it is apparent that the choice of strategy is likely to depend on the type of service and the nature of the business environment. For example, services which require a high degree of interpersonal interaction (people-processing services) will probably be most suited to a multidomestic strategy, particularly if cultural or regulatory differences between markets are significant. In contrast, services that have limited requirements for interpersonal interaction (information or possession-processing services) will be more suited to global or transnational strategies. The choice between the two will then be driven by the extent to which customer needs differ and the ability of the organisation to deliver a differentiated service.

In addition to thinking about the right strategic approach to adopt for international operations, there are three other important decisions that require consideration: which markets to enter, how to enter those markets and how to market services within those markets. Each of these will now be considered in turn.

8.5.1 Which markets to enter?

In very simple terms the choice of markets to enter is based on identifying those which offer the best long-term returns. Superficially this may sound like a straightforward decision. In reality, it is potentially very complex. The factors discussed in Chapter 4 as being the basis for an evaluation of target market attractiveness domestically will all be relevant to the choice of target market internationally. Cultural proximity is frequently a major factor in determining international developments, at least during the early stages of a strategy for overseas expansion. Moving to a market that is familiar is generally considered to be more straightforward and lower risk than moving to a market which is very different.

More generally, the market selection decision does require careful consideration of risks, particularly with the move to very different markets. Carpenter and Vellat (2009) for example, highlight the challenges associated with assessing the risks associated with market entry in a planned economy, using the example of China. Greater government involvement and control of the domestic industry, difficulties in gathering information and uncertainties around the operation of regulation can all present particular risks for foreign entrants. And, of course, broader macro influences must also be considered and factored into the market selection decision. Factors such as size of population, levels of income and rates of growth will have important implications for the attractiveness of a market. One of the reasons why both India and China are attractive to many financial services organisations is that they are large markets, and although income levels are relatively low, economic growth rates are high suggesting considerable long-term potential. Many countries in Africa and South America are seen as similarly attractive for the same reasons.

Economic variables are important in determining the attractiveness of a market, but it is equally important to consider the feasibility of operating in a particular market. Infrastructure is one important consideration and would encompass quality and capacity of communications networks, access to essential supporting services (e.g. market research) and the ability to access suitable premises. Given the importance of people in a service business, it is also important to consider the availability of appropriate quality staff and this may be of particular relevance in cases where there are marked cultural difference between home and target market. In financial services, understanding the nature of domestic market regulation and its implications for the conduct of business is essential. Finally, of course, it is important to remember that some international markets may be strategically significant and that irrespective of the other factors, firms need to have a presence in those markets. For banks operating internationally, a presence in the key markets of London, Hong Kong, Tokyo and New York would probably be essential quite simply because customers and competitors would expect to see them there.

8.5.2 Method of market entry

Methods of market entry are normally divided into three categories: export, contractual and investment. In very simple terms we can think about these forms of market entry as being distinctive in terms of cost and control (see Figure 8.4) with exporting at one extreme seen

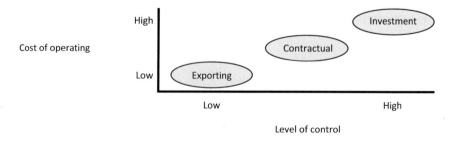

Figure 8.4 Options for market entry

as offering low cost but low control and investment being high cost but high control. The choice of entry mode can then be thought of in terms of the extent to which the firm needs to control the marketing and delivery of its products and services to customers and the extent to which it wishes to control costs. Exporting is often presented as being the first stage in internationalisation, because it involves a relatively low resource commitment. As firms build up experience, they are thought to move on to more complex and high commitment method of market entry such as a contractual arrangement or direct investment in overseas markets. In practice, of course, the choices are rarely that straightforward and the nature of financial services does tend to constrain the choice of mode of market entry. A helpful overview of the complexities associated with internationalisation and methods of market entry is provided by Whitelock (2002).

- Exporting: Exporting involves supplying goods from the home country to customers located in international markets. Provider and customer essentially remain at arms' length. Different regulatory systems and customer preferences for a physical presence make this form of market entry difficult for providers of financial services, although deregulation within the EU has sought to encourage increased trade in financial services through a system of mutual recognition. Moreover, it has been suggested that high levels of information intensity in some financial services, combined with the ability to digitise have increased the potential for service exports (McLaughlin and Fitzsimmons, 1996). Certainly the global securities business, which relies heavily on digitised information, depends on growing volumes of export-style activities with, for example, an investment house in New York dealing with a securities house in Hong Kong who will then provide a service remotely, based around information.
- Contractual: A contractual entry mode involves some form of partnership arrangement with a domestic provider which typically does not involve any shared ownership. Contractual entry modes are rather more costly than exporting but also provide rather more control. The most immediately recognisable forms of contractual entry are franchising and licencing. Both these arrangements grant an overseas firm the right to use some of the knowledge and expertise associated with the firm wishing to internationalise and because they draw on local managerial expertise they can be of particular value when there is a need to be sensitive to and adapt to local culture. Licencing arrangements are common in the physical goods sector: a variety of different types of soft drinks and food stuffs available worldwide are manufactured "under licence" – i.e. using licenced recipes, manufacturing processes, etc. Franchising extends the licencing concept to cover not just the product but to cover a broader business format. Service businesses such as Hertz, Hilton Hotels and McDonald's rely heavily on franchising as a method of market entry, but it is relatively less popular in the financial services sector for internationalisation, although it is used in domestic markets for activities such as financial advice and broking.
- Investment: Investment-based entry describes any type of operation in which a control is established over physical assets in an international market. It is the highest cost mode of entry and requires considerable commitment, but it also offers the highest level of control over the conduct of business. Investment-based entry may involve wholly new developments (sometimes referred to as greenfield developments), some form of joint venture or strategic alliance or merger/acquisition. Greenfield developments are costly, but allow the organisation to do exactly what it wants. Citibank's entry to the Japanese market in the 1980s, for example, was managed as a wholly new development. Joint

ventures and strategic alliances are less flexible because they entail working with local partners, but they do ensure access to organisations with local knowledge (which can be very important in some markets). In many countries, government regulations require that foreign entrants operate in a joint venture, so new market entrants may simply not have a choice. Mergers and acquisitions can be attractive as routes to market because they provide speedy access to an existing customer base and save the new entrant the difficulty of building up the business from nothing. Axa Group has relied heavily on acquisition as a means of expanding internationally. The Spanish bank, Santander, also relied heavily on growth through acquisition. Now one of the largest banks in the world, its international acquisitions include Banco Español in Chile, First National Bank of Puerto Rico, Abbey, Alliance and Leicester, and Bradford and Bingley in the UK, Banco Real in Brazil and CC-Bank in Germany. However, there are clear challenges associated with integrating the staff and systems of two or more businesses and this can make mergers and acquisitions difficult to manage. In general, investment entry modes have been widely used in financial services; there are numerous examples of joint ventures where regulations and market conditions require many of the largest international financial services organisations to have reached their position through a series of mergers and acquisitions. For example, Deutsche Bank became a global bank through the acquisition of Banca d'America e d'Italia in 1986 (Italy), Morgan Grenfell in 1989 (UK), Bankers Trust in 1999 (USA), Scudder Investments in 2002 (USA), Rued Blass & Cie in 2003 (Switzerland) and United Financial Group in 2006 (Russia).

The choice of method of market entry is subject to a variety of influences including the nature of the service, the internal resources and capabilities of the firm, the regulatory environment and the host country environment. This means that it can be difficult to generalise about the best mode of market entry for any given service, but investment modes do appear to be the preferred route to market for most financial services providers, reflecting perhaps the importance of a physical presence in the market, regulatory considerations, the value of local knowledge and the need for control over the service itself and the way in which it is delivered.

8.5.3 How to market in international markets

Once a method of market entry has been selected and implemented, the issue of marketing needs to be addressed. Discussions of international marketing traditionally revolved around the debate between standardisation and customisation, i.e. should an organisation operate with the same marketing strategies and tactics across all markets or should strategy and tactics be tailored to the local market. In basic terms, this can be thought of as directly analogous to the choice between a global strategy (low levels of local responsiveness) and a multidomestic strategy (high levels of local responsiveness). Although this debate has attracted much attention in academic literature and international marketing textbooks, most academics and practitioners would recognise that some degree of customisation is unavoidable and that sensible approaches to international markets will involve standardising where possible (the brand, advertising messages, logos, use of colour, methods of distribution) and being prepared to customise where necessary (product features, creative presentations, use of language, price). The leading global financial services providers such as Standard Chartered Bank, American Express, HSBC and Citibank all provide examples of how this is done. Some marketing activities are adapted to the specific context, but there remains considerable standardisation in terms of the marketing communications, thus ensuring that the brand is recognisable worldwide.

8.6 Summary and conclusion

This chapter has introduced some of the major issues relating to internationalisation in the financial services sector. Although it is commonly assumed that financial services are very much domestic markets because of regulatory frameworks and consumer expectations regarding a physical presence, many aspects of the industry are highly international. A variety of factors may encourage internationalisation. At a micro level, we can distinguish those factors which "push" an organisation overseas and those which "pull". At a macro level, variations in the environment can make international operations more or less attractive.

A series of broad strategic approaches to international activity can be identified based around the degree to which there is pressure for integration to exploit economies of scale and the degree to which there is a need for local responsiveness. As well as establishing a broad strategic approach to operating internationally, organisations must also give careful consideration to the choice of markets in which to operate, the method of market entry and the right approach to marketing its services once established.

Learning outcomes

Having completed this chapter, you should be able to:

1. **Identify the key drivers of internationalisation in the financial services sector.** At the level of the individual firm, the motives for expanding beyond the domestic market by a given provider may be divided into push and pull factors. Push factors are essentially domestic market conditions which will tend to encourage a firm to look outside its national markets. Pull factors are features of non-domestic markets which encourage a firm to consider expanding operations overseas. Push factors focus essentially on conditions in the domestic market which may in some way inhibit a firm from achieving its strategic goals. Probably the commonest pull factor is the size and growth potential of markets in other countries. At the macro level, there are a series of developments in the business environment which make internationalisation an increasingly attractive activity. Yip (1994) originally identified these as market, cost, technology, government and competition drivers.

2. **Understand the factors influencing the choice of internationalisation strategy.** Ghoshal and Bartlett (1998) suggested that the right approach to internationalisation would depend on the extent to which there were pressures to integrate activities and pressures to be locally responsive. Pressures to integrate activities across markets are essentially cost/competitive pressures. They will encourage organisatons to exploit economies of scale (which keep costs low) and offer a relatively standardised product which leverages around particular assets or competences. Pressures to be locally responsive, entail adjusting and adapting a service offer to local (country specific or regional) needs.

   Based on the extent to which these pressures are high or low, organisations may consider four broad strategic approaches according to where these pressures are high or low. These four basic options for internationalisation are multi-domestic, international, global standardisation and transnational.

3.   **Explain the marketing implications associated with internationalisation.**
     Key decisions that require consideration in developing specific international marketing strategies are: which markets to enter, how to enter those markets and how to market services within those markets. In very simple terms the choice of markets to enter is based on identifying those which offer the best long-term returns with an acceptable level of risk. This will require consideration of economic, social/cultural, technological and political factors. Methods of market entry are normally divided into three categories: export, contractual and investment. In very simple terms we can think about these forms of market entry as being distinctive in terms of cost and control with exporting at one extreme seen as offering low cost but low control and investment being high cost but high control. The choice of entry mode can then be thought of in terms of the extent to which the firm needs to control the marketing and delivery of its products and services to customers and the extent to which it wishes to control costs. Once a method of market entry has been selected and implemented, the issue of marketing needs to be addressed. Discussions of international marketing traditionally revolved around the debate between standardisation and customisation, i.e. should an organisation operate with the same marketing strategies and tactics across all markets or should strategy and tactics be tailored to the local market.

Review questions

1. Why are banks more international than financial advisors? Why are corporate financial services more international than retail financial services?
2. What are the benefits to HSBC of the development of a global brand?
3. Compare and contrast exporting and investment modes of market entry for financial services. Why have investment modes of entry been more widespread?

Notes

1   www.revolut.com/news/revolut_surpasses_30_million_retail_customers_worldwide/   (accessed January 2024)
2   www.linkedin.com/pulse/foreign-banking-landscape-changing-india-tamal-bandyopadhyay/ (accessed January 2024)
3   www.spglobal.com/marketintelligence/en/news-insights/latest-news-headlines/why-do-foreign-banks-expand-in-china-despite-weakening-profitability-64778421 (accessed January 2024)
4   Convenient acronyms used to describe some of the most attractive emerging economies – the earliest term was "BRICS" to describe Brazil, Russia, India and China. Following the BRICS, the next identified rapidly developing economies were described as the CIVETS (Colombia, Indonesia, Vietnam, Egypt, Turkey, South Africa) or the Next-11 (Bangladesh, Egypt, Indonesia, Iran, Mexico, Nigeria, Pakistan, Philippines, Turkey, South Korea and Vietnam).
5   See www.db.com/hongkong/en/content/history.html, (accessed February 2017)
6   www.kormany.hu/en/ministry-of-foreign-affairs-and-trade/news/fund-management-company-blackrock-to-establish-innovation-centre-in-budapest-and-create-500-new-jobs.(Accessed December 2023)
7   www.ey.com/en_uk/news/2022/03/ey-financial-services-brexit-tracker-movement-within-uk-financial-services-sector-stabilises-five-years-on-from-article-50-trigger (accessed January 2024)

References

Cardone-Riportella, C. and Cazorla-Papis, L. (2001). The internationalisation process of Spanish banks: A tale of two times. *International Journal of Bank Marketing*, 19(2), pp. 53–67.

Carpenter, S. and Vellat, M. (2009). The application of a Planned Economy Country Risk Model to the assessment of market entry into the Chinese banking sector. *Journal of Financial Services Marketing*, 13(4), pp. 345–56.

European Commission. (2006). *The Internal Market*. Available at http://europa.eu.int/comm/internal_market/index_en.htm (accessed 4 March 2006).

EU. (2023). 'Financial Services Policy', Fact Sheets of the European Union, available at (https://www.europarl.europa.eu/factsheets/en/sheet/83/financial-services-policy#:~:text=Progress%20has%20come%20in%20phases,post%2Dcrisis%20reform%20(from%202007, (accessed 30 January2024).

Ghoshal, S. and Bartlett, C. A. (1998). *Managing Across Borders*. New York: Random House.

House of Commons Library. (2016). *Brexit and Financial Services*, 1 November 2016. http://researchbriefings.parliament.uk/ResearchBriefing/Summary/CBP-7628.

James, S. and Quaglia, L. (2023). "Three challenges the UK faces in de-Europeanising financial services policies after Brexit", LSE Blog (available at https://blogs.lse.ac.uk/businessreview/2023/05/09/three-challenges-the-uk-faces-in-de-europeanising-financial-sector-policies-after-brexit/, (accessed on 29 January2024)

Lovelock, C. H. and Yip, G. S. (1996). Developing global strategies for service businesses. *California Management Review*, 38(2), pp. 64–86.

McLaughlin, C. P. and Fitzsimmons, J. A. (1996). Strategies for globalizing service operations. *International Journal of Service Industry Management*, 7(4), pp. 43–57.

Neilson, L. and Chadha, M. (2008). International marketing strategy in the retail banking industry: The case of ICICI Bank in Canada. *Journal of Financial Services Marketing*, 13(3), pp. 204–20.

Odindo, C. O., Diacon, S. and Ennew, C. (2004). *Outsourcing in the UK Financial Services Industry: The Asian Offshore Market, CRIS Discussion Paper*. Nottingham: Nottingham University Business School. (CRIS Discussion Paper Series – 2004.I).

The Economist. (2016). From Big Bang to Brexit, October 29. www.economist.com/news/britain/21709333-financial-services-industry-considers-its-future-outside-european-union-big-bang.

Tobin. (2023). 'UK-EU Relationship in Financial Services', House of Lords Library – in Focus, UK Parliament, London.

UNCTAD. (2023). Handbook of Statistics, 2023, available at https://hbs.unctad.org/total-trade-in-services/#:~:text=In%202022%2C%20global%20services%20exports,2019%2C%20except%20travel%20and%20construction.

Wang, T. (2004). China's Entry Into the WTO: Implications for Market Access of European Banks in China and Chinese Banks in the EU. Master of European Affairs Thesis. Lund University.

Whitelock, J. (2002). Theories of internationalisation and their impact on market entry. *International Marketing Review*, 19(4), pp. 342–47.

World Trade Organisation. (2016). International Trade Statistics. WTO (available at www.wto.org/english/res_e/statis_e/its2015_e/its2015_e.pdf, (accessed 1 February 2017).

Yip, G. S. (1994). Industry Drivers of Global Strategy and Organization. *The International Executive (1986–1998)*, 36(5), pp. 529. http://0-search.proquest.com.pugwash.lib.warwick.ac.uk/scholarly-journals/industry-drivers-global-strategy-organization/docview/232066933/se-2

Part I

Case studies

The following case studies are provided in relation to Part I of this book and they focus particularly on issues addressed in this section. They serve to complement the examples provided in each chapter through "marketing in practice" and can also be used for more extensive discussion of a range of marketing issues. Each case is provided with an indicative set of questions which may be useful for individual self-study or for group work and assessments.

- Case 1: Microinsurance
- Case 2: China Merchants Bank: *We are here just for you.*
- Case 3: Liiv
- Case 4: Prudential: international marketing strategy

DOI: 10.4324/9781003398615-11

Case study CS1

Microinsurance

Microinsurance has been defined in various ways by authors, practitioners, regulators, and others. While the term was coined in the late 1990s, some argue that microinsurance already existed in the 19th and 20th centuries under the labels of "industrial insurance", "cooperative insurance", and "mutual insurance". In those days, such terms were synonymous with insurance services catering to lower income workers and small businesses. Notable examples include the "working man's" life insurance policies targeted at factory workers in United States in the 1870s, and, more recently, life insurance sold to Saskatchewan farmers after WWII by a cooperative life insurer initiated in 1945 by the farmers themselves. Today, microinsurance broadly refers to products designed to protect low-income populations and their economic activities in developing countries. Recognising that low insurance penetration is more about access to insurance rather than just income level, the segment has expanded to use the term "inclusive insurance" to describe insurance targeting those without access to insurance at all income levels. The two terms are used interchangeably with inclusive insurance becoming more common.

The number and variety of microinsurance products has increased rapidly since the new millennium following a widespread realisation that insurance services were a vital complement to most other types of poverty alleviation activities. More generally, it is seen to provide access to financial risk protection services for a vast segment of the world's low-income populations that otherwise would not have any. Once bought, it lessens the financial setback following harmful events and thus reduces the number of households spiralling into a new cycle of poverty following such events.

Initially, microinsurance was supplied by relatively few insurers, and not surprisingly, a significant proportion of those were mutual or cooperative based. Commercial companies entering the market for the first time often did not develop new products but merely scaled down their existing ones to a level deemed affordable by this market. This approach did not work well since the modified products remained too complex and were misaligned with the market needs which often differ from those of traditional insurance customers.

In countries such as Bangladesh and Philippines, the gap in demand and supply for suitable products resulted in a proliferation of self-insured programmes within cooperatives, NGOs, MFIs, and other organisations that were already providing other services to the poor. While these programmes were typically built on market-based needs, they generally lacked professional risk management and were embedded with other business activities. Although such programmes were not approved by regulators, they were largely tolerated because of their valuable contribution to an underserved market and with the recognition that existing insurance regulations were unfavourable for microinsurance development. Much more work

DOI: 10.4324/9781003398615-12

needs to be done through organisations such as the Access to Insurance Initiative (a2ii) to assist regulators in creating access to the microinsurance market.

Today, it is more widely understood that microinsurance can only succeed if it covers the insurable risk events that the target market faces, is simple to understand and easy to enrol, is readily accessible by most with minimal restrictions, and provides good financial value. Requirements for sustainability include reliable and sufficient data from the market, technical capacity to monitor and calculate commensurate premium rates, an efficient delivery channel, constant monitoring, and professional insurance management using key performance indicators for monitoring. All of this can be more readily accomplished if insurance risk is transferred to a formal insurer or where microinsurance regulations permit, formalisation and regulation of existing informal programmes.

Since microinsurance products must be purchased, the poorest of the poor cannot afford them. Hence, microinsurance is most suited for those sectors that are able to generate a small annual disposable income for purchasing cover. Occasionally governments and donors provide subsidies in a bid to expand cover to the most needy, but these are mostly temporary.

For those that can afford microinsurance, it is rarely possible to buy complete protection against all risks. Hence choices must be made. A successful product is client focused, in the developmental stages and after implementation, to ensure the product is meeting the clients' needs. This begins with market research and involves soliciting constant feedback from the clients even after the product launch with the aim of establishing: a) the priority risks to be covered through microinsurance; b) the amount of premium that the majority of households can afford; c) the minimum amount of benefit expected; d) priority with regards to which members of the household should be covered; e) effectiveness of the distribution channel and; f) the understanding clients have of insurance, their coverage and how to make a claim.

The effectiveness and cost efficiency of delivery channels are key components to a successful microinsurance product. It is imperative that delivery channels have established access to the target market. The clients must be familiar with the distributor and have a strong level of trust in the delivery channel. Given the high usage of mobile phones, mobile networks have become desired channels by reducing administrative costs, and ability to reach millions of clients. Technology and insurtech have become effective strategies to reduce administrative costs, collect premiums, process claims, complete enrolment and interact with the client. In the process of increasing client retention, value and awareness, providers are keeping in contact with clients through sales and enrolment practices that include some human contact, either face to face or through customer calls in service centres, to provide more information and explanations. SMS messages are also used to maintain contact with the client by providing product information, renewal alerts and even health/crop disease prevention practices.

The risks most commonly covered through microinsurance are premature death of household members, sickness, accident and disability, and destruction of property. Hospital cash products have become a popular product offering for health microinsurance. In 2020, it is estimated that health microinsurance covered the most lives with over 50% of the market, followed by personal accident and life products (see Figure CS1.1).

Agriculture products are becoming increasingly popular and have the potential for protecting low-income of farmers (both land-based and aquatic) and enhancing food security. These products, however, are highly subsidised in all countries to date and this is not likely to change. Weather indexed or parametric-type products which pay based on pre-determined levels of wind speeds, rainfall, or other parameters are technologies being used to advance the development of agriculture, property or disaster (or calamity) products. Parametric

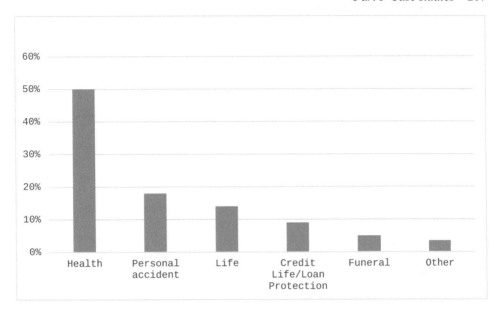

Figure CS1.1 Microinsurance covered lives

Source: Microinsurance Network, The Landscape of Microinsurance 2021[1]

insurance addresses the consequences of climate change and therefore has recently grown in importance as a way to help microinsurance clients. Growth in parametric insurance is expected as more are paying attention to the protection needs of the population impacted by climate change.

To conclude, market potential for microinsurance at this time of writing remains vast. In the Philippines, favourable regulatory development boosted micro-insurance coverage from covering 3 million in 2010 to around 49 million in 2021[2] although micro-insurance premiums accounts for just 3%[3] of the total insurance market[4]. Insurers who have been competing fiercely for a limited upscale market are increasingly venturing into the much greater down market and while this is challenging, these companies are gaining new learnings and skills such as innovative product development, more efficient delivery through alternative channels, and so on in order to succeed. These gains carry over into their traditional lines of business which results in improved performance and fresh advantages in their traditional markets.

Denis Garand FSA, FCIA, John Wipf, Donna Swiderek

Case study questions

1. Which groups within your own country could benefit from access to micro-insurance?
2. What sort of needs would they have and what kind of insurance products would be of benefit to them?
3. What special safeguards would be necessary to ensure they would be treated fairly and not likely to suffer any detriment?
4. What challenges do you think might apply to the regulation of micro-insurance in your country?
5. How is the marketing mix used in the microinsurance market?

Case study CS2

China Merchants Bank: *We are here just for you.*

The combination of government-instigated reform and a growth in domestic and international competition has transformed the banking sector in China over the past 30 years. The first policy initiatives to liberalise the Chinese economy appeared in 1978 and since then, the banking system has experienced three main phases of reform. During the first stage (1978 to 1993), the mono-bank system was dismantled and the four state-owned commercial banks (SOCBs) were established as independent entities (Bank of China [BoC], China Construction Bank [CCB], Agricultural Bank of China [ABC] and Industrial and Commercial Bank of China [ICBC]). In the second stage (1994 to 2000), the SOCBs transitioned to become more independent and the numbers of joint-stock and commercial banks expanded. During the third stage of reform (post-2001), further liberalisation was put in place as China worked towards and finally joined the World Trade Organisation (WTO), an important milestone in the process of opening up the country's financial markets.

One of the Chinese financial system's most visible features is that it is dominated by the banking sector. According to statistics from the China Banking Regulatory Commission (CBRC), in 2010, the banking system included two policy banks and the China Development Bank, five large commercial banks, 12 joint-stock commercial banks, 147 city commercial banks, 85 rural commercial banks and 40 locally incorporated foreign bank subsidiaries. Altogether, there were 3,769 banking institutions with approximately 196,000 outlets and 2.9m employees in China's banking sector. In 2023, the number of banks had increased to 4,561 with the growth essentially coming from the smaller banks. The "Big 4" State owned Commercial banks (Industrial and Commercial Bank of China, Bank of China, China Construction Bank and Agricultural Bank of China) dominate the banking sector and are in the top 4 positions of "The Bankers" global ranking. Although their market share has been decreasing year by year, they still hold a dominant position, although in an increasingly challenging market. And they are not alone – half of the top twenty largest Banks globally are Chinese including China Merchants Bank, Postal Savings Bank, Industrial Bank, Shanghai Pudong Development Bank and China Citic Bank. Figure CS2.1 shows the growth in the number of banking institutions in China between 2009 and 2023.

Traditionally, Chinese banks had lent mainly to large, mostly state-owned enterprises. While this group continues to dominate, target customers have increasingly included smaller and private enterprises as well as retail consumers. Indeed, retail banking is becoming a major growth area. As capital markets develop and provide an increasingly large proportion of corporate financial needs, the retail market is becoming more and more important to the banks. From 2000 to 2004, for example, it is estimated that retail banking grew around 40% per year; by 2020, annual growth rates were closer to 10% and forecasts for the remainder of

DOI: 10.4324/9781003398615-13

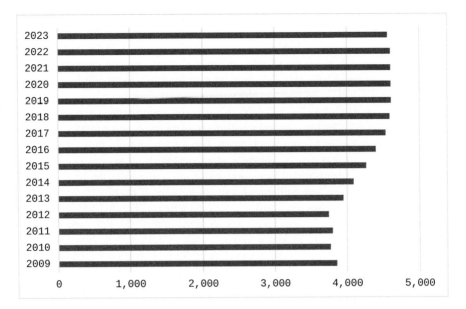

Figure CS2.1 Number of banking institutions in China

the 2020s suggest a further slowing in growth to around 5%. And while this is a significant slowdown, it still represents an attractive market.

In China, we see the combination of one of the highest savings rates in the world and a rapidly developing and increasingly sophisticated middle class; together these create significant demand for a range of financial services. There are a variety of different growth opportunities. For example, while markets in the main Tier 1 cities are well developed, there is thought to be considerable potential in the Tier 2 cities which, increasingly, are home to a growing number of affluent consumers. And the rural market offers perhaps even more dramatic potential in the longer term; a large proportion of the Chinese population is still based in rural areas and the dominantly cash economy presents real opportunities for market development. There are also growth opportunities in relation to product holdings. For example, Statista.com reports that the number of credit cards in China has increased from around 50m in 2006 to around 800m in 2021. In the debit card market, holdings were reported at over 8 billion in 2022 suggesting that each individual was holding an average of 5 cards.

The CMB approach

Following China's entry into the WTO and the end of the five-year transitional period, competition in the domestic market intensified as access for foreign banks became so much easier. While retail banking continued to be dominated by the four major SOCBs with their extensive branch networks, some of the more agile privately owned banks were able to establish strong challenger positions in a rapidly growing marketplace. One such bank was China Merchants Bank (CMB). CMB, China's first joint-stock commercial bank, was established in 1987 in Shenzhen and was subsequently listed on the Shanghai Stock Exchange in 2002. From its origins as a small bank with one branch, 30 employees and a capital of around 100m yuan, CMB has grown to rank among the world's top 100 banks and in 2016 it was named as China's Bank of the Year. In 2023 it was listed as the 11th largest bank in the world and the

5th largest in China with a 7% share of the market according to Statista.com. Market research suggests that CMB is relatively more popular with millennial customers, customers living in mega cities and customers with medium household income. CMB's income has been growing, partly through increases in interest-earning assets, interest margins and interest spreads, but also because of a growth in non-interest income (effectively fees) from credit cards, certain banking products and wealth management services.

CMB argues that its willingness to adopt effective and appropriate business practices has been key to its success. The bank has established a modern governance structure with a clear separation of ownership and control and clearly specified responsibilities for the Board of Directors, the Board of Supervisors and the management team. It has invested heavily in IT and systems, creating a bank-wide IT platform which allowed it to be the first Chinese bank to offer nationwide deposit and withdrawal and real-time funds transfer. With respect to the management of its human resource, CMB was to break with tradition in China and abolish the "three-guarantee mechanism" (guaranteed job, guaranteed position and guaranteed salary). This was replaced with a more adaptable system which permitted promotion or demotion on the basis of ability, flexible remuneration and allowed for employees to be dismissed.

CMB has been identified as one of a small number of "world-class" Chinese brands and is arguably the most influential commercial bank brand in China. Its achievements have been recognised with a string of awards from the press including the *Financial Times* and *Euromoney*:

- Best Commercial Bank of China,
- Best Retail Bank in China,
- Best Private Bank in China,
- China's Best Custody Specialist.

The strategic development of CMB has been driven by a focus on the outcomes of "Profit, Quality, Scale" and underpinned by certain core values including "Service, Innovation and Stability". Indeed, the Wall Street Journal's "Asia 200" survey in 2009 highlighted the strength of CMB's financial and corporate reputation, its high-quality services and its innovativeness in responding to customer needs. Although it services both retail and corporate markets, CMB's business places a particular emphasis on the retail sector and in 2010 this accounted for around one-third of its total lending. Estimates suggested that CMB had around 25% of the personal consumer finance market in China. In addition, non-interest income was expanding through growth in credit card , wealth management, personal banking and insurance services.

One of CMB's earliest innovations was the multifunction All-in-One Card which provided a range of banking services via a single card and rapidly become one of the most popular bank cards in China. A range of modifications has subsequently enhanced the card and it now offers a current account and deposit facilities in multiple currencies, telephone and online banking, foreign exchange trading, bill payment, self-service loan applications and mobile phone top-ups. The related online banking platform – All-in-One.Net – was China's first such service. Other significant innovations include the first dual-currency credit card, the launch of its Sunflower VIP Platinum card and the development of China's first full private banking service. Indeed, its success in this area has earned it the title of "Best Private Bank" in China.

In a subsequent innovation, CMB partnered with the Chinese equivalent of Facebook – RenRen to launch a co-branded credit card. This new card takes advantage specifically of the

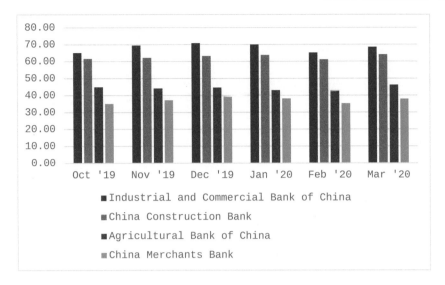

Figure CS2.2 Numbers of mobile banking app users (millions)

localisation features offered by the social network. Card holders who choose to "check-in" from selected locations will be eligible for promotional offers from CMB merchants located nearby. The card also includes a loyalty programme with both CMB and RenRen offering customer specific benefits.

In 2017, China Merchants Bank was recognised in the Asian Banker Technology awards for is mobile banking app which offered a range of tailored services and enhanced customer experience. The app – available via Apple and Android also offered improved security. And while the big four banks continue to dominate mobile banking in China, as Figure CS2.2 shows, CMB has built a significant market share.

Alongside product innovation, CMB has been noted for its willingness to pioneer online banking services. As a relatively new bank, CMB's branch network was limited compared to those of the major SOCBs. In 2010, it reported only 82 branches and 763 sub-branches in 96 cities. Consequently, as part of its growth strategy, CMB concentrated on trying to offset this potential disadvantage by developing alternative delivery channels (online, ATM, telephone). As an unexpected bonus the development of these alternative delivery channels also enabled CMB to attract a relatively large number of high-value customers who appreciated the greater convenience that such channels offered. By the first half of 2011, almost half of general over-the-counter services and around 80% of retail banking transactions were completed either online or by telephone. And by the end of that same year, CMB's mobile banking platform had over four million users. At the same time, CMB recognised the need to invest in developing its physical presence and by 2022 it had some 1800 branches including an international presence to support its wealth management business.

Case study sources:

CMB Company Information (undated), www.english.cmbchina.com.
Wall Street Journal. (2009). http://online.wsj.com/article/SB125078753306946803.html.
www.thebanker.com/China-s-banks-forced-to-learn-new-operational-rules-1688716621
www.statistia.com

Case study questions

1. Critically evaluate CMB's marketing strategy to date.
2. What options are available for CMB to continue its growth in the future?
3. What are the challenges for a bank operating at this size and scale? How can it sustain a high level of innovation?
4. Explore CMB's digital presence – how well does it work and how difficult is it to under-take this evaluation if you do not understand Chinese?

Case study CS3

Liiv

In 2016, Interbrand helped KB Financial Group (based and operating in South Korea) launch a mobile financial platform designed to support customers in every aspect of their financial lives. As the top brand in traditional banking, KB was seeking to address the challenges posed by players venturing into the arena from the world of information technology, chiefly Kakao and Toss.

Daunting as it might have been, the ambition was also straightforward: to replicate KB's footprint in the fintech sector. The original press release helps give a flavour of the product: "The application provides users with the calendar service so they can easily link their transactions with their daily schedule. Users can create a club and share the club's meeting schedule, store important dates like birthdays and a dues ledger with other members. Also, users can purchase mobile gift certificates and use the application as a travel card. Through its 'go Dutch' function, users can easily split bills and transfer money... the application also has a function for foreign exchange, allowing users to change currencies when the rate is favourable for them".

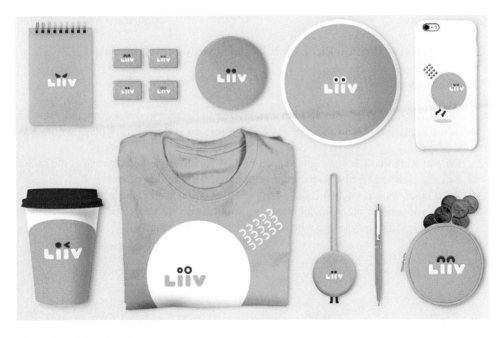

Figure CS3.1 Liiv brand appearance

DOI: 10.4324/9781003398615-14

The KB brand's legacy within the arena was clearly a blessing – but also a curse. The strategy to overcome this was to avoid stretching the brand into this new competitive space, but rather to create a new brand equipped to become the most relevant in its space to the younger generations – MZ (millennials and GenZ). Winning this bet would be the most promising path to fulfil the ambition.

Interbrand worked across three phases:

1. Diagnosis and Strategy,
2. Verbal and Visual Identity,
3. Moves.

Uzin Hwang and Eunice Min, respectively Chief Creative Officer and Chief Contents Officer of Interbrand's Seoul office, recall: "The original value proposition was around 'living in fintech'. The issue, however, was that consumers were having trouble understanding what that actually meant and what it could do for them. And with plenty of mobile and digital platforms, we really had to convey the idea that this was about making things easier and more convenient. This is why our Trajectory was to build GenMZ'z 'Life Finance Platform'".

That trajectory inspired the new brand's name, Liiv – which was acronymised at launch as encompassing the ideas of "life styling, integrated, interesting and valuable". The visual system was an engaging take on the world of e-games and social media – a deliberate way of capturing the eyes, minds and hearts of the younger generations. What however brought the trajectory to life was an intentional use of moves – from enrolling as ambassadors then pop sensation and teen idols all-girl band I.O.I. to making the Liiv Concert an annual ritual, all the way to building proprietary emoticons and a free chat app.

"This is an example of how our approach, involving the right strategy, the right design and the right moves build brands that would otherwise cost billions of dollars to launch," Hwang and Min observe.

Case study source: Manfredi Ricca, Global Chief Strategy Officer, Interbrand

Case study questions

1. Take some time to research KB Financial Group and, thereby, develop an understanding of the organisation's business strategy. What role do you think Liiv plays within KB's strategy?
2. Do you think that KB was right to position Liiv as a lifestyle brand aimed at the millennial and GenZ segments? What arguments support your point of view?
3. What other options might KB have explored to position itself in the fintech marketplace?
4. When you look at other fintech banks in South Korea do you consider that Liiv has a clear competitive advantage with its approach to positioning?

Case study CS4

Prudential: international marketing strategy

Prudential Plc was founded in London in 1848 to provide loans and savings options for working and professional people. Its name and brand visuals come from "prudence" which, in Graeco-Roman tradition, is one of the four cardinal virtues: Prudence, Justice, Fortitude and Temperance. If something is described as prudent it is generally interpreted as being wise, based on foresight, intelligence and memory and hence grounded in an awareness of the past, present and future – exactly the image that Prudential wished to project. Its logo incorporates a Graeco-Roman head with the company name alongside in a distinctive and easily recognised red font.

In 1854 Prudential pioneered a new type of insurance, targeted to working class customers, sold at a premium of typically a penny a month with premiums collected by sales staff who went out to their clients' homes. So significant was the impact of the distribution innovation that the premium collectors were immortalised in popular culture as "the man from the Pru" which was eventually to become an integral component of advertising for a number of years. The acquisition of several key competitors in the 1860s helped to establish Prudential as the UK's leading life company. Its growth continued over the years with moves into related financial services including general insurance in 1919 and pensions in 1929. Growth continued through a mix of acquisition and organic development. In the UK, key acquisitions included Scottish Amicable and M&G.

Prudential's international strategy dates back to the period just after the First World War. In 1921, Prudential established an agency in France, then in India in 1923 and thereafter in Canada, Malta, Africa, Australia, the Middle East and Malaya. Jackson Life was acquired in 1994 to give the company a position in the US market while Prudential Asia was set up in 1996 to enable Prudential to significantly grow the business that had dated back to its establishment of overseas offices in Malaysia and Singapore. It is listed on the stock exchanges of Hong Kong, Singapore, London and New York.

In 2016 Prudential focused on the following areas

- Prudential Corporation Asia – where it had businesses in Hong Kong, Taiwan, Japan, South Korea, Singapore, Malaysia, Philippines, Thailand, Vietnam and Indonesia and a range of joint ventures including ICICI Prudential in India and CITIC Prudential Life in China.
- Prudential Africa – which expanded through the acquisitions of Express Life, the Ghanaian life insurer in 2013 and subsequently Shield Assurance of Kenya. Both were rebranded under the Prudential name. Prudential also operated in Uganda and Zambia.

DOI: 10.4324/9781003398615-15

- Eastspring Investments, focusing on asset management across 10 Asian markets serving both business and retail clients. It has over $140bn in funds under management.
- M&G – an asset management company with over £240bn of assets under management. M&G offers both investment management and retail fund management and is the UK's second largest provider.
- Jackson National Life Insurance Company – one of the US's largest life insurers which it purchased in 1986.

In 2017, Prudential demerged M&G Prudential and in 2020 it parted company with Jackson, thus sharpening its focus on Asia and Africa, both of which were identified as highly attractive collections of markets because of their significant savings and protection gaps. These two regions give Prudential access to a total population of around 4 billion people.

Prudential currently operates in 16 countries in Asia and 8 in Africa, serving 18 million customers in total. The company's largest life insurance businesses are in Mainland China, Hong Kong, Indonesia, Malaysia and Singapore. In Malaysia, Prudential, via its joint venture with Bank Simpanan Nasional is one of the country's largest providers of Islamic insurance products (Takaful) and in 2022 the company launched a standalone Shari'ah compliant insurer in Indonesia. In both Asia and Africa, Prudential relies on an integrated multi-channel distribution strategy and the company boasts more than 120,000 active agents and more than 200 bancassurance partners with access to over 27000 branches.

Asia has a growing and increasingly affluent middle class, estimated to be about half of the middle class globally in 2020. Insurance penetration levels are still relatively low and Prudential has identified considerable market potential for savings, protection and health products. Spending on life insurance may have grown quite significantly in the past decade but is still well below levels in the UK and the US.

Africa is expected to have a population close to a billion in 20 years' time and the levels of penetration for insurance and savings products are particularly low on average (although with considerable variation across markets). Prudential has grown largely by acquisition and now serves eight markets with a population of almost 400 million.

Core to the Prudential marketing strategy is the aspiration to be seen as a trusted partner for its customers. The company aims to deliver this through enhanced understanding of customer needs built around life stage segmentation. In turn this should enable the development of innovative and accessible product solutions for a broad market in the areas of health, well-being and wealth. The company plans to further develop its digital activities and is building a digital platform to support end-to-end customer journeys. Customer engagement will be delivered through both an expansion in social media and Prudential's partnership eco system to ensure personalised customer engagement. Prudential's aim is to secure significant growth in customer acquisition and retention given that the markets in which it operates have significant long-term growth potential. Distribution plays a key role in delivering to this ambition. Prudential's approach has two core components – its extensive agency network and its strategic partners in bancassurance.

Prudential is a leader in agency-based distribution and it looks to support agents to ensure that they are able to deliver the desired level of customer engagement. A franchise model helps to attract and retain the best agency talent and they are supported by Prudential's agency platform – PruForce – to enable them to deliver a positive customer experience.

Prudential is also a leading Bancassurance partner and its ambition is to be the bank partner of choice across the markets it serves. Given the significance of cross selling and the extent to which its bank partner has a broad based customer view, Prudential is emphasising the development of a digitally enabled model to help them (and their partner banks) reach underserved markets.

On its website, Prudential summarises its overarching approach as follows:

> **Our purpose** is to be partners for every life and protectors for every future. At Prudential, it is our mission to be the most trusted partner and protector for this generation and generations to come, by providing simple and accessible financial and health solutions.

> **Our strategy** comprises of three strategic pillars: enhancing customer experiences, powering our distribution with technology and transforming our health business model. We will execute this strategy with renewed focus and discipline using three group-wide enablers: open-architecture technology platform; engaged people and high-performance culture and wealth and investments capabilities. Our approach will ensure we're accelerating value for our employees, customers, shareholders and communities.
>
> (https://www.prudentialplc.com/en/about-us/our-company)

Case study sources: www.prudential.co.uk/, www.prudential.co.uk/~/media/Files/P/Prudential-Corp/business-presentations/2016/Group-Strategy-and-Performance.pdf, www.prudentialplc.com/~/media/Files/P/Prudential-V13/reports/2022/prudential-fact-sheet-2022a.pdf.

Case study questions

1. To what extent do you think Yip's drivers of globalisation help to understand the evolution of insurance globally?
2. How would you characterise Prudential's approach to international markets?
3. What might Prudential focus its future growth plans on given its current country and product coverage?
4. What role do you think ESG considerations could or should play in Prudential's international marketing?

Part II
Customer acquisition

9 Customer acquisition and the marketing mix

Learning objectives

At the end of this chapter, you should be able to:

1. Understand the relationship between marketing strategy and the marketing mix,
2. Understand the role played by the marketing mix in attracting new customers to the firm,
3. Understand the challenges associated with developing a financial services marketing mix,
4. Appreciate the ways in which the digital world is impacting upon the use of the marketing mix,
5. Understand some of the ethical considerations in the management of the marketing mix.

9.1 Introduction

Discussions of marketing have traditionally focused attention on how to attract new customers – a process typically described as customer acquisition. Increasingly, it has been recognised that the retention of existing customers may be every bit as important as the acquisition of new ones. The elements of marketing used for acquisition and retention are in many respects very similar, but the ways in which they are used can be quite different. In Part II of this text we focus upon aspects of marketing management which are particularly concerned with the acquisition of new customers. Specifically, we focus on the well-established concept of the marketing mix which is introduced in this chapter and explored in more detail in the following chapters.

9.2 The marketing mix

The marketing mix is a term used to describe the marketing tools that a manager controls. Managers must make decisions about these different tools to create a clear competitive position in the market that is consistent with the nature of the overall marketing strategy. By convention, the tools that make up the marketing mix are often referred to as the 4Ps – product, price, promotion and place – although in services marketing this is often extended to 7Ps

DOI: 10.4324/9781003398615-17

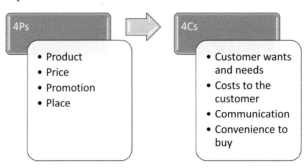

Figure 9.1 Translating the 4Ps into the 4Cs

Source: Lauterborn, R. (1990). New marketing litany: Four Ps pass: C-Words take over, *Advertising Age*, 61(41), p. 26

with the addition of people, process and physical evidence. However, it is often suggested that the 4P paradigm represents a view of the marketing mix that is unduly product focused with a bias towards tangible products. Admittedly, the augmentation of the 4Ps to the 7Ps by Booms and Bitner (1981) by the inclusion of people, process, and physical evidence represented a valuable attempt at reflecting the particular characteristics associated with marketing services as opposed to tangible products. Nevertheless, this still does not seem to reflect the particular challenges posed by marketing financial services. It is also perhaps not the best way of reflecting how the marketing mix is being impacted upon by the digital world and neither does it address contemporary thinking regarding customer value and customer experience. Writing in *Advertising Age*, Lauterborn (1990) had similar misgivings about the 4Ps and proposed, instead, the 4CS, namely: customer needs and wants, cost to the customer, convenience, communication. They read across from the 4Ps as follows (see Figure 9.1):

Lauterborn contends that the 4Ps are unduly producer, or supply-side, focused and pay insufficient attention to the demand side, i.e. the customer. To quote from Lauterborn's original article in *Advertising Age*:

> Forget product. Study Consumer wants and needs. . . . Forget price. Understand the consumer's cost to satisfy that want or need. . . . Forget place. Think convenience to buy. . . . Forget promotion. The word is communication. All good advertising creates a dialogue.
>
> (p26)

Lauterborn recognised that *place* was perhaps more about the ease with which a product provider can gain access to customers and with what would be most convenient for customers. It is a term chosen perhaps more in the interest of alliteration than accuracy and relevance to marketers in the digital age. Moreover, Lauterborn was very prescient when he asserted the need for promotion to be replaced by communication, and by communication that involves a dialogue between provider and customer. This is something that the functionality afforded by digital has now made a reality as social media and other forms of digital communication allow for genuine engagement between product providers and their customers and, indeed, the wider marketplace.

In the contemporary world of digital and disrupters, the additional 3Ps of Booms and Bitner (people, processes, and physical evidence) are less additional stand-alone components of a marketing mix for services than aspects of the core 4Cs. For example, people are often a core aspect of how *customer wants and needs* are satisfied in financial services. Similarly, people are also vital in many parts of the processes associated with *convenience to buy*. It can also be argued that whereas the 4Ps are highly pertinent in the context of new customer acquisition, they are somewhat less useful as a concept when considering the marketing mix for the ongoing delivery of customer service. Therefore, in this book, we have sought to adapt Lauterborn's 4Cs to devise an umbrella conceptual approach to the marketing mix for financial services that we consider best reflects the characteristics of this particular commercial sector as well as digital developments and the likely direction of travel over the strategic time horizon. And so, we propose a marketing mix for financial services we are calling the 2P2C mix, and it comprises:

Product and Consumer needs
Price and Cost to the Consumer
Convenience and Distribution
Communication and Promotion.

These four components of the marketing mix may lack the alliterative attractions of the 4Ps or 4Cs but we believe it best reflects the imperative of aligning the synergistic interests of both the supply and demand sides of this particular market.

It is through the marketing mix that strategy takes practical effect. In other words, the marketing mix is the practical expression of the marketing strategy. Consumers have little or no knowledge of, or interest in, strategy. What concerns them is the utility they experience from the contact they have with the marketing mix. It is important to recognise that decisions about the marketing mix have both strategic and tactical dimensions. The strategic dimension of the marketing mix is primarily concerned with decisions about the relative importance of the different elements it comprises. For example, communication and promotion, and particularly television advertising, may play an important role in the marketing mix for many retail financial services, but may be almost irrelevant for specialised corporate financial services. Equally, a mass market financial service such as a standard bank account or mortgage will need a distribution system that makes it easily available (convenient) to a large proportion of the population, whereas a highly specialised product can rely on a far more selective system of distribution. In contrast, the tactical dimension of the marketing mix is concerned with specific decisions about the individual marketing tools. Thus, for example, once a decision has been taken about the general approach to pricing (e.g. premium pricing), a specific decision is required regarding the actual price to be set.

Since the start of this new millennium we have seen momentous changes to the nature of the marketing mix owing to the development of the internet's functionality and the emergence and rapid development of digital marketing, and which, for the rest of this book, we will refer to simply as *digital*. Digital is a true game-changer which is having an enormous impact at both the strategic and tactical level. Arguably it is the most radical development that the world of business has ever encountered and its impact must not be underestimated. Indeed, the unprecedented ways in which technology is impacting on every aspect of contemporary life has been dubbed the Fourth Industrial Revolution. Klaus Schwab, Chairman of the World Economic Forum writing on the 11 October 2016 observes:

> Unprecedented . . . advances in artificial intelligence, robotics, the internet of things, . . . quantum computing and others are redefining industries, blurring traditional boundaries, and creating new opportunities. We have dubbed this the Fourth Industrial Revolution, and it is fundamentally changing the way we live, work and relate to one another.[1]

In the early days of digital, in the late 1990s, it was seen as an innovative addition to the array of channels that marketers could use to reach customers, on a par with the introduction of telephone-based forms of distribution such as telephone banking that had emerged a decade earlier. Given the then state of functionality, technical issues such as narrow bandwidth and limitations of hardware at that time, such a viewpoint was reasonable. It is also fair to say that consumer competence in using this emerging technology and capability was in its infancy. However, advances in software, hardware, information and communication technology(ICT) architecture and consumer competence have developed at an unprecedented pace. Consider the fact that when the first edition of this book was published just back in 2007 aggregator sites (price-comparison sites) were just emerging, social networking was in its infancy, and the iPhone and iPad had yet to appear in the marketplace. The introduction and adoption of these and other manifestations of the digital world have been truly breathtaking. Of particular note is the speed with which the adoption of new forms of digital experience by consumers seems to be accelerating. According to Rohit Shewale of DemandSage[2],ChatGPT already has more than 100 million users. In fact, so fast has been its adoption that it managed to gain 1 million users in its first five days following its launch in November 2022. Total page visits have already exceeded 10 billion with 88% of traffic being direct-to-site and 4.22% directed from social media platforms. Roughly 60% of users are male and 40% female. General public awareness of ChatGPT has also grown dramatically, indeed, as of May 2023 some 58% of US adults claim to be familiar with it according to Pew Research Centre. That's all remarkable given that Facebook took about one year to get to one million users, X (Twitter) almost two years, and Netflix more than three and a half years.

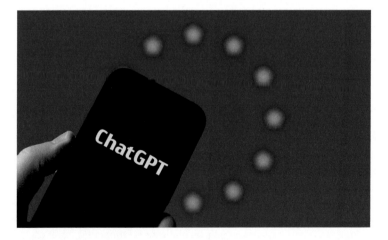

Figure 9.2 ChatGPT revolutionising AI

Given what we now know about the impact of digital on consumer behaviour, and its possible potential, it would be foolish merely to view it prosaically as just another channel alongside, say, the branch, telephone and direct sales force. Indeed, it requires us to think radically not only about the structures of marketing functions but also about the implications of digital for the way a business is organised and structured. As commented earlier, new business models are emerging to a growing degree based upon what are termed "disruptive technologies".

Thus, the purpose of this chapter is to provide an overview of the marketing mix for financial services, paying particular attention to the way in which it may be used for customer acquisition. The four core components of the marketing mix are discussed more fully in the following chapters. The chapter begins with a brief discussion of short-term, annual marketing planning, to set a context for discussion of the mix elements. Section 9.3 explores some of the core issues associated with managing the marketing mix while Section 9.4 considers the components of the financial services marketing mx in a little more detail. The role of the marketing mix in relation to customer acquisition in financial services is covered in Section 9.5, and Section 9.6 explores some of the broader challenges and opportunities arising from digital developments. The chapter closes with a discussion of some of the ethical dimensions of customer acquisition,

---

Progress check

- The marketing mix is the means by which customers experience a company or product.
- Interaction between provider and customer results in how a customer receives value, ie: the mix is about delivering value and utility.

9.3 Short-term marketing planning

In Chapter 4 we considered strategic marketing planning and recognised that its primary role is to set direction over the medium to long term, typically three to five years. It is upon the platform of the strategic marketing plan that major policy decisions are made such as selecting which segments are to be served and establishing how the organisation will differentiate itself in delivering value to customers and thus achieve competitive advantage. To complement the strategic marketing plan, best practice dictates that an organisation should have an "annual marketing plan". If the strategic marketing plan is about the setting of long-term direction and the determination of competitive advantage, the annual marking plan is about achieving a joined-up and coordinated approach to achieving short-term marketing objectives.

In the way that there is no universally agreed process and template for strategic marketing planning, there is no such model for the annual marketing plan. However, it is important that there is consistency between a given organisation's strategic and annual marketing plans. Moreover, it is important that organisations that comprise a number of individual strategic business units (SBUs) or business lines adopt a common approach to marketing planning. For example, a broad-based financial services provider such as HSBC could choose to, say, produce an annual marketing plan for its range of mortgage and property finance products. This could be quite separate from, for example, its pension product range. Whilst each of these two product groups will be guided by the overall corporate positioning statement of being"the world's local bank", a brand positioning statement it adopted in 2002, they nonetheless operate in quite distinct marketplaces. Therefore, each will have quite different requirements in respect of the market specific objectives that they specify, the elements that need to be considered when analysing the marketing environment and the characteristics of the segments that they identify and target. For example, the competitor set that applies to pensions products will vary greatly to that of the mortgage area. This is an important point as there are real dangers of conducting a marketing plan at too aggregate a level. There are no straightforward solutions to this difficulty other than to say that all organisations must approach the issue in a way that best suits their particular circumstances such as product range, scope and organisational structure.

The conduct of the annual marketing plan comprises two components, namely the process and the written plan itself. It must be borne in mind that there should not be a strict one-size-fits-all approach to the annual marketing plan. Rather, it should be tailored to suit the particular characteristics of any given organisation. However, the following model, Figure 9.3, represents a sound core structure for the ultimate output of the planning process.

The plan should make clear where responsibility and accountability lies for marketing objectives and the successful completion of marketing mix activities. Ownership should be made clear and unambiguous and sole ownership for delivery should always be sought. It is common to encounter a plethora of shared accountabilities which result in an unclear sense of ownership. Indeed, well-defined accountability is a necessary prerequisite of an appropriate appraisal system and performance review. This section of the plan can also be used to summarise the array of key performance indicators (KPIs) that arise from the marketing mix activities.

In the discussion of strategic marketing planning in Chapter 4, explicit reference was made to internal communication. The lack of sufficient emphasis upon this issue is a major contributory factor to the failure of marketing plans to achieve their objectives. It is very rare for a marketing objective in the field of financial services to be accomplished without the

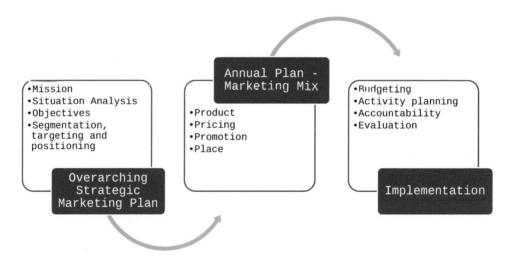

Figure 9.3 Annual marketing plan

involvement of people in other functions. In the case of an insurance company there may be a sales force to consider, a building society must take care to inform branch staff, and even for a digital provider there will be people involved in the provision of service. In all types of financial services companies it is vital that administration staff are made fully aware of marketing activities that will impact upon their work. Similarly, IT and business systems colleagues need to know how plans for new products or new product features should be factored into their own functional plans.

A central component of any annual marketing plan will be decisions about the marketing mix and details about how key marketing variables will be managed and controlled. The remainder of this chapter will explore, in more detail, the concept of the mix as it applies in financial services.

9.4 The role of the financial services marketing mix

It is vital to grasp the point that the marketing mix is what determines the customer experience. Thus, it is the role of the mix to deliver customer value and satisfaction, and it should result in a stream of margin that delivers shareholder value. A purchase decision is made by the consumer based on the overall service offer and how well this meets their needs. A service offer can simply be deconstructed into the elements of customer benefits, charges, communication and channels (and even people, process and physical evidence) and these form the basis of the marketing mix. Marketing managers make decisions about these variables to enable them to implement a marketing strategy – in particular, they use these variables to create a clear market position and demonstrate how their product meets consumer needs in the target market. This process is shown in Figure 9.4.

The remaining chapters in Part II address in detail those aspects of the mix that are instrumental in acquiring new customers. It must be borne in mind that the same elements of the mix also have a part to play in the retention of customers, and the nature of the mix in this context will form the focus for Part III.

Each chosen target customer segment should be the subject of a tailored marketing mix. Unless the organisation has chosen to follow an undifferentiated strategy, the mix must be adjusted to suit the characteristics of each individual segment. In addition to segmentation,

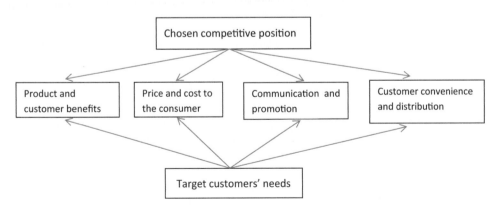

Figure 9.4 Customer needs and the marketing mix

the strategy will identify the basis of the company's competitive advantage. The chosen form of competitive advantage provides a reference point for the marketing mix designed for each target segment. Thus, there must be consistency in the design of segment-specific mix to ensure that the core competitive advantage is in evidence across the employed range of mix. All elements of the marketing mix must be designed, presented and delivered in ways that are mutually reinforcing and faithfully reflect the company's chosen basis for differentiation.

In practice, there are a range of different marketing tools that marketing managers can use. Thus, when we refer to the idea of 2C2Ps it is necessary to remember that each element encompasses a range of different marketing tools. Some examples of these are as follows:

- Product and consumer benefits: includes range of products offered, features, brand, quality, packaging, warranties, terms and conditions, the processes that deliver customer value;
- Price and cost to the consumer: includes product charges, listed prices, discounts, payment periods, credit terms;
- Communication and promotion: includes all forms advertising and social media, personal selling, sales promotion, publicity, public relations, other forms of physical evidence that provide some sense of tangibility;
- Consumer convenience and distribution: includes channels of distribution, location, access (opening hours), the people who deliver service features.

In managing the marketing mix, we should note that each decision about a particular tool will send a message to consumers. A high price, for example, may be interpreted to mean high quality. A limited number of outlets for a product or service may imply that it is exclusive and so too might advertising in expensive magazines with limited circulation. Thus, if the marketing mix is to be used to create the organisation's desired competitive position there are two key requirements:

- **Consistency with position**
  The decisions about each mix element must be consistent with the position that has been chosen. Thus, for example, when Maybank decided to promote a youthful lifestyle image in Malaysia, it supported that decision with a major promotional event that included a live band, promotional offers for mobile phones and a competition with a VW Beetle as the major prize. These were all activities that were seen as consistent with a youthful image. If the same event had included a performance by a string quartet and a Volvo as the competition prize, many consumers would have found this inconsistent with the image being portrayed and the promotional event would have been much less successful.
- **Synergy from mix elements**
  As well as ensuring that an element of the mix is consistent with the chosen position, it is also important to ensure that all the mix elements are consistent with each other. This is important because each element of the mix presents customers with a very clear message about the organisation and its products and services. There are very real synergies generated when each element of the mix conveys the same message to consumers. Equally, if elements of the mix send different messages then consumers may be confused. For example, the American Express Platinum charge card is associated with high income consumers and symbolises prestige and success. It is the fact that it is

exclusive that makes it attractive. A press campaign in mass market media is likely to be perceived as being in conflict with the desired position for the product. In contrast, more tailored promotion in partnership with exclusive hotels and restaurants and advertising in high-end magazines would serve to reinforce the association with prestige and success.

Thus, an effective marketing mix must aim for consistency and synergy – consistency with strategic position and synergy from the individual elements. Individual elements of the mix should not be viewed in isolation; constant cross-referencing is essential to ensure consistency with other elements in the mix.

 Stop and think?

What are the limitations of the 4Ps for financial services?

Why is the 2P2C model better suited to financial services providers?

What is the relationship between the strategic marketing plan and the annual marketing plan?

9.5 The financial services marketing mix: key issues

In Chapter 3 the distinguishing features of financial services were identified and their marketing implications discussed. The main differences between financial services and physical goods were listed as:

- Intangibility – financial services have no physical form and are often complex and difficult to understand;
- Inseparability – financial services are produced and consumed simultaneously, they cannot be stored and there needs to be significant interaction between customer and supplier;
- Heterogeneity – the quality of financial services is highly variable because of differences between consumers and a heavy dependence on people to provide the service;
- Perishability – services cannot be inventoried, they have to be produced on demand.

To address intangibility, marketing activities might consider:

- Making the service more tangible by providing consumers with some physical evidence (or at least a tangible image),
- Building trust and confidence through the people that help deliver the service.

To address inseparability, marketing activities might consider:

- Training to ensure that staff are friendly and responsive,
- Developing processes for service delivery that are customer oriented.

Figure 9.5 Brank branches give tangibility to an intangible product

Source: "PayPal employee shuttle" by Richard Masoner / Cyclelicious licensed under CC BY-SA 2.0

To address heterogeneity, marketing activities might consider:

- Standardising service delivery processes,
- Managing and training staff to encourage a high and consistent level of quality.

To address perishability, marketing activities might consider:

- Automating services features via processes for remote access,
- Managing demand through careful use of staff rosters or by using special price mechanisms.

Thus, the provision of physical evidence, staff management (people) and the systems for delivering service (process) are all likely to be important elements of marketing decision-making for financial services. This led Booms and Bitner in 1981 to propose that people, processes and physical evidence should be added to the traditional 4P framework to create what is termed the extended marketing mix (7Ps). The remainder of Part II will be structured around the 2P2C approach to the marketing mix (product and consumer needs, price and cost to the consumer, communication and promotion, consumer convenience and distribution), but a brief description of the elements of the extended marketing mix that Booms and Bitner posited is provided below in sections 9.5.1–9.5.3.

9.5.1 Process

Process is concerned with the way in which the service is delivered, including business policies for service provision, procedures, the degree of customisation, etc. There are several reasons why process is important. First, the heterogeneity of services raises the issues of quality management and control. Second, inseparability suggests that the process of pro-viding the service may be highly visible to the consumer and will need to be flexible enough to accommodate potential demand variations. Third, the intangibility of services means that the process by which the service is provided will often be an important influence on the con-sumers' assessment of service quality. Given that "process" focuses on the way things are done, then in the 2P2C approach to the marketing mix, process is effectively a component of "customer convenience and distribution" as well as having some overlap with "price and customer costs".

In developing distribution systems for financial services, the intangible nature of the product means that there is nothing physical to supply to the consumer; the consumer is paying only for a bundle of benefits and the delivery process will need to emphasise these benefits. Furthermore, the variability of service quality leads to pressure for automation in service delivery wherever possible, something that is becoming increasingly possible with digital developments. Even apparently complex services such as financial advice are being transformed because of developments in artificial intelligence.

Although process is important in relation to distribution, it is also relevant to price through its impact on the monitoring and measurement of production costs. Careful attention to the process of delivering a service can be of value in understanding the nature of costs and thus developing a sensible approach to pricing.

In the digital world that we now inhabit, process is assuming growing importance. Mobile technology really does condition the consumer to be able to transact their financial services requirements anytime, anyplace, anywhere and across multiple channels, adding to the pressures for effective and customer-focused processes.

9.5.2 Physical evidence

Physical evidence refers to anything tangible that is associated with a given service; it may be the buildings that an organisation occupies, the appearance of staff, the look of the organisation's website, cheque book holders or wallets that are provided for documents. In other words, physical evidence is part of the wider issue of how corporate brands, their products and services are communicated to the wider marketplace and the firm's customers.

The need for physical evidence within the marketing mix arises directly from the typic-ally intangible nature of the service. It is generally recognised that physical evidence can be subdivided into two components;

- Peripheral evidence which can be possessed by the consumer but has little independent value (e.g. a document wallet),
- Essential evidence, which cannot be possessed by the consumer but has independent values (e.g. a bank branch).

The provision of physical evidence has traditionally been most relevant to the "product and customer needs" and "customer convenience and distribution" components of the marketing mix but it is also increasingly relevant to "communication and promotion". In the product element of the marketing mix, brand building is important in the process of tangibilising a service. Building an image and a brand is seen as increasingly important in the finan-cial services sector because the brand is a way of reducing risk and emphasising quality. Traditionally, brands were accompanied by a variety of forms of peripheral evidence (cheque books, plastic cards, document wallets, etc.) to reinforce the brand's message.

The need for physical evidence is also significant in the context of communication. The particular problem facing suppliers of financial services is that they have no physical product to present to consumers. Thus, from a marketing perspective, communication must try to develop a message and a form of presentation which makes a service seem more tangible. It is also interesting that the more successful forms of sales promotion have tended to be those offering tangible items as free gifts (calculators, watches, etc.) and competitions rather than simple price promotions.

9.5.3 People

The "people" factor in the marketing mix emphasises the important role played by individuals in the provision of financial services. Staff may be involved directly in the customer-acquisition process as, for example, direct sales staff working face-to-face in branches or staff interacting with customers online or by phone through service centres. They may well be involved in after-sales service by handling customer queries and, crucially, can have a vital role to play in delivering key benefits to customers through activities such as handling insurance claims.

Consumers will often find the precise details of a financial service difficult to understand; they often do not see anything tangible for their expenditure and the benefits from many financial services may only become clear at some time in the future. Furthermore, the provision of information and the purchase of a financial service depends on the interaction between the consumer and representatives of the organisation. These features of financial services mean that the purchase decision may be heavily influenced by way in which consumers perceive the staff that they deal with and how they interact. The people who provide a service affect the way in which customers see the product, how it is promoted and how it is delivered.

In particular, the people component of services marketing is most commonly associated with personal engagement which relates to both the "communication and promotion" and "customer convenience and distribution" elements of the marketing mix. It is also relevant to the product element of the mix because it can have a significant impact on the quality of service. It is also true to say that "people" as a component of the mix is central to the role played by branch outlets in that branch staff provide a form of human interaction which customers seem to value. Metrobank is a fine example of the careful use of people as a core component of the marketing mix. Similarly, the real-time human interaction provided by service centre staff should be viewed as part of the marketing mix and managed accordingly. Indeed, a number of financial institutions have reversed their previous policy of offshoring various aspects of customer service by bringing call centre facilities back to the home country of the customer. This is in response to adverse feedback from customers regarding their perceptions of less-than-satisfactory service from overseas-based facilities.

9.6 Customer acquisition and the financial services marketing mix

Thus far, this chapter has given an overview of the key elements associated with the marketing mix for financial services. This section focuses on the challenges which might confront organisations when trying to manage these elements with a view to the acquisition of new customers. In Marketing in practice 9.1 we see how CIC insurance in Kenya has effectively integrated its marketing strategy and marketing mix to promote customer acquisition.

Marketing in practice 9.1: developing the marketing mix at CIC Insurance, Kenya

CIC is one of Kenya's largest insurance companies and offers life and non-life insurance products as well as investment and wealth management. It also operates in South Sudan, Uganda, and Malawi and is the leading cooperative enterprise and micro-insurer in Africa. CIC's purpose is to provide its customers with financial security and peace of mind and it shows a strong commitment to safeguard the interests of individuals and businesses by paying claims promptly. CIC's consistent adherence to the motto "We keep our word" has made it one of the fastest-growing insurance companies in Kenya.

A streak of product innovations such as M-Bima, a mobile phone-based insurance premium remittance platform, has seen the group emerge as a leading provider of microinsurance. CIC has had a standing objective to become a household name and a one-stop shop for all the insurance needs of the low-income households in the country. The marketing approach used by CIC to achieve its ambition is as follows:

Product strategy

Following the development of microcredit life insurance, CIC progressed into designing products covering the end consumer directly against insurable risks. These products include health, a life and personal accident policy for security guards, a low-cost personal accident policy, group funeral expense policy, an endowment life policy, and a pension plan. As well as offering a broad product range, CIC focuses on products being simple and inclusive. For example, the health microinsurance product is designed as a family cover being offered at a single annual premium regardless of family size.

Pricing

Given the nature of the market for micro insurance, the pricing strategy emphasizes affordability: For example, the endowment product is designed to allow for premiums of as little as US$0.25 per day paid on a weekly basis at no transactional cost to the insured member.

Distribution and promotion

As well as enabling delivery through a customers' mobile phone, CIC's micro-insurance products are distributed through the partner-agent model where CIC partners with organisations that already have a relationship with the end user to distribute and sell the products. These partners include MFIs, Sacco societies, welfare associations, religious and self-help groups.

To make the partnerships work, CIC invests in raising consumer awareness, education and promotion, often working with the Ministry of Cooperatives for inclusion in the cooperative societies' education days. CIC sponsors awareness campaigns through local radio stations and organises roadshows, participative games, song, dance, local comedy performances and competitions for instant CIC-branded prizes. All of this is reinforced by comprehensive advertising campaigns through the mainstream media, particularly the regional radio stations that communicate to the market in their local dialect.

Service delivery and new brand promise

Since micro-insurance is based on trust, efficient service delivery is critical. CIC works with a strict turn-around time of five days for all customer cover confirmations and endorsements. New business is processed immediately where all details are available and a policy document issued as the customer waits. Renewal reminders for all open policies are sent to the members through their insured groups three, two and one months before the due date. Further, a renewal reminder is sent directly to the customer through an SMS on their mobile phone. Any complaint or customer query is addressed within 48 working hours.

Source: Detail provided by Tom Gitogo, Group Chief Executive, CIC, Kenya and https://cic.co.ke/

Progress check

- Inappropriate financial behaviours can be hugely damaging at the international, national, and individual levels. In managing the marketing mix, we should note that each decision about a particular tool will send a message to consumers.
- The provision of physical evidence, staff management (people) and the systems for delivering service (process) are all likely to be important elements of marketing decision-making for financial services.
- In the digital world that we now inhabit, process is assuming growing importance.

However, not all financial services providers have been so successful in managing the mix for consumer acquisition. Historically, the financial services sector has received considerable criticism for tending to focus on new customer acquisition to the detriment of existing customers. Indeed, claims of the cynical practice of offering unsustainably attractive benefits to consumers at the time of acquisition which are subsequently worsened remains a feature of certain parts of the industry. It is undoubtedly true that companies have the right to use promotional pricing as part of its new customer acquisition activities. Promotional pricing is prevalent in virtually every category of consumer goods and service marketing, so why should financial services be exempt? Promotional pricing does indeed have a perfectly legitimate role to play in financial services. However, it must be used with care given the complexity of the products, the timescale over which they operate and limited consumer understanding. With the one-off purchase of, say, a television or a holiday, the consumer clearly understands the net price they have to pay and is in a position to make a well-informed choice. When "buying" a deposit account from a bank or a building society the consumer may well be in possession of the facts regarding the short-term price promotion, but she may not be able to judge long-term competitiveness of the interest rate. In the field of mortgages an attempt has been made to factor-in the effect of special introductory offers through the introduction of the Annual Equivalent Rate (AER). The key point to grasp is that care must be taken with the use of new customer price promotions to ensure the appropriate management of expectations.

In addition to concerns about the way in which marketing mix variables are used, we must also recognise that the specific features of the financial services sector may create additional challenges. Chapter 2 devoted considerable attention to the array of products that comprise the domain of retail financial services. In Chapter 10 we present key models and concepts concerning the successful management of products. Meanwhile it is important to appreciate that the relationship between product and process is particularly close in the case of financial services. When a person "buys", say, a current account, she is seeking to secure access to a range of service benefits on a continuing basis. The availability of online banking facilities may be perceived as a product feature or a process associated with the consuming of the product. However, in the context of customer acquisition, the focus of this part of the book, we should consider process in terms of how one first becomes a current account customer of a given provider. It must be borne in mind that the processes associated with customer acquisition comprise information that the organisation chooses to require as well as information requirements which are imposed by external agents such as the regulator. To continue with the example of a current account, many countries have strict rules regarding money laundering. This results in the need to provide original forms of documentary evidence as proof of identity and address. It adds a degree of complexity to the new customer acquisition process; it may cause frustration for the customer but cannot be avoided and this must be explained and managed.

A further aspect of the mix that may be challenging in a financial services context concerns channels. In the conventional consumer goods context channels is pretty straightforward; it concerns the means by which the consumer gains access to buying the product, i.e. the channel of distribution. This meaning of the term also applies in the case of financial services. For example, Independent Financial Advisers (IFAs) represent the primary means of distribution by which a consumer gains access to the products of Standard Life, the Scottish-based insurance company. However, having become a customer of Standard Life, ongoing service contact is likely to be directly with the company via the telephone, for example. Thus, channel is a somewhat ambiguous concept since it can refer both to the channel of distribution that consumer uses to become a customer and also to the means by which a customer engages in service interactions with the provider company.

Owing to the economics of new customer acquisition, it is becoming increasingly important for companies to market themselves on the basis that there will be an ongoing customer relationship in which several products will be bought by the customer over a prolonged timescale. In other words, the profit is in the lifetime value of a new customer and not necessarily in the profitability of the first product purchased. Customer profitability is determined to a large extent by a surprisingly small group of variables that apply consistently to most forms of financial services products. Consider the case of, say, a loan that is secured on the value of a consumer's home. This type of loan is sometimes referred to as a second mortgage because, in law, the lender can only gain access to the property's security value once any first mortgage debt has been discharged. The profitability of a new second mortgage customer is a function of:

- The amount of money loaned,
- The term of years over which repayment of the loan takes place,
- The likelihood of the customer defaulting on the loan,
- Interest margin,
- The purchase of other products from the lending company.

Relatively small changes, either positive or adverse, in one or more of these variables can exert significant impact on profitability, and the gearing effect can be dramatic if all five variables are affected. This model works equally for first mortgages and unsecured loans.

In the life insurance sector an analogous model has profitability determined by:

- The value of the sum assured,
- The term that the policy remains in force,
- The likelihood of a claim being made,
- Policy margins,
- The purchase of other products from the insurance company.

Again, the cumulative impact of positive or adverse variances with respect to these key variables has a compounding effect upon customer profitability. These variables should be factored into the plans that are designed to achieve targeted level of new customer acquisition. The logic of this thinking indicates a balanced scorecard approach to new customer target setting. To target crudely based on maximising new customers or products sold in a given budget year is to play a pure numbers game that invites considerable long-term commercial risks.

9.7 Digital marketing and customer acquisition

The 21st century has witnessed nothing less than a digital revolution. The financial services sector is endeavouring to adapt to meet the needs of the marketplace as consumers are increasingly comfortable researching, purchasing and servicing online. In many cases, customer expectations are becoming increasingly hard to meet as digital developments elsewhere impact on what consumers think might be available for financial services. The pace of technological change also creates pressure for organisations to not only create products and services utilising new technology, but also ensure they're up to date and evolve. If a particular app doesn't and isn't consistent with customer needs, then customers will often simply withdraw. We have moved from a situation in which financial services providers considered it sufficient simply to have a presence online (as recently as 2010, this was limited to broadcast "PR-style" content) to one in which a full online service proposition is a basic expectation. People are now comfortable buying online via smartphones and tablets, and concerns over online purchasing and online security have been vastly reduced. Consumers are far more aware of the value their data holds and are willing to share it with organisations they trust to gain a more personalised and relevant proposition. However, the Accenture 2019 Global Financial Services Consumer Study showed that while consumers trust their providers with their data, issues over data security i.e. a breach, is is also the top reason they would switch providers.

Financial services providers cannot afford to underestimate the shift in the mindset of consumers; they expect their needs be fulfilled in a timely and convenient manner regardless of whether they are interacting with an online retailer or bank. There's a risk that financial services providers focus overly on the destination, i.e. product. Instead, they must shift focus to the journey, or route to product, seeing that in a competitive marketplace convenience for the customer is increasingly a key differentiator. This is particularly true in a climate where neobanks and fintechs are launching compelling digital propositions. Acquisition for financial services is increasingly about being seen as a trusted, authoritative and accessible brand. Digital activities that promote brand engagement in the social space are particularly effective and are yet currently underestimated. Communications, conversations and communities all have the potential to positively impact upon marketing engagement. This is something that Asset Managers Investec have really demonstrated in their leveraging of LinkedIn to promote events and connect with this important professional network.

In this section we will explore in more detail the ways in which digital developments impact on the ways organisations manage their marketing mix for the purposes of customer acquisition, considering both the implications for consumers (their needs, segmentation) the challenges for providers (managing processes) integrating across platforms and integrating off- and online.

9.7.1 Context and convenience

In a time-poor society, value is being increasingly placed on convenience. Not only is there an expectation that digital interaction spans all devices, but decisions over who to do business with are often based on which service provider can fulfil the end user's needs in the most efficient manner.

Digital bank Chase UK was launched by parent company JP Morgan in 2021 has to date amassed two million customers and £15 in deposits[3]. Opening an account is straightforward; download the app and verify identity with a passport or United Kingdom (UK) driving license and start using the account via the app immediately. It's a purely digital proposition which services customers through its app, however interestingly their unique selling point (USP) is that live chat is not powered by chatbots, rather it is serviced 24/7 by real people in an Edinburgh-based call-centre. Thus, it offers customers the advantages and agility of a digital bank, with human servicing, and the peace of mind of being backed by one of the big 4 dominant US banks.

CEO Sanoke Viswanathan observed "The market structure in the U.K. is such that you have to generate economies of scale; there are profits to be made but if you subscale or have a high-cost infrastructure, you're not going to make it work," Thus the lack of branch network and investment in technology is the brands key strategy, with the ability for its platforms to support multiple products and easily scale to more customers and markets once established. Interestingly, while there's an option to use the current account switching service to transfer payments from old accounts automatically, a 2023 YouGov survey[4] highlighted that only 8% of their customers use Chase as their main bank account. The majority of their customers, 81%, prefer to hold multiple accounts, a far higher percentage that the 53% of public who hold multiple accounts. Chase customers may like the efficiency and accessibility it offers but aren't quite ready to commit to it being their primary bank, showing that convenience doesn't trump established authority yet.

People like to feel empowered by choosing how they consume information. For example, City Index sought to meet this need by developing "Daily Market News" which offers timely relevant information in a mass consumption friendly way.[5] Similarly, JPMorgan's podcasts share information in a way that is more engaging than just a piece of text on a web page; it also offers the opportunity to download content that can be consumed at a time which is convenient to the user, for example on the tube commute to work where there is no fast phone signal.[6]

These organisations have recognised that content is king, and that by creating rich, authoritative content in an easily accessible and consumable manner, they increase the "stickiness" of their sites (propensity of visitors to remain on site and return) and their overall value add. Lloyds TSB employed a similar tactic with its mortgage advice video on their branded YouTube channel. By producing non-biased, generic videos Lloyds has managed to circumnavigate compliance issues by avoiding any element of financial promotion while still "owning" the message and generating a buzz associated with its brand. It has created a niche whereby it is a go-to for general mortgage advice information, the secondary payoff being it naturally boosts its reputation as a thought leader, increases brand trust and indirectly promotes its mortgage offering.[7]

Decisions are based on both rational and emotional responses. The bigger the decision, the more emotional it becomes, e.g. saving money towards your child's university education. Financial decisions generally fall into this significant category, particularly when it comes to products such as savings and investments, mortgages and life assurance. Where organisations offer intangible products such as financial services, it becomes even more important to engage with the target audience and understand what is motivating them. HSBC's "What's next on the horizon for you" campaign did this particularly well in this regard by framing products according to possible consumer motivations.

A paradox of financial services is that while customers love simplicity, financial services providers love complexity. This is because they believe it mitigates risk; arguably, however, this is not always the case, particularly when compliance regulation and terms and conditions intended to protect the customer serve to cause confusion and frustration. This reinforces the message that financial services must keep the customer journey (and the ease with which it should be undertaken) at the forefront of their minds. A key challenge will be proactively anticipating customers' needs and offering them convenient solutions. Arkadi Kuhlmann, founder of ING Direct, wanted banking to be as simple as buying a cup of coffee and used YouTube to explains his desire to remove barriers and increase transparency and simplicity.[8]

Financial services providers need to be mindful of customer expectations that they stay abreast of technological innovations and provide up-to-date solutions that offer them easy ways to manage their money in a timely and simple manner. An S&P report[9] showed 38.7% of consumers switched banks for a better mobile experience, interestingly scoring just slightly ahead of the 37.9% who reported they had switched to get better customer service. Covid-19 accelerated the shift to online, and the decline in branch-based banking during the pandemic resulted in an increased number of branch closures in 2021; McKinsey reports "In developed markets, banks closed 9 percent of their branches in 2021, the largest reduction in five years, as they reevaluated existing approaches to sales and service."[10] Contactless payments are facilitating the move towards a cashless society; UK Finance predicts that by 2031 only 6% of transactions will be cash[11]. However, while digital capabilities are certainly a key influencing factor, they must still form part of a blended, omni-channel experience.

> While there is no doubt we are moving towards a digital world, this shouldn't and doesn't mean that traditional channels are 'dead'. For consumers, digital simply means a new way to communicate whether that be their bank, insurer or their favourite retailer – in whatever way suits them. 'Traditional' methods and face-to-face interaction still have a place in modern-day banking and insurance. Providers that will be successful will be the ones who modernise their back office to integrate these various channels to create 'banks and insurers of the future' that provide their customers with all options.[12]
>
> Francois Fleutiaux, Senior Vice President and Head of Sales,
> EMEIA, Fujitsu

Consumers are happy to share their data if it's used sensitively to offer them truly useful, compelling solutions to their banking needs. Attitudes to innovation have impacted data sharing. The vast majority (97%) of the European Fujitsu Banking on Change survey[11] respondents reported they were happy for banks or insurers to use their data to offer them a wider range of services as long as they're relevant and maximise convenience to the client.

- 47% are happy for their data to be used to offer recommendations on other relevant products and services,
- 44% would like their data to be used to provide easy visibility on their spending habits and offer relevant advice,
- 59% are happy for their mortgage provider to lower their premium based on data insights.

Artificial Intelligence (AI) offers opportunities for end-to-end digital onboarding and authentication which can dramatically simplify banking processes and increase customer convenience and satisfaction. It's also particularly important where the application starts online that there is a continuing, robust online experience through application, onboarding and servicing. Generative AI can offer significant benefits here; onboarding communications can be highly personalised based on data insights and individual customer activity during the onboarding period, positively impacting the customer experience.

9.7.2 Segmentation and targeting

Digital marketing offers the potential for major developments in relation to segmentation and targeting. Personalised service is different to relevant service; it needs to go beyond basic cross-sale messages of "if you browse this online, we'll email you these similar products", to really understanding customers' needs and providing them tailored, value-add service. With the vast amounts of data now available, CRM systems must be able to capture information from multiple disparate sources to provide a holistic view of the customer and facilitate easier segmentation. Generative AI enables targeting in real-time, enhancing traditional behavioural segmentation. It powers dynamic content, where web content changes based on users' live online behaviour patterns, enabling truly personalised experiences at an individual level.

Multivariate testing (MVT), based on the behaviours of people from the same category, allows businesses to serve specific content to different audiences based on criteria such as age, gender, geodemographics and previous behaviour in order to provide an experience most likely to convert into a purchase. With the use of cookies, companies can serve returning customers content that most closely suits their perceived needs, based on their site activity history across different browsers and devices. With cookie-based behavioural email targeting there is also the opportunity to trigger emails to site visitors when they perform certain actions. For example, if an IFA that a company holds the email address for visits a particular fund page and downloads a related piece of literature from their site, this action can trigger an email to the IFA offering more information about the fund or trigger an email to a member of sales to follow up with the IFA as a lead.

9.7.3 *Managing the process*

Usability, i.e. the ease with which online interfaces are used, is key to successful online marketing, particularly when it comes to new customer acquisition. There is a danger that organisations place more weight on style over substance. Innovation and design are important; however, the basic use of a tool must be intuitive and, more importantly, make the action you want the visitor to perform as simple as possible. This must be borne in mind across all electronic modes of interaction and businesses must ensure that users find it equally easy to engage via website, tablet or smartphone, thus making the purchase process as simple as possible.

Driving people to a website and then asking them to download and post in a form breaks the purchasing path and is likely to drive them to seek to complete the transaction with a competitor which does provide online fulfilment. The Retail Insight Network report that 84% of UK consumers cited digital usability as important and 49% would switch provider for an easier experience[13]. People have become less brand loyal and more driven by convenience. The rise of price comparison sites gives weight to this; people are willing to invest time shopping around for a best deal and "satisfice" with a provider who is *good enough* to fulfil their immediate needs. The point of using online for the user is to save time – we need to fulfil this requirement if we are to evolve in the online space.

There is a real risk that new entrants will steal market share and poach customers from traditional financial services providers who are unwilling to fully embrace and adopt digital practices. PayPal emerged as a direct result of banks feeling anxious about people using bank details online. Ironically, PayPal was established at the banks' behest and now has its own banking licence and is hugely successful in its own right. Atom Bank, Octopus and PayPal in particular, are excellent examples of innovation in banking. None of these services had banking licences to start with (all now do). They highlight that innovation in banking is coming from outside traditional banking services and it is these nontraditional newcomers to the banking space who are driving the greatest change. They don't suffer the same issues as large established banks with regards to heavy legacy systems, spanning multiple business units which are costly to replace. Their lightness and agility gives them a huge advantage and ability to move at pace to satisfy customers' technological expectations. Covestor was established in 2009 as a pioneering platform for investment management allowing members to mirror real transactions of knowledgeable and successful investors. It is an excellent example of innovation in the investment banking sphere which financial services should be cultivating[14]. It was acquired in 2023 by Interactive Brokers Group, the largest US electronic broker, a testament to Covestor's cachet.

Figure 9.6 PayPal digital payment platform

Source: "PayPal employee shuttle" by Richard Masoner / Cyclelicious licensed under CC BY-SA 2.0

Looking at recent digital versus offline retailers, traditional incumbents have struggled to compete with emergence of digital. For example, Borders could not compete with Amazon for book sales, and likewise Virgin Megastore could not compete with iTunes. There is a risk that banking could move in the same direction with new business models offering greater convenience making all the running.

This may take shape in form of hybrids where innovative new digitally driven front-end banking institutions are serviced by traditional banks at the back end, such as the Simple app, which delivers a banking interface which adds value to the underlying banking functions supplied by The Bankcorp Bank. What is clear is that financial services cannot ignore the impact of technology and the resulting shift in consumer behaviour.

Progress check

- The 2P2C mix comprises:
  - product and consumer needs
  - price and cost to the consumer
  - convenience and distribution
  - communication and promotion
- Consumers expect their needs be fulfilled in a timely and convenient manner regardless of whether they are interacting with an online retailer or bank.
- Artificial intelligence (AI) offers opportunities for end-to-end digital onboarding and authentication which can dramatically simplify banking processes and increase customer convenience and satisfaction.

9.7.4 Migrants, natives and social media

Digital migrants – who have moved to an online world as technology has developed – may view online offerings as a convenient addition to the core traditional marketing and servicing channels. However digital natives, those born post-1990, and who grew up interacting with digital technology, have a different perspective and attitude. They demand 24/7/365 access in the manner most convenient to them. Rather than passively accepting channels on offer, they "own" the relationship; banking has shifted from a B2C model to C2B, and banks have to cater to the resultant shift in expectations. They feel no sense of gratitude that a financial services organisation is offering them digital interaction as an ancillary service to a core offline proposition.

There is no silo approach in the mind of a digital native; they see the organisation's variety of touchpoints as one single brand, offering them their choice of interaction modes. Thus, if the online proposition of a financial services organisation does not fulfil their needs, this will impact their view of the brand as a whole and they will be less likely to explore investing with that organisation through traditional means.

Digital interactions offer the opportunity for a more engaging experience with traditionally corporate organisations. People like tools and widgets that make the journey more interesting and this, in turn, will also drive positive word of mouth (WOM) and repeat business. Consumers expect their financial services providers to offer up-to-date technological banking solutions. Many of these innovations are actually being supplied not by banks, but in the form of interfaces designed by tech start-ups which work alongside existing traditional bank accounts to enhance the customer experience. Clinc is a voice-activated platform that allows user to interact with their bank account using natural search queries, such as "can I afford a new jacket?" as opposed to "what's my balance?" with the aim of removing the perception of banking as stuffy and obstructive, and making it more natural and applicable to customers' lives. Similarly, AI-powered chatbot Plum connects to users' bank accounts and analyses their spending habits. It then uses this information to assess how much they can afford to save and regularly deposits money from their bank account into a savings account. The aim being is that Plum will encourage saving habits by starting with micro-saving that doesn't impact the users' lifestyle.

Digital natives are also more likely to research and share experiences via online word of mouth. For financial services, where transactions often involve investing with and trusting an organisation with large sums of money, this is particularly pertinent. People are naturally risk averse and this, combined with the recent economic climate, compounds low levels of trust in financial services. Thus, there is an increased propensity for people to research online and trust the experiences of their peer group. Social media has played a key role in the shift towards greater consumer power. Poor experiences are easily shared via social networking sites, blogs and forums and this means that bad experiences quickly gain viral momentum and visibility, and this can have a real impact on brand perception.

In an increasingly online WOM-centric world, it could be argued that financial services have the most to gain from social media and blogging; however, they frequently lag behind other industries in terms of adoption. It is an ideal way to build engagement, visibility and, most importantly, trust, as it requires timely responses and complete transparency. People seek transparency and social media facilitates this, explains intent and garners feedback, all of which result in making organisations appear more credible, passionate and willing. It is very easy to spot when organisations try to hide or mislead customers the public domain, so by being open to dialogue and feedback – both positive and negative – there is scope to gain the trust of consumers. Social media also has the benefit of ensuring that organisations are aware of what is being said about them. They need to be realistic and understand that consumers are going to share poor experiences online regardless of whether they want them to. The key question financial services organisations should be asking themselves is: how can they gain customer advocacy in a social world?

Digital media can also be used to make conventionally boring elements of financial services fun, and this in turn can have a really positive impact on brand perception and marketing engagement. For example, Skandia recorded comedian Clive Anderson reading out their terms and conditions and broadcast it on YouTube. This rather cute approach elevated a rather dry compliance requirement to a quirky viral[15].

Organisations should not make the mistake of thinking that by not having a Facebook or Twitter page they will mitigate the risk of negative comments being posted. Comments will still be posted online, but, more worryingly, without the organisation's knowledge, which removes any power from them to manage, diffuse or rectify the situation. By owning the platform that consumers share feedback on, organisations have the opportunity to manage the situation and rebalance negative experiences. This can have a really positive eventual outcome for business and also provides rich insight into real-time customer sentiment and feedback which should be crucial to ongoing business development.

The peer-to-peer money lending network Zopa has developed a strong social model. They use their blog to try to connect and engage with people. Their X (formerly Twitter) account demonstrates a highly positive online customer engagement experience. They also service prospective and current customers via Facebook which is a great aid to transparency. The highly social model they employ reinforces research which implies that the psychology of this kind of lending via social networks is radically different to traditional bank loans. This is because there is a person at the other end of the transaction, not a faceless banking institution.

In 2010 New Zealand Bank ASB claimed to have launched the world's first Facebook branch in a bid to appeal to the increasing number of social media users in their prospective customer base. Their app allows customers and prospects, private and secure real-time interaction with customer service representatives during business hours. The Facebook "branch" launch came a year after they launched an X (formerly Twitter) service channel which was, they claimed, an invaluable asset in terms of interacting with their online community. While their Internet Banking service remains at the core of their online transactional business, X and Facebook provide a complementary means for customers and prospects to interact with the bank.

9.7.5 Integrating on- and offline

The manner in which financial services organisations are traditionally structured are often a legacy of digital migrant attitudes. Digital teams are often separate to the marketing department, frequently being viewed as sitting under group operations or even information technology (IT). There is often little synergy between the public relations (PR) team and digital marketing, and this lack of knowledge sharing and integration results in an inefficient digital offering which lacks synergy and cohesion with the overall brand and marketing message. This is evident from many examples of fantastically executed offline marketing campaigns which are entirely unrepresented online, thus breaking the continuity of the user journey. If a customer has engaged enough to follow the campaign online and then receives no visual cues to continue this, the momentum and impact is lost.

An omni-channel marketing planning and execution strategy is optimum to present a cohesive customer experience, regardless of which touchpoint a consumer accesses. Carrying the message consistently across all physical and digital media will reinforce the impact of a campaign and reinforce the brand credibility and values. The use of augmented reality print advertising by Commonwealth Bank in Australia provides a good example of joined-up on- and offline advertising. The bank ran a full-page advertisement in the Sunday papers in Brisbane and Adelaide, as well as in a free commuter paper. Users had to download the Commonwealth Bank 3D reader onto their iPhones. When they viewed the newspaper advert through their iPhone, it offered a tour around a fictitious neighbourhood called "Cherryford Hill". The aim was to give people an idea of Commonwealth Bank's property guide iPhone app and engage them in an interesting and fun advertising experience[16].

Many organisations are still siloed which means their marketing tends to be product based as opposed to customer based. They need to embrace technologies to enable a 360 view of customers in order to serve them better in this new C2B world. Customers can have a positive digital experience with an organisation, but only within one particular silo; if they move outside of this and try to interact with another part of the organisation or different channel, the customer experience often becomes fractured and confused.

Online transacting and servicing is far cheaper for business to maintain; banks should be driving traffic to these sources with offline activity and encouraging people to engage with them, rather than confusing them with poor campaign alignment. A key part of this is the need for organisational structure change – digital is merely another marketing channel and arguably the most significant from a user-engagement point of view. Customers do not see the organisation in terms of individual channels, thus organisations need to ensure all activity is integrated, meaningful and working towards a common marketing purpose.

In conclusion, the recent shift in consumer behaviour as a result of digital innovations and an expansion of the digital touchpoints is a trend that financial services cannot afford to ignore. The development of satisfaction and trust can be hugely significant to customers' commitment to a brand and their willingness to pay a premium for brand reassurance. Not only does trust have a particularly positive effect on commitment but it also manifests itself in "behavioural intentions" such as WOM, repurchase and long-term engagement with a brand.

9.7.6 Digital organisational structure

Customers expect a seamless, joined-up, omni-channel experience when they interact with a brand, intelligently recognising previous interactions and tailoring future engagements in light of this behavioural data. This is what creates a value-add proposition and builds trust. Many traditional financial services organisations are undergoing the not so insignificant task of redefining themselves for the digital age. This is costly and time consuming, not only involving the replacement of heavy legacy systems but the reordering of internal structures. This is a huge operational challenge, as it's a far harder task to try and retrofit a new mode of working into an existing framework of diverse platforms and business units than to rebuild from scratch.

Consultancy firm Deloitte's have commented that:

> Refining the customer experience will be the main driver for technology that drives core transformation, digitisation, and automation. . . . As technology upgrade cycles continue to shorten, banks may finally demonstrate a willingness to retire legacy systems for cloud-based platforms.[16]

There are three key factors in attaining digital marketing success: recognising complexity, addressing speed and meeting expectations. In an increasingly tech-savvy world, organisations have to invest in both the right technology and people in order to achieve these goals. There needs to be cultural change to drive a more seamless customer experience and in order to be effective, it must be driven by top-down, board-level buy-in. CEOs need to consider how to transform their whole business rather than just digitise part of it. They need to enforce policies to employ staff with the right skill sets, and pay to bring in the right systems to overcome legacy issues. The rise of chief digital officers and chief customer officers signifies that businesses are appreciating the necessity of having decision makers at the senior level looking at how the business can interact best with customers across products, channels and organisational silos. Organisations also need to adopt technological solutions that enable a horizontal view of the customer; to enable a more customer-centric view and proposition.

This organisational change should mean that not only analysts, but employees right across the organisation understand what clients are thinking by reading into the meaning and context behind their data. They need to employ and develop a culture of broad-based marketers who can think strategically, linking the customer back to the data. However, while data is undoubtedly crucial, customers should not be viewed as just data; marketers need to understand their clients and prospects' motivations, what they're doing and why, in order to truly connect and engender a positive customer experience. Hargreaves Lansdown's digital mission statement phrases it succinctly: "The best people, with access to the best tech, deliver the best experience for our clients."

As the fintech industry has grown, financial organisations have also been challenged in attracting the right kind of talent. They are incentivised to change their internal structures and processes not only in a bid to attract and keep customers, but also to attract and keep staff who will likely find the prospect for working for an agency start-up more appealing than a traditional bank. Both Barclays and Blackrock have rethought their office layouts and dress codes, adopting a more relaxed, agency feel; open plan floors, hot desks as opposed to permanent desks, casual dress codes and flexible working hours. This open plan feel lends itself to more collaborative working relationships and makes moving people around and pooling people to brainstorm easier.

This was crucial in attracting particularly millennials who want a different working structure and a non-linear reporting line and career path. Beyond the working environment they expect decent work–life balance, access to good mentoring and the ability to be able to move around and work on cool things and different projects. Blackrock responded to this demand by creating an annual hackathon; HACK:BLK, launched in 2012. It brings together people from across the back and front end of the business and empowers them to be innovative; creating solutions through technology that meet needs of clients and sales teams. It has the added benefit of providing the opportunity for employees to work on a variety of projects that interest them, engendering a culture of innovation across the business[17].

The shift in consumer behaviour because of digital innovations and an expansion of the digital touchpoints is a trend that financial services have had to embrace at pace to meet consumer expectations and remain competitive. The development of online satisfaction and trust can be hugely significant to customers' commitment to a brand and their willingness to pay a premium for brand reassurance.

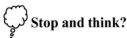 **Stop and think?**

What are the ways in which you think AI will enrich the marketing mix for financial services providers?

Think of 3 examples of fintech companies, how do you believe they use digital media to acquire new customers?

What do you think might be the implications of digital-based business models on corporate cultures?

9.8 Customer acquisition and ethical behaviour

A common criticism of the marketing practices of financial services companies in many parts of the world is that the interests of the supplier take precedence over those of the customer. The most obvious manifestation of this is the enormous scale of compensation costs arising from the mis-selling of a range of products over many years in the UK. Whilst regulation clearly has a role to play in mitigating such detriment to the consumer interest, ultimate responsibility must be borne by the companies that provide financial products and services. Corporate culture has a vital role to play in providing guidance which will inform marketing teams how to use the marketing mix in an ethical and responsible manner. What follows are some valuable insights from the Institute of Business Ethics into what is meant by the term "business ethics" and advice about how to put it into practice.

 Marketing in practice 9.2: promoting an ethical culture

Institute of
Business Ethics

Promoting an ethical culture

The marketing function in any organisation can be a key source of ethical lapses. Research into reasons why some employees behave unethically indicates that pressure is brought on staff to behave in a manner that is inconsistent with the organisation's values. To try and combat this, written guidance to staff, usually in the form of a code of ethics may be provided. Too often, this is a dull formal document, given to a new employee on joining the company with occasional reminders of the necessity of doing business by the standards set out in the booklet. It is usually stressed that this is required to safeguard the reputation of the organisation.

In practice, departmental cultures can deviate from the ethical standards that are promulgated by the main board or senior leadership which is often referred to as "the tone from the top". If this tone is not accepted in a corporate unit away from the head office or in a country with a different way of doing things, choices made may work against the company's stated ethical values. This can and often does have significant consequences. No matter what communications come from Head Office, employees will share their own stories regardless. So, for example, the organisation may say that retaliation against those who "speak up" about something that concerns them, will not be tolerated; but the reality may be that employees believe the opposite because of the stories which are told of what happened to say, Meera from the insurance sales team, when she dared to raise a concern, she had about sales methods.

Ethics is personal. Just as everybody thinks they have a good sense of humour, so everybody tends to think they are ethical. That is why it can be a challenge for companies to communicate to employees what they mean by "doing business ethically".

Communicating ethical values is not as simple as informing employees about laws, regulations and procedures and checking they are compliant. Ethics goes beyond compliance and springs from intrinsic values – like honesty, fairness, openness – that underpin behaviour. That is why discussions about ethics at work must start with a concept that everyone understands. A good starting point is what is known as the Golden Rule "Treat others as you would like them to treat you". This ethical "Norm" is generally accepted throughout the world!

Case studies and scenarios are now recognised as one of the most effective means of communicating an organisation's ethical values. The point is that they are stories and as stories they engage and inspire people. This makes them an effective tool for influencing behaviour and attitudes. Using scenarios allows employees to talk openly about ethical dilemmas and "voicing values" thereby giving them the confidence to act appropriately when faced with real-life challenges. Scenarios offer new ways of thinking about ethical issues and can show how and why situations can escalate out of control.

The stories can either relate to a success where somebody acted in a way that preserved the company's integrity, or a story about proven misconduct that shows people the consequences of doing wrong. One of the key benefits of using scenarios to communicate ethical values is their flexibility: they can be used in lots of ways: to bring a training session to life; inserting brief Q and As in a code of ethics; including fictionalised case studies in a staff newsletter; having them printed on a pack of cards for team leaders to use throughout a business; or even introducing dramatised performances at an away-day. To communicate ethical values effectively to embed an ethical culture, these stories need to evolve into positive ones, where doing the right

thing is celebrated and rewarded. So, the stories we tell should, where possible, cast employees as the heroes. One CEO put it this way: "We should celebrate the guardians of the company's ethical culture. Employees are the protectors of our reputation. They need support, not rules, to help them do the right thing".
    @IBEUK

Source: Ian Peters, Director, Institute of Business Ethics, London

9.9 Summary and conclusion

The effectiveness of any marketing strategy depends on the development of an effective marketing mix. The marketing mix consists of all the marketing tools that can be used to communicate an organisation's service offer to its target markets. To be effective, the elements of the marketing mix must be consistent with the organisation's chosen position and consistent with each other. In financial services the marketing mix must recognise and respond to the distinctive features of service products. When managing the elements of customer benefits, charges, communication and channels, marketers in the financial services sector need to pay particular attention to the people delivering the service, the process by which the service is delivered and the physical evidence which represents the service. Events of the recent past have put into sharp relief the importance of making an astute assessment of the trade-offs associated with new business volumes and the quality of those customers and sales. All too often the headlong dash for growth in market share has resulted in the acquisition of value-destroying customers and business; as one sage has commented, "market share is vanity, profitability is sanity".

  In the context of customer acquisition, digital marketing has had far-reaching consequences for financial services, creating wholly new business models and calling for completely new ways of looking at how products and services are marketed. Of particular importance is the need to ensure that off- and online activities are properly integrated to provide a seamless customer experience.

Learning outcomes

Having completed this chapter, you should be able to:

* **Understand the relationship between marketing strategy and the marketing mix**
  The marketing mix is a term used to describe the marketing tools that a manager controls. Managers must make decisions about these different tools to create a clear competitive position in the market that is consistent with the nature of the overall marketing strategy. Strategy concerns the vision that a company has for achieving long-term goals and the marketing mix concerns the specific tools aimed at delivering the strategy in practical terms that impact on the market and its customers. It is through the marketing mix that strategy takes practical effect. In other words, the marketing mix is the practical expression of the marketing

strategy. Consumers have little or no knowledge of, or interest in, strategy. What concerns them is the utility they experience from the contact they have with the marketing mix.

- **Understand the role played by the marketing mix in attracting new customers to the firm**

  The marketing mix for financial services is termed as the 2P2C mix and it comprises:
  - Product and Consumer needs
  - Price and Cost to the Consumer
  - Convenience and distribution
  - Communication and Promotion

The role that each of the above four components have in the acquisition of customers has been presented and practical examples given.

- **Understand the challenges associated with developing a financial services marketing mix**

  Alternative approaches to the marketing mix, such as the 4Ps, have been discussed and their strengths and weaknesses assessed in the context of financial services. The distinctive characteristics of financial services presented in Chapter 3 result in the need for a more nuanced model of the marketing mix, those characteristics comprise:
  - Intangibility
  - Inseparability
  - Perishability
  - Heterogeneity
  - Fiduciary responsibility
  - Contingent consumption
  - Duration of consumption

The above results in the need for the 2P2C mix in order to address the challenges they pose both to providers and consumers of FS.

- **Appreciate the ways in which the digital world is impacting upon the use of the marketing mix**

  The emergence of digital has impacted every aspect of the 4Ps. The internet and ubiquity of mobile devices means brands can reach a global audience, 24/7, with banks increasingly servicing customers online as opposed to in-branch. Promotion spans multiple mediums in an omnichannel marketing approach, whereby traditional channels are complemented by online activity across website and social media. Product design is being shaped by insights gleaned from connected devices and wearables, with the insurance industry in particular tailoring products based on data. Aggregator sites have made it easier for customers to compare prices and shop around for the cheapest deal, and the efficiencies of AI are enabling cheaper and faster servicing of customers which in turn can have a positive impact on pricing. The digital world has accelerated the pace and scope of data-driven marketing, which along with generative AI, is enabling brands to target personalised communications more effectively in real-time.

- **Understand some of the ethical considerations in the management of the marketing mix**

  The characteristics of FS referred to above present opportunities for abuse by unscrupulous product providers and those involved in the distribution process. All too often the interests of providers and distributors have taken precedence over those of customers. This has resulted in ever more demanding regulation and for the need for providers to conform to the spirit of regulation as much as the latter. As recently quoted:

  "We should celebrate the guardians of the company's ethical culture. Employees are the protectors of our reputation. They need support, not rules, to help them do the right thing".

Review questions

1. Why is consistency important in the development of an effective marketing mix?
2. What makes the marketing mix for financial services different from the marketing mix for physical goods?
3. What are the major challenges for financial services providers when developing a marketing mix for customer acquisition?
4. Which practices on the part of a financial services provider undermine consumer trust, and which practices and activities can enhance trust?
5. Describe the ways in which digital marketing has been adopted by financial services providers in your country as a means of attracting new customers. What opportunities are there for a greater degree of application of digital marketing techniques? Give specific examples of where you feel they could have greater impact.

Notes

1 Four leadership principles for the Fourth Industrial Revolution, World Economic Forum, 11 Oct, 2016
2 www.demandsage.com/chatgpt-statistics/ (accessed September 2023)
3 https://thefinancialbrand.com/news/digital-banking/chases-success-with-its-u-k-digital-bank-could-become-a-global-model-146936/ (accessed January 2024)
4 https://business.yougov.com/content/45763-uk-chase-has-tapped-younger-and-richer-audiences-w
5 www.cityindex.co.uk/market-analysis/ (accessed January 2024)
6 https://am.jpmorgan.com/us/en/asset-management/gim/adv/podcasts (accessed January 2024)
7 www.youtube.com/watch?v=YbqvCt8qlhk&feature=plcp (accessed January 2024)
8 www.youtube.com/watch?v=iMvicTIF974&feature=related (accessed January 2024)
9 www.spglobal.com/en/research-insights/featured/markets-in-motion/the-future-of-banking (accessed January 2024)
10 www.mckinsey.com/industries/financial-services/our-insights/best-of-both-worlds-balancing-digital-and-physical-channels-in-retail-banking (accessed December 2023)

11 www.ukfinance.org.uk/news-and-insight/press-release/contactless-makes-third-all-payments-while-cash-use-falls-again-in#:~:text=We%20expect%20cash%20usage%20to%20continue%20to%20fall,was%20but%20remains%20valued%20and%20preferred%20by%20many. (accessed January 2024)

12 www.fujitsu.com/lu/about/resources/news/press-releases/2016/lu-emeai-160504-banking-on-change-consumers-drive-digital.html (accessed March 2017)

13 www.retail-insight-network.com/news/uk-consumers-likeliest-abandon-retail-platforms-complex-logins/?cf-view (accessed January 2024)

14 www.youtube.com/watch?v=O4yBxiGpgR4. (accessed January 2024)

15 www.youtube.com/watch?v=kEeoD2r0inE&feature=relmfu (accessed January 2024)

16 www.youtube.com/watch?v=ZEYLalzacyU (accessed January 2024)

17 https://careers.blackrock.com/2023/11/13/category1/how-blackrocks-hackathon-empowers-employees-to-be-innovative/ (accessed January 2024)

References

Booms, B. H. and Bitner, M. J. (1981). Marketing strategies and organisation structures for service firms. In: J. Donnelly and W. R. George (eds.) *The Marketing of Services*. Chicago, IL: American Marketing Association.

Lauterborn, R. (1990). New marketing litany: Four Ps pass: C-Words take over. *Advertising Age*, 61(41), p. 26.

10 Product and consumer needs

Learning objectives

At the end of this chapter, you should be able to:

1. Explain the nature of financial services products and the ways in which they deliver customer benefits,
2. Outline the issues influencing product policy,
3. Provide an overview of issues relating to the management of existing products,
4. Outline the issues associated with the development of new products and new ways to meet consumer need.

10.1 Introduction

In many respects, product is fundamental to any marketing activity since it is through consuming the product that a customer experiences enjoyment and value. In effect we use the term "product" to describe a collection of components which together satisfy a set of customer needs. Clearly, a product which does not offer what consumers want at a price they are prepared to pay will never succeed. Decisions about the products that an organisation offers are both strategic and tactical decisions. The strategic issues associated with the management of the product portfolio were introduced in Chapter 4 and these were discussed further in relation to segmentation, targeting and positioning in Chapter 7. Alongside these strategic level decisions about the product, there are also important tactical issues which must be considered. These relate to the development, presentation and management of products which are offered to the marketplace in order to satisfy certain customer needs. Thus, the product element of the marketing mix deals with issues such as developing an appropriate product range and product line as well as considering decisions relating to the attributes and features of individual products. In this context, the issue of branding is of particular significance both for individual products as well as for the organisation as a whole. The product element of the marketing mix also deals with issues relating to new product development. Extending product ranges and product lines, either by new product development or through the modification of existing products is increasingly important for organisations that wish to remain competitive by continuing to deliver in relation to a range of customer needs.

DOI: 10.4324/9781003398615-18

This chapter begins by providing an overview of financial services products, the benefits they offer and the associated marketing challenges. The next section examines the factors that will influence decisions about the development of the product element of the marketing mix. Here we revisit the product life cycle concept and consider its uses and limitations in further detail. Subsequent sections deal specifically with aspects of the product range strategy and the process of new product development in the financial services sector.

10.2 The concept of the service product

In the tangible goods domain, the notion of what constitutes a product is pretty straightforward as it comprises palpable physical characteristics. However, the situation is perhaps less straightforward when it comes to financial services because *product* comprises both utility features and service features. The former concerns the primary customer need for which the product was bought, e.g. a personal pension to provide an income in retirement. Amongst the utility features associated with a pension may be a choice of investment funds, the ability to switch between funds, and an option for income drawdown. Services features are somewhat analogous to the process element of the extended marketing mix of the 7Ps. In the case of a personal pension it could include ability to access a fund's value and make additional contributions online, or perhaps the access to information and assistance via a 24/7 call centre or even a chatbot. Often, the boundary between the two types of feature can appear to be somewhat blurred.

An additional dimension to appreciate is the role played by service features where third-party intermediaries form part of the distribution processes for a product provider. In such cases real competitive advantage can be achieved by providing intermediaries with a range of helpful and responsive service features such as the ability to input new cases online and the provision of connectivity between the information technology (IT) systems of the provider and intermediary.

Thus, when we refer to terms such as product, product management and product development in the context of financial services we must ensure that both utility and service features are given due consideration.

Products are only purchased because they provide these benefits to the consumer. So, in order to understand products and how they should be managed, it is important to understand what those benefits are and how they are provided. Understanding the nature of the service product requires an understanding of both the needs of customers and the organisation's ability to meet those needs.

10.2.1 What customers want

The majority of organisations offer a range of products to a variety of customer groups in order to meet a variety of customer needs. In financial services, the prime customer groups are personal customers, institutional and corporate customers. In personal markets, financial institutions will often separate high net worth individuals (HNWI) from other customer groups. In the corporate markets, banks will typically separate large corporations from small- and medium-sized enterprises. These customer groups have a wide variety of financial needs as was shown in Chapter 2 and again in Chapter 7. The diversity of customer needs outlined in Chapter 2 can be classified under six main headings as Figure 10.1 shows:

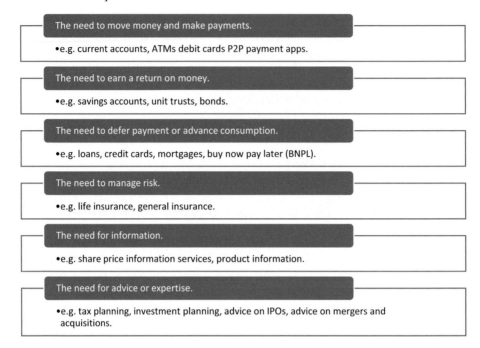

The need to move money and make payments.

•e.g. current accounts, ATMs debit cards P2P payment apps.

The need to earn a return on money.

•e.g. savings accounts, unit trusts, bonds.

The need to defer payment or advance consumption.

•e.g. loans, credit cards, mortgages, buy now pay later (BNPL).

The need to manage risk.

•e.g. life insurance, general insurance.

The need for information.

•e.g. share price information services, product information.

The need for advice or expertise.

•e.g. tax planning, investment planning, advice on IPOs, advice on mergers and acquisitions.

Figure 10.1 Customer needs and associated products

And as Figure 10.1 shows there are a range of ways in which these generic needs can be satisfied. Marketing in practice 10.1 outlines how one particular set of customer needs – students' need to access finance for international higher education – can be addressed through the development of a new loan product.

Marketing in practice 10.1: the development of innovative loans for international students

The demand for international higher education has grown significantly over the past 2 decades, with students seeing the opportunity to study in another country as an investment in their future career and earnings. Historically, international higher education had been largely the domain of either those students whose families were able to fund the costs or to those who were exceptionally able and could access a limited number of highly competitive scholarships. But the attractions of the international experience are such that a growing number of students have started to look at financing their studies through loans. They recognise that their international qualifications should enable them to secure significantly higher future earnings and that these have the potential to more than cover the cost of taking out a loan.

There have long been traditional lenders (banks) who were willing to make study loans, particularly in the US and also the UK, relying on some form of collateral or guarantee from borrowers to protect against the risk that the student would not ultimately repay the loan. This approach effectively restricted the opportunity to borrow to those students who were already relatively affluent; the potential market for student loans was much greater based on the demand for higher education but a new approach was required to reach the students who wanted an international education but could not access traditional loans.

New players, with venture capital or investment bank backing have moved into this market to exploit its growth potential – and with a model that deals rather differently with risk and does not require collateral or co-signature. The current leaders in this market are MPOWER Financing (www.mpowerfinancing.com/) and Prodigy (https://prodigyfinance.com/).

Both companies focus on the future earnings potential of students rather than on collateral or guarantees; they aim to lend only to students in certain countries, and institutions. They use their own algorithms to assess the future creditworthiness of applicants based on information about graduation rates, post-study employment and alumni earnings.

MPOWER Financing was started in 2014 by 2 former international students with a vision to broaden the opportunity for students to access international education. The company offers loans to international students studying at eligible institutions in Canada and the US; it currently offers loans of $2000-$100,000 with competitive fixed rates across a range of subjects and qualifications. While studying, students make only interest payments on their loans but on graduation they start to repay both principal and interest.

Prodigy currently provides loans to students studying graduate courses at 1800 institutions in 18 countries worldwide and focuses on a subset of subjects – those that have particularly good career prospects.

In both cases, the interest rates on loans are higher than might be the case for collateral-backed funding because the risk is higher, but a growing number of students are willing to accept the higher repayments in return for the ability to access finance to boost their future earnings potential.

Source: https://monitor.icef.com/2021/09/private-finance-companies-are-expanding-loans-for-international-students/ (Accessed 12 December 2023)

Organisations in the financial services sector concentrate on the development of products and services which meet these particular needs. However, to be successful, it is not enough to just have products that meet these very basic needs. Organisations must also seek to understand broader customers wants and preferences and identify ways in which they can ensure that their products deliver those requirements and convince the customer to purchase. In order to understand how organisations can make their products attractive to customers, we must understand the nature of the product itself.

10.2.2 What organisations can provide

Organisations provide products to meet customer needs. One common way of thinking about products is to see them as a series of layers around a central core.

- **Core**
  The core product represents the basic need that is being provided – in the case of a bank current account, the core product is money transmission. At the core product level, all organisations in the market are basically the same – all current accounts offer money transmission, all credit cards offer the opportunity to delay payment and all unit trusts provide an investment opportunity.
- **Tangible**
  The next layer of the product is usually described as the tangible product and at this level, the organisation will make the product identifiable by adding certain features, facilities, brand name, etc. At this level, the products of different organisations will be slightly differentiated, although from a consumer perspective, all the features offered in this layer are what they would expect as a minimum before purchasing. This suggests that it may be difficult to really differentiate products at this level.
- **Augmented**
  The third layer which is described as the augmented product is usually used to refer to those features which organisations add to make their products distinct from the competition such as the special customer service offered to holders of platinum credit cards. It is at this level that an organisation would hope to gain a competitive edge by offering attractive features that competing products do not offer. Of course, as was explained in Chapter 3, this is difficult because of the ease with which the features of financial services can be copied.
- **Potential**
  The final layer of the product is described as the potential product. This refers to features that are either very new or not yet available, but which can potentially be added to a product to make it very distinct.

An illustration of the different layers of a product is shown in Figure 10.2. Here, the financial service being illustrated is an investment platform (a service that allows customers to invest in a range of different types of investment including unit trusts, exchange traded funds, etc). The core element of an investment platform is that it provides customers with a way of investing their existing wealth and generating a return in the future. The tangible elements might include an association with a specific supplier (branding), range of funds, choice of investment realisation method (income vs capital growth) and the ability to manage a portfolio online or via an app. The augmented element might then incorporate additional features which go beyond those that would be expected by the consumer. In the case of a unit trust, this might include the option to invest only in responsible funds (often described as ESG – environmental, social and governance). Finally, the potential product might include a feature such as fractional capital protection which may not currently be available but is technically possible and might respond to identifiable customer needs.

Based on this way of thinking about products, marketing managers must:

- Understand the core benefit that their product offers and the needs of customers;
- Identify the tangible elements which consumers would expect the product to offer;

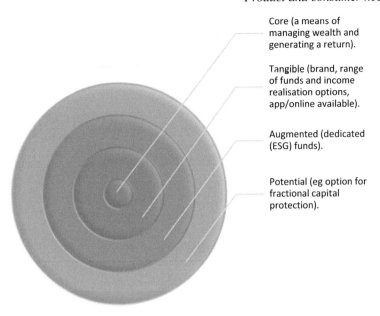

Core (a means of managing wealth and generating a return).

Tangible (brand, range of funds and income realisation options, app/online available).

Augmented (dedicated (ESG) funds).

Potential (eg option for fractional capital protection).

Figure 10.2 The different layers of a product

- Identify augmented product features which would provide the basis for differentiating the product;
- Monitor developments that could provide the basis for potential value-adding features in the future.

In performing these tasks, it is important to be aware of the distinctive features of services discussed in Chapter 3. In particular, there is a clear need to create some tangible representation of the product for consumers and also to address the issues that arise in relation to the variability in quality.

 Stop and think?

Think of the financial services you currently have – what are the core, tangible and augmented elements. What features are not yet provided but which would be really valuable. Do you think there is a reason why these are not currently offered?

10.3 Influences on product management

Financial services organisations will look to develop services which meet some or all of the financial needs for some or all customer groups. Some organisations will concentrate on serving a subset of customers (what was described in Chapter 7 as market specialisation). Some organisations will focus on a subset of needs (described in Chapter 7 as product

Figure 10.3 Sample product range at KB Kookmin Bank, South Korea

Source: Adapted from https://omoney.kbstar.com/quics?page=C020979 (accessed 15 January2024)

specialisation). A small number of organisations – typically the major banks, will attempt to serve the majority of customer groups and meet the majority of customer needs.

To meet selected needs of selected customers requires a range of differing products. A simple example of the product range which might be offered to personal customers is presented in Figure 10.3 for KB Kookmin Bank in South Korea.

The width of the range refers to the number of different broad product types or lines (savings, deposits, funds). Each type or line will consist of a number of related products and the number of such products determines the length of the line. In the case of KB Kookmin, the deposits product line consist of 3 sub-lines with the instant access and regular savings lines being the longer ones. In contrast, the e-banking line consists only of two products. Financial services providers looking to serve a broad market will tend to have a wide product range (to meet a diversity of generic needs); they have relatively short lines if they are choosing to complete on cost and keep their product offer simple. Longer product lines tend to be more common with differentiated strategies that seek to target a range of different market segments. Malaysian Bank, Maybank, for example, has a long product line in credit cards. At the time of writing, the bank offered 29 cards in total; these target two broad markets – Islamic and conventional – and then there are further points of differentiation structured around product features – namely, cashback, travel privileges, online shopping benefits, sustainability, rewards and points and no annual fee. Many other banks offer relatively long credit card lines – partly because there is a diversity of customer needs but also because the different combinations of features can be offered cost-effectively.

A key aspect of product management is to make decisions about the development of this range to ensure that the organisation continues to meet customer needs. As explained in the introduction, this involves both strategic and tactical decisions and covers a broad range of activities. For the purpose of this discussion, product management will be discussed under two broad headings:

- **Management of existing product lines**
  Existing products need to be managed and refined to ensure they deliver the benefits that customers expect. This includes product design (features, quality, brand, points of differentiation, etc.) and product modification (checking product performance and making adjustments to product design where necessary) and product line management (addition of new variants of existing products). These issues are discussed in detail in Section 10.5.
- **Product range management**
  This focuses on the overall choices about the range of products to offer – and therefore the diversity and range of customer needs to satisfy. Of particular importance in this area is the introduction of new products and the removal of older, poorer performing products. These issues are discussed in detail in Section 10.6.

While each of these aspects of product management will be considered separately, it should be recognised that they are necessarily interdependent; product attribute decisions have implications for the product range and decisions relating to the product range will also have implications for aspects of the new product development process and for product elimination.

The concept of the product life cycle (PLC), was introduced in Chapter 4 (see also Figure 4.9) as a way of thinking about the overarching product portfolio but it may also have value (if used sensibly) to support thinking about some of the more tactical aspects of product management. The PLC has many detractors whose issues with the concept are threefold.

- First, there are those who argue that the progress of a product through the stages from growth to decline and extinction have more to do with poor quality marketing of the product than with any immutable law concerning the natural life of a product. The impact of poor quality marketing is often seen in companies that use direct sales force distribution. A new product gets launched and, if successful, the product manager responsible is promoted and the product loses its champion. Additionally, with perhaps an annual rate of sales force turnover of 40%, within a couple of years most of those present at the initial product launch have left the company. Meanwhile, another new product has been launched to a largely new sales force and the previous "new product" loses a major part of its distribution capability. Unsurprisingly, the previous "new product" goes into rapid decline.
- The second group of critics are often to be found in the packaged-goods domain and simply see no reason why, so long as there is a need for the product and it is properly marketed, it should not achieve growth on an indefinite basis. The Mars company

has always been of the view that the PLC does not apply to its brands. Having been launched in the UK in the early 1930s, the Mars bar continues to flourish as a brand over 70 years on. Mars ensures that successive generations of brand managers conform to what might be termed a policy of "brand husbandry" to ensure that the legacy of the brand is maintained to ensure its continuing success. Arguably then, it is effective marketing that is sustaining the product over a particularly long-life cycle.

- The third issue that detractors from the PLC concept cite is that with an established product it is very difficult to determine at precisely what stage in the life cycle a product has reached. For example, if a product's sales level is at roughly the half-way point in the growth phase of Figure 4.9, how can you tell whether it is about to enter its maturity phase or has several years of continued growth to look forward to?

Nevertheless, the PLC has its uses when handled with due caution as a conceptual device to determine how to structure and make adjustments to the marketing mix in support of a product. For example, the pre-launch mix may place a great deal of emphasis upon gaining distribution and staff training. During the launch phase there will be heavy use of the promotional elements of the mix to achieve awareness and encourage a desire to find out more about the product. In the tangible goods field this is a phase when there may be a lot of money spent on sampling and special price promotions to encourage trial purchase. As growth continues there may come a time when additional features could be introduced to the product to refresh it and revitalise interest by distributors and consumers. A prolonged period of flat sales may indicate the need to reposition the product, possibly in conjunction with product performance improvements.

Like any aspect of marketing, the product management process will be influenced by a range of external factors; in particular it will be important for organisations to regularly monitor customers, competitors and the environment to identify new ways of meeting consumer needs. Equally of course, product management must be based on a clear understanding of the organisation's strengths and weaknesses. Each of these is considered in turn.

- **Consumers**
  Consumer needs, wants and expectations are a major influence on product management. In personal markets, factors such as customers' tastes and preferences, lifestyles, patterns of demographic change and income levels will be of particular importance. For corporate customers, marketing managers must focus on the objectives and strategies of customers and on understanding the environment in which customers' businesses operate in order to identify likely financial needs.

  Understanding consumers, particularly retail consumers can be very difficult. Financial services are often complex, often seen as uninteresting and so difficult to research. One important factor to take into consideration is the idea of trying to understand changing lifestyles and the implications that these will have for customer financial needs. For example, an awareness of the increasing time pressure on many consumers and the increased desire for flexibility should lead banks to consistently look for ways of delivering service in a more flexible and convenient fashion. Marketing in practice 10.2 explores some of the interrelationships between technology developments and evolving customer needs.

Marketing in practice 10.2: technology and customer needs

Technology enables financial services (FS) providers to meet customer needs in a personalised, accessible, timely and tailored manner. Customers want easy, secure mobile banking to facilitate quick payments and product applications, such as mortgages, while retaining confidence that their data is being protected. Banks must balance this demand for speed and convenience with security. Customer expectation is changing at pace; passwords are already viewed as passé with biometrics increasingly becoming the expected access norm. Access to mobile banking apps via facial, thumbprint and voice recognition is commonplace, and Amazon Echo allows users to bank from their own home using voice ID biometrics, which are also in use by Capital One and Moven. Banking is becoming seamlessly integrated into our lives – virtual, constantly available, and highly personalised.

Banks are taking advantage of technology's ability to allow them to help customers manage their money, track spending and maximise saving in real time, as opposed to the "rear-view" information gained from traditional statements. Banking interface Simple allows customers to annotate their spend reports to help track how they spend and identify patterns. Similarly, the Moneybox app helps first-time investors save and invest small increments. Like a digital piggy bank, users can link the app to as many of their bank accounts as they wish, and Moneybox will round up their everyday spending to the nearest pound and invest the change in a stocks and shares individual savings account (ISA). Users can choose the level of risk they feel comfortable with: cautious, balanced or adventurous, in order to balance the risk and return of their investment across a range of investment strategies. As techworld.com comments "It's small change, but given the average user makes 120 transactions per month and rounds up on average 28p per transaction, that's about £36 saved each month and about £440 saved per year, according to their figures".

Customers want added value; banks sending push reminders when they need to pay a bill and enabling the transaction with a single tap, money transfers being made instantly without the traditional three-day clearing period.

The ability to help customers manage their money not only builds consumer confidence and trust, it creates opportunities for banks to cross-sell products which fulfil customers' specific needs, based on their financial situation and goals. This is only possible if banks move away from siloed data management. A holistic view is not only crucial for effective customer management from a business perspective, more importantly it also enables them to offer customers a dashboard view across their financial holdings with that bank.

Banks need to be proactive and creative in anticipating how customers will want to interact with them as technology evolves. There has been a dramatic evolution in the payment space driven by technology since the introduction of the first credit cards (1958 in the US and 1966 in the UK). This has gathered pace significantly in recent years with a relatively short time frame between contactless payments being launched in the noughties, to sole biometric payments being available in 2017. Apple Pay already makes use of biometrics to enable users to approve payments using face ID (as do many bank accounts, e.g. Barclays, to access banking apps). In 2017, trials of direct biometric payments began, where the user's bank account is linked to their unique finger vein pattern and enables them to make payment using solely their finger, without the need for a mobile app middleman. With the odds of two people sharing the same vein pattern being 3.4bn to 1, it offers solid security benefits as well as convenience to the customer in terms of not needing to carry a card or remember a PIN. Biometric startup FinGoPay, launched the product in 2019 to Copenhagen Business School students in Denmark and Brunel University in the UK, enabling them to make payments at campus cafes and convenience stores. In 2019, Natwest bank in the UK trialled the use of biometric cards; payment cards which have in-built fingerprint readers. They offer an alternative to using mobile wallets, but unlike phones they will never run out of battery. Alipay, the financial arm of Alibaba has allegedly invested $420m developing Smile-to-Pay, technology which, true to its name, enables facial recognition payment at in-store point-of-sales machines and has been deployed across China. One step further, the IFuree self-service super-market in Tianjin, 3D camera scans all customers upon entry to measure the width, height and depth of their faces, and when they checkout it automatically charges their linked payment account. As aptly reported by the BBC "It was only [2016] that just about all smartphones could be used as wallets. Now, biometrics. Your body as a bank card."

FS organisations need to consider not only the physical way consumers interact with banks and how to leverage technology to fulfil this, but also the actual products and services they offer. They should use the data they hold about customers' finances to proactively meet needs the user isn't aware of yet; paying bills before they're overdue, transferring savings to maximise interest, proactively offering finance or insurance that can be completed at the tap of a button when it detects a customer is in a car-showroom or an automatic pre-approved mortgage offer based on increased child spending or maternity grants being detected.

As banking takes advantage of emerging technologies such as AI and voice ID to fulfil customers' routine needs, their role undergoes a transformation from the traditional bank that customers directly interact with, to a resource that automatic-ally understands and facilitates their lifestyle choices and needs. While there has been much discussion regarding the threat of new entrants to the baking space, conversely there may be an opportunity for banks to move into non-banking territory. Already trusted by consumers to safeguard their money, this confi-dence could be leveraged to market them other products and services. The 2015 Fujitsu "Walking the Digital Tightrope" report found that a third of respondents would consider buying personal data storage and home energy from their finan-cial services provider and 30% would buy broadband services from their bank, and suggested the landscape of products offered by FS organisations could be set to open up greatly. An interesting concept, but the reality thus far is FS providers' focus is on how they can leverage technology to improve their core product and service offering.

- **Competitors**
  The regular monitoring of competitors is an important source of information for product managers for several reasons. First, changes in a competitors' product range and product features will indicate a possible change in the pattern of competition. Second, because it is relatively easy to copy financial services, monitoring what competitors do can be an important source of new product ideas.
- **External environment**
  The importance of the external environment and its influence on marketing strategy was discussed at length in Chapter 5. Marketing managers must be aware of general trends in the environment so that they can identify new threats and opportunities. For example, China's accession to the World Trade Organisation (WTO) created a major opportunity for non-domestic financial services providers to access a market with one of the highest savings rates in the world. The technology changes discussed in Marketing in practice 10.2 are a perfect example of the way in which external changes could create opportunities for a range of different approaches to satisfying customer needs.
- **Internal factors**
  As explained in Chapter 4, understanding internal factors is important because it defines what is possible. To make good product decisions, managers must have a clear understanding of the resources available to the organisation and its particular strengths and weaknesses in order to understand how best to respond to a particular opportunity or threat. Thus for example, Prudential's strengths and track record in life insurance and investment management give the company a strength which it has been able to match to emerging market opportunities in countries such as Vietnam, Thailand, Indonesia and the Philippines.

This analysis of self, customers, competitors and the external environment is a continual process. Marketing managers must keep abreast of these factors and consider how best to respond to key changes. It is not operationally or financially feasible for an organisation to react to every change in the marketing environment; at the same time, no organisation can afford to miss key opportunities which may be presented by legislative, social or economic change.

Progress check

- One common way of thinking about products is to see them as a series of layers around a central core – typically these layers are core, tangible, augmented and potential. These different layers can be developed based on an understanding of current and future consumer needs.
- Product management includes considerations relating to the management of product lines (the number of variants of a particular product offered) and the management of product ranges – the variety of broad product types being provided.
- As well as being driven by customer needs, product management must also take into consideration the competition, the broader external environment and the internal environment.

10.4 Managing existing product lines

The management of existing product lines covers two broad areas; the first deals with decisions about the features to attach to a particular product; the second deals with product line management and in particular issues relating to product modification and line length modification.

10.4.1 Product attributes

One of the most basic sets of decisions relate to the choice of product attributes (features, brand name, quality, etc.). These attributes are used to create a tangible or augmented product as described earlier in this chapter. So, the generic service product (life insurance, for example) has to be developed into some tangible or augmented form (General China's GC Living Assurance Plan) through the addition of various features such as cover for total and permanent disability, premium waivers in the event of disability and so on.

The features that are offered as part of a particular service product are one means of differentiating the service. Thus for example, the UK's NatWest offers, as part of its current account product line, an Everyday bank account and a Reward Account. The Everyday account offers no monthly fee, savings round-ups, spend tracking and budgeting and a split-the-bill facility. The Reward account offers cash back for direct debits, for logging on and for spend with partner retailers, but charges a monthly fee. In addition, the bank offers accounts for students and for children and teens.

However, the actual range of distinct features which can be attached to a particular financial service is limited and may not provide a long-term basis for differentiation since such features are easily copied. Offering interest payments on chequeing accounts will be an extra attraction for customers but it is one that would be easily copied by competitors. So, it becomes very difficult to differentiate in terms of product attributes. Thus, any attempt to differentiate a product at the expected or augmented level must look beyond simple product features and consider instead issues such as quality, branding and organisational image.

Quality is regarded as an increasingly important product feature and refers to the ability of a product to perform its intended task. As is explained in Chapter 15, quality in the service sector in general and financial services in particular can be a rather more complex concept. Some researchers suggest that customers assess service quality based on both technical and functional quality.

- Technical (or outcome) quality is concerned with how the product performs (e.g. does a capital growth investment trust provide an acceptable rate of capital growth).
- Functional or (process) quality is concerned with the way in which the service is delivered and might include factors such as the way staff behave towards customers, and the speed of response to questions. Often, the way the service is delivered (process) can be every bit as important as the technical quality of the product itself.

Branding is well developed in the marketing of products and is now increasingly important in financial services. Branding has particular value because it provides a means of creating a clear identity in a competitive marketplace. This process is discussed in some detail in Chapter 7 and Marketing in practice 10.3 provide an example of branding in practice, focusing on the development of a corporate rather than a product brand. It is important to recognise that branding is more than just creating a memorable name. Effective branding aims to create a relationship between the organisation and the customer; when that relationship exists, the brand provides a means of communicating information about quality, differentiating the organisation from its competitors and encouraging customer loyalty. For many financial services providers it is the perceived strength of their brand that provides a justification for the move into bancassurance. Frost Bank was able to build on its brand to support its move into insurance in 1998; similarly, the strength of the Banco Santander brand in Spain provides a basis for customers to choose insurance-related products from the bank as opposed to dealing with a specialist insurance provider.

Marketing in practice 10.3: Frost Bank's community focused brand

Frost Bank in San Antonio, Texas traces its history back to the 1860s when it was established to support its community providing a range of services to those settling, living and working in the area. It formally associated with the Federal Reserve Board in 1919 and despite widespread bank closures during the great depression, Frost Bank survived and prospered. It was the first Texan bank to offer ATMs in 1979 and in 1998 it moved to offer insurance alongside banking services. In 2000 it introduced its online banking service and launched its banking app in 2013 with debit card alerts added in 2014. Frost Bank reported assets of close to $50 billion in 2023, placing it in the top 50 banks in the US and it now offers a broad range of services to corporate and retail customers including banking, insurance and investments across Texas.

As a local institution, Frost Bank prides itself on being embedded in its community and has built its brand around this principle. Frost Bank uses its name, its heritage and a range of community support programmes to build a distinctive brand. Its web presence stresses its commitment to being a good corporate citizen:

> At Frost, everything we do is aimed at making people's lives better. And for over 150 years, that commitment has steadily guided our approach to our employees, our planet and the communities we proudly serve.

This branding has been translated into practice through both marketing programmes and through corporate programmes. Marketing activities in support of the brand include:

- Niche marketing campaigns to demonstrate the way in which Frost wanted to be viewed. One such examples in 2004 was the sponsored touring exhibition "Revealing Character" based around photographs of working Texas cowboys.
- Sports sponsorship – when corporate sponsorship of National Basketball Association teams was first permitted, Frost Bank put its name on the jersey of local heroes, the San Antonio Spurs.
- Building naming – in 2003, Frost took the naming rights for a major downtown tower block in Austin, giving it a distinctive and visible presence on the city's skyline.

- The Frost Bank Center – continuing a longstanding link to the San Antonio Spurs, in August 2023, Frost Bank announced a partnership with the Spurs based on naming rights for the Spurs' arena.

Key to all these activities is the intention to demonstrate that Frost is fully embedded within the San Antonio and broader Texas community. These campaigns are complemented with corporate programmes focused on:

- Supporting nonprofits in the area where Frost's employees and customers live and work.
- Volunteering programmes that work locally to mentor young people, support nonprofits, care for the elderly, and contribute to a range of related good causes.
- Community Reinvestment Act (CRA) – commitments to meet the whole community's credit needs in line with the CRA.
- Administering scholarship applications for Texas students.

Perhaps the best summary of the approach to building the brand comes from comments made by Phil Green, Frost's Chairman and CEO when announcing the partnership with the Spurs.

> *We believe in San Antonio – it's our hometown. We want this relationship with the Spurs to demonstrate our unwavering sense of pride for San Antonio's rich history and its bright future. The longevity and success of both the Spurs and Frost Bank are rooted in our shared values of integrity, caring and excellence. These values ultimately help strengthen and shape our entire community.*

Source: West, P. (2024), https://www.frostbank.com/about-us (accessed 31 January 2024)

In the financial services sector, it is arguably the customer's image of the organisation which is the most important type of branding available. Most financial products are identified primarily by the supplier's name and where individual product brands are created, such as Maybank2u Savers and Maybank2u Premier – these are typically a combination of both company name and product name. The company name is seen as being of particular importance in branding because of relatively high levels of recognition in the marketplace and the potential to exploit overall corporate reputation.

Despite the undoubted importance of brand in financial services, the financial services sector appears to struggle with branding. In Interbrand's ranking of "Best Global Brands"[1], the highest ranked financial services brand is JP Morgan at 26 followed by American Express at 28. Research in the UK suggests that many traditional financial services brands are seen by consumers as relatively weak, lacking relevance and that they fail to build a strong emotional bond with target markets (Devlin and Azhar, 2004). This research highlights the importance of thinking carefully about the best way to connect with customers and differentiate a brand from the competition.

Making a connection with customers relies on emotional appeals as well as appeals based on functional values of products and most financial services organisations have not adequately developed such appeals (Dall'Olmo Riley and de Chernatony, 2000, O'Lauglin, Szymigin

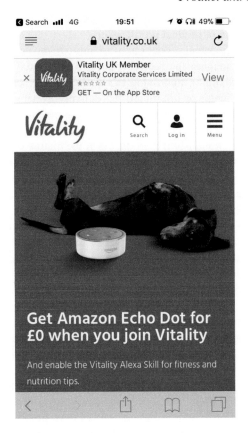

Figure 10.4 Vitality insurance app with health focused giveaways
Image by Steve Bowbrick licensed under CC BY 2.0

and Turnbull, 2004). Traditionally, financial services organisations have relied very heavily on functional values such as size and longevity. While these are clearly important in building trust and confidence, they may not always be enough to create a real connection with consumers. Indeed, the relative success of nontraditional entrants into financial services is often explained by brands that are much better developed, much more clearly differentiated and much more able to connect with customers. For example, the Virgin Group in the UK has seen significant success in the financial services sector, building on its brand image of unconventional customer champion. Similarly, Vitality, a relative newcomer to the UK insurance market has built a distinctive brand based on its shared value insurance model and quirky marketing campaigns including the use of a distinctive shade of pink and the image of a young and healthy dog (see Figure 10.4).

10.4.2 Product modification/product development

Once a product is established, there are two broad areas that require attention – product modification and product development. Product modification is concerned with changing the attributes of a product to make it more attractive to the marketplace. Product development involves creating a new variant of an existing product and it is typically associated with either product line stretching or product proliferation.

Product modification in financial services aims to improve the performance of an existing product. This may mean making the service easier to use (fixed annual repayments on existing mortgages, for example), improving the quality of the service (personal account managers for corporate clients) or improving the delivery system (redesigning an online banking site to make it more useable). With increases in competition and with high consumer expectations, product modification is important for organisations seeking to maintain and expand the customer base. Obviously if a product is at the mature or decline stage in its life cycle, then additional expenditure on that product may be risky. At the same time, trying to develop completely new products is also risky, so an approach which concentrates around modifying existing products can be very attractive. For example, Vitality is one of the UK's larger health insurers[2]. Their app (see Figure 10.4) promotes insurance that seeks to incentivise members to follow a healthy lifestyle. The core product offered is fairly standard but what makes Vitality's variant distinctive is the modification it has introduced. It encourages members to be active and healthy by gamifying fitness. Members who are willing to demonstrate a healthy lifestyle (e.g. via Apple Watch, Fitbit) can collect rewards based on their levels of activity which include meals, drinks and cinema tickets. They are also able to track their fitness and health, get well-being advice, healthy recipes and connect with others in the app community. This represented a significant (and effective) change to the traditional health insurance model, creating a value-add proposition and cultivating an ongoing relationship with customers (members) as opposed to interaction being solely limited to the purchase and redemption of policies.

Product line stretching or product proliferation involves adding new services to an existing service line and has traditionally accounted for much of the new product development activity in financial institutions. One widespread example of this form of activity is the development of premium bank accounts providing customers with a range of additional services. For example, in addition to its Regular Savings Account, HDFC Bank in India offers a SavingsMax Account, a Women's Savings Account, a DigiSave Youth Account, a Senior Citizens Account and several more, each of which offers a slightly different set of features and attributes. Customer feedback provides invaluable insights for product development – whether it is the addition of new attributes or the introduction of new service variants. Digital bank, Monzo uses a Trello Board to capture suggestions from its loyal customer base (see https://trello.com/b/ID7Li0ni/monzo-extraordinary-ideas-board). The rationale for stretching a product line is to further differentiate existing products in order to appeal to more specific segments of the market. Since line stretching is a form of new product development in a market with which the organisation is familiar, the risks tend to be relatively low.

 Stop and think?

Consider the example of Maybank credit cards earlier in this chapter and that of HDFC. Does having such a large choice of product variants make it easier or more difficult to find the right product? Do online comparison tools help?

However, there are dangers with line stretching. In particular, it is possible to identify a large number of segments among the consumers of financial services and develop variants of existing products to meet the needs of these segments. However, if these segments are not large enough or distinct enough to be viable, then the effect of line stretching may be to increase costs but not increase revenue. The organisation will have too many different variants of a product, the product line will be long and difficult to manage, and this can cause confusion amongst consumers who almost face too many choices. Accordingly, product line management must be aware of the need to consider withdrawing existing products as well as introducing new ones.

Withdrawing products can be difficult in some areas of financial services owing to the extended lives of many products. For example, a company might launch a new mortgage product (let's call it the maxi mortgage) and then some time later launch another new mortgage (the mega mortgage). Unlike the tangible goods marketplace, the company cannot simply cease manufacturing, run down stocks and remove the maxi mortgage from its product range. Instead, it has to maintain the product for those customers who have already bought it and may well wish to continue using it for, say, the next 25 years. Such a product is known as a legacy product and the world's established financial services companies are frequently burdened with the costs of running a plethora of legacy systems. This is why new entrants to financial services can often be highly cost effective compared with their established rivals – they do not have to carry the legacy system cost burden. The implication of this is that new product development and launch needs to be based upon significant new products that can be expected to have a prolonged life for the provider. It is also important to design products and contracts in such a way as to facilitate migration of current products onto newer variants in order to mitigate the legacy cost problem.

Progress check

- The management of existing product lines will include first, decisions about the features to attach to a particular product and second, issues relating to product modification and line length modification.
- The features that are offered as part of a particular service product are an important mechanism for differentiating the service offer.
- Product modification is concerned with changing the attributes of a product to make it more attractive to the marketplace. Product development involves creating a new variant of an existing product and it is typically associated with either product line stretching or product proliferation.
- Stretching a product line helps to further differentiate existing products and appeal to more specific market segments. In effect it is a form of new product development in a market with which the organisation is familiar, the risks tend to be relatively low.

10.5 New product development

Developing new products is an important aspect of product management because it ensures that the range is up to date, innovative and meets changing consumer needs. The term New

Product Development (NPD) covers a range of types of innovation; some new products are genuinely new, but other new products are actually developments of existing products as discussed above. It should be borne in mind that innovation can be in areas concerning service features as well as utility features. In this section we will consider two specific types of new product development, namely major innovations and new service lines.

10.5.1 Major innovations

These are products which are new to the organisation and new to the market. As such, while they offer great potential in terms of returns, they are more risky since they will typically require a much higher level of investment, the use of different and new technologies, and may involve the organisation moving into areas in which it is comparatively inexperienced. Such major innovations are rare in financial services. Critical illness insurance launched in the 1980s was one such product as was the launch of the Virgin One offset account in the 1990s, both having spawned a range of variants. Marketing in practice 10.4 provides an example of a major potential source of product innovation for financial services.

 Marketing in practice 10.4: blockchain

Blockchain is a type of distributed ledger, made up of secure blocks of data held across a network of computers known as a chain. These blocks of information are cryptographically bound together so they can't be altered, tampered with or counterfeited. As it's collectively managed and no one person or entity owns the system, it's harder for it to be corrupted or hacked. It can be used to record all data of value, not just financial transactions. Don Tapscott summarises its benefits well in his paper, "Blockchain Revolution":

He describes blockchain as a global spreadsheet which can record financial transactions alongside "virtually everything of value and importance to humankind: birth and death certificates, marriage licenses, deeds and titles of ownership, educational degrees, financial accounts, medical procedures, insurance claims, votes, transactions between smart objects, and anything else that can be expressed in code". Proponents of blockchain suggest that blockchain replaces the need for trust because of the high degree of data integrity it offers.

Blockchain offers financial services some interesting opportunities. Its ability to hold a historical, public record of interaction and transactions offers transparency to customers, providers and regulators. This single source of truth is particularly valuable to FS providers and is already being used to speed up processes, verify identities and validate account/policy applications and insurance claims. This drives efficiencies for FS organisations, and reduces processing times and costs for customers, which in turn can increase satisfaction, trust and retention. Accenture and the World Economic Forum created the following tool to identify the value of distributed ledger technology:

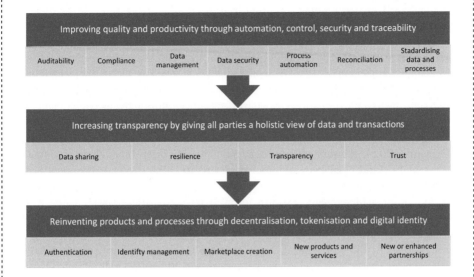

Figure 10.5 Evaluating blockchain's benefits

Source: Building Value with Blockchain Technology: how to evaluate Blockchain's benefits. Accenture and WEF

The insurance market is already making good use of blockchain technology. Smart contracts have terms written directly in code and automatically self-execute when certain pre-defined conditions are met. They enable customers to purchase directly from underwriters, bypassing reinsurers. US Insurtech, Lemonade, uses AI and blockchain to deliver home, car and pet insurance, and set a world record in 2023 for settling a claim in 3 seconds.

Between 5:49:07 and 5:49:10, A.I. Jim, Lemonade's claims bot, reviewed Brandon's claim, cross-referenced it against his policy, ran 18 anti-fraud algorithms on it, approved it, sent wiring instructions to the bank for the transfer of $729, and informed Brandon of the good news. 3 seconds: it took you longer to read the previous sentence.

Blockchain facilitates the automation of lengthy and outdated process, enabling all parties involved in a claims process to record, track and verify data from a single source. This immutable record also helps reduce fraud, as data cannot be tampered with, and claims will only be paid out if recorded circumstances are met. The fact blockchain ledgers are decentralised means they are almost impossible to hack and alter; extremely useful for an industry whose profitability is based on the veracity of data. Nationwide Insurance in the US are members of the "The RiskBlock Alliance", a blockchain platform set up to provide proof of insurance. They use this technology to gain real-time verification of insurance coverage which reduces fraud and speeds up the insurance claims process. The global market for blockchain in the insurance industry has grown from US$64.5 million in 2018, to US$473.4m in 2023. It is projected to reach US$3643.66 by 2029, which would demonstrate a compound annual growth rate 41.32%.

Cryptocurrency currency, such as Bitcoin and Ethereum, uses blockchain technology to be transferred globally, its unique selling point (USP) being its decentralised nature and the fact that no banks are involved. As it allows oversight of trades and payments, it removes the need for intermediaries (exchanges, clearing houses, etc.) and significantly speeds up money transfer processes. In 2015, Santander posited systems like this could save banks up to $20bn by 2022. Pioneers in the field, in 2016, Santander became the first UK bank to launch blockchain tech for international payments, in 2018, they introduced international payments app "One Pay FX" and in 2019 issued the first blockchain bond. Many banks are exploring the use of blockchain technology in trade finance, supply chain management, securities and payments, working collaboratively on consortiums to understand its viability and potential. In December 2024, Reuters reported that the " 'world's first' blockchain payments at Bank of England" had been completed by Fnality, a blockchain payments firm for shareholders Lloyds Banking Group, Santander and UBS. In 2023, JPMorgan launched Onyx, a blockchain platform for B2B payments transactions, using it to facilitate its first live settlement transaction (with Blackrock and Barclays) to be used in a derivatives trade. Citibank announced their blockchain initiative, Citi Token Services, in 2023, allowing institutional customers to convert cash into digital tokens which are more easily traded when markets are closed. Shahmir Khaliq, Global Head of Services, explained:

> Digital asset technologies have the potential to upgrade the regulated financial system by applying new technologies to existing legal instruments and well-established regulatory frameworks. The development of Citi Token Services is part of our journey to deliver real- time, always-on, next generation transaction banking services to our institutional clients.

Blockchain is still in its infancy in terms of widespread consumer understanding, acceptance and trust; it's a "Big leap into the unknown. The thought of replacing a large secure central service with public records held across the net is a big stretch". Its decentralisation is both an advantage and a disadvantage – for all the flack big banks have taken over the financial crises, people still have base level trust that they will protect their money. There needs to be more confidence in it before people will have enough faith to place their finances in this type of technology. However, the fact it is already in use by many financial heavyweights is an indication of the potential direction of travel. Blockchain is something of a silent revolution; it is already being used across FS in ways consumers aren't aware of but are benefitting from. As it gains momentum and people hear more about its use by established brands, the more comfortable they will become. Regulation of blockchain varies widely across different international markets; as yet there is no global standard framework. Regulation of cryptocurrencies is discussed in Chapter 2.

It is interesting to note that governments have often been the source of major new product developments for the industry. For example, in the UK, the Thatcher government of the 1980s was largely responsible for the huge growth of the personal pension market. Similarly, that same government also devised the Personal Equity Plan (PEP) and the Tax Exempt

Savings Account (Tessa). Not to be outdone, the government of Tony Blair introduced the Stakeholder Pension, the Individual Savings Account (ISA), and the Child Trust Fund. And in 2008 the Pensions Act introduced auto-enrolment which required employers to automatically enrol all eligible staff into a workplace pension scheme, a process which started in October 2012 and was progressively rolled out to a range of employers.

Britain is not alone in this as governments around the world play a major role in product development. The Polish government has introduced the IKE personal pension account. The IKE is one of the forms of the Polish government's third level of pensions, and can be in a form of a life insurance policy or different kinds of bank investments or investment funds. There are tax allowances, for example, no capital gains tax is payable when you receive your accumulated fund once you retire, but if you want to withdraw money beforehand you pay the tax. In 2023, the Financial Services Commission in South Korea and the Ministry of Agriculture, Food and Rural Affairs announced that specialist pet insurance providers would be allowed to operate in the local market. The number of pets was estimated to be close to 8 million in 2022 but the penetration of pet insurance stood at around 1%. The change aims to encourage greater competition and a greater diversity of products in what is currently a relatively under-developed market[3].

As well as being responsible for the introduction of new products, governments also influence product policy in other ways. For example, in the UK, regulations have had a major impact, notably at the service feature level for a range of investment products, by introducing rules such as hard disclosure of charges and commissions, and rules regarding fact finding.

Arguably, it is in the area of service features that innovation has had the most noticeable effect upon the customer experience. For example, digital innovations have probably affected customers more profoundly and directly than utility feature innovation in recent years. And if developments in AI, such as those outlined in Marketing in practice 10.5, are anything to go by, this is a trend that might be expected to continue.

Marketing in practice 10.5: developments in artificial intelligence (AI)

AI is not new to the financial services space. The use of technology to automate tasks previously carried out by humans has been in place since the mid-twentieth century and, in particular, has long been used for fraud detection, offering organisations the ability to respond to fraudulent activity in real time. As bank branch closure numbers increase, investment in AI to help meet the increasing demand for online and call centre support is essential. It's also been highly successfully applied in the provision of automated robo-advice in the wealth management space. Its capabilities to assist in personal banking are now surfacing, with a range of new banking apps and interfaces coming to market in recent years. In 2017, a study carried out by Narrative Science and the National Business Research Institute reported that "32% of financial services executives surveyed confirmed using AI technologies such as predictive analytics, recommendation engines, voice recognition and response." The 2024 State of AI in Financial Services Report states 91% of FS providers are either already using, or assessing AI for use.

Andrew Power, partner at Deloitte comments,

> The big issue in the UK is that customers don't engage in their investments very well . . . so people don't save enough and AI can help. AI is good at trend and pattern recognition, so one of the applications is to monitor spending and how much you can save.

Launched in the UK in January 2016, the Plum is a Facebook-powered chatbot that operates off the messenger interface, so it doesn't require customers to download yet another app (although they can download the Plum app if they wish). It connects to a user's bank account, analyses it to learn the individual's spending habits and uses this knowledge to make savings deposits on the users' behalf, within their financial limits. Primarily aimed at millennials and Generation Z, it aims to help them develop saving habits through "micro-saving" in the easiest way possible. Founder Victor Trokoudes explains:

> Rather than pulling money out once a month we try to save regularly between five to seven times a month, the whole idea being you're not feeling the fact that money came out as much as if it had all in one go . . . it's small, negligible."

Technology company Clinc, have created a conversational AI tool to provide a voice-activated platform which allows users to interact with their bank account using natural language queries such as "Can I afford dinner out tonight?" and "Have I spent more on coffee this month than last?" instead of "What's my current account balance?" The aim is to break down traditional banking jargon barriers and facilitate a more value-add relationship which encourages users to gain better control of their finances and promotes saving habits. Isbank in Turkey used this technology to build their chatbot, Maxi, which services its 8.2m mobile app users via written and spoken conversational AI, enabling payments, transfers and spending advice.

Recent years has seen the evolution of generative AI (GAI); ChatGPT launched in 2022 and saw 57m users in its first month. While traditional AI solves specific problems using machine learning algorithms, GAI analyses vast quantities of data to produce new and original content that doesn't exist anywhere else. It is, in theory, able to apply a human-like lens to problem solving and fulfil tasks that usually need human intelligence and has enormous potential to support complex tasks and workflows. Right across FS, GAI could radically shift consumer expectations and internal business operations, driving efficiency and accessibility through GAI virtual assistants able to collate and present highly personalised propositions. This will increase product-ivity and reduce the cost-to-serve by increasing the speed of content generation and decreasing human effort. Integrating GAI into a firm's processes will help them stay relevant and competitive and potentially reduce costs.

The Schroders Pulses report 73% of IFA firms plan to integrate GAI into their processes, recognising benefits it offers namely increasing efficiencies, identifying client needs, screening, and reducing overheads by automating processes which frees up human IFA and paraplanner time for more profitable activities. FS providers are already using GAI across multiples use cases; Goldman Sachs are experimenting with how GAI can help with the writing of software code and Morgan Stanley rolled out a GAI assistant to its financial advisers in 2023. Head of Analytics, Data and Innovation for Morgan Stanley commented:

> AI @ Morgan Stanley is about helping our advisors service their clients more effectively and to deliver differentiated advice...In 2023, human engagement remains our most important driver of growth. AI is about helping our advisors do better, not a replacement for them.

Lemonade insurance company famously used blockchain and generative AI to settle a claim in just 3 seconds in 2023[xxv]. A report by Opinium and insurtech Sprout. ai found:

> a surprising number (59%) insurance companies are leveraging generative AI. AI is here to stay, and if insurers aren't using it to their benefit, they run the risk of falling behind. Other insurers must keep up to stay competitive and in the game.

JPMorgan Chase is developing a generative AI tool that offers investment advice to customers to help them select financial securities. They applied to trademark the name "IndexGPT" in April 2023 and will plan to launch the product within 3 years of approval to secure the trademark, meaning they may be the first major FS provider to launch a GAI product directly aimed at the customer market.

The use of GAI in FS continues to evolve as organisations explore the benefits it offers across virtual assistants, coding, synthetic data, semantic search, employee self-service, and customer services. As GAI tools that enhance FS product and service offerings become more commonplace, organisations will need to embrace and innovate GAI in order to meet customer expectations and remain competitive.

10.5.2 New service lines

These refer to products which are new to the organisation but not new to the market. Sometimes they are referred to as "me too" products, and this aspect of product development has been more in evidence than wholly original product development during the past. Since there are competing products already established in the market, the potential returns may be lower, but at the same time, the organisation is moving into an area with which it is considerably more familiar, either in terms of the technology or the markets. It is probably one of the most common forms of NPD in the financial services sector, particularly so as regulatory changes have reduced some of the restrictions on what organisations can do. For example, a number of competitors have copied the offset account that was originally devised by Virgin. Indeed, it is impossible to recollect a single new product that has not been taken up by any number of rival companies. The same goes for product features and fund variants. No sooner was the first ethical fund launched in the late 1980s then a range of analogues gradually entered the market.

10.5.3 The new product development process

Whether considering genuine innovations or the addition of new service lines, there are many benefits from operating a structured process to consider which developments are most suitable. The basic components of a new product development process are outlined in Figure 10.6.

New product development strategy

A clear strategy is important to ensure that all those involved understand the importance of NPD and what the organisation wishes to achieve. For example, it is essential that all those involved should understand whether the process of NPD is to be oriented towards taking advantage of new market segments, whether it is seen as crucial to the continued competitiveness of the organisation, whether it is required to maintain profitability, whether it is designed to reduce excess capacity or even-out fluctuating demands. The ideas that should be considered are likely to vary according to the purpose of the NPD programme.

Idea generation

Ideas may be generated from both inside an organisation and from outside. Ideas may be generated internally from specialised NPD teams, from employee feedback or suggestions. Externally, ideas may be generated based on customer feedback, market research, specialist new product development agencies or by copying competitors. One common failing in idea generation is a tendency to focus on what is possible rather than what the market wants – this has been particularly apparent with new technology-based products where too much attention has been paid to what the technology can do and not enough to what consumers want.

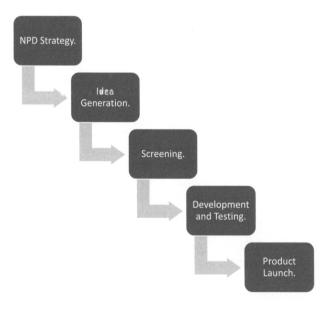

Figure 10.6 The new product development process

Screening

The variety of ideas produced at the idea generation stage must be screened to check that they are suitable. This usually means deciding, in advance, a set of criteria to be used when ideas are evaluated. The sort of criteria used can vary but are likely to include the following:

- Does the idea fit with the organisation's strategy?
- Does the idea fit with the organisation's capabilities?
- Does the idea appeal to the right market segments?
- Is the idea viable in terms of cost and profit?

Often, the screening process passes through several stages; initially all ideas are screened, using simple criteria to eliminate any obviously unattractive suggestions. The remaining ideas are then screened much more thoroughly and this involves a more detailed examination of their operational and financial viability, and often some product-specific market research.

Development and testing

Ideas which have survived the screening process are then worked up into specific service concepts – that is to say the basic idea for the new product must be translated into a specific set of features and attributes which the product will display.

At this stage it is common to test this newly defined product and to identify consumer and market reactions in order to make any necessary modifications to the product before it is launched. The problem with test marketing in the financial service sector is that it gives competitors advance warning of an organisation's latest ideas and it offers competitors the opportunity to imitate. As a consequence, test marketing of financial services is comparatively unusual. Many organisations argue that the actual costs of developing a new product are often low but the losses from giving advance warning to competitors may be quite high.

Product launch

The product launch is the final stage and the true test of any newly developed product; it is the point at which the organisation makes a full-scale business commitment to the product. At this stage, the major decisions are essentially of an operational nature – decisions regarding the timing of the launch, the geographical location of the launch and the specific marketing tactics to be used in support of that launch.

Effective new product development is clearly important to the maintenance of a competitive position. Consequently, the process of developing new products has been extensively researched and a number of important practices that contribute to success have been identified:

- Maintaining regular contacts with the external environment to identify changes in market characteristics and customer requirements,
- Encouraging a corporate culture which is receptive to innovative ideas,
- Operating a flexible approach to management to stimulate and encourage the NPD process,
- Identifying key individuals with specific responsibility for the NPD process,
- Encouraging supportive environments,
- Ensuring support and commitment from head office/senior managers,
- Effective communications both internally and externally,
- Choosing a product which fits well with the company,

- Developing strengths in selling,
- Offering product quality,
- Using market knowledge and customer understanding.

These practices cannot guarantee success, but it is clear that an open, supportive and flexible approach to NPD augmented by good marketing at product launch can contribute significantly to the success of NPD activities.

10.6 Conclusion

The key to successful product management is the development and maintenance of an appropriate product range. This requires a financial service be developed with a set of features which correspond to consumer requirements and that this range is constantly monitored so that existing services can be modified and new services can be developed. The process of new product development in the financial services sector has tended to concentrate on the redesign of existing products within an organisation's portfolio and the development of products which are new to the organisation, though not necessarily new to the sector. The perennial problem which faces the provider of financial service products is the ease with which such products may be copied and the consequent importance of ensuring rapid market penetration in the desired segment when new products are launched.

Learning outcomes

Having completed this chapter, you should now be able to:

1. **Explain the nature of financial services products and the ways in which they deliver customer benefits.**
    Financial services comprises both utility features and service features. The former concerns the primary customer need for which the product was bought, e.g. a personal pension to provide an income in retirement. Amongst the utility features associated with a pension may be a choice of investment funds, the ability to switch between funds, and an option for income drawdown. Services features are somewhat analogous to the process element of the extended marketing mix of the 7Ps. In the case of a personal pension it could include ability to access a fund's value and make additional contributions online, or perhaps the access to information and assistance via a 24/7 call centre or even a chatbot. Often, the boundary between the two types of feature can appear to be somewhat blurred. The idea of a product as comprising multiple layers (core, tangible, augmented and potential) is useful in thinking about how to meet customer needs and how to differentiate the offer.
2. **Outline the issues influencing product policy.**
    Like any aspect of marketing, the product management process will be influenced by a range of external factors; in particular it will be important for organisations to regularly monitor customers, competitors and the environment to identify new ways of meeting consumer needs. Equally of course, product management must be based on a clear understanding of the organisation's strengths and weaknesses.

3. **Provide an overview of issues relating to the management of existing products.**
   The management of existing product lines considers both product attributes/features and issues relating to product modification and line length modification. One of the most basic sets of decisions relate to the choice of product attributes (features, brand name, quality, etc). The generic service product (life insurance, for example) has to be developed into some tangible or augmented form (General China's GC Living Assurance Plan) through the addition of various features such as cover for total and permanent disability, premium waivers in the event of disability and so on. Once a product is established, there are two broad areas that require attention – product modification and product development. Product modification is concerned with changing the attributes of a product to make it more attractive to the marketplace. Product development involves creating a new variant of an existing product and it is typically associated with either product line stretching or product proliferation.

4. **Outline the issues associated with the development of new products and new ways to meet consumer need.**
   Developing new products is an important aspect of product management because it ensures that the range is up to date, innovative and meets changing consumer needs. The term New Product Development (NPD) covers a range of types of innovation; some new products are genuinely new, but other new products are actually developments of existing products. New product development can comprise either major innovations or new service lines. Both will benefit from a structured process (i.e. a clear strategy, careful idea generation, screening of ideas, development and testing of product concepts and planned launch). Major innovations are high risk and consequently much of the NPD focuses on the development of new service lines.

Review questions

1. Choose a product with which you are familiar. Identify the different layers in that product and decide what you think is the main point of differentiation between this product and other competing products.
2. Why is line stretching an important part of product management? What are the risks associated with this approach to product management?
3. What are the key stages in the NPD process? Why is it useful to have an organised process for developing new products?

Notes

1 https://interbrand.com/best-global-brands/ (accessed January 2024)
2 Vitality was launched in the UK in 1997 and is a subsidiary multinational financial services provider, Discovery Ltd which operates in 30 countries worldwide with over 20 million customers.
3 www.koreatimes.co.kr/www/biz/2024/01/602_361236.html#:~:text=Pet%20insurance%20plans%20to%20be%20diversified%20in%20Korea&text=A%20convenient%20one%2Dstop%20system,as%20early%20as%20next%20summer.(Accessed January 2024)

References

Dall'Olmo Riley, F. and de Chernatony, L. (2000). The service brand as relationship builder. *British Journal of Management*, 11(2), pp. 137–51.

Devlin, J. F. and Azhar, S. (2004). Life would be a lot easier if we were a Kit Kat: practitioners' views on the challenges of branding financial services successfully. *Journal of Brand Management*, 12(1), pp. 12–30.

O'Lauglin, D., Szymigin, I. and Turnbull, P. (2004). From relationships to experiences in retail financial services. *International Journal of Bank Marketing*, 22(7), pp. 522–39.

West, P. (2024). "How a Texas Bank Anchors its Brand in Local Communities", *The Financial Brand*, January 17. https://thefinancialbrand.com/news/bank-marketing/how-a-texas-bank-anchors-its-brand-in-local-communities-174014/?edigestT2 (accessed 17 January2024)

11 Communication and promotion

Learning objectives

At the end of this chapter, you should be able to:

- Explain the essentials of communication for financial services marketing,
- Outline the process of planning a promotional campaign,
- Provide an overview of the strengths and weaknesses of different approaches to marketing communications for financial services,
- Understand the impact of new media on the management of marketing communications.

11.1 Introduction

The term "communication and promotion" refers to the range of methods used by an organisation to communicate with actual and potential customers in order to influence the way in which a customer thinks and feels about a service (or a service provider) and to influence behaviour (most commonly to encourage purchase). A commonly used alternative description of this activity is "marketing communications" (marcoms) and for many this is a better term as it captures the breadth of this element of the marketing mix. For many of us, marcoms are the most visible element of marketing and indeed it is not unusual for people to think of marketing as being purely about promotions and communications. As explained in Chapter 3, internal marketing and specifically communications with staff play a key role in the delivery of high-quality service and so the "communications and promotion" aspect of the marketing mix may also focus attention on employees as well as customers. And, of course, with the widespread use of social media, communication and promotion increasingly happens between consumers and separately from the service provider. Word of mouth (whether positive or negative) has always been recognised as an important method of communication but developments in digital technology mean that it is happening in a way and on a scale that is very different to traditional one-to-one exchanges. Social media fin-influencers (financial influencers) can reach large audiences and what they say about a brand or a service can have a major impact on prospective and actual customers. Barclays campaign with Big Zuu (popular British rapper and TV personality) on managing money and spending habits performed extremely well with the target Gen Z audience (those born 1997–2012)[1]. Santander UK have a long-standing partnership with Ant & Dec (British TV personalities)

DOI: 10.4324/9781003398615-19

who recently fronted a TikTok campaign called "Scammer Time" to raise awareness of scamming through humour[2].

As an element of the marketing mix, communication and promotion encompass a broad range of tools that convey messages to consumers – whether through traditional media (e.g. broadcast, print, physical environments) or through digital media (social media, websites, apps). The most recognisable tools include advertising, publicity/public relations, personal selling, sales promotion and direct marketing and while organisations will look to control and manage the messages being conveyed and the tools being used, they cannot control all communication – word-of-mouth between consumers, for example, can be difficult to manage but an important source of information. And even where communication can be significantly controlled, marketers need to be sensitive to the impact of "noise" – unplanned and sometimes unexpected occurrences that can confuse or even undermine messages. For example, debates about a brand's "green" credentials and fossil fuel financing can have significant reach via social media and undermine brand Environmental, Social and Governance (ESG) messaging. Campaigning charity, Greenpeace have been highly critical of Barclays[3] and HSBC have been accused of "greenwashing" because of their claimed involvement in raising funds for the expansion of oil and gas production having previously pledged to end funding for new oil and gas fields[4].

Effective promotion relies on ensuring a high degree of coordination and integration between these different elements of the communications mix. The importance of clear positioning has already been emphasised in Chapter 7 and Chapter 9. Positioning provides an overarching framework that outlines the way in which an organisation, brand or product should be perceived by the market. Communications play a key role in ensuring that the chosen position is presented to the target market in a way that is aligned with all other elements of the marketing mix. And of course different promotion tools must themselves be aligned and consistent with the brand and position.

This chapter addresses the issues surrounding the development of an effective communication strategy in financial services. It begins with an overview of the essentials of marcoms for financial services and briefly outlines some of the tools and the challenges that financial service providers may face. The next section examines the development of promotion campaigns. The chapter then proceeds to discuss the relative merits of the different forms of promotion the financial services organisations use. The final main section explores digital marcoms in much greater detail. A summary and conclusions are presented in Section 11.6.

11.2 Financial services communications: the essentials

From a marketing perspective, the term "communications" refers quite simply to the way in which organisations try to send messages to target markets. The marketing communications process is most commonly thought to be concerned with telling consumers about the features, benefits and availability of a particular product and attempting to persuade them to make a purchase. Increasingly, however, it is being recognised that communication has a rather broader role to play. In addition to stimulating consumer interest in a product, the communications process is also concerned with the way in which an organisation projects itself and the image and identity it seeks to create with various stakeholders. And it is also of relevance in guiding consumers in terms of how best to use products and services to ensure maximum value. As will be explained in the next section, when considering who to target through a particular campaign and what message to try to convey, a fundamental question is whether the campaign is focused strategically around positioning the organisation/brand or whether it is to be focused more tactically on specific products and customer groups. In the case of the former, the campaign is likely to be concerned with influencing the way in which a broad customer group thinks about and feels about the organisation and the extent to which they see it as distinct from the competition. An example of this type of campaign is the HSBC "Together we Thrive" campaign (part of their overarching branding), and this is a sample of the copy used in the United Kingdom (UK) which seeks to highlight the importance of cultural diversity and cross-cultural engagement.

> **We are not an island. We are a Colombian coffee drinking, American movie watching, Swedish flat-pack furniture assembling, Korean tablet tapping, Belgian striker supporting, Dutch beer cheering, tikka masala eating, wonderful little lump of land in the middle of the sea. We are part of something far, far bigger.**

This campaign uses a range of marketing tools and focuses on a message about the overall positioning of HSBC. HSBC had previously presented itself as "The World's Local Bank", but following its withdrawal from a number of markets after the financial crash, it struggled to justify this position (see also Chapter 8). While being "glocal" remained an important part of the underpinning ethos of the organisation, HSBC needed to position itself differently. The new campaign was launched in 2018 with a central position for the logo and a message that stressed the bank as an organisation that was genuinely global and yet connected to and comfortable with a diversity of places worldwide.

Design themes developed for broad-based brand and positioning campaigns are typically reflected in product specific advertising with a combination of colour, logo and where possible theme. The red colour used by HSBC is instantly recognisable globally as is the blue used by Barclays and the yellow used by Maybank. The creative detail and copy will then be more specifically targeted to the product type.

Nationwide Bank (Figure 11.1) is similarly distinctive with its combination of red, blue and white. The message displayed here is part of a wider campaign that is integral to the

Figure 11.1 Nationwide Building Society's commitment to its branch network

Source: Reproduced with permission from Nationwide Media Centre (www.nationwidemediacentre.co.uk/resour ces/f/images/campaigns)

Nationwide brand and emphasises its commitment to its community and its commitment to its branch network at a time when digital channels have led to widespread branch closures creating access problems for some consumers. (See also Chapter 13).

As well as determining the purposes of marcoms, it is also essential to consider what communications methods (or tools) are to be used. In the same way as we think about a marketing mix – elements of marketing that are blended together, we often also talk about a promotional mix. Typically, marketers consider 4 broad components of a promotion mix.

1.   Advertising is defined as any paid form of non-personal presentation and promotion of ideas, goods or services by an organisation (whether through television, radio, internet, newspapers).
2.   Personal selling is defined as a process of encouraging and persuading potential customers to purchase a good or service, or to respond to any idea presented orally.
3.   Sales promotion covers activities which mainly provide short-term stimulation to purchase through the use of incentives (e.g. contests, coupons, rebates, gifts, etc.).
4.   Publicity/public relations describes any form of communication about the organisation which is basically not paid for and not personal. Good examples of public relations include significant news about the organisation or its services in the media, speeches, reports, etc. Sponsorship is often also seen as a form of public relations.

Finally, direct marketing is often considered to be a fifth tool; in some respects, it overlaps with advertising and sales promotion and entails a direct approach to customers with a personalised marketing message and a request for action. The message may be personalised at the level of the market segment; increasingly organisations are able to personalise the message to the individual. Because direct marketing has a focus on both communication and securing action from the consumer, it also overlaps with the distribution element of the marketing mix and is discussed in more detail in Chapter 13.

 Stop and think?

How many different examples of financial services communications have you seen in the past day? Which one has been most memorable and why?

Most campaigns will use a mixture of these tools as will be discussed below; each has strengths and weaknesses, and their value will vary according to campaign purpose and product life cycle stage. Campaigns will need to consider the right mix of communications tools, when they should be used, where they should be placed (e.g. which types of media should be used) and ensure that the elements of a campaign are consistent and integrated.

Communications and promotions for financial services are very similar to promoting physical products in many respects. However, financial services organisations do face some significant challenges. As explained in Chapter 3, they have no physical product to present to consumers and consequently a major requirement of the communications process is to develop a message and a form of presentation which allows the organisation to make their offer seem more tangible. Furthermore, financial services can be difficult to differentiate and this can make it challenging for an organisation to develop a clear message about the superiority of its own products. Finally, consumers tend to be relatively uninterested in financial services and this suggests that there may be a greater need to attract attention and so developing creative approaches to communication may be particularly important for financial services organisations.

While these issues are discussed in some detail in Chapter 3 and Chapter 6, Table 11.1 provides a brief reminder of the issues that financial services marketers need to be sensitive to when developing their marcoms. As you look through the table – and as you look back at chapters 3 and 6 you will realise that many of the suggested marketing actions will enable markers to address multiple characteristics of financial services.

Table 11.1 Marcoms responses to the characteristic of financial services

Characteristic	Marketing Challenges	Possible Marcoms Responses
Intangibility	The lack of physical form meaning that there is nothing tangible to show. In additional products may be difficult to understand and are often uninteresting to consumers.	• Try to visualize the service (e.g. Direct Line's red telephone). • Emphasise different forms of physical evidence (e.g. branch networks). • Use tangible names. • Rely on staff or recognisable individuals to represent the service. • Tell stories about the experiences of others who have used a particular service.
Inseparability & Perishability	Consumer evaluation is difficult because services are effectively produced and consumed simultaneously. This also means they cannot be stored for future consumption.	• Try to build trust and confidence in the organisation providing the service. • Endorsements from independent organisations can reassure consumers. • Pay attention to customer service skills for front line staff.
Heterogeneity	Variability in quality and in the service experience means it's difficult to make clear promises to consumers.	• Focus on staff and their concern to ensure that customers have a positive experience. • Emphasise the value and consistency of automation.
Fiduciary Responsibility	The potential impact of consumption on the consumer and on others often means that providers cannot provide a product to anyone who wishes to buy.	• Ensure that marcoms are carefully targeted to those consumers who are likely to be able to access the service. • Emphasise a responsible approach to customers, stressing honesty and prudence. • Ensure front line staff and sales people clearly understand which customers to target and which customers might not be eligible for a service.
Long term	Many products are for a long duration and benefits may not be realised for decades.	• Make use of storytelling to show what the future will look like and the benefits that will accrue.
Contingent Consumption	Products often have little direct value themselves – their real value is indirect through other forms of consumption or reassurance.	• Make use of storytelling to demonstrate future benefits – including reassurance in relation to risks as well as future purchases.

Marketing in practice 11.1 provides an example of how one organisation attempted to deal with some of the challenges of pensions marketing. In this case personalised video helped both to tangibilise the product and provide reassurance in the context of a product that is long term. In Canada, Home Equity Bank used a similar approach for an equity release product led by Peter Mansbridge – Canadian icon and trusted author and journalist. He participates in a question-and-answer session with an audience of Peter Mansbridges in a campaign entitled "Ask Yourself". Hello Bank, the digital bank owned by BNP Paribas, uses a humorous story telling approach to demonstrate the real benefits offered to consumers and the tag line "You make enough compromises" and the message that with Hello, you don't have to[5].

Marketing in practice 11.1: BBVA – an innovative pensions marketing campaign

Pensions provide a significant challenge in terms marcoms. The products relate to a future (getting older) that many customers would like to ignore and a purchase decision requires consumers to give up current consumption in favour of promised future consumption (at some unspecified date but expected to be a long time in the future). As the discussion in Chapter 6 around behavioural economics and finance illustrated, many consumers have a bias to the present and may undervalue future benefits such as retirement income. Across a range of markets internationally, it is widely recognised that many individuals are not saving for their retirement and those who are, may not be saving enough.

The difficulty associated with developing an effective marketing campaign (one that will encourage greater saving for retirement) is how best to convince individuals to sacrifice something today in order to enjoy income in the future. Historically, many companies relied on personal selling to actively persuade customers, but this can be a relatively expensive approach. Many customers prefer to avoid a selling context and for those who don't, personal sales can often have greater value at later stages in their decision process.

Banco Bilbao Vizcaya Argentaria – generally known as BBVA – is among the largest financial services providers in the world with a big presence in Latin America but also across Europe and pensions are a significant part of their product range. In developing a pensions campaign, BBVA decided on an approach which would show customers a future and their future selves would thank them for the existing contributions and encourage an increase in savings. To give the campaign maximum impact, BBVA targeted digital clients and personalised a video-message. Using a secure platform provided by idomoo they were able to bring together video creative and personal data (name, age, current levels of savings to send the customer a message from their future self. One such example script goes as follows:

Hello Chris Do you know who I am? You know me very well because I am you 20 years from now. I am sending you this message from 2042 because I want to thank you for thinking of me. Well, thinking of me in 2018. And I want to help you

*make the right choice – a choice that has allowed me to live comfortably in retire-
ment. As you've already made a contribution to you pension at BBVA this year,
I encourage you to contribute to the maximum of €12,500, which is the limit for
those who, like you, are over 50 years old. Let me give you a piece of advice – continue to live life intensely, but also remember your future. Time flies.*

As an indicator of the effectiveness of this campaign, BBVA saw savings from digital
clients increase faster than those for non-digital clients with estimates suggesting a
high level of engagement amount viewers and a 78% increase in pension savings.

Source: www.idomoo.com/en-gb/blog/bbva-pension-video-campaign-shows-savers-their-fut
ure-self/ (accessed 31 January2024)

Thus, an effective communications strategy requires careful thought and planning to
ensure that the organisation has a clear and coherent message to present. This message must
be clear, simple, honest and believable. Finally, of course, it is important that any promotional activity does not promise something that the organisation cannot deliver. Apart from
any legal implications that this might have from the point of view of advertising standards,
etc., promising what cannot be supplied will lead to consumer dissatisfaction with the purchase and the potential loss of future consumers.

In the UK, the Advertising Standards Authority is responsible for UK media complying with
the rules of advertising (The Advertising Code). It is a self-regulatory body – so it is funded by
the industry that it regulates, although it does also work with the UK's communications regulator. Like good marketers, the ASA[6] recognises the value that responsible advertising brings
and it may ban advertising that is irresponsible, hurtful, misleading or offensive. Indeed in 2022
it reports dealing with around 33,000 complaints on about close to 22,00 adverts. But some
of the challenges in marcoms are not simply about poor and misleading campaigns – even
when campaigns are accurate the way in which they are presented may impact on consumers.
Research insight 11.1 highlights some of the challenges associated with the way in which commonly used messages around the past performance of investment products are presented (or
"framed") and shows how different message framing may impact on consumer choice.

**Research insight 11.1: consumer reactions to the presentation of
past performance information**

Existing research on the performance of investment funds generally suggests that prior
performance of market-based financial services (e.g. equity funds, bond funds, etc.)
is of little use to investors as it does not serve to predict future performance; nonetheless, it remains widely used by providers and customers alike. Financial services
regulators have long been concerned about the ways in which companies selling such
products can present information on past performance selectively in order to create
a more favourable (and perhaps unrealistic) view of the future performance of the

products they offer. Prior performance is often presented in a graphical format, but the information can be represented in many different ways.

Research by Diacon and Hasseldine (2007) used prior performance charts in a controlled experiment to assess the impact on respondents of different forms of presentation and the use of data over different timescales. Their survey showed respondents a pair of past performance charts for a low-risk/low-return fixed-interest fund and an equity fund, where performance was presented as an index of the day-by-day fund value (relative to a base year with value =100). Respondents were then asked which fund they would recommend to a friend who wished to make regular contributions to a savings plan, over at least ten years. The exercise was then repeated with the same prior performance represented instead by percentage annual yield bar charts, using the same timescale combination as the pair of index charts.

Diacon and Hasseldine's results suggested that the presentation format of prior performance influenced the respondents' choice of fund (that is, between fixed interest and equity funds) and their perceptions of the investment risk involved. In particular, when past performance was charted using annual percentage yields, respondents were less likely to recommend an equity fund to their friend. Of those respondents who had recommended an equity fund when shown information based on an index of fund values, around half changed their mind when shown the same information using annual percentage yield figures. Furthermore, the use of annual percentage yield figures as a measure of prior performance was also found to increase the perceived investment risk, particularly of the equity fund.

In commenting on the implications of their findings, Diacon and Hasseldine made three main points. First, the fact that the format of prior performance clearly influenced respondents' recommended fund suggests that past performance charts have a role in investors' decision-making – perhaps because they convey information about the investment risk involved. Although past performance may have little value in predicting future returns, it may still be of use in judging future risk. Second, presenting past performance solely in terms of annual percentage yields is likely to deter investment in higher-risk equity funds, and therefore deprive investors of the higher average returns that equity funds generally produce over a longer period. Finally, one way of avoiding the impact of a particular presentation format on investment choice is to present prior performance in more than one alternative format.

Source: Diacon and Hasseldine (2007).

11.3 Planning a promotional campaign

There are arguably three core components to any promotional campaign – the tools that are being used (advertising, personal selling, sales promotion, public relations and direct marketing), the media that are selected and the message to be conveyed. These components are then used by financial providers to communicate with a target market and as Fill (2006) has suggested, using the acronym DRIP (see Figure 11.2), they are specifically expected to help the organisation to:

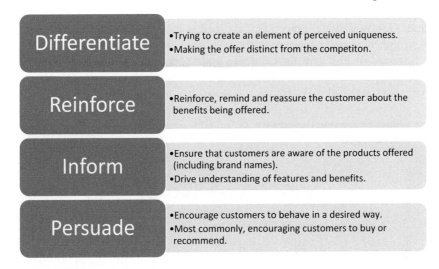

Figure 11.2 The purposes of marketing communications

Source: Adapted from Fill (2006)

Marketing in practice 11.2 outlines the way in which price comparison website "Comparethemarket.com" secured differentiation from the competition through a particularly effective marketing communications campaign.

Marketing in practice 11.2: Differentiation through promotion: Comparethemarket.com

There are a number of apps and websites which effectively distribute financial services to the retail market by gathering together information about a large number of product options in response to a specified consumer request. Customers can then compare different product offers across a range of attributes and then click through to the chosen supplier to progress a purchase. Differentiation is difficult for these price comparison sites because each does essentially the same thing and service innovations are relatively easy to copy.

UK-based "Comparethemarket.com" (see Figure 11.3) wanted an advertising campaign which would provide it with distinctiveness and drive traffic to its website, without incurring some of the very high costs associated with pay-per-click advertising. It engaged VCCP ("We make your brand shine brighter") to undertake this work and has now worked with them for some 14 years. The agency identified "market" as being a key element of the company name and looked to develop a campaign based around that word. The creative team focused on the similarity between "market" and "meerkat" and created an advertising campaign focusing on the experiences of Russian oligarch, Aleksandr Orlov, a meerkat. Launched in January 2009 in the UK, the campaign was phenomenally successful; the objectives specified for a 12-month period were delivered in less than three months and "comparethemarket.com" moved to become the top brand in its area in terms of spontaneous recognition. In 2013 the same campaign was launched in Australia.

Figure 11.3 Comparethemarket.com

Source: Shutterstock

The campaign gained momentum as the personality of Aleksandr Orlov (and his assistant, Sergei) captured the public imagination; advertising campaigns evolved to tell the story of his family, Orlov himself engaged with consumers via Twitter and Facebook. Orlov became the public face of the brand and created a genuinely distinctive position for "comparethemarket.com". Building on this success, the campaign has been sustained with a number of developments including customer reward in the form of a cuddly meerkat toy; the meerkat movies campaigns (rewards in the form of 2-for-1 cinema tickets) and meerkat meals. The pandemic and long periods of social distancing significantly devalued these two initiatives but the brand responded with meerkat music, reuniting iconic band "Take That" for a streamed online show, watched initially by over 600,000 people. In the latest development, launched at the start of 2023, the campaign introduced a new, non-meerkat character – Carl, the wombat. Whenever bumbling Carl gets involved in anything he invariably makes matters worse. Bringing in a new character was risky, but Carl proved to be in immediate success and a very effective way of refreshing a long-standing campaign.

Financial services advertising rarely stands out in the marketplace. The "compare the meerkat" campaign is arguably one of the great success stories of advertising – a campaign that has run for close to 15 years with consistently highly positive rating from audiences and a dramatic impact on the reputation of "comparethemarket".

Source: Baines, Fill and Pagel, (2010); Curphey, (2011)

The component elements of marketing communications need to be carefully planned and managed to ensure that any campaign is effective. Careful planning is also important to ensure that the different methods of marketing communications are sending consistent messages and that marketing communications are aligned with other elements of the marketing mix.

11.3.1 Stages in communications planning

The simplest way to think about the planning of a promotional campaign is to think of it as a series of stages as shown in Figure 11.4.

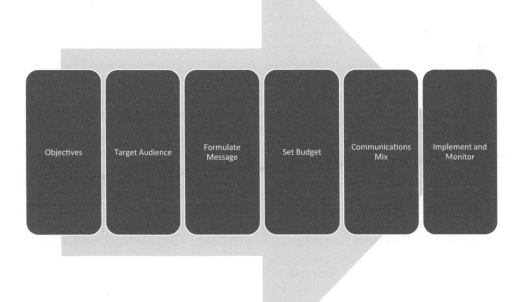

Figure 11.4 Planning a promotional campaign

Objectives

Defining objectives is important so that all involved in a promotional campaign know what they are trying to achieve. Often objectives are specified in terms of an increase in sales but other objectives may concern themselves with raising awareness, creating a particular image, smoothing patterns of demand, etc. In general, there are two broad types of objectives which may underpin any promotional campaign – one focuses more on behaviour and specifically purchase behaviour; the other focuses on attitudes – and particularly on thoughts and feelings:

• **Positioning and differentiating – building a brand (strategic)**
  Many promotional campaigns are directed towards creating and maintaining a particular corporate image. Such campaigns have been particularly noticeable in the financial services sector because the characteristics of financial services (as discussed in Chapter 3) mean that organisations must pay particular attention to their brand and reputation. Campaigns of this nature may focus on building awareness for new brands, while for more established brands, the aims are more likely to focus on developing positive thoughts, feelings and beliefs.
• **Influence consumers through decision process (Tactical)**
  Promotions may be directed explicitly towards influencing the level of demand for a service or range of services. Normally, this would imply increasing the level of demand through attracting new customers away from competitors, increasing usage by existing customers, or encouraging customer referrals.[7] This type of promotional activity is primarily concerned with influencing how actual or potential customers behave through prepurchase (inform, encourage), purchase (call to action) and post purchase (reinforce post purchase).

As far as possible, objectives should be quantified. The guidelines given in Section 4.3.3 regarding the criteria for a suitably robust marketing objectives are equally relevant for promotional objectives. This may simply mean specifying a target for increased sales volume or value. Alternatively, in the case of image-based objectives, targets may be set based on levels of awareness of the organisation or on attitudes towards the organisation.

Target audience

The next stage in promotional planning requires the identification of consumer groups who are the target of the promotional activity – who to communicate with. At one level, this may simply involve defining the target market for a specific service or specifying "the general public" (if the promotion is concerned with positioning, image and organisational reputation). But it is always worth remembering that the organisation's communications will also be seen by employees and other stakeholders (as secondary audiences). Messages will be crafted for the primary audience, but it is important to ensure that these primary audience messages are consistent with other communications that might have reached secondary audiences.

It is also important to recognise that there will be differences between consumers in terms of their knowledge and awareness of an organisation's image and range of services (and indeed as shown in Chapter 6, consumers may be at different stages in a decision process).

In particular, researchers have suggested that consumers pass through a number of different stages when considering a purchase. One example of this is known as the AIDA model because consumers are expected to move from Awareness to Interest to Desire and finally to Action. A related Hierarchy of Effects framework proposes that consumers pass through six stages (awareness, knowledge, liking, preference, conviction, purchase). The process of defining the target audience should consider which stage in the AIDA/Hierarchy of Effects sequence consumers have reached. A promotional message and medium which is concerned with creating awareness of, or interest in, a product is likely to differ from one which is trying to create a desire to purchase or stimulate an actual purchase.

Formulate message

Having identified the target audience the next stage is to establish what form the message will take. Any message can be divided into two key components – the message content and the message form. The message content relates to the basic ideas and information that the organisation wishes to convey. It should make clear why the product is different, what benefits it offers and why the consumer should buy this product rather than one of the available alternatives.

Once the basic content of the message has been established, the next stage is to consider the form this message should take. It is at this point that the creative input from outside organisations such as advertising/communications agencies becomes important. This process involves finding the most appropriate combination of verbal, audio and visual signals which will present the content of the message in a form which is most suitable for the target audience. Great care must be taken with the construction (encoding) of the message to avoid possible misunderstandings. At the same time, the information must be presented in a form which will attract attention and maintain sufficient interest in an advertisement or a leaflet to enable the potential consumer to absorb the information being conveyed. Increasingly, this is a major challenge given the changes to reading and viewing habits and the ease with which consumers can skip past advertising messages. Often, to attract attention, creative teams will make use of humorous sketches, indirect comparisons with competitors or it may simply focus on imaginative presentations of the product or the organisation itself. We have already seen (in Marketing in practice 11.2) how effective the creation of a meerkat character – Aleksandr Orlov – was for price comparison site "comparethemarket.com". In South Africa, Standard Bank promoted its sponsorship of the Joy of Jazz with an advertising campaign that feature freestyle jazz, played by pigeons in Johannesburg's Pigeon Square[8]. In the US, CO-OP Financial Services tried to attract customer attention with a humorous press campaign that provided examples of embarrassing or awkward work situations accompanied by the strapline "making money is hard but putting it in the right place doesn't have to be"[9]. And in the example of Hello Bank discussed earlier, the humour theme was again used to grab the interests of viewers. In a rather different approach, but one that is also designed to grab attention through an emphasis on responsibility, insurer Allianz France launched a campaign focusing on accident prevention in winter sports. The campaign launched in 2024 on TikTok and Instagram using high impact videos of skiing accidents with the theme of "Same causes, same consequences". Implicitly. Allianz, which offers winter sports insurance was hoping to reduce the risk to consumers (and in turn) the risk of claims.

Stop and think?

How effective is humour in messaging for financial services? Will customers find it engaging or is there a risk that it may undermine the serious aspect of the product?

Budget

A budget must be established for the communications exercise as a whole, and, at a later stage for the individual components of the promotional mix. There are no hard and fast rules for determining the size of the communications budget and even within the same broad market, organisations will vary enormously in terms of promotional expenditure. There are a number of different approaches to the formulation of communications budgets including:

- The affordable method
  This simply suggests that the organisation's expenditure on promotion is determined according to what the overall corporate budget indicates is available. The organisation basically spends what it thinks it can afford.
- Sales revenue method
  This approach sets the communications budget as some percentage of sales revenue. By implication this means that sales "lead" promotion rather than promotion "leading" sales which is what might be desired. That is to say, the size of the promotional budget will be dependent on past sales rather than desired future sales.
- The incremental method
  The budget is set as an increment on the previous year's expenditure. This is widely used, particularly by smaller firms. However, it does not allow for feedback from the market-to-communications spend and does not allow promotional or marketing objectives to guide the level of expenditure.
- The competitive parity approach
  This approach focuses on the importance of promotion as a competitive tool and entails setting budgets to match those of competitors.
- The objective/task method
  This is probably the most logical approach to the establishment of communications budgets, but perhaps also the most difficult to implement because of the complexity of many of the calculations. As a consequence it is not used widely. It relies on specific quantified objectives and then requires that a precise cost is calculated based on the activities required to achieve these objectives. The budget is then based on these costs, so that marketing managers have a precise budget which should allow them to achieve their stated objectives.

A growing number of researchers argue that the marketing budget in general and a communications budget in particular should be seen not as an annual cost but rather as an investment (see for example, Doyle, 2000). This approach argues that many marketing activities, and particularly advertising, have a cumulative effect and pay a key role in building the brand. If the effects of communications expenditure have an impact over a number of years, then it would be misleading to focus on costs on an annual basis.

Communications mix

Having determined the appropriate level of communications expenditure this must be allocated between the various promotional tools available to the organisation – namely, advertising, personal selling, sales promotion, public relations and direct marketing. This mix will vary across organisations, products and markets. While it is difficult to generalise, retail markets will often make more use of mass communication methods such as advertising, sales promotion and public relations/publicity, while personal selling will be more important to corporate customers. In financial services, as is explained in Chapter 13, personal selling is relatively widespread in retail markets for more complex financial services. However, mass forms of communication remain popular for the less complex products such as credit cards, current accounts and savings accounts.

There is a high degree of substitutability between promotional tools so organisations must consider the strengths and weaknesses of different methods of communication and choose the combination that is most appropriate to the particular product and market. The individual components of the promotional mix will be examined in more detail in the next section.

Implementation and monitoring

As with any plan, the final stage concerns the process of implementation and monitoring. Implementation concerns itself with the allocation of tasks and the specification of timescale. Monitoring focuses on the regular evaluation of the progress of the promotional campaign and the identification of any areas where changes may be necessary. The problem that faces many organisations is the difficulty of measuring the effectiveness of promotional activities. There are a number of approaches that might be used to assess the effectiveness of promotional campaigns as outlined in Figure 11.5.

Thus, evaluating campaigns can be difficult and ideally organisations would use several different sources of information and undertake detailed research with consumers. In practice, the costs of different types of research often lead to a reliance on general, commercial studies and an acceptance of some loss of detail and relevance in the evaluation.

Progress check

- From a marketing perspective, the term "communications" refers quite simply to the way in which organisations are able to send messages to target markets.
- The tools used for communications are typically classed as advertising, promotion, personal selling and publicity/PR. Direct mail is sometimes seen as a fifth.
- Developing promotional campaigns must take into account the distinctive characteristics of services and think about the best way to really engage actual and prospective customers.
- To do this effectively, a structured approach is important and when messages are developed, they need to take into consideration the target market, where they are in terms of decision making and their level of engagement with the product (See AIDA/hierarchy of effects)

Pre-Testing

- Demonstrate the campaign to selected consumers.
- Amend the campaign based on audience responses, assess likely impact.
- Does not guarantee effectiveness and many successful advertisements have failed pre-tests.

Live-Testing

- Digital enables organisations to get campaign performance feedback in almost real time.
- Uses a range of analytical techniques to determine which messages drive the desired consumer response.
- Retire and replace low-performing messages with speed and efficiency.

Ex post commercial market research

- Using commercial market research to determine levels of recall and comprehension once a campaign has started.
- Recall and comprehension surveys can indicate whether the basic message has been conveyed to the target audience.
- Less suitable for assessing how effective a campaign has been in terms of encouraging purchase. Simply because people say that they have recalled an advertisement or are aware of or interested in a product does not mean they intend to buy it.

Statistical Analysis

- Essentially,this involves a comparison of sales before the campaign with sales after the campaign.
- The findings of such studies can often show a change in sales after the campaign but it is difficult to demonstrate that the campaign actually caused the change to occur.

Figure 11.5 Approaches to assessing the effectiveness of promotional campaigns

11.3.2 Integrated marketing communications

As the discussion above has demonstrated, the process of managing marketing communications involves bringing together a mix of different tools and media to target particular consumer groups in pursuit of specified objectives. Integrated marketing communications (IMC) is an approach to managing promotional activity that focuses on ensuring that all communications activity is integrated, providing a consistent and unified message (see for example Fill, 2006). This involves using the different promotional tools in an integrated fashion, deploying each for the purpose for which they are most effective. It also entails ensuring commonality of message across different tools and media and of course a consistency in the appearance of advertising. As discussed earlier in the chapter with the examples of Barclays, HSBC, Nationwide and Maybank (see Figure 11.6), consistency in colour, in imagery, in style and in message is fundamental to ensuring impact. Apart from the obvious benefits in terms of delivering a consistent message, integrated marketing communications can also offer greater efficiency with the costs of creative work being spread across a larger range of activities.

11.4 Forms of communication

As the previous section has indicated, there are a range of different communications tools available to suppliers of financial services. This section discusses some of the more important

Figure 11.6 Maybank's use of colour in advertising

Source: "We'll be there when her daughter borrows the sari for her own wedding. Maybank." by myahya licensed under CC BY-SA 2.0

methods of promotion in greater detail, highlighting their strengths and weaknesses. The particular role of new media in financial services is addressed in more detail in the next section.

11.4.1 Advertising

Advertising is a form of mass communication which is paid for and involves the non-personal presentation of goods/ideas. As such, it covers television, radio, internet and press advertising and some would also include other approaches such as direct mail and direct-response advertising, although these are treated separately here. How and why advertising works continues to be the subject of some debate. While some researchers argue that advertising of different types can play a key role in terms of driving individuals through a hierarchy of effects from awareness through to action (purchase), others would suggest that advertising has a more limited role of maintaining brand awareness and reinforcing existing attitudes.

Advertising is usually classified as being of two types, above-the-line and below-the-line.

- **Above-the-line**
  Above the line advertising refers to all forms of advertising where a fee is payable to an advertising agency and includes press, TV, radio, internet, cinema and poster advertising. The major advantage of above-the-line advertising is that it enables an organisation to

reach a large and diverse audience at a low cost per person. A further strength is that the sponsor (i.e. the organisation) retains a good degree of control over the message content, its presentation and timing. A potential disadvantage is that messages are highly standardised and as such advertising can be an inflexible promotional tool. It may also be wasteful because it reaches a large number of individuals who are not potential consumers.

- **Below-the-line**
  Below-the-line advertising describes forms of advertising for which no commission fee is payable to an advertising agency and includes direct mail, direct-response advertising, exhibitions and point-of-sale material. In comparison with the types of media advertising described above, these methods tend to be much more focused, they reach a smaller number of people at a higher cost per person, but this is often counterbalanced by the higher degree of accuracy associated with such methods.

Advertising is one of the most widely used promotional tools in retail financial services because of its ability to reach large numbers of customers cost effectively. However, the features of financial services do present some difficulties when developing advertising. As mentioned earlier, financial services are intangible so there is little to show in an advert. Furthermore, customers often require large amounts of information in order to make purchase decisions but many forms of above-the-line advertising are not very effective at making this information available. Press advertising can provide more information than TV, radio, cinema and poster advertising, but the quantity of information is still limited. The internet can provide rather more information to consumers once they have clicked on a particular advert.

Financial services are some of the largest spenders in the digital advertising arena. In the US, for example, in 2022, digital ad spending by the financial services sector was estimated at 16% of total spend with a value of around $11billion and an estimated 32% return on investment[10]. The automation of buying and selling digital media, known as programmatics, has made a significant contribution to the efficiency of online advertising and aided its continued growth. Initially, there were concerns that digital advertising may not prove an effective medium for the financial sector; however in practice, this has not been the case. Combined with effective CRM, digital offers organisations an opportunity to target prospects and clients with extremely focused and bespoke advertising. Social media offers a powerful advertising opportunity, for example Facebook advertising allows brands to target particular segments based on demographics such as age, gender, interests and location. As well as advertising on their own sites, cookies enable organisations to employ retargeting to reconnect with customers who have bounced off the brand's site prior to converting. As the visitor continues to surf the web, they will be served ads relating to the product or service they browsed on the brand's own website. Because the target is already familiar with the brand and product or service, there tends to be a higher conversion rate for retargeting campaigns.

Because customers will often need a lot of information in order to make a decision, above-the-line advertising is often thought to be more suited to the process of raising awareness and generating interest while other promotional tools are used to encourage desire and action (remember the AIDA and Hierarchy of Effects models discussed earlier). For example, many unit trust companies will operate campaigns to raise awareness of their fund performance and encourage consumer interest. These adverts provide minimal information – rather their aim is to encourage a sufficient level of interest that the consumer will think about approaching the company for a prospectus or alternatively will respond positively if a prospectus is mailed to them.

Above-the-line advertising can also be particularly effective in building organisational reputation and image because this type of communication does not require detailed information but rather focuses on a broad general message. An example of this latter type of advertising would be Great Eastern's "Great Trust Great Confidence" campaign which involved minimal information, just a logo and a message. Equally, HSBC's campaign illustrated how the bank's local knowledge is used worldwide and has played a major role in building the HSBC brand.

Advertising financial services is carefully regulated in many countries because of its potential to mislead. The combination of product complexity and limited consumer interest mean that some forms of creative presentation can be misleading. Interest rates are a particular area of concern because many consumers do not fully understand different forms of presentation such as APR and AER and their relationship with headline rates (Buch, Rhoda and Talaga, 2002). The presentation of investment performance is another area of concern. Many adverts rely heavily on figures about past performance to demonstrate the quality of their products and then accompany such adverts with a disclaimer in small print to indicate that past performance is no guide to what will happen in the future. In addition, the actual formats used to present investment performance figures may result in the same real performance being interpreted differently according to style of presentation as was outlined in Research insight 11.1.

Thus advertising can take many forms and the type of advertising used by a financial services organisation will be influenced by the stated objectives and the nature of the target audience. Whatever type of advertising is used, particular attention must be paid to trying to make the service more tangible, reducing customer perceived risk, being transparent and trying to build trust and confidence.

11.4.2 *Personal selling*

Personal selling is discussed in more detail in Chapter 13. Personal selling has a dual role to play in the marketing of financial services. It is a channel of distribution and also a method of communication. Personal selling is probably most common in corporate markets, but is also widely used in personal markets in relation to some of the more complex financial services – and indeed, with the options that digital technologies present (e.g. chatbots, live chat), personal interactivity may even increase in the retail environment.

One of the major benefits of personal selling as a form of communication is that it allows immediate feedback from consumer to the organisation. Other forms of communication are basically one-way, but personal selling is two-way. The customer can raise queries with the salesperson and those queries or concerns can be dealt with immediately. This means that the information communicated can be accurately tailored to the needs of particular individuals. Furthermore, because personal selling allows queries and response, it is often thought to be very effective towards the end of the AIDA/Hierarchy of Effects process – in encouraging action (purchase).

Thus, although personal selling can be a valuable and effective form of promotion, it is also very expensive. Thus, it tends to be used more heavily for relatively high value products and more heavily when customers are close to making a purchase. As well as being expensive, it is also a form of promotion that can be difficult to manage. Increasingly, some organisations are trying to manage the costs of personal selling through the use of technology. Avatar technology is being used to create virtual customer service representatives and advisors, although the effectiveness of these initiatives is still unproven. More effective is the use of video banking. Barclays UK offers this service via their mobile banking app, allowing customers to have a confidential conversation with a banking relationship manager (free over Wi-Fi), as a convenient alternative to visiting a branch. In Spain, Bankinter uses specialist advisor capacity at one branch to provide advice to customers at another branch. Financial services are getting wise to the potential of artificial intelligence to not only process large volumes of back-end data, but also to be used to provide robo-advice (see Chapter 13 for more on this topic). This enables the provision of fast, cheap and unbiased financial advice based on automated and algorithmic analysis of a specific customer's financial situation, arguably more accurate than a human advisor could provide. Hybrid models are also available where customers can receive a blend of both robo and human advice for more complex financial decisions. This is already a well-established offering from established brands such as Blackrock and HSBC as well as new players to the robo-investing space such as Moneyfarm, Atom and Nutmeg.

11.4.3 Publicity/public relations

Publicity is normally defined as being any form of non-paid, non-personal communication, and like advertising, it involves dealing with a mass audience. For this discussion, we broaden the concept of publicity to include an additional element, namely public relations. Public relations is paid-for whereas publicity is assumed to be "free". However, it is included under this heading because it is concerned more generally with building and maintaining an understanding between the organisation and the general public.

When Metro Bank launched its new banking service in the UK, it briefed a communications agency to create a genuine level of interest and excitement that would ensure positive media coverage when the first new branch opened. The strategy involved a range of press briefings, regular news stories ahead of the launch and profiles of key individuals. The messaging focused on the novelty of the Metro Bank offer (long opening hours, innovative branch design) and the fact that Metro Bank was the first new UK high street bank in 100 years. The campaign generated a high level of media coverage which was both positive in tone and which reflected Metro Bank's key messages. Indeed, public relations (PR) was the only form of marketing communications used by Metro Bank and it underpinned a successful launch, a high level of brand awareness and an accelerated branch-opening programme.[11]

Publicity offers a number of benefits to the organisation. It has no major time costs, it provides access to a large audience and the message is considered to have a high degree of credibility, not least because the information is seen as coming from an independent or quasi-independent source rather than from the organisation itself. However, it is also one of the more difficult forms of promotion to implement and to control since the final presentation and timing of information about the organisation will usually be edited by the media such as television, newspapers and online news providers.

Traditionally, publicity and public relations were seen as being centred around producing regular, informative press releases and building up good contacts with journalists. As a consequence, their importance has often been underestimated. However, with increasing pressure on advertising space and costs, the importance of publicity seems likely to increase. Two areas merit particular attention – namely the creation of a corporate image and sponsorship.

- **Corporate image**

  The importance of corporate image and organisational branding was mentioned earlier in this chapter. The development of a suitable corporate image is an aspect of public relations which is of particular importance to financial services organisations because the reputation or image of the company has a major impact on consumer choice. Indeed, corporate image is often seen as one of the most important forms of branding that is available to a financial services organisation. Each December the magazine *PR Week* reports on corporate reputation based upon the extent and nature of public relations coverage that businesses receive in the UK and similar reports are found in many other parts of the world. It is unusual for financial services companies to feature in the upper echelons of such surveys. Interbrand's survey of the best global brands has no financial service provider in the top 20. The highest positions for financial services organisations in 2023 were JP Morgan at 26, American Express at position 28 followed by Allianz at 31 Visa at 37 and Paypal at 40[12].

The factors that contribute to the creation of a favourable image are many and varied. A clear corporate identity is important to make the organisation instantly recognisable. An organisation's corporate identity can be represented by a variety of visual symbols associated with promotional material, the branch network and staff appearance. Other forms of communication can be used to help create an image and personality. Internal marketing can be used to encourage staff to commit to the corporate identity and believe in the image that the organisation wishes to create.

- **Sponsorship**

One increasingly important aspect of public relations and the creation of a desirable corporate image has been the growth in sponsorship. The extent to which this method of communication is used varies considerably across organisations, but with increased competition for advertising slots on television and rising media costs in general, sponsorship is seen as an important and effective way of projecting the image of the organisation.

Particular features of the usefulness of sponsorship include the ability of the sponsoring brand to be associated with the characteristics of the sponsored activity (the so-called presenter effect), and the facility to be used for corporate hospitality. The latter feature is why sponsorship is often favoured by financial services companies involved in B2B marketing. Financial services organisations are involved in sponsorship of a variety of events including sports events (e.g. football), entertainment (e.g. music concerts), and cultural events (e.g. art exhibitions). This type of sponsorship can be very effective at getting the organisations noticed by retail customers and Marketing in practice 10.2 demonstrated how Frost Bank used this sort of sponsorship as an integral component of its brand building work. For corporate customers, the sponsorship of local business seminars is also a widely used technique. The advantage of sponsorship, apart from its cost-effectiveness, tends to be that it is viewed less cynically by the consumer than more traditional forms of advertising.

11.4.4 Sales promotion

Sales promotions are usually described as being demand-pull methods. Demand-pull promotions are concerned with providing consumers with a direct incentive to try and buy a product. The use of sales promotions as part of a marketing campaign has increased considerably in recent years as has been evidenced by the rapid growth in the volume of business conducted by specialist sales promotion agencies.

There are a variety of techniques available although the most popular are probably:

- **Benefits tied to product use**

This is one of the most popular forms of promotion used in financial services and in many other sectors. If the consumer uses or buys a particular product or service, he or she receives a free or discounted gift. Barclays has offered new personal pension customers the equivalent of three months' free contributions as an incentive to encourage new customer acquisition. The campaign was supported by in-branch promotional material and reinforced by branch staff in their interactions with customers. Cashback websites have grown in popularity, particularly within the insurance space, with aggregators and cashback sites such as Moneysupermarket and Quidco offering cashback incentives when users purchase a product through their site. Loyalty schemes which provide rewards such as Air Miles based on the level of spend on a credit or charge card are widely used in financial services and are another example of promotion based on product-use benefits. Some of these schemes are discussed in more detail in Part III of this book.

- **Reduced price**
  This constitutes the most direct method of sales promotion in that it simply involves offering the product to the consumer at a reduced price. It is similar to couponing (see below), but it is available to anyone rather than being restricted to those consumers with a coupon. For example, Citibank offered a one-year fee waiver as a promotional device when they launched their Citibank Blue Credit Card. Savings accounts often offer time-limited bonus rates when a customer opens an account.

- **Competitions**
  Competitions are a popular and easy-to-manage form of promotion. Consumers of the product are offered the opportunity to enter a competition to win attractive prizes. Citibank's "99 Wishes" campaign was a competition which allowed card holders to send their top nine wishes from a list of 99 and if their list matched the popular list for that day, the customer's number one wish was fulfilled. As only Citibank customers were able to enter, this can be seen as the kind of competition which would encourage new customers to Citibank as well as generating publicity. Similarly Standard Chartered offered prize-draw entry to anyone who signed up for the Standard Chartered Motorists Club Visa.

- **Couponing**
  Money-off coupons are probably the technique which is most commonly associated with sales promotions. It is less common in financial services, although a number of companies will offer discounts through direct mailing to certain target customers and this can have a similar effect in that it should encourage purchase. A related concept is that of the introductory offer and a growing number of financial services providers are offering either initial discounts on credit products or introductory interest premia on savings products. These introductory interest rates (sometimes described as "teaser rates") can be very successful in attracting new business but there are concerns that they may also mislead vulnerable customers who maybe attracted by the headline rate and may not fully appreciate the impact on their savings when the introductory rate comes to an end.

Sales promotions can be very effective towards the final stage of the AIDA/Hierarchy of Effects process as they are designed to encourage the consumer to actually make the purchase.

11.4.5 Direct marketing

Direct marketing (and the associated technique, direct-response advertising) involve direct communication from the organisation to actual or prospective customers with a view to stimulating a purchase, referral or other related behaviour. Both these techniques are discussed in more detail in Chapter 13 because as well as being a means of communication, they are also a method of distributing financial services.

The particular advantage of both direct mail and direct-response advertising is that they can provide customers with a lot of the detail necessary to make a final purchase decision. Indeed, direct mail which is accurately targeted to the right customer group can be very effective at generating new business, as well as cross-selling to existing customers. Accordingly, these methods of advertising are likely to be more effective in encouraging the final stage in the AIDA/Hierarchy of Effects model – namely the purchase (action). In addition, direct mail has the advantage that it is effectively invisible to competitors. However, the ability to use direct mail effectively does depend on the organisation having good, accurate and up-to-date customer databases and this can present a problem for many financial services organisations.

Progress check

- Advertising is a form of mass communication which is paid for and involves the non-personal presentation of goods or ideas. Advertising is thought by many to be more effective in building brand awareness and modifying or reinforcing existing attitudes.
- Personal selling has a dual role to play in the marketing of financial services. It is a channel of distribution and also a method of communication. It is more common in corporate markets, but is also widely used in personal markets for more complex financial services.
- Publicity is normally defined as being any form of non-paid, non-personal communication. Publicity and public relations deal with a mass audience. Both tend to be most effective for awareness and reputation building.
- Sales promotions are demand-pull methods of promotion specifically concerned with providing consumers with a direct incentive to try and buy a product.
- Direct mail is personalised communication but also serves as a method of distribution.

11.5 The digital effect

Digital disrupts how customers interact with organisations. Financial services providers need to understand how to leverage this disruption and use customer data to facilitate the shift in consumer expectations. The "Uber effect" has led consumers to expect physical world experiences to offer the same seamless experience as the digital world. However, while customers are more empowered when they come to organisations to interact, they still want reassurance that the innovations on offer will benefit them specifically, as well as society as a whole. Thus, financial services organisations must ensure their marketing communications are delivered in a manner that responds to these concerns.

As the digital media available have expanded (voice-activated banking, mobile, wearables, Internet of Things, etc.) consumers are now bombarded with brand messages across all forms of media, on every device. They expect to be able to interact with brands through the medium of their choice and brands must ensure their communications span the new connected, internet-enabled world as well as more traditional channels. Brands also need to be sensitive to the ways in which users will respond to communications through different media. For example, while mobile is one of the most popular methods of accessing the internet, SMS messaging is often too intrusive and off-putting. Organisations should aim to target customers rather than devices and ensure they employ sequential messaging across all channels and devices in order to deliver an effective omni-channel experience.

Marketing in practice 11.3 explores some of the ways in which fintechs have been particularly effective in their digital marketing. Content marketing is an approach that has been widely used, especially by the neobanks and has also been widely adopted by traditional players as a highly cost-effective way of attracting customers to a web site and engaging them by providing material that helps the customer to answer a particular question.

 Marketing in practice 11.3: Fintechs and digital marketing

Digital marketing (and specifically digital engagement) is an area in which the new fintech and insurtech start-up have excelled – in part because they do not have some of the same legacy practices of some of their more traditional competitors and in part because their digital expertise is often a core competence.

Analysis by digital media shop GA Agency (reported in The Financial Brand) looked specifically at Revolut and Monzo – two of the best know UK neobanks; Ally Bank in the US is an equally good example of how digital marketing can be employed to best effect. Key features of the digital engagement activities of these neobanks include:

- **Search Engine Optimisation (SEO)**
  Search engines are a critical mechanism through which consumers assess market offers and consequently a lot of the work in digital communication is about how to get an organisation's name as high up a search engine results page (SERP). In addition to brand bidding (see below), marketers will also bid for more generic keywords that prospective customers might use. And while bidding on their own names is often criticised as paying to reach customers who are already interested, it can help raise an organisations visibility on the SERP.

- **Brand Bidding and Keywords.**
  Since 2019, Google has eased its previous restrictions on bidding for key words. It is now possible for one brand to bid for another's branded keyword. This approach is increasingly seen as a key part of any pay-per-click strategy. Brand bidding means that when a customer searches for a competitor they can be presented with the opportunity to click through to the bidder's web site. Revolut are thought

to have invested heavily in this approach, although it can be expensive. Digital marketing specialists recommend careful monitoring of impact, bidding on your own as well as competitor's brands and thinking carefully about advertising copy that grabs attention.

- **Developing appealing content to bring traffic to a web site.**
  In addition to targeted search, customers may be attracted to a web site by the presence of content that is interesting and engaging. Typically, this takes the form of blogs and videos on topics linked to the organisation's broad business area. For example, Monzo has a number of blogs providing generic financial advice and which could attract the interest of potential customers and bring them to the Monzo site. This approach is becoming increasingly popular as a growing number of traditional providers have developed their own content-based strategies.

- **Manging the Web: testing and ease of use.**
  Some of the best digital marketing organisations rely on the use of different landing pages for different queries and/or different types of leads. This makes tracking and understanding the effectiveness of different routes to the web pages more straight forward as well as enhancing the customer experience.

[i] https://thefinancialbrand.com/news/bank-marketing/digital-marketing-banking/inside-the-digital-marketing-strategies-of-top-neobanks-revolut-monzo-148400/ (accessed 10 January2024)

Table 11.2 provides an overview of some of the main tools being used by financial services marketers and their distinguishing features.

Getting marketing content right has a huge impact on its success and the ability to generate a greater emotional connection with consumers. This is what ultimately builds the brand relationship and longer-term profitability. The timelines with which content is delivered is also of huge importance. Customers look to financial services providers as authoritative, so their communications need to be timely and relevant in order to reinforce their position as a "go-to" provider. Lastly, the way content is conveyed online is paramount, and this explains the explosion in recent years of user-experience teams and customer-journey managers.

Organisations face a challenge to deliver the right content, in the right context, and the right time, and data is the key to that success. They need to view themselves as being in the customer experience (CX) business; this means having enough data available in real time to be able to deliver a relevant proposition, in a personalised manner. Digital workflows are crucial; organisations need to employ the right people to manage content generation and curation, push content out through the correct channels and test and optimise based on analytics, as exemplified in the RBS "Superstar DJ" in Marketing in practice 11.4.

Table 11.2 Digital communications tools

Email	Offers fast and simple distribution.
	Ideal cross- and upsale (CS and UP) opportunities.
	Highly cost effective, scalable and measurable.
	Offers customer insight through engagement assessment.
	Encourages instant response.
	Easily personalised and targeted specifically to suit recipients' needs and optimise retention.
	Allows regular contact to keep data set informed of brand activity, promotions, offers increasing brand awareness, engagement and brand benefits.
	Ideal for A/B testing to maximise optimum response (test layout, Calls To Actions (CTA), subject line, sender, time of day/week).
	Ideal for sharing viral campaigns and also driving traffic to blogs, forums, communities and websites.
A/B & multivariate testing (MVT) – i.e. testing different content variations with website users	Offers opportunity to trial varying creative propositions on different segments of the market allowing message to be specifically tailored to audience's needs.
	Low cost to run (post-implementation).
	Ideal for targeting customers with bespoke content to suit their needs: through cookies can serve tailored content to existing customers.
	Also allows testing of different messages, imagery and CTAs to determine which has greatest uplift.
	Highly measurable and accurate as users vote with their clicks which means marketers can respond quickly to trends and hone creatives to drive retention.
	Provides detailed insight into the behaviours of users and what motivates them to perform certain actions, i.e. obtain a quote or purchase.
	Click-stream analysis identifies the customer journey path which can be used to XS and UP to existing customers with MVT used to establish the most successful strategy.
Mobile websites and app marketing	High penetration of mobile usage in UK makes this an ideal marketing medium both in terms of mobile websites and SMS marketing.
	Offers ideal medium for purchases that are based on quick quote tools.
	Maintain accessibility to encourage brand engagement.
	Increases convenience to user as always available.
SMS mobile marketing	SMS broadcast marketing is highly scalable, cheap and easily measured.
	Can be personalised and has fast delivery time, making it extremely responsive.
	Offers a "push" opportunity, rather than having to rely on users visiting websites and apps or engaging in social media.
	Prime cross- and upsale opportunities.
QR codes	Promote a quick response.
	Removes need for reprinting costs when campaign details need to be changed mid-way through.
	Wide adoption of mobile phones means there is a huge market for developing this type of technology.
	Offers instant information: QR codes show offline communications success immediately and without the need for follow-up surveys.
	Cost-effective
Social media	Increases brand presence online.
	Offers easy route to market for company press releases and viral activity.
	Aids SEO through effective link building.
	Optimises word-of-mouth advocacy.
	Peer-to-peer approach in building advocacy is perceived as more credible than B2C marketing.

Table 11.2 (Cont.)

	Provides extra and more convenient options for customer support. Social media monitoring offers opportunity to gain direct customer insight in order to provide solutions. Use of social sharing buttons across all online brand assets increases propensity for users to share information with their peer group and gain reach. Offers ideal engagement platform to enable two-way dialogue with prospects and increase transparency. Ideal platform for video and influencer marketing which has seen exponential growth.
Podcasts	Endorsement by a trusted source the audience has chosen to listen to is powerful. Highly targeted as the podcast market covers many niches markets. Opportunity to sponsor episodes or series offers flexibility. Option of dynamic insertion ads which can be added/removed from recordings in the future, or baked in ads which are part of the original recording and can't be removed and replaced by another brand. Paid interviews with the podcast host offers more airtime, and a sense of content collaboration, which increases credibility, brand awareness and trust.
Online customer service	Live chat function offers instant online response. Online iFaqs are dynamic and specific. Email a query or request a call back allows further opportunity to ask questions and get help on customers' own terms. Aids conversion process through effective problem solving and advice in purchase path.
Viral marketing	Ideal word-of-mouth opportunity. Highly scalable. Easily integrated into wider digital retention strategy, especially email. Engages customers with brand.
Affiliate advertising	Offers a wider arena to market product; more websites = more customers = more scope for sales. Payment model is customisable: runs on a commission basis of cost per click, sale or lead. This is defined by the organisation. Low cost to implement and run, merely requires placing a hyperlinked advert on an affiliate website: acts as an "extension" to in-house sales teams. Cheap to run after initial set up as operating on either pay-per-click, pay-per-lead or pay-per-sale basis. Opportunity to win sales without spending time searching for customers. Advertising cost and energy is passed to affiliate.
Display advertising	Can be highly targeted to specific audiences: using cookies can serve bespoke content to users who have visited the website for research but not yet converted. Cost effective as generally PPC – there cost only incurred for clicks through to the website. Highly trackable and therefore able to be tested and honed to optimise conversion. Ideal for raising brand awareness and promoting the brand message across the web. Can have a positive impact on subsequent search behaviour by raising brand awareness.

(*continued*)

Table 11.2 (Cont.)

Natural search	Relatively low cost as it can be implemented in-house as well as externally. Natural list ranking is free so can be very cost effective. High rankings increase brand awareness and have a positive effect on brand credibility. Responsive to consumers' needs. Website retains complete control of their content and ranking information, no third-party interference. Perceived greater trust in high natural listings as opposed to paid search listings.
Paid search	Simple and quick to implement; listing appears within a matter of hours. Results measurable and fast so enables campaign tweaks for improved conversion. Reliable in terms of guaranteed visibility in listings. Stable advertising, not susceptible to fluctuations like SEO. Although natural search is more trusted, there is a lack of distinction between paid and natural search listings, so guaranteed visibility is an advantage regardless of type.

 Marketing in practice 11.4: RBS and the superstar DJ programme

The RBS "Superstar DJ" programme was set up to drive change in the company's approach to digital communications. Powered by analytics, it was a super-charged optimisation process run by 50 journey managers whose sole focus was testing the consumer experience (CX), continuously monitoring performance so it can be honed and optimised to the greatest degree of accuracy. The focus was on understanding the customer and delivering messaging to best suit their needs. Interestingly, one of the benefits of the programme has been that it has helped drive cultural change and produce innovation, as well as optimise the customer journey.

> "We used the theme of a top DJ feeling connected to the audience he was playing to, and gauging what they needed. He would experiment with new content and instantly see if it was going down well. If it wasn't he would change it almost instantly. He was cognisant that audiences change depending on where they come from and over time. Most importantly he had the tools and the skill to do it all himself".
>
> (Giles Richardson, Head of Analytics, RBS)[13]

Despite this being about the optimisation of a digital journey, the key to its success has been the human factor. The journey manager's knowledge and scrutiny of every part of the optimisation process has meant they have been able to pick-up on and contextualise certain human trends that automated analysis may have missed. For example, the RBS allows users to withdraw emergency cash from ATMs using their banking app if they happen to have lost their card, but journey managers noticed they "don't see that much true 'emergency' use. Instead, they see a sharp uptick in non-card withdrawals on weekends, specifically late at night in high-traffic locations – when the pubs are closing".[14]

The wide penetration of smartphones meant that optimising marketing communications for mobile technologies has become an important element of marketing communications. Users increasingly prefer to read news, access social media, watch media, email and purchase from their mobiles,[15] with the average person reportedly touching their phone 2,167 times per day[16]. Mobile search behaviour is different to desktop; mobile searchers tend to use more keywords than in PC search and these search terms are timelier and more specific with users having a particular idea of what they're looking for. As such there is huge weighting on results immediately meeting user needs and directing them to a mobile, user-friendly site. Travel insurance is a product that is commonly purchased last minute, and indeed sometimes at the start of a journey. Such last-minute purchases are increasingly likely to take place using mobile devices, ensuring that the purchase process is optimised for such devices is a key consideration.

Mobile solutions need to be simple and have minimum requirements for form filling where possible, particularly for applications and quick quotes. Phone numbers should be prominent and business should ensure mobile-friendly versions are available across all mobile devices, thus not restricting their reach. Bearing these factors in mind when designing a mobile solution will reduce the propensity to abandon quotes and seek a solution with a competitor.

Apps provide a means of ensuring a positive consumer experience (CX) because the interface is tailored for the specific device and marketing communications can be appropriately customised. NatWest's easy-to-use iPad app helped to ensure an increase in the number of customers using its online services. WestPac's "Big Red Button" was an innovative impulse savings app. Users can save on impulse by simply pressing a big red button on their iPhone.[17] Interestingly the promotion of this and many other similar apps still relies significantly on traditional media, exemplifying the importance of a joined-up marketing approach.

New market challenges have emerged with digital innovations; content velocity, personalisation, authenticity and engagement. As soon as a brand seeks to create a personalised experience for customers, they uncover an immediate demand for relevant content. Brand content can be viewed as too advertorial, but user-generated content (UGC) leads to increased perceptions of authenticity and positively influences customer journeys. Organisations should focus efforts on how they can easily surface UGC and publish it effectively to complement brand content. The challenge is to identify UCG and use it in a timely and meaningful way, bringing customers in from third-party social media platforms and carrying on the conversation on their own channels.

Digital offers financial services huge advantages in the delivery of highly relevant, optimised communications to drive marketing success. Communications can be increasingly personalised through the use of conditional content, for example contextual emails that display content that is appropriate and assessed in real time, depending on when and where a user opens it. Similarly, generative artificial intelligence (AI) offers capabilities for marketing tools to self-learn based on consumer behaviours and interactions and craft highly personalised communications. However, it's worth noting that to be truly successful, customer experience must be consistent across all customer touchpoints – a poor physical (human) CX can undermine all good digital CX work.

11.6 Summary and conclusion

Promotional strategy deals with all aspects of communication between an organisation and its customers, its employees and other interested parties. Four main promotional tools are available to an organisation, specifically, advertising, publicity, sales promotion and personal selling. The balance between these tools will vary according to the nature of the overall marketing strategy, the characteristics of the product, the resources of the organisations and the nature of the target market. Whatever promotional mix is chosen, the effectiveness of the communications process depends on the development of a clear and unambiguous message that is presented to the right target audience, at the right time and through the most appropriate medium.

Promotion has always been important in financial services but, if anything, its importance is increasing. The market for financial services is going through a period of rapid change and levels of competition are increasing. Deregulation, increased consumer sophistication and technological developments have encouraged a rapid growth in marketing and particularly in promotional activity. Financial services institutions now spend significant amounts on communicating a variety of product and brand messages to a range of target audiences. With promotion attracting a significant level of marketing expenditure, it is important that promotional activity is carefully planned and implemented and that it is consistent with the rest of the organisation's marketing activities.

Learning outcomes

Having completed this chapter, you should now understand:

1. **The essentials of communication for financial services marketing.**
   From a marketing perspective, the term "communications" refers quite simply to the way in which organisations are able to send messages to target markets. A fundamental question is whether the campaign is focused strategically around positioning the organisation/brand or whether it is to be focused more tactically on specific products and customer groups. Whatever the approach, it is also necessary to consider what communications methods (or tools) are to be used (advertising, personal selling, sales promotion and publicity/public relations). In the same way as we think about a marketing mix – elements of marketing that are blended together, we often also talk about a promotional mix.

   Communications and promotions for financial services are very similar to promoting physical products in many respects, but their distinctive characteristics (discussed in chapters 3 and 6) suggests that marketers need to think about how to develop a message and a form of presentation which allows the organisation to make their offer seem more tangible, how to develop a clear message about the superiority of its products and how to engage customers, many of who tend to be relatively uninterested in financial services.

2. **The process of planning a promotional campaign.**
   The component elements of marketing communications need to be carefully planned and managed to ensure that any campaign is effective. Careful planning is also important to ensure that the different methods of marketing communications

are sending consistent messages and that marketing communications are aligned with other elements of the marketing mix. The simplest way to think about the planning of a promotional campaign is to think of it as a series of stages as shown in Figure 11.4, progressing from objective setting, defining a target audience, formulating a message, setting a budget, determining the mix of promotional tools and then implementation and monitoring.

3. **The strengths and weaknesses of different approaches to marketing communications for financial services.**

Advertising is a form of mass communication which is paid for and involves the non-personal presentation of goods or ideas. As such, it covers television, radio, internet and press advertising and some would also include other approaches such as direct mail and direct-response advertising. Some researchers argue that advertising of different types can play a key role in terms of driving individuals through a hierarchy of effects from awareness through to action (purchase), others would suggest that advertising has a more limited role of maintaining brand awareness and reinforcing existing attitudes.

One of the major benefits of personal selling as a form of communication is that it allows immediate feedback from consumer to the organisation (or its representative). Furthermore because personal selling allows queries and response, it is often thought to be very effective towards the end of the AIDA/Hierarchy of Effects process – in encouraging action (purchase). Although personal selling can be a valuable and effective form of promotion, it is also very expensive.

Publicity is any form of non-paid, non-personal communication, and like advertising, it involves dealing with a mass audience. Public relations is similar in many respects, but is paid for whereas publicity is assumed to be "free". Both are concerned more generally with building and maintaining an understanding between the organisation and the general public.

Sales promotions are demand-pull methods of promotion. Demand-pull promotions are specifically concerned with providing consumers with a direct incentive to try and buy a product. The use of sales promotions as part of a marketing campaign has increased considerably in recent years and they can be very effective in encouraging a final purchase decision.

Direct mail and the associated direct-response advertising can potentially provide customers with a lot of the detail necessary to make a final purchase decision. Indeed, direct mail which is accurately targeted to the right customer group can be very effective at generating new business, as well as cross-selling to existing customers. Accordingly, these methods of advertising are likely to be more effective in encouraging the final stage in the AIDA/Hierarchy of Effects model – namely the purchase (action).

4. **The impact of new media on the management of marketing communications.** Digital disrupts how customers interact with organisations. Financial services providers need to understand how to leverage this disruption and use customer data to facilitate the shift in consumer expectations. As the digital media available have expanded, consumers are now bombarded with brand messages across all forms of media, on every device. They expect to be able to interact with brands through the medium of their choice and brands must ensure their communications

span the new connected, internet-enabled world as well as more traditional avenues. Brands also need to be sensitive to the ways in which users will respond to communications through different media. For example, while mobile is one of the most popular manners of accessing the internet, SMS messaging is often too intrusive and off-putting. Organisations should aim to target customers rather than devices and ensure they employ sequential messaging across all channels and devices in order to deliver an effective omni-channel experience.

Review questions

1. Think of an advertising campaign that your organisation has used. Explain the different stages in the communications process using this campaign as an example.
2. What do you understand the term AIDA to mean? How can this framework be used to help choose the best method of promotion for a particular financial service?
3. Explain the difference between above- and below-the-line advertising. Which do you think would be most effective for the marketing of a unit trust?
4. Explain the strengths and weaknesses of the five main promotional tools.

Notes

1 https://theelephantroom.net/casestudy/barclays-x-big-zuu/ (accessed January 2024)
2 www.youtube.com/watch?v=mYK73McI_v4 (accessed January 2024)
3 www.greenpeace.org.uk/news/barclays-banks-climate-change-fossil-fuels/ (accessed January 2024)
4 www.itv.com/news/2024-01-19/hsbc-duping-public-after-helping-raise-37bn-for-new-oil-and-gas-fields?irclickid=Tc9W0IQxpxyPW%3AuX4IR6PSqsUkHw2nw1nTS-xA0&utm_medium=affiliate&utm_source=planit&utm_id=Tc9W0IQxpxyPW%3AuX4IR6PSqsUkHw2nw1nTS-xA0&utm_campaign=svodacquisition_planit&utm_marketing_tactic=41097&irgwc=1&im_rewards=1 (accessed January 2024)
5 Many of these campaigns are visible online – see for example www.adsoftheworld.com/campaigns/online-and-better for the Hello Bank example. (accessed January 2024)
6 www.asa.org.uk/about-asa-and-cap/about-regulation/about-the-asa-and-cap.html (accessed February 2024)
7 Schmitt, Skiera and Van den Bulte (2011) report on a study undertaken with a bank in Germany and provide evidence to suggest that customers who have been referred to the bank are more valuable in the short and long term than customers acquired through other routes.
8 See http://adsoftheworld.com/media/ambient/standard_bank_joy_of_jazz_2012 pigeon_jazz. (accessed August 2017)
9 See http://adsoftheworld.com/media/print/coop_financial_services_ex. (ccessed August 2017)
10 https://zipdo.co/statistics/financial-services-digital-marketing/(accessed January 2024)
11 Financial Services Forum. (2011). Not just any bank, this is MetroBank. *Argent*, 37, thefsforum.co.uk.
12 https://interbrand.com/best-global-brands/ (accessed January 2024)
13 Brighton, J. (2015). Digital Analytics and Optimisation: An interview with a superstar DJ. https://blogs.adobe.com/digitaleurope/personalisation/digital-analytics-and-optimisation-interview-superstar-dj/. (accessed June 2017)
14 Lindsay, K. (2015). Superstar DJs Are Changing the Face of Optimization https://blogs.adobe.com/digitalmarketing/personalization/superstar-djs-changing-face-optimization/. (accessed June 2017)
15 https://techreport.com/statistics/mobile-vs-desktop-usage-statistics/#:~:text=All%20mobile%2C%20desktop%2C%20and%20tablet%20devices%20have%20seen,3.36%25%2C%20while%20it%20was%201.53%25%20for%20mobile%20users. (accessed February 2024)

16 https://dscout.com/ (accessed February 2024)
17 Mckenna, I. (2014). Has True Potential cracked investment micro payments? https://www.
    moneymarketing.co.uk/ian-mckenna-has-true-potential-cracked-investment-micro-payments/.
    (accessed February 2024)

References

Baines, P., Fill, C. and Page, K. (2010). *Marketing*. Oxford: Oxford University Press.

Buch, J., Rhoda, K. and Talaga, J. (2002). The usefulness of the APR for mortgage marketing in the USA and the UK. *International Journal of Bank Marketing*, 20(2), pp. 76–85.

Curphey, M. (2011). Who's chasing Aleksandr Orlov. Argent, 37, thefsforum.co.uk.

Diacon, S. and Hasseldine, J. (2007). Framing effects and risk perception: The effect of prior performance presentation format on investment fund choice. *Journal of Economic Psychology*, 28(1), pp. 31–52.

Doyle, P. (2000). Value-based marketing. *Journal of Strategic Marketing*, 8(4), pp.299–311. https://doi.org/10.1080/096525400446203

Fill, C. (2006). *Marketing Communications: Engagement, Strategies and Practice*. London: Financial Times/Prentice Hall.

Schmitt, P., Skiera, B. and Van den Bulte, C. (2011). Referral Programs and Customer Value. *Journal of Marketing*, 75 (January), pp. 46–59. https://doi.org/10.1509/jm.75.1.46

12 Price and cost to the consumer

Learning objectives

At the end of this chapter, you should be able to:

1. Explain the role of pricing in the financial services marketing mix,
2. Understand the different approaches and methods of setting price,
3. Appreciate and understand the complexities associated with pricing in financial services and why "charges'" is a more appropriate term in this context,
4. Appreciate the ways in which technology is empowering consumers to shop around for better value.

12.1 Introduction

In the context of the traditional marketing mix, *price* is often the most problematic for marketing executives to manage. Unlike all other constituent parts of the mix, price is concerned with the determination of revenue and plays a crucial role in the derivation of product margins and profit. Indeed, it is not uncommon for other business functions, typically finance, to bear the primary responsibility for setting price, and some organisations may even have an arbitrary margin or mark-up that is applied as a default when setting the price of new product introductions. It is easy to appreciate the inherent tensions which exist between, say, the sales and finance divisions of a company. Sales personnel like to be able to offer low, or at least competitive, prices to maximise sales. Finance directors, on the other hand, are rather partial to high prices since they equate such an approach to high margins and, therefore, high profits (and the avoidance of a loss). Thus, the setting of product price is often a process which is political in nature and the subject of considerable negotiation among the stakeholder functions within the company.

In the context of the financial services sector, price and the setting of prices is no less contentious and in many such organisations price is the one element of the mix that is not under the control of the marketing function. To add to the challenge for marketeers, and to consumers for that matter, price is a term that is somewhat obscure and lacking in transparency within the domain of financial services. As we shall see in Section 12.3, the actual word *price* is rarely used, and a plethora of other terms are used to express the cost that consumers incur as consideration for the benefits they receive from their transaction. For this

DOI: 10.4324/9781003398615-20

reason, it is perhaps more appropriate to use the term *charges* when referring to price so far as financial products are concerned. Charges represent the costs incurred by the customer in return for the product benefits they receive. Thus, charges represent the income the company receives from the products and services it provides and, once all costs have been attributed to its corporate activities, determines the profits it reports. That is somewhat of an oversimplification as, depending upon the sector in question, income can also be derived from other sources such as, say, in the case of an insurance company, income that arises from its investment activities. However, for the purpose of this text, we will view charges received from customers as the principal source of income and the basis upon which business models are designed. From a consumer point of view, there is much to be gained by thinking of price in terms of charges when assessing competitive offerings as it facilitates a more effective appreciation of the range of costs they might incur in exchange for their custom and the way in which they fulfil their obligations as customers. However, we see no need to be unduly prescriptive when deciding when to use price and charges and so will tend to use both terms depending upon the context of the discourse.

It is commonplace for the marketing team to have no influence in the setting of prices but for them to be passive recipients of price set in other parts of the organisation. In the case of an insurance company, prices are often prescribed by one of the actuarial functions. In banks, prices are often set by the finance or treasury division, whilst in building societies it is often the prerogative of the finance team. Thus, as is often the case in the wider commercial sphere, pricing and the determination of product and service charges is often the source of much internal organisational politicking and, therefore, must be handled with care to ensure that all relevant parties participate in the process in a suitably joined-up fashion.

Pricing represents no less a challenge from the consumer perspective too. Ultimately, it is the price of a product or service that is used to denominate value. For consumers to be able to judge what is the best value from the competing products assumes a degree of numeracy on the part of the consumer and transparency on the part of the product provider that are all too often found wanting. In particular, the pricing policies of providers are often unclear, and this problem is reinforced by the fact that many consumers struggle to understand exactly how pricing works for financial services. Thus, marketers of financial services must pay due regard to these factors when determining pricing policies and the ways in which the price of their products are displayed, presented and explained. Failure to do so can result in the provider organisation incurring hefty costs in terms of compensation and fines imposed by their regulatory authority. It is for this reason that the current authors have a preference for placing more emphasis on charges than prices.

This chapter provides an overview of charges and pricing in relation to financial services. It begins with a brief discussion of the role and characteristics of pricing and then moves on to explore in more detail some of the challenges associated with pricing in financial services. Subsequent sections consider approaches to price setting, the issues associated with price discrimination, the process of price determination and the nature of overall pricing strategy.

12.2 The role and characteristics of price

Price has been defined as the value of a good or service for both the buyer and seller in a market exchange. For our purposes price is expressed as a monetary value and as such is the metric by which the financial performance of an organisation is evaluated. Thus, price is a measure of value for both buyers and sellers, or, rather customers and providers. From the customer's point of view, price performs several functions:

- It is used as a yardstick to compare competing options.
- It is how value is assessed.
- It may be used as an indicator of product or service quality.
- It represents the cost of the good or service.
- It can influence the frequency of purchase or quantum of an individual purchase.

As far as providers are concerned, price is important for the following reasons:

- It is a crucial determinant of margin and profit.
- It influences the level of demand for its products and services.
- It plays a key role in affecting relative competitive position.
- It can be adjusted quickly, under certain conditions, to enable the provider to achieve short-term volume or margin priorities.
- It can be varied at different stages in the product life cycle in conjunction with other elements of the marketing mix.

In general marketing texts it is customary to observe that price can be changed quickly in response to events in the marketplace or opportunistic situations. However, for some financial services the changing of price can be extremely time-consuming and costly. For example, in the life assurance arena the implementation of a price change can be a complex matter requiring major resource inputs from actuarial and systems departments. Depending upon the prevailing systems architecture, a price change can require as much resource and lead time as the launch of a new product. However, there are other products that are highly flexible and responsive to urgent deadlines such as certain interest-rate driven products.

12.3 The challenges of pricing for providers of financial services

For the marketers of packaged goods, pricing is a relatively straightforward matter whereby the cost to the customer is simply the price she pays. It is similarly straightforward as far as the customer is concerned. The emergence of profit is similarly simple to grasp, it is the purchase price minus all direct and indirect costs. However, pricing is far more complex for financial services; indeed, the terminology associated with pricing is itself a complex and diverse issue. For example, consider the following products and the ways in which price may be expressed for conventional financial services (a different set of terms may apply for Islamic financial services where interest payments are not relevant):

Product	Terms associated with price
Whole of Life Assurance Policy	Premium
	Bid: offer spread
	Initial charge
	Annual management charge

Product	Terms associated with price
	Policy fee
	Early surrender penalty
	Market value adjustment
	Cost of advice
	Reduction in yield
	Premium loadings
Mortgage	Arrangement fee
	Interest rate
	Average equivalent rate (AER)
	Early redemption penalty
Unsecured loan	Interest rate
	Annual percentage rate (APR)
Current account	Overdraft rate
	Charges – overdraft arrangement fee
	Charges – unauthorised overdraft fee
	Charges – additional statements
	Charges – cheque representation fee
Personal pension	Contribution
	Initial charges
	Bid offer spread
	Charges
	Policy fee
	Annual management charge
	Cost of advice
	Reduction in yield
	Early surrender penalties
Credit card	Annual fee
	Annual percentage rate (APR)
	Average equivalent rate (AER)
	Late payment charge
	Interest charge
General insurance	Premium
	Excess charge

Progress check

- Price is concerned with the determination of revenue and plays a crucial role in the derivation of product margins and profit.
- It is commonplace for the marketing team to have no influence in the setting of prices but for them to be passive recipients of price set in other parts of the organisation.
- Pricing is far more complex for financial services; indeed, the terminology associated with pricing is itself a complex and diverse issue.

From the above set of examples, it can readily be appreciated that customers are faced with the need to develop a familiarity with a wide range of terms used for expressing the charges they will incur from the transaction. Additionally, the overall cost to the customer is often arrived at through the accumulation of several differently expressed charges. In the case of several products there is the added confusion that arises because the notional amount of money paid into certain products represents an investment by the customer from which certain charges will be deducted. Thus, the *contributions* paid into a pension, the *premiums* paid into an endowment savings plan, the *investment* made in a mutual fund represent sums of money that are being invested on behalf of the customer. They do not strictly represent *price*, where price means the sacrifice made by the customer. In these cases, *price* is represented by the various charges that are deducted by the product provider. However, in the case of general insurance products such as home contents and motor insurance, the premium does represent the price to the customer. In such cases there is no investment content incorporated into the premiums and thus no return of funds at the expiry of the contract period. Indeed, there may well be additional charges levied on the customer such as the payment of an *excess charge* should a claim arise.

The difficulties which consumers face in fully appreciating the price they pay for certain financial services products are compounded further by a combination of complexity and the accumulation of charges. We have already observed how complexity arises from the range of terminology that applies to financial services pricing and from the added confusion surrounding the treatment of the sums of money that the consumer invests in one form or another. A further issue that must be appreciated is the way in which charges accumulate during the period of the life of the product. Consider the case of a personal pension.

Let's assume that a consumer undertakes to contribute £300 per month to a personal pension (PP) and does so during a 30-year period. Let us also assume that the PP comprises the following charging structure:

Initial charge – 5% is deducted from each contribution made.
Policy fee – a fee of £2 per month is deducted.
Annual Management Charge – an AMC of 1% of the consumer's fund value is deducted per annum.

Thus, during the 30-year term the consumer will have incurred the following charges:

Initial charges (£300 x 5% x 12 x 30) = £5,400
Policy fees (£2 x 12 x 30) = £720
AMC (assumes average annual growth of 7.5%) = £32,730
Total costs = £38,850.

And so, during the course of the 30 years that the personal pension has been in force, the consumer will have paid £38,850 in total charges. Attempts are made to present the cumulative impact of charges during the lifetime of an investment policy. One method is called the *reduction in yield* (RIY). RIY operates by showing the impact of charges in terms of how it reduces average annual returns on the consumer's investment. For example, if the cumulative impact of charges on a personal pension has a RIY of 2.8%, it means that instead of the consumer receiving annual growth of, say, 7.5% from their contributions, she receives an actual return of 4.7%. Looked at another way, the effect of the 2.8% RIY is to reduce the return on investment by 37% (2.8 ÷ 7.5 x 100).

The complexity and confusion already discussed contributes to a relative lack of transparency regarding costs and pricing. Drake and Llewellyn (1995) suggest that, when considering the pricing of financial services, it might be helpful to distinguish between two main forms of pricing, namely explicit or overt pricing and implicit or covert pricing.

- **Explicit or overt pricing**
  This approach makes the price paid for the service very clear. The consumer is presented with clear and precise figures about what they will pay for this service. When a bank charges for an ATM withdrawal or a credit card company charges an annual fee, this is an example of explicit pricing. This approach has the advantage of being very clear to both consumer and to supplier. The supplier is likely to be more able to predict likely revenue and the consumer is much more obviously aware of what the service costs. Furthermore, an explicit price allows the organisation to signal costs of different services and use price as a way of influencing consumer behaviour. For example, if branch-based transactions were priced relatively high (because of their high costs) and internet transactions were priced relatively low (because of their lower costs), the organisation could use pricing to try and encourage consumers to move from branch-based transactions in favour of the internet. However, to operate a good and efficient system of overt pricing does require a thorough understanding of the cost base and principles of cost allocation. As explained earlier, this can be a difficult area for financial services organisations as what may be termed explicit prices may, nonetheless, be lacking in transparency and comprehensibility from the customers' point of view.
- **Implicit or covert pricing**
  This is a system of pricing in which the actual price to the consumer is unclear and appears not to be paid by consumers. The bank that offers free banking but pays no interest on credit balances is pursuing an implicit pricing policy. The consumer may not be aware but he or she is effectively paying a price based on the size of any outstanding credit balances. Similarly, an organisation providing a regular savings product may not explicitly charge for its services but will take a share of the initial payments to cover costs and contribute to profit.

Implicit pricing has the advantage of being very simple for both the organisation and the customer and it is relatively low cost to administer because it does not necessarily require the same sort of detailed understanding of costs. However, there are significant disadvantages to this approach. First, both the price paid by the customer and the revenue paid by the bank will vary according to the interest rate or the amount that consumers wish to save or invest. Second, there is no incentive for consumers to move to lower-cost services because all services offered appear to be free of charge. Third, implicit pricing creates potential for cross subsidisation. Thus, for example the customer with significant positive credit balances will pay a much higher price for a given service than the customer with a minimal credit balance. In effect the customer with a large credit balance subsidises the service provided to the customer with a small credit balance.

12.4 Methods used for determining price

A number of elements of economic theory are helpful in enabling us to understand how price levels are arrived at. The demand curve is useful as an aid to understanding the relationship between price and demand. As we see in Figure 12.1, in simple terms the lower the price of the given product the greater the level of demand for that product.

In Figure 12.1, as price increases from £P1 to £P2, demand falls from Q1 volume to Q2 volume. From the supply side, the higher the price the greater will be the volume of output that manufacturers and product providers are willing to supply. However, this is an oversimplification since it assumes economic rationality on the part of consumers and an ability to clearly identify best value. It also implies that high price is a proxy for high margin from the supplier's point of view. Indeed, the basic economic theory of price implies the characteristics associated with perfect competition. Fundamental to the notion of perfect competition is consumer sovereignty whereby the consumer is both highly knowledgeable about all aspects of the product in question and has full and unhindered access to all forms of information regarding the entire universe of suppliers. In practice such conditions seldom

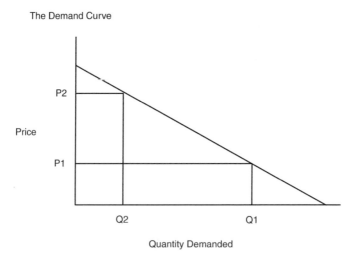

Figure 12.1 The demand curve

apply in the field of financial services and the term *information asymmetry* is commonly used to describe the balance between consumer and provider knowledge.

Nevertheless, under certain circumstances there is little doubt that demand is stimulated by price reductions and that price increases can be used to lessen demand. For example, in the run-up to the end of the government's tax year it is customary for investment management firms to offer special deals with lower charges as a means of encouraging investors to make use of their tax allowances under the United Kingdom (UK) government's individual savings account (ISA) scheme. Pension providers engage in similar price promotions as the tax year draws to a close.

Shapiro and Jackson have proposed three core approaches to the determination of price, namely:

* Cost-based,
* Competitive,
* Market-oriented.

Let us consider each of these approaches in turn.

12.4.1 Cost-based pricing

In simple terms, the cost-based approach to pricing operates by identifying the costs associated with a given product and then adding on a profit margin to arrive at a price. In practice, one encounters two main variants of the cost-based approach to pricing namely: full-cost pricing and marginal-cost pricing. Whereas full-cost pricing takes account of all components of cost (overhead as well as direct or variable costs), marginal-cost pricing relates just to the direct costs associated with the manufacture of the good or service in question. Two examples will help to illustrate these two alternative approaches.

Full-cost pricing example

Fixed overhead costs	£100,000
Variable (direct) costs per unit	£25
Forecast sales	5,000 units
Profit margin mark-up	20%
Total costs	£1000,000 + £125,000 (5,000 × £25) = £225,000
Full cost per unit	£45 (£225,000 ÷ 5,000)
Mark-up (20%)	£9
Price	£54

The advantage of full cost pricing is that it should ensure that profit is achieved and that all costs have been covered. However, it suffers from the potentially major disadvantage that it can result in an uncompetitively high price. Such a situation can arise from two perspectives. First, the adoption of a cautious approach to forecast sales will limit the extent to which fixed costs can be attributed to units of output. In the above example, suppose we had forecast sales volume of 20,000 units instead of 5,000. We would arrive at a materially different set of costs and price as can be seen in the following:

Fixed overhead costs	£100,000
Variable (direct) costs per unit	£25
Forecast sales	20,000 units
Profit margin mark-up	20%
Total costs	£1000,000 + 500,000 (20,000 × £25) = £600,000
Full cost per unit	£30
Mark-up (20%)	£6
Price	£36

The difference in the two examples is explained by the reduction in overhead cost per unit from £20 to £5. Had the provider been more bullish about sales it would have opted for a higher sales forecast and thus set a price some 36% lower than the price based upon the cautious forecast of 5,000 units. The second weakness is that we do not know the price level that applies to the nearest competitor. If we assume a competing product is priced at £45 it seems reasonable to assume that a £54 price tag will be unattractive.

Marginal cost-based price is arrived at by adding a profit margin onto the direct, variable costs of manufacture. To take the earlier example:

Direct cost per unit	£25
Mark-up (20%)	£5
Price	£30

Marginal costing results in a much lower price than the full-cost approach because no account is taken of overhead cost attribution. It is sometimes used in highly competitive situations on the basis that so long as the price at least covers direct costs it is making a contribution to the fixed-cost overhead. However, in practice it means that the price is set at an unrealistically low level and other products will, in effect, be subsidising the direct cost-based product. It is an economic fact of life that overhead must be paid for somehow, and there has to be a compelling commercial reason to use marginal cost as a basis for pricing decisions.

Cost-based pricing assumes that the product provider has a robust and accurate appreciation of the costs associated with any given product. This is a straightforward matter for manufacturers of tangible goods but represents far more of a challenge to the service sector in general and financial services in particular. To take a simple example, branch-based organisations often have difficulty in arriving at an accurate apportionment of fixed costs to individual products. Banks typically have very wide, diverse product ranges, and determining what proportion of branch costs should be allocated to individual products is fraught with difficulties. Nevertheless, some arbitrary cost allocation bases can be used to ensure that an appropriate contribution be made to overhead costs. At a more complex level, there are long-standing concerns that insurance and pension companies have not priced their products based upon a sufficiently realistic appraisal of the costs that apply to a range of risk-related factors. It is argued that the unrealistic valuation of assets and liabilities distorts pricing and, in the long-term, is disadvantageous to the consumer interest. This argument has resulted in the European Union introducing the Solvency II regime with effect from 1 January 2016.

Solvency II aims to address this long-standing issue by addressing the amounts of capital that insurance companies must hold (something which represents a significant element of their costs). Replacing the previous Solvency I regime, Solvency II was introduced primarily to improve the protection of policyholders, and has been further amended in 2023. Readers wishing to learn more about Solvency II are encouraged to read Professor Karel Van Hulle's paper *Solvency II: A realistic approach to pricing for risk and safeguarding company solvency* in the Support Material for this book.

 Stop and think?

What role does price play in the marketing mix from the point of view of a) the company and b) the customer?

What makes the price of FSPs difficult for consumers to understand?

What is the difference between explicit and implicit pricing?

12.4.2 Competition-based pricing

Rather than set price based on cost, with the disadvantages that have been identified, price can also be based upon one's competitors' price levels. Two variants are commonly encountered, namely: going-rate pricing and competitive bidding.

Going-rate pricing implies that there is little heterogeneity between competing products and that providers are, in effect, price takers rather than price setters. The idea of going-rate pricing seems at odds with strategies based upon product and service differentiation. Indeed, it suggests a largely commoditised marketplace with little scope for premium pricing. However, it is undoubtedly true that what we might term benchmark pricing applies in many commercial areas. There has to be a very good reason for a price premium being charged in the real estate market, for example where a 1.5% fee is a common benchmark. Sometimes governments and regulators can establish going-rate pricing, such as the 0.75% charge cap on the Stakeholder Pension in the UK.

The second basic approach to competition-based pricing is competitive tendering. In this case prospective suppliers are invited to submit their most competitive bid to the prospective customer. Such an approach to pricing is rarely encountered in the domestic marketplace and is more a feature of the business-to-business environment. As can be readily appreciated, such a method is fraught with the twin dangers of bidding too high on a price and failing to get the business or bidding too low and damaging margins. Success in an area that involves competitive tendering requires great expertise in understanding one's own cost base and those of one's competitors. It can be remarkably difficult to achieve differentiation and premium pricing in marketplaces that are characterised by competitive tendering. Once successful with a bid, the service or product provider can render themselves vulnerable to the customer who can assume a great degree of power.

12.4.3 Marketing-oriented pricing

The limitations associated with cost and competition-based pricing have resulted in the development of marketing-oriented pricing. Marketing-oriented pricing sets out to reflect a broad range of variables in the determination of price. Significantly, it recognises that price

Figure 12.2 Marketing-oriented pricing

has a strong strategic dimension in being closely implicated in issues such as positioning and competitive advantage. David Jobber (2004) identifies an array of ten components of a marketing-oriented approach to pricing (see Figure 12.2).

Each of these ten components will now be considered in turn:

Marketing strategy

Pricing presents valuable opportunities for a company to craft extremely subtle approaches to the implementation of its marketing strategy. This is, in part, made possible by the multivariable nature of financial services pricing. Consider the example of level term assurance (LTA). This is one of the simplest types of life assurance and the costs associated with providing the product, and, therefore, its price (premium) varies from customer to customer depending upon the following customer attributes:

- Amount of sum-assured
- Duration of term
- Age
- Gender*
- Smoker, non-smoker
- Health status
- Occupation
- Leisure pursuits

The maximum number of permutations, and hence individual prices, that arises from the above variables will run into thousands. An insurer must make choices regarding where it wants to position itself with regard to its competitors for those thousands of individual prices. Amongst the choices to be made are which competitors to benchmark against. This is far from straightforward as different groups of competitors are to be found in different parts of the market for LTA. The answer lies in adopting a pricing policy that is designed to complement the marketing strategy regarding target segments and positioning. Let us consider two hypothetical providers of LTA and the ways in which they can use pricing in ways that are consistent with their respective strategies.

Since the end of 2012, European law has prohibited insurers in European Union (EU) member states from factoring gender into health, life, and auto insurance premiums. See Factsheet: EU rules on gender-neutral pricing in insurance, 20 December 2012[1].

 Marketing in practice 12.1: Hallmark Insurance

Hallmark Insurance is an insurance company that is based on the eastern seaboard of the USA. It specialises in providing LTA on high sums assured for terms of up to ten years. A particular field of expertise is the use of Hallmark's LTA as a loan-protection policy for a small and medium-sized enterprise (SME) company directors who are taking out high value loans for purposes such as corporate buy-outs and acquisitions. As such they target corporate financiers and investment banks to promote their products and services. Hallmark has designed a pricing strategy to enable it to be competitive in the following areas:

- Sums assured from $1 million to $20 million
- Terms of five to ten years' duration
- Individuals aged 35 to 55

Table 12.1 shows where Hallmark has set its pricing in terms of quartile ranking on the key variables indicated above. By the term "quartile" we mean 25%, thus the first quartile means the top 25% of companies ranked based on price competitiveness.

Table 12.1 Hallmark's LTA price positioning in preferred sectors of business

Price Quartile	Sums Assured $US million			
	1–5	*5–10*	*10–15*	*15–20*
Q1				Hallmark
Q2			Hallmark	
Q3		Hallmark		
Q4	Hallmark			
No of competitors	200	50	25	10

It can be seen that Hallmark has set its stall out to be highly competitive for higher sums assured. Note how the number of competitors falls as sums assured increase, thus making positioning even more important.

Marketing in practice 12.2: Everyman Insurance, a subsidiary of Everyman Bank

Everyman Insurance is based in Melbourne in Australia and is the bancassurance arm of one of Australia's leading high street banks. An important part of its strategy is that it seeks to support the bank's small business operation which has the goal of trebling the size of its loan book during the next five years. The small business banking operation enjoys close relationships with its customers who show a high degree of loyalty to the bank. Part of the Everyman Bank strategy is that its small business owners go on to become owners and directors of much bigger businesses in due course.

Everyman Insurance has designed a pricing strategy to enable it to be competitive as part of an overall Everyman loan and insurance package to its small business customers. Thus, it seeks to be particularly competitive in the following areas:

- Sums assured from $50,000 Au to $250,000 Au,
- Terms of five to ten years,
- Individuals aged 30–40 years.

In the table below we see where Everyman Insurance has positioned its prices in quartile ranking terms according to its preferred business profile.

Table 12.2 Everyman Insurance's LTA price positioning in preferred sectors

Price Quartile	Sums Assured $Aus 000				
➤	25–50	50–100	100–200	200–400	>400
Q1			Everyman		
Q2		Everyman		Everyman	
Q3	Everyman				Everyman
Q4					
No. of competitors	75	75	75	75	70

Everyman Insurance has structured its price positioning to become increasingly competitive as the sums assured increase to its optimum position, i.e. sums assured in the range of Au$100,000–200,000. At these levels of sums assured the number of competitors remains almost static. Everyman's price positioning in non-target areas of sums assured, term and age are typically pitched at the mid-point of the third quartile. This enables them to achieve good margins on business they do not seek to chase.

The Hallmark and Everyman examples give a clear indication of how pricing can be organised to fit the overall marketing strategy. In a study of the UK term assurance market conducted on a private basis by one of the authors it was noteworthy how random price positioning appeared to be. Of some 20 insurance companies studied, only one demonstrated the kind of logical coherent approach illustrated by Hallmark and Everyman. There is scope for pricing to be used in a thoughtful and commercially astute manner in a way that is consistent with the company's approach to market segmentation, but often such opportunities are missed.

Price-quality relationships

Consumers form a judgement about the relationship between price and quality. It is understood that a high quality, personalised service will incur higher costs to the provider than an undifferentiated basic form of commoditised service.

Product line pricing

Product line pricing refers to the need for integrity between all of the products that comprise an overall product range. Thus, an investment management company will be expected to charge more for a personalised portfolio management service than it does for managing a packaged portfolio of investments.

Negotiating margins

Negotiating margins apply in circumstances where customers expect to be able to haggle over prices. Thus, an extra margin is included in the basic list price to allow for negotiation. The inclusion of negotiating margins is a particular feature of B2B marketing where sellers are faced with professional buyers. Such buyers are skilled at conducting negotiations and usually have personal objectives to achieve which include successful negotiation of procurement activities.

Political factors

Government policy frequently impacts upon the pricing of financial services whether through impacts on costs or through the imposition of certain constraints on what is or is not permitted. For example, interest rates are set by central banks and, in turn, these will impact on the rates of interest charged on mortgages and other types of loan products because they drive the costs associated with those products. As an illustration of policy determined constraints or limits on pricing, the EU has directed that car insurance premiums cannot be differentiated based solely on gender. In a slightly different example, when the UK government introduced the Stakeholder Pension, it mandated a price cap initially of 1% of fund value. Providers were free to charge less and could still compete on price but could not charge above this threshold.

Costs

Clearly, costs must be considered when setting price if the company is to avoid making a loss. As previously mentioned, financial services present particular problems in respect of the allocation of variable as well as overhead costs to individual products. This problem is further exacerbated in circumstances where the marketing team is on the periphery of the pricing process. In such circumstances marketing staff can miss out on the opportunity to develop a keener sense of commercial judgement. Organisations that view pricing as a responsibility of the marketing team can be expected to benefit from marketing executives who have a solid grasp of costs and of how profit emerges.

Effect on distributors and retails

Distribution channels can have a profound effect upon pricing since they require a level of remuneration that motivates them to work in a vigorous and committed manner on behalf of the product provider. This argument applies both to direct and indirect distribution channels. Some forms of distribution become too costly for product providers to be able to satisfy the remuneration needs of the distributors and their own profit requirements. It is common for, say, banks and insurance companies to decide not to market certain products, such as Stakeholder Pensions, because their cost bases do not leave enough margin for their distributors to earn what they consider to be an appropriate level of remuneration.

A common dilemma for product providers is that distributors seek to maximise their remuneration from their distribution activities yet want to be able to offer a competitive price to their end customers. We see this in the grocery domain where supermarkets seek to negotiate good margins for distributing products yet want to offer consumers the lowest possible prices. This has tipped the balance of power very much in favour of the supermarkets and resulted in a weak position for producers. Thus, brokers might also expect to receive high levels of commission for distributing, say, motor insurance but want to offer low premiums to their customers. This dynamic has been a major catalyst for the development of remote, IT-based distribution methods in a number of areas such as motor insurance.

It is fair to say that the ability to make sound judgement calls in respect of setting a price that optimises distribution margin and customer attraction is a crucial marketing competence. The preferred approach is to argue that lower customer prices will result in such a high volume of demand that distributors will ultimately earn more cash, albeit at a lower margin per unit, than they would from selling a lower volume at a higher margin. Such an approach assumes elements of a perfect market and price elasticity of demand that are not necessarily in evidence universally in the financial services sector.

Competition

In some respects, the pricing of financial services has been less influenced by competition than many other product categories. Until comparatively recently, life, pension and investment products were priced more to secure distributor support than to ensure competitive value-for-money. Importantly, the complexity and lack of transparency of financial services pricing act as inhibitors to highly competitive pricing. Fortunately, a combination of regulatory, legislative, technological and competitive developments is acting to achieve a significant increase in the role played by competition in the pricing of financial services.

Competition exerts its most powerful effect in circumstances characterised by product simplicity, consumer knowledge and confidence, low perceived risk from buying largely based on lowest cost option, limited product differentiation, simplicity of purchase process, ease of switching and wide number of competing providers. Thus, it can be appreciated that motor insurance is influenced by competition to a far greater degree than the provision of banking services to small companies or critical illness insurance. The internet has had profound consequences for financial services as price comparison sites (also known as aggregator sites) have increasingly empowered consumers to shop around for the best deal to suit their personal circumstances. Indeed, according to market research company Mintel, some 73% of UK adults had used a financial comparison website in 2022[2]. This resonates with a similar survey carried by YouGov, in which some 70% of consumers use aggregators when considering buying a financial product. There seems to be a presumption on the part of consumers that this type of shopping behaviour will result in a good deal, a view supported by research by Equifax research that showed 38% of respondents believe they always get a good deal using price comparison sites.

In the following Marketing in practice vignette Ian Hughes CEO of Consumer Intelligence identifies some of the key factors that are acting as drivers of change when it comes to the pricing of financial services in today's market environment. He also shows how important aggregator sites have become in the context of shopping around for general insurance products such as automobile and household insurance.

 Marketing in practice 12.3: how insurers are addressing present day pricing challenges

The transformation of insurance pricing: a historical perspective

Historically, insurance pricing in the UK was characterised by relative stability, with annual policy renewals and price adjustments based on broad demographic factors and claims history. This approach offered predictability for both insurers and consumers. However, the advent of the digital age and increasing market competition have ushered in a new era of dynamic pricing strategies.

Technological advancements: enabling real-time pricing

The introduction of advanced data analytics and machine learning algorithms has been a game-changer in the insurance industry. These technologies enable insurers to analyse vast amounts of real-time data, allowing for more nuanced risk assessments and pricing adjustments. Consequently, insurers can modify premiums based on immediate risk factors, market conditions, and individual consumer behaviour, moving away from the traditional monthly or annual price-setting model.

Consumer behaviour and pricing sensitivity

The modern insurance consumer is more informed and price-sensitive than ever before. The proliferation of online resources and comparison tools has empowered consumers to compare policies and prices quickly, fostering a culture of price sensitivity and comparison shopping. Insurers must now consider this heightened consumer awareness in their pricing strategies, ensuring competitiveness while maintaining profitability.

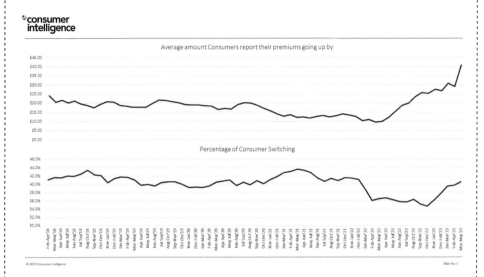

Figure 12.3 Consumer-reported premium increases, graphed against propensity to switch

The role of Price Comparison Websites (PCWs)

PCWs have revolutionised how consumers shop for insurance. These platforms aggregate pricing information from multiple insurers, presenting it in a user-friendly format that facilitates easy comparison. The impact of PCWs on pricing strategies cannot be overstated. Insurers are now compelled to offer competitive prices to feature prominently on these sites, knowing that a significant portion of their customer base will be influenced by the information presented on these platforms.

Regulatory changes influencing pricing

Regulatory bodies have played a pivotal role in shaping pricing strategies in the insurance market. Initiatives like General Insurance Pricing Practices and Consumer Duty have been implemented to ensure fair pricing practices and protect consumers from discriminatory pricing models. These regulations have forced insurers to re-evaluate their pricing strategies, ensuring compliance while staying competitive.

Pandemic-induced market fluctuations

The Covid-19 pandemic has introduced unprecedented volatility into the insurance market. Changes in consumer behaviour, such as reduced vehicle usage during lockdowns, have impacted risk assessments and pricing models. This has been coupled with rapid changes in costs caused by a lack of replacement parts and increased labour costs. Insurers have had to rapidly adapt their pricing strategies to these new risk profiles, balancing the need for financial sustainability with consumer expectations during a challenging economic period.

Balancing risk and reward: The insurer's dilemma

Insurers face the perpetual challenge of balancing risk with profitability. Accurate risk assessment is crucial to setting competitive premiums and reflecting the actual risk. This balance is further complicated by the need to maintain customer satisfaction and loyalty. In a market where consumer loyalty is increasingly influenced by price, insurers must be careful not to alienate existing customers with significant premium hikes while also attracting new customers with competitive offers. General Insurance Pricing Practices (GIPP) means that they must offer the same prices to new and existing customers, but as the price change and switching graph shows, pushing higher prices to existing customers will push them to ship around and switch.

Impact of external factors on pricing

External factors such as climate change, economic fluctuations, and technological developments continually impact insurance risk assessments and pricing. For instance, the increasing frequency of extreme weather events has forced insurers to recalibrate their risk models for property insurance, subsequently affecting pricing. Similarly, advancements in vehicle technology and telematics have influenced motor insurance pricing. Over the coming years Internet of Things technology both in the home and on the road (think self-driving vehicles) will again change the price of risk and this will mean that future versions of this chapter might be radically different.

Innovative pricing models: telematics and usage-based insurance

Adopting telematics and usage-based insurance models represents a significant shift in pricing strategies. These models utilise real-time data to assess individual risk profiles, allowing insurers to offer personalised premiums based on actual usage patterns and driving behaviours. This approach provides more accurate pricing and encourages safer driving habits among consumers.

The future of insurance pricing: predictions and trends

The insurance industry is on the brink of exciting developments in pricing strategies. The integration of advanced data analytics and artificial intelligence (AI) will bring about more personalised and dynamic pricing models. Insurers are expected to bundle additional services with standard policies to create more comprehensive and attractive offerings in response to the growing importance of customer experience and value-added services.

Ethical considerations in pricing

As pricing models become more sophisticated, ethical considerations come to the forefront. There is a growing concern about the potential for discriminatory pricing practices, especially as algorithms become more involved in decision-making. Insurers must navigate these ethical waters carefully, ensuring their pricing strategies are transparent and fair.

Conclusion: navigating the evolving pricing landscape

In conclusion, the UK's insurance pricing landscape is characterised by its dynamic and evolving nature. Insurers must continuously adapt to changing market conditions, consumer behaviours, and regulatory environments. The future of insurance pricing promises further complexity and innovation, challenging insurers to stay agile and responsive to maintain competitiveness and profitability in a rapidly changing market.

Source: Ian Hughes, CEO, Consumer Intelligence

Explicability

By explicability we mean the ability to explain and justify why a product is significantly more, or indeed less, expensive than competing offerings. Products that are materially cheaper than the norm may attract consumer suspicion in product areas that are typified by relative consumer ignorance and the risks associated with making a poor choice. A corollary to this is that under conditions of consumer ignorance and perceived riskiness, a price higher than the norm may be seen to imply quality and instil consumer confidence. This is somewhat akin to the so-called Giffen effect coined from the eponymous Victorian economist Sir Robert Giffen. According to the Giffen effect, under certain circumstances demand increases as prices rise. This may in part explain the attractiveness of certain exclusive or designer label goods. For several years L'Oreal has used the tag line "because I'm worth it" as a means of justifying a premium price for its cosmetic and beauty products.

Explicability is more difficult to achieve the closer market conditions approximate to perfect competition. The implication for marketers is that those seeking to achieve a premium price position must invest in an appropriate level of product/service differentiation to justify the price premium. It is interesting to note that several high street banks have attempted to market higher net worth current account banking services at a premium price in recent years such as Barclays and Lloyds TSB. The impression conveyed is that neither has been particularly successful as consumers fail to place sufficient value on the premium price they are charged. Bank of America customers in the USA who maintain an average daily balance of $20,000 or more have access to its Premium Solution current account. Chase offers two premium accounts in addition to its basic chequing account options: Premier Plus, which does not charge a fee on up to four withdrawals from non-Chase ATMs per statement period. Additionally, the account earns interest and, like Bank of America, fees for money orders, cashier's cheques and travellers cheques are waived. You can also link two other Premier Plus accounts to your account. It requires the customer to maintain an average daily balance of $15,000 in linked deposits/investments or make automatic payments to your Chase first mortgage to avoid the $25 monthly fee. Chase also offers its Premier Platinum chequing account which has all of the same features as the Premier Plus but adds more free services. For example, you can link as many as nine accounts, and you receive priority customer service over the phone. However, it requires an average daily balance of at least $75,000 to avoid the fee, which is $25 per month ($35 in Connecticut, New Jersey and New York). In order to qualify, deposits and investments can be linked to it but not mortgage payments. In India, HDFC Bank offers a range of premier banking options under the brand names of Imperia, Preferred and Classic.[3]

Value to customer

Progress check

- Three core approaches have been proposed for the determination of price, namely: cost-based, competitive, market-oriented.
- Marketing-oriented pricing sets out to reflect a broad range of variables in the determination of price. Significantly, it recognises that price has a strong strategic dimension in being closely implicated in issues such as positioning and competitive advantage.
- Competition exerts its most powerful effect in circumstances characterised by product simplicity, consumer knowledge and confidence, low perceived risk from buying largely based on lowest cost.

The ultimate test of a price must be the extent to which customers feel they are receiving fair value and will maintain a mutuality advantageous relationship with the provider. As discussed earlier, customer value (from the provider's perspective) is a function of a remarkably discrete set of variables such as, in the case of a loan:

- Value of sum borrowed,
- Duration of loan,
- Incidence of default,
- Cross-sale/purchase of other products.

The retention of customers based upon their perceptions of the value-for-money they enjoy is assuming ever greater importance in companies' marketing strategies.

12.5 Price differentiation and preferred lives

In many marketplaces one can encounter rules and regulations concerning price discrimination. This refers to a product or service being offered to a buyer at a lower price than applies to other buyers. Implicit in price discrimination has been the notion that the buyer presented with the higher price is being treated unfairly. In practice, there is a growing recognition that the charging of differential pricing is a legitimate and, indeed, desirable feature of a consumer-oriented marketplace. As a component of the marketing mix, price can be adjusted to suit a range of buying situations. Such variations in price may be a reflection of genuine lower costs that apply to differing buying scenarios. In the consumer goods domain for example, buying, say, soft drinks in bulk quantities involves genuine cost savings to the distribution channel that can be reflected in a lower cost per unit to the end consumer.

Similarly, bulk discounts are a defensible aspect of the pricing structure that applies to the distribution channels associated with the soft drinks market. A retailer committing to buy a million cases of Pepsi Cola should expect to receive a better price than one buying just a dozen cases at periodic intervals.

Equally, it seems perfectly reasonable for a railway company to stimulate higher levels of off-peak usage of its trains by charging a lower price than applies during the rush-hour period. In this way, differential pricing serves the interests not only of the supplier and customer, but those of the wider community, by using resources in a more efficient manner. In turn, this contributes to the goal of sustainability, an issue that is assuming ever growing importance in a wide variety of contexts.

Deliberately disadvantaging one group of customers through price discrimination represents a highly undesirable practice. Referred to earlier, in 2012 the EU outlawed the practice of differential pricing based on gender on the grounds that it was unfair. In practice, women often pay lower premiums than men on, say, car insurance but that is a consequence of their better risk-related behaviour. For example, they tend to drive fewer miles per annum, drive at lower speeds, and are less likely to drive expensive high-performance cars than do men. It is those lower risk behaviours that result in lower premiums and not their gender. Price differentiation, on the other hand, has several positive features that serve the interests of a wide range of stakeholders. Differential pricing can be based upon several factors reflecting both genuine commercial considerations on the part of providers, and customer characteristics including:

- Lower costs associated with bulk purchase.
- Costs that vary according to factors such as geographical variation in labour costs, and rents for example.
- Costs that vary according to buyer characteristics. For example, people with a poor credit history indicate a greater propensity to default on loans and therefore may pay a higher rate of interest.
- Utilisation of off-peak capacity.
- Demographic factors – age, employment status, gender.

Arguably, price differentiation is particularly well-advanced in the field of financial services. The most graphic example is life assurance where prices vary according to age, sex, occupation and health status. Price differentiation in this case is based upon genuine cost/risk-related factors concerning mortality costs that vary with age and so on. Annuities are a good case in point as individuals with serious chronic medical conditions can benefit from what are termed impaired life annuities. The harsh reality is that the annuitant (consumer) can benefit from a larger pension payment on the basis that they will not live for as long as other annuitants who enjoy better health status and, thus, longer life expectancy.

Differential costs associated with different types of customers have acted as the basis for what are termed *preferred lives* insurance companies. This is a form of niche marketing where the company targets a specific segment based upon clearly defined cost advantages that are in evidence. For example, SAGA Financial Services offers relatively low premiums on motor insurance because it only sells to the over-50s, an age cohort that has relatively low claims experience. By excluding younger drivers from its book of business, SAGA is reducing the costs associated with their higher incidence of claims.

The preferred lives approach can be applied in several situations where clear customer characteristics have a direct and material bearing upon customer value. In health insurance, for example, a company might choose to target just those individuals that have favourable health status. It should be borne in mind that there are some marked differences around the world regarding the acceptability of preferred lives insurance. For some people and political organisations preferred lives insurance is seen as an oxymoron in that insurance should be about the use of pooling to best serve the overall public good. This philosophical principle underpins the approach of the French health mutuals whose premiums do not discriminate based on age. In South Africa there is hostility to the concept because consumers do not like to divulge the kind of information that would be needed to adopt a preferred lives approach on a mass market basis. Preferred lives insurance is at its most advanced in the USA insurance market.

Pricing policies can also be designed to reflect the relative riskiness of a consumer's behaviour and lifestyle. Consider motor insurance premiums where, to a growing extent, drivers who have committed a number of offences over time, such as speeding, are experiencing significant increases in their premiums at policy renewal time.

12.6 Price determination

Some form of process is required for an organisation to arrive at the finally agreed selling price. In Section 12.3 we considered the three main bases upon which price can be developed, namely, cost-based, competition and marketing-oriented. However, whichever basis is used, several steps need to be considered when setting price. The nature of these steps will vary according to whether the cost-based, competition and marketing-oriented approach is used. Figure 12.4 outlines a process that might be applied when setting price in accordance with the marketing approach.

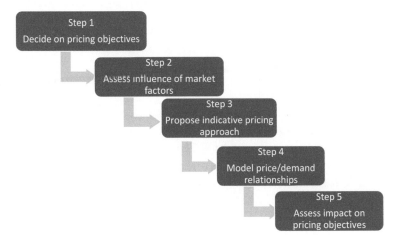

Figure 12.4 Price determination process

- Decide on pricing objectives
  At the outset there needs to be clarity regarding the financial and non-financial object-ives that are being sought. Typical financial objectives might include:
- Sales value,
- Margin,
- Profit,
- Return-on-capital.

Non-financial objectives may comprise one or more of the following:

- Sales volume,
- Market share,
- Market position,
- Customer value.
- Assess influence of market factors
  Having formed a view on the desired pricing objectives, it is important that an assessment be carried out of how Jobber's ten influences on pricing (see above) might be expected to exert an influence on the final price.
- Propose indicative pricing approach
  Armed with a clear set of price objectives, and an assessment of relevant influences, one is in a position to propose an indicative price. This stage in the process can be relatively complex in the case of insurance-related business where there is a huge array of indi-vidual premiums to be calculated. In such a case it is recommended that a number of spe-cific headline premiums be proposed that are indicative of key market positioning. For other sectors of financial services, mortgages for example, it can be far more straightfor-ward as it may simply be a case of proposing a single rate of interest.
    This is also the stage where factors such as special promotional pricing are considered. For example, it is commonplace for companies seeking new depositors to offer a bonus rate of interest, say, for the first six months, although such promotional prices often give rise to concerns that consumers may not fully appreciate that an attractive rate of interest may not last.

 Stop and think?

Marketing strategy is one of the issues to consider when determining price according to the market-oriented approach to pricing. How do you think this might relate to the subject of positioning that was presented in Chapter 7?

How important do you believe aggregator sites are in your country? Do you think consumers get a better deal from companies listed on aggregator sites than those that avoid using them?

Other aspects of price that might also be addressed at this stage are:

- Status requirements, e.g. no claims bonuses on motor insurance, income, occupation previous financial history and track record;

- Volume-related factors, e.g. lower rates of interest charged for high value loans;
- Allied charges, e.g. penalty fees on overdue payments, unauthorised overdraft charges;
- Customer contributions, e.g. the level of excess payments on general insurance contracts, early settlement penalties on, say, fixed-rate mortgage loans.
- Model price/demand relationships

  It is advisable to model how price elasticity of demand might operate given the proposed price. This can be used to make various trade-offs such as whether a lower price could result in significantly enhanced results in terms of market share or sales volumes. Such outcomes will need to be judged in the light of their impact upon the break-even point and emergence of profit. For a life assurance policy this could have a material impact upon new business strain and hence capital requirements.
- Assess impact on pricing objectives

  The modelling carried out in step 4 is a key input to assessing the likely impact of the indicative price on the achievement of the desired pricing objectives. An unfavourable outlook may result in the need to make changes to the pricing objectives or indicative pricing approach. It is advisable to ensure that relevant parties are aligned at this stage before committing further resources to the overall process.
- Assess competitor and distributor responses

  To some extent certain aspects of this stage will have already been incorporated into steps 3, 4 and 5. However, this is the point at which a more explicit assessment needs to be made. Scenario planning may be a useful approach to adopt as a means of considering the range of distributor and competitor options.
- Gain internal agreement to price

  It is expected that an appropriate level of consultation and collaboration will already have taken place. Many companies have formal pricing and credit committees whose endorsement is required before the price can be finally agreed.
- Set-up implementation project

  There is a wide range of complexity when setting prices in financial services and in some cases extensive project management will be required. It is especially important that pricing events involving a significant amount of IT resources are planned well in advance, probably well before step 1 of this process. Systems resources are usually key elements on the critical path and the availability of relevant personnel must be scheduled at an early stage if target launch dates are to be met. Staff from other functions may have an equally significant role to play, pricing actuaries for example, and so the expectation of their availability must be suitably planned for. Due regard must be paid to gaining the timely involvement of appropriate administration staff. It is by no means uncommon for them to be treated as somewhat of an afterthought in such activities; such oversights must be avoided. Other requirements that need to be factored into the implementation plan include price lists, documentation and rate books, computerised illustration systems, aggregator site content, trade communication, customer communication, and staff training. Finally, price changes on existing products need to take account of cut-off dates regarding pipeline business.

12.7 Pricing strategy and promotional pricing

It is axiomatic of all components of the marketing mix that they interact in a complementary and consistent manner to support the chosen product or corporate position. Thus, a premium quality service can be expected to yield distinctive value-added features to its customers and should be promoted in a manner that is in keeping with its high-quality market position and

Table 12.3 New product-pricing strategies

		Promotion	
		High	Low
Price	High	Rapid skimming	Slow skimming
Price	Low	Rapid penetration	Slow penetration

attract a price that reflects its superior characteristics. Pricing must, therefore, be consistent with a product or corporate position as well as achieving its financial objectives. Indeed, the two are closely inter-related. In this way strategies in respect of the use of price must align with the wider marketing strategy. However, any such adjustments must be made by paying due regard to overall product positioning and not be used superficially in response to possible tactical pressures. At the very outset of a new product's life, it can be helpful to consider the following options with regard to pricing strategies.

The consideration of the four options presented in Table 12.3 need to pay due regard to product characteristics, such as the degree and value of any competitive advantages it enjoys, as well as market characteristics, such as the likely timescale over which demand may be expected to materialise. It also depends upon the expectations of the company regarding return on investment.

An aspect of pricing strategy that is often a source of contention concerns the relationship between prices charged to new, as opposed to existing customers. In effect this is a further variant of price differentiation discussed earlier in this chapter. This practice is especially common in the field of savings, loans and credit and poses real dilemmas. Take the case of savings deposit accounts. It is commonplace for deposit-takers to offer higher rates of interest to new depositors than those that apply to existing depositors.

Arguably, the premium rates frequently offered to new depositors are unsustainably high and imply a degree of cross-subsidy on the part of current depositors (sometimes referred to as the "book") or that, in due course, the rate offered to the new depositors will be reduced to a substantially lower rate of interest. In effect, the advantageous price offered to new customers is an example of promotional pricing and is a variant of the rapid penetration strategy shown in Table 12.3. A similar approach can often be observed when new credit card customers are offered, say, a zero rate of interest for the first six months. In the mortgage market it is commonplace for new mortgage borrowers to be offered lower repayment interest rates for a period. In the UK, the Financial Conduct Authority has introduced rules that ensure that customers renewing home and motor insurance policies are quoted prices that are no more than they would be quoted as a new customer through the same channel.

In practice, many consumers choose not to take a long-term view and are attracted by headline rates offered to them as new customers. Once the promotional pricing period is over, buyer inertia sets in and the customer reverts to a lower rate (having become part of "the book"). Alternatively, some consumers become serial new customer deal chasers, regularly changing providers in search of best rates. These customers take advantage of special offers on credit cards and deposit accounts in particular to gain maximum advantage. Promotional pricing aimed at stimulating demand has become more commonplace in financial services as the sector attempts to mimic the promotional approaches more typical of the mainstream consumer goods and retail markets.

12.8 Impact of digital marketing on charges and pricing

Consumers, and particularly younger ones, increasingly don't discriminate between how they interact with retailers, be that fashion, grocery shopping or financial services. There is an elevated expectation of how products and services should be accessed regardless of sector. Consumers expect an omni-channel experience. They no longer follow a linear purchase path and increasingly expect to interact with service providers on their terms; banks are only useful if they're able to deliver what customers want, when they want it, and via the medium the customers choose. Banking is no longer B2C, it's C2B; the power has shifted, and consumers are now increasingly in control.

This evolution in buyer behaviours and expectations will only increase as technology advances and consumers' lives become more connected through the Internet of Things. In the noughties, aggregator sites drove a real change in the way insurance was researched by customers and distributed by organisations. As it became quicker and easier to compare policies across different providers, price became the key purchase decision point. Consumers can shop around online for the best deal, wherever they are, from their mobile devices. This is no longer seen as a nice to have, it's an assumed norm.

In the general insurance space, the better insurers can understand the data behind both claims and non-claims, the better they will be able to assess and price risk and more efficiently set premiums. The Internet of Things enables organisations to create a multitude of different policies specifically based on each customer's specific needs, fuelled by data. Forbes have reported that connected devices have helped some insurance companies lower their premiums by as much as 25%.[4]

The emergence of insurtech – the use of technology to disrupt and streamline insurance – has been a catalyst for change in the industry. Smart technologies: doorbells, home surveillance cameras, locks, lights and heating to name a few, are an increasingly common feature of modern homes. Insurers can price policies based on information provided by connected devices. Home insurance claims historically relied on information disclosed by the customer, but with the advent of smart homes – where utilities are controlled remotely by app – insurers can predict with greater accuracy both the likelihood, and the veracity of claims, which could reduce premiums and insurance fraud. LeakBot is an app-controlled device, that when clipped to a water pipe close to the stopcock, it monitors water usage to identify leaks at inception, preventing major leaks and water damage. Given escape of water is the most common home insurance claim it's unsurprising that several major UK insurers already offer LeakBot free of charge to their customers. Smart heating systems can maintain a constant temperature when homeowners are away, reducing the likelihood of pipes freezing and bursting. Similarly, turning lights on remotely makes houses seem more inhabited and less likely to be burgled. Historically insurance premiums have been calculated based on average groupings of data plus factors such as presence of a burglar alarm. Insurtech allows insurers to use specific real-time data to build personalised risk profiles and set pricing accordingly. Insurtech faces similar challenges to fintech; it's challenging for startups to compete with the large incumbent brands who already hold the market share and are more likely to be trusted. However, again similar to fintech, younger consumers are demanding greater personalisation and in-app servicing, which may help shift the dial on insurtech adoption. Established brands evidently see the benefits; home insurance market leaders Aviva acquired a majority share in insurtech brand Neos Ventures Ltd in 2018 to help them modernise their offering.

The car insurance industry has also seen pricing impacted by GPS technology that provides data on how, when and where people drive; known as telematics. This data is used alongside traditional factors such as age and home address to build personalised risk profiles and set premiums. The premise being that the safer the driver, the more they can save, with some insurers offering up to 40% discounts.

Within the health insurance arena, integrations between medical-tech and fintech are being used by insurers, such as Vitality, to set premiums and validate claims. The rise in wearables – smart devices that track daily activity levels, heart rate, sleep, blood pressure and ECG readings – provides a steady stream of real-time data that helps build an accurate health profile. A study by German multinational insurance company Munich Re found that "steps per day can effectively segment mortality risk even after controlling for age, gender, smoking status, and various health indicators".[5]

Health data from wearables enables insurers to price appropriately and moreover, allows them to potentially forecast health issues and flag them to customers. Early intervention has obvious advantages to the customer in preventing potential severe health outcomes, and to the insurer in reducing policy claims. Real-time health data also reduces health insurance fraud, ensuring claims are genuine and based on tangible data. As ever, firms need to be mindful of data storage and privacy, as well as data accuracy, ensuring for example that activity isn't over or under reported.

The reach may go beyond underwriting insurance to the lending and mortgage space, with banks using health data from connected devices such as FitBits to assess the ability of customers to repay loans. Similarly, business banking could gauge the ability of a commercial customer to repay loans based on data about the number of customers who enter their shop premises on any given day.

Digital has also had a significant impact on the asset management space, where robo-advice has successfully filled a gap left by human advisors. Consumers are now able to shop around in the wealth management space in a transparent manner, accessing information that previously was the preserve of financial advisors. AI provides timely, cheap, and unbiased advice which arguably is more consistent and accurate than human advice. As the public becomes increasingly comfortable with wearable tech, there is an expectation that their insurers should also be just as invested in utilising it to benefit their customers.

12.9 Summary and conclusion

This chapter has highlighted the importance of pricing in the marketing process. Pricing is the only element of the marketing mix that contributes to revenue rather than cost, so its importance must not be underestimated. For any organisation, the pricing decision is influenced by a range of internal and external factors. Financial services organisations do face some additional challenges when dealing with pricing decisions because of the greater complexity of costing, the need to deal with risk, the problems of variability and the difficulties that consumers have in understanding price.

The role played by price in determining value-for-money cannot be overestimated. Regulatory bodies on a global basis will expect ever higher standards of transparency and fairness when reviewing the pricing policies and practices of financial services companies. Technology will assume an ever-greater role in empowering consumers to compare competing offerings when seeking best-value solutions to their needs.

Learning outcomes

Having completed this chapter, you should now be able to:

1. **Explain the role of pricing in the financial services marketing mix.**
   Unlike all other constituent parts of the mix, price is concerned with the determination of revenue and plays a crucial role in the derivation of product margins and profit. Thus, price is a measure of value for both customers and providers. As far as providers are concerned, price is important for the following reasons:
   • It is a crucial determinant of margin and profit.
   • It influences the level of demand for its products and services.
   • It plays a key role in affecting relative competitive position.
   • It can be adjusted quickly, under certain conditions, to enable the provider to achieve short-term volume or margin priorities.
   • It can be varied at different stages in the product life cycle in conjunction with other elements of the marketing mix.
2. **Understand the different approaches and methods of setting price.**
   We learned that there are two basic approaches to pricing, namely explicit or overt pricing and implicit or covert pricing. The former approach makes the price paid for the service very clear in that the consumer is presented with clear and precise figures about what they will pay for this service. As far as implicit pricing is concerned, this is a system of pricing in which the actual price to the consumer is unclear and appears not to be paid by consumers. For example, the bank that offers free banking but pays no interest on credit balances is pursuing an implicit pricing policy.
      In terms of specific pricing processes we considered three, namely, cost, competition, and marketing-based methods of arriving at a price.
3. **Appreciate and understand the complexities associated with pricing in financial services and why "charges" is a more appropriate term in this context.**
   From the customer's perspective, pricing is far more complex for a financial product than for a typical consumer good or service, indeed, the terminology associated with pricing is itself a complex and diverse issue. We identified some 37 different ways of expressing what a customer pays to receive a financial product, none of which involved the use of the word *price*. This results in confusion and makes it difficult for a non-expert financial product consumer to determine relative value for money and make effective choices. It was asserted that the term *charge* is perhaps the best way of helping the consumer to understand the financial sacrifice they make in return for the utility they gain from the product or service.
4. **Appreciate the ways in which technology is empowering consumers to shop around for better value.**
   Consumers are more informed and price-sensitive than ever before. The proliferation of online resources and comparison tools has empowered them to compare policies and prices quickly, fostering a culture of price sensitivity and comparison shopping. It can be expected that the integration of advanced data analytics and AI will bring about more personalised and dynamic pricing models. Product providers are expected to bundle additional services with standard products to create more comprehensive and attractive offerings in response to the growing importance of customer experience and value-added services.

Digital has also had a significant impact on the asset management space, where robo-advice has successfully filled a gap left by human advisors. Consumers are now able to shop around in the wealth management space in a transparent manner, accessing information that previously was the preserve of financial advisors. AI provides timely, cheap, and unbiased advice which arguably is to be more consistent and accurate than human advice.

Review questions

1. Explain the role that pricing pays in the marketing mix.
2. What are the particular difficulties that marketing managers face when trying to set prices for financial services?
3. Which type of pricing strategy do you consider most appropriate for banking services?
4. To what extent do you believe that the price promotion techniques of the fast-moving consumer goods and retail sector transfer to the world of the high street bank?
5. Critically appraise the contribution made by the internet in furthering consumer interest regarding the value consumers obtain from financial services. How do you see this contribution evolving in years to come?

Notes

1 Factsheet: EU rules on gender-neutral pricing in insurance, European Commission.(ccessed December 2012)
2 UK Price Comparison Sites in Financial Services Market Report 2023 (mintel.com) (accessed November 2023)
3 www.hdfcbank.com/personal/HNW_Banking/hnw_banking (accessed January 2024)
4 www.forbes.com/sites/blakemorgan/2018/05/16/heres-how-iot-will-impact-the-insurance-claims-process/?sh=13f15ec8366e (accessed January 2024)
5 www.munichre.com/content/dam/munichre/marc/pdf/wearables/stratifying-mortality-risk-using-physical-activity/Stratifying_Risk_Using_Wearable_Data.pdf/_jcr_content/renditions/original./Stratifying_Risk_Using_Wearable_Data.pdf (accessed January 2024)

Reference

Drake, L. and Llewellyn, D. T. (1995). The price of bank payment services. *International Journal of Bank Marketing*, 13(5), pp. 3–11. DOI:10.1108/02652329510147319

13 Customer convenience and distribution

Learning objectives

At the end of this chapter, you should be able to:

1. Explain the different types of channels used by financial services providers,
2. Evaluate the strengths and weaknesses of different distribution channels,
3. Appreciate how the internet and mobile capability are revolutionising the distribution of financial services,
4. Understand how AI is impacting on the access to financial services,
5. Appreciate that the consumers' interaction with channels forms part of the customer experience.

13.1 Introduction

In any marketing mix, the component that addresses channels of distribution is concerned with making sure that a product reaches the target market at a convenient time and place. In relation to physical goods, distribution decisions are concerned with both channel management and logistics. Channel management refers to all those activities involved in managing relationships and linkages between the producer and the various organisations that distribute the product (e.g. wholesalers and retailers). Logistics is concerned with the physical movement of products from the place where they were made to the place where they will be purchased. Of course, with financial services there is no physical product, so the logistics element of distribution is of little relevance. Instead, channels of distribution in financial services marketing concern how the service is delivered to the consumer, making sure that it is available in a location and at a time that is convenient for the customer. It is yet another aspect of how an element of the marketing mix delivers value to the customer by providing access that is convenient and may also involve the provision of information and expertise to that is of help in making a decision. In chapters 3 and 9 we saw the ways in which financial services products differ from tangible goods and those differences have important implications when developing channel strategies and deciding upon routes to market. For example, by virtue of their intangibility, financial services do not involve the logistical aspects of supply chain management. Similarly, the characteristic of perishability obviates the need for warehousing and inventory management. Other important features of financial services such as duration

DOI: 10.4324/9781003398615-21

of consumption, uncertainty of outcome, contingent consumption, lack of transparency and fiduciary responsibility all have important implications for the distribution of financial services as this chapter will demonstrate.

This chapter provides an overview of the nature and management of distribution channels for financial services. The chapter begins by exploring the distinguishing features associated with channels of distribution and then moves on to examine in detail the different channels that may be used to deliver financial services to the target market and discusses their advantages and disadvantages. New to this edition is material on the ways in which AI is impacting upon how consumers gain access to financial services.

13.2 Channels of distribution: distinguishing features

As far as financial services are concerned, distribution channels fulfil the following roles:

1. The provision of appropriate advice and guidance regarding the suitability of specific products.
2. The provision of choice and a range of product solutions to customer needs.
3. The means to research product types and compare prices, most notably via the internet.
4. The means for purchasing a product.
5. The means for establishing a client relationship.
6. Product sales functions.
7. The provision of information concerning relevant aspects of financial services.
8. Access to the administration systems and processes required for the ongoing usage (consumption) of the product or service.
9. The means for managing a customer relationship over time.
10. The cross-selling of additional products to existing customers.

During this current chapter, we will largely focus upon the ways in which distribution channels address the first seven roles noted above. In Part III we will devote specific attention to items, 8, 9 and 10 above.

As a component of the marketing mix, distribution has several distinctive features that distinguish it from the other elements of the mix.

* **Cost**

  The costs associated with distribution channels may well dwarf the combined costs of all the other components of the mix. For example, the real estate and staff costs of a branch-based retail bank may be between 40 and 60% of a bank's total costs, hence the reason why so many branches are being closed. For a life assurance company, the costs associated with developing and maintaining a direct sales force of scale will incur an annual operating cost of well over one hundred million pounds.

  The use of the internet may appear to offer dramatic cost savings to a potential new entrant to the banking or insurance sector. However, these savings may well be nullified by the heavy costs associated with marketing communication and promotion aimed at generating awareness and demand, and establishing trust and credibility. Clearly the costs associated with channel strategy have major implications for pricing and profitability.
* **Timescale**

  The development of certain channels can take a considerable period to come to fruition. Obvious examples of this are the timescales associated with the creation of a branch infrastructure or of a direct sales force of scale. Similarly, once commenced, the timescales associated with certain third-party distribution arrangements can place limitations on strategic options over a protracted period of time.

- **New business strain and capital requirements**

The costs associated with the distribution and set-up of a range of investment-related products can impose significant pressure upon capital. Take the case of personal pensions. A new personal pension policy may well not achieve its break-even point until the policy has been in force for many years. Until break-even point is achieved, each policy sold will represent a deficit in cash flow terms to the product provider. This deficit is referred to as *new business strain* and an appropriate amount of capital is required to finance the strain until a surplus begins to be generated.

Thus, product features and the costs associated with certain channels of distribution will have major implications for capital. This, in turn, will influence the structure of the product range, the source of product supply, and method of distribution. For example, some while back, Barclays took the decision to cease being the sole supplier of its life assurance and pensions products and entered into an agreement with Legal and General for the manufacture of such products. Whilst Barclays would doubtless forego the underwriting profits arising from these products in the long-term, it would reduce the need for capital to fund the associated new business strain. Thus, it could enhance its internal return on capital or divert the capital so saved into other potentially more attractive aspects of its business.

- **Contractual arrangements**

The involvement of third parties in the distribution of an organisation's products may require a commitment to a contract term lasting many years. Whilst this can facilitate a degree of certainty and assist long-term planning, it does involve a degree of inflexibility during the term of the contract.

- **Loss of control**

Product providers who distribute their products through third parties such as insurance brokers, finance brokers and appointed representatives, risk being unable to exert the required degree of control with consistency amongst all distribution channel members. This may result in damage to the product provider's reputation should a material degree of customer dissatisfaction arise. Additionally, it may add to costs if substandard documentation occurs and can weaken the quality of an overall tranche of business if a broker introduces relatively poor value customers to the provider.

As an aside, the UK pensions mis-selling scandal saw product providers having to accept full responsibility for compensation in cases where policies had been mis-sold through sales agents directly in their employ. However, consumers who had been mis-sold by IFAs had to seek redress from the IFAs concerned. In such cases product providers could not be deemed to be in a position to have controlled the selling practices of IFAs.

- **Interdependencies with other mix elements**

The choice of which routes to market to employ has potentially far-reaching implications for all other elements of the marketing mix. These implications arise in the form of capability, resources, and costs and, amongst other factors, timing and responsiveness.

For example, a general insurance company planning to adopt a purely internet-based method of distribution might, at least in theory, have the opportunity for a highly competitive pricing structure. However, such a strategy means that the organisation restricts its potential market solely to individuals that have ready access to the internet and are willing to transact their insurance requirements in this way. This is becoming less of a problem as more people become accustomed to transacting business via the internet. It also results in the need to have well-developed skills and competencies regarding the use of the promotional mix. Esure is a good example of a general insurance brand that has adopted this approach to the distribution of its products.

The case of telesales as a channel of distribution places heavy demands upon the *people* and *process* elements of the mix. It may also be coordinated with a major investment in the use of direct mail as a means of both stimulating inbound enquiries for quotations as well as fulfilling post-quotation requirements. This calls for significant expertise in the use of direct mail and, possibly, direct-response advertising in the press.

- **Product interface**
  There is an extremely close relationship between product characteristics and route to market. It is in the very nature of certain products that they lend themselves towards certain types of channels or, indeed, rule out other options. Pensions are a classic case of the need for a channel strategy that involves face-to-face interaction between customer and seller/adviser (not necessarily product provider). For a whole number of reasons consumers appear, for the most part, to be unwilling to buy a personal pension on a remote basis whether via the internet, or, indeed, telesales. Issues concerning trust, uncertainty of outcome, timescale for delivery of outcome, and consumer financial illiteracy mean that the consumer feels a strong need to be advised by a suitably qualified individual in a face-to-face setting. This seems to be an obvious example of risk-reducing behaviour on the part of consumers. As yet, no pension product producer has built a book of business of any scale, by relying solely on remote channels of distribution. On the other hand, motor insurance distributed via remote channels has been an enormous success. Again, this is very much a function of factors such as the greater degree of familiarity that consumers have with motor insurance and the low level of perceived risk that they associate with this type of product.

Progress check

- Channels of distribution in financial services marketing concern how the service is delivered to the consumer, making sure that it is available in a location and at a time that is convenient for the customer.
- This aspect of the marketing mix concerns not only the processes of acquiring a new customer but also how that customer gains access to the services associated experiencing the product.
- The issue of control lies at the heart of whether a product provider should make use of intermediaries.

13.3 Distribution methods and models

13.3.1 *Direct versus indirect distribution*

In purist terms, direct distribution concerns the provision of a good or service from manufacturer/provider to customer in the absence of an intermediary that is under separate ownership, management and control. Therefore, it is channel ownership rather than the structure of the distribution channel that determines whether distribution is *direct* or indirect. In the case of a direct route to market, all the steps which are involved in acquiring a customer and selling a product are owned by the product provider. Indirect distribution, on the other hand, involves the use of agents of one form or another that are owned by a third-party organisation. As can be imagined, direct distribution facilitates a far greater degree of control over the customer experience than does indirect distribution. However, that degree of control may be bought at the price of a lower level of sales than might occur if some form of indirect distribution is employed. A range of factors must be considered when addressing the issue of direct versus indirect distribution. These factors are summarised here:

Direct distribution

POTENTIAL ADVANTAGES

- Control of brand values,
- Control of customer experience,
- Control of corporate reputation,
- Maintenance of competitive advantage from unique products and features,
- Control of regulatory obligations,
- Freedom of action,
- Strategic flexibility,
- Clarity and consistency of internal communication.

POTENTIAL DISADVANTAGES

- Limited distribution coverage,
- Restricts sales volumes,
- Limits market share,
- High cost,
- Managerially intensive.

Indirect distribution

In many ways the potential advantage and disadvantages are the obverse of those given above. However, it is helpful to see them presented as a discrete list.

POTENTIAL ADVANTAGES

- Enables provider to focus on core competencies, of which distribution may not be one;
- Ability to focus on product quality and costs;
- Avoidance of set-up costs associated with new forms of distribution;
- Allows for rapid penetration of markets, nationally and internationally;
- Access to higher sales volumes may result in lower aggregate costs that could feed into enhanced price competitiveness;
- Added cachet of having products distributed by high-profile intermediaries with strong brand reputations;
- Flexibility to experiment with new sales channels within limited cost parameters:
- May limit access to marketplace by competitors;
- Can enable provider and major distributors to test a working partnership that could ultimately result in a merger.

POTENTIAL DISADVANTAGES

- Loss of control over brand values, customer experience and reputation;
- Regulatory risks;
- Long-term distribution contracts can limit strategic options;
- Lengthy and variable communication arrangements can slow down reactions to tactical events;
- Can result in undue reliance on dominant distributors.

Elements of direct and indirect distribution models are to be encountered in most areas of financial services. However, some areas display a greater tendency towards one than others. For example, retail banking remains overwhelmingly direct. The sale of new life assurance and pension policies in the UK has become increasingly indirect and now most of the new individual life and pensions business is distributed by financial advisers.

13.3.2 Whether products are bought or sold

Before presenting an overview of currently available methods it is important to grasp the thorny issue of whether financial products are bought or sold. Although the needs expressed for the range of financial services are easily understood and readily appreciated, the motivation on the part of consumers to engage in proactive product search and buying behaviour is more muted. We can all grasp the benefits of enhanced income in retirement from buying a pension or the security a family gains when the breadwinner buys a critical illness insurance policy. However, the level of expressed demand and proactive purchasing behaviour is of a relatively low order. A range of factors is implicated in this reluctance not least of which is affordability. Additionally, there is the opportunity cost to current consumption of other more pleasure-inducing goods and services. Undoubtedly there are circumstances in which the consumer does actively seek to buy; this is most apparent with mortgages and motor insurance. In the latter example there is simply a legal obligation for motor vehicle owners to ensure they have at least third-party insurance coverage.

Whilst it is certainly the case that some products are predominantly *bought* whilst others fall more generally into the category of being *sold,* it is far from a product specific issue. Rather, it is a complex and multifaceted matter which involves the interplay of product, customer, and situational considerations. An individual might proactively *buy* into, say, a mutual fund on one occasion; equally she might well decide to make an unplanned purchase on another occasion because of proactive sales activity on the part of a product provider or intermediary.

 Stop and think?

Distribution channels fulfil 10 roles for financial services provider (FSP)s, can you name them all?

What do you think are the two primary aspects of distribution regarding the customer's experience of an FSP?

What are the main advantages and disadvantages of direct forms of distribution?

A financial services sector based purely upon products distributed to proactive buyers would be of a materially smaller scale than one which engages in proactive selling. It is in the interests of all parties (consumers, providers, intermediaries, regulators and governments) that proactive sales activity is fully appropriate to the customer's circumstances. In other words, great care must be taken to ensure that the rights of all parties are respected. It is similarly important that all parties are aware of their responsibilities and act in ways that are commensurate to those responsibilities.

Although the role played by intermediaries is notable within the context of life and general insurance, indirect channels play an important role in other areas including:

- Mortgages,
- Credit cards,
- Secured loans,
- Unsecured loans,
- Health insurance,
- Creditor protection insurance,
- Hire purchase,
- Share dealing,
- Credit.

13.4 Distribution channels

There is a diversity of channels used in the distribution of financial services. These include:

- Specialist financial services branch outlets such as banks, building society branch offices, credit union offices, and some insurance companies for example;
- Non-financial services retailers such as supermarkets, electrical goods, motor dealers, clothes shops, department stores;
- Quasifinancial services outlets such as post offices, real estate agents;
- Face-to-face sales channels such as financial advisers, direct sales forces, credit brokers, insurance agents;
- Telephone selling via both outbound call centres and inbound call centres;
- Internet: provide direct, aggregator sites;
- Direct mail;
- Direct response advertising including newspapers and magazines, commercial radio and television;
- Affinity groups such as employers, trade unions, football clubs, universities, etc.

Each of the above methods of distribution will now be addressed in turn.

Bank and similar branch-based outlets

The branch outlet has until recently been the dominant means of gaining access to the mainstream products associated with banking and mortgages. In these contexts, the branch has performed the dual roles of acting as a retail outlet in which buying and selling activities could take place as well as providing a range of processing functions to facilitate the ongoing administration of products. The importance of the branch network in retail banking is evidenced by the fact that there are very few banks worldwide which operate without a branch network. However, that situation is in a process of flux as many new entrants to banking now operate on a purely remote basis. That trend is likely to continue as traditional banks maintain their branch closure programmes. For example, HDFC Bank in India draws attention to the rapid development of its branch network as a key factor behind its successful market penetration strategy. However, with the development of bancassurance, bank branches have become oriented more towards being product sales outlets and less involved in administrative functions. This transition from the branch as essentially a customer services outlet to one of being a customer sales outlet has not been without its difficulties. For established branch networks, the culture of the branch has had to undergo a major transformation as staff have had to adapt to a new sales-oriented role, a process which many traditional banks' staff have found challenging (Knights, Sturdy and Morgan, 1994).

The branch itself is a complex environment. It is an area where consumers make routine transactions, where staff may try to make sales and where a range of back-office tasks may be accomplished. Traditional branch designs placed very heavy emphasis on back-office processing and the traditional bank branch provided a relatively unwelcoming environment. Recent developments in branch design have placed much greater emphasis on ensuring a customer-friendly environment and increasing the amount of space available for customers. Thus, banks rely on open plan layouts and decoration which is themed according to the bank's corporate identity. For example, when redeveloping its Singapore network, Citigroup used the same firm that had designed Apple's stores to create a more relaxed and welcoming environment. Over a decade ago, BNP Paribas opened a "concept store" in Paris which featured flat screen TVs, bean bag couches, and iPads to browse while sipping coffee (*Economist*, 2012d).

The Swedish-based bank Handlesbanken has an interesting business model whereby the great majority of its service functions are carried out within the client's local branch. This is in stark contrast to most banks which over many years have pursued a policy of stripping service and administrative functions out of branches and into large, centralised service centres supported by call centres which are often offshored. Founded in Stockholm in 1871, Handlesbanken now has 461 branches in Sweden as well as 408 other branches in some 24 other countries. The UK is now Handlesbanken's second largest market after Sweden and its branch network has grown from 26 outlets in 2006 to more than 200 by 2023.

Many banks have also introduced "zoning". This means that the floor area is divided up so that there are distinct areas for different types of banking transaction. Thus, for example, a bank may have a separate "self-service" area for basic money transmission, balance enquiries, etc. – often relying only on ATMS. A different area of the branch will then be dedicated to standard products such as account opening, credit card applications and basic loans. Finally, a third area may be set aside for customers looking for more complex products requiring more detailed discussions with a member of the branch staff.

Quite often banks look to expand the range of services available via the branch in order to make more efficient use of their network. Again, a prime example would be Standard Chartered Bank's Financial Spa, which is presented as a one-stop financial management centre or "financial supermarket".

Branch-based banking can be expected to undergo enormous changes from now on in response both to changes in patterns of consumer behaviour and rapid advances in information and communication technology (ICT). These twin phenomena of consumer behaviour and ICT are interconnected and synergistic. The rate of adoption of internet banking has been rapid across the globe and has served to question the future viability of the traditional branch-based model. Other developments such as the steady reduction in the use of cheques

Advantages	Disadvantages
•Represent physical evidence of intangible services •Provide reassurance and represent solidity of the provider •Give confidence to customers that they can gain access to services features and help •Achieves reinforced awareness of brand •Provides access to face-to-face service and advice •Allows complex transactions to be easily conducted	•Rural and poor communities often poorly served •Limited opening hours restrict access to services •Branch geography based on historical usage patterns •High costs •Pressure on staff to achieve cross-sale targets can cause customer dissatisfaction

Figure 13.1 The advantages and disadvantages of branch-based distribution

are also serving to undermine the primacy of the branch. Branch reduction programmes have been a feature of UK banking for many years, but the rapid uptake of internet banking would appear to have accelerated the process of late. According to consumer lobby group Which? HSBC had a network of almost 1200 branches as recently as 2012 but by mid-2023 that had shrunk to little more than 320. This is a phenomenon that applies to all mainstream traditional banks in the UK. As of September 2023, some 5,355 branches have closed, or are planned to close, since 2015. This seems to be a worldwide issue, indeed, according to S&P Global Market Intelligence over 10,000 bank branches have closed in the USA since 2019 as more customers have turned to digital services. The picture is similar in Australia as between June 2017 and June 2022 banks shut more than 1,600 branches.

Commenting on its branch closure programme in 2022, HSBC noted that the number of people visiting its branches had fallen by 65% during the past 5 years, with some branches serving fewer than 250 customers a week. In 2022 it was estimated that 93% of UK adults were using on-line banking and by 2023 some 24% had a digital-only bank account, up from just 9% in 2019. The Covid-19 pandemic of 2020-2022 has also been an important catalyst to the closure of bank branches.

The advantages and disadvantages associated with specialist financial services branch outlets as a means of acquiring customers are summarised in Figure 13.1.

Internet-based distribution

It's now possible to transact digitally from anywhere, on any internet connected device. Banking is no longer restricted to visiting branches, writing cheques, carrying physical cash or, with the emergence of contactless, even a bank card. While the impact of the internet on banking was initially somewhat inflated – with some of the more extreme forecasters predicting that the internet (clicks) would make the branch (bricks) redundant within a five-year period, it has undoubtedly driven a dramatic shift in the way we bank over the past 30 years.

The internet has provided many consumer benefits in the form of greater access to financial services with the introduction of online banking and trading and a greater choice of 24/7/365 services. It has also resulted in the introduction of products that offer better value-for-money in areas such as loans and deposit taking. Moreover, digital, and particularly mobile banking has obvious advantages in countries with geographically dispersed populations and where branch networks are patchy. Research insight 13.1 outlines the development of mobile payments in the context of India where lower levels of urbanisation have presented particular challenges in terms of access to payments systems. This opens up access to banking products in parts of the world where it would be impossible to serve with any form of physical branch. In the case study section that completes Part II we see how Turkey's Aktif Bank has innovated access to credit through an internet-based solution called NKolay Kredi.

Research insight 13.1: the emergence of the Indian mobile payments market

This study uses a theoretical perspective from institutional theory along with evidence from a range of secondary sources and a series of interviews to analyse the emergence and development of the market for mobile payments in India.

An initial review of the opportunities in this area by the regulator – Reserve Bank of India (RBI) in 1998 prompted interest from banks and from telecoms providers. One of the early movers was HDFC who, (working in partnership with a major mobile phone provider) started to use its ATM network to accept utility bill payments. State Bank of India and ICICI were also relatively early adopters of mobile payments. The model at this stage was limited, the banks were clear leaders and telecoms companies were thought of as the more junior partners. The period 2004 – 2010, saw the emergence of specialised payment companies – a process facilitated by new legislation in 2007. This was the period that saw the emergence of the first digital wallets – perhaps the earliest example being mCheck, launched by ICICI in collaboration with Visa and Airtel. The uptake of mobile phones during this period was significant and by 2010 the mobile subscriber base was close to 600m.

During the early phases of the emergence of the mobile payments market, the dominant logic was very much about security and this meant that the banks played a leading role. Telecoms companies were typically more oriented to inclusiveness – their mobile subscriber base was considerable larger than the customer base of the leading banks. And indeed, from a regulatory perspective there was growing interest in the opportunities to provide payment services to a large, often unbanked, rural population.

As a consequence, during the first half of the next decade the telecoms companies became increasingly active. The banks had a limited rural presence, but the telecoms companies were able to access a much wider customer base. Security considerations required that they continued to partner with banks, and during this period a number of different types of mobile wallet emerged – the open and semi open were highly flexible and accepted by multiple retailers. The closed and semi closed were more restricted but also simpler and more secure.

The balance between inclusiveness and security shifted further after 2015 in the second half of that decade with RBI approving the formation of payment banks which allowed telecoms companies and specialist mobile payments companies to provide basic banking services – particularly reaching out to the unbanked rural population.

Payment banks offer basic deposits and payments but no provision for credit, so the business model relies on transactions fees and merchants fees.

The authors highlight the way in which the mobile payments market has been shaped by the changing balance between what they describe as the "secure or banking logic" and the "inclusiveness or telecoms logic". They also draw attention to the key role of the regulator in shaping the re-balancing. On the consumer side, the demographic of the market place (large numbers of young consumers) and the active engagement of merchants in accepting mobile payments we particularly influential in securing high levels of customer engagement with this payment mechanism.

Source: Shekhar, S., Basak, S. and Manoharan, B. (2019).

The digitisation of financial services is mutually beneficial, offering greater ease of access to the client and vast quantities of valuable client data to financial organisations. Financial institutions can supplement owned customer transactional data with the users' online browsing habits, location and social shared data should the customer use social media sign-on. All this data is crucial to enabling financial services to create an ever-more tailored customer experience to improve trust, customer satisfaction, loyalty and advocacy. The emergence of biometrics offers the opportunity for greater financial inclusion, enabling people with no or low credit history or lacking formal documentation to confirm their identity. This could be hugely beneficial in Sub-Saharan Africa where 30% of the potential mobile-money account holding population are unbanked due to lack of documentation.[1]

Consumers are increasingly comfortable with online banking; the digital banking statistics study by Finder[2] reported 86% UK adults used online banking, and digital-only banking use had grown from 24% at the start of 2023, to 36% in just 12 months. A significant acceleration given just 9% of the UK adult population had adopted digital-only banking in 2019. Almost half of respondents intending to open a digital-only bank account cited convenience as their motivation, something of which traditional providers should be mindful. Interestingly almost a quarter, 24%, of traditional bank customers don't trust digital-only banks and a third of UK adult population don't plan to open a digital-only account. Indeed, digital-only banks may have seen an uptick in new accounts, but retention figures aren't as positive, with over 20k digital-only accounts being lost in the first half of 2023. They may attract customers who want an ancillary account to make cheap payments abroad as opposed to being used as a primary bank account.

The Covid-19 pandemic accelerated the shift to digital banking, with limited opportunities to engage in banking in any other format. Santander UK reported an increase of 18% in digital transactions over 2020[3] and 89% of eligible payments in the UK were contactless[4]. Global data tells the same story; Fidelity Information Services (FIS), which works with 50 of the world's largest banks, detailed a 200% increase in mobile banking registrations in April 2020, with mobile banking traffic increasing by 85%.[5] Data from the World Bank estimated that 67% of the adult global population held an account with a bank or mobile financial service provider in 2021[6].

The pandemic also had a big effect on how people make purchases, with contactless payments jumping by 40% worldwide since the start of the pandemic. The World Bank reports that after the start of Covid-19, 80 million adults in India and 100 million adults in China made their first contactless payments.[7] The pandemic exemplified the benefits of consumers being able to manage their finances without having to visit a physical branch.

There has been much focus on the closure of bank branches and the impact this has on communities and those reluctant or unable to make use of digital channels. Banks are embracing "phygital", a blend of physical and digital services to best serve customer needs in the ever-evolving world. This could include anything from video banking whereby real-people service customers via a video banking app to Barclays Eagle Labs repurposing closed bank branches into shared workspaces for the entrepreneur community, offering mentoring and SME banking advice. A 2023 study showed that 16% of UK adults who opened digital-only bank accounts, did so because of the lack of local bank branches[8], an interesting warning to the big banks that "out of sight, out of mind" may be prescient. Leveraging machine learning is also to financial services (FS) providers' advantage; chatbots are able to offer highly tailored guidance on complex customer needs. Using technology to deliver personalised services and products will help fulfil customer needs and increase conversion rates and market share. It also reduces the risk of customers suffering "flavour-blur" when too many unnecessary options and information are presented and going to a competitor's site to complete the task, something a reported 40% of FS customers have done[9].

On a fundamental level, banks need to ensure basic services can be delivered digitally. Deloitte report that less than 60% of the largest traditional banks in Europe enable accounts to be opened fully online[10] let alone allow people to apply for personal loans or mortgages online. The term "neobank" has emerged in recent years, and while it's often used interchangeably with the term fintech, they are actually a subset of fintechs. Like fintechs, they are solely digital, with no physical branch presence. Neobanks do not hold banking licenses and thus usually partner with other organisations to be able to offer banking solutions, whereas fintechs can hold banking licenses and operate autonomously. Neobanks offer simple banking solutions such as current accounts, credit cards and loans, whereas fintechs provide a more diverse set of features such as peer-to-peer payments and robo-advice, and actively seek to disrupt the traditional banking landscape and offering.

Below we see how neobanks are making inroads into the Indian banking market.[11]

 Marketing in practice 13.3: neobanks in India

Neobanks are fintech firms that function like banks and operate digitally – a collection of financial apps and services. Every transaction is done online and is entirely safe, customised, and more convenient in several aspects compared to traditional banks. Neobanks break old banking traditions such as cash deposits, bulky documentation, and personal interaction with a bank official.

The primary purpose of neobanking in the economy is to provide cutting-edge financial services and facilities through fintech and artificial intelligence (AI) at a lower cost. It's a gap that the current applications of traditional banks don't fill!

There are no conventional brick-and-mortar branches of neobanks. Although not directly regulated by RBI, neobanks in India have banking partners such as ICICI, HDFC, and other banks which are registered with RBI.

Digital allows financial services suppliers to set up completely new online-only organisations with discrete brand identities, such as The Cooperative owned bank Smile.com. It's also prompted the creation of wholly new business models such as Zopa, an online marketplace which matches people who need a personal loan with people who have money to lend. By cutting out the middleman Zopa sets out to offer lower interest rates to borrowers and better returns to investors. In the UK, new digital only banking brands in recent years have included Starling, Atom Bank and Monzo. Also based in the UK but operating internationally is what is termed the global neobank and financial technology company Revolut. In India the top 12 neobanks have been identified by Freo. It is estimated that roughly 35% of the Indian population were using internet banking as of 2023; this amounts to some 355 million people.

Whichever strategy is pursued, there can be no doubt that online is able to achieve dramatic cost savings, especially with regard to routine administration functions such as making payments and funds transfers. The emergence of blockchain digitised ledger transaction technologies that are secure and tamperproof offer even greater scope for cost efficiencies. They facilitate the immediate transfer of funds and remove the need for intermediaries from the transaction process. Santander's 2015 Fintech 2.0 paper,[12] created in collaboration with Oliver Wyman and Anthemis Group, made bold claims regarding the impact blockchain technology could have on banking costs within the next seven years:

> Cutting operational costs is not the only benefit in securities trading. Distributed ledgers can increase investor confidence in products whose underlying assets are now opaque (such as securitisations) or where property rights are made uncertain by the role of central authorities. Our analysis suggests that distributed ledger technology could reduce banks' infrastructure costs attributable to cross-border payments, securities trading and regulatory compliance by between $15–20 billion per annum by 2022.

This is backed up by Santander's decision to launch blockchain technology for international payments up to £10,000 in May June 2016, the first UK bank to have done so. In December 2024, Reuters reported that the "world's first' blockchain payments at Bank of England" had been completed by Fnality, a blockchain payments firm for shareholders Lloyds Banking Group, Santander and UBS[13].

Traditional current account banking has been revolutionised with the emergence of mobile banking apps, contactless payments, money transfer tools such as Ping.it and voice-activated banking through Amazon Echo. Digital technology has been leveraged to give customers greater access to, and oversight of, not only their money but their spending and savings habits. Apps such as Moneybox and Plum link current accounts to the users' savings goals and encourage them to invest in order to reach them.

As the Internet of Things (IoT) continues to gather momentum (see also Chapter 5), there is serious potential for this to revolutionise FS. It has already impacted the insurance industry; car insurance premiums are being calculated on real-time information gathered from vehicle's usage, the condition it's kept in, its service history, etc. In the future cars may even have their own digital wallets, enabling them to purchase their own insurance or identify when a part is faulty, order it directly from the garage and pay for the parts and labour with its own digital wallet. IoT has the potential to nullify many transactional interactions consumers would traditionally have to manage themselves which could dramatically impact how consumers view and interact with banks. IoT is discussed in more detail in Chapter 5.

Advantages	Disadvantages
•Provides customer access anywhere, anytime •Enables providers to gain universal distribution •Complements other channels •Permits cost-effective pro-active communication with existing customers •Low administration costs •Can be a low-cost purchase channel •Encourages diversity and choice through easy entry by new providers •Allows consumers to transact business in a completely impersonal and remote manner •Results in lower prices •Can allow new products and services to be piloted at low cost and thus encourages innovation •Allows providers to react quickly to changes in the marketplace •Enables customer research to be conducted easily and cheaply •Can enable providers to bespoke customer services and move towards more finely-tuned segmentation •Can facilitate development of close relationships through customised communication •Lessens demands placed on branch networks and face-to-face sellers and advisers	•Disenfranchises people who do not have access to internet and thus exacerbates financial exclusion •Concerns regarding security and fraud inhibit consumer purchasing via internet •Difficult-to-use sites cause consumer dissatisfaction •Not well-suited to complex products and customer encounters requiring person-to-person conversational interaction •Requires a well-known existing brand or high cost marketing communication programme for new customer acquisition and product purchase

Figure 13.2 The advantages and disadvantages of internet-based distribution

Some complex products such as mortgages are now able to be applied for and purchased online. Other products, such as pensions still rely on offline service and support, with face-to-face advice. There is a shift however, as is evidenced through the success of robo-advice, offering unbiased, fast and low-cost investment guidance. There is an argument that algorithm driven programmes offer a superior service for more complex digital advice as they don't suffer the same partiality and inconsistency as humans. As consumers become more comfortable with digitised advice and familiar with the start-up brands which are now offering banking services, there may be a greater shift away from traditional bank branch networks and the big five banking brands.

The advantages and disadvantages of the internet as a channel for new customer acquisition are shown in Figure 13.2.

Robo-advice vs the personal touch

One of the most controversial developments in financial services of recent years has been the emergence of robo-advice, attracting enthusiasm and cynicism in equal measures. The very term robo-advice makes some recoil because it stirs up images of a dystopian future; problematic given the importance of winning trust and public acceptance within the financial services arena.

In the simplest terms, robo-advice is the replacement of human-to-human advice with algorithm-powered online financial guidance and execution, commonly known as machine learning. It has quickly established itself, with several stand-alone robo-advisory businesses having been set up in the UK in recent years, attracting the attention of consumers and established human-based advisers in equal measure.

After the banking crisis, financial services had to manage increased regulation with consumers' demand for better advice at lower costs. This resulted in many low-value customers being left orphaned, as large organisations struggled to service them in a profitable manner. Robo-advice filled this gap, providing algorithm-powered automated technology to offer personalised advice.

US online investment advisory service, Betterment, was one of the first to adopt this approach, positing that as investing is inherently formula and data driven, robo-advice is the natural investment solution.

It offers an efficient and low-cost way for financial organisations to offer personalised advisory services while fulfilling consumers' desire for quick, inexpensive, unbiased advice, particularly attractive to millennial and mass affluent customers.

This was supported in Accenture's "Financial Services Global Distribution & Marketing Consumer Study"[14] which explored the transformation of retail financial services across 33,000 financial services consumers across ten markets. Respondents to the survey highlighted three main attractions of robo-advice as "the prospect of faster (39%) and less expensive (31%) services, and because they think computers/artificial intelligence are more impartial and analytical than humans (26%)."

The Accenture report presents an increased propensity for trust in robo-advisory service; seven in ten respondents welcome computer-generated advice and services for banking, retirement and insurance planning, and almost four out of five are open to robo-advice for traditional investing. Conversely, the study also found that nearly two-thirds of respondents still value and expect a personal service, particularly for more complex product advice and complaints handling. Thus banks are challenged to provide a blended offering, utilising robo-advice to fast-track and streamline basic banking needs while freeing up human resource to facilitate the value-add transactions.

Piercarlo Gera, Senior Managing Director of Accenture Financial Services cautions that:

> Successful financial services firms will therefore need a "phygital" strategy that seamlessly integrates technology, branch networks and staff to provide a service that combines physical and digital capabilities and gives consumers a choice.[15]

Progress check

- A financial services sector based purely upon products distributed to proactive buyers would be of a materially smaller scale than one which engages in proactive selling.
- The branch has performed the dual roles of acting as a retail outlet in which buying and selling activities could take place as well as providing a range of processing functions to facilitate the ongoing administration of products.

> •   Digital, and particularly mobile banking, has obvious advantages in countries
> with geographically dispersed populations and where branch networks are patchy.
> This provides access to banking products in parts of the world where it would be
> impossible to serve with any form of physical branch.

Most robo-advice propositions allow access to an actual person within the user journey, ranging from help when a potential client may get a little lost online, through to bringing in an adviser for final confirmation of a financial plan and recommendations, though this could be by telephone or video link. Other offerings involve a combination of the two, where talking to a person is an intrinsic part of the process covered by definitions such as the futuristic sounding cyborg-advice or, in one very bullish recent statement from an advice firm, bionic advice.

In its report "Advice Goes Virtual: How New Digital Investment Services Are Changing the Wealth; Management Landscape", consultancy Ernst and Young point to the tremendous potential offered by robo-advice. E&Y estimate that the current market share of digital wealth firms is just 0.01% of a US$33 trillion global industry. The report identifies that the USA, as the world's largest market for financial services, represents a considerable opportunity for a set of common foundational wealth services like financial planning, asset allocation and investment management across a range of sectors. The report calculates fees for automated advice to be typically around 0.25% to 0.5% of assets compared with 1–2% for a human adviser.

Writing in *Financial Adviser* on 4 January 2017, Damian Fantato provides a further example of just how international robo-advice is becoming with the announcement that Novofina intends to launch its "state-of-the-art" algorithms onto the UK market in 2017. The first products it plans to launch are Novofina 7plus and Novofina 20plus; the company claims that based on past simulations, these products aim to offer average net returns of 7% and 20% respectively.

A report published in mid-2015 by consultancy A. T. Kearney entitled "Hype vs. Reality: The Coming Waves of 'Robo' Adoption" [16] asserted robo-advisory services would become mainstream among US investors over the next three to five years with total assets under management (AUM) increasing by 68% annually to about US$2.2 trillion by 2020. In reality, global AUM in the robo advisor market hit US$97.70bn in 2020, a lower trajectory than predicted. However, growth has increased exponentially with global AUM expected to hit US$1,802.00bn in 2024, and US$2,274.00bn by 2027. In 2017 there were 2.6m global users of robo-advice. This grew to 31m global users in 2023 with sizeable year-on-year increases, however, this is predicted to level out in the coming years, with projected global users of 34m by 2027. [17] In 2023 Brandon Russel of IFAmagazine.com posited a theory as to why robo-advice hadn't quite fulfilled initial projections: [18]

> Robo "advice" falls down because it's not advice. And this is predominantly why it
> hasn't engaged consumers with larger sums. In its current form it doesn't satisfy the
> more complex analysis of all of a client's holdings (investments, pensions, property,
> earnings etc) that are required to give advice.

It is worth noting that there are some key regulatory discrepancies between these markets, which make a like-for-like comparison unfeasible with the UK, being subject to more stringent regulation. It could be argued that the low-cost US advice offerings represented are an American version of digital guidance but with the addition of a recommendation. FCA regulations in the UK specify that it can't be guidance if it involves making a recommendation to the client to pursue a specific course of action. That rule may keep guidance separate from execution-only sales and frustrate applying digital to this element of distribution.

Regulatory concerns aside, bearing in mind the success of robo-advice in the US, it's easy to understand why the UK market might be anxious to adopt these lessons and practices. Nutmeg is perhaps the best-known UK stand-alone robo-advisory service, but there are a plethora of others including Moneyfarm, InvestEngine and Wealthify as well as new entrants set to come to market soon, such as Moola.

However, these stand-alone businesses have not been without their critics. Alan Miller, founder of passive fund specialist SCM Direct, has suggested a break-even point may not be reached for 11 years given the cost of client acquisition. Miller cites the increasing cost of internet marketing and the relatively small amounts a typical millennial has to invest as primary drivers for the increased acquisition cost.

Two robo-businesses have been bought by larger financial concerns – insurance and pension mutual insurer LV bought Wealth Wizards in August 2015, to power its retirement advice offer in the wake of the pension freedoms. Among other things, this demonstrates that firms are prepared to offer fully regulated digital advice beyond the investing stage. Aberdeen Asset Management bought Parmenion Capital Partners, a firm that offered discretionary fund management, a fund platform and robo-advice for £50m at the beginning of 2016. LEBC, an advisory and corporate advisory firm, says it has raised £500m from its bionic service, i.e. robo plus telephone advice. Such numbers may make others sit up and take notice.

It's likely that it may take some time for consumers to really understand what is on offer from robo-advice and for the market to mature. It could be that initially they merely experience increased efficiency among technology-enabled advisers rather than true robo-advice. There is nothing wrong with this if it helps more clients and the businesses involved.

It is yet to be seen whether robo-advice will be truly disruptive and represent an extinction event for other channels in the way that aggregator sites killed off most high street insurance brokers. However, human beings' main weakness is their humanity, as a species inconsistent by nature and prone to behavioural shifts and mistakes. Robo-advice and artificial intelligence is inherently more consistent and reliable.

Generative AI (GAI) has emerged in recent years and offers an evolution in robo-advice. The best-known tool, ChatGPT, launched November 2022. GAI is an evolution of machine learning that produces new and original content, as opposed to simply surfacing responses based on algorithms. It is in theory able to apply a human-like lens to problem solving and fulfil tasks that usually need human intelligence. It has certainly gained a great deal of public interest, with ChatGPT attracting 57m users in its first month, and over 100m weekly users.[19] In 2023, Citywire reported that a UK IFA firm was using ChatGPT in lead generation, to identify and screen prospective clients.[19]

As when robo-advice first launched, there have been concerns raised around the risk of GAI replacing IFAs and paraplanners; if consumers are able to get advice from ChatGPT and other similar GAI tools for free, why pay IFA fees? The Schroders Pulse reported 43% of advisors view GAI as a threat and 27% never plan to integrate GAI into their processes.[20] However, it's more likely that the threat comes from firms not understanding the benefits integrating with GAI offers; increasing efficiencies, identifying client needs, screening, and reducing overheads by automating processes which frees up human IFA and paraplanner time for more profitable activities. In theory, this could mean IFAs could take on more clients and increase profitability and market share. It is likely that GAI is only a threat to those who don't embrace it and that in reality, it's essential they do it in order to remain competitive.[21]

> The biggest worry for advisers may not necessarily be generative AI itself replacing them, but rather other advisers or companies utilising generative AI to enhance their services and outperform competitors. Financial advisers should be more concerned about not integrating AI within their processes for greater efficiency and productivity, as the risk lies in others employing generative AI to reduce fees, improve service quality, and increase responsiveness.[22]

GAI isn't able to replace emotional intelligence quite yet and financial advice is based on more than just raw data, it's about nuance and understanding the "needs, values, goals and important relationships" of clients.[23] However, the nature of GAI is that it is constantly learning and evolving so who knows how well it may be able to meet this challenge in the future.

The predicted wealth transfer from baby boomers to millennials and Gen Z is somewhere in the region of £5-6tn. Given the generational discrepancies in digital fluency and trust, it is likely this will drive a demand for more tech-savvy services which GAI is well placed to support.

One thing to be mindful of is how regulation will keep up with the pace of change in GAI. There needs to be a balance between protecting the interests of customers, whilst ensuring innovation isn't hampered. Brett King of Moven states "For me, advice is the next big disruption. For instance, in banking you do need real-time advice. The ability of humans to provide that is poor and, as humans, we're inconsistent and we make mistakes. Artificial intelligence will not." [24] The advantages and disadvantages of robo-advice as a channel for new customer acquisition are summarised in Figure 13.3.

Advantages	Disadvantages
•Lower fees for consumer •Reduced costs for providers by removing human manpower element •Impartial; removes human bias •Can reduce level of risk as portfolio is automatically monitored and adjusted •Removes risk of conflict of interest (advisors recommending certain funds they may benefit from) •Provides far speedier service •Offers access to tools previously the preserve of financial advisers •Low investment minimums so caters for smaller accounts •Ease of access; 24/7/365 availability •Convenience; able to be accessed across all digital mediums	•Lack of personal touch and an inability to offer the tailored kind of advice human interaction allows •Rules based algorithm creates an element of inflexibility which may not benefit the consumer in unpredictable market conditions •Less sophisticated robo-advisors may offer one-size-fits-all solutions which do not benefit consumers with complex investment needs •Limited by their pre-programmed questions when creating a portfolio •May requires more hands on management by customer to ensure portfolio adapts to any life changes

Figure 13.3 The advantages and disadvantages of robo-advice

Table 13.1 Examples of typical NFSRs

Retail Outlet	Typical Financial Services Distributed
Supermarkets	Current banking accounts, general insurance: motor health, holiday, unsecured loans, credit cards
Motor dealers	Car loans, creditor protection insurance
Home improvement companies	Finance, creditor protection insurance
Electrical goods retailers	Hire purchase, extended warranties, creditor protection insurance

Non-Financial Services Retailers: NFSRs

A wide range of retail outlets have some involvement in the distribution of financial services as an adjunct to their core business. Some of these outlets are involved in the direct distribution of their own manufactured products whereas others act as agents for third-party product providers. Additionally, some retailers are hybrids in that they distribute their own products (direct) as well as distributing products manufactured by other providers on an agency basis. A characteristic of most forms of NFSRs is that financial services are not their core business. Examples of typical NFSRs are given in Table 13.1.

Other forms of retailers have provided various forms of finance, such as hire purchase, for many years. Indeed, for many it represents a significant source of margin. In Brazil, the home appliance retailer Magazine Luiza provides finance for purchases by almost 75% of its customers across a retail network of over 600 shops (*Economist*, 2012d). However, in being a non-core part of the mainstream business there are certain limitations on the scope of financial services that can be distributed in this way. For example, it tends to be a single product provided by a single provider, such as car finance distributed via an automobile dealership. In this case, motor vehicle finance is viewed by the consumer as a credible adjunct to the dealer's own business of automobile sales. The resonance between a car dealership and automobile finance is reasonably viewed as being salient or representing a good fit. However, the relationship between the car dealership and other forms of financial services may not be viewed as having the same degree of saliency. For example, if the car dealership was considering selling, say, mutual funds, consumers might be expected to be somewhat resistant because the product (mutual funds) is not readily associated with the provider (car dealer).

The issue of brand saliency plays a role in the case of supermarkets. They have made material progress in distributing relatively straightforward products, such as motor and holiday insurance, but have yet to register a significant breakthrough as a vehicle for distributing products such as pensions and investments. It is interesting to speculate on why major retailer branches have stretched into simple financial services products but not, as yet, into more challenging areas of financial services. The answer to this issue may have less to do with brand saliency than with the issue of whether products are bought or sold. Arguably, brands such as Virgin, Tesco and Sainsbury can stretch successfully into product areas characterised by the *bought* mode of acquisition, but do not yet have the capability to operate effectively in the *sold* mode.

There is evidence from research by Devlin (2003) that consumers are willing to place their trust in brands that are primarily not financial services oriented as a source of financial products. This suggests that, at least in the UK, nontraditional financial services brands could leverage their brand associations into the financial services arena. However, it is yet

Advantages	Disadvantages
•Well respected consumer brands can create high levels of trust and imply value and dependability. •The physical branch presence facilitates low-cost promotional displays •The branch facilitates access to help and assistance •Face-to-face help can be provided at relatively low marginal cost •In their role as intermediaries, they can provide access to high volumes of new customers •Well suited to distribution of complementary products (eg: car finance via car dealers •Can be a relatively low cost means of distribution •Convenience and ubiquity	•May not be seen as credible providers of financial advice •May not be seen as credible providers of complex products such as pensions, mortgages and investment funds •Loss of control over quality of business introduced •Loss of control over quality of customer experience •Potentially high costs of commission paid to introducers •Over-dependence on high volume producing agents can make a supplier vulnerable

Figure 13.4 The advantages and disadvantages of NFSRs

unclear the extent to which brand saliency or selling capability lies at the heart of the current limitations on the penetration of major retailing and consumer brands into complex financial services product areas. Research carried out by Opinium on behalf of 3R Insights in August 2016 showed that while consumers have a range of concerns regarding the intentions and behaviours of traditional product providers such as banks, insurance companies and investment companies, they are doubtful whether others could do any better. Indeed, when asked whether consumers thought that companies from other major consumer goods sectors would serve the customer interest better than established providers, only 20% thought they could. Some 18% answered firmly "No" whilst an overwhelming majority of 62% were unsure.

The advantages and disadvantages typically associated with NFSRs as a means of new customer acquisition are summarised in Figure 13.4.

 Stop and think?

Do you believe that the physical branch will still have a role to play 10 years from now?

Why do you think that supermarkets seem not to have fulfilled the ambitions initially expected of them?

To what extent do you believe that AI will make face-to-face financial services redundant?

Quasi-financial services outlets: QFSOs

This term refers to channels that, whilst not being traditional financial services outlets, have a strong affinity with them. The best examples of QFSOs are post offices and real estate agents. Throughout the world, post offices are often the channel through which state social security payments are made and this positions them as having a money transmission role. As well as making cash payments of state benefits, post offices are typically used for providing access

Advantages	Disadvantages
•Highly localised branch network of post offices provides ready access to all consumers •Post offices seen as trustworthy and secure •Post offices handle cash sums and have systems capability for a range of money transmission options •Post offices often have extended opening hours compared with banks •Post offices can play a vital role in facilitating financial inclusion •Relatively low value customer traffic •Real estate agents can provide access to high value sales opportunities •Branch outlets conducive to face-to-face advice and assistance	•Although well-suited to simple products, may be less suited to distribution of complex products where advice may be required •There is often a lack of privacy which consumers find inhibits the nature of their transactions •Often limited space for effective point-of-sale promotion •Queues are often a feature of post offices and this inhibits their usefulness as distribution outlets •Real estate agents often suffer from a poor reputational image which may undermine consumer trust •Real estate firms are often led by strong local characters with a highly independent approach •Potential loss of control re compliance with regulations and customer experience

Figure 13.5 The advantages and disadvantages of QFSOs

to state-owned savings institutions such as National Savings & Investments in the UK. Thus, they may well be limited in their ability to distribute products supplied by the private sector. However, in an era of deregulation of financial markets worldwide, this may become less of a hurdle in the future.

We consider real estate agents as QFSOs rather than NFSRs because of the complex nature of real estate finance. The financing of a real estate purchase involves, potentially, the interplay of a range of complex financial products including mortgages, endowment insurance schemes, life protection policies, pensions and critical illness insurance. Thus, the real estate channel has the potential to be a highly profitable method of customer acquisition given the bundle of products that can be packaged together. Indeed, this was an important part of the rationale of major banks and insurance companies acquiring real estate chains in the late 1980s and early 1990s. Many of those acquisitions foundered as the new owners failed to properly value the chains they acquired and recognise the competencies needed to run businesses that were outside of their previous experience. Unfortunately, it also coincided with a dramatic recession in the UK housing market.

The advantages and disadvantages of QFSOs are summarised in Figure 13.5.

Face-to-face sales channels

Direct sales forces have been the backbone of the life assurance industry throughout the world for decades. However, it is the conduct of many of those individuals engaged in delivering face-to-face advice that has been the source of a great deal of controversy and, arguably, much of the mistrust that has bedevilled the industry in numerous parts of the world. For example, writing in Harvard Business School's Working Paper 12–055 in October 2015, Anagol, Cole and Sarkar[25] report on a research project they carried out into the sales practices of financial advisers in India. They conducted a series of field experiments to evaluate the quality of advice provided by life insurance agents in that country and concluded that:

Agents overwhelmingly recommend unsuitable, strictly dominated products, which provide high commissions to the agent. . . . We also find that agents appear to focus on maximizing the amount of premiums (and therefore commissions) that customers pay, as opposed to focusing on how much insurance coverage customers need.

In the UK, insurance company business models as well as the role, culture, and style of working of financial advisers have changed radically over time and this has had the effect of dramatically reducing the numbers of people working as financial advisers. For example, during the 1980s it was estimated that in excess of 200,000 people in the UK were registered with the then regulator of life assurance direct sales forces (LAUTRO; the Life Assurance and Unit Trust Regulatory Organisation). According to a Nextwealth report[26] there were 27,839 people advising on retail investment products as at the end of 2021, the vast majority of whom are Independent Financial Advisers.

The USA represents the largest market for financial advice in the world. According to US Labor Statistics data there were more than 330,000 financial advisers as at the end of 2021. With a population of 332m that's one financial adviser for every 1,006 people and compares with one to every 2,418 in the UK. It is estimated that the number will continue to grow in response to the needs for financial advice presented by the growing number of baby boomers requiring financial planning help as they approach retirement. Demand will be further increased as people live longer and, therefore, require financial advice over a protracted period in retirement.

Historically, a key driver of the direct sales force model was the notion that life assurance, investment and pension products had to be sold rather than be bought. Although there is undoubtedly a given level of business that is *bought*, the adherents to the *sold* model argue that it is in the nature of life, pension and investment products that a significant element of demand is latent rather than expressed. The primary role of the direct sales force is to turn latent demand into real new business through its capability to prospect for new customers. Thus, the capacity of a direct sales force to work as a powerful means of prospecting has been seen as key to its success. The traditional prospecting direct sales force was underpinned by a funnel model as follows in Figure 13.6.

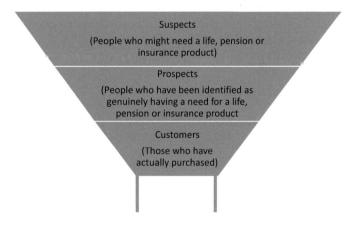

Figure 13.6 The prospecting funnel

It has not been uncommon for the ratio of suspects to prospects to customers to be of the order of 100:10:1, i.e. it takes one hundred suspects to produce ten prospects and then just one customer. Hence, direct selling has sometimes been seen as essentially a numbers game. Until the rigours of financial regulation and control began to take effect, the direct sales force was driven to increase its headcount year on year, since, so the theory went, the bigger the sales force, the greater the sales volumes. Unsurprisingly, direct sales forces can often experience extremely high rates of staff turnover; indeed, historically in the UK it was often more than 40% per annum. Thus, a company with a direct sales force of three thousand advisers would have to recruit twelve hundred new salesmen per annum (assuming a 40% turnover rate) just to stand still. As can be imagined, the recruitment of one hundred new salesmen each and every month is a challenging task. For this reason, sales managers would spend a disproportionate amount of time sourcing new recruits relative to the time spent training and developing their existing salesmen and women.

Such a model is clearly highly inefficient and has resulted in unsustainably high distribution costs. It is a model which is predicated by the notion that life, pension, and investment products are fundamentally sold rather than bought and results in the costs associated with overall prospecting activities being borne by the customer who buys. Thus, in the example of the prospecting funnel given earlier, the costs associated with the 99 people who do not buy are loaded onto the one person who does. This has resulted in distribution-related costs that have been criticised for delivering poor customer value.

The means by which direct sales forces are remunerated has been the subject of much controversy and debate. In essence there are two basic approaches, namely commission or salary plus bonus. However, a number of variations based upon these two basic approaches are to be found. In the commission-based approach, the salesperson receives payment purely based on sales made. Thus, an individual who works diligently but fails to make a sale will receive no income. This may well seem to benefit the provider company since it results in the avoidance of certain overhead costs associated with the sales force. Critics of this method of remuneration argue that it places undue pressure upon the salesperson to make a sale, which, in turn, results in coercive sales practices to the detriment of the consumers (Diacon and Ennew, 1996).

Adherents of the salary-based model argue that this method of remuneration is more consistent with present-day employment philosophies by recognising the professionalism of the salesperson. Importantly, it is argued that a salaried approach reduces the pressure on the salesperson to make a sale and that this, in turn, results in better quality of business and greater levels of customer satisfaction. However, the costs associated with time spent prospecting must still be paid for, and these costs are loaded onto the customer who buys in much the same way as on the commission-based approach. Arguably, the costs are even higher in the salaried model than the commission-based model since it results in a higher level of fixed cost to the provider.

Progress check

- It is yet to be seen whether robo-advice will be truly disruptive and represent an extinction event for other channels in the way that aggregator sites killed off most high street insurance brokers.

- The issue of brand saliency plays a role in the case of supermarkets. They have made material progress in distributing relatively straightforward products, such as motor and holiday insurance, but have yet to register a significant breakthrough as a vehicle for distributing products such as pensions and investments.
- The commission-based sales model which is predicated by the notion that life, pension, and investment products are fundamentally sold rather than bought. This results in the costs associated with overall prospecting activities being borne by the customer who buys.

The discussion regarding remuneration so far assumes that the advisory function provided by the salesperson is available free of charge to prospective customers. A contrary point of view is that financial advice should be seen to be a professional service in much the same way as the advice given by a lawyer or an accountant. Accordingly, the argument runs that prospective customers should be offered the opportunity to pay a fee for advice, whether or not they subsequently make a purchase. Ultimately, it is presumed that the distribution costs loaded onto product charges will fall as actual purchasers are relieved of the cost burden associated with prospecting activities. This may well sound good in theory, but in practice customers are not always willing to pay up-front fees for advice as we saw from the observation of Rick Kahler in India noted earlier.

There are instances where salespeople are paid purely on the basis of a flat rate salary with no sales value or volume-related bonus. The advantages claimed for this approach are that it frees the salesperson from any pressure to sell and results in good quality sales and high levels of customer satisfaction. However, the prevailing corporate orthodoxy maintains that some degree of incentive is necessary to encourage high performance and thus remuneration based upon sales results remains the norm.

It is worth commenting a little upon the cultural differences that apply to commission and salaried direct sales force since they have far-reaching implications. Commission-based sales organisations revere high-performing individuals and have been accused of almost encouraging the cult of the sales prima donna. Such organisations position the role of the salesperson as a self-employed businessperson who enjoys considerable freedom to act. In extreme cases the salesperson enjoys the freedom to organise their work very much as would an independent contractor. The value of what are termed renewal commissions can be commuted to achieve a capital value that high-performing advisers can realise in much the same way as small entrepreneurs can sell their business and realise a capital gain. Notwithstanding the rigours of regulation, the self-employed commission-based sales adviser sets their own levels of sales performance at a level that satisfies their personal lifestyle aspirations. They are often disdainful of their sales managers who they consider to be their inferiors in the highly charged field of life assurance sales.

The culture of the salary-based direct sales force represents a far more controlled business environment. Because he or she is an employee, the individual salesperson is expected to conform to the values, style, and processes of the employer company in much the same way as other employees such as those working in administration or IT. A more traditional approach to the managerial hierarchy is in evidence whereby top performing advisers are not encouraged to feel they have a direct line to the Chief Executive (unlike top-performing commission-based salesmen). Importantly, strict standards are laid down for the achievement of input-oriented performance such as the number of appointments carried out per day or per week.

Bancassurance

As the name implies, this is a form of distribution that has its origins in France. In simple terms it concerns the provision of life, pension and investment products by a banking organisation. Indeed, in many parts of continental Europe bancassurance has become the dominant distribution channel for products of this nature – in countries such as France and Spain, bancassurance may account for 60–80% of insurance sales.

According to Imarc Group, in its assessment of the outlook for bancassurance in Europe (having reached US$ 588.2 billion in 2022 it expects the market to grow to US$ 792.7 billion by 2028, a compound annual growth rate of 5.3%. It attributes this growth to:

> The regulatory changes promoting collaboration, customer trust in banks, evolving financial goals, personalized solutions, and enhanced accessibility through extensive networks and digital innovation are among the key factors driving the market growth.[27]

Bancassurance has also become an important channel for distribution in Latin America, in Australia, Malaysia, India and in China. Indeed, in Hong Kong, bancassurance accounts for over 50% of premiums, while in Singapore it has reached 33%. Bancassurance emerged in India at the end of the 1990s when the life insurance sector was privatised. New insurance entrants into both India and China are using bancassurance models to compete against established insurance companies with their own extensive branch networks. Both countries are expected to continue to display significant growth in bancassurance-based distribution over the next ten years, partly because of the impact of foreign entrants to the domestic market and partly through the growing use of this channel by domestic insurers.

The real power of the bancassurance model derives from its ability to achieve the following:

- Low customer acquisition costs,
- Maximise cross-selling opportunities,
- Utilisation of relevant customer data.

Bancassurance comprises elements of both the *bought* and *sold* aspects of customer acquisition addressed earlier. We might term these the *passive* and *active* models of bancassurance. The passive model is demonstrated in Figure 13.7.

It can be readily appreciated that this passive model operates reactively to the instigation by the client. Two notable consequences arise from this model. First, the mix of life, pension and investment products displays a marked bias in favour of loan-protection insurance policies. Second, it fails to engage that proportion of the total current account customer base who do not proactively use the branch to engage in suitable problem-solving behaviour.

The limitations of the passive model of bancassurance gives rise to the *active* model. In this model, the bancassurer recognises the need to achieve the dual goals of optimising sales opportunities presented by the current account customer base as a whole and achieving a well-balanced product sales mix. The bancassurance model can only begin to achieve its full potential when it adopts the active model. However, this requires a different approach

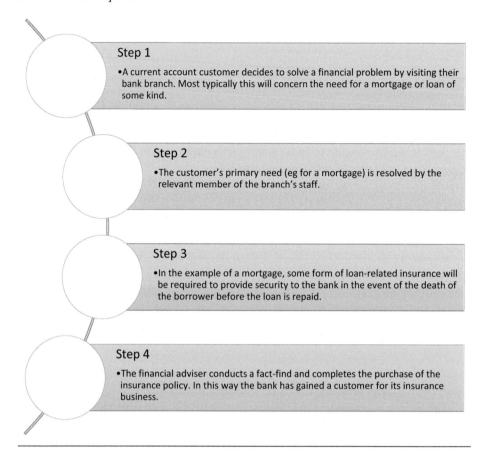

Figure 13.7 Passive model of bancassurance

to the passive model as the organisation seeks to make the transition from a customer-pull method of distribution (the *bought* approach) more towards a supplier-push method (the *sold* approach).

A key issue to grasp when adopting the active model of bancassurance is the relationship between the insurance and branch banking operations. Although a wide range of organisational structures are encountered, there is usually some form of structural boundary that separates the two entities of insurance and branch banking. A typical model is one in which cashiers and other branch-based customer service staff perform the role of introducer of prospective customers to the sales advisers of the bancassurance operation. Therefore, it is of paramount importance that excellent working relationships are fostered between the two. Indeed, it is the norm that branch staff have a balanced scorecard of objectives to achieve and the bancassurance advisers should work closely with them to achieve the valuable synergies which exist. This requires a high degree of mutual understanding and respect. Organisations that fail to recognise the importance of managing the introducer–adviser interface are unlikely to succeed in achieving their aspirations for bancassurance. The advantages and disadvantage of bancassurance are given below in Figure 13.8.

Advantages	Disadvantages
•Access to high volumes of good quality potential customers •High levels of adviser sales productivity •Potentially lower acquisition costs then prospecting sales forces •Backed by the reputation of the core bank brand •Permits face-to-face advice in the branch, the home or office •Current account data and transactions can provide triggers for sales opportunities •Potential for developing a bundled pricing approach involving bank and lpis products •On-going administration synergies	•A poor banking reputation can limit customers' willingness to buy its life, pension and investment products •A bank brand may not convey sufficient sallency regarding certain products i.e. may lack a degree of credibility •Over-zealous telephone prospecting harms core banking relationships •Over zealous prospecting in branch harms core banking relationship •Face-to-face advice can be expensive for low margin products •The passive model fails to achieve expected success

Figure 13.8 The advantages and disadvantages of bancassurance

 Stop and think?

To what extent do you think the bancassurance model relies upon customers being physically present in bank branches?

How might the rapid expansion of internet banking have an impact upon bancassurance?

Do you think that bancassurance is a viable business proposition for neobanks?

Telephone-based distribution

The telephone has become a powerful means for the achievement of a range of purposes in the field of retail financial services. At its simplest it can act as a cost-effective means of prospecting for potential new customers by seeking to secure sales leads. At its most complex it can provide a fully functional banking service. In between these two extremes sits the use of the telephone as a highly successful means of product distribution, especially for general insurance products.

During this current section we will focus primarily upon the role of the telephone as a channel of distribution in the context of new business acquisition. The role played by the telephone in managing ongoing customer relationships will be addressed in Part III of this text.

It was during the 1980s that the telephone began to assume major significance as a distribution channel in financial services. Prior to that it had been employed typically as a promotional tool associated with canvassing for leads for salespeople. However, as the '80s progressed, advances in telecommunications capability and data processing facilitated a far more integrated approach to the use of the telephone as a distribution channel. Throughout the world, these advances have seen the development of a teleworking industry on an enormous scale. Telemarketing has become truly global with major telephone call centres established in India and other parts of Asia. Indeed, Indian-based telephone call centres have formed the core of the fast-evolving offshore outsourcing of financial services.

Two terms that are commonly encountered in the context of telemarketing are *outbound* and *inbound*. By *outbound* we mean that the call centre proactively seeks to contact people by initiating the telephone contact. This could take a variety of forms such as cold calling from telephone lists or in response to an initial contact prompted by, say, a direct mail shot. In essence, outbound telemarketing is about generating leads with a view to those leads being followed up by salespeople as the next step in the sales process. This issue was addressed more fully in Chapter 11 where we learned how telemarketing has had to evolve in response to the growth of on-line means of leads generation. Indeed, it has been estimated that between 75% and 90% of financial services searches begin online.

Inbound calls, as the name implies, relate to call centre responses to a call initiated by the consumer. The consumer may well be calling in response to some forms of stimulus from the provider company such as a television, magazine, or internet advertisement.

The economics of *outbound* calling have presented major difficulties. This arises from practical problems such as low daytime response rates and the relatively high incidence of engaged lines. Again, technology has helped with the advent of the predictive dialler that automatically dials a list of numbers and presents a call to an agent only when the phone has been answered by the consumer. Even so, *outbound* calling tends to be more limited than *inbound* calling.

As a distribution channel, the telephone has been especially successful with relatively simple products such as motor insurance using the *inbound* approach. Originating in 1985 using only telephone-based distribution, Direct Line has grown to become a major player in the direct insurance market. Direct Line has evolved its strategy in response to the growth of internet usage and began to distribute its products online in 1999.

Telephone-based distribution permits real-time person-to-person interaction without the need for expensive branch networks or direct salesforces. However, there are limitations on the nature of business that consumers are willing to transact on this remote basis. It remains firmly based upon relatively simple, low-risk transactions. However, there is growing use of this form of distribution for a range of investment products and services on a purely outbound basis such as broking services and investing in wine, commodities, and the other non-mainstream asset classes. The advantages and disadvantages of telephone-based distribution are given below in Figure 13.9.

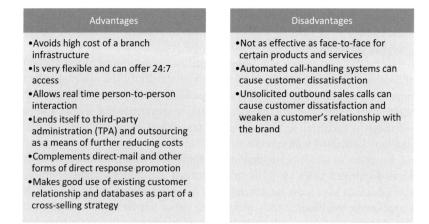

Advantages	Disadvantages
•Avoids high cost of a branch infrastructure •Is very flexible and can offer 24:7 access •Allows real time person-to-person interaction •Lends itself to third-party administration (TPA) and outsourcing as a means of further reducing costs •Complements direct-mail and other forms of direct response promotion •Makes good use of existing customer relationship and databases as part of a cross-selling strategy	•Not as effective as face-to-face for certain products and services •Automated call-handling systems can cause customer dissatisfaction •Unsolicited outbound sales calls can cause customer dissatisfaction and weaken a customer's relationship with the brand

Figure 13.9 The advantages and disadvantages of telephone-based distribution channels

Direct mail

In contrast to the internet, direct mail (DM) is one of the longest established forms of distribution. It may seem to have fallen out of fashion as newer, digital distribution and lead generating methods have risen to prominence so dramatically, but it is argued that it continues to play a vital role of an integrated approach to marketing. It has been argued that direct mail helps to combat digital overload, it now faces less competition for consumers' attention than previously and can provide an element of tangibility which can be useful in a market where products are intangible.

Clearly, direct mail performs several roles from simple awareness raising and information giving, through sales lead generation and onto the actual closing of a sale. The use of direct mail by the financial services sector has grown on a worldwide basis. In certain respects this medium has a particularly important role to play within the context of financial services. For example, product complexity coupled with regulatory requirements lends themselves to the need for hard-copy communication in many cases.

Advances in the use of databases and the technology associated with direct mail have facilitated a high degree of personalisation. In conjunction with these developments, companies can use direct-response mail both with respect to their existing customers and prospective customers with a greater degree of accuracy and efficiency than ever before.

Direct mail is a highly controllable means of distribution that lends itself to rigorous analysis of key performance measures such as: cost per individual mailer, conversion to sale rate, and cost per sale. Although direct mail is frequently referred to somewhat pejoratively as junk mail with high wastage rates, it can, nonetheless, be a highly cost-effective means of obtaining sales. Indeed, a number of organisations use it as the primary method for new business acquisition. The successful use of direct mail hinges upon a quite small array of KPI's:

- Accuracy of lists used,
- Creative appeal and impact of the individual mailing piece,
- Speed and follow-ups to responses,
- Quality of response follow-up.

There is a rapid rate of decay from the .time at which the recipient of the mail shot provides her or his response and their motivation to engage in any subsequent follow-up activity on the part of the originator of the mail shot. This is especially important where a two-stage mailing process is being used whereby the first mail shot is aimed at stimulating an enquiry and the follow-up mail shot seeks to complete the actual purchase.

This rapid decay rate also applies where the initial direct mail communication is intended to generate a sales lead which is to be followed up on a person-to-person basis either by a direct salesperson or telephone sales agent. As a rule of thumb, direct mail responses should be followed-up by the product provider within 48 hours of the receipt of the response. It is essential that the user of direct mail has the necessary resources, infrastructure, systems and processes to ensure rapid follow-up to prospective customer response. The longer the delay in the follow-up contact the lower the ultimate sales conversion rate and greater the cost per sale.

It is argued that DM is in a state of evolution as it responds to the digital world. Its proponents contend that it has not suffered any marked decline in the face of the rapid growth of social media. According to UK direct mail company PostGrid:

Many marketers may be overlooking direct mail as a marketing tool. It is not just its ability to generate a response from the recipient but also its significantly higher ROI. When compared to some of the advanced digital marketing campaigns, direct mail still manages to beat many of them in terms of ROI. This is why the industries that never gave up direct mail marketing still hold on to it despite the majority of businesses switching exclusively to digital marketing.[28]

According to PostGrid, advertising mail volume has increased by 87% and expenditure has increased by 118%. The company goes on to affirm that DM growth appears to be all the more impressive given that whilst the advertising market grew as a whole by 16% in the last five years, DM grew by 42%. The advantages and disadvantages of direct mail-based distribution are given below in Figure 13.10.

Other distribution channels

Direct-response advertising using methods other than direct mail include: direct-response radio, television, press, magazine and poster advertising. These forms of direct response are less controllable and easily targeted than direct mail but offer their own discrete creative advantages. For example, direct-response television advertising using daytime schedules has become commonplace for organisations targeting the retired sector of society. Equity release schemes, and simple forms of life insurance plans are of particular note in this regard. Direct-response press advertising is used extensively by organisations marketing secured loans (sometimes called second mortgages). The preferred media are those aimed at the mass market such as the *Sun, Star* and *Daily Mirror* in the UK. At the other end of the societal

Advantages	Disadvantages
•Can communicate a great deal of detail	•Is a common source of consumer irritation and dissatisfaction
•Can communicate detailed regulatory warnings and requirements	•Can place heavy demands upon the literacy skills of recipients
•Can be retained for future reference	•Regulatory requirements can result in a large amount of copy and information that diverts prospects from core sales messages
•Is a means of providing physical evidence of an intangible product	
•Volumes can be controlled to match resources for follow-up	•Low response rates can make it uneconomic
•Messages can be highly personalised	•No opportunity to discuss problems and concerns
•Lends itself to a multi-segment marketing strategy	•Often suffers from a poor image which can undermine trust in a brand
•Costs and efficiency can be finely monitored	
•Can complement other channels such as telesales, direct sales	
•Can take advantage of opportunities presented by the behavioural cues of existing customers	
•Permits low-cost entry into a market	
•Allows for experimentation at low cost	

Figure 13.10 The advantages and disadvantages of direct mail-based distribution

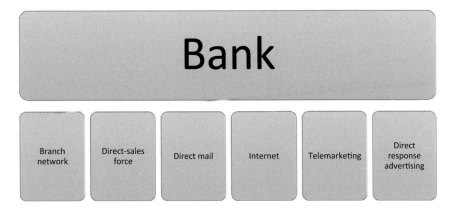

Figure 13.11 Multi-channel approach for banks

continuum we see investment products such as investment trusts, mutual funds (unit trusts and OEICS) and bonds distributed on a direct-response basis using titles such as *The Daily Telegraph* and *The Sunday Times*.

A final form of distribution is the use of affinity groups such as trade unions and sports clubs. These often provide a means of access to people using methods such as telesales, direct mail and direct sales. As such, they are not so much a distribution channel as a means of generating sales leads and, therefore, should be more correctly viewed as forming part of the promotional mix.

Multi-channel distribution

During this chapter, we have sought to provide a pragmatic insight into the real world of financial services distribution. Although the major methods of distribution have been discussed as individual channels, it is important to appreciate that to an increasing extent companies are simultaneously employing a range of channels. Thus, multi-channel distribution strategies are now the norm for most mainstream, mass-market financial services organisations. For the typical clearing bank, such a multi-channel approach will comprise the elements shown in Figure 13.11:

A typical mass market life assurance company will employ a multi-channel distribution strategy (as shown in Figure 13.12).

Increasingly, marketers are using the term "Omni channel" to reflect the requirement not just for multiple channels but also the importance of seamless integration across channels so that customer experiences are consistent and structured which ever channel is used.

13.5 Summary and conclusion

This chapter has argued that channels of distribution play a central role in the marketing of financial services because distribution channels provide the opportunity for a purchase or sale to be made. As such, they are part of the overall process by which the marketing mix

Figure 13.12 Multi-channel approach for life insurance

yields value both to customers and to the provider of products and services. It is important to emphasise the value-conferring dimensions of marketing rather than view in cost terms. Financial services organisations often employ a multi-channel strategy, using a number of different distribution channels to reach various target markets. These channels may be the organisation's own direct channels or they may involve the use of intermediaries (indirect distribution). The range of possible distribution channels available is determined partly by technology and partly by regulation. Cost, customer, and competitor influences will determine which channels are actually chosen.

Of the different distribution channels available, the branch network remains the most important for traditional current and savings accounts, but a moot question is for how much longer as neobanking continues to grow? Personal selling is probably the most common method of distribution for pensions and investments. However, fintech and new electronic based channels are developing rapidly and are likely to increase in importance over the next five years. Already, ATMs, phone and web-based distribution systems are well established. Web-based distribution is expected to experience the most growth with the most important developments being concerned first with the method of access and second with what can be done via the web. In terms of method of access, it is anticipated that there will be a much greater variety of ways of accessing the web with interactive digital TV being one of the most significant. In addition, as bandwidths increase and infrastructure improves, there will be the potential for customers to engage in face-to-face interactions with sales staff via the internet. Such a development will have major implications for the distribution of financial services because it will mean that traditional face-to-face selling falls in cost and becomes much more convenient to customers. Furthermore, for many customers the prospect of dealing with someone face to face may reduce some of the resistance to using online distribution.

Of particular note at this moment is the way in which AI will impact upon many aspects of product distribution and access.

Learning outcomes

Having completed this chapter, you should now be able to:

1. **Understand the distinctive nature of distribution channels in financial services.**
   In financial services, channels of distribution concern how the service is delivered to the consumer, making sure that it is available in a location and at a time that is convenient for the customer. It is yet another aspect of how an element of the marketing mix delivers value to the customer by providing access that is convenient and may also involve the provision of information and expertise that is of help in making a decision. Other important features of financial services such as duration of consumption, uncertainty of outcome, contingent consumption, lack of transparency and fiduciary responsibility all have important implications for the distribution of financial services as this chapter has demonstrated.

2. **Explain the different types of channels used by financial services providers.**
   We considered the characteristics and relative merits of direct and indirect methods of distribution. A detailed examination of the eight principal forms of distribution spanning the gamut from those which are branch-based to those which are fully remote was carried out.

3. **Evaluate the strengths and weaknesses of different distribution channel.**
   Each of the eight methods of distribution was summarised according to their strengths and weaknesses. We also explored how a multi-channel approach is used in order to best serve the needs of customers.

4. **Appreciate how the internet and mobile capability are revolutionising the distribution of financial services.**
   The digital world enables brands to reach customers globally, 24/7. This has broadened the reach of organisations and changed their operating model; increasingly banks are servicing customers online and physical branch closures are accelerating. Online banking is now a basic requirement for customers, as is the ability to quickly make payment, transfers and purchase new products digitally. Aggregator sites make it easier for customers to shop around to the compare the prices and features across various products, and digital claims processing has streamlined the customer experiencing. The emergence of AI powered investment platforms makes investing more accessible to a wider customer-base and cuts out the middleman and their associated additional fees.

5. **Understand how AI is impacting on the access to financial services.**
   The use of chatbots that provide 24/7 customer support for routine queries has become ubiquitous across the FS industry. The emergence of generative AI that can provide human-like responses is facilitating better targeting and more personalised advice. Natural Language Processing (NLP) enables AI-powered interfaces to understand colloquialisms and respond to queries via speech, democratising access to FS for people who may have visual or accessibility issues.

> **6. Appreciate that the consumers' interaction with channels forms part of the customer experience.**
>
> Distribution concerns the means by which someone, or an organisation, becomes a customer of an FSP, and those initial encounters set the tone and manage expectations of what the on-going customer experience will feel like. The nature of the *channels* aspect of the marketing mix concerns the actual processes that are used to deliver the on-going service and, thus, represents a key part of the customer experience. Indeed, it could be argued that, that is *the* key aspect of the customer experience.

Review questions

1. Explain the difference between direct and indirect distribution; provide one example of each form of distribution channel for a financial services organisation.
2. Which channels of distribution does your organisation use? Which are direct and which are indirect? Which is the dominant channel and why?
3. Outline the factors which influence the choice of distribution channels for a bank and for a life insurance company.
4. What are the advantages and disadvantages of distributing financial services through a branch network?
5. What are the advantages and disadvantages of distributing financial services using the internet? Why might some customers be unwilling to use the internet to manage their financial affairs?
6. To what extent do you believe that AI will revolutionise the way in which financial advice is made available?

Notes

1 www.worldbank.org/en/news/press-release/2022/06/29/covid-19-drives-global-surge-in-use-of-digital-payments (accessed August 2023)
2 Digital banking statistics 2024: How many Brits use online banking? (finder.com) (accessed September 2023)
3 santander_uk_strategic_report_2020_3.pdf (ccessed September 2023)
4 Digital banking statistics 2024: How many Brits use online banking? (finder.com) (ccessed September 2023)
5 www.fisglobal.com/en-gb/insights/what-we-know/2021/march/one-year-on-the-impact-of-covid 19-on-mobile-banking (accessed January 2024)
6 www.theglobaleconomy.com/rankings/percent_people_bank_accounts/ (accessed January 2024)
7 www.worldbank.org/en/news/press-release/2022/06/29/covid-19-drives-global-surge-in-use-of-digital-payments (accessed January 2024)
8 Digital banking statistics 2024: How many Brits use online banking? (finder.com) (accessed January 2024)
9 www2.deloitte.com/content/dam/Deloitte/uk/Documents/financial-services/deloitte-uk-hp-the-fut ure-of-retail-banking.pdf (accessed January 2024)
10 www2.deloitte.com/content/dam/Deloitte/uk/Documents/financial-services/deloitte-uk-hp-the-fut ure-of-retail-banking.pdf (accessed January 2024)
11 Freo freo.money/guides/neobanks-in-india/ (accessed January 2024)
12 https://www.oliverwyman.com/our-expertise/insights/2015/jun/the-fintech-2-0-paper.html (accessed January 2024)

13 https://www.reuters.com/world/uk/fnality-completes-worlds-first-blockchain-payments-bank-england-2023-12-14/ (Accessed January 2024)
14 "Financial Services Global Distribution & Marketing Consumer Study" exploring the transformation of retail financial services. https://d.adroll.com/cm/index/outhttps://d.adroll.com/cm/n/outht tps://www.accenture.com/t20170111T041601__w__/us-en/_acnmedia/Accenture/next-gen-3/ DandM-Global-Research-Study/Accenture-Financial-Services-Global-Distribution-Marketing-Consumer-Study.pdf (accessed September 2018)
15 https://newsroom.accenture.com/news/seven-out-of-10-consumers-globally-welcome-robo-advice-for-banking-insurance-and-retirement-services-according-to-accenture.htm   (accessed Jan 2024)
16 https://www.atkearney.com/documents/10192/7132014/Hype+vs.+Reality_The+Coming+Waves+of+Robo+Adoption.pdf (Accessed September 2018)
17 www.statista.com/outlook/fmo/wealth-management/digital-investment/robo-advisors/worldwide#assets-under-management-aum (accessed January 2024)
18 https://ifamagazine.com/advisers-will-be-replaced-by-generative-ai-chatgpt-but-not-those-that-embrace-it-says-advicebridge/ (accessed January 2024)
19 https://citywire.com/new-model-adviser/news/chatgpt-lead-generation-raises-control-questions-for-advisers/a2413000 (accessed January 2024)
20 www.schroders.com/en/global/individual/media-centre/schroders-uk-financial-adviser-pulse-survey-2023/ (accessed January 2024)
21 https://ifamagazine.com/advisers-will-be-replaced-by-generative-ai-chatgpt-but-not-those-that-embrace-it-says-advicebridge/ (accessed January 2024)
22 www.ftadviser.com/your-industry/2023/07/17/can-generative-ai-truly-replace-a-financial-adviser/?page=2 (accessed January 2024)
23 www.nerdwallet.com/article/investing/chatgpt-wont-replace-financial-advisors-yet   (accessed January 2024)
24 https://thefinancialbrand.com/news/data-analytics-banking/artificial-intelligence-ai-banking-big-data-analytics-63322/#:~:text=He%20told%20Narrative%20Science%2C%20%E2%80%9CFor,Artificial%20intelligence%20will%20not.%E2%80%9D   (Accessed February 2024)
25 Understanding the Advice of Commissions-Motivated Agents: Evidence from the Indian Life Insurance Market, Santosh Anagol, The *Review of Economics and Statistics* (2017) 99 (1): 1–15, MIT Press Direct.
26 Delivering Operational Leverage, Nextwealth. (accessed November 2023)
27 www.imarcgroup.com/europe-bancassurance-market (accessed January 2024)
28 www.postgrid.co.uk/direct-mail-statistics/(accessed September 2023)

References

Devlin, J. F. (2003). Brand architecture in services: The example of retail financial services. *Journal of Marketing Management*, 19(9–10), pp. 1043–65.
Diacon, S. R. and Ennew, C. T. (1996). Ethical issues in insurance marketing in the UK. *European Journal of Marketing*, 30(5), pp. 67–80.

Part II
Case studies

The following case studies are provided in relation to Part II of this book and they focus particularly on issues related to customer acquisition. They serve to complement the examples provided in each chapter through "marketing in practice" and can also be used for more extensive discussion of a range of marketing issues. Each case is provided with an indicative set of questions which may be useful for individual self-study or for group work and assessments.

- Case 5:Aktif Bank
- Case 6: HDFC Bank
- Case 7: HUK24
- Case 8: Nat West Accelerator

DOI: 10.4324/9781003398615-22

Part IV

Case study CS5

Aktif Bank – N Kolay Kredi

Background

Aktif Bank was restructured in 2007 with a new vision and mission. By investing its revenue in manpower and systems, Aktif Bank became a full-service bank in 2010, offering service in all areas with its strong infrastructure. During the process of restructuring, Aktif Bank increased its total assets 41 times and became Turkey's fastest-growing bank.

Aktif Bank focused on a tri-banking model calling it "New Generation Banking":

- Direct banking: instead of investing in a branch network, Aktif Bank provided technology-based products regardless of time and location constraints with convenient and attractive prices. The strategy was to offer full retail banking services throughout the country without opening physical branches.
- City banking: Aktif Bank provided customised financial and non-financial products and services for the different needs of city-based customers.
- Regional banking: Creating synergy with its foreign based subsidiaries, Aktif Bank aimed to expand trade relations as a financial actor in the Balkans, the economies of central Asia and the Middle East.

The Turkish banking sector had long been dominated by commercial banks operating through large-scale branch networks across the country. In order to compete with the top commercial banks, Aktif Bank concentrated on working with the largest physical network provider in Turkey, Turkish Post Office (PTT). In 2010 Aktif Bank created the "Aktif Online" system in the PTT and transformed itself into the organisation with the widest distribution network in Turkey, aiming to reach the unbanked population as well as the 17 million people who visit the PTT every month.

Creating Aktif Online

Before the "Aktif Online" system was created and integrated, the PTT was working offline with 18 banks only for credit card and retail credit payment collections. The staff were not sales oriented and did not have experience in banking products. Despite these challenges Aktif Bank was determined to create a success story. The goals of "Aktif Online" project were to become the most inclusive bank sales organisation without opening branches. This required:

- Integration of full-service banking activities,
- Money transfer products,

DOI: 10.4324/9781003398615-23

Figure CS5.1 Aktif Bank Logo

- Retail credits,
- Insurance products,
- Using a third party effectively as a sales and marketing channel with minimal marketing budget.

The first phase of the project was the implementation of the "Aktif Online" structure, the first and only online real-time platform between bank networks and the PTT. This phase took three months and was completed at the beginning of 2010.

In the second phase, the UPT (money transfer) system was implemented. This project and product was completed and launched in Q1 2010. Before the launch of the product, 1,500 PTT staff all around Turkey were given hands-on training in 23 cities by the Aktif Bank project teams.

The marketing consisted of in-store billboards, brochures and LCD screens in PTT locations and advertisements in national newspapers and TV channels. The motto was "Goodbye EFT, Welcome UPT – The cheapest method to transfer money between banks and PTT". Even with this limited campaign, UPT quickly gained acceptance. By the end of 2012, the total UPT had exceeded 3 million transactions, totalling $1 billion.

Following the completion of the money transfer programme, the consumer credit system project started and the credit and insurance products were launched in June 2010. The marketing was limited to in-store billboards and brochures. In eight months, 25,000 retail credits (35% of whom were previously unbanked customers) with a total amount of US$80 million were granted. At the end of 2016, 874,385 credits with US$1.5 billion had been sold, and PTT succeeded to be the twelfth bank in the credit market. The credit sales volume is also paralleled by life insurance sales, where a unique life insurance product for pensioners aged up to 80 years has been co-developed; this sector soon reached close to 1million policies sold.

Aktif Bank's projects with the PTT have proved that complex financial products like a retail credit application can be processed through a non-financial third party, including simple and assistive application entry and an online decision-making system which requires no credit expertise from PTT's staff. Integrated campaign management and payment plans which are differentiated according to customer segment, an intelligent document management system which automatically prepares the necessary documentation for customer signature at the PTT offices in a way that is secure (no fraud) and fast (five minutes from application to payment to customer), have all contributed to a very low NPL (0,08%), and a lean (low operation error and cost) operation.

Aktif Bank reached its goals and successfully implemented the PTT as its primary physical distribution channel with the "Aktif Online" system. The "Aktif Online" system was up and running successfully, while UPT and credit volumes increase day by day. With these developments, investment products could be accessible by 1.5m PTT customers. With all these products, Aktif Bank is meeting the financial needs of PTT customers and building long-term customer relationships with them.

Next Steps: N Kolay Kredi from Aktif Bank

In today's digital world, customers demand easy and quick processes, more transparency and autonomy for their financial transactions, so success at Aktif required continued innovation. The result was the development of a next generation online lending platform: "N Kolay Kredi" (www.nkolaykredi.com), which translates to "what an easy loan", in English.

NKolaykredi.com is a next generation online retail lending platform that provides instant, easy, and transparent cash loan service 365 days and 24 hours. This new platform has introduced many new features to the market:

- Firstly, it is not limited to the bank's own customers since Aktif have established an alternative legal process for wet-signature requirements – Aktif confirms the applicant's personal information by using several digital integrations to the e-government platforms, authorises the phone number by confirmation and originates the loan digitally.
- Secondly, the entire process takes only seven minutes as Aktif designed a user-friendly platform compatible with all types of mobile and desktop instruments.
- Thirdly, the platform is open 24 hours, weekends and even on national holidays.
- Pricing is highly transparent, with no bundled product requirements, no obligations for life insurance, no hidden commissions such as account fees or money transfer fees. What Aktif offers is a straightforward consumer loan.
- Finally, Aktif do not just reject the customers as other banks do. When the bank's response is negative Aktif offers free personal advice about the techniques that could help to improve the applicant's credit score.

The existing digital retail lending platforms of Turkish market suffers from two major deficiencies:

- Bundled product requirements (life insurance, bank account) make things complicated and result in a lack of transparency in terms of pricing.
- Approval rates are excessively low (only around 5%) because there is no thin-file solution or sub-prime program. When an individual gets rejected by a bank, they are likely to face rejections from all others as well.

Nkolaykredi.com is designed to address all those deficits and put itself in a different standpoint in the playground.

There are 4 unique aspects of N Kolay Credit that makes it distinctive among other players:

- Aktif offers totally free banking with no hidden costs, surprises, or mandatory bundled products. This is a unique offering in the market; no free banking proposition and simple pricing is available in the retail lending market.
- When a loan application is rejected, Aktif suggests a free personal advice service about the techniques for improving their credit score – unique by far. Other banks say simply "NO" to the rejected customers.
- Customers who use an N Kolay loan receive an internet branch password where they can make transactions with their "N Kolay accounts".
- Customers can call the "N Kolay call center" anytime for any other needs. "N Kolay" is not just another loan campaign brand; it is a comprehensive banking proposition unique to Aktif Bank and tailored for N Kolay customers.

The success of N Kolay is clear from a series of post-launch outcomes.

- Since 2016, Aktif has received more than 98 billion TL in application. 8.1 million unique people have visited the website and 1.6 million people received an offer.
- Aktif has successfully engaged bank's customers through pre-approved loan offers; 29% of the nkolaykredi loan portfolio comes from cross-selling to existing bank customers, while 71% are new customers.
- Loan performance data show that the product Non-Performing Loan (NPL) rate is 2% lower than the probability of expected default rate of the credit program. ROA (Return of Assets) is around 6-7%. This new digital loan product has become the most profitable product of the bank and the cost of loans is three times cheaper than the other loans sold by physical channels.
- TikTok has been used effectively for marketing purposes. In the first half of 2023, TikTok marketing activities have resulted in a net cost of sale of approximately USD$1.9.
- Aktif conducts quarterly surveys to measure customer satisfaction and gather feedback. Compared to the previous year, customers' net promoter score (NPS), which measures their likelihood to recommend Aktif to friends and relatives, increased from 31 to 39, representing a 26% increase.

Case study source: Tugce Iskenderoglu, Canan Sayin, Aktif Bank

Case study questions

1. Carry out some research into the Turkish banking market and describe which markets and customer needs Aktif sets out to serve.
2. What limitations in the conventional bank lending market does nkolay kredi aims to address?
3. How would you describe nkolay kredi's use of the marketing mix? How might you make better use of its marketing mix?
4. If you were devising a perceptual mapping grid for nkolay kredi what two core product features would you choose as a way of positioning the brand to achieve competitive advantage?

Case study CS6

Customer acquisition at HDFC bank

Introduction

Until the 1990s, the banking sector in India was dominated by two main types of institution – the public sector banks and the international banks. The former served the mass market, but with a limited range of products and services, poor customer service and little differentiation. The latter offered superior quality products but only to wealthy segments and were typically highly selective in terms of accepting new customers. The liberalisation of the Indian banking sector during the 1990s paved the way for the influx of new private sector providers, the first of which was HDFC Bank (short for Housing Development Finance Corporation), launched in 1995. In 2022 HDFC Ltd, which had focused on housing finance, and HDFC Bank announced their intention to merge.

Establishment and growth through customer acquisition

As a new entrant and a market challenger, HDFC needed to concentrate on cost-effective customer acquisition – attracting customers from the established players. The bank's research had identified a significant middle-class market, which expected a high quality of service and was willing to pay for it. To date these customers had banked with the public sector banks but resented the poor service and long queues. At the same time, switching to one of the international banks was not an option because they were outside the very high-income segments that were targeted by those banks.

Customer acquisition was the principle that guided marketing decisions, HDFC needed to develop a marketing mix in order to target these customers and persuade them to move to HDFC. The basic value proposition that underpinned HDFC's approach was that of "international levels of service at a reasonable price". Specific marketing mix decisions were as follows:

- *Product and customer needs*
  To meet the needs of the chosen mid-market segment, HDFC offered a comprehensive range of banking services, comparable to the product range of international banks. This was supported by the targeting of specific products to subsegments based on differences in needs, expectations and behaviours. For example, HDFC developed a diverse set of current and savings accounts, each with different features designed for different customer segments. But, the focus wasn't just on products; staff were recognised as being of

DOI: 10.4324/9781003398615-24

considerable importance, particularly those on the front line and the bank paid particular attention to recruiting staff with good customer service skills.

- **Price and customer cost**

  HDFC offered its initial bank account with the requirement for a minimum balance of Rs 5,000, significantly below the typical international bank requirement of Rs 10,000 and so significantly cheaper, but still higher than the public sector requirement of Rs 500. This ensured that HDFC had the margin to support the delivery of superior service, while remaining significantly cheaper than the international banks.

- **Communication and promotion**

  HDFC supported its product and service offer with the usual range of above- and below-the-line marketing promotion with direct mail, email and SMS initially being of particular importance. A significant innovation was the use of sophisticated analytical techniques to test and evaluate campaigns. This enabled HDFC to gain a better understanding of how customers respond to marketing promotions and use this information to develop increasingly effective campaigns. In addition, the analysis has enabled HDFC to target its communications more effectively, thus reducing marketing spend and reducing the costs of acquisition.

- **Customer convenience and distribution**

  HDFC initially focused attention on the ten largest cities in India which accounted for close to 40% of the population, and the bank concentrated on gaining maximum market share in those areas before expanding on to other cities. The decision to operate with a central processing unit allowed the bank to keep the cost of establishing a branch network relatively low and this supported a sustained growth in branch numbers reaching over 4,000 by 2015. The bank paid particular attention to developing a leading position in relation to technology-enabled service provision, thus ensuring that it could offer customers both convenience and flexibility. By 2015, HDFC could boast almost 12,000 ATMs in over 2,500 cities countrywide.

Acquisition marketing was essential to enable HDFC to establish itself in the marketplace, but sustainable growth required complementary strategies to focus on retaining and cross-selling to newly acquired customers. With this in mind, HDFC invested heavily in marketing analytics, to support segmentation and improved targeting of existing customers. Cross-selling to existing consumers helped to reduce acquisition costs for new sales as well as strengthening relationships with existing customers.

The success of HDFC was evidenced in initial growth rates of 30% per annum, consistently good financial performance and a string of awards from AsiaMoney, Forbes Global, Euromoney and many others. In 2014 it was rated as India's most valuable brand by Millward Brown, and it consistently features as one of India's best and largest private banks.

Digital developments

HDFC had considerable success with its approach to customer acquisition and while the market was growing it continued to pay attention to how best to attract further new customers. But with a strong customer base, managing the customer lifecycle became increasingly important. The overarching HDFC strategy for future growth is outlined in Figure CS 6.1.

HDFC's marketing continues to focus on customer acquisition to support growth while also being attuned to the importance of both retention and making the most of cross selling opportunities.

Acquisition	• Government and business (digitisation of transacting). • Digital marketing (build awareness, engagement and loyalty). • Commercial and rural banking (range of key business services). • Corporate cluster (value-added and industry specific solutions).
Product and service delivery	• Retail assets (best in class digital lending). • Expanding wealth management (targeting afffluent and mass affluent segments). • Leadership in payments business (issuing, accepting and financing).
Relationship Management	• Technology and digital (increasingly digital-led). • Reimagining the branch - integrating digital and physical ("phygital"). • Virtual relationship management (provide sealess customer experience).

Figure CS6.1 HDFC's strategic approach to marketing

Source: HDFC Strategy in Action

They offer a comprehensive range of services for both retail and business customers with a range of different options within each of its broad product categories. These categories include Payments, Savings Investments, Borrowing and Insurance. Within the insurance category, for example, HDFC then offers life, health and accident, vehicle, home, cyber, pay and pension products. While these products are accessible through branch networks, many are easily purchased through digital channels.

While digital delivery has become increasingly important to HDFC, a physical presence continues to be of particular significance (hence the use of the term "phygital" – to reflect the need to integrate the physical and the digital). In 2023, HDFC Bank had almost 8,000 branches and over 2,000 ATMs across close to 4,000 towns and cities. This network is augmented by the various offices and outlets of HDFC Ltd. The branch network is supported and underpinned by an omni channel mindset to integrate branch-based delivery with website, mobile, SMS, social media and WhatsApp channels.

Digital marketing has played a key role in building the HDFC brand. It has also provided better insights into customer behaviour and customer journey enabling HDFC to personalise product offers to customer circumstances. HDFC has invested significantly in customer analytics to enable a deep understanding of customer behaviour and to understand the impact of different marketing approaches and different marketing interventions. The bank has tried to prioritise a user-friendly design for its digital channels and multiple channels enhance accessibility.

HDFC continues to operate a premium pricing strategy reflecting its position as a premium banking institution. As was the case at launch, it continues to require relatively high minimum deposits compared to its competitors. For example, the Regular Savings Account requires Rs.10,000 as a minimum deposit for customers in urban branches. For the SavingsMax Account the requirement is that holders maintain an average monthly balance of Rs.25,000. These minimum balances are part of the price that account holders pay for the facility, its interest rates and associated services.

As is the case with distribution, marcoms at HDFC combine both traditional and digital channels with a common "underpinned by the bank's brand livery, look and feel", with the logo and colour scheme being instantly recognisable. Examples of the diversity of campaigns that HDFC has delivered in recent years include:

- Mooh Band Rakho – a campign to raise awareness of fraud and the importance of protecting banking information. The most recent implementation saw campaign messages backed-up by workshops, and with a particular focus on the youth segment who were thought to be most vulnerable.
- Bounceback – a campaign launched by HDFC Life which focused on the importance of the customer trying to secure their financial future. The impact of the Covid-19 pandemic and human resilience in responding to the challenges created provided the backdrop for this campaign. One of the key creative elements was based on the experiences of a couple looking back on their journey towards success. They reflect on how they dealt with multiple setbacks and the impact of their early financial preparedness in helping them navigate these difficulties and "bounce back".
- HDFC Festive Treats – the fifth annual campaign was announced in the lead up to the holiday season in India with the theme *"Iss Tyohaar No Intezaar"*, (no waiting this festive season). As the campaign title suggests "Festive Treats" is structured around a range of special offers to customers including discounted loans, discounts on processing fees and offers based on partnerships with leading retail brands including Samsung, Apple, IKEA, Sony and HP.

Figure CS6.2 HDFC's Branches remain important

Individual campaigns are supported by and delivered through a number of channels including HDFC's social media presence. On Facebook, HDFC boasts 2.8m likes and 2.9 m followers; the site includes content marketing such as commentary on financially relevant news (e.g. the budget) and opportuinities for customer engagement, and the delivery of marketing communications. HDFC's Instagram account has 350,000 followers and focuses on visuals of HDFC advertising including #FestiveTreats and #MoohBandRakho and social campaigns such as the #StopMithani campaign to promote blood donation.

The merger between HDFC Bank and HDFC Ltd has made HDFC one of the largest banks in the world. To date, its marketing activity has been impressive, and the merger gives it the benefits of considerable scale. But mergers bring with them their own challenges – particularly in relation to the integration of two organisations and the identification of routes to deliver additional value to customers. HDFC executives are often heard to talk of HDFC as evolving into a technology company that is into banking. HDFC Ltds focus on housing finance certainly creates new opportunities for bunding products for customers and for cross selling.

Case study sources:
Saxena. (2000),
Interview with Ajay Kelkar, available at www.exchange4media.com/Brandspeak/brandspeak.asp?brand_id=81#1,.
HDFC Bank, www.HDFCBank.com,
DeFelice, A. (2006). *Return on Rupees*, www.destinationcrm.com/Articles/Columns/Departments/REAL-ROI/Return-on-Rupees-47676.aspx.
HDFC – Strategy in Action.

Case study questions

1. How well does HDFC's marketing mix support customer acquisition – what might need to change to strengthen the focus on longer term customer relationships?
2. How valuable as social campaigns – such as #MoohBandRakho and #StopMithani in helping HDFC build its brand?
3. Review HDFC's social media channels – how engaging are they? What changes would you recommend to enhance their user engagement?
4. What are business commentators saying about the HDFC Ltd-HDFC Bank merger? What do you see as the marketing implications and the challenges associated with delivery?

Case study CS7

HUK24: Managing the customer experience for online insurance

Introduction

The HUK-COBURG Insurance Group is the leading German insurer offering a comprehensive range of insurance products for all private households. More than 13 million customers have already put their trust in HUK. Since its foundation in 1933, the parent company HUK-COBURG which is at the top of the insurance group has been operating according to the principle of mutuality.

The group consists of five property and casualty insurers – among them one online-only insurer (HUK24) – two life insurers, two health insurers and one assistance company.

The majority of insurance business in Germany is offline, however, given the dramatic shift toward digital interaction brought on by Covid-19, the shift to digital in insurance is underway—with increasing pressure to automate in order to realise efficient cost structures and therefore be able to offer competitive prices, and to meet the immediacy that customers expect from other industries. If they want to compete with digital natives, traditional insurers will have to adapt—and there is a lot of progress to be made.

The launch of HUK24

In the late 90s the dot-com bubble reached its climax. Internet entrepreneurs experienced enormous rises in stock prices and therefore moved faster and with less caution than usual. Many companies relied on venture capital (and especially initial public offerings of stock) to pay their expenses without having any income at all. In due course, many of the dot-coms ceased trading after burning through their capital, many having never made a "net" profit. The HUK-COBURG Insurance Group did not participate in the immediate internet hype in the late 90s but was watching it attentively. Of course, HUK recognized the huge opportunities offered by the commercial usage of the internet and was convinced that pure online distribution in the insurance sector could be a successful business case. It would remain a market niche in the mid-term, however, with increasing importance in certain market segments. But management at HUK avoided the early internet hype. They resisted the pressure to launch an immediate "quick to market" solution and instead prepared a well-considered market entry strategy based on careful analysis of customer needs and technological capabilities. Following an extensive analysis, a realistic business case was built and approved.

HUK24 was finally launched in October 2000 – just at the time that the dotcom bubble was beginning to burst. Defining itself as a pure online insurer without any supporting sales organisation, HUK24 was targeting a new segment of customers: people with high internet

DOI: 10.4324/9781003398615-25

Figure CS7.1 HUK24

affinity preferring a pure online supply of insurance cover without any personal counselling. Research suggested that this target market would be price conscious, comfortable with standardised products (non-life insurance – motor insurance in particular) and comfortable to make decisions without specialist advice. In short, they were the ideal group to adopt online insurance purchasing.

From the very beginning HUK24 offered a comprehensive range of insurance products – nonlife insurance but also life and health insurance products at extremely favourable rates. Now, HUK24 is probably Germany's largest direct motor insurer.

The company's success is widely attributed to a strategy that focuses on customer experience and particularly on simplicity throughout the customer journey. Since its launch, HUK24 has dedicated its service delivery thinking to automating as much of the customer experience as possible.

HUK24 was an early entrant – and has described itself as a "digital-native insurer", but now faces new competitive threat from the rise of InsurTechs (the insurance variant of fintechs) and the possibility that digital specialists such as Amazon may look to move into their market. Having launched with a pure online offer, HUK24 was able to sidestep the challenges of established competitors – it did not have to worry about legacy systems or channels or mindsets. While the digital business model brings with it many advantages, it also foregrounds the importance of customer-centricity. In particular, what HUK24 understood was that, in an online environment, every customer touchpoint was both potential point of sales and a risk point. If the process wasn't easy and didn't meet customer expectations then it only required a click for customer to "walk away". With the customer in the driving seat, ensuring a satisfying digital experience was essential for success.

HUK24 monitors the customer journey, with a view to looking for those points where consumers struggle or indeed are lost. Being customer centric would be fundamental to success. The view of HUK is that to sustain and grow their success they need continuous improvement, and they need to continuously re-visit customer wants and expectations and continue to deliver the right products through simple digital solutions and competitive prices. They respond with technical solutions to process problems but also use this analysis to develop new products and services (e.g. digital cancellation for a customer's existing policy). And where data permits, HUK24 looks for opportunities to link sales opportunities to key life events (e.g. if someone has just bought a house, they will need property insurance).

At the heart of HUK24 is an "insurance engine" which automates the process of understanding customer needs and recommending suitable products. This "engine" brings together existing databases and a range of relevant customer data (subject to privacy considerations and permissions), with advanced analytics to generate product recommendations and these can be fed into AI-based chatbots. As an illustration, if a customer is flagged as being especially price conscious, the "engine" will focus on products that will give the consumer the ability to keep costs low – so products that use telematics to monitor driving behaviour (and thus risk) or those where costs are directly link to the level of car use.

Customers can only engage with HUK24 directly via email, chatbot or the customer portal, although it is worth noting that for the crucial element of claims, the full claims service of HUK-COBURG – without any restrictions – also applies for HUK24 customers.

As an indicator of the extent to which HUK24 has succeeded in delivering a genuinely customer-centric experience, satisfaction levels are comparable to those of traditional face-to-face insurers.

HUK24's philosophy is defined in four bullet points bullet points.
HUK24 means…

- Standardised and scalable insurance products, tailored to online customers' needs
- Extremely attractive premiums
- Easy and safe handling of all insurance issues via huk24.de without human interaction
- Personal counselling in case of claim (claims handling by HUK-COBURG; providing full service without any restrictions)

A communication strategy was designed to meet market needs. Using the brand awareness of the parent company, HUK24 focused on internet users only. The intention of the communication transported the picture of a young, innovative, online insurer with a traditional and trustworthy "big player", HUK-COBURG in its background.

After market launch of HUK24, marketing activities mainly focused on building brand awareness. More than 90% of HUK24's marketing budget was spent online on visual advertisement, e.g. online banners. With the increase of the brand awareness of HUK24, the strategy was adapted to a performance-based marketing concept.

Fully automated processes have been part of HUK24's DNA right from the start. An additional key factor for further growth is meeting today's customer expectations for digital customer journeys – which are shaped by e-commerce – while achieving a fully automated interaction that still feels "personal". This leads to the vision of a personal insurance engine.

With customer centricity and a profit-oriented growth strategy, HUK24 is on its path to creating a personal insurance engine. Essential aspects include a clear focus as the starting point for further growth, cost advantages and further automation, the best price/performance ratio, as well as a superior customer experience (+ data experience).

Technological advancement provides the opportunity to deliver this personal insurance engine, particularly with the aid of data analytics and artificial intelligence (AI). HUK24 is already using AI in fully automated digital interaction and is continuously working to expand this.

HUK24 today

At present HUK-COBURG insurance group has more than 12 million insured vehicles in its portfolio which makes HUK to the market leader in car insurance in Germany. HUK24 is one of the most trustworthy insurance brands in Germany with a strong growth, especially in motor insurance, private liability insurance and household insurance. Gross Written Premiums in 2022 were €1,121.7m. HUK24 stresses guaranteed price competitiveness as a central product feature. HUK24 offers online-only access; no personal or phone counselling in contract matters.

HUK24 captures new market segments for the HUK-COBURG Insurance Group.

HUK24 is a market leader in online insurance and on its way to realise a digital personal insurance engine.

A strong brand, focus and cost leadership (through automation) are still very important, and must be combined with an excellent customer experience and personal interaction (i.e. via Chatbots) based on data analytics and AI.

Case study source: HUK24, 2023 Mr.Detlef Frank and Dr. Uwe Stuhldreier, www.mckinsey.com/industries/financial-services/our-insights/revolutionizing-insurance-the-personalized-insurance-engine, Interview with Dr. Uwe Stuhldreier, March 2021 (accessed 08 January 2024)

Case study questions

1. How important do you think the mutual and cooperative insurance sector is in Germany?
2. In what ways do you think its mutuality helped HUK24 to achieve success in the German insurance market?
3. How would you describe HUK24's segmentation, targeting and positioning strategy?
4. What do you consider to be Strengths, Weaknesses, Opportunities and Threats that apply to HUK24?
5. What opportunities can you identify for an internet-based insurer such as HUK24 to use AI to: a) improve the customer experience and, b) to achieve greater operational efficiency?

Case study CS8

NatWest Accelerator programme

Introduction

NatWest Group is the largest SME (small and medium enterprise) bank in the UK with over one million business customers. Enterprise is the cornerstone of success and the lifeblood stimulating economic growth of the wider UK economy. At NatWest, we want to remove barriers to enterprise and champion anyone starting or growing a business. However, we know that, for many, this remains harder than it should be.

NatWest Accelerator

The NatWest Accelerator supports and empowers UK entrepreneurs to scale their businesses to the next level. Our free Accelerator programme specialising in wrap around support provides:

- one-to-one coaching with our experienced Acceleration Managers,
- a programme of thought leadership and events,
- access to a network of like-minded peers, supported by our Ecosystem Managers,
- focused support with access to experts from across your specialism,
- use of our modern co-working spaces in one of our nationwide hubs.

We now currently have 13 hubs across the UK, in Belfast, Birmingham, Bristol, Cardiff, Edinburgh, Glasgow, Leeds, London, Manchester, Milton Keynes, Newcastle, Southampton and Warwick.

Eligibility

If you're a business with ambitions to expand, the NatWest Accelerator programme could help. You may be looking to build your team, venture into new markets or seeking further investment. The programme could help you gain the knowledge and skills to excel in a range of business areas:

- accessing new markets,
- attracting talent and building an effective team,
- access to growth funding,
- leadership development,
- developing a scalable infrastructure.

DOI: 10.4324/9781003398615-26

Figure CS8.1 NatWest

Our current Accelerator programmes are open to all business owners, you do not have to be a NatWest customer.

Impact and outcomes

As a purpose-led bank, our ambition is to help businesses to thrive and to become the biggest supporter of start-ups in the UK. In 2022, we supported 53,000 individuals and businesses through 269,000 interventions to start, run or grow a business. We engaged 48,000 young adults in enterprise and entrepreneurship activity.

In 2022, we supported 1,300 entrepreneurs through the NatWest Group Accelerator programme, of which 50% were female-led businesses. We expanded our footprint to 13 Enterprise Hubs across the UK to further enhance local and regional ecosystems and networks, and provide modern co-working space for entrepreneurs. During 2022, we continued to deliver our Accelerator Programme through in-person and virtual coaching sessions, workshops, thought-leadership and events.

Case study source: Mike Johnstone, NatWest Commercial Banking

Case study questions

1. How visible is the NatWest Accelerator Programme? If you were running a small business, would you be aware of what it offers?
2. How should NatWest develop its marketing campaign?
3. Does the NatWest Accelerator have enough potential to support customer acquisition?

Part III

Managing customer relationships and the future of marketing

14 Customer relationship management principles and practice

Learning objectives

At the end of this chapter, you should be able to:

1. Understand the importance of relationship marketing and customer retention in financial services,
2. Understand the interactions between customer acquisition, customer retention and marketing activities,
3. Understand the nature and significance of the concept of customer lifetime value,
4. Appreciate how digital marketing and the use of social media is impacting on customer-relationship marketing strategies,
5. Have an appreciation of some of the ways in which artificial intelligence (AI) is impacting upon the customer service experience.

14.1 Introduction

Until comparatively recently, there had been a presumption that marketing was principally concerned with the processes surrounding the creation of customers for a commercial organisation. Thus, decisions concerning the use of the marketing mix were largely geared to this end. In part this explains why marketing and sales are often viewed as being one and the same thing. It is undoubtedly true that customer acquisition has historically been the dominant purpose of marketing in the field of financial services. However, in the contemporary world, marketing skills and resources are used increasingly in the context of the existing customer base – that is to say, organisations have increasingly focused attention on marketing their services to their existing customers – encouraging them to either purchase more of the same product or to purchase different products from the organisations' product range. In part, this reflects the increase in costs associated with acquiring new customers. According to research carried out by Frederick Reichheld of consultancy firm Bain & Co[1], increasing customer retention rates by 5% increases profits by 25% to 95%. We shall return to this issue in Section 14.3.

This process is described in several different ways. Some will simply use the generic term "relationship marketing"; others will refer to customer retention or customer base marketing. Increasingly, the term Customer Marketing has come to replace CRM – customer-relationship

DOI: 10.4324/9781003398615-28

marketing (or management as some prefer to call it) as the preferred way to describe this form of marketing. Whatever term is used, the important thing to remember is that we are dealing with that branch of marketing which concerns the contribution of marketing inputs once the customer acquisition phase has ended. During the third and final part of this book we will focus upon marketing as it concerns the retention, management, and development of existing customers. Thus, this section completes the triangle of strategy and planning, customer acquisition, and customer management that forms the basis of this book. This first chapter of Part III provides an overview of some of the key issues associated with the management of customers. Subsequent chapters will deal with issues relating to service quality, value, customer satisfaction and, finally, attention is turned to the environmental, social, and governmental issues (ESG) that are increasingly impacting on marketing strategy.

14.2 Drivers of change

It is often suggested that by the very nature of the products concerned, providers of financial services have always had continuing relationships with their customers and that financial services marketing is inherently relational. For example, someone buying a personal pension can be expected to maintain a relationship with their product provider for several decades whereas, arguably, the typical consumer goods purchase is a one-off transaction. While there is much truth in this view, it is also the case that financial services providers have traditionally not managed these relationships well in a mass market context. This is clearly changing. A range of environmental factors have contributed to the growing concern about customer retention and development of customer-base (or relationship) marketing in financial services including:

- Slowdown in economic growth,
- Rising costs of customer acquisition,
- Increasing focus upon customer value,
- Competition,
- Consumerist practices,
- Regulation and legislation,
- Technological innovation,
- Development of relationship marketing in other sectors,
- Easier product switching,
- Impact of social media.

In what follows we provide an overview of how the above factors have influenced the growth of relationship marketing in financial services.

- Slowdown in economic growth

Between the beginning of the 21st century and the financial crisis of 2007/8, the world economy grew at an unprecedented rate and, even allowing for the impact of the financial crisis, by 2011 the Gross Domestic Product (GDP) of the top 20 economies had more than doubled from $28.09 billion to $57.99 billion in constant prices according to IMF data. Unsurprisingly, financial services grew apace across the world particularly in developing countries as an increasing proportion of their populations became customers for the first time of financial services companies. However, the situation has changed markedly since 2011 as economic growth has stalled globally. The World Bank's 2023 report *Falling Long-Term Growth Prospects*[2] notes that growth has declined sharply for emerging markets, developing economies, and advanced economies (EMDEAEs) alike during the past decade. To quote from the report:

> Global growth declined from a recent peak of 4.5 percent in 2010 to a projected low of 1.7 percent in 2023. The slowdown was widespread: in 80 percent of advanced economies and 75 percent of EMDEs, average annual growth was lower during 2011-21 than during 2000-10.

Figures 14.1 and 14.2 show growth rates at the aggregate and per capita levels respectively from 1990 to 2024. Global growth had already been slowing in the years up to 2019 but the Covid pandemic served to amplify that trend and the invasion of Ukraine by Russia has only served to exacerbate the problem.

Figures 14.1 and 14.2 show trends in GDP growth[3]

When economies slow down it becomes more difficult to pursue strategies based upon acquiring new customers; indeed, it can be difficult to retain the customers you already have.

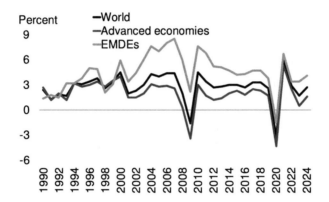

Figure 14.1 GDP Growth 1990–2024

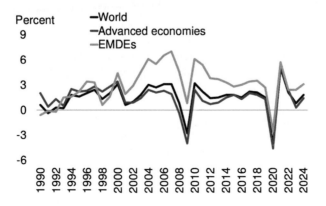

Figure 14.2 Per Capita Growth in GDP 1990–2024

Thus, modest levels of economic growth should be expected to be the norm for most countries for the foreseeable future so far as strategic planning assumptions are concerned. For these reasons, the potential for acquiring wholly new customers has been severely curtailed and increasing emphasis is being placed upon the retention of existing customers and finding new ways to leverage the value of those customers.

• **Rising costs of customer acquisition**
As the market penetration rate rises (i.e. the proportion of the total market that is already purchasing a product or service), the marginal costs of acquiring new customers increases. Since the 1980s the penetration rates in most product categories in developed economies have steadily grown and this has resulted in higher marginal acquisition costs. At the same time the value of customers at the margins of a segment can be expected to be lower than the value of those already served. Rising costs of customer acquisition have affected some areas more than others, especially regarding regulation-induced cost increases.

• **Increasing focus on customer value**
The economics of marginal customer acquisition referred to above have acted as a catalyst for an increased focus upon customer profitability as opposed to product profitability. That is not to say that the management of product margin is not important, but both measures of value have a role to play in determining commercial performance. However, it is in the nature of financial services products, notably the characteristics associated with longevity and time-scale, that individual product margins are of lesser significance than long-term individual customer value. It makes more sense to appraise the value of a business by reference to its aggregate customer worth, rather than simply the sum total of its in-force product margins.

• **Competition**
The retail financial services sector is dynamic and diverse with relatively few barriers to entry. Innovation in fields such as third-party administration (TPA), web-based distribution, call centre functionality, AI, and access to capital enable new entrants to participate in what are already highly penetrated market sectors. Additionally, the previous factors make it relatively easy for existing financial services organisations to diversify into new areas as has happened with, for example, insurance companies setting up banks.

The continual development of the competitive environment in market sectors that are already highly penetrated means that one company's newly acquired customer is increasingly likely to be the lapsed customer of a rival organisation. Under such circumstances the retention of existing valuable customers becomes even more important. In an era of increasingly sophisticated technology the absence of old, cumbersome and expensive-to-maintain legacy systems gives new entrants tremendous advantages over incumbent players. This competitive threat poses new challenges to customer retention and adds further weight to the importance of this aspect of marketing.

• **Consumerist pressures**
Organisations representing the consumer interest such as the Which? and Consumer Focus in the UK, the Consumers Union in the US or the Consumers Federation of Australia have long campaigned to improve the ways in which the financial services industry serves the interests of consumers. Their campaigns have addressed a range of issues including product charges, the use made of orphan funds, mortgage endowments, payment protection insurance and overarching matters of how boards of directors are accountable for serving customer

interests. As a result, companies have become more sensitive to accusations that they attract new customers with attractive propositions only to be subjected to detriment once they have become customers. This has provided further impetus to the need to develop more effective and sophisticated marketing policies and practices regarding existing customers. The increasing importance of social networks and the prevalence of blogging have also served to add further impetus to the forces of consumerism.

- **Regulation and legislation**

The range of regulatory and legislative developments that have occurred since the mid-1980s has had far-reaching implications for the industry, most immediately by adding to costs. There is an aspiration that, in the long run, such costs will be compensated for by the avoidance of costly mis-selling compensation and more persistent, and hence profitable, product sales. Meanwhile, the costs of new customer acquisition have been impacted upon by the costs associated with sales adviser training, competence, and supervision along with an enormous array of other provisions included in the rule books of regulators around the world.

In addition to their impact upon costs, developments in this area have also impacted upon pricing and charging policies and mechanisms. This issue is becoming increasingly important, especially in areas such as life assurance and pensions.

- **Technological innovation**

Innovation in telecommunications, database management, and digital has had a dramatic impact upon customer management. The careful and detailed capture of appropriate data during the customer acquisition process provides an organisation with the ability to manage the relationship to far greater effect than was hitherto possible. And so it is fair to say that technological innovation has been a major facilitator of customer base marketing. What has now become known as eCRM will be addressed in detail in Section 14.8.

- **Development of relationship marketing in other commercial sectors**

Arguably, the B2B sector pioneered the concept and practice of relationship marketing owing to the importance of forging genuine buyer–seller partnerships. The information asymmetry that is said to characterise retail financial services is far less in evidence in the B2B context. This is because buyers are often professional procurement executives and are considerably more empowered than the typical financial services domestic consumer. Indeed, the B2B business areas of major banks have themselves long practised effective relationship marketing processes in the handling of major corporate client relationships.

Customer management (CM), which is essentially technology-enabled relationship marketing, is now a vital element of the marketing approach in many consumer goods markets and the retail sector. The rapid expansion of customer affinity schemes by supermarkets such as Tesco's Clubcard are perhaps the best example of this form of marketing in practice. The extensive use of relationship marketing across the B2B,FMCG (fast moving consumer goods) and retail sectors has added further impetus to its adoption by financial services organisations.

- **Easier switching**

Policymakers are devoting increasing attention to ways in which switching providers can be made easier as the removal of barriers to switching is an important principle of good regulation. Again, the internet has been an important enabler as websites such as uSwitch make the process of comparing options and making a switch from one bank or insurance company to another much simpler. Long-standing accounts tend to earn lower rates of interest than new accounts, but consumers are put off switching because of perceived hassle and also a lack of understanding; both in terms of the fact their money isn't working as hard for them as it could be, and also the available alternatives that could offer them a better deal. As a result, the Financial Conduct Autthority (FCA) proposed various measures to promote transparency around rates of interest and any changes to them, ease of comparison between different accounts and reduced barriers to switching. There is evidence that UK consumers are showing a greater propensity to switch bank accounts. According to Matthew Boyle of Finder.com[4]

- In the first half of 2023 there were nearly 700,000 current account switches.
- The number of current account switches was up by 76% in April-June 2023 compared to the same period in 2022.
- Current account switching rates were up by 26% in 2022 compared to 2021.
- 41% of people swith current accounts to get better online or mobile app banking.
- Impact of social media

The rise of AI, blockchain and crypto has increased the pace of change in FS. As the industry becomes ever more digital, SM is a key medium to engage and influence customers and prospects, particularly younger audiences. The Covid-19 pandemic highlighted the importance of an active online presence with increasing numbers of customers seeking answers and information online when access to physical branches wasn't an option.

Social media (SM) offers companies an excellent platform to communicate with customers in a timely, open and transparent manner. FS providers were initially circumspect to entering the social media arena, primarily due to concerns around the visibility of the medium, compliance and privacy issues as well as concerns about the levels of controls in the social space. However, as consumer engagement with SM has increased FS providers have had to get onboard to avoid missing out on an increasingly influential communication opportunity; reportedly 75.4% of people use SM for brand research with almost a quarter actively following a brand they are considering buying from pre-purchase[5]. The Edelman trust barometer ranks FS as the least trusted industry[6] and SM provides an opportunity to humanise brands which can be particularly helpful for an industry that promotes intangible products that are often functional as opposed to desirable.

Social media is a powerful and influential communication channel. It offers opportunities for customer service, information sharing, brand awareness, social listening and relationship building, all of which can enable brands to better connect with customers and help build trust. SM platforms are ever evolving, with new formats, tools and content types being released regularly. The current main players leveraged by FS companies are LinkedIn, Facebook, X (formerly Twitter), Instagram, YouTube and TikTok, each offering unique benefits in terms

Figure 14.3 Social media engagement ring"social media engagement ring" by pro1pr licensed under CC BY 2.0

of audience targeting. Facebook has been around for a while, and tends to have an older audience; Millennials, Gen X (born 1965–1981) and Baby Boomers (born 1946–1964). Online loans provider SoFi generated a 39% increase in loan applications from a mobile ad campaign it ran across Facebook and Instagram[7]. Facebook is a community-based platform. It allows users to connect with loved ones and join groups of like-minded individuals to engage in conversations about shared interests. Superfan communities are prevalent in this platform. From a customer acquisition perspective this means that targeting capabilities are very strong. Facebook allows brands to identify prospects that are interested in things related to their brand – creating a tight approach to targeting from an acquisition perspective. For example, if a consumer joins a group about sharing make-up tips, this is a strong indicator to any beauty brand that this group of consumers may be interested in their products.

Instagram is a visually engaging platform, most used by Millennials (born 1981–1996) and Gen Z (born 1997–2012). It allows users to share photos and videos with followers, and follow accounts related to their interests. It allows scalable reach to provide a visual newsroom for brands. Video is allegedly better at holding peoples' ever dwindling attention span[8], and YouTube offers the perfect platform to leverage this. It's often used to extend the reach of TV advertising. TikTok is a predominantly Gen Z-based platform with trend-savvy users and is gaining traction amongst millennials and Gen X-ers. The key format is short-form videos to share; while predominantly an entertainment channel with organic reach (not paid for media), social trends often originate from TikTok. And so, if brands can utilise these trends in the right way, TikTok is a powerful tool to build brand reputation and build a younger customer base.

X, formerly known as Twitter, is a blend of social media, blogging and texting, the restriction on the number of characters that can be on used the platform promotes a clever use of language. X is where conversation happens, and where customer service-based comms usually take place. Simple digital bank uses its @Simplify X handle as both a primary customer service channel and also an idea-generation platform to garner real-time user feedback for product development. Rather than deal with call centre queues and automated phone systems to raise queries and complaints, customers can immediately post comments in a social space. This (hopefully) generates a prompt response and resolution from the organisation in question and allows organisations to gauge customer sentiment quickly and take immediate remedial actions. By being able to handle this in a public forum, it is possible for companies to turn around a negative situation through prompt and sympathetic handling which can garner positive sentiment in the long run.

HSBC staff are encouraged to engage with SM (through its approved publication mechanism) which has had a positive impact on engagement and followers. There are huge opportunities for brands to use their staff base to act as brand advocates, actively engaging with their official channel posts and promoting it to their own audiences, thus amplifying the messages to broader audience. This is useful for promotion of brand, products, services, and sponsorships, and also recruitment. Sharing active vacancies is commonplace on LinkedIn, and it makes sense to tap into your employees own SM networks. Linkedin is the leading platform for professional networking and thought leadership in the B2B space. It offers insight into clients lives and needs which can be useful in building relationships within the advisory world. Reportedly almost 95% of advisers who use social media, use it for direct messaging and lead generation[9], with HubSpot reporting LinkedIn is "277% more effective for lead generation than Facebook and Twitter"[10]. The channel driving the most engagement in banking in general is LinkedIn, particularly with regards to senior leaders being highly visible and regularly posting about key messages; 92% of professionals report they are more likely to trust a company whose senior leaders are on LinkedIn. The FTI FTSE 100

LinkedIn 2023[11] report highlighted the importance executive voices on the channel play in building trust and brand reputation; the number of CEOs engaging on social media doubled from 2021–2023, with 55% of FTSE 100 CEOs now active on LinkedIn. Two FS companies feature in its list of top 10 most impactful FTSE 100 executives; Barclays at position 3 and HSBC at position 4. The report found CEOs drive the greatest engagement but those companies who have a broad range of ExCo senior leadership regularly publishing content on LinkedIn derive the greatest success and impact; brands with more than 4 leaders active on SM, saw a 38% increase in their FTI Impact Score.

> For companies to unlock the greatest impact on social media, they need to look beyond the CEO and also activate the broader senior leadership team. Developing bespoke and cohesive social media strategies for each member of the leadership team is now a critical component of corporate communications.
>
> Claire Twohill, MD Digital and Insights, FTI[12]

 Marketing in practice 14.1: Monzo Wrapped campaign

Fintech Monzo ran an end of year wrap up campaign, "Monzo Wrapped" which gave regional and personal insights to its customers on how they were spending. This was a holistic campaign that ran across all forms of physical and digital media, for example regional billboard and poster advertising such as "London, you were literally the only place that went to Pret more than Greggs".

This was complemented with a personal wrap up for customers via the app "This is the story of how you Monzo'd your way through 2023 like nobody else," showing their money habits across 2023; what categories they spent the most on, where they liked to eat and shop, etc.

The campaign was very clever in managing to engage communities in its broader regional advertising as well as targeting individual customers with their personal spending habits. It was a highly visual campaign that worked equally well across traditional and digital media and was created to be shared.

SM offers financial services a significant opportunity to display their values and communicate with customers and prospects in an open and transparent manner. Barclays regularly focuses on major events through its social channels, such as Black History Month, International Women's Day, and Pride. These focussed campaigns allow the brand to show what's important to them and is indicative of the culture they aim to foster and the clients and colleagues they seek to attract. It is also an excellent tool for listening to the market and identifying trends that can influence product development and help companies understand what is important to their customers and what drives their decisions. Jeff Bezos, founder of Amazon, described brand as "what people say about you when you're not in the room." SM monitoring allows brands to tap into this and really listen to the market. This could be crucial information to drive differentiation in the crowded financial services space.

14.3 Customer persistency – acquire the right customers

A feature of many businesses is that they simultaneously acquire new customers for their organisations whilst losing a number of existing customers. Such a process of acquisition and attrition can result in a business working incredibly hard to stand still as far as its numbers of customers are concerned. This has been referred to as the *bucket theory of marketing*, a term attributed to James L Schorr, a former Executive Vice President of Holiday Inn.

It is axiomatic of any organisation that it seeks to achieve growth in the number of new customers it acquires, a reduction in the number of customer defections and, thereby, achieve net growth in its customer base. Unfortunately, the prevalence of the bucket theory can make it a slow and expensive process.

Faced with this problem, there is an understandable response whereby a company devises a detailed, and costly, customer retention programme. However, such programmes can be misplaced if they result in the retention of relatively poor value, and possibly negative value, customers. Some customers have a greater propensity to maintain a relationship with a product provider than others. From the provider's point of view, it is desirable to try to identify customer characteristics that are associated with a high likelihood of lapsing. The need to do this applies to organisational as well as domestic customers because differential lapse rates apply to customers in both the B2B and B2C domains.

The identification of customer characteristics that are associated with a relatively high propensity to lapse, or to persist for that matter, is an important marketing activity. It requires the determination of which aspects of customers themselves, as well as of the marketing mix, are causally related to relative persistency. This is by no means an easy and quick procedure to accomplish. Rather, it calls for thoughtful and detailed analysis of possible causal factors over a protracted period. Thus, it could take years rather than weeks or months to yield truly valuable insights. In the long run it can have a profoundly beneficial impact upon the bottom line by increasing average customer value and reducing wasteful marketing and administration spend. A decision to conduct a customer persistency measurement programme requires the capture of data that influences persistency. Such data must be captured during the customer acquisition process and be supported by the development of appropriate systems for analysis and reporting. The characteristics associated with persistency, both causal and correlated variables, differ according to marketplace, customer segment, purchasing situation and so on; there is no one-size-fits all solution. However, likely candidates for consideration as possible persistency factors are:

Customer characteristics

- Age,
- Income level,
- Occupation,
- Previous history in consuming a given product type.

Acquisition process characteristics

- Strength of real need by customer,
- Whether product was bought or sold (degree of customer proactivity in acquisition process),
- Distribution channel used,

- Individual, distributor or salesperson,
- Date of acquisition.

Other marketing mix characteristics

- Usage of a sales promotion,
- Source of sales leads,
- Special price offers,
- Product feature variants.

The above list is purely indicative of possible factors; each company must resolve to determine what is appropriate given its particular circumstances. Ultimately, such analysis should inform marketing planning and result in focusing customer acquisition activities upon customers who are more likely to be persistent. Thus, the key to effective customer retention is the acquisition of customers who can be presumed to be persistent in the first place.

14.4 Retaining the right customers

The reasons why customers cease their relationships with product providers fall into the following four basic types:

- **Customer self-induced**: the original need no longer exists. For example, a mortgage loan has been repaid early and, therefore, the loan-protection policy is no longer required. Another example could be that the customer wants immediate access to cash and so surrenders an insurance endowment policy.
- **Customer-environment-induced**: the customer has lost her job and is unable to maintain the, say, premium/contribution, interest payments.
- **Provider-self-induced**: poor service (service failure) has caused a level of dissatisfaction that causes the customer to sever the relationship. Alternatively, pricing changes may have caused the customer to seek a different supplier.
- **Provider-environment-induced**: an increase in prevailing base interest rates results in some customers lapsing. A fall in stock markets causes customers to cash in equity-based investments. It might also be the case that an appealing competitor offer has induced a desire to switch providers.

Progress check

- Customer management has become increasingly important as costs of new customer acquisition have escalated.
- Higher levels of customer retention result in significant growth in profits.
- Social media has been transformative as a new medium for developing customer relationships.

The implications of the above factors are that providers must identify those factors over which they can exert some influence whilst developing contingency plans for factors outside of their control. Ideally, customer-self-induced defections are best mitigated by careful selection of customers during the initial acquisition process. Where they do arise, it is probably best to deal with their request to "leave" as efficiently and swiftly and at as little cost as possible.

Provider-self-induced customer lapsing is a particular cause for concern from a marketing perspective since it is associated with a failure to deliver the right service experience or, possibly, clumsy practices regarding renewal premiums in the case of, say, motor insurance. Research to date has suggested that switching/exit is a process rather than a response to specific individual events (Stewart, 1998). Triggers for exit are usually charges, facilities, information, and service encounter and usually there is an accumulation of negative experience prior to exit. The fact that exit appears to be a cumulative process would suggest that opportunities do exist for relationships to be rebuilt (and the ability to respond effectively to complaints is often one very important part of such a process as will be discussed in Chapter 15), although the extent to which financial services providers have been able to capitalise on these is more debateable. As commented earlier in this chapter, the internet has presented new and highly convenient ways for disgruntled customers to check out the competition and, if desired, switch providers. One major challenge associated with customers who are lost through provider-self-induced lapsing is the potential for negative word of mouth. As mentioned above, increases in motor insurance premiums have been a particular source of customer dissatisfaction. Customers are frequently baffled when, for example, their car insurance premium is raised by anything up to 400% at renewal without explanation. This bafflement can turn to outright anger and hostility when they discover they can obtain the same insurance cover for no more, and sometimes less, than they had been paying for the previous year's cover from their incumbent provider. Policy lapse and negative word of mouth are inevitable consequences of such practices.

Customer-environment-induced cases also need to be managed with care. Difficulties associated with the loss of a job may be insurmountable and should be dealt with in a suitably sensitive yet efficient manner. However, unemployment tends to be a temporary matter and measures such as contributions to holiday or policy loans may enable the customer to maintain her product until she is in employment again. Careful analysis of key customer variables such as income level, occupation, duration of customer relationship and other products held is essential in enabling a sound judgement to be made. It makes no sense to allow a customer–product relationship to lapse automatically when a request is received from a customer. Administrative staff must be trained to appreciate the important role they can play in retaining valid customer/product relationships. This calls for the development of suitable management information systems and customer analytics capability to match product lapse cues with relevant customer data. Such cues might include a missed monthly payment or, say, a request for a valuation or early surrender value in addition to written requests to cancel.

Customer defections brought about through the actions of competitors present particular challenges for financial services companies. This is likely to be encountered more in some areas than others. For example, credit cards have become a fiercely competitive arena where customer acquisition is commonly based upon transferring a consumer's outstanding balance to the new provider at a highly attractive rate.

The argument that it is much cheaper to retain existing customers than to attract new ones (sometimes referred to as the "economics of customer retention") is a powerful driver of increased interest of the management of customer relationships. However, it is important to note that this does not imply that all retained customers are profitable and that all customers should be retained. As will be explained later in this chapter, the lifetime value of customers varies. In research outside of financial services, Reinartz and Kumar (2002) identified a class of customers who they described as "Barnacles" – customers who were retained/loyal but unprofitable because they were relatively costly to serve and did not generate significant revenues. Thus, the challenge for marketers is not customer retention across the board but the retention of profitable customers.

14.5 Customer retention strategies

Zeithaml,Bitner and Gremler (2008) have built upon the framework proposed by Berry and Parasuraman (1991) to develop a useful model for the development of a customer retention strategy. Zeithaml and Bitner's model posits that excellent service quality and value must provide the basis for an effective retention strategy. They proceed to identify a sequence of four bonds which, when operationalised by means of the marketing mix, should result in a high probability of retaining valuable customers and are summarised as follows:

- **Level 1 financial bonds: volume and frequency rewards, bundling and cross-selling, stable pricing**

At level 1 the intention is to tie the customer to the provider through the provision of a range of financial incentives. In this way the provider is reflecting the perceived worth of the customer relationship by increasing the economic value that the customer gains. A straight-forward example of this is to be found in the frequent flyer programme operated by airlines such as Singapore Airlines. In the financial services area one encounters companies such as Fidelity offering discounts on initial charges to existing customers when they make subsequent purchases of a mutual fund. General insurance companies will offer discounts to customers who have, say, a home contents policy when they buy a building's insurance policy too. Credit card companies frequently offer special deals on a range of other services such as air travel, hotel accommodation and car hire. American Express provides air miles to its customers as a means of encouraging retention. Stable pricing refers to a provider shielding its customers from general price increases as a means of lessening the impact of customer defections.

Financial bonds are relatively easy to implement and straightforward to communicate. For these reasons they are easily copied by competitors and therefore have immediate limitations as a means of achieving long-term differentiation.

- **Level 2 social bonds: continuous relationships, personal relationships, social bonds among customers**

The types of actions proposed in level 2 represent an attempt by the provider to recognise the individuality of the customer. It is based upon interactions that build upon the financial incentives provided by level 1 to create a sense of affiliation with the provider. A classic example of this is to be found in the life assurance sector where advisers endeavour to meet clients on a regular basis to review their circumstances and needs. Well-established financial advisers frequently report that of the order of two-thirds of their new product sales each year are derived from existing customers. In addition, a further fifth of their sales arise from referrals that they receive from their existing customers. Thus, sales to wholly new customers account for less than one-fifth of the total new product sales of advisers who have invested in developing successful long-term customer relationships.

 Stop and think?

Why has customer retention become a more important aspect of marketing?

What is meant by the term customer churn?

What factors influence a person's decision to stop being the customer of a financial services provider(FSP)?

The development of social bonds is a particular feature of the B2B area of financial services. A range of forms of hospitality are frequently encountered including the use of sponsorship of sporting and cultural events. Such sponsorship activity can be a highly effective means of not only building bonds between the provider and its client, but also amongst the actual client community itself. It is much more difficult for a competitor to replicate the social bonds that a rival provider may have formed with its customers.

- **Level 3 customisation bonds: customer intimacy, mass customisation, anticipation/innovation**

Level 3 strategies involve the two-way flow of information between provider and customer with the aim of creating a marketing mix that is tailored to the particular needs of the customer. Although elements of this process of customising are in evidence in levels 1 and 2, in level 3 the boundaries are pushed out as detailed knowledge of individual customer requirements are translated into customer-specific mix components such as product and service features.

Historically, the costs associated with the development of level 3 strategies meant that they were a particular feature of the B2B environment. However, advances in customer database technology have allowed the concept of mass customisation (i.e. marketing to a segment of 1) to become a cost-effective reality within the B2C arena. The internet has been instrumental in further advancing customisation bonds by acting as a highly efficient means of communicating with customers.

- **Level 4 structural bonds: shared processes and equipment, joint investments, integrated information systems**

The creation of structural bonds between provider and customer represents the greatest challenge to competitive activity and, in conjunction with activities carried out under levels 1, 2 and 3, can achieve long-term differentiation and competitive advantage. One observes examples of this in the way that IT suppliers integrate their systems with a range of financial services companies. Level 4 strategies afford the potential for significant synergies to occur as each partner contributes its expertise to create unrivalled value. From a customer perspective there is the risk that such an integrated relationship will place her at a disadvantage over the long term. Safeguards should be considered to ensure that the customer can mitigate any potential long-term detriment. Ultimately, a commercial judgement must be made about the costs, risk, and benefits of forming structural bonds with a supplier. Indeed, this type of risk can work both ways in that a powerful customer may be able to exert a high degree of power over the product-service provider in contract negotiations over the long-term.

14.6 The customer-relationship chain

So far in this chapter emphasis has been placed upon the interrelationships between getting and keeping customers. It has been established that getting the right customers in the first place is instrumental in keeping them. Thus, it is helpful to conceptualise the process associated with customer acquisition and management as forming component elements of an overarching process that we call the "customer-relationship chain", shown diagrammatically in Figure 14.4.

- **Suspect**
A suspect is an individual who has been identified as being a member of one of the company's target market segments. The company will use its marketing mix to try to attract a suspect's attention and interest to engage them in some form of dialogue.

- **Prospect**
Once a dialogue has been established the suspect becomes a prospect. There is a wide range of behaviours associated with this link in the chain. For example, a television advertisement aimed at suspects could invite contact via a free telephone number to find out more about the provider company or a given product. Alternatively, a mail shot aimed at suspects could invite a response to request a personal financial review.

- **Customer**
Becoming a customer is the obvious outcome of effective prospecting activity. It may be that the prospect has agreed to buy, say, an insurance policy, or, as can also be the case, has registered to become a customer without having made a product purchase. This frequently happens in the case of stockbroking firms.

- **Repeat customer**
The evidence indicates that an individual who has bought a financial services product has a high probability of buying a further product within 18 months of the initial purchase. If the

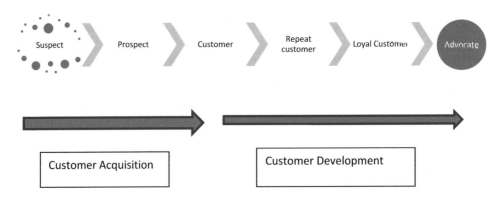

Figure 14.4 The customer-relationship chain

initial product provider has not secured that subsequent purchase, the relationship weakens, and a stronger affiliation is likely to be struck up with the provider of the subsequent purchase. In such a situation the customer will, in all probability, cease to be a *warm customer*. Indeed, there is evidence to suggest that such customers become no more responsive to the marketing efforts of the initial provider company than completely new suspects.

• Loyal customer
A loyal customer is one that has two or more products with a given provider and, when the need arises, takes the initiative to invite their current provider to offer a solution to that need. The customer may well contact other potential providers too and may not necessarily buy from the current provider. However, they will have experienced a sufficiently high level of satisfaction and confidence in the current provider to give them the first chance of securing the additional business. Customer-initiated proactive behaviour is what defines the loyal customer.

• Advocate
An advocate is a customer who expresses such a high level of trust in their provider that she recommends it to any member of their personal reference group should such a third party raise the fact that they have an appropriate need. Thus, friends, family members, workplace colleagues and social contacts represent opportunities for advocacy to take place. Personal recommendations are considered to represent a particularly important aspect of consumer choice in the field of financial services. Just consider the potential power offered by having, say, 10% of your customers becoming advocates. A company with a customer base of two million people could have 200,000 people recommending that company to their respective reference group contacts.

The customer-relationship chain is applicable in both the B2C and B2B domains. Indeed, in the latter case the financial consequences of the loss of a valuable customer will be far more significant than applies to the former case.

14.7 Lifetime customer value

The notion of lifetime customer value is central to the concept of retaining and developing customer relationships. It moves the thinking about profitability on beyond mere one-off product margins, important though they are, and onto a much broader appreciation of customer value. It is entirely possible that attempts to maximise short-term product margins may not result in optimal long-term profitability. For example, an investment fund with a relatively expensive charging structure may offer the potential for high product margins in the short term, but if customers are unconvinced of the benefits offered, they may withdraw from the fund. In contrast, a lower-priced fund may offer smaller margins, but may retain customers for longer and generate much better margins for the provider over the customer's lifetime. Therefore, it is axiomatic that strategies based upon the existing customer base are firmly grounded in a robust model of lifetime customer value.

In simple terms, lifetime customer value involves making a set of assumptions regarding the following variables in Figure 14.5.

Knowledge about the likely revenue, cost and referral variables that apply to the array of consumer and organisational customer types will have already been reflected in a company's segmentation strategy. This can be further fine-tuned through the careful analysis of the performance of customer groups over time. The resultant data can be used to inform the

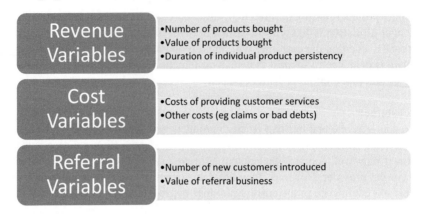

Figure 14.5 The variables affecting lifetime customer value

development of a lifetime customer value model. An illustrative example of what this might look like is given below:

Motim Manufacturing revenue scenario

Motim Manufacturing has a relationship with Beta Broking, a general insurance broker that began when Motim sourced a public liability policy via Beta. A year later Motim decided to source its directors liability cover from Beta. The following year its all-risks buildings and plant policy came up for renewal and Beta secured the business in competition with the incumbent provider. This was followed by the provision of motor insurance to its fleet of 15 vehicles. The value of premium income secured by Beta with Motim during a 15-year period is as follows:

Revenue variables
(assuming no annual policy increase for illustrative purposes)

	Annual Premiums (£)	*Term Years*	*Total Premiums (£)*
Public liability policy	2,200	15	33,000
Directors' liability	4,750	14	66,500
Buildings & plant	12,250	13	159,250
Motor vehicles cover	7,500	12	90,000
Total			**348,750**

The total "lifetime premium income" was therefore £348,750, and value of commission income generated at 20% of annual premium was £69,750.

Referral variables
- Number of new clients introduced by Motim
  (one per year)   15

- Value of referred business
  (assuming same profile and product mix as Motim itself)   £2,158,000
- Commission earned from referrals   £431,600

Thus, the lifetime value to Beta Broking of its relationship with Motim Manufacturing amounts to commission earnings of some £501,350 over the 15-year period. This illustration gives some idea of the real value of making that initial sale of a £2,200 public liability policy that generated just £440 in commission. It also underlines vividly just how valuable it is to follow through the customer-relationship chain to achieve customer advocacy. Indeed, in this example the real value is derived from referrals; during the 15-year period of the example, 88% of the lifetime value accruing to the Motim relationship is accounted for by the resultant referrals.

A similar approach can be applied to the consumer marketing domain. It is simply a case of identifying the relevant revenue, cost and referral variable data and computing the resulting value. For both final consumers and business consumers the development of a suitable model of lifetime customer value is essential for the development of effective customer management strategies.

Progress check

- The identification of customer characteristics that are associated with a relatively high propensity to lapse, or to persist for that matter, is an important marketing activity.
- Provider-self-induced customer lapsing is a particular cause for concern from a marketing perspective since it is associated with a failure to deliver the right service experience.
- Zeithaml and Bitner's model posits that excellent service quality and value must provide the basis for an effective retention strategy, and identify a sequence of four bonds which, when operationalised by means of the marketing mix, should result in a high probability of retaining valuable customer.

14.8 Digital marketing and its impact on CRM

14.8.1 Context

As society becomes more technologically literate the role of digital marketing becomes increasingly crucial as a key component of an omni-channel marketing strategy. Digital natives tend not to use email for personal use, preferring to use SMS, IM, VOIP and social media. FS providers need to evolve at the same rate as their future target market's expectations, cognisant of how Gen Z expect to interact with them and meet their needs. It must be easy to connect socially, and for customers to like, follow, subscribe to, and share information, including social sharing buttons across their sites as standard, particularly in real value-add areas such as thought leadership which can really differentiate organisations from their peer group. In an increasingly digital social world, leveraging online to boost brand engagement and positive word of mouth (WOM) is a priority for providers or to stay competitive.

The digital revolution has brought a plethora of customer touchpoints (see also Chapter 5), particularly with the emergence and growth in popularity of mobile devices which have now overtaken laptops as the most popular route for UK users to get online. The Ofcom[13] 2022 "Adults Media Use and Attitudes" report showed 66% of UK adults own a smartphone, a significant rise from 39% in 2012, and a third of internet users stated that their smartphone is their primary method of accessing online. Tablets have also increased in popularity, 54% of UK homes having one, compared with just 2% in 2011. Ofcom also identified that a majority of smartphone users make use of their mobiles whilst shopping, in a range of ways such as taking pictures of products, making comparisons online and researching product features. Thus, it is evident that mobile technology has radically changed customers' expectations of how they interact with brands. Their perception of customer service has shifted; if they are able to check in for a long-haul flight via mobile, why can't they complete all their banking needs via mobile? M-pesa is a mobile phone-based banking solution used in Kenya[14]. It allows users to deposit, transfer and access money via SMS. Customers can access cash from the bank via mobile or from a cash point by typing in their mobile phone number; they'll then receive an instant SMS containing a pin to type in and can then withdraw cash as usual.

This is far more evolved than the UK where we still employ bank cards to withdraw cash and it is still commonplace to make payments and account deposits using account numbers and sort codes. Square, a facility which allows mobile point of sale, is an excellent example of mobile innovation (https://squareup.com/). Such simple methods of transacting serve to increase the appetite for mobile transactions by consumers. This has been accelerated with contactless payment technologies like Apple Pay and BPay, which allow users to make payments from mobile devices, connected watches and key fobs. Biometrics is an area of increasing focus with facial recognition payments already available and live trials of payments links to users' vein patterns (more in Chapter 10). Banks and other financial services providers will need to match this kind of innovation as they become more commonplace and the expected norm by customers.

It understood that to be successful and truly meet the needs of the customer, banks' marketing messages need to be personalised, timely and relevant. However, there remains a gap between banks' ability to meet these aspirations. The primary challenges they face relate to internal structure and internal systems.

Digital is still finding its natural fit within organisations; there is no consistent approach, sometimes it sits within IT, at others it is a digital team separate from marketing and sometimes it is viewed as merely another channel within the overall marketing department. Arguably the latter aligns more closely with the customer perspective; it is merely another communications touchpoint. Regardless of where digital sits, organisations must be willing to move away from outdated data sources and marketing methodologies to maximise digital potential. Banks need to use internal and external data to ensure customer needs are not only met but exceeded. Traditional data is no longer enough: marketers need to look beyond demographics, transactions and product holdings and make use of online activity logs, email interaction and social media engagement to build a truly personalised profile of each customer. The volume of data marketeers have access to has, and continues, to grow exponentially. Their challenge is collecting this data in a centralised system and having the correct tools and skill set to analyse it effectively. Traditional analytics provides an historical view of customer activity; advanced analytics provides real-time insight and an opportunity to predict the opportunities which may lie ahead.

Figure 14.6 Traditional banks face legacy challenges

"(1)HSBC building George Street Sydney" by Sardaka (talk) 08:27, 6 October 2014 (UTC) licensed under CC BY 3.0.

Banks' heavy legacy systems and lack of agility is a real risk. By their nature they hold a great deal of rich personal and transactional data, but the structure of financial organisations is often siloed resulting in no single view of the customer. This puts them at a real disadvantage when compared with light and more agile start-ups. While the threat of "new" banks has not been realised over the past 20 years, the changing perception of millennials towards placing their money in the care of nontraditional banks, combined with their ability to move quickly and embrace lighter infrastructure, means these challenger banks may finally present a real threat.

The key to true personalisation is data. In order to succeed, banks need to leverage the data they have access to, deliver compelling messages in real time to touchpoints across multiple channels. Banks must work harder to achieve customer satisfaction and need to look beyond their competitors to their comparators. Customers expect expert advice and recommendations like other retailers such as Amazon and Facebook where needs are not just met but anticipated.

The use of advanced analytics and AI allow marketers to identify product or service needs before even the customers are aware they have that need. This can assist in providing a consistent experience across multiple channels. Data obtained via social media single-sign-on (SSO) can be used not only to build out customer profiles in terms of basic data and preferences, but also to learn about life events and to gain greater insight into customers' attitudes and behaviours. This can be used to build targeted marketing campaigns and predictive models which will resonate more keenly.

Greater use of analytics and profiling is a mutually beneficial experience for both bank and customer; through use of advanced analytics, banks improve their predictive modelling and reduce the volume of overall data they have to process as well as reducing marketing efficiency and costs. The customer benefits from more targeted messaging which improves their customer experience, satisfaction and trust.

The following sections will explore some of the implications of developments in mobile and digital technologies for the way in which existing customer relationships are managed. It will outline the nature of the underpinning data that facilitates effective customer-relationship management and that highlight the need to carefully integrate online and offline CRM. The potential for digital technologies to deliver high degrees of personalisation will be explained and the implications for the development of eCRM will be outlined.

14.8.2 Customer data management and analytics

The capability to collect, store, analyse and act upon meaningful customer data is now firmly established as a critical marketing competency. Indeed, some would argue that in an era of digital marketing and eCRM, customer analytics is the most critical marketing competency. Allied to this is the ability to monetise or place a financial value on customer data. Technology has facilitated the means by which vast arrays of data can be processed to identify events in the provider–customer relationship that have meaning and implications for both parties.

Storbacka and Lehtinen (2001) conceptualise the collection and organisation of customer data as the creation of "customer-relationship memory". To quote from the authors themselves: "This customer relationship memory differs from ordinary databases in that it is the memory of a specific customer relationship." This emphasises the uniqueness that can be attributed to customer base marketing and the role played by technology in making it cost effective to market to a segment of one. Clearly this relates to the importance of being able to have a single view of each customer. Data can be used to create knowledge about a customer that results in unique value being created for that customer; it provides the basis for a long and mutually beneficial relationship. The notion of a customer memory referred to by Storbacka and Lehtinen indicates the need for an organisation to create customer knowledge through the analysis of appropriate inputs of data and information. The platform for the formation of customer knowledge, and hence, if you like, a customer memory, is the customer database.

The core elements of a customer database are as follows:

*   Customer fact file,
*   Customer product file,
*   Customer transaction file,
*   Customer brand interaction file,
*   Customer insight file.

The relationship between these files is shown in Figure 14.7.

• Customer fact file
This comprises what might be termed the customer's demographic profile and thus contains data such as name, postal address, telephone number, email address, gender, age, data of birth, occupation, salary, marital status number of children, gender, and ages of children.

• Customer product file
Data regarding the products held with the provider is held here and includes information such as product name, optional features selected, value of product-holding funds selected. It could also store data on financial products held with other providers.

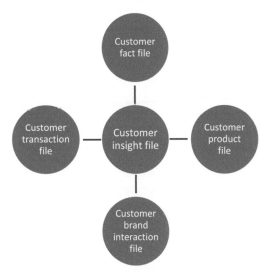

Figure 14.7 Top level structure of the customer database

- **Customer transaction file**

This is where data is stored that provides an audit trail of the interactions that take place between the provider and customer. It might include information such as a frequency of using an ATM, amount of cash withdrawn per transaction, whether an acknowledgement of transaction is requested, place at which ATM was used. It would also store written communication between the provider and customer and provide a log of all telephone-based contact for example.

- **Customer brand interaction file**

This file collates data based on digital behaviours and contact. This may include activity such as website browsing history – such as pages visited, pdf downloads, time on site and online applications and queries – as well as social media interactions, viral, display advertising and pay-per-click (PPC) engagement, webinars attended, email opens and click-through rates, online surveys and digital events invitations and registrations.

- **Customer insight file**

In this file we record data that gives insights into how the customer views her or his relationship with the provider. For example, information resulting from the customer's involvement in a customer satisfaction survey would be stored here. Any complaint-related feedback would also be found in this file, and it allows staff to record customer preferences and dislikes.

The customer insight file should benefit from inputs from the other four files. Thus, events in the customer's life act as a trigger for the creation of customer insights and the generation of appropriate actions on the part of the provider to add value to the relationship.

It is important that suitable systems and procedural architecture be devised to allow for the capture of data to populate the five files shown in Figure 14.7. Clearly there are cost implications to consider when developing such a framework for the management of customer information. Thus underlines the importance of targeting customers with the required commercial potential as part of the customer segmentation strategy.

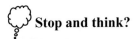 **Stop and think?**

How do you think digital marketing impacts upon the ability of a company to create customer advocates?

14.8.3 Integrating on- and offline for effective CRM

To achieve high rates of retention, organisations must adopt an integrated, omni-channel marketing approach incorporating both offline and online techniques to deliver a consistent message. As discussed, customers interact with brands across multiple mediums, thus an omni-channel marketing approach will maximise campaign success. Taking advantage of a variety of complementary communications approaches will not only maximise exposure but reinforce the message and create a halo effect of high-brand value. To develop an effective retention strategy, brands should follow integrated marketing communications theory as summarised by Pickton and Broderick (2001):

- Coherence: logical synergy between marketing mediums.
- Consistency: integrated approaches work together to reinforce common aim.
- Continuity: all techniques remain consistent in the goal they seek to achieve as they evolve over time.
- Complementary: sum of overall marketing activity is magnified compared to individual components.

Different communications approaches are levers which prompt a response; often the action of one leads the user to seek out another communications method which will build upon the previous marketing tactic; for example, a billboard advert may stimulate its audience to log onto the website. Brands should use different communications techniques as stepping stones, leading the customer to their ultimate objective of purchase. As different audiences respond to different stimuli, this increases the significance of an integrated and consistent message being delivered across all communications approaches. It's not possible to predict which message will be viewed first and what action it will prompt, if any. To achieve the greatest success, organisations should ensure they combine their traditional and eCRM data into a single system that enables a holistic view of prospects and customers. This will enable them to better target marketing with appropriate products and services, at the optimal time, via the optimal medium.

14.8.4 Personalisation

Good marketing practice dictates that organisations get as close to the recipient's individual needs as possible, ideally marketing to an audience of one. We know that "a one-size-fits-all" approach is not optimal, and personalisation is essential. Organisations need to make their marketing messages as relevant as possible to make the most of each contact point. Effective CRM enables companies to target differing segments in a unique way, fostering ongoing relationships with long-term customers. It is important to recognise that not all customers are of equal value and as such, it makes good business sense to target them with this in mind.

CRM not only benefits the customer, it also allows organisations to target different customer segments in a bespoke manner – for example, sending one message to the most profitable segment, and another to the remaining customers. Each customer an organisation holds marketable data for represents an asset. Smart, targeted marketing should seek to leverage the value of these assets to their maximum potential.

Personalisation remains a top priority for banks. One of the biggest challenges financial institutions face is their siloed nature, resulting in customer data spread across multiple business units. The hallowed single view of customers necessary for effective targeting and personalisation requires synchronisation between databases as well as staff who can collect and interpret data effectively. SaaS systems offer valuable data collation and segmentation capabilities. As does artificial intelligence, with its capability to facilitate the back-end processing of vast volumes of data at speed from a wide variety of sources, and front end robo-advisory services who use algorithms and automation technology to offer personalised wealth management.

Email is a prime eCRM device, being highly cost effective, scalable, and measurable whilst also easy to personalise and target to specifically suit customers' needs, thus optimising retention. The ability to maintain regular contact with customers via eNewsletters and updates provides an ideal opportunity to build relationships. Email contact strategies based on a series of communications (welcome message, engagement messages, then cross-sell message) are among the most common online retention techniques. Providing customers with a facility to be able to manage the types of emails they would like to receive is another important factor within eCRM. To ensure organisations provide value-added communication – recipients should be able to select the types of emails they receive (eNewsletters, events, fund updates, etc.) and the frequency (weekly, monthly, quarterly) in preference centres linked to eCRM systems.

Customer preferences should also extend to online browsing using multivariate testing. It is now standard practice for websites to offer highly personalised user experiences using targeting software that surfaces specific content, displayed in a particular order and manner based on data gathered in the current and previous browsing sessions (cookie data allowing). For example, surfacing customised content based on previous visit history, or links to frequently viewed areas, such as fund prices. Enabling customers to customise areas of the site could further add value by allowing them to create a bespoke hub of information most useful to them. Personalisation of websites creates a "sense of ownership" from the customers' perspective (Chaffey and Smith, 2008). This capability also adds value by saving the user time and allowing them to access key information quickly and conveniently, particularly useful, for example, to investment professionals who must access key fund information regularly. In a saturated market, a facility like this could be a key differentiator and significantly increase retention. The rise of generative AI has huge implications for personalisation with its ability to process vast quantities of data and use it to present highly targeted recommendations and communications in real-time (covered more in Chapter 10).

14.8.5 *Social CRM*

As discussed earlier in this chapter, people are increasingly comfortable interacting with organisations via social media (SM) channels. Social CRM is about building relationships with customers who expect a more meaningful connection with brands, on terms most convenient to them and specifically via the SM network of their choice e.g. Instagram. It offers benefits in terms of meeting customer needs and expectations with immediacy. It is particularly important in the context of futureproofing for the customers of tomorrow, with digital natives being very comfortable engaging with customer service in this manner. It provides an opportunity for instant engagement and response which is becoming more important as customers expect brands to respond quickly, via their preferred interaction platform. Financial services were traditionally cautious of interacting in this space, with the risk it poses for private customer information to be shared; however, neobanks offering SM servicing and the Covid-19 pandemic has made it a basic customer service expectation that traditional banks have had to meet. Banks should recognise that SM offers them a valuable and immediate insight into customer sentiment and trending topics which they can use to their advantage. Moreover, while social CRM allows issues to be highly visible in a public space, arguably it also aids transparency. The way an organisation responds to customer service queries via SM offers them an opportunity to publicly rectify a situation or complaint and turn a negative situation into a competitive advantage.

Marketing in practice 14.2: M&G Bond Vigilantes

Investment company M&G created their "Bond Vigilantes" blog to build stronger bonds with its audience of investment professionals, using it to broadcast "cutting edge fixed interest commentary, straight from the fund management floor". The blog is aimed at the IFA audience, offering topical and regular updates from the Fixed Income Desk Fund Managers and Investment Specialists as well as contributions from guest bloggers from the M&G Institutional desk. The aim of the blog was as an alternative digital marketing tool to promote our expertise and knowledge within the fixed income space and reinforce the M&G Bond brand without pushing M&G funds. It was originally UK centric but now targets institutional clients in Europe with content available in German, Spanish, Italian and French. The blog offers clients the opportunity to engage directly with their fixed income team, led by Jim Leaviss and allows M&G to share unique insight into the minds of their funds, fund managers, and how they manage their funds without actually pushing any of the fixed income funds.

> This blog is here for us to share our views on the things that matter to bond investors – inflation, interest rates and the global economy – as well as to talk about the bond markets themselves. Over the past few years we have blogged about value in high-yield bonds, the outlook for emerging market debt, and new developments in the inflation-linked bond markets. We'll also make sure we let you know our views on the traditional investment grade corporate bond markets – being a good bond vigilante should also be about identifying deteriorating trends in corporate behaviour, as well as that of governments.
>
> Jim Leaviss, fund manager and head of M&G fixed interest

The blog enables M&G to show a different "personality"; the style is straight talking and informal in order to ensure the content is engaging and rich enough to increase the "stickiness" of the site. Engagement relies on the audience finding relevant and entertaining content based on clear editorial guidelines. Each year for Halloween the team produces "It's Halloween. Here are some scary charts" which has seen good success being shared on social media

While the primary motivation of launching the blog was a space for the Fixed Income team to share their thoughts on market developments, it also offers the opportunity for the audience to interact directly with the team. Feedback and comments are encouraged, as are recommendations for future blog topics. The success and longevity of the blog relies heavily on interaction and debate with the audience, which in turn provides transparency and builds trust. Bond Vigilantes cemented M&G as a leading bond house by encouraging debate and demonstrating innovative investment thinking in a public space, which in turn has had a positive impact on the M&G brand. Moreover, the higher the relevance and engagement, the more likely users are to share the blogs with their peer group. As promotion of the blog has been minimal, its success has primarily been built on its credibility and value within the investment professional space and being shared via word of mouth, social sharing buttons onsite and re-Tweets. It has fostered trust and engagement with the investment professional audience which is essential in ongoing customer-relationship management.

Social media offers customers a voice in the marketplace, providing an opportunity for them to listen and share information with other customers. This customer community approach can be leveraged by organisations by building branded communities. The importance of community management has evolved beyond simply responding to comments and messages. Whilst not a traditional pillar of CRM marketing activities, community management has become an important function in the social space to ensure positive relationships with customers. There are two key parts to community management: proactive monitoring and engagement, and crisis management. Collectively, these duties enable positive interactions with customers, via social channels. Social communities offer a content rich space for brands to promote forums, blogs, competitions, offer advice and interaction, providing ideal insight into the target retention market. Moreover, it offers two-way interaction between the user and organisation and is an ideal platform to promote customer benefits in one area and allow peer-to-peer advocacy. The opportunity to tap into the retention market and garner feedback to improve the customer experience should aid customer satisfaction and loyalty. People who participate in branded chat rooms are most likely to be already engaged with the brand. Thus, they offer an ideal opportunity to strengthen the relationship with this core segment of already loyal customers, who are also more likely to act as word-of-mouth brand advocates.

Social media plays a huge role in managing and maintaining 1-2-1 customer relationships, Meta (Formerly Facebook Inc) platforms in particular. CRM data can be input into both Facebook and Instagram to allow brands to connect with customers through social channels extending the traditional CRM reach. This requires paid media investment however it offers a more diverse and integrated approach to management of customer relationships and the ability to use sequential messaging across multiple channels to enhance storytelling. Showing the same messaging across multiple channels to ensure that messages are being seen by customers aids a cohesive customer experience and reinforces the brand. When customer data is input into social channels, targeting is reliant on an email address match between the CRM system and the email address associated with the social platform customer login. Additionally, the correct marketing permissions must also be captured for that email address. Match rates can vary significantly based on quality of first party data, permissions and which social platforms are being used.

14.8.6 Digital tools – CRM systems

Digital communication tools and data enable businesses to easily mass personalise and customise their marketing messages. Core to CRM is developing a clear understanding of customers' needs and using this information to create targeted campaigns. By segmenting their audience, organisations can create specific groups, or personas that have common characteristics. Persona-based segmentation allows marketers to group customers into segments based on certain digital behaviours, as well as offline data and demographics. This then allows them to focus certain offers at segments who are closest to their target group. The trends that these groups demonstrate can also be leveraged to predict common cross-sell and upsell opportunities.

The use of electronic customer-relationship management (eCRM) tools greatly help an organisation's ability to collate customer information, such as personal and profile data, transactional data and communications data. As discussed in previous chapters, marketers have more channels than ever at their disposal to reach customers: direct mail, search, online ads, print ads to name but a few. Maintaining a single view of customers is incredibly important as it ensures communications are sensitive to the customers' needs and make sense in the context of the overall communications strategy. With so many touchpoints, there is a risk that if marketing is not joined up, it can create confusion and a negative brand impression with the end consumer. For example, a common tactic of banks is to use necessity products such as bank accounts or insurance as "gateway" products to gain new customers. Once acquired, the aim is to cross-sell longer-term, more profitable savings and investment customers. If the eCRM systems for these two business areas are not integrated, then there is a total lack of synergy of information.

Financial services companies need to be aware of the importance of not only introducing CRM systems but must also ensure there is a synergy between different internal CRMs. They can hold and capture information at a granular level – be it sporting preferences, favourite colour or birthday, all of which can be used to create targeted marketing messages that resonate with the recipient to a greater degree. If, for example, you know a particular customer loves golf, using that as a theme in a marketing email subject line just may be the differentiator that prompts them to open the communication. CRM systems also provide a central view of programmes that are connected to sales. If CRM is integrated with an organisation's websites, information on which web pages customers visit,[cxxiii] can be fed back into the CRM. Organisations can personalise future web visits based on information gleaned from a customer's previous behaviour on the site, such as pages visited, pdfs downloaded and self-reported information in data capture forms. An email can be triggered to the customer promoting the product they were viewing, or alternatively to the sales team for them to follow up with a call. The vision with CRM systems is to provide a 360 view of touchpoints between organisations and clients, to build a mutually beneficial enhanced view of the customer's needs. This will facilitate businesses providing only information that is of real value to the customer, reducing inappropriate marketing and making future communications relevant and more welcome.

Often there can be resistance to the introduction of CRM systems and its adoption by sales teams. Rather than viewing it as a tool to better enable their client relationships, they resist change, preferring to continue using existing, familiar and disparate personal data collection methods, e.g. Excel. As CRMs log all client interactions, they may feel it is a mechanism for management to monitor their performance. Or, perhaps they may be concerned that by

Figure 14.8 Neobank brands
Source: Shutterstock

centralising customer data, it allows other staff access to client relationship information which could be used to poach their client (particularly in organisations which use a single CRM system across multiple boutiques, such as BNY Mellon). In the case of sales support staff, they may feel threatened by the introduction of systems that they fear do their role and could potentially make them redundant. Organisations need to present CRM systems as a vital tool to assist success, not a method of monitoring performance. Part of a CRM system roll out should involve consultation with the sales team to understand the way they work and how it can be best implemented to assist them to execute leads in the easiest manner. Organisations would also be wise to embed CRM use in the marketing sales funnel and refuse to reward bonuses for leads and sales not captured in the system.

14.8.7 Data privacy and cookies

Having collected and stored data in a useable manner, it is important that contact strategies are enforced to avoid the same people being repeatedly hit with communications. Identifying a particular segment as prime can mean that they are sought by a variety of internal business areas, a particular issue within many financial services organisations. There is a fine balance between communicating enough to build a relationship and remain front of mind and saturating them with marketing. If, for example, a particular segment receives too many emails from a single brand, it will lead to disengagement and possibly to them unsubscribing from all future email communications. Therefore, there needs to be a robust internal contact strategy that illustrates how frequently data contacts are contacted, and which business area "owns"which data, particularly in businesses where there is a great deal of cross-over with regards to audiences.

Effective implementation of CRM is reliant on safety and effective protection of private consumer data. eCRM relies on the quality of data held; the better the data, the better the individualised service organisations can offer to its customers. However, consumers can tend to be wary of sharing personal data and allowing organisations to hold information beyond that which is strictly necessary to the relationship. Reportedly 90% of people want their bank to understand their needs, but only a third believe they actually do. Moreover, 86% of global banking customers would share their data if they felt they would get a more personalised experience as a result[15] and 83% are more willing to share data so long as brands are transparent about its use[16]. Conversely 72% Americans report concerns about being tracked online and how their data is used[17]. The reality is consumers want to know their data is safe and secure and those organisations they entrust it to will use it in a controlled manner that is to their benefit not their detriment. Banks need to utilise data elegantly and stay away from "faux" personalisation experiences with crude recommendations that are neither accurate nor relevant and ensure they deliver truly value-add experiences.

 Stop and think?

To what extent do you believe that concerns about data security have been overcome by the financial services industry?

Do any significant causes of data insecurity concern you?

The quality of an organisation's website is a key influencer of consumer trust and the likelihood of web visitors to transact and share personal information on an organisations' website. Cookies are commonly used to track and capture user information and behaviour on websites, as well as tailoring repeat visit experiences with multivariate testing, thus this data is fundamental in terms of retention marketing to repeat visitors. Cookies are text files containing information which is downloaded to the user's browsing device when they visit a website. They capture information about the visit, such as pages visited, user preferences, data entered into forms, disclaimers selected, and items saved to shopping basket. If the cookies used are persistent, this data can be used to serve targeted advertising as well as tailoring subsequent website visits (as opposed to session cookies which only apply for the duration of a single visit). So, for example, an asset management website may have different areas of the site specifically designated for consumers or investment professionals. UK Compliance regulations dictate that any information suitable for the professional audience must sit behind a disclaimer page, advising them the content they are about to view is suitable for investment professionals only. Rather than having to navigate to the relevant section and tick the disclaimer upon each visit, a returning cookied user will be directed to the relevant pages automatically, bypassing the barrier page. This creates a seamless and faster user journey, particularly advantageous for audiences who access certain pages daily, for example IFAs and daily fund prices. Third-party cookies are tracking cookies that have been passed on or sold to third-party websites and infringe on user privacy. The third-party cookie ban came into effect in 2020 when the major browsers started blocking all cookies set by third-party domains. Brands will instead have to maximise first party data and zero party data – data that is proactively and voluntarily shared with a brand e.g. via polls or quizzes. As well as adhering to data protection principles, since 26 May 2012, UK websites must adhere to the EU Cookie Directive. This principle states that websites must make users aware if they use cookies, offering them the opportunity to opt out should they wish. There are levels of blocking, ranging from a full block of all cookies, only allowing "trusted" sites to set them to session cookies for solely the site they are currently on. There is ongoing debate about the extent to which cookies infringe on privacy. While their purpose is to capture information about the behaviours of web users, giving rise to potential concerns about individual privacy, they also offer benefit to the user, not least in terms ease of navigation and use. Consumer rejection of cookies can result in a lower level of web intuitiveness and a poorer user experience, but the EU Directive was designed to offer individuals an opt-out to protect their privacy should they so wish. Data privacy is hugely important for effective customer relationship management. Aside from the regulatory consents that must be adhered to, it incredibly important proponent of trust and brand reputation. This is particularly significant given the growing number of connected devices users which are all sharing increasing amounts of data about highly personal subjects such as users' health. Clear and transparent practices when it comes to how brands use and store data are key, with highly visible data privacy policies available across all digital mediums. Naturally, given the nature of the industry, FS providers must have robust data security processes and systems in place to protect any information they hold on customers and prospects. Marketers must ensure they balance ethical and transparent data practices with appropriate levels of personalisation as they seek to maximise marketing effectiveness.

14.9 Relationship marketing in specific contexts

Arguably, the provision of financial services in B2B contexts has always been characterised by a focus on long-term relationships. In mass B2C markets, the focus on building customer relationships and encouraging customer retention has been a more recent, occurrence and has been hastened by the ubiquity of social media. Discussions thus far have highlighted the importance of the careful management of customer relationships from acquisition through to long-term retention, highlighting the importance of understanding and focusing attention on those customers who are likely to be profitable. While these principles have general relevance, their application can vary according to context. This section focuses attention on two specific contexts, namely marketing via intermediaries and marketing internationally.

14.9.1 Relationship marketing and the role of intermediaries

Particular challenges are presented in using relationship marketing where there is the involvement of third-party intermediaries. Typical examples might include high street general insurance brokers, independent financial advisers (IFAs).

There are inherent conflicts of interest with the accompanying potential for mistrust. Much of this surrounds the thorny question of 'who owns the customer?'. This often depends upon whether any given request by a customer is likely to result in additional sales revenue/ commission or lead to the incurring of some administrative task, and the accompanying costs. The incentive structure (additional sales means revenue, administration implies costs) means there is a risk that intermediaries will display a preference to think that they 'own' the customer when a new sale is in prospect, or a potential policy lapse that could result in commission claw-back. By contrast, such intermediaries may defer customer owner-ship in favour of the core product provider where a non-income-related task is indicated. Insurance, pensions, and investment companies have had to negotiate this contentious issue for many years as they cautiously walk the tightrope between the ultimate customer and the third-party introducer. Often the customer finds themselves neglected as brokers fail to meet their ongoing service needs adequately while the product provider fails to act in the customer's interest for fear of offending and alienating the broker who originally introduced the business.

It is important to grasp that companies that distribute via brokers may have spent decades building and maintaining a culture in which the intermediary is viewed as *the* pri-mary customer. Indeed, one can be forgiven for thinking that the needs of the broker took precedence over those of the end customer. Therefore, there is a strong cultural dimension to the development of a relationship or CRM-based approach, whereby the intermediary sales branches of provider companies must learn to view brokers and their relationship to customers in a new light, with the needs of the end consumer taking precedence over those of the broker. This may seem straightforward enough, but for some companies and their broker sales support staff it can represent a radically different way of thinking and behaving.

Thus, where intermediaries are involved, a customer management model is required that comprises the following features:

- Positions the end customer as the ultimate beneficiary of the product/service provided and clearly establishes the primacy of their interests;
- Has a robust set of protocols that establishes the respective rights and responsibilities of the provider and intermediary. A suitable level of security must be guaranteed such that there are no compromises either to the data protection rules that apply in any given country or from commercial sensitivities between intermediaries;
- Clearly identifies the array of possible events in the life of the customer relation-ship and specifies the respective roles of provider and intermediary in handling those events;
- Is a CRM programme geared specifically to address the interests of the intermediary sector in addition to the CRM programme designed for the end consumer.

14.9.2 Relationship marketing: some international perspectives

In Chapter 8 we considered some of the ways in which operating across national boundaries impacts upon marketing strategy and planning. Operating internationally can give rise to a range of new opportunities and threats and will require the development and maintenance of a new set of competences. Similarly, each country will present its own unique set of oppor-tunities and threats to be matched with the appropriate set of strengths and weaknesses. Clearly, this adds a material degree of complexity to strategy development and use of the marketing mix. Doole (1998) has identified three features that are associated with the strategies of organisations that have competed successfully in international markets:

- A clear competitive focus based upon in-depth knowledge of each respective market, a strong competitive positioning, and a truly international marketing strategy;
- Well-managed organisations characterised by a culture of learning, innovativeness, effective monitoring and control procedures, and high levels of energy and commitment to international markets;
- An effective relationship strategy, based upon strong customer relationships, the commitment to quality products and services, and a high degree of commitment to customer services across all international markets.

We observe elements of all three of these features in brands such as Singapore Airlines, Ritz Carlton Hotels and American Express. In the case of financial services, particular consideration must be given to issues such as regulation and culture, as they can vary widely from country to country and be of profound significance, as Kaspar, Van Helsdingen and de Vries (1999) observe:

> Formulations of relationship marketing based on contemporary western interpretations may fail if transplanted to overseas countries, where the cultural and economic environments differ significantly from the country for which a relationship policy was originally formulated.

These differences may be of particular significance to retail consumers, but they are still likely to have relevance in the business-to-business domain. Again, relationship management is a particularly important feature of the B2B market. Technology and process innovation have presented new threats and opportunities to financial services organisations that operate on a global basis. Additionally, deregulation and the opening-up of markets to new forms of competition have added to the value attached to effective international CRM strategies for financial services companies involved in the B2B domain. It is instructive to consider the four relationship bonds proposed by Berry and Parasuraman (1991) and discussed by Zeithaml and Bitner (2003) presented earlier in Chapter 14. These have particular relevance in the B2B context where financial, social, customisation and structural bonds can be developed in a cost-effective and potentially meaningful way. There are particular opportunities for the development of customisation and structural bonds, these being less easy and cost effective to employ in the B2C context.

In both the B2B and B2C contexts, decisions regarding the development and execution of international CRM programmes must take account of issues such as:

- Segmentation – Which groups of customers are in sufficient numbers and of a value that it makes sound economic sense to make them the focus of an international CRM programme (ICRMP)?
- Cultural proximity – Do the desired target segments for an ICRMP display sufficient cultural proximity to make the programme a practical proposition?
- Devolution – Deciding which aspects of an ICRMP should be determined and managed centrally, and what should be devolved to local management.
- Competition – How can an ICRMP protect valuable customers from the overtures of overseas competitors?

- Rewards – How transferable are individual rewards in influencing behaviours by members of the target segment on an international basis?
- Partnerships – How can reward-scheme supplier relationships be leveraged for mutual benefit, preferably on a global basis?
- IT – How can IT be used to increase the cost-effectiveness of an ICRMP, preferably by achieving interconnectivity between local national customer databases and central management facilities?
- Commercial – Does it make strategic and financial sense?

The above set of factors are neither exhaustive nor mutually exclusive but, nonetheless, provide a firm basis for considering the development of an ICRMP. American Express has acquired significant expertise in managing customer loyalty programmes on a global scale. In many respects this is an understandable response to the phenomenal growth of competition in the credit card market across the globe. Case Study 14.1 shows how Amex uses its international loyalty programme to reinforce the relationship it has with its higher value customers.

14.10 Summary and conclusions

This chapter has outlined the environmental factors that have resulted in the development of customer-relationship marketing. It has demonstrated how the characteristics associated with financial services have a marked resonance with the features associated with CRM. For example, the Gen Z long-term nature of many financial services products makes them a natural context within which CRM programmes can be particularly effective.

The crucial importance of carefully selecting the *right* customers in the first place was presented as a prerequisite of customer longevity and lifetime value. A range of factors was discussed that are implicated in customer persistency. Strategies aimed at facilitating customer retention were explored, notably Zeithaml and Bitner's model concerning the four levels of bonds.

This chapter also introduced the concept of the customer-relationship chain which explains how the marketing mix can be used to facilitate the progression of both domestic consumers and business customers from suspect to advocate. The value of the customer-relationship chain was augmented with a demonstration of the importance of focusing on lifetime customer value.

While the principles associated with managing customer relationships are general, developments in technology have created new opportunities for their implementation. More sophisticated systems of gathering and processing customer data, combined with the use of channels such as mobile phones. Email, the internet and social media have all created opportunities for genuinely marketing to a segment of one. The growth and adoption of generative AI into FS is enabling FS brands to target more effectively, using real-time data to truly understand customer needs and wants, and service them in a timely manner with personalised products and services before they may even be aware they need them.

Such highly targeted marketing, if managed carefully and thoughtfully should enable the development of higher-value customer relationships, improved retention, and better long-term benefits for both customer and provider.

Consideration was given to the implications of the use of intermediaries when adopting a CRM-based approach. This led onto some of the particular issues that need to be addressed when considering the use of international CRM programmes. Finally, the significance attached to the role played by data was discussed. Here we gained an appreciation of the need for appropriate systems functionality, competence in data analysis and interrogation within any organisation seeking to pursue a customer development strategy.

Learning outcomes

Having completed this chapter, you should now be able to:

1. **Understand the importance of relationship marketing and customer retention in financial services.**
   Relationship marketing concerns the contribution of marketing inputs once the customer acquisition phase has ended. During this third and final part of this book we are focussing upon marketing as it concerns the retention, management, and development of existing customers. Thus, this section completes the triangle of strategy and planning, customer acquisition, and customer management that forms the basis of this book. Until relatively recently FSPs have seen marketing primarily as a discipline that is about getting customers. However, we identified a wide ranging array of factors that have acted as drivers of change that have focussed ever greater importance on marketing as a discipline aimed at managing relationships with a company's existing customer base. Among those drivers of change were: the slowdown in economic growth, rising costs of customer acquisition, and technological innovation to name but three.

2. **Understand the interactions between customer acquisition, customer retention and marketing activities.**
   A feature of many businesses is that they simultaneously engage in acquiring new customers for their organisations whilst losing a number of existing customers. Such a process of acquisition and attrition can result in a business working incredibly hard to stand still as far as its numbers of customers are concerned. This has been referred to as the *bucket theory of marketing* and is a highly inefficient strategy for business growth. For this reason we explored the importance of targeting customer acquisition resources onto customers who have a greater propensity to remain a customer in the long-term.

3. **Understand the nature and significance of the concept of customer lifetime value.**
   We identified the importance of customer lifetime value and examined the kind of variables that can help determine its quantum. We considered revenue, cost, and referral variables. Of note were factors such as value of purchase, number of products held, duration of product holding, and likelihood of cancelling a product contract. We saw how the work of Zeithaml and Bitner, as well as Berry and Parasuraman have been instrumental in the development of customer retention strategies. Zeithaml and Bitner's model posits that excellent service quality and value must provide the basis for an effective retention strategy. They proceeded to identify a sequence of four bonds which, when operationalised by means of the marketing mix, should result in a high probability of retaining valuable customers.

4. **Appreciate how digital marketing and the use of social media is impacting on customer-relationship marketing strategies.**

    Social media (SM) offers companies an excellent platform to communicate with customers in a timely, open and transparent manner, particularly younger audiences. It can be utilised for customer service, information sharing, brand awareness, social listening and relationship building, all of which can enable brands to better connect with customers and help build trust. It also offers customers a voice in the marketplace, providing an opportunity for Brands to listen and garner customer sentiment on what's important to them. Brands should employ an omni-channel approach, ensuring marketing campaigns work equally well across all media including SM, and leverage the opportunity it offers for social shares to increase reach. They should also ensure their CEO and ExCo are active on social, particularly LinkedIn which drives significant benefits in terms of brand reputation and trust.

5. **Have an appreciation of some of the ways in which AI is impacting upon the customer service experience.**

    AI solves specific problems using machine learning algorithms and is used effectively across FS for servicing via chatbots. Generative AI (GAI) has evolved in recent years and analyses vast quantities of data to produce new and original content that doesn't exist anywhere else. It is in theory able to apply a human-like lens to problem solving and fulfil tasks that usually need human intelligence and has enormous potential to support complex tasks and workflows. Right across FS, GAI could radically shift consumer expectations and internal business operations, driving efficiency and accessibility through GAI virtual assistants able to collate and present highly personalised propositions. This will increase productivity and reduce the cost-to-serve by increasing the speed of content generation and decreasing human effort. Integrating GAI into a firm's processes will help them stay relevant and competitive and potentially reduce costs.

Review questions

1. Discuss the extent to which CRM is a feature of the financial services sector in your own country.
2. What do you consider to be the relative importance of marketing's role in customer acquisition compared with customer development?
3. Explore the respective merits of product profitability and customer lifetime value as measures of new business contribution.
4. In what ways might the design of a customer development marketing mix vary between the B2B and B2C marketplaces?
5. Identify which innovations in the field of ICT have impacted upon CRM practices. Discuss how these innovations are being adopted by financial services providers in your country. Do you think that good progress is being made with the adoption of new ICT capabilities? Use examples to justify your views.

Notes

1 The value of keeping the right customers; Amy Gallo, *Harvard Business Review*, 29 October 2014
2 Falling Long-Term Growth Prospects: Trends, Expectations, and Policies. Washington, DC: World Bank. License: Creative Commons Attribution CC BY 3.0 IGO Accessed January 2024

3 Kose, M. Ayhan (ed.); Ohnsorge, Franziska (ed.). 2023. Falling Long-Term Growth Prospects: Trends, Expectations, and Policies. © World Bank: Washington, DC. http://hdl.handle.net/10986/39497 License: CC BY 3.0 IGO." Accessed August 2023

4 Source: Matthew Boyle, Finder.com, www.finder.com/uk/current-account-statistics, Accessed August 2023

5 https://blog.hootsuite.com/social-media-financial-services/ Accessed January 2024

6 https://www.edelman.com/trust/2022-trust-barometer Accessed August 2023

7 https://www.smartinsights.com/digital-marketing-strategy/financial-services-social-media-strategy-trends-and-recommendations/ Accessed January 2024

8 https://www.flyingvgroup.com/why-your-business-needs-video-marketing-and-video-content/ Accessed January 2024

9 https://www.putnam.com/advisor/business-building/social-media/ Accessed February 2024

10 https://blog.hubspot.com/blog/tabid/6307/bid/30030/linkedin-277-more-effective-for-lead-generation-than-facebook-twitter-new-data.aspx Accessed February 2024

11 https://fticommunications.com/beyond-the-ceo-the-power-of-leadership-voices-on-social-media/ Accessed February 2024

12 https://fticommunications.com/beyond-the-ceo-the-power-of-leadership-voices-on-social-media/ Accessed February 2024

13 https://www.ofcom.org.uk/__data/assets/pdf_file/0020/234362/adults-media-use-and-attitudes-report-2022.pdf

14 https://www.vox.com/future-perfect/21420357/kenya-mobile-banking-unbanked-cellphone-money Accessed December 2023

15 https://www.bjss.com/industry-insights/how-can-banks-balance-ai-powered-personalisation-with-data-privacy#:~:text=Eighty-six%20percent%20of%20global%20banking%20customers%20would,exchange%20their%20data%20for%20a%20more%20personalised%20experience. Accessed January 2024

16 https://www.zdnet.com/article/four-out-of-five-consumers-will-trade-data-for-personalisation/ Accessed January 2024

17 https://www.pewresearch.org/internet/2019/11/15/americans-and-privacy-concerned-confused-and-feeling-lack-of-control-over-their-personal-information/#:~:text=Prevalence%20of%20tracking%3A%2072%25%20of%20Americans%20report%20feeling,some%20of%20what%20they%20do%20is%20being%20tracked. Accessed January 2024

References

Berry, L. L. and Parasuraman, A. (1991). Marketing Services, Competing Through Quality. New York: Free Press.

Chaffey, D. and Smith, P. R. (2008). eMarketing Excellence: Planning and Optimizing Your Digital Marketing. 3rd ed. London: Elsevier Butterworth-Heineman.

Doole, I. (1998). Benchmarking the competencies and capabilities of SMEs successfully competing in international markets. PhD working papers. In: I. Doole and R. Lowe (eds.) International Marketing Strategy: Analysis, Development and Implementation, 2nd ed. International Thomson Business Press, London.

Kaspar, H., Van Helsdingen, P. and de Vries, W. J. (1999). Services Marketing Management: An International Perspective. New York: John Wiley & Son.

Reinartz, W. and Kumar, V. (2002). The mismanagement of customer loyalty. Harvard Business Review, 80(7), pp. 86–94.

Pickton, D and Broderick, A (2001) Integrated Marketing Communications. Harlow: Pearson Education.

Stewart, K. M. (1998). An exploration of customer exit in retail banking. *International Journal of Bank Marketing*, 16(1), pp. 6–14. DOI:10.1108/02652329810197735

Storbacka, K. and Lehtinen, J. (2001). *Customer Relationship Management: Creating Competitive Advantage through Win–Win Relationship Strategies.* New Jersey: McGraw Hill.

Zeithaml, V. A, Bitner, M. J. and Gremler, D. D. (2008). *Services Marketing: integrating customer focus across the firm*. New Jersey: McGraw Hill.

15 Service delivery and service quality

Learning objectives

At the end of this chapter, you should be able to:

1. Explain the importance of service quality in the marketing of financial services,
2. Understand the basic principles of the service-profit chain,
3. Understand the nature of quality in financial services,
4. Review approaches to the management of service quality,
5. Understand the importance of service recovery.

15.1 Introduction

The previous chapter highlighted the importance of developing and managing customer relationships and the importance of customer retention. Central to any approach to build and maintain good customer relationships is the management of service delivery to ensure quality and minimise the risks of service failure. The ability to deliver a high-quality service that meets the needs and expectations of customers is key to building a competitive advantage in financial services sector. It is difficult for financial services providers to gain a sustainable competitive edge just by offering new products or new product features; in contrast, the quality of the service that an organisation provides is much harder to copy. And indeed a study by Almquist, Senior and Block (2016) stressed the central role of quality as a driver of customer value. Furthermore, research suggests that high levels of quality will lead to higher levels of customer satisfaction and higher levels of loyalty. The economics of customer retention argues that retained customers will be important to financial services providers for two reasons. First, retained customers are usually cheaper to serve because they are known to the organisation and the level of marketing expenditure required to keep them is much lower than the cost of acquiring new ones. Second, loyal customers can generate more revenue because they tend to be less price sensitive, because they are likely to buy additional products and because they will engage in positive word of mouth. While recognising that some aspects of this argument may apply to many markets, there are good grounds for believing that loyal customers are particularly important in financial services where cross-selling is a major strategic thrust. The delivery of a high-quality service is essential to ensuring that customers maintain a productive relationship with a financial services provider

DOI: 10.4324/9781003398615-29

and in that sense, service quality can be expected to have a positive impact on organisational performance. Some research would also suggest that high levels of service quality can contribute to employee satisfaction as well, since staff are typically happier in their work when delivering a good customer experience.

This chapter provides an overview of service delivery in financial services and highlights some of the issues associated with managing quality. The chapter begins by introducing the concept of the service profit chain as a way of thinking about the service delivery process and its impact on customers. Thereafter, the discussion focuses more specifically on quality and begins by defining service quality and highlighting its key features. The next sections discuss models of service quality, the service delivery process and the areas where problems may arise with respect to service delivery. The final section in the chapter examines the outcomes of service quality paying particular attention to the issue of service failure and service recovery.

15.2 The service profit chain

The process of delivering service, generating customer loyalty and improving profitability has been conceptualised in the service profit chain (Heskett et al., 2008), which is illustrated in Figure 15.1. The starting point is internal service quality which refers to the extent to which an organisation is able to provide the right quality of support to employees to enable them to serve customers effectively. Included in the general concept of internal service quality would be factors such as job design, working environment, reward systems, training and support systems. Internal service quality will result in higher levels of employee satisfaction, productivity and retention. Employees who are satisfied in their job and well motivated will deliver a high-quality service to customers. This high quality is the foundation for delivering enhanced service value. Value will, in turn, lead to increased levels of customer satisfaction and retention. Given the economics of customer retention (Heskett, Jones, Loveman and Sasser (1994) improved revenues and profit are the expected consequences. In essence, the service profit chain highlights the important links between how an organisation manages itself internally, the impact of this on the experience of customers and the benefits in terms of organisational performance.

The logic of the service profit chain (SPC) is very appealing and the model has been widely adopted by consultants and managers; in particular, it has been used to guide a range of managerial interventions, most notably in relation to internal organisation and management and its usefulness has been demonstrated in a variety of settings including South West Airlines, Xerox, Taco Bell (Heskett et al., 1994) and Sears (see Rucci, Kirn and Quinn, 1998). By

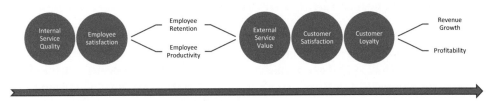

Service Delivery System

Figure 15.1 The service profit chain
Source: Adapted from Heskett et al. (1994, 2008)

contrast, in a retail setting, Silvestro and Cross (2000) noted that that store profitability tends to be negatively rather than positively correlated with employee satisfaction, although they did find evidence to support the customer dimension of the service profit chain. Systematic research to test this model has proved difficult because of the complexities of data collection.

 Stop and think?

Does the service profit chain make sense to you – think about it from your position as a customer? Does it make sense if you think about the relationships from the perspective of an employee?

In the financial services sector, one of the first and most comprehensive studies using the SPC was undertaken in relation to retail banking in the US. Loveman, (1998) used secondary, branch-level data and found that, internally, reward systems, the organisation's customer focus and the quality of management had a positive impact on employee satisfaction. There was rather limited evidence for a link between employee satisfaction and loyalty. Employee length of service was found to affect customer satisfaction but the relationship between employee satisfaction and customer satisfaction was weak. Customer satisfaction had a positive impact on loyalty to the bank and loyalty in turn was found to have an impact on financial performance. Overall, Loveman's evidence provided tentative support for the key relationships that underpin the SPC. Using data from Brazil, Kamakura, Mittal and de Rosa (2002) found evidence to suggest that all major links in the SPC were significant. An examination of SPC in a longitudinal study demonstrated links between customer metrics (satisfaction, quality, share of wallet) and performance metrics (retention and profitability) but also pointed to the complex nature of some of the relationships (Larivière, 2008). Similarly, in a study of banks in Ghana, Acheampong and Asamoah (2013) find evidence at least to partially support the links from managerial interventions through to bank performance. And moving out of the face-to-face environment, Chicu et al. (2016) evaluate the SPC in a series of call centres across a range of countries and services (including financial services). The results of a large-scale survey suggest that even in nontraditional settings the core relationships that characterise the model are still relevant. Research insight 15.1 outlines some of the latest thinking on the contribution of this widely used approach to thinking about service delivery.

 Research insight 15.1: the service–profit chain

The service–profit chain (SPC) provides a compelling conceptual argument that draws on various strands of management research (HR, operations management and marketing) to integrate internal service quality, external marketing and organisational performance. It has attracted considerable interest from researchers working in the area of services marketing, it has been widely cited and there have been numerous attempts to evaluate its impacts in empirical settings. In practical terms, many organisations have strengthened their focus on managing employee roles in service delivery with a view to improving the experience of their customers and enhancing their performance. This study provides a review of existing work, identifies areas for further research and considers how the SPC should be developed in the context of: first, dramatic increases in digital service delivery and the growing role for AI; second, the growing interest in employee wellbeing and third, the impact of major external shocks to organisations operations (including the Covid-19 pandemic).

As noted above, the availability of comprehensive data sets does provide challenges for empirical testing of the framework. While some of the early studies produced variable results in terms of whether or not the model was supported, later studies were more positive, particularly those that focused on subsets of the chain. Overall, the authors conclude that there is general support for the relationships proposed within the SPC, although the size of the impacts vary and some of the relationships are considered to be possibly non-linear or contingent.

Based on their analysis of existing studies and the different approaches that have been adopted they argue that there may be a case for developing the SPC in 5 key areas. First, they suggest that there is a need to take a more holistic view of human resource management practices rather than simply focusing on internal service quality. Second, they suggest that wellbeing for employees and customers might be a better way of thinking about their levels of engagement (rather than just satisfaction). Third, they argue that more attention should be focused on loyalty including paying attention to the object of loyalty – is it the organisation, the customer that an employee serves, the manager for whom an employee works or the employee that serves a particular customer. Indeed they suggest that these different ways of thinking about loyalty could complement or offset each other. Fourth, they suggest that better results may come from using more sophisticated empirical approaches to recognise that some links in the chain may be contingent and some may be non-linear. This latter point is thought to be of particular significance in especially turbulent imarket environments. Finally, they recognise that with the growth in digital delivery, there may be a need to for the SPC to think beyond human-to-human interaction and accommodate digital engagements.

Source: Hogreve, Iseke and Derfuss,(2022)

Of course, the SPC concept has its critics. Perhaps the most general concern is that the SPC does not explicitly address issues relating to the cost of quality and it focuses more on revenue than profit. A further concern is that retention may be behavioural rather than attitudinal and thus a reflection of inertia rather than positive attachment (see for example Colgate and Lang, 2001). Others have pointed out that that satisfaction alone is not sufficient and that what really creates loyalty is customer "delight". And of course, Reinartz and Kumar (2002) have challenged the idea that loyalty is always of financial benefit because loyal customers may actually be more demanding and more expensive to serve.

Notwithstanding these concerns and limitations, SPC is a model which tries to provide a simple representation of the complex chain of causality that runs from managerial decisions, via employee responses and consumer experiences through to financial performance. Given this complexity, it is probably no surprise that researchers have identified gaps and failings. Perhaps the real value of the model is that it highlights the importance of quality and value in managing the customer experience and the central role of the organisation's employees in delivery. What it does not do is provide a detailed insight into that nature of service quality and the ways in which it should be managed. This will be the focus of the rest of this chapter. The concept of value (as the relationship between quality and costs) and the concept of satisfaction will be addressed in more detail in the next chapter.

Progress check

- The service profit chain highlights the important links between how an organisation manages itself internally, the impact of this on the experience of customers and the benefits in terms of organisational performance.
- It highlights the importance of delivering high quality service to ensure customer satisfaction and retention. Higher levels of satisfaction and retention in turn are expected to lead to enhanced organisational performance.
- There is a growing body of empirical evidence to support the various links that comprise the service-profit chain.

15.3 Defining service quality

Quality is much more difficult to define for a service than it is for a physical good. With a physical good, quality can often be measured by specifying certain physical features that the product should possess. For example, the quality of a laser printer can be specified in terms of the number of pages that will be printed each minute and the quality of the printed output. This serves as an objective standard – if the printer reaches this objective standard, then it is considered to be of a particular quality. In financial services, it is much more difficult to specify objective standards because service encounters can vary and the needs of customers can vary.

There are a range of different perspectives on quality. Garvin (1988) suggests that these can be organised under five main headings as shown in Figure 15.2.

When thinking about service quality, the most common view is that service quality is subjective – that is to say it is based on the customer's perception of how well the service matches their needs and expectations. Service quality is what consumers perceive it to be.

15.4 Models of service quality

While recognising that the user-based view of service quality means that quality is defined by the customer, any attempt to manage service quality requires an understanding of how customers evaluate the service they receive, and which elements are most important. Because we have adopted a subjective view of service quality, the most common way to think about how consumers evaluate a service is the idea that consumers will have expectations about the sort of service that they will receive. They will compare the actual service with the expected service. If the actual service meets or exceeds the expected service, then the level of quality will be seen to be relatively high. If the actual service is below what was expected, then consumers will perceive that the quality of service is poor.

Figure 15.2 Perspectives on quality

Source: Garvin, (1988)

While it is widely agreed that service quality will involve a comparison of expectations and actual service performance, there are different views about the aspects of service that are important. In general, there are two main ways of looking at the elements of service quality. In broad terms, attempts to define and understand service quality have developed in two distinct directions – one stream of research originated in Europe (largely Scandinavia) while the other developed in North America. The European stream of research is often described as the Nordic School and originates in the work of Christian Grönroos (see for example, Grönroos, 1984; 1988). This approach tends to be more qualitative and emphasises the overall image of the organisation, the outcome of the service (technical quality) and the way in which it is delivered (functional quality). The North American stream of research developed from the work of Parasuraman, Zeithaml and Berry (see for example, Parasuraman, Zeithaml and Berry, 1985; 1988); it explicitly defines service quality as the difference between perceptions and expectations and measures quality across five main dimensions, namely Reliability, Assurance, Tangibles, Empathy, Responsiveness (RATER). Specifically Parasuraman, Zeithaml and Berry (1985; 1988) proposed a method of measuring service quality using a measurement model called SERVQUAL. This has since been the most widely used approach to the measurement of service quality and SERVQUAL has been applied to a variety of different services, in a variety of different countries. Each of these two approaches will be discussed in more detail below.

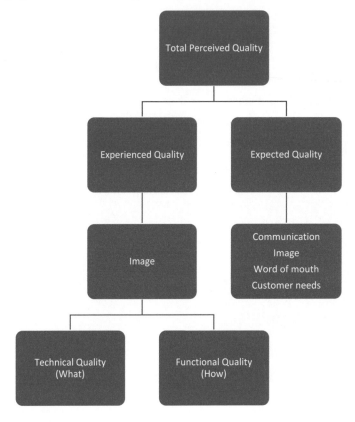

Figure 15.3 The Nordic perspective on service quality

Source: Adapted from Gronroos (1984)

15.4.1 The Nordic perspective on service quality

The framework developed by Grönroos is outlined in Figure 15.3. In this framework, it is proposed that customers form expectations and make evaluations of service delivery in relation to both functional and technical quality.

- Functional quality – this is concerned with the way in which the service is delivered and will cover things such as friendliness, helpfulness, politeness, pleasantness, understanding, etc. It deals mostly with the way in which a service encounter happens. In the case of say a financial planner, functional quality would be concerned with the way in which he or she treats their customers.
- Technical quality – this is concerned with the quality of the service outcome – that is to say it is concerned with the extent to which the service is done correctly and accurately. In the case of a financial planner, technical quality would be concerned with the quality of the actual advice.

Perceptions of functional and technical quality combine to create an image for the organisation and this drives overall perceptions of quality.

Because overall service quality will be dependent on both functional and technical quality, to deliver a high-quality service will require not just good technical skills but will also require good interpersonal skills. In many cases, research in financial services has suggested that functional quality may often be more important than technical quality. It has already been suggested that many personal customers find financial services complex and difficult to understand. In such situations, there will be a tendency for evaluations to be based on the quality of the interaction with the financial services provider rather than the intrinsic quality of the financial service itself.

 Stop and think?

Think about your bank current account? What do you think are the technical dimensions of that service and what are the functional ones? How easy is it to separate these two aspects of quality?

15.4.2 The North American perspective on service quality

The North American perspective on service quality is based on the work of Parasuraman, Zeithaml and Berry (1985; 1988). They explicitly proposed that quality evaluations were based on a comparison of consumer expectations of what they should receive and consumer perceptions of what they did receive. They proposed that such comparisons would be made in five main areas. These are shown in Figure 15.4:

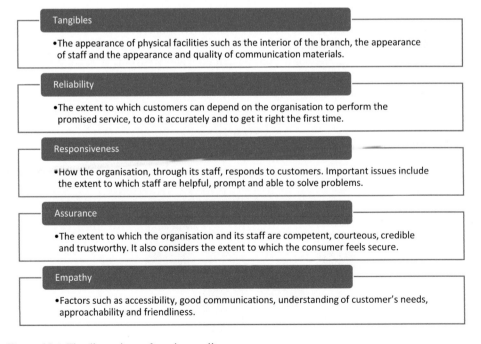

Tangibles
•The appearance of physical facilities such as the interior of the branch, the appearance of staff and the appearance and quality of communication materials.

Reliability
•The extent to which customers can depend on the organisation to perform the promised service, to do it accurately and to get it right the first time.

Responsiveness
•How the organisation, through its staff, responds to customers. Important issues include the extent to which staff are helpful, prompt and able to solve problems.

Assurance
•The extent to which the organisation and its staff are competent, courteous, credible and trustworthy. It also considers the extent to which the consumer feels secure.

Empathy
•Factors such as accessibility, good communications, understanding of customer's needs, approachability and friendliness.

Figure 15.4 The dimensions of service quality

Source: Parasuraman, Zeithaml and Berry (1985, 1988)

In order to measure service quality, data should be collected about customers' expectations in each of these areas and about their perceptions of the quality that they receive. Indeed, Parasuraman, Zeithaml and Berry developed a questionnaire – known as SERVQUAL – specifically to collect data on these five aspects of service quality. By looking at the difference between the level of performance and the customer's expectations, an organisation can identify the areas in which it should focus its attention. Consider the example in Figure 15.5. The graph plots the value of perceptions minus expectations for each of the five dimensions of service quality. Positive scores indicate that performance is above expectations and negative scores indicate that performance is below expectations. In the case of this organisation, the tangibles dimension is fine, as is empathy – both exceed customer expectations. However, performance with respect to reliability and responsiveness is clearly well below customer expectations. These findings would suggest that in managing the delivery of service quality, attention should be focused on reliability and responsiveness as areas most in need of improvement.

These five dimensions of service quality (often referred to as the RATER dimensions) are by their nature very generic to enable them to be used in a diversity of contexts and have been widely used in studies of service quality in financial services. Ladhari (2009) used SERVQUAL in a study of Canadian banking and identified responsiveness and empathy as the most important elements of overall service quality. Wong et al. (2008) use the scale to examine service quality for business customers in Australia and draw attention to the continuing importance of reliability as a driver of service quality and also as an area of relative weakness in provision. Mersha et al. (2012) employ the SERVQUAL approach in a study of retail banks in Ethiopia and report that perceptions fall short of expectations in all five dimensions, with the biggest gap arising in relation to empathy.

Researchers focusing on service quality in specific online contexts have identified a need to develop more context specific measures. For a general online context, Zeithaml, Parasuraman and Malhotra (2002) proposed a five dimension measure (e-SQ) based on information availability, ease of use, privacy, graphic style and reliability which was subsequently reduced to four dimensions, namely efficiency, fulfilment, availability and privacy (Parasuraman, Zeithaml and Malhotra, 2005). Herington and Weaver (2009) use a modified version of this scale in a banking context and identifies four specific dimensions to e-service quality based on personal needs, site organisation, user-friendliness and efficiency.

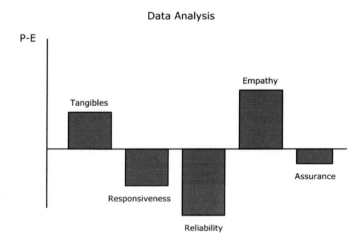

Figure 15.5 Service quality perceptions and expectations

Although the SERVQUAL framework has been used extensively in academic and business research it has also attracted a significant amount of criticism (see for example Buttle, 1996). A particular cause for concern has been the idea that service quality is a difference score (i.e. the difference between perceptions and expectations [P-E]). Implicit in this approach is the idea that when a score is negative it indicates poor quality. However, some researchers have suggested that consumers may still perceive a high level of quality despite recording negative difference scores – for example if expectations are very high and scored at 7 while perceptions are positive but scored lower at 6. In addition, difference scores do not distinguish between a situation in which P=7 and E=6, which indicates very positive evaluations and one in which P=2 and E=1 which indicates very poor evaluations. Both would result in the same quality rating – i.e. 1. Other criticisms have been concerned with the generalisability of the SERVQUAL questions across very diverse services and the adequacy of the coverage of the core service features. Consequently many researchers have supplemented SERVQUAL with additional service-specific questions.

In response to criticisms, Parasuraman, Zeithaml and Berry continued to develop SERVQUAL. One important development related to the interpretation of expectations. The initial work on SERVQUAL treated expectations as being ideal – i.e. measures of what consumers think they should get. In recognition of the possibility that such ideal expect-ation could be unrealistically high, Parasuraman, Berry and Zeithaml (1991) proposed the concept of a "zone of tolerance". This approach suggested that consumers might have two types of expectation – ideal (or should) expectations and adequate (or will) expectations. In effect, it was argued that consumers would distinguish between their ideal standard of service and a realistic standard of service. Whereas the latter concerns the minimal accept-able standard that will provide a solution to their need, the former represents the level of services that they would like to experience.

In between the desired and the adequate levels of service, resides the zone of tolerance. This represents a range of service performance that the customer will consider satisfactory. Figure 15.6 provides an example of perceptions measured against zones of tolerance.

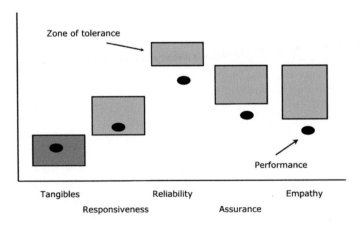

Performance with respect to tangible and responsiveness is within the zone of tolerance. Performance with respect to reliability, assurance and empathy is a cause for concern because all lie below the zone of tolerance.

Figure 15.6 Zones of tolerance

Consider the following example. A building society customer wishes to deposit some cash in her savings account and expects the entire service encounter, from entering the branch premises to leaving it, to take four minutes (the desired service level). However, the customer appreciates that a range of other variables might result in a somewhat longer service encounter. For example, there may be a number of other customers waiting to be served, one of whom may have a particularly large amount of coins and cash to deposit. Our customer may be willing to accept a total service encounter time of 12 minutes based upon her expectations of likely factors. In this case the difference between 12 minutes (the adequate service level) and four minutes (the desired service level) represents the zone of tolerance. A service encounter that is of a duration within the zone of tolerance will result in a positive assessment of service quality. However, a service encounter that is quicker will result in a highly favourable impression of the quality of service delivered. Conversely, a service encounter falling below the adequate level will result in a negative assessment.

Progress check

•   In the context of services marketing, the best way of thinking about quality is in relation to the ability of an organisation to deliver what consumers want and expect.

•   There are different models of service quality. The European (Nordic) perspective focuses on difference between technical (what is delivered) and functional quality (how it is delivered).

•   The North American model focuses on five key dimension (Reliability, Assurance, Tangibles, Empathy and Responsiveness) and looks to measure quality based on comparisons of what customers expect and what they receive.

As can be imagined, the zone of tolerance is a highly flexible concept which varies not only from customer to customer and according to the nature of the given transaction, but may also vary for the same customer depending upon the circumstances surrounding a given transaction. Zones of tolerance vary across individuals because of different personal situations, differences in past experience and also different service philosophies. The zone of tolerance also varies across the five key dimensions customers use in evaluating a service, namely reliability, tangibles, responsiveness, assurance and empathy. Reliability, or keeping the service promise, is thought to have a far narrower zone of tolerance than other aspects of a service. Zones of tolerance may also be affected by service context – for example, when faced with an emergency situation, zones of tolerance may be narrower than in a non-emergency situation. And finally, marketing activities may affect the size of the zone of tolerance marketing communications place an important role in creating expectations – overpromising in marketing communications can raise the level of "adequate" expectations and this can reduce the size of the zone of tolerance. Research insight 15.2 provides an illustration of the use of the zones of tolerance concept in understanding service quality for life insurance and stockbroking in Singapore.

The practical consequences of this model are manifold. For example, the development of customer advocacy is likely to result from customer experiences that are consistently above the upper limit of the zone of tolerance. Companies would do well to develop a firm grasp of the relative importance of zones of tolerance in respect of the more critical encounters

Research insight 15.2: using the zone of tolerance concept to understand the impact of service quality on loyalty and satisfaction

Notwithstanding all of the arguments and evidence about the benefits of service quality, there is still research that points to the fact the customers who claim to be satisfied will still defect (Jones and Sasser, 1995). Specifically, it has been suggested that those customers who report themselves as being "satisfied" as opposed to "very satisfied" are less likely to be loyal and more likely to defect.

Durvasula, Lobo, Lysonski and Mehta (2006) argue that we may be able to gain a better insight into this phenomenon by looking at the dimensions of service quality in more detail and particularly by exploring the dynamics of expectations and perceptions by using the concept of the zone of tolerance and the distinction between the desired level of service quality and the adequate level of service quality. Specifically, they seek to explore whether delivering the desired level of service quality rather than just an adequate level will increase satisfaction and reduce intention to defect.

The authors argue that using the zone of tolerance and the associated Measure of Service Superiority (MSS – based on desired expectations) and Measure of Service Adequacy (MSA based on adequate expectations) will provide more of a better and more reliable measure of service quality. These measures will contain more diagnostic information and as such will enable a better understanding of the relationship between service quality, satisfaction and behavioural intention.

Empirical evidence was collected from customers in Singapore and focused on life insurance and stockbrokerage. All respondents had purchased these services within the previous 12 months.

The initial analysis confirmed that service quality was appropriately represented by the five RATER dimensions. In terms of perceived quality, the data suggested that stockbrokers performed best in terms of assurance aspect while life insurers scored highly on both assurance and reliability. In general, customer perceptions and expectations of service quality were higher for life insurers than for stockbrokers.

Specific attention was then focused on MSS (which measures the gap between perceived quality and desired expectations) and MSA (which measures the gap between perceived quality and adequate expectations). Stockbrokers were found to have marginally negative MSA scores (i.e. provide less than adequate service) in the areas of tangibles, reliability and responsiveness while life insurers have negative MSA scores in relation to assurances. MSS was negative for all dimensions for both industries indicating that that actual service is consistently poorer than desired service. The differences between the two industries are small and not statistically significant.

While MSA was positive or marginally negative (perceived service quality was close to adequate expectations), MSS was clearly negative (perceived quality significantly less than desired expectations) suggesting considerable scope for service quality improvements.

A correlation analysis suggests that the relationship with relevant outcomes (e.g. satisfaction, attitudinal loyalty and behavioural loyalty) is stronger for quality perceptions than it is for quality expectations. The impact of expectations appears to be stronger for stockbrokers than it is for life insurers. Both MSA and MSS have a stronger impact on outcomes in life insurance than they do in stockbrokerage. At a more disaggregated level, reliability had a particularly strong relationship with the outcome variables for stockbrokers, while for life insurance the strongest relationship was observed for assurance.

Source: Durvasula, Lobo, Lysonski and Mehta (2008).

of primary target segments. As a rule of thumb, the more crucial a given service feature, the narrower the zone of tolerance and the greater the likelihood of engendering customer negative evaluations of the service. By knowing what the critical service encounters are, a company can take action to ensure high standards of delivery.

What this highlights is the importance of being able to monitor customer experiences of service quality. As well as using frameworks such as SERVQUAL to gather quantitative assessments of customer experiences, there are other approaches and Marketing in practice 15.1 explains how Nationwide developed its customer experience tracker to ensure that it has a good understanding the way in which consumers evaluate the service quality they receive.

 Marketing in practice 15.1: Nationwide's Experience Tracker

Historically, Nationwide has been well-regarded as a financial institution in the UK. Its brand is significant in the public imagination, which is at least in part down to its mutual status and unique position as the world's biggest building society. But to maintain this position, it's important that the business understands the varied needs of its customers and members so as to remain relevant in an increasingly competitive UK banking market.

When the Covid-19 pandemic hit, tactics that had developed over many years to understand what their customers wanted became obsolete overnight. It was clear a new solution was needed. For Nationwide, this was the Nationwide Experience Tracker, or ET: a bespoke, real-time customer sentiment and feedback platform.

ET is a tool which processes responses from Nationwide customers with advanced text analytics, helping to inform decision-making around the building society's customer service in call centres, in-branch and online. As lockdowns progressed and the UK went through one of its biggest ever peacetime crises, the role of financial services firms and the way people used money changed – meaning that when it became more difficult for businesses to understand what customers wanted, it was becoming even more important to do just that.

ET, which was designed and built by Kantar, mines data from customer feedback across a range of channels. During 2020, these insights helped Nationwide to:

- Adapt to the changing world. Nationwide was able to change opening times and introduce self-service capabilities so people could continue to use branches safely. Elsewhere the real-time feedback helped branches make social distancing more comfortable – for example, branch staff were able to provide shade and water for customers who felt tired and dehydrated while queuing in the summer. Customer satisfaction with in-branch experience rose from 69% to 81%.
- Further improve its online services. During the Covid period the loss of the ability to go to branch led to frustration from customers about the need to use digital channels instead, which led satisfaction with Nationwide's digital services to fall to a low of 66%. ET identified the issues for new users, which the building society could address such as difficulties logging in and problems with reliable connection. Since then, continual investment in digital services has led the same satisfaction statistic to hit 80.7% in August 2023.
- Introduce a "Close the Loop" function, where dissatisfied members were contacted directly by branch staff to respond to their feedback with a human touch. This approach resulted in 75% of those members reporting an improvement in experience with Nationwide.
- Continue its Tea and Tech education initiative throughout the pandemic, which helped people who struggled with the digital alternatives to face to face banking that the Covid pandemic temporarily imposed on them.

Ultimately, ET's contributions helped Nationwide drive changes which reduced the proportion of members contacting the building society with Covid-related questions from 14.1% in April 2020 to zero that August.

As restrictions eased across the economy, it became clear that the lessons learned from the experience tracker would be valuable in hitting future corporate objectives and in understanding how Nationwide was performing against its core purposes: to support communities and provide a good way to bank.

Source: The People Experience Team, Nationwide Building Society

In addition to identifying the areas that would be important to consumers when evaluating service quality, Parasurmanan, Zeithaml and Berry (1985) also developed a model of service delivery to help managers understand how problems might arise in the service delivery process and how service delivery could be managed to ensure high levels of quality. This will be discussed further in the Section 15.5.

15.4.3 Integrating the Nordic and the North American perspectives

The Nordic and North American perspectives share many similarities in the way in which they view service quality. In 2001, Brady and Cronin proposed a framework which sought to integrate the key components of the major models of service quality; this proposed a

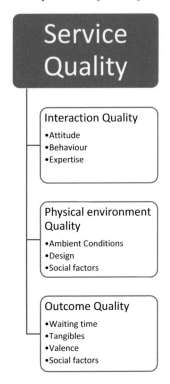

Figure 15.7 Integrating perspectives on service quality

Source: Adapted from Brady and Cronin (2001)

hierarchical approach to the assessment of service experience by consumers as shown in Figure 15.7.

Brady and Cronin propose that there are three primary determinants of perceived service quality, namely interaction quality, the quality of the physical environment, and the quality of the outcome of the service experience. Interactive quality is viewed as being a function of how employees' attitudes, behaviours and expertise influence the quality of a service interaction. This component of the model illustrated the importance attached to the people element of the marketing mix, an issue that will be discussed further in Chapter 18. The role played by the physical environment quality is held to be a function of the design and layout of the environment, the nature of the usage level taking place (social factors) and the atmosphere that is perceived (ambient conditions). The ambient conditions are determined by mood-setting devices such as lighting, music and interior design. As discussed earlier, with the changing role of bank branches, more attention is being paid to design issues to create an environment which actively attracts customers. When Metro Bank launched in the UK, it paid particular attention to branch design creating a welcoming and relaxed environment which tried to remove any artificial barriers between staff and customers.

Finally, outcome quality is held to be a function of waiting time, tangibles and value. Waiting time is self-evident and the above explanation regarding zones of tolerance well illustrates how these impact upon customer perception. Tangible evidence closely relates to the physical evidence component of the marketing mix.

"Valence" is a term used by Brady and Cronin to express whether the customer considers the ultimate outcome of the service experience to have been good or bad. This judgement is an overarching evaluation by the customer irrespective of how they evaluate other components of the service encounter. For example, consider the case of a consumer approaching a bank for a home improvement loan. Her perceptions of the interaction quality and physical environment will be of no consequence if her loan application is refused. In other words, the appraisal of whether the core need was satisfied (valence) takes precedence over the other eight elements that influence the consumer's perception of service quality. It should be noted that the reliability, responsiveness and empathy components of the SERVQUAL model have been incorporated into the model as descriptors of the nine sub-dimensions of quality in themselves.

 Stop and think?

When you think about the quality of the service you experience, what are the aspects that matter most to you? Are these consistent with any of the models that you have encountered here?

Brady and Cronin have subjected their model to empirical analysis and the results provide support for its validity. In that sense, they have succeeded in consolidating a range of service quality conceptualisations into a robust, comprehensive and multi-dimensional framework. It provides a useful platform for practitioners as they seek to raise levels of perceived quality. Managers can use the model as a means of enabling them to identify what defines service quality, how service quality perceptions are formed, and the significance attached to the place in which the service experience occurs.

15.5 The gap model of service quality

We have already explained the idea that service quality can be based on a comparison between expectations and performance. Where there is a gap between what customers expect and what they get, this gap can be related to four other gaps in the service delivery process. In simple terms, if the delivered service does not meet customer expectations (GAP 5), this can be explained by any of four other gaps in the service delivery process; these are:

- misunderstanding expectations (Gap 1),
- wrong specifications (Gap 2),
- failure to deliver (Gap 3),
- overpromising (Gap 4).

The service delivery process and the gaps are outlined in Figure 15.8.

Delivering a quality service requires a good understanding of what customers expect. Given their knowledge of what customers expect, managers must then set appropriate standards for the service and ensure that staff will deliver a service of the specified standard. It is important to ensure that what is promised to customers by the organisation's marketing communications is consistent which what the organisation is able to deliver. Gaps in the

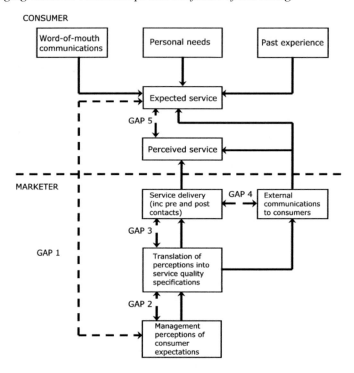

Figure 15.8 The Gap Model of service delivery

Source: Adapted from Parasuraman, Zeithaml and Berry (1985)

service delivery process can arise at key points throughout this process as Parasuraman, Zeithaml and Berry (1985) explain. Each of the four main gaps will be discussed in turn.

• **Misunderstanding expectations (Gap 1)**
This gap arises when senior management do not understand what consumers actually expect from the service. There are a number of reasons why this might happen. A failure to undertake market research may lead to a poor understanding of what customers actually want. Equally important as a cause of Gap 1 may be poor upward communication – front line employees are in regular contact with customers and probably have a good understanding of their needs and expectations. However, if management are unwilling to listen to front line staff, then this knowledge and understanding will be wasted. Where organisations have good relationships with their customers, Gap 1 is less likely to occur because the organisation will have built up a high level of knowledge about customer needs and expectations.

Clearly then, to deal with Gap 1, attention must be paid to increasing understanding of consumers through additional market research, through encouraging flows of information from front line staff and to building stronger relationships with customers.

• **Wrong specifications (Gap 2)**
The second gap arises if service specifications are not consistent with the expected service. This would imply that the company specifies and designs a particular service but the features, are not what customers would expect. There are several reasons why this gap may arise. Some services may be very difficult to standardise, managers may think that customer

expectations are unreasonable and cannot be met. In some cases, the commitment to service quality may be missing and consequently there will be a lack of interest in setting sensible services specifications. Closing Gap 2 means ensuring that the service that is specified matches the service that consumers expect. To do this, it is essential to ensure that top management is committed to providing service quality. Once that commitment is present, it is necessary to ensure that customer service expectations are part of the design process – that they are built into service development. Key service features must be identified (what is important to the consumer) and sensible specifications identified based on consumer priorities. Thus, for example, if customers expect a quick service when making a loan application, then managers must identify what "quick" means (is it a response in one day or in one week?). If customers also expect low interest rates and flexible repayments, then the relative importance of these should be identified and more attention paid to the feature that is most important. Where services can be standardised, they should as this allows one set of standards to be used rather than multiple sets of standards.

Senior managers do play a key role with respect to Gap 2. Demonstrating a firm commitment to setting and using customer-defined performance standards can have a major impact on closing service quality Gap 2.

• Failure to deliver (Gap 3)
Service quality Gap 3 arises when the actual service that is delivered does not match up with the service that was specified. Even if a sensible, customer-driven specification is in place, there is no guarantee that the service that is delivered to the customer will meet this standard. There are many reasons why Gap 3 (failure to deliver) might arise. To deliver to a certain specification requires that appropriate resources (people, systems, and technology) exist and are supported. Broadly speaking, Gap 3 may arise because of problems with human resource policies, because of problems with customer participation, because of problems with intermediaries and because of problems with respect to managing supply and demand. If employees are not committed, willing and able to do their job well, then problems will arise with respect to the delivery of the service. If customers do not understand what they are meant to do, then there will be problems with the service that is delivered. If a service provider relies on an intermediary to distribute the service, then there may be difficulties in controlling the quality of what the intermediary does. Finally, if the organisation cannot manage supply and demand, then it may be difficult to deliver that appropriate quality when levels of demand are high and staff are under pressure.

Closing Gap 3 requires that considerable attention is paid to staff. To get a high level of performance and ensuring that high quality service is delivered requires that the organisation:

- Recruits the right people – with the skills and knowledge to delivery quality service,
- Ensures that there is a sensible reward system, so that employees receive rewards (monetary and non-monetary) for delivering high quality service,
- Ensures that there is a good fit between technology and people – i.e. that people have the right technology for the job,
- Encourages empowerment and teamwork so that staff can adjust and adapt to differences in customer needs.

Equally importantly, the organisation must make sure that customers know what they should be doing and how they should contribute to the delivery process. This requires effective communication to ensure that customers know what they should do – for example, what information they need to provide, what forms they need to complete, etc.

Finally, attempting to synchronise demand and supply will be important to ensure that resources are not overstretched and quality standards can be maintained. Equally important is the need to ensure good cooperative working relationships with intermediaries to ensure that they will be motivated to deliver the standard of service that the organisation expects.

• Overpromising (Gap 4)

The fourth gap arises when the organisation promises a better service than it actually delivers. This raises customer expectations and when the delivered service does not match those expectations, quality will be assessed as poor. A failure to deliver what was promised may arise for a number of reasons. The two most important are first, poor information and second, pressure to overpromise. Poor information flows between marketing and the rest of the organisation may result in marketing having a poor understanding of what the organisation will be able to do and thus the claims that marketing makes will be inaccurate. Equally, there may be a tendency to overpromise in marketing communications, to outperform competitors and to make the organisation appear in the most favourable light. Addressing Gap 4 requires that attention is paid to ensuring good, accurate communications between marketing and those involved in the service delivery process. This communication should provide clear and accurate information about what consumers can expect and this information should then be integrated into all marketing communications to ensure that customers receive a consistent and honest message.

If the management of the service delivery process can focus on these potential gaps and identify ways of addressing them, then the potential for the organisation to be able to deliver the kind of quality that customers expect will be much greater.

Progress check

- In order to think about how best to manage service delivery, the Gap Model presents overall service quality as the gap between expectations and perceptions of the service and links this to four other gaps.
- The service delivery gaps relate to first, a misunderstanding of what consumers want, second, a failure to appropriately specify the service, third a failure to deliver the specified service and fourth a failure to communicate what customers can expect.
- Understanding these gaps and addressing them will enable an organisation to deliver the level of quality that customers want and expect.

15.6 The outcomes of service quality

As the introduction mentioned, if an organisation can deliver a high quality of service, its customers will receive better value and are more likely to be satisfied. In turn, satisfied customers are more likely to be retained and to be loyal. The nature of customer satisfaction and its measurement are discussed in more detail in the next chapter, as is the nature of value. Loyalty is seen as a particularly significant outcome of service quality, value and customer satisfaction because of its impact on profit, as mentioned earlier. Marketing in practice 15.2 explores how Nationwide uses information from its Experience Tracker to improve what it delivers to its customers and secure positive service outcomes.

Marketing in practice 15.2: Nationwide – using the ET and the members-only ISA

The Nationwide Experience Tracker (ET) dashboard is regularly reviewed by the CEO to monitor the level of satisfaction with the business and its services and the dashboard's insight is referred to daily in making decisions across the business.

For example, during the pandemic frustration increased among longstanding members due to a perceived neglect of savings rates for loyal members. This informed the design of Nationwide's members-only ISA, which led the market in interest rates when it was launched in March 2021. By contrast to high street banks, which at the time were mainly seeking to bring in new customers, Nationwide's understanding of its members led it to distinguish itself in the market with this product.

The result was a record ISA season for Nationwide, despite a challenging interest rate environment – to the point that the volume of applications led to delays in processing. The knock-on effect on satisfaction was picked up by the ET in May 2021 and led to targeted action on processing times, staff knowledge, and the provision of adequate materials to members, leading to a rapid recovery in satisfaction scores over the following months.

As well as helping set the course for the development of new products, the ET is used to help analyse the impact of business decisions on member sentiment. Nationwide's Fairer Share initiative was launched in 2023 to reinvest the building society's profits in direct payments to its members. Given its mutual structure, Nationwide has no need to pay dividends, and so introduced the scheme to share £340m of its profits in £100 payments to eligible members with both a current account and a savings or mortgage product.

The initiative was a success, with positive media coverage and social media discussion. ET statistics showed that within a week 71% of customers were aware of Fairer Share, with a satisfaction rate of 84.3% -- with FS providing a 13.2% increase in satisfaction. 51% of members felt more positive about Nationwide after becoming aware of the initiative.

Despite this success, there were still questions to be answered. The ET flagged concerns among a small minority of members about eligibility – with some ineligible customers feeling they should have received payments. The ET found that these complaints were flagged most often through Nationwide's digital services, which helped inform the decisions the team made about how best to make online communications as clear as possible. As well as these kinds of subtle changes, insight from the experience tracker helped inform considerations of how the proposition could evolve in any future iterations.

These changes, made in-flight during the wider campaign, allowed the business to tailor its comms strategies for these members and maintain the high level of satisfaction felt with the Fairer Share initiative on an ongoing basis.

As of 2023, Nationwide has been number one for customer satisfaction in the UK for eleven years running. The building society also measures its position for satisfaction across all sectors and as of January 2023 had placed in joint 28th position out of 267 major organisations, with a score that was 4.9 points ahead of the all-sector average.

The lessons learned from the experience tracker have ultimately helped to cement Nationwide's position as a leading brand in the UK financial services market – especially with Nationwide's mutual status, which allows the business to continue to sharpen its focus on member experience rather than shareholder profits, both now and in the future.

Source: The People Experience Team, Nationwide Building Society

	Retained customer	Customer not retained
Positive attitude to provider	Loyal/apostle	Mercenary
Negative attitude to provider	Hostage	Defector/terrorist

Figure 15.9 Attitudinal and behavioural loyalty

Source: Adapted from Jones and Sasser (1995)

The Nationwide example highlights the importance of engaging productively with existing consumers – loyal consumers. Loyalty is potentially a complex construct – it has both attitudinal dimensions (i.e. what the customer thinks or feels about an organisation) and a behavioural dimension (i.e. what the customer does – and whether they repurchase). Customers may feel very positively towards an organisation and thus be attitudinally loyal, but their situation may mean that no further purchases are made. Conversely, a customer may feel very negatively about an organisation (be attitudinally disloyal) but continue to purchase, perhaps because of the lack of alternatives (see for example Dick and Basu, 1994). The different configurations of attitudinal and behavioural loyalty are outlined in Figure 15.9.

Customers classified as "Loyal/Apostle" are those who have positives views about their experiences with the organisation and continue to make purchases. "Mercenaries" may have positive evaluations of an organisation but choose not to repurchase for a variety of reasons. Consumers buying mutual funds may, for example, choose to spread their business across a number of funds to spread risk, despite having very positive experiences of a given investment company. Other customers may move savings around between different providers in search of the best rates and not because they have any negative views of the service provided by an individual organisation. Customers in the "Defector/terrorist" category have both a negative evaluation and decide not to repurchase. Such customers have clearly had very poor experience with an organisation and thus more likely to engage in negative word of mouth as a result of their experiences. The final category, "hostages", are those customers who have negative attitudes to the organisation but continue to repurchase because of a lack of alternatives. Such customers appear to be loyal (because they continue to purchase) but are not and are potentially vulnerable to attractive offers from competitors. For example, many bank current account customers are thought to fall into this category – they do not have a positive view of the service they receive but do not switch their bank account because the process is too complex and they perceive few differences between competing banks.

To realise fully the benefits of loyalty depends on having customers who both continue to repurchase and also have positive attitudes. With such customers, there are a variety of potential financial and non-financial outcomes which provide the basis for arguments around the "economics of customer retention":

- Better knowledge of customer needs – which means that the organisation is better able to meet customer needs and at lower costs (because there is no need to gather new information);

- Positive word of mouth – customers who are attitudinally loyal are likely to say positive things about the organisation and this can be an important (and cost effective) form of marketing – particularly in financial services;
- Spread costs of acquisition – financial services organisations spend a lot of money (marketing expenses) to acquire customers. When a customer is behaviourally loyal, those costs can be spread out over a much longer relationship and over more transactions;
- Less price sensitive – attitudinally loyal customers are thought to be less price sensitive because they value the relationship with the organisation;
- Cross-selling – attitudinally loyal customers are more likely to purchase additional products from a particular organisation.

Overall, then, creating customers who are both attitudinally and behaviourally loyal can mean reduced costs and higher revenues and thus can have a positive effect on profitability as argued in the service profit chain framework. Discussions in previous chapters have noted that it may be unwise to assume that all retained customers are profitable. In particular, Reinartz and Kumar (2002) have suggested that some retained customers will be "barnacles" – retained but unprofitable. This may arise because such customers are more rather than less price sensitive; that they are aware of their potential value to the organisation and demand special treatment making them more rather than less expensive to serve. If such customers do not engage in positive word of mouth, then the benefits of retention to the organisation may also be curtailed. While it is important to be aware that not all retained customers are profitable, this should not detract from the importance and value of customer loyalty and retention to financial services organisations.

As shown in Chapter 14, there is a developing body of research in financial services that seeks to highlight the beneficial outcomes of service quality. The evidence for service quality having an impact on financial performance is partial, although Loveman (1998) has pointed to a positive relationships between service quality/customer satisfaction and profitability in banking. Yeung and Ennew (2001) use data from the American Consumer Satisfaction Index (ACSI) and show that customer satisfaction with financial services providers has a significant positive impact on a variety of measures of financial performance across the period 1994–99. Other researchers have demonstrated that service quality does have a positive impact on satisfaction (e.g. Crosby and Stephens, 1987; Herington and Weaver, 2009), retention (e.g. Miguel-Dávila et al., 2010) willingness to recommend and willingness to continue purchasing (e.g. Ladhari, Ladhari and Morales, 2011). Thus, while there may be some debate about the precise nature of the outcomes of service quality, there is strong evidence to suggest significant benefits for organisations that focus attention on the delivery of high-quality customer service.

15.7 Service failure and recovery

Of course, we should remember that however much attention is paid to ensuring a high quality of service, there will be service failures – something will go wrong, a mistake may be made and customers may complain. For example, there may be a genuine mistake, staff may be absent meaning that a particular customer cannot be dealt with properly, some aspect of technology may fail, etc. A poor service (service failure) will result in customer dissatisfaction and this in turn will prompt a variety of responses which may include complaining, negative word of mouth and decisions not to repurchase. If it is impossible to avoid service failures and dissatisfaction, then it becomes essential for organisations to understand how to minimise their adverse effects. There is a growing body of evidence to suggest that effective service recovery can generate a range of positive customer responses with complaint handling being seen as a key element in service recovery. Responding effectively to consumer complaints can have a significant impact on satisfaction, repurchase intentions and the spread of word of mouth.

In order to be able to deal with service failure, an organisation must first be aware that a failure has occurred, and this means making it easy for customers to complain. All too often, customers experience a service failure but for some reason – too much effort or the expectation that nothing will be done – they may choose not to complain to the provider. They may simply switch to another provider and/or engage in negative word of mouth. The absence of a formal complaint means that the organisation has no opportunity to address the individual customer's dissatisfaction and no opportunity to learn from that customer's experience. Thus, it makes sense for an organisation to make it easy for customers to complain – perhaps by providing free phone numbers and complaints hotlines, etc. Thus for example, ICICI bank in India promotes its 24-hour customer care hotline and promises customers "We aim to respond to your complaint with efficiency, courtesy and fairness. You can expect a response to your complaint within two business days". Similarly African Bank Investments in South Africa stress a commitment to responding to complaints and provide customers with a three-stage process for lodging a complaint. Such guidance and encouragement is increasingly common as organisations recognise the value of responding to and learning from service failures. In addition to making the complaint process transparent and straightforward, organisations may also consider active research to check that the service delivery has gone well – this again provides the consumer with an opportunity to complain if necessary.

If an organisation is to learn from service failure, then, in addition to knowing that a failure has occurred it is important to have a clear understanding of the type of service failure. If the failure arises in relation to the service delivery, then the appropriate focus of attention may be service operations and design. In contrast, if the failure is a consequence of employee behaviour, then the appropriate response may be to reconsider human resource management policies and practices. Service failure can take many forms. Bitner, Booms and Tetreault (1990) used the critical incident technique to identify and classify three main types of service failure – namely service delivery failures, failures to respond to customers and unsolicited employee actions.

• **Service delivery failures**

Failures in the service delivery system failures generally fall into three categories. First, the service may simply be unavailable – an ATM or website may not work or a key member of staff may be unavailable to serve a particular customer. Second, unreasonably slow service covers any delivery experience which is slow and includes long queues, a website that is slow to respond and any other delay in providing service to a customer. The third category, other core service failures, is deliberately broad to encompass a range of core failures including, for example, errors in money transmission, errors in claims handling and errors in processing service applications.

• **Failure to respond to customer needs**

Customers may have a variety of needs and requests in relation to a particular service – whether explicit or implicit. The second category of failures relates to failures to respond to these needs. Implicit needs are not formally articulated by customers but are nevertheless important. A failure to inform customers about a change in the terms and conditions of a service would constitute a failure to respond to implicit needs. Explicit needs are generally considered to be of four types: (1) special needs, (2) customer preferences, (3) customer errors, and (4) disruptive others. A failure by a financial advisor to select a product that matched an investor's risk preferences would constitute a failure to respond to the special needs of that individual. Similarly a failure to amend the delivery system at the customer's request, as might occur when a customer requests a different schedule of loan repayments, would be a failure to respond to customer preferences. The third type of explicit request occurs when the customer makes an error and the employee fails to respond appropriately as could occur with a lost credit or ATM card or a failure to make a payment on time. Finally, service failures may occur when employees are required to resolve a dispute between customers.

- **Unprompted and unsolicited employee actions**
Service failures may also occur when employees engage in behaviours that fall outside the normal, expected service delivery system. Included in this category of service failure would be behaviours such as poor employee attitudes, rudeness, ignoring customers, discriminatory behaviour, unfairness and dishonesty.

There are a variety of recommendations about the best way to manage service recovery. For example, Bell and Zemke (1987) suggested a five-stage strategy for dealing with customer complaints:

- Apology: preferably a first-person apology rather than a corporate apology. Should acknowledge that a failure has occurred.
- Prompt response: once a failure has been recognised, then a speedy response to attempt to rectify the situation is essential, as far as is possible.
- Empathy: the process of dealing with the customer's complaint should be characterised by an understanding of the customer's situation.
- Symbolic atonement: the customer should be offered some form of compensation that is appropriate to the nature of the failure (e.g. refunding service charges, small gifts, discounted or free services in the future).
- Follow-up: monitoring customer satisfaction with the recovery process.

Bitner, Booms and Tetreault (1990) suggested a similar approach focused on four key elements.

- Acknowledgement of the problem,
- Explanation of the reason for the failure,
- Apology where appropriate,
- Compensation such as a free ticket, meal or drink.

In the banking sector, research by Lewis and Spyrakopoulos (2001) highlighted the importance of ensuring that service recovery resulted in consumers getting what they originally expected, even if this required exceptional treatment. Empathy and speed were also identified as important elements in the recovery process. This study suggested that consumers' recovery expectations were generally reasonable, although customers with long-standing relationships with their bank tended to be more demanding when they experienced service failures. In a more recent study, Jones and Farquhar (2007) look at minor service failures in banking and the impact of service recovery on loyalty. They report low levels of satisfaction with service recovery and consequent negative impacts on switching intentions and intention to recommend. Failures in the area of charging and general account management were found to have a particularly negative impact.

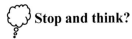 **Stop and think?**

Have you ever complained about a financial service or indeed any kind of service – or do you know someone who has? What prompted the complaint? How well do you think it was resolved? What worked and what didn't?

A particular theme in service recovery research has been the role of perceived justice in understanding the effectiveness of service recovery strategies (e.g. Tax, Brown and Chandrashekaran, 1998). Perceived justice focuses on the extent to which customers perceive the process and outcomes of service recovery to be just. Where levels of perceived justice are high, consumers are more likely to be satisfied. The three dimensions of perceived justice are the fairness of the resolution procedures (procedural justice), the interpersonal communications and behaviours (interactional justice) and the outcomes (distributive justice). These are demonstrated in Figure 15.10.

A growing number of empirical studies have applied perceived justice to examine consumer responses to complaints. Blodgett, Hill and Tax (1997) used retail-based scenarios to demonstrate the importance of interactional justice as an influence on subsequent consumer behaviour. In a cross-sectoral study, Tax, Brown and Chandrashekaran (1998) present evidence for the importance of all three dimensions of perceived justice in generating positive evaluations of complaint handling.

One factor that is key to effective service recovery is ensuring that front line staff are empowered and encouraged to deal with customer complaints and problems as they happen.

Procedural justice

• Factors such as the delay in processing the complaint, process control, accessibility, timing/speed, and flexibility to adapt to the customer's recovery needs.

Interactional justice

• The manner in which people are treated during the complaint handling process including elements such as courtesy and politeness exhibited by personnel, empathy, effort observed in resolving the situation, and the firm's willingness to provide an explanation as to why the failure occurred.

Distributive justice

• Focuses on the perceived fairness of the outcome of the service encounter. In effect, distributive justice is concerned with the level and nature of apologies and compensations.

Figure 15.10 Dimensions of perceived justice

Source: Tax, Brown and Chandrashekaran, (1998)

They should be able to use their judgement and take the initiative in solving customer problems. Indeed, one of the things that distinguishes many of the world's best service providers is the ability of their staff to deal efficiently and effectively with service failure. Like service quality, there are good reasons for investing in service recovery. Successful service recovery can have a positive impact on customer loyalty. In addition, the process of dealing with and resolving customer complaints can provide valuable insights into the nature of the service delivery process and help the organisation to identify areas that may require further attention and development.

15.8 Summary and conclusion

This chapter has focused attention on service quality as a central component of service value. It has explained that service quality is increasingly important in financial services as it provides a source of competitive advantage. It can also contribute to higher levels of profitability because high levels of quality can increase customer satisfaction and loyalty. These benefits mean that organisations must pay considerable attention to managing service delivery and ensuring that customers experience a high-quality service.

In services, quality is based on the customer's perception of what is delivered. In particular, the consumer's assessment of service quality is based on a comparison of the service that was expected with the actual service received. There are different ways of making this comparison; one approach suggests that consumers will consider both functional and technical dimensions of service quality. Another approach suggests that consumers will make comparisons across aspects of service such as tangibles, assurance, reliability, empathy and responsiveness. Whichever approach is adopted, the assessment of service quality across these dimensions can help managers identify the areas in which improvements should be made.

To determine how best to manage the delivery of service, it was suggested that we should think about quality as being a gap between customer expectations of a service and the service actually received. This gap could then be related to four problem areas (gaps) – namely misunderstanding customer expectations, failure to get the right service specifications, failure to deliver to specifications and overpromising about the quality of the service. To manage the delivery of a high-quality service requires the careful management of people, processes and systems to attempt to ensure that managers understand what customers want, that they specify the right service, that staff are able to deliver to specifications and that the market makes accurate promises. This management process should lead to a high level of service quality; it is probably impossible to guarantee that the organisation will always get its service delivery right. Some service failures are bound to occur and organisations must have a clear strategy for dealing with failures and solving customers' problems.

Learning outcomes

Having completed this chapter, you should now be able to:

1. **Explain the importance of service quality in the marketing of financial services.**
    Service quality plays a central role in the marketing of financial services. It is effectively the customers overall assessment of what they receive both the core service and the broader customer experience.

2. Understand the basic principles of the service-profit chain (SPC).

The starting point for the SPC is the extent to which an organisation is able to provide the right quality of support to employees to enable them to serve customers effectively (usually described as internal service quality). Employees who are satisfied in their job, who are well-motivated and empowered will deliver a high-quality service to customers. This high quality is the foundation for delivering enhanced service value. Value will, in turn, lead to increased levels of customer satisfaction and retention. Retained customers bring value to organisations (they are often easier to serve, may generate better margins and will act as advocates). Satisfied and retained customers generate higher margins and better profits. In essence, the service profit chain highlights the important links between how an organisation manages itself internally, the impact of this on the experience of customers and the benefits in terms of organisational performance.

3. Understand the nature of quality in financial services.

Quality in financial services is most commonly viewed from a consumer perspective and their assessments of the service they receive. Customer perceptions are what matter. There are different models of service quality. The European (Nordic) perspective focuses on difference between technical (what is delivered) and functional quality (how it is delivered). The North American model focuses on five key dimension (Reliability, Assurance, Tangibles, Empathy and Responsiveness) and looks to measure quality based on comparisons of what customers expect and what they receive.

4. Review approaches to the management of service quality.

One of the simplest ways of thinking about the management of service quality is to start from the idea that poor quality arises when what customers reasonabley expect is not what is delivered. This gap in a customer's service experience can be related to four other gaps: a failure to understand what customers really want, a failure to specify an appropriate service, a failure to deliver the planned service and a failure to accurately communicate to customers what they should expect. Once these gaps are identified and understood, organisations can focus on how best to eliminate them via their marketing and operational processes.

5. Understand the importance of service recovery.

However well service delivery is managed there will always be some service failures – something will go wrong, a mistake may be made and customers may complain. A service failure will result in dissatisfaction and this in turn will prompt a variety of responses which may include complaining, negative word of mouth and decisions not to repurchase. If it is impossible to avoid service failures, organisations must understand how to minimise their adverse effects. There is a growing body of evidence to suggest that effective service recovery can generate a range of positive customer responses with complaint handling being seen as a key element in service recovery. Responding effectively to consumer complaints can have a significant impact on satisfaction, repurchase intentions and the spread of word of mouth.

Review questions

1. Why is service quality so important in financial services?
2. What is the difference between functional and technical quality?
3. Explain the difference between Gap 1, Gap 2 and Gap 3 in the gap model of service quality.
4. What are the benefits of customer retention?

References

Acheampong, I. and Asamoah, K.A. (2013). Service delivery and business growth among banks in Ghana using the service profit chain model. *International Journal of Global Business*, 6(2), p.57.

Almquist, E., Senior, J. and Block, B. (2016). The elements of value. *Harvard Business Review*, September (available at https://hbr.org/2016/09/the-elements-of-value).

Bell, C. R. and Zemke, R. (1987). Service breakdown: The road to recovery. *Management Review*, 76(10), pp. 32–35.

Bitner, M. J., Booms, B. H. and Tetreault, M. S. (1990). The service encounter: diagnosing favourable and unfavourable incidents. *Journal of Marketing*, 54(1), pp.71–84. https://doi.org/10.1177/002224299005400105

Blodgett, J. G., Hill, D. J. and Tax, S. S. (1997). The effects of distributive, procedural, and inter-actional justice on post-complaint behaviour. *Journal of Retailing*, 73(2), pp. 185–210.

Brady, M. K. and Cronin, J. J. (2001). Some new thoughts on conceptualising perceived service quality: A hierarchical approach. *Journal of Marketing*, 65(3), pp. 34–49.

Buttle, F. (1996). SERVQUAL: Review, critique, research agenda. *European Journal of Marketing*, 30(1), pp. 8–32.

Chicu, D., Valverde, M., Ryan, G., and Batt, R. (2016). The service-profit chain in call centre services. *Journal of Service Theory and Practice*, (26:5), pp. 616–641.

Colgate, M. and Lang, B. (2001). Switching barriers in consumer markets: An investigation of the financial services industry. *Journal of Consumer Marketing*, 18(4), pp. 332–47.

Crosby, L. and Stephens, N. (1987). Effects of relationship marketing on satisfaction, retention, and prices in the life insurance industry. *Journal of Marketing Research*, 24(4), pp. 404–11.

Dick, A. S. and Basu, K. (1994). Customer loyalty: Toward an integrated conceptual framework. *Academy of Marketing Science Journal*, 22(2), pp. 99–113.

Durvasula, S., Lobo, A., Lysonski, S. and Mehta, S. (2006). Finding the sweet spot: A two industry study using the zone of tolerance to identify determinant service quality attributes. *Journal of Financial Services Marketing*, 10(3), pp. 244–59.

Garvin, D. A. (1988). Managing quality. *McKinsey Quarterly*, 3, pp. 61–70.

Grönroos, C. (1984). A service quality model and its marketing implications. *European Journal of Marketing*, 18(4), pp. 36–44

Grönroos, C. (1988). Service quality; the six criteria of good perceived service quality. *Review of Business*, 9(3), pp. 10–13.

Herington, C. and Weaver, S K (2009) E-retailing by banks: E-service quality and its importance to customer satisfaction. *European Journal of Marketing*, 43(9/10), pp. 1220–31.

Heskett, J. L., Jones, T. O., Loveman, G. W., Sasser, J. and Schlesinger, L. (1994). Putting the service profit chain to work. *Harvard Business Review*, 72(2), pp. 164–74.

Heskett, J. L., Jones, T. O., Loveman, G. W., Sasser, J. and Schlesinger, L. (2008). Putting the serviceprofit chain to work. *Harvard Business Review*, 86(7/8), pp. 118–29.

Hogreve, J., Iseke, A., & Derfuss, K. (2022). The service-profit chain: Reflections, revisions, and reimaginations. *Journal of Service Research*, 25(3), 460–477. https://doi.org/10.1177/1094670521 1052410

Jones, H., and Farquhar, J. (2007). Putting it right: service failure and customer loyalty in UK banks. *International Journal of Bank Marketing*, 25(3), pp.161–172. https://doi.org/10.1108/0265232071 0739869

Jones, E. O. and Sasser Jnr, W. E. (1995). Why satisfied customers defect, *Harvard Business Review*, November/December, pp. 2–14.

Kamakura, W. A., Mittal, V., and de Rosa, F. (2002). Assessing the service-profit chain. *Marketing Science*, 21(3), pp. 294–317.

Ladhari, R. (2009). Assessment of the psychometric properties of SERVQUAL in the Canadian banking industry. *Journal of Financial Services Marketing*, 14(1), pp. 70–82.

Ladhari, R., Ladhari, I. and Morales, M. (2011). Bank service quality: Comparing Canadian and Tunisian customer perceptions. *International Journal of Bank Marketing*, 29 (3), pp.224–46, https://doi.org/10.1108/02652321111117502

Larivière, B. (2008). Linking perceptual and behavioral customer metrics to multiperiod customer profitability: A comprehensive service-profit chain application. *Journal of Service Research*, 11(1), p. 3.

Lewis, B. R. and Spyrakopoulos, S. (2001). Service failures and recovery in retail banking: The customers' perspective. *International Journal of Bank Marketing*, 19(1), pp. 37–48.

Loveman, G. W. (1998). Employee satisfaction, customer loyalty and financial performance. *Journal of Service Research*, 1(1), pp. 18–31.

Miguel-Dávila, J., Cabeza-García, L., Valdunciel, L., and Flórez, M. (2010). Operations in banking: The service quality and effects on satisfaction and loyalty. *Service Industries Journal*, 30 (13), pp. 2163–2182.

Mersha, T., Sriram, V., Yeshanew, H., and Gebre, Y. (2012). Perceived service quality in Ethiopian retail banks. *Thunderbird International Business Review*, 54(4), pp. 551–65.

Parasuraman, A., Zeithaml, V. and Malhotra, A. (2005). E-S-QUAL: A multiple-item scale for assessing electronic service quality. *Journal of Service Research*, 7(3), pp. 213–34.

Parasuraman, A., Berry, L. L. and Zeithaml, V. A. (1991). Refinement and reassessment of the SERVQUAL scale. *Journal of Retailing*, 67(4), pp. 420–50.

Parasuraman, A., Zeithaml, V. A. and Berry, L. L. (1985). A conceptual model of service quality and its implications for future research. *Journal of Marketing*, 49(4), pp. 41–50.

Parasuraman, A., Zeithaml, V. A. and Berry, L. L. (1988). SERVQUAL: A multiple item scale for measuring consumer perceptions of service quality. *Journal of Retailing*, 64(1), pp. 14–40.

Reinartz, W. and Kumar, V. (2002). The mismanagement of customer loyalty. *Harvard Business Review*, 80(7), pp. 86-94. https://hbr.org/2002/07/the-mismanagement-of-customer-loyalty

Rucci, J. A., Kirn, S. P. and Quinn, R. T. (1998). The employee – customer – profit chain at Sears. *Harvard Business Review*, 76(1), pp. 83–97.

Silvestro, R. and Cross, S. (2000). Applying the service profit chain in a retail environment: Challenging the 'satisfaction mirror'. *International Journal of Service Industry Management*, 11(3), pp. 244–68.

Tax, S. S., Brown, S. W. and Chandrashekaran, M. (1998). Customer evaluations of service complaint experiences. *Journal of Marketing*, 62(2), pp. 60–76.

Wong, D. H., Rexha, N., and Phau, I. (2008). Re-examining traditional service quality in an e-banking era. *International Journal Of Bank Marketing*, 26 (7), pp. 526–545.

Yeung, M.C.H. and Ennew, C. T. (2001). Measuring the impact of customer satisfaction on profitability: A sectoral analysis. *Journal of Targeting, Analysis and Measurement for Marketing*, 10(2), pp. 106–16.

Zeithaml, V., Parasuraman, A. and Malhotra, A. (2002). Service quality delivery through websites: A critical review of extant knowledge. *Journal of the Academy of Marketing Science*, 30, pp. 362–75.

16 Satisfaction, value, trust and fairness in customer relationships

Learning objectives

At the end of this chapter, you should be able to:

1. Understand the nature of customer satisfaction and customer value,
2. Be aware of the issues associated with measuring and monitoring customer satisfaction,
3. Understand the importance of trust and trustworthiness in organisations' interactions with its customers,
4. Understand the importances of fairness and the implications for marketers.

16.1 Introduction

One of the fundamental principles of marketing is that an organisation can enhance its performance by ensuring that it responds to and satisfies customer needs. This simple idea is at the heart of the service profit chain as outlined in the previous chapter. In the long run, businesses that fail to deliver customer satisfaction go out of business. Thus, there should be no contradiction between seeking to align the interests of owners and consumers. Problems often seem to occur when attempts are made to satisfy the short-term needs of one group to the detriment of the other. For example, a company might seek to achieve above-trend profit growth by a combination of price increases with cost reductions on the input side (e.g. reducing the number of staff, using less well-trained staff). Product margins might receive a short-term boost but competitors and consumers will gradually figure out what is happening and customer defection will occur. On the other hand, a company that is favouring customer preferences for higher quality at lower prices can be expected to achieve short-term growth in market share but will jeopardise the business's long-term viability if profitability is eroded in the process.

The previous chapter introduced the concept of the service profit chain and argued that the quality of service delivered to consumers is one of the main determinants of customer satisfaction because of its impact on value. Satisfaction is then expected to result in increased customer loyalty and improved profits and revenues.

Given that the purpose of marketing is getting and keeping customers, it is axiomatic that marketing's success must be judged in terms of how well customer needs and wants are met. It is not sufficient to rely upon levels of sales as a proxy for customer satisfaction. A business may

DOI: 10.4324/9781003398615-30

well present a superficial appearance of continuing success based upon performance measures that are essentially financially based. Although financial performance measures such as sales value and product margins are clearly important, they are merely financial reflections of consumer behaviour. A bank, for example, may be reporting healthy customer retention rates in a market where there is little competition even though its customers actively dislike the company. However, the appearance of a competitor that is capable of providing better value-for-money and higher customer satisfaction could well steal significant share from the incumbent bank.

Therefore, it is vital that organisations develop the means by which they can acquire a well-founded knowledge of how they are viewed by their customers. Indeed, information about customer perceptions can yield valuable insights well in advance of the impact upon levels of sales. This chapter will explore consumer evaluations of a service with particular reference to both satisfaction and value. The chapter will begin by defining satisfaction and value and will then move on to examine specifically how organisations approach satisfaction measurement. The second part of the chapter then examines issues relating to trust and fairness and their implications for the way in which organisations engage with their customers.

16.2 Consumer evaluations: value and satisfaction

The successful management of relationships with customers depends on ensuring that consumers have good experiences when they consume a service, that they evaluate that service experience positively and thus have a reason to maintain a relationship with a provider and make future purchases. The previous chapter focused attention on service delivery, on customer evaluations of quality and on service recovery. Consumer evaluations of the quality of service provided are clearly an important aspect of their evaluation of the overall experience of dealing with an organisation. More significantly perhaps, the evaluation of service quality is also an important determinant of value and of satisfaction and these latter two outcomes are the focus of attention in the following discussions.

However, it is important to note that there is sometimes a degree of interchangeability, if not indeed confusion, regarding terms such as customer satisfaction, product and service quality and value. All three terms concern the ways in which customers appraise the benefits they receive from engaging in a customer–supplier relationship. Service quality is an evaluation of a particular service offer, judged in relation to customer expectations of the type of service that should be received (i.e. the judgement is made in relation to the consumers' expectations of "excellence"). Quality is generally recognised as an antecedent to customer satisfaction. Value is commonly treated as an outcome of service quality and involves a comparison of the benefits received (including service quality) relative to price or cost. This recognises the possibility that something which is relatively low quality may still deliver value if the costs associated with consumption are equally low. Satisfaction is also an evaluation of a service experience and is commonly conceptualised as a comparison of expectations and perceptions. Unlike quality, expectations are based around what the customer expects that he or she will actually get during consumption, thus giving rise to a judgement of the extent to which consumption has provided fulfilment.

16.2.1 Customer value

Zeithaml (1988) observes that the determination of value is not a simple task in that consumers use the term in a number of different ways about a wide range of attributes and components. She proposes that customers define value in one of four basic ways as shown in Figure 16.1.

> **Low price**
>
> • Value is viewed as being about low price, or what we might call cheapness. Customers buying on the basis that value is low price focus upon the basic functional aspects of a given goods or service, expect a degree of similarity across different product offers and thus focus attention primarily or even exclusively on low price. It might be argued that in motor insurance this particular approach to value is dominant.

> **Everything I want from a service**
>
> • Value is about the extent to which a good or service most closely satisfies a customers wants as well as their needs. Value *as low price* concerns basic need satisfaction, value as "everything I want" is at the opposite end of the spectrum and concerns the satisfaction of a potentially complex and multifaceted set of desires. Private banking is an example of an aspect of financial services where this concept of value might be most relevant.

> **The quality I get for the price I pay**
>
> • This combines the previous two approaches to value. It involves the customer making a trade-off between the range and quality of benefits they receive and the financial sacrifice they make. For example, when buying household contents insurance, the customer might want to ensure they have 'new-for-old' cover, and pay accordingly for it, but be unwilling to pay for comprehensive accidental damage cover for carpets and upholstered furniture.

> **Value is what I get for what I give**
>
> • Value is considered in a measurable way. The customer considers all of the benefits they receive in detail, as well as all of the elements of sacrifice they make. The component of sacrifice comprise time and effort as well as money. For example, a customer might decide that the additional time costs incurred searching for the single best mortgage deal are sufficiently high that they may actually reduce the value associated with the 'best' product. Such a consumer may perceive themselves to have obtained good value by obtaining acceptable product features with little or no search costs and a reasonable price.

Figure 16.1 What does value mean?

Zeithaml (1988) suggests that looking at these somewhat different perspectives on value, that the most appropriate of view of value is one which recognises the trade-off between benefits and costs, defined in their broadest sense, as follows:

> Perceived value is the consumer's overall assessment of the utility of the service based on perceptions of what is received and what is given.

Precise measurement of value is more problematic and exactly how benefits and costs combine to product value is unclear (is it simply the difference between benefits and costs or is it a ratio?). However, what is clear is that value can be increased by either increasing the quality of what is offered or reducing the costs of consumption or a combination of the two. In both cases, it is important to recognise that benefits and costs must be thought of in their broadest sense. For example, benefits are not just functional, they are also emotional – a strong brand that inspires trust and confidence in consumers (and thus reduces risk) can be an important benefit in financial services and may deliver higher value even in the presence of a price that is high relative to the competition. Similarly, on the cost side, we should consider not just price paid but other non-monetary costs of consumption – the increased convenience that smartphone banking offers to certain market segments is effectively enhancing value by reducing the non-monetary costs of consumption.

Organisations need to respond to the value consumers place on their time and convenience and data safety. They want their banks to provide value-add services and products such as spending visualisation tools that help them manage their money better. The provision of such additional, helpful tools arguably creates a sense of higher-lever trust. Consumers trust banks to keep their money safe (base-level trust) but the value-add creates the feeling of well-being and the sense that the bank truly understands their needs and aspirations and will work to provide tools to enable them to reach their financial and life goals.

As discussed in Chapter 13, consumers expect financial services to facilitate and power their lifestyles with minimal effort and interaction needed from them; they just want to be able to trust it's working for them in the background. Financial services providers should be wise to the shifting expectations of customers in an ever more connected world. Consumers are increasingly familiar with purchase processes that are voice driven, app based, paid for with facial recognition and delivered the next few minutes. In comparison, many financial service process can seem old fashioned and dated. The emergence of AI-powered robo-advice, apps that monitor and analyse customer spending and make useful suggestions, micro savings tools such as Moneybox and Plum, all support the demand for convenient, value-add, time-saving products by customers. This expectation will only grow with the development and wider adoption of the Internet of Things. Organisations that can fulfil the value-add expectation with robust data security provision will gain real competitive advantage.

16.2.2 Customer satisfaction

On the face of it, one might imagine that customer satisfaction is a pretty straightforward concept that readily lends itself to evaluation. However, upon further consideration it turns out to be a complex and multifaceted concept which has attracted enormous attention from both the academic and practitioner communities, not least because it is recognised as being of great significance to the well-being of individuals, firms and the economy as a whole. Although it is a crude indicator, Google Scholar returns over 400,000 results for a search of "academic research on customer satisfaction".

Satisfaction is generally recognised as a pleasurable outcome, "a desirable end state of consumption or patronization" (Oliver, 1997, p10). Precise definitions of satisfaction vary but common themes emphasise that it is customers' judgement of the consumption experience formed through some kind of psychological process that involves some form of comparison of what was expected with what was received. This does not preclude the possibility that interim judgements of satisfaction can be made (i.e. part way through the consumption process) and also allows for the possibility that satisfaction judgements may be made after specific transactions or in relation to an accumulated series of transactions. For example, a customer may form a satisfaction judgement relating to a specific encounter with a financial adviser and a satisfaction judgement relating to the overall relationship with that adviser. Similarly, consumers may form satisfaction judgements about specific attributes of a service (e.g. the responsiveness of staff, the amount information provided, branch opening hours, etc.) or about the service overall.

The term "fulfilment" is commonly used in discussions of satisfaction. However, there is a danger in interpreting such a term too narrowly – rather than thinking of satisfaction as simply meeting basic customer requirements, there is an increasing tendency to see satisfaction as being concerned with positive, pleasurable experiences. Some commentators go a stage further and suggest that marketers should go beyond satisfaction and instead focus attention on "delighting" customers (Berman, 2005). Satisfaction will involve a positive experience and the delivery of a service that matches (or possibly exceeds) customer expectations; delight goes a stage further, delivering beyond expectations and generating a stronger emotional response.

What is evident in most discussions of satisfaction (or even delight), is that consumer judgements are made by comparing the service that is experienced against some pre-existing standard. One of the commonest bases for comparison is that of perceptions against expectations (what the consumer predicted he or she would get). This is commonly referred to as the Disconfirmation Model of Satisfaction. In simple terms, when perceptions are less than expectations, the result is a negative disconfirmation resulting in a negative evaluation and a lack of satisfaction. Confirmation of expectations or a situation of positive disconfirmation (performance exceeds expectations) will result in a positive evaluation, usually satisfaction but perhaps also delight. There are clear similarities between this perspective on customer satisfaction and the idea that service quality is derived from the gap between expectations of what should be received and perceptions of what is actually received. The key difference arises in the way in which expectations are specified. As discussed in Chapter 15, in the case of service quality, the starting point for a comparison is some notion of "ideal" expectations (what should I get); in the case of customer satisfaction, the starting point is predicted expectations (what will I get). Expectations are only one comparison standard, although probably the most commonly used. Other comparison standards which may be relevant in satisfaction judgements include customer needs and a sense of what is fair/reasonable (equity theory).

The emergence of online has meant that organisations are able to gain immediate insight into customer sentiment and levels of satisfaction. As discussed in Chapter 14, the social media space allows for transparent and real-time opinion and experiences of brands to be shared. Wise organisations will leverage this in two ways. First, through the use of social media (SM) monitoring software that tracks and reports what is being said in relation to the brand (and other tags should they wish), thus enabling the organisation to listen to what's really being said about them. Second, through the creation and use of proprietary SM channels to allow them to directly engage with customers and drive satisfaction through positive interactions. As consumers often utilise SM to express dissatisfaction, a brand can turn this to their advantage through swift response and resolution, ultimately driving customer satisfaction in a public forum.

16.3 Managing customer expectations

From the discussion so far, it is evident that quality, value and satisfaction are all influenced by the customer's expectations and perceptions in some form or another. While perceptions are effectively a product of the service encounter and should be managed by careful management of service delivery (as discussed in Chapter 15), expectations (whether ideal or predicted) are formed in advance of experiencing the service. As Parasuraman, Berry and Zeithaml (1991) have shown, there are a variety of factors which will affect customer expectations.

The previous experience that the customer has had will be of importance in determining expectations. Poor service experiences will tend to reduce expectations, good past experiences may raise them. However, previous experience may not necessarily relate directly to the exact product or service in question, but may relate to analogous consumption experiences. Even when experiencing a service for the first time, a consumer may form expectations based on experiences elsewhere or their knowledge of the experiences of others. The customer visiting a financial adviser for the first time may draw on experiences with their bank in forming expectations about the nature of the service she will receive and the nature of interactions with the adviser. It is also the case that customers have become accustomed to higher standards of quality, choice and convenience in certain areas of commerce that create benchmarks for completely different product and service categories.

Third-party communication also impacts upon the formation of expectations. This may arise from a number of sources including word-of-mouth information and impressions gleaned from family members, friends, acquaintances and work colleagues. It also includes the views expressed by journalists and media commentators regarding the positive and negative aspects of a product, service or company. Other forms of third-party communication might include evaluations carried out by consumer interest organisations such as Which?. In January 2006 for example, Which? achieved wide publicity for the research it carried out into home equity release products and the resultant comments on their true costs and pitfalls. This information will inevitably have impacted on the expectations of many customers considering the purchase of such products. Similarly, stockbrokers and analysts produce reports on general industry sectors and the prospects for individual companies that inform the expectations of the investment management community.

Zeithaml and Bitner (2003) draw attention to the idea of explicit and implicit service communication as having a role to play in forming expectations. Explicit service communications refer to the formal written and broadcast messages that a company communicates regarding the nature of product and service quality and performance it provides. The danger here is that a company may make claims about its products or services that it does not deliver in practice. There is a well-developed research-based body of literature that demonstrates the ways in which consumers punish companies that overpromise and under-deliver.

Implicit service communication refers to the range of subtle cues that organisations put out about the nature of what they do and how they do it. Included in this are the physical conditions and state of business premises. For example, an untidy financial adviser's office with poorly produced and displayed promotional material could convey an impression of disorganisation and amateurishness that may impact upon negatively customer expectations. Conversely, the elegant marble entrance halls associated with many traditional bank branches may enhance expectations relating to confidence, reliability, trustworthiness, etc.

The values and beliefs system of the individual consumer will also have a bearing upon their expectations for a given company. Clearly, these influences are highly variable and subjective. A customer who attaches considerable importance to social responsibility may have particularly high expectations of this aspect of a financial service provider's behaviour. Equally, an individual with a strong belief in personal service will typically have high expectations of the nature of service provided to customers. Other individual-specific factors may also affect expectations. Expectations may vary according to temporary personal circumstances. For example, a consumer who has lost a credit card may have particularly high expectations about speed of service because of the desire to get the card replaced. A customer experiencing financial difficulties may have high expectations regarding the flexibility of loan repayments.

A financial services provider may believe that it offers a high-quality service to its customers and one which meets their needs at a competitive price. However, customer evaluations are the ultimate arbiter of quality, value and satisfaction. For this reason, it is vital that organisations have in place a strategy for managing customer expectations and perceptions. Ultimately, perceptions are managed through the process of delivering the service to the customer as explained in Chapter 15. The management of expectations is equally important. The discussion of the gap model drew attention to Gap 4 – the difference between what an organisation promised, and what it delivered and highlighted the importance of having a strategy to manage customer expectations. Such a strategy should comprise the following components:

Objectives	How does the organisation want to be perceived by its primary customer segments (think of positioning as discussed in Chapters 7 and 9).
	Consider both aggregate perceptions for the customer experience as well as specifically considering benefits and sacrifice.
Delivery	Ensure that expectations of customers are reflected in product design and planning for the service encounter.
	Ensure that staff understand the required service standards and are supported and motivated to deliver an excellent customer experience.
	Ensure clarity about what customers can and cannot expect from the service, both benefits and sacrifice.
Recovery	Clear policies and procedures are required to ensure effective recovery following a failure to deliver with regard to both benefits and sacrifice.
	Effective service recovery can result in the creation of customer advocacy if handled well. Indeed, quality failures should be seen as valuable opportunities to demonstrate empathy, and responsiveness.
	All too often poor recovery policies and procedures (or indeed their complete absence) served to make a bad situation worse.
Communication	Expectations regarding benefit delivery and sacrifice should be established at the outset and this requires careful communication. It is not sufficient for a company to assume that customers will simply know what to expect.
	Similarly, customers may need to be told when a company is holding prices steady for an additional year or giving them preferential treatment regarding the purchase of an additional product.
Measurement	Processes that facilitate the tracking of perception over time in order to identify positive or adverse trends are necessary.
	Ideally data should be gathered from a range of sources including: customers (formal surveys, complaints, informal) feedback from staff and feedback from external sources such as the media.
	The latter is important given the capacity of the media to have a material impact upon corporate reputations.
Feedback	The results of customer value and satisfaction measurement should be fed back into relevant parts of the organisation and, as appropriate, communicated to customers.
	If measurement shows that a company is delivering high levels of satisfaction to customers and outperforming competitors, this is a positive and reassuring message to customers, staff and other stakeholders.

16.4 The measurement of satisfaction

Most discussions of satisfaction measurement focus primarily on the measurement of customer satisfaction because of its importance as a performance metric. However, as the service
profit chain shows, both employee satisfaction and customer satisfaction may be relevant as
performance metrics, and both will be considered in this section.

16.4.1 Customer satisfaction

So far in this chapter we have established that customer satisfaction is a multifaceted concept and far from one-dimensional. As such, individual managers must form a view on the
nature of satisfaction for their own organisation with regard to factors such as: the need being
fulfilled, degree and variety of competition, segment variations, and how the resultant data
will be used.

As a rule, customer satisfaction is measured by the use of some form of quantitative
survey. It is in the nature of customer satisfaction, and the use that is made of its data,
that it is required to be statistically reliable and robust. For example, its outputs may be
used as the basis for major investment in time, money and systems resources in upgrading
elements of service delivery. Managers responsible for deciding upon and implementing
such investments must only do so on the basis of valid and reliable information. Thus, the
sample size and structure of a customer satisfaction survey must be of a scale and scope that
engenders the necessary confidence.

The starting point for any customer satisfaction survey must be the identification of relevant, business-oriented objectives that will produce clear, unambiguous results. A useful
starting point is deciding which business decisions need to be made and require knowledge
regarding customer satisfaction. In common with any data capture and analysis exercise,
there is no point in doing it unless it plays a role in influencing a business decision. Thus,
customer satisfaction should form an integral part of senior management information flows.
In this way it can influence a range of decisions such as:

- What do we need to do to improve customer retention?
- What do we need to do to get customers to place more business with us?
- Which competitors pose the greater threat and what do we need to do to counter those
  threats?
- What do we need to do to increase market share?
- What opportunities are there to reduce operating costs without harming customer
  satisfaction?
- What should form the basis of future competitive advantage?

The above six business decisions are simply indicative of the range of issues that customer
satisfaction information can inform, as there are many others. Nevertheless, it illustrates the
point that such information lies at the very core of the big issues that determine sustainable
organisational success. The implications of this are clear: first, the conduct of effective customer satisfaction measurement is non-negotiable; second, the highest level of management
must actively engage with the results of such surveys and be prepared to act upon them.
Common failings are either the absence of appropriate customer satisfaction measurement or
the lack of visibility of its findings and ineffective follow-through.

Therefore, the objectives for a customer satisfaction survey (CSS) must be grounded in the nature of the business decisions it will inform. The following list gives an indication of the kind of objectives that might be considered for a CSS:

- What do customers expect from the services we provide?
- To what extent are customers' expectations met by the services they receive from us?
- What level of satisfaction do our customers experience from the individual components that comprise our service?
- Which of our competitors do our customers also use for the provision of services and what levels of satisfaction do they express for each competitor?
- How do levels of customer satisfaction with our services compare with those of our rivals?
- How do customers rate the value-for-money they receive from our services compared with our competitors?
- Which elements of our service do we need to improve in order to achieve higher levels of customer satisfaction?
- Which aspects of our services do customers gain little value from and consider to be of little relevance to their experience as a customer?
- How does satisfaction vary by customer segment?
- How have customers' expectations changed since we last surveyed their perceptions?
- How are customers' perceptions of our service quality trending over time?

The final objective is interesting in that it introduced the concept of trends over time. It is in the identification of performance-related trends that have important consequences for the organisation that CSS has a major role to play. For this reason it is important that, at the outset of a CSS programme, a view is taken of which variable the organisation wishes to track over the long-term. Thus, such variables will be clearly addressed by the initial study in order to establish benchmarks. Additionally, subsequent surveys should be designed to ensure that wording is entirely consistent to ensure that any resulting trend data can be relied upon. In a similar vein, it is important that the sample frame used over time is consistent with its predecessors.

Once an organisation has some clarity regarding the purpose and objectives it requires from a CSS it must then consider the process and methodology deemed most appropriate. A basic question concerns whether the survey should be conducted using one's own in-house resources or be subcontracted to an experienced agency such as SPSS in the USA or YouGov or MORI in the UK.

Using a specialist agency is often the best option owing to the expertise they possess in questionnaire design, data capture, data analysis, interpretation and presentation. Furthermore, they introduce a necessary degree of independence and detachment. Most such agencies also conduct staff satisfaction surveys (which really should be conducted on an independent basis) and there is a strong logic to combining both forms of survey within the same external agency.

In-house may be a viable option where the customer base is relatively small. This might apply in certain parts of the B2B domain such as where a provider of company pension schemes wishes to assess levels of satisfaction among its large corporate clients. Indeed, in such circumstances it may be desirable to measure satisfaction levels for all customers given the higher proportion of business accounted for by each corporate client. Although the logistical and analytical aspects of such CSS activities may be of a scale that would allow it to be conducted on an in-house basis, the need for independence and impartiality argues in favour of outsourcing to a specialist agency.

Whether conducted on an in-house basis or via outsourcing, a written brief is essential. In addition to specifying objectives it should address issues such as:

- Which individual issues it requires data on such as the specific aspects of service it wishes to investigate (the nine components of service quality proposed by Brady & Cronin might form the basis for this);
- Which categorisations of the customers it wishes to use as a basis for cuts of the data such as: specific, segments, length of customer relationship, light, moderate or heavy users of the service, image of certain competitors;
- Demographic classification criteria such as: age, gender, occupation, income, geographical location;
- The format of the presentation of results;
- Timescale and costs.

Once these issues have been fully resolved the most appropriate methodology can be considered. Data can be captured in a variety of ways, most commonly by postal questionnaire, telephone interview or, in recent times, via the internet. Face-to-face interviewing is often encountered with regard to high-value B2B situations which may involve discussions with a number of people comprising the decision-making unit (DMU) and user community. Each of these four principal methods of data capture has its respective advantages and drawbacks and must be considered in the light of the requirements specified in the brief. For example, the telephone allows the researcher to speak directly with the customer and respond to any issues of ambiguity which might arise. However, it is best limited to calls of no longer than ten minutes as a rule and can present some problems regarding the use of certain rating scales. Written surveys administered by the post can permit a greater array of issues to be investigated. It can also allow certain forms of visual stimuli to be used, as well as relatively complex rating scales. However, it can result in low response rates and skewed respondent profiles. The internet offers much of the functionality of the postal questionnaire but is low-cost and lends itself to speedy, flexible and cost-effective data analysis. User group bias may be an issue particularly in parts of the world or among segments where usage of the internet is patchy.

Whichever method of data capture is preferred, it is strongly recommended that an initial pilot study be carried out. The scope of the pilot study is such that it not only tests the appropriateness of the means of data capture and the nature of the individual questions themselves, but it should also test the format of results presentation. Leading on from the final point should be a simulation of the likely outputs. This will enable the organisations to judge the extent to which the survey as proposed will answer the objectives. As a result of the pilot study, reconsideration may be made of the means of data capture wording of individual questions, or, indeed, the number and nature of the questions included. In this way there is a much greater likelihood that the CSS will achieve its objectives.

A high degree of rigour is necessary when carrying out CSS activities as it is by no means uncommon for research exercises of this nature to be subject to scope creep and redirection of emphasis in the absence of due rigour and control.

As a final point, the results of customer satisfaction surveys should not only be communicated extensively among the organisation's own staff but consideration should be given to communicating the results back to customers. This is especially important in the B2B context which often involves face-to-face interviews with client staff. In such circumstances there is usually a strong presumption that such individuals will receive feedback on the survey in consideration of the time they have contributed to the actual survey.

A customer group that requires particular consideration in the context of financial services are intermediaries and brokers. In many areas of financial services, mortgages and pensions for example, brokers are of fundamental importance and the satisfaction they gain from supplier relationships and service must be assessed.

16.4.2 Employee satisfaction

A complementary activity to customer satisfaction measurement is that of the assessment of staff satisfaction. In the same way that the acquisition and retention of customers is important to an organisation, so too is the hiring and retention of good quality staff. Thus, staff satisfaction surveys can yield valuable insights that can assist the development of staff attraction and retention policies and practices. Given the importance of staff morale and motivation to the provision of good quality service, it is important that a company possesses a solid knowledge of staff feelings and perceptions.

As with CSSs, staff surveys should be subject to due rigour with regard to their planning and execution. This means that objectives need to be clearly articulated, data sets specified, and classification categories defined. It is particularly important to incorporate questions regarding aspects of customer service into staff surveys. For example, staff should be asked what they believe to be the appropriate expectations of customers with regard to the role they and their department perform.

A common belief surrounding the use of staff surveys is that senior management will not act upon them. Indeed, far from facilitating better staff morale and motivation, poorly executed staff surveys that are badly communicated can do more harm than good. One company made the results of a staff survey available on its intranet for a period of one week and then it was forgotten about. Worryingly, the perception of middle-ranking and junior staff was that senior management appeared to have treated it as a cynical exercise of "going through the motions".

Nationwide Building Society whose customer research was explored in more detail in Chapter 15 also provides an example of good practice when it comes to assessing, communicating and acting upon its staff satisfaction survey. Further detail on this is shown in Marketing in practice 16.1, again featuring Nationwide Building Society.

Figure 16.2 Nationwide Building Society branch

Marketing in practice 16.1: Nationwide Building Society's ViewPoint process

Nationwide is Britain's biggest building society – and with over 18,000 employees, it's important to the business' ongoing success that senior managers understand the experiences of their colleagues and direct reports.

Historically this took the form of a single employee opinion survey, ViewPoint, which Nationwide conducted each April. The concept was largely similar to other employee listening systems – giving Nationwide colleagues a platform on which to confidentially have their voices heard about their work, working environment and the manner in which they are led, managed and developed.

The most important part of the employee opinion process is ensuring that colleagues feel heard – as failure to do so would lead to a loss of confidence in the survey, declining engagement, and a loss of usefulness as the data becomes less statistically significant.

The annual ViewPoint survey always led to proactive actions within the business – but only having one opportunity a year to speak up meant that some colleagues still felt unheard, while others who had recently joined wouldn't have the opportunity to share their fresh perspectives for months on end. It was clear a new solution was needed.

Over time, the ViewPoint process and Nationwide's listening strategy was refined to provide a more detailed understanding of the business's culture. The new strategy was to run a "Culture Survey" every six months, along with a partnered "mid-point survey" spaced three months between culture surveys. The culture survey measures progress against a range of customer-focused behaviours consistently, to provide a clear sense of progress within the business. Meanwhile, the midpoint surveys offer the opportunity for a "deep dive" on any specific issues or cultural challenges within the business at any given moment in time.

While the culture surveys and midpoint surveys are strongly encouraged, they are not mandatory and are also kept as brief as possible to encourage colleagues to take the time to fill them out. Leaders and managers are not held to account for response rates or engagement scores on the monthly sentiment checks, as to do so would risk placing pressure on both managers and their staff, thus undermining the quality of the data.

The surveys include a space for colleagues to leave confidential verbatim commentary for leaders. This helps build a sense of psychological safety among the workforce, which also allows colleagues to feel comfortable to flag their concerns in person or use the company's internal whistleblowing processes should these tools be needed.

There are benefits to running a regular survey, for both junior and senior colleagues. If a colleague feels especially strongly about a particular issue or recent business decision, they can choose to flag via the survey which feels right for them – which means that colleagues are more satisfied that their concerns are being heard, as well as providing real time data.

The response rates speak for themselves: when the Culture Survey was first launched, the response rate was just 48%, but six months on the response rate had increased to 74%.

The faster turnaround for data allows business leaders to better understand the trends underlying sentiment in real time, informing their long-term decision-making. These have been used to inform communications internally, especially around cultural matters – such as a recent drive to focus internal behaviours more closely on customers, which needed buy-in from every colleague in the organisation. Infographics drawn from the Culture Survey and regular touchpoints were used to make it easier to understand colleague feedback so the comms plan could be tailored on an ongoing basis to encourage the uptake of the customer-focused behaviours.

These changes to understanding colleagues put Nationwide in a strong position to continue to refine their internal listening approach and gain an even sharper view of colleague sentiment in the future – allowing for the thoughtful development of colleague engagement plans and an even stronger starting point for the building society's initiatives.

Source: Alex Brammer, Nationwide Building Society

16.5 Trust

While understanding satisfaction and value are key to any assessment of relationships with customers, the notion of trust has for many years attracted the attention of researchers and practitioners. At various stages reference has been made to the issue of trust and we have seen how the characteristics of financial services, coupled with varying levels of consumer financial literacy and infrequency of purchase, present the consumer with particular challenges when it comes to decision-making. As we saw in Chapter 6, consumers employ several strategies to assist their decision-making and, thereby, mitigate the likelihood and extent of any detriment that may occur. Trust has been cited as a heuristic (decision-making short cut) and companies and brands that enjoy high levels of consumer trust enjoy an important source of competitive advantage. This is because under conditions of unfamiliarity with a particular product type consumers will place their confidence with an organisation they trust. In this way the consumer is seeking to manage the asymmetry of information and knowledge between herself and potential product providers.

However, although the use of the word *trust* is ubiquitous in connection with financial services, and indeed many other areas of the consumption of goods and services, it is a poorly understood concept. Thus, although the issue of trust attracts considerable attention and appears to be a cause for concern in the industry, our understanding of the construct of trust can be both variable and imprecise. Its importance as a means of ensuring stability within social systems and facilitating economic transactions is well accepted; its precise meaning is open to rather more debate. As previously seen, there is a considerable amount of research that deals with issues of trust in an organisational context; in contrast, marketing researchers have acknowledged the key role played by trust, modelled its impact on relationships but paid relatively little attention to the precise nature of the construct. In this section we seek to investigate what precisely are the properties associated with trust and to provide a robust conceptual basis upon which to discuss, measure and manage it.

16.5.1 The meaning of trust

Much of the discussion about the meaning of trust has its origins in literature relating to organisations and organisational analysis. Within this body of research, trust has attracted the interests of psychologists, sociologists, economists and management researchers; as a consequence, there are a variety of different approaches to understanding the construct of trust (Rousseau, Sitkin, Burt and Camer 1998). Much of the confusion that sometimes arises in relation to an understanding of trust can be viewed because of the variations between different disciplinary styles and approaches.

Alongside these different disciplinary perspectives are a variety of approaches to trust that emphasise different forms. McAllister (1995) for example, is of particular interest in the way he draws a distinction between cognitive and affective trust. Cognitive trust is essentially based on some level of knowledge and belief about others; it represents a conscious choice on the part of an individual and is likely to be based on attributes such as the competence, reliability, and dependability of exchange partners. In contrast, affective trust is essentially based on emotional ties in relationships and is likely to be structured around elements such as care and concern for others. Writing in the *Journal of Financial Services* in 2015 Devlin et al. observe that:

> When considering trust, certain core themes emerge regardless of the disciplinary perspective adopted. . . . Trust involves exchange relationships and interdependence; the existence of risk and vulnerability; and confident expectations about future behaviour.

The cognitive trust of McAllister and the calculative trust of Darley are similar to the economists' concept of trust based around rational assessments of costs and benefits. A consumer may calculate that he or she can trust an organisation because the loss of reputation, the direct financial costs, etc, that would be associated with a breach of trust are so high that there is every incentive for the organisation to behave in a trustworthy fashion. The roll call of businesses whose reputations have been tarnished by a sudden loss of trust is lengthy. Historically, product defects and their impact on customer expectations and experience have accounted for the great majority of cases of lost trust. However, in this developing era of CSR and ESG, non-product-related aspects of corporate behaviour are having an increasing impact on trust and corporate reputation. For example, in recent times Uber suffered a major loss of trust when company officials were accused of sexual harassment and other forms of abusive behaviour towards staff. Loss of trust in a company or brand can have far-reaching reputational and financial consequences. Take the relatively recent experience of Volkswagen. This is a salutary example of the way in which the loss of trust can have huge financial consequences. In September 2015 the German car maker admitted that it had installed software in its cars that cheated emissions tests in 11 million vehicles in the USA. The impact on sales was immediate and in the first quarter of 2016 the company experienced a reduction in revenues of 3.4% and a fall in profits of 20%. In April 2016 VW recorded its first annual loss in more than 20 years after setting aside 16.2 billion euro to provide for compensation costs. According to *Auto Express* in January 2017

> The total penalty for the Volkswagen emissions scandal will now exceed $19.2bn. Six VW executives have been indicted for their role in the scandal.

The affective and non-calculative forms of trust probably have more in common with the social psychologists' perspective on trust, and both emphasise the significance of having the trustor's interests at heart. For the consumer, this form of trust would depend on a belief that an organisation, or an individual, will seek to act in what might be the best interests of the consumer. This is perhaps the form of trust that might be most associated with interpersonal relationships, but Darley and others would also argue that it will have relevance in an organisational context whether through relationships between staff within an organisation or relationships between organisations and their customers.

16.5.2   Measuring trust: the Trust Index

Nottingham University Business School in the UK has been a pioneer in developing our understanding of the nature and determinants of trust and trustworthiness. In 2003 the then Financial Services Research Forum (FSRF) developed an approach to conceptualising trust (see Ennew and Sekhon, 2007). The FSRF has since merged with other specialist groups within the business school to create the Centre for Risk, Banking and Financial Services (CRBFS). It conceptualises that trust is in essence two-fold in nature comprising cognitive and affective elements. Cognitive, or low-level trust as it has become known, concerns the trust that a person has in the competence of a person or organisation to carry out expected tasks to a given standard of performance. Affective, or higher-level trust, concerns the trust that an individual has in the intentions of another person or organisation to demonstrate genuine concern for their interests and well-being. Arguably, the CRBFS Trust Index provided the most comprehensive measures of the levels and determinants of consumer trust in relation to retail financial services to date. The data was collected from 2004 until 2015. It enabled the tracking of consumer perceptions across different types of trust and trustworthiness, permitted analysis by consumer and institution characteristics and enabled a comparison of consumer evaluations of the industry as a whole with their evaluations of their own provider.

An index ranging from minus 100 to plus 100 was devised, whereby an index score of 0 represents a neutral viewpoint, indicating that consumers perceive that the financial services institution (FSI) concerned is neither particularly trusted, nor particularly untrusted. Values above 0 would range from moderate to strong perceptions of trust and values below 0 would range from moderate to strong perceptions of a lack of trust on the part of consumers. The survey data was collected by the specialist polling and market research agency YouGov using its extensive panel of consumers. This ensured an even spread of responses across institution types and ensured a representative distribution of consumer types. Each respondent was asked to respond for one FSI only and to respond to a battery of attitudinal questions that related either to their own FSI or to FSIs in general. Each wave of data collection generated some 2,000 responses.

Figure 16.3 shows the aggregate Trust Index based upon the sample's assessment for "All FSIs" (as opposed to the group which rated their own FSIs). Whilst this shows that, on balance, the industry as a whole is not trusted (scores consistently below the neutral point of zero) it seems to reveal an improving trend.

The CRBFS's Trust Index results consistently showed that Base Level Trust (i.e. trust that is based on competence-related notions of dependability and reliability) is greater than High Level Trust (trust based on concern about the customers' best interests). This demonstrated that consumers have more confidence in the functional capabilities of product providers than they do in their intentions to act in the best interest of their customers. The implications for

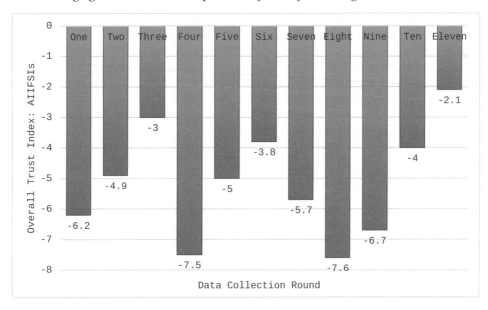

Figure 16.3 Trust in all financial services institutions 2009–2015

companies wishing to become more trusted is that they need to be able to identify which aspects of their activities impact upon the consumer's assessment of their competence, and what affects the consumer's views on the company's genuine desire to put customers first. In other words, what levers can the company pull that will result in customers rating it more highly in terms of Base-Level and High-Level trust. The CRBFS refers to this aspect of corporate behaviour as trustworthiness and this will be discussed shortly.

Progress check

- Companies and brands that enjoy high levels of consumer trust enjoy an important source of competitive advantage.
- Cognitive trust represents a conscious choice on the part of an individual and is likely to be based on attributes such as the competence, reliability, and dependability of exchange partners.
- Affective trust is essentially based on emotional ties in relationships and is likely to be structured around elements such as care and concern for others.

It should be noted that although consumer trust in the financial services sector as a whole is poor, consumer trust in their own FSI tends to be around 10 points higher than their trust in FSIs in general. Indeed, the data shows wide disparity in the ratings attributed to individual companies by their own customers with some achieving high trust ratings whilst others perform particularly poorly.

The data is also cut and presented by each of seven sub-sectors that comprise the retail financial services domain and in Figure 16.4 we see how this has trended over time.

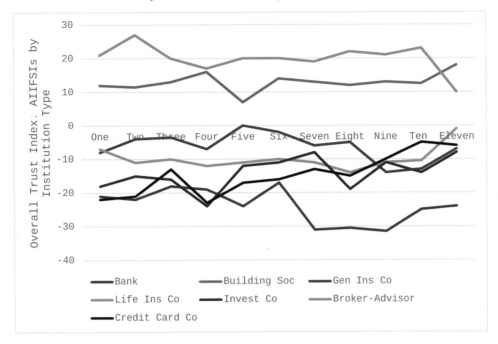

Figure 16.4 Trust and institution type over time

In Figure 16.4 the challenge faced by banks is clearly in evidence, but it also shows that the broker/adviser channel would appear to have challenges of its own to address. This will be discussed further in the next section relating to fairness.

16.5.3 *Trustworthiness*

Trust is a property of what is termed the *trustor* and in the case of a commercial transaction we would call this the customer, i.e. the party that makes the decision whether to trust another person or organisation who might provide them with a product or service. Trustworthiness, on the other hand, is a property of the *trustee*, namely, the party in the relationship who wishes to be trusted, say a bank or an insurance company. Devlin et al. put it succinctly as follows:

> Trustworthiness is the characteristic of the counterparty (known as the trustee) that may lead others to trust it. . . . Given the fundamental difference between trust and trustworthiness, it is important to note that trustworthiness may be influenced directly by the strategies and actions of a trustee in a way in which trust cannot.

In 2014 Sekhon, Ennew, Kharouf and Devlin (2014) described how they developed and tested a model that aimed to identify the independent variables associated with trustworthiness that are key determinants of trust. In the event, by adopting a robust empirically based methodology, they identified five corporate characteristics which they assert are the primary determinants of trustworthiness and which, in turn, drive the high- and low-level trust discussed in the previous section, and they are shown below in Figure 16.5:

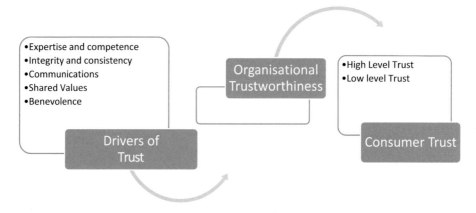

Figure 16.5 Drivers of trust

This is an important piece of research as, to the authors' knowledge, it is the first time that key antecedents of trustworthiness have been identified and the strength of their impact measured on an empirical basis. This model provides marketing executives with an insightful approach to the development of policies, practices, processes and procedures that they can manage as a way of engendering higher levels of trust by their customers and, indeed, other stakeholders whose opinions impact upon a company's reputation. The above drivers of trustworthiness may be defined as follows:

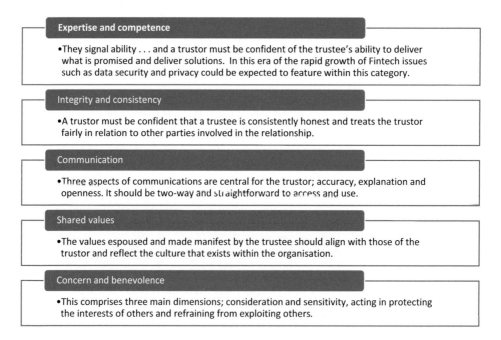

Figure 16.6 Drivers of trustworthiness

Trust can be developed by building trustworthiness between the organisation and its customers, by working with the five drivers of trustworthiness. Concern and benevolence is probably the most important factor in the model, but all of the specified drivers can be shown to have a significant and substantial impact on trustworthiness (Ennew and Sekhon, 2015).

 Stop and think?

What is the difference between cognitive and affective trust?

What is meant by trustworthiness, and what do you think determines it?

What are the factors that influence you to trust a financial services provider (FSP)?

16.5.4 How trust is won, retained and lost

The CRBFS has carried out qualitative research in conjunction with YouGov to develop insights into what behaviours on the part of product providers appear to engender higher levels of trust and what behaviours appear to reduce trust in a financial services provider. The findings are summarised as follows:

Consumers trust because

- We believe can rely on an organisation to perform consistently;
- We believe an organisation to be honest and truthful – it has integrity.

How is trust maintained?

- Reliability – it does what it says it'll do;
- Nothing goes wrong or if it does it's corrected;
- No breaches of confidentiality;
- Good communication;
- No unfair charges;
- Fairness – there is notification of better products if available.

How is trust lost?

- By being seen to be greedy and incompetent;
- Service failures that are not adequately addressed;
- Not appearing to care about its customers;
- Providing misleading information;
- Charging unfairly, not informing, appear to be dishonest;
- Trying exploit customers, focusing on profit;
- Poor performance;
- A lack of integrity.

The findings of the CRBFS are reflected in the work of the Edelman organisation[1] which identifies that five main areas are material for consumer trust to be built in the financial services sector and these are as follows:

1. Engagement with customers and employees is essential and this means communication that is both frequent and honest and involves listening to customer needs.
2. Provider companies must display excellent standards of integrity through the adoption of an ethical and responsible approach to how they conduct their business.
3. Products and services should be both innovative and of high quality.
4. Companies must act with a sense of purpose that includes social as well as commercial dimensions.
5. Companies must at all times deliver excellent standards of service and deliver consistent returns for investors.

Whilst Edelman surveys organisations across the globe and in a wide array of sectors in its *Most Trusted Brands 2022* report it observes that:

> Trust and data privacy are the pillars of financial services relationships and that to consumers: trust, honesty and data privacy matter more in financial services than in almost any other industry (with the sole exception of Health care in respect of trust and honesty- data privacy still mattered more with regard to financial services).

Edelman also identifies that financial services is the industry which consumers are most likely to report never using a brand again after losing trust in it. Whilst acknowledging the growing importance of ESG policies within business, Edelman notes that bad customer service experience and perceptions of lower product quality are the most common reasons given for discontinuing a relationship with an FS company. In the *Most Trusted Brands 2022* report, the financial services brand that was consistently ranked among the most trusted was Visa.

Figure 16.7 Visa – a highly trusted brand
Source: Shutterstock

There can be little doubt that it is easier to manage aspects of corporate behaviour and practices concerning cognitive rather than affective trust. However, the evidence suggests that real competitive advantage is more likely to be secured based upon affective trust. Brands and companies that have wavered from time to time in terms of perceptions of cognitive trust (based, say, upon service or product failings) and that have a fund of affective trust are much better able to recover their reputations than those that do not enjoy a high level of affective trust.

16.5.5 *Trust in a digital world*

Trust is gained when consumers feel providers have a genuine concern for them and their needs, and they can transact with confidence. FS companies that demonstrate transparency, operate in an ethical manner, meet regulatory requirements and implement robust technology security programmes, will put themselves in the best position to engender consumer trust.

Customers expect to be able to trust their bank is protecting both their money and their data. The use of data driven marketing, Customer Relationship Management (CRM) and personalisation to create a coherent and truly joined-up, omni-channel experience goes a long way to build consumer trust. It reassures the customer that their financial provider knows them and understands their financial needs and that this is consistently applied regardless of how they interact with them (direct mail, email, mobile, desktop, social media, etc.). Using real-time data gathered from online behaviours and social media interactions, brands can engage and respond to customers in an incredibly specific and targeted manner. Moreover, they can optimise the creation of trust by using customer data to have a two-way dialogue, as opposed to a traditional broadcast marketing approach. Through use of digital, banks can move away from a reactive to a proactive customer engagement model, which, if done correctly, is the antecedent of trust.

As mentioned earlier in this chapter, banks and others can build trust through the provision of value-add apps that demonstrate they truly understand their clients' financial needs and can help support them reach their financial goals. Trust is won by adding value and surprising and delighting customers with personalised and helpful financial recommendations. Well-designed digital platforms that are intuitive, user-friendly, easy to navigate and that enable visitors to complete the tasks they need to i.e. open an account or transfer money, will increase short-term customer satisfaction, and enhances trust.

One of the primary benefits of digital is that it aids transparency. As discussed in Chapter 14, the Financial Conduct Authority (FCA) has proposed various measures to surface information on interest rates and make comparisons between accounts and providers easier and clearer, both of which can be easily facilitated through digital means. The availability of this type of account information combined with the provision of easier switching services should lead to fairer treatment of customers. Ultimately, if customers feel they are being treated fairly, they will also have a greater propensity to trust their provider and recommend them to peers. Transparency is also important when it comes to how data is collected, stored, and used; given the increasing number of connected devices and data being shared, customers need to be reassured their personal data is securely managed.

Treating customers fairly is more transparent in the social space so, in theory, brands' adoption of social media (SM) should drive fairer treatment. Banks need to engage in SM seriously, investing in staff who can engage appropriately with customers on a human basis, not just provide stock responses.

One of the other key drivers of trust is data security. Banks need to address and allay customer fears over data vulnerability and security. Research carried out by India-based MicroSave highlighted that while 85% of online financial services customers said they would recommend digital banking to peers, they still thought of it as a "Plan B" due to misgivings over trust of security.[2] 2024 Digital Banking Statistics reported 21% of UK adults hadn't opened a digital bank account due to fear around security and data breaches, with more older customers citing this as concern; 24% of baby boomers and silent generation as compared with 17% of millennial and Gen Z.[3] To build trust, providers must demonstrate robust measures to mitigate concern; multi-step authentication, encryption and use of biometrics. One of the major issues banks must contend with are phishing, lookalike, and scamming sites masking themselves as a genuine brand to steal customer data and ultimately their money. There was a hope that branded top-level domains (bTLDs) offered a potential solution, enabling brands to create their own domain (e.g. .com) which they fully owned and governed. This offered a marketing opportunity to reassure customers that if a website sits on a bTLD, it could be trusted to be 100% genuine, and customers should never use or input data into a website that doesn't sit on their bTLD, e.g. www.[subdomain].[brand]. In France, BNP Paribas made the bold move of migrating their entire domain ecosystem to the bTLD in summer 2015. Barclays was the first UK bank to launch a bTLD, adopting a more cautious approach and migrating its corporate site from www.barclays.com to www.home.barclays in June 2015, with plans to move its transactional sites over in due course, however, this never came to fruition. State Bank of India followed suit, launching www.bank.sbi in 2017. For a brief time, it seemed bTLDs were going to be a big deal, however, they never realised mass adoption. A brand would also have to undergo a full migration of their existing top-level domain ecosystem to the bTLD before they could promote the trust marketing message. The cost of migrating huge established online ecosystems, particularly complex customer log-in portals, was prohibitive. There would also be a significant impact on SEO in the short-medium terms while the new domains gained credibility and authenticity with search engines, impacting revenue. Lastly, bTLDs weren't widely understood by the public, and FS providers were cautious of committing to such a major change until they potentially gained mainstream recognition through their use by FMCG brands, something which hasn't occurred.

Progress check

- Given the fundamental difference between trust and trustworthiness, it is important to note that trustworthiness may be influenced directly by the strategies and actions of a trustee in a way in which trust cannot.
- Consumers trust an organisation because they believe they can rely on it to perform consistently, and because they believe it to be honest, truthful and having integrity.
- Through use of digital, banks can move away from a reactive to a proactive customer engagement model, which, if done correctly, is the antecedent of trust.

The evolution of fintech has acted as a catalyst for the further study of trust since round about 2015. Whilst fintech's core proposition is based upon convenience and simplicity, the new business models which it has spawned do not possess many of the characteristics that consumers are used to associating with product provider trust. There are no branches which can act as physical evidence of dependability, no face-to-face service that can provide reassurance and, no call centres to solve problems. Moreover, there are concerns regarding data security and privacy. This has led to renewed interest in the study of trust in the field of financial services. For instance, writing in the Journal of Consumer Sciences in 2020 Nangin et al[4] drew attention to the increased level of security threats posed by the rapid development of fintech and the challenges they pose to customers and providers alike. They comment on the importance of addressing these challenges to engender the necessary degree of trust, given the tremendous potential of fintech to address the unmet demand for financial services in many parts of the world and its ability to allow for greater financial inclusion.

For many years the Edelman organisation has produced surveys on trust and in 2020 reported on its findings that there was broad mistrust of fintech. It identified four key areas of concern, namely:

- Data privacy
- Fear of the unknown
- Limited regulation
- Sector scandals

The author of the Edelman report, Andrew Wilde, concludes by saying:

> Fintech is at a crossroads. There are many reasons to believe that the sector should be the standard bearer for business as we move into a post-Covid era and some areas of historical distrust in fintechs are now receding. However, widespread adoption will ultimately depend on fintech's collective ability to bridge the trust gap between themselves and the larger names in finance.

In 2022 a Chinese study entitled *What makes consumers trust and adopt fintech? An empirical investigation in China*[5] underpined the role played by trust as a heuristic by people to help form judgements about the likelihood of a desired outcome from a relationship or transaction. To quote from the study:

> We found that consumer trust in fintech either fully or partially mediates the effects of perceived security and perceived privacy on consumer attitude. These findings imply that trust plays a key role in online environments and e-commerce services based on digital technologies.

Also in China, in 2023 Xia et al[6] published their study *Trust in Fintech: Risk, Governance, and Continuance Intention** which was based on the three constructs of institutional trust, technology trust, and interpersonal trust. Institutional trust relates principally to ways in which wider environmental factors, such as regulation, and generally held beliefs about the safety of on-line transacting, act to engender trust. Technology trust concerns the trust that an individual has in the reliability, and functionality of a given piece of technology to perform as required. Interpersonal trust relates to the expectations that an individual has of another party based upon their experience of that party, and their use of language, behaviours, and intentions.. The research provides empirical support to the importance of all three forms of trust in providing the conditions for the adoption and progress of fintech business models.

 **Stop and think?**

To what degree do you believe trust influences consumers decisions to open and switch bank and other financial products?

16.6 Treating customers fairly

Closely related to the concept of trust is the need to ensure that customers feel they have been treated fairly. Indeed, there is a close connection between the notion of fairness and trust in that people display a willingness to trust individuals and organisations they consider act in ways that are fair. The corollary to this is that resentment and mistrust are the consequences of customers being exposed to what they consider to be unfair practices. Set within the context of managing ongoing customer relationships, it is imperative that organisations endeavour to build trust through being seen to act fairly. To quote from Berry and Parasuraman (1991):

> Trust requires fair play. Few customers wish to build and continue a relationship with a firm they perceive to be unfair.

The concept of fairness has assumed growing significance in a range of contexts throughout the world. For example, fair trade products have become a feature of various markets and product categories such as fresh fruit and vegetables, packaged food and beverages and clothing. In essence fairness has to do more with adherence to the *spirit* of what is the right thing to do rather than conformance with the *letter of the law*. In an environment characterised by fairness, organisations must increasingly strive to avoid hiding behind punitive and unfair contractual terms.

Following the abolition of the Office of Fair Trading 2014, fairness has established itself firmly as part of the agenda of the FCA in the UK. Indeed, this is nothing new as the requirement to treat customers fairly is clearly laid out in Principle 6 of its Principles for Business which states: "A firm must pay due regard to the interests of its customers and treat them fairly." Cartwright (2008), has reviewed the literature regarding fair treatment of consumers on behalf of the Financial Services Research Forum (now the CRBFS at Nottingham University Business School referred to in Section 16.7). He observes that the FSA (the FCA's predecessor) conducted research aimed at helping it to understand consumers' perceptions and views of what constitutes fair treatment by product providers. Ultimately, the FSA identified a set of six principles that would appear to summarise its perspective on fairness, and we present them diagrammatically as follows:

In the event, the FCA has chosen to address the issue of fairness through a principles-based approach and has identified six "consumer outcomes" which relate to the product life cycle as follows[7]:

- Consumers can be confident that they are dealing with firms where the fair treatment of customers is central to the corporate culture.
- Products and services marketed and sold in the retail market are designed to meet the needs of identified consumer groups and targeted accordingly.

Figure 16.8 FSA (now FCA) principles regarding fair treatment of customers

- Consumers are provided with clear information and are kept appropriately informed before, during and after the point of sale.
- Where consumers receive advice, the advice is suitable and takes account of their circumstances.
- Consumers are provided with products that perform as firms have led them to expect and the associated service is both an acceptable standard and as they have been led to expect.
- Consumers do not face unreasonable post-sale barriers imposed by firms to change product, switch providers, submit a claim or make a complaint.

The FCA has advised the organisations it authorises that the treating customer fairly (TCF) principles should be embedded in all parts of the organisation and at all levels and be evidenced by way of a formal review of its performance in respect of its TCF obligations on an annual basis. Rather than view this as yet another imposition that will add to the burden of overhead costs, the FCA is of the opinion that the industry will ultimately benefit from embracing TCF in the form of:

- More repeat business,
- Greater confidence in the industry,
- Fewer rules
- Fewer complaints upheld by the Financial Ombudsman Service.

In Chapter 1 reference was made to the FCA's new initiative concerning Consumer Duty that was introduced in 2023. It would appear that the FCA is disappointed by the inability of its TCF arrangements to provide sufficient safeguards against consumer detriment. Indeed, in its work on Consumer Duty the consultancy KPMG comments as follows[8]:

The FCA has highlighted that it continues to see practices that cause consumer harm, including:

- Firms providing information which is misleadingly presented or difficult for consumers to understand.
- Products and services that are not fit for purpose in delivering the benefits that consumers reasonably expect.
- Products and services that do not represent fair value.
- Poor customer support and other practices which hinder consumers' ability to act, or which exploit information asymmetries, consumer inertia, behavioural biases or vulnerabilities.

Whereas the six core principles of TCF provided expectations that the FCA had of product providers, Consumer Duty is more prescriptive in terms of how the regulator will operationalise fair treatment and the actions it will take to intervene where it deems an FSP has not been fair in its treatment of customers. To quote from the FCA website[9]:

> Our new Duty sets higher and clearer standards of consumer protection across financial services and requires firms to put their customers' needs first.........We expect the Consumer Duty to improve outcomes for consumers in all areas of business between firms and customers.

The Duty's four outcomes cover the key elements of the firm-consumer relationship. The Duty means consumers should get:

- communications they can understand,
- products and services that meet their needs,
- products and services that offer fair value,
- the customer support they need when they need it.

The new rules took effect in July 2023 and rather than simply address its requirements to the financial services industry the FCA has produced a version aimed at addressing consumers directly in the following terms[10]:

Under the Duty, firms should be open and honest, avoid causing foreseeable harm, and support you to pursue your financial goals. You should expect:

- **helpful and accessible customer support**, so it's as easy to sort out a problem, switch or cancel your product, as it was to buy it in the first place
- **timely and clear information** you can understand, so you can make good financial decisions. This means important information shouldn't be buried in lengthy terms and conditions
- providers to offer **products and services that are right for you**, rather than pushing products and services you don't need
- **products and services to provide fair value**. This should mean you won't be ripped off or have to pay costs you didn't expect. But while your provider should offer you a fair price, it doesn't mean it will be the best deal for you, so you should still shop around
- firms to consider if you're in a **vulnerable situation** when dealing with you. This could be due to poor health or financial troubles, for instance

These rules apply to all new and existing products and services that are currently on sale. For older products that are no longer on sale, the rules will apply from 31 July 2024.

 Stop and think?

What does fair treatment of customers mean to you?

What measures has your country's regulator introduced to safeguard the fair treatment of consumers?

Peter Cartwright has emphasised the ways in which information asymmetries serve to disadvantage the consumer. Quoting from the Cruickshank Report (Cruickshank, 2000), in which it states:

> Knowledgeable consumers provide the best incentive to effective competition. With the right information, consumers can take responsibility for their own financial well-being, shop around and exert the pressures on suppliers which drive a competitive and innovative market.

Cartwright comments that, in reality, many markets fall short of Cruickshank's ideal, and he proposes an approach to addressing fairness in the context of financial services that is based upon justice theory (Smith, Bolton and Wagner, 1999) which is in turn adapted from equity theory and social exchange.

Devlin has developed a conceptual framework for the measurement of fairness on behalf of the CRBFS. Commenting on survey findings, Devlin (2015) observes:

> The CRBFS has been measuring perceptions of fairness of financial institutions from the perspective of consumers since 2009. Each time we have collected data in exactly the same manner and have used identical questions, hence allowing us to analyse trends accurately. When measuring fairness, taking our cue from theories of justice, we measure the following dimensions:

- **Procedural fairness**, which is fairness of a firm's policies and procedures (made up of Impartiality, Refutability, Explanation and Familiarity);
- **Interactional fairness**, which is the fairness of interpersonal treatment and communication (made up of Bilateral Communication and Courtesy and Respect), and;
- **Distributive fairness,** which concerns resource allocation and the outcomes of exchange, or how "the pie" is shared out. [11]

The CRBFS's Fairness Index uses data collected using a standard five-point scale (1=strongly disagree – 5=strongly agree) and converts overall scores to an index score from minus 100 to plus 100. The interpretations of the index are directly analogous to those outlined for the Trust Index earlier in this chapter. Figure 16.9 shows how the aggregate Fairness Index for "All FSIs" has trended since 2009 from which it can be seen that from wave 1 in 2009 until wave 11 the index was in negative territory, i.e. consumers do not believe they are treated fairly by the industry. However, data presented from wave 9 would appear to suggest that somewhat of a tipping point may have been achieved as the index closed rapidly towards positive territory. The breakthrough seems to have taken place in 2015 when, for the first time, the index broke through the neutral point to register a small positive result.

One can only speculate on what factors may be at play in explaining this improvement. Possible explanations include the greater muscularity of the FCA compared with its predecessor, as well as the principles associated with Treating Customers Fairly gaining more traction. Additional factors to consider are that feelings of anger regarding the role of the industry in causing the financial crisis of 2008–2010, may be waning. Another issue to bear in mind is that publicity regarding the PPI mis-selling scandal probably peaked in 2014. This is borne out by data from the Financial Ombudsman Service (FOS) which shows that having

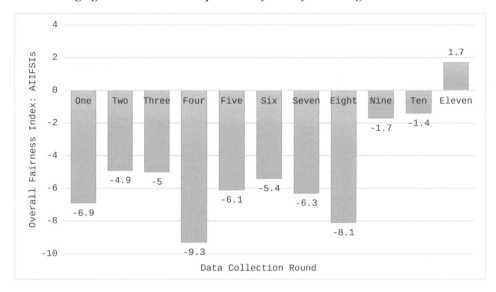

Figure 16.9 Fairness Index for all financial services institutions

Source: Devlin (2015)

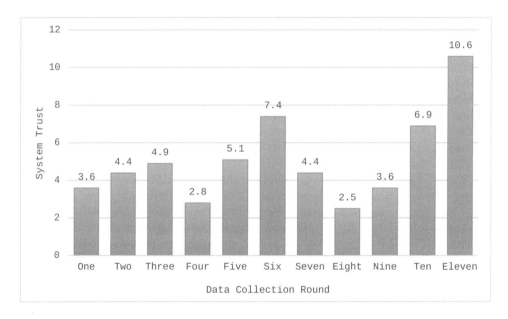

Figure 16.10 Trust in the UK regulatory system

Source: Devlin (2016)

received 627,814 consumer enquiries regarding possible detriment in 2007 the number swelled to a peak of 2,357,374 in 2014. The evidence seems to support the view that public confidence is growing in the ability of regulation to address consumer concerns regarding fair treatment and overall trust in the system. This is shown in Figure 16.10.

Whichever country the reader resides in, it is likely that some form of TCF or Consumer Duty initiative will arise, if indeed it has not already done so.

Regulators aside, it is axiomatic of good marketing strategy and execution that fairness is firmly embedded as a core principle. In any event, TCF fundamentally concerns the issue of consumer vulnerability and how to avoid detriment. We have seen how information asymmetry is complicit in this regard but there are other factors that can result in consumer detriment and need to form part of any organisation's approach to dealing with its customers fairly. Writing on this subject again, Cartwright (2011) encourages us to rethink how we conceptualise vulnerability by proposing what he calls a new taxonomy of vulnerability, to quote from his paper on the subject:

> This is a novel framework consisting of a set of elements which, taken together, help to identify where vulnerability is liable to exist. The elements are classified by the paper as:

- Information vulnerability,
- Pressure vulnerability,
- Supply vulnerability,
- Redress vulnerability, and
- Impact vulnerability.

Cartwright proceeds to articulate the nature of each of these forms of vulnerability and proposes remedies. This forms a highly practical and actionable approach which companies can readily adapt to suit their individual strategies for treating customers fairly; readers are to be encouraged to consider this thoughtful yet pragmatic contribution to the topic of fairness and how to facilitate it.

Over a number of years the FCA has also made an important contribution to the issue of consumer vulnerability. Its activities in this area began in 2015 with its report "Consumer Vulnerability in Financial Services, Occasional Paper No. 8". That landmark paper moved thinking on by introducing the notion that we should think of vulnerability in terms of consumers in vulnerable circumstances rather than as types of individuals who are inherently vulnerable (such as those with learning disabilities or infirmity). The implications of this approach are that anyone may find themselves in a situation of vulnerability at one or more times in their life and, therefore, companies need to be more expansive and imaginative in how they develop policies and practices and procedures about vulnerability. In 2021 that was followed up with *FG21/1*[12] *Guidance for firms on the fair treatment of vulnerable customers* which defined a vulnerable customer as someone who, due to their personal circumstances, is especially susceptible to harm, particularly when a firm is not acting with appropriate levels of care. The document goes on to make highly pertinent observations about the antecedents of corporate behaviours that in the view of the FCA are implicated in causing harm:

> In our approach to supervision we outline our focus on business models and culture as the key drivers of harm in firms. We explain that when we assess culture, we look at what drives behaviour in a firm. We address the key drivers of behaviour which are likely to cause harm. These include:

- The firm's purpose, as understood by its employees.
- The attitude, behaviour, competence and compliance of the firm's leadership.

- The firm's approach to managing and rewarding people, such as staff competence and incentives, and
- The firm's governance arrangements, controls and key processes, such as for whistleblowing or complaint handling.

Progress check

- Set within the context of managing ongoing customer relationships, it is imperative that organisations endeavour to build trust through being seen to act fairly.
- Principles concerning the fair treatment of customers should be embedded in all parts of the organisation and at all levels and be evidenced by way of a formal review of its performance in respect of its TCF obligations on an annual basis.
- Customer detriment is likely to be found where there is Information vulnerability, pressure vulnerability, supply vulnerability, redress vulnerability, and impact vulnerability.

In the following marketing in practice, Ian Hughes, CEO of Consumer Intelligence, gives his views on just how momentous the FCA's Consumer Duty regulations will be for marketing practitioners.

Marketing in practice 16.2: Consumer Duty – a fundamental shift in financial services marketing?

The introduction of Consumer Duty by the Financial Conduct Authority (FCA) signifies a landmark shift in the UK financial services industry. Rooted in Policy Statement PS22/9 and further elucidated in Finalised Guidance FG22/5, this regulatory framework became operational on 31st July 2023. It envisions a financial landscape where firms are mandated to prioritise the welfare and interests of their customers, thereby redefining the industry's approach to consumer protection and service delivery.

Key components of Consumer Duty

Consumer Duty is built on a foundation that includes:

1. **Consumer principle**: firms must act to deliver good outcomes for consumers, effectively prioritizing their best interests.
2. **Cross-cutting rules**: these rules mandate firms to avoid foreseeable harm, act in good faith, and enable consumers to pursue their financial objectives.

3. **Four outcomes**: focusing on precise and comprehensible communications, offering products and services that meet consumer needs, providing customer service that supports consumers, and ensuring price and value considerations.

Integration with Drucker's philosophy

The ethos of Consumer Duty aligns with Peter Drucker's marketing philosophy from the 1950s, which places the understanding of customer needs at the forefront. Drucker posited that effective products should naturally meet consumer demand, echoing the FCA's guidance that financial services and products should be inherently consumer centric.

Impact on financial services marketing

The emergence of Consumer Duty demands a transformation in marketing tactics within the financial industry. Companies must now guarantee complete transparency and communicate the advantages and drawbacks of their products clearly. The FCA's measures against unfair practices in sectors such as car leasing, GAP insurance, and PPI demonstrate its dedication to enforcing these criteria.

Opportunities and challenges post-2023

Looking ahead to the period after 2023, the financial services industry is poised for innovation. This is due to the potential for new entrants like Amazon and Apple to disrupt traditional banking models with their customer-focused, technology-driven solutions. However, this also presents significant challenges for existing financial institutions, which must adapt to remain competitive.

Risks of non-compliance

Non-compliance with the principles of Consumer Duty can lead to severe consequences, such as regulatory penalties, damage to reputation, and a decline in consumer trust. In today's age, where consumers are becoming more knowledgeable and selective, it is essential to follow these standards to maintain a firm's position in the market and protect its reputation.

Conclusion

Starting from the end of July 2023, the UK's financial services industry will undergo a significant change in the form of Consumer Duty. This regulatory framework will prioritize the well-being of customers over everything else. It is not just about compliance, but a strategic shift towards more ethical, transparent, and customer-oriented business practices. Companies that adopt this new approach are likely to enjoy greater customer loyalty and business sustainability, while those that fail to adapt may face significant setbacks. The Consumer Duty era marks a new phase in financial services, emphasising the importance of aligning business operations with consumer interests and ethical standards. Drucker would be delighted and so should we as marketers.

Source: Ian Hughes, CEO, Consumer Intelligence

16.7 Summary and conclusion

Central to the marketing concept is the idea that an organisation can enhance its overall performance by taking a customer-oriented view of its business and focusing on the delivery of customer satisfaction. This general idea is encapsulated in the concept of the service profit chain. Satisfaction and value are both seen as important evaluations of the service experience and as determinants of customer retention and loyalty. Satisfaction is concerned with the extent to which a service is able to deliver against customer expectations while value is concerned with the range of benefits offered by the service relative to its associated costs. As with service quality, consumer evaluations of satisfaction and value play a major role in the development of relationships with financial services providers. Customer dissatisfaction and/or poor value are potential reasons for terminating any financial services relationship.

Careful measurement of satisfaction is an important element of any relationship marketing/ CRM programme. Indeed, in some of the best examples, the measurement of customer satisfaction would be accompanied by the measurement of employee satisfaction as the latter can serve as an important determinant of the former. While there are a variety of approaches available to measuring satisfaction, there are many benefits to be gained for the use of an external and independent agency for data collection and analysis. However, the value of such exercises is crucially dependent on the organisation's willingness to use the information that is generated. Simply undertaking customer and employee satisfaction surveys without a serious commitment to act upon their results will be of little value in managing customer relationships.

In financial services in particular, the management of customer relationships is increasingly focusing attention on the concept of trust and the need to treat customers fairly. Although such initiatives have been prompted by regulatory bodies and are probably most developed in the UK, it seems likely that the trust and fairness agendas will increasingly become part of good relationship management across the financial services sector worldwide.

Learning outcomes

Having completed this chapter, you shold now be able to:

1. **Understand the nature of customer satisfaction and customer value.**
   Readers have been made aware that satisfaction is a complex and multifaceted concept which has attracted enormous attention from both the academic and practitioner communities, not least because it is recognised as being of great significance to the well-being of individuals, firms, and the economy as a whole. Consumer judgements of satisfaction are generally thought to be made by comparing the service that is experienced against some pre-existing standard. One of the commonest bases for comparison is that of perceptions against expectations (what the consumer predicted he or she would get). This is commonly referred to as the Disconfirmation Model of Satisfaction. In simple terms, when perceptions are less than expectations, the result is a negative disconfirmation resulting is a negative evaluation and a lack of satisfaction. Confirmation of expectations or a situation of positive disconfirmation (performance exceeds expectations) will result in a positive evaluation, usually satisfaction but perhaps also delight.
2. **Be aware of the issue associated with measuring and monitoring customer satisfaction.**

Given that customer satisfaction is a multifaceted concept and far from one-dimensional, individual managers must form a view on the nature of satisfaction for their own organisation with regard to factors such as: the need being fulfilled, degree and variety of competition, segment variations, and how the resultant data will be used. In this chapter we saw that, as a rule, customer satisfaction is measured by the use of some form of quantitative survey. It is in the nature of customer satisfaction, and the use that is made of its data, that it is required to be statistically reliable and robust. For example, its outputs may be used as the basis for major investment in time, money and systems resources in upgrading elements of service delivery. Managers responsible for deciding upon and implementing such investments must only do so on the basis of valid and reliable information. Thus, the sample size and structure of a customer satisfaction survey must be of a scale and scope that engenders the necessary confidence. We also saw how the results of customer satisfaction surveys should not only be communicated extensively among the organisation's own staff, but consideration should be given to communicating the results back to customers. This especially important in the B2B context which often involves face-to-face interviews with client staff.

3. **Understand the importance of trust and trustworthiness in organisations' interactions with its customers.**

In Chapter 6 we were introduced to behavioural economics in the context of consumer decision-making. We saw that trust is one of several unconscious decision-making strategies known as heuristics which human beings deploy to deal with the uncertainties that attend many decision-making situations. Heuristics act as short cuts and are particularly useful under conditions of uncertainty and limited previous experience of the type of decision needed to be made. People use trust as a proxy for the extent to which they can rely upon a person or organisation to perform according to their expectations of them. This implies a degree of vulnerability on the consumers part when they place their trust in a financial services company to deliver the outcomes they require and expect. Put simply, we are more likely to do business with a company we trust than with one we don't. For this reason, it is vital that marketeers take seriously their responsibilities to use the marketing mix, in order to engender consumer trust.

Trust is a property of what is termed the *trustor* and in the case of a commercial transaction we would call this the customer, i.e. the party that makes the decision whether to trust another person or organisation who might provide them with a product or service. Trustworthiness, on the other hand, is a property of the *trustee*, namely, the party in the relationship who wishes to be trusted, say a bank or an insurance company. Companies should aim to adopt policies, behaviours, and activities that enhance their trustworthiness and, thereby, encourage consumers to trust them.

4. **Understand the importance of fairness and the implications for marketers.**

Related to the concept of trust is the need to ensure that customers feel they have been treated fairly. Indeed, there is a close connection between the notion of fairness and trust in that people display a willingness to trust individuals and organisations they consider act in ways that are fair. The corollary to this is that resentment and mistrust are the consequences of customers being exposed to what they consider to be unfair practices. Regulators such as the FCA take fairness seriously and have developed principles, policies and exacting rules that require companies to treat their customers fairly or be sanctioned for failing to do so.

Review questions

1. Why should financial services organisations be concerned about delivering customer satisfaction?
2. What is customer satisfaction and how does it differ from service quality and value?
3. What role do expectations play in relation to customer satisfaction? How should organisations seek to manage customer expectations?
4. What are the key steps in developing an effective consumer satisfaction survey?
5. Why is trust so important in the marketing of financial services?
6. For a company of your choosing, what could it do to become more trustworthy and, thereby, become more trusted by its customers and other stakeholders?
7. In which areas of marketing is treating customers fairly of greatest significance?

Notes

1 http://www.edelman.com/insights/intellectualproperty/2014-edelman-trust-barometer/trust-in-business/trust-in-financial-services/, accessed August 2015
2 www.centerforfinancialinclusion.org/building-trust-and-growing-digital-financial-services-a-look-at-jumo
3 www.finder.com/uk/digital-banking-statistics (ccessed January 2024)
4 The Effects of Perceived Ease of Use, Security, and Adoption on Trust and Its Implications on Fintech Adoption, Nangin M. A., Barus I.R.G., and Wahyoedi S., Journal of Consumer Sciences 2020, Vol. 05, No 02, 124-138
5 Taewoo Roh, Young Soo Yang, Shufeng Xiao & Byung II Park 26 January 2022, https://doi.org/10/s10660-021-09527-3)
6 Huosong Xia, Duqub Lu, Boqiang Lin, Jeretta Horn Nord & Justin Zuopeng Zhang (2023) Trust in Fintech: Risk, Governance, and Continuance Intention, Journal of Computer Information Systems, 63:3, 648-662, DOI: 10.1080/08874417.2022.2093295
Link: https://doi.org/10. 1080/08874417.2022.2093295
7 www.fca.org.uk/firms/fair-treatment-customers,last updated: 13/03/2023 (accessed January 2024)
8 kpmg.com/xx/en/home/insights/2022/05/what-are-the-drivers-behind-consumer-duty.
9 www.fca.org.uk/firms/consumer-duty (accessed January 2024)
10 Source: www.fca.org.uk/news/news-stories/consumer-duty-higher-standards-financial-services
11 Page 13 (accessed January 2024)
12 Guidance for firms on the fair treatment of vulnerable customers, FCA.,FG 21/1, February 2021 (accessed January 2024)

References

Berman, B. (2005). How to delight your customers. *California Management Review*, 48(1), pp. 129–51.
Cartwright, P. (2008). Fairness, Financial Services and The Consumer in an Age of Principles-Based Regulation: Position and Consultation Paper. Nottingham: Financial Services Research Forum.
Cartwright, P. (2011). *The Vulnerable Consumer of Financial Services: Law, Policy and Regulation.* Nottingham: Financial Services Research Forum.
Cruickshank, D. (2000). Competition in UK Banking: A Report to the Chancellor of the Exchequer, Her Majesty's Stationery Office, Norwich.
https://webarchive.nationalarchives.gov.uk/ukgwa/20050301221631/http:/www.hm-treasury.gov.uk/documents/financial_services/banking/bankreview/fin_bank_reviewfinal.cfm
Devlin, J. (2015). Trust and Fairness in Financial Services: 2015 Report CRBFS, Nottingham University Business School, Nottingham. https://www.nottingham.ac.uk/business/who-we-are/centres-and-institutes/gcbfi/documents/crbfs-reports/crbfs-paper-7-trust-fair-2015.pdf
Ennew, C. T. and Sekhon, H. (2007). The trust index. *Consumer Policy Review*, March/April, 17(2), pp. 62–68.

Ennew, C. T. and Sekhon, H. (2014). Trust and trustworthiness in retail financial services: An analytical framework and empirical evidence. In: T. Harrison and H. Estelami (eds.), *The Routledge Companion to Financial Services Marketing*. Vol. 1, p. 576. London: Routledge.

McAllister, D. J. (1995). Affect- and cognition-based trust as foundations for interpersonal cooperation in organizations. *Academy of Management Journal*, 38, pp. 24–59.

Oliver, R. L. (1997). *Satisfaction: A Behavioural Perspective on the Consumer*. London: McGraw-Hill.

Parasuraman, A., Berry, L. L. and Zeithaml, V. A. (1991). Refinement and reassessment of the SERVQUAL scale. *Journal of Retailing,* 67(4), pp. 420–50.

Rousseau, D., Sitkin, S., Burt, R. and Camer, C. (1998). Not so different after all: A cross-discipline view of trust. *Academy of Management Review*, 23(3), pp. 393–404.

Sekhon, H., Ennew, C. T., Kharouf, H. and Devlin, J. F. (2014). Trust and trustworthiness: Influences and implications. *Journal of Marketing Management,* 30(3/4), pp. 409–30.

Smith, A. K., Bolton, R. N. and Wagner, J. (1999). A model of customer satisfaction with service encounters involving failure and recovery. *Journal of Marketing Research*, 36, pp. 356–73.

Zeithaml, A. V. (1988). Customer perceptions of price quality and value: A means-end model and synthesis evidence. *Journal of Marketing*, 52(3), pp. 2–22.

Zeithaml, V. and Bitner, M. J. (2003). *Services Marketing: Integrating Customer Focus across the Firm*. London: McGraw Hill/Irwin.

17 Corporate social responsibility (CSR) and environmental, social and governance (ESG)

Learning objectives

At the end of this chapter, you should be able to:

1. Appreciate that financial services companies inhabit a wide social, economic, and environmental ecology in which good corporate citizenship is vital for sustainable success in the ever-changing marketplace,
2. Understand what is meant by the terms CSR and ESG and how they relate to each other,
3. Understand marketing's wider contribution within the contexts of corporate social responsibility and ESG,
4. Appreciate some of the ways on which FSCs are fulfilling their ESG responsibilities and the implications for marketing.

17.1 Introduction

In this chapter we will consider marketing's role in the discharging of an organisation's corporate social responsibility (CSR). Importantly, we'll look at how marketing can contribute to the sustainability agenda which is assuming ever more significance. It is contended that the adoption of a more values- (as opposed to value) based approach to marketing strategy, and one that fully integrates the organisation's corporate social responsibilities within its programmes, will resonate with the needs and expectations of the marketplace of the future. In this 4th edition we include new material on ESG (environmental, social and governance) and how it is gaining traction as a concept that is building on the earlier, and, arguably, less muscular CSR. This chapter deliberately gives prominence to what is happening in the real world of financial services and ESG and includes many inspiring examples of what is already being achieved. By so doing we have been able to present the latest thinking regarding ESG, but first, let's begin by considering some of the antecedents of the subject.

17.2 The origins of CSR

The origins of CSR as we currently understand it can be traced back to the 19th century when industrialists on both sides of the Atlantic engaged in a range of philanthropic activities. In

DOI: 10.4324/9781003398615-31

1889, Andrew Carnegie set out his beliefs about the use of wealth in the *North American Review*. Of particular note was the following passage:

> This, then, is held to be the duty of the man of Wealth:.............. to provide moderately for the legitimate wants of those dependent upon him; and after doing so to consider all surplus revenues which come to him simply as trust funds, which he is called upon to administer, and strictly bound as a matter of duty to administer in the manner which, in his judgment, is best calculated to produce the most beneficial results for the community--the man of wealth thus becoming the mere agent and trustee for his poorer brethren, bringing to their service his superior wisdom, experience and ability to administer, doing for them better than they would or could do for themselves.[1]

Carnegie made his fortune in the steel industry and during his lifetime gave away some $US 350 million to philanthropic causes. Others followed in Carnegie's wake including such names as John D Rockefeller, while in Britain chocolate tycoon Joseph Rowntree and textile magnate Sir Titus Salt were but two among many 19th century industrialists who wished to use their wealth for the common good. It was not until 1953 that the term corporate social responsibility was first coined with the publication of *Social Responsibilities of the Businessman* by American economist Howard Bowen.

The development of "stakeholder theory" (Freeman, 1984, 2010) had a major impact on thinking about CSR and continues to be hugely influential today. Freeman's argument was essentially that focusing purely on profit is a short term perspective and that business needs to recognise that it depends not just on owners (shareholders). Long term success depends on the recognition that a business has a range of stakeholders and must think about how to balance engagement with and the interests of all of these. In discussing marketing we have already highlighted the importance of a customer focus. But Freeman and others working in this tradition would also point to the importance of engaging with and understanding the interests of employees, suppliers, regulators, communities, the media and even competitors. Recognising and understanding responsibilities to and dependence on a range of stakeholders is essential for reputation, for legitimacy and for long term sustainability. In a stakeholder world, CSR is part of the responsibility that a business has to stakeholders.

In identifying that business enterprises exercised great power that could have a tangible impact on society he argued that business leaders are under an obligation to pursue policies for the benefit of the common good. A major step forward in the interest in CSR came in the 1990s as globalisation held sway in the wake of the collapse of the Soviet Union and its communist satellites. Of particular note were the agreement to the United Nations Framework Convention on Climate Change[2], and the Kyoto Protocol[3]. These events served to increase the concerns of multinational corporations for the impact of their operations on the world as a whole.

17.3 The evolution of CSR

Since the beginning of this millennium, many authorities have commented on the range of factors that have been responsible for profound changes in the operating climate for contemporary financial service organisations including the following and many of these have been flagged earlier in this book:

- Globalisation and/or regionalisation,
- Marketisation and/or public private partnerships,

- Speed and transparency of communications,
- Shift to a service economy,
- Retreat from, or constraint of, public welfare in favour of private provision.

Whole business models have been created by digital disruption and AI now presents global opportunities and challenges. At the same time, there has been an increased demand from various stakeholders, including national governments, international bodies, and regulators, for a greater focus on corporate ethics and social responsibility. Between 17–20 January 2017, the 47th World Economic Forum (WEF) Meeting met in Davos in Switzerland to address the theme of *Responsive and Responsible Leadership.* To quote from the WEF itself:

> Responsive and Responsible Leadership requires recognizing that frustration and discontent are increasing in the segments of society that are not experiencing economic development and social progress. Their situation will only become more uncertain with the onset of the Fourth Industrial Revolution and its impact on future employment. Responsive and Responsible Leadership therefore entails a deeper commitment to inclusive development and equitable growth, both nationally and globally. It also involves working rapidly to close generational divides by exercising shared stewardship of those systems that are critical to our prosperity. In the end, leaders from all walks of life at the Annual Meeting 2017 must be ready to react credibly and responsibly to societal and global concerns that have been neglected for too long.[4]

Thus, governments worldwide are now looking to create greater transparency, openness, and responsiveness in the business sector by introducing both "hard" and "soft" legislation to improve standards of corporate governance in the boardroom and social responsibility towards internal and external stakeholders. Despite these demands being made more urgent by several high-profile scandals, major problems surround the very definition of corporate social responsibility, added to which is a lack of any consensus as to whether it should be a central part of business policy and practice. Jackson and Nelson (2004) address this issue constructively by proposing what they term a values-based approach to strategy observing that:

> Companies today are under intense pressure to rebuild public trust and to be competitive. ....To do this they must act with greater accountability, transparency and integrity, while remaining profitable and innovative....Applied broadly, this values-driven approach offers companies new opportunities for value creation, benefitting not only shareholders, but employees, communities, and society at large. (Jackson and Nelson, 2004, p1)

Based on a study of 60 multinational companies they propose a set of seven business disciplines for delivering profits with principles:

- Harness innovation for the public good,
- Put people at the centre,
- Spread economic opportunity,
- Engage in new alliances,
- Be performance-driven in everything,
- Practice superior governance,
- Pursue purpose beyond profit.

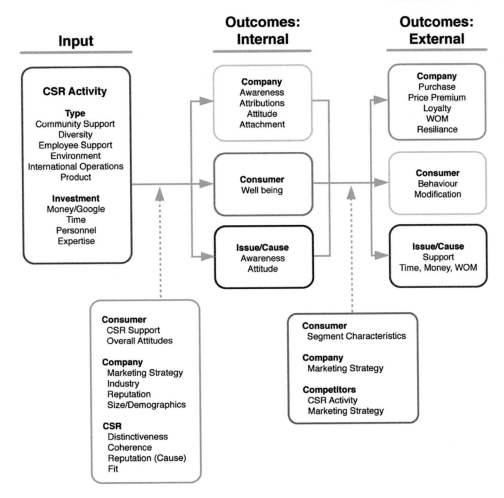

Figure 17.1 A contingent framework for integrating CSR

Source: Adapted from Bhattacharya and Sen (2004)

The notion of integrating what might be seen as stand-alone CSR-related activities into overall marketing strategy is echoed in the work of Bhattacharya and Sen who propose what they refer to as Contingent Framework of CSR as shown in Figure 17.1.

This is a very practical approach to leveraging the investment made in CSR activities and identifies several ways in which a range of attitudinal and behavioural outcomes can be achieved. The model also identifies several multiplying factors that serve to enhance the value gained from the range of inputs cited. These factors include what are termed consumer-related effects such as the characteristics of the segment to which they belong and their attitudes towards the input activity. Company characteristics such as the industry it represents, and its corporate reputation, also exert multiplying effects.

A number of researchers have explored the impact of CSR practices on business and specifically financial services. A detailed review was undertaken by Zainuldin and Lui (2022). Research insight 17.1 provides an overview of one study which identified the positive consequences of CSR in financial services.

Research insight 17.1: the impact of CSR on bank performance in China

This is an empirical study that aims to assess the extent to which corporate social responsibility affects organisational performance, using data from China's banking sector. The study draws on stakeholder theory (Freeman 1984, 2010) discussed earlier in this chapter and treats CSR as a broad based responsibility to a range of stakeholders (not just communities).

Data was collected for banks and from managers within banks. Seven key aspects of CSR were measured – based on responsibility to employees, to customers, to suppliers/business partners, shareholders, community, environment and to government. Organisational culture was also measured, and respondents were also asked to evaluate organisational performance relative to competitors. Responses were obtained from over 400 managers in banks based on a convenience sample and a structural model was estimated to explore the relationships between CSR (and the seven aspects mentioned above), organisational culture and competitive performance.

The results suggest a strong relationship between CSR and competitive performance and the most influential aspects of CSR were responsibility to employees, to customers and to government. Organisational culture also shown to be important and enhanced the relationship between CSR and competitive performance arguably because of its impacts on organisational productivity. Given the reliance on a convenience sample, the results need to be interpreted with some caution.

Source: Waheed, Zhang, Zafar, Zameer, Ashfaq and Nusrat (2021)

The notion of a new commercial narrative centred upon a values-based approach to strategy is also reflected in the work of Michael Willmott in his book *Citizen Brands* (Willmott, 2003). Core to Willmott's arguments is that a range of environmental factors are steadily undermining the trust that consumers have in brands and companies whose business strategies are focused narrowly on the maximisation of shareholder returns. Through an array of closely argued points, supported by vivid examples, he makes a compelling case in favour of citizen brands that display a strong set of core values that relate to their roles in, and relationships with, society. He asserts that:

> To build competitive and sustainable brands, companies need to understand the mindset, apprehensions and concerns of the consuming public by engaging in a much more pro-active way with society and its citizens. They need to become Citizen Brands-building up a stock of goodwill and trust to maintain their reputation in the challenging and uncertain times ahead.[5]
>
> (Willmott, 2003, p262)

17.4 Towards a sustainable future

In many respects marketing and consideration of the future are inextricably linked. This relationship is in evidence in marketing's role in seeking to understand the forces that will shape the marketplace of the future. Strategic marketing planning describes the processes which formally assess environmental trends and present scenarios for responding to those trends to sustain an organisation's future survival and success. Customer marketing is based upon the notion of continuity and responding to the changing needs of the individual customer over an extended period. Thus, the term sustainability has a particular resonance in the context of marketing. Its significance extends beyond marketing and strikes at the very core of the organisation's future survival.

It is our view that marketing can contribute to the issue of sustainability in two ways. First, it has a crucial role to play in ensuring the survival and future success of the organisation itself through the role it plays strategically and tactically. Second, it can play a role in contributing to wider issues regarding social and environmental sustainability. Let's call the former *internal sustainability* and the latter *external sustainability.*

As far as internal sustainability is concerned, marketing plays a vital role in maintaining the strategic triangle referred to at various points in the book. Of note is the importance of marketing's role in environmental scanning. It is only by continually refreshing one's knowledge of the forces that will shape future demand and supply that organisational survival can be safeguarded. For this reason, it is vital that environmental scanning is suitably wide-ranging to provide the necessary breadth of vision. This is particularly important in the case of multinational players. For example, if we consider the demographic profile of the world's major groupings, we observe that the population of North America, Europe and Japan (what we might call the old economies) amount to the order of 800 million people. The population of China is some 1.36 billion and the combined populations of the Muslim world stretching from the Atlantic coast of Africa eastwards to the Indonesian archipelago is greater than 2 billion. Major cultural differences apply between these three basic groupings and, clearly, multinational organisations must be especially well-tuned to their respective drivers of change. Scenario planning is a technique that is particularly useful as a means of endeavouring to identify possible opportunities and threats in a macro-environment of the multinational organisation. Such an approach can serve as a means of stimulating new insights that challenge received wisdom and the status quo. A world view based purely upon the conventional mindset of the G8 capitalist democracies may be woefully inadequate as a basis for shaping strategies in future.

Additionally, marketing has an obligation to discharge its responsibilities in respect of its use of the marketing mix such that it does not endanger the prospects of the organisation it seeks to serve. This involves an acute awareness of the risks associated with marketing activities on the one hand, and the need to exercise sound commercial judgement on the other hand. As far as the former is concerned, it calls for a thorough-going appreciation of regulatory and legal requirements as well as sound husbandry of corporate resources. Consumers are aware to an increasing extent of how companies are responding to the challenges posed by ESG. In her online article *Social Media in Financial Services: Benefits, Tips, Examples* in May of 2022 Christina Newberry[6] comments that;

Financial services brands now have to show they're about more than financial returns.

64% of respondents to the 2022 Edelman Trust Barometer survey said they invest based on beliefs and values. And 88% of institutional investors "subject ESG to the same scrutiny as operational and financial considerations."

Newberry also notes that younger investors have a particular interest in sustainable investment and points to a Harris Poll in the USA on behalf of CNBC in which a third of millennials, 19% and 16% of generations Z and X respectively either often or exclusively use ESG-focussed investments in their decision making.

Progress check

- CSR has its origins in the philanthropic industrialists of the nineteenth centuries. The term CSR was first coined in 1953.
- Globalisation in the 1990s gave renewed impetus to CSR, and UN Framework Convention on Climate Change and UN Kyoto Agreement resulted in a step change in the commitment of business globally to take ESG seriously.
- Marketing can contribute to sustainability in two ways. Firstly, by ensuring the survival and future success of the organisation itself through the role it plays strategically and tactically. Secondly, it can contribute to wider issues regarding social and environmental sustainability. Let's call the former *internal sustainability* and the latter *external sustainability.*

Finally, let us turn our attention to the issue of external sustainability. Again, it should fall to marketing to appreciate the interrelationships between the organisation and variables at play in the external environment beyond the micro-environment referred to earlier in Part I. One is beginning to observe gathering evidence of an appreciation of how marketing can contribute to broader issues concerning the social and physical environment. The avoidance of practices that involve polluting the atmosphere, and the efficient use of natural resources, for example, have a role to play in contributing to environmental sustainability. A particularly compelling example from the world of financial services is the Swedish insurance company Folksam. Folksam was one of 19 Insurance companies in the world to become the first signatories of the UNEP Statement of Environmental Commitment. The Statement now has more than 180 signatories from the insurance industry and the number is growing steadily. The following marketing in practice provides some interesting insights into Folksam's approach to environmental well-being and sustainability.

 Marketing in practice 17.1: sustainability at Folksam

Folksam

Folksam is a mutual company whose vision states: " People should feel secure in a sustainable world." With over four million customers, and managing over SEK 600 billion of assets on their behalf, Folksam is one of the largest insurance and pension providers in Sweden.

Towards net-zero emissions in own operations by 2030

Folksam has a goal of achieving net-zero emissions from its own operations by the year 2030. This means that we need to have reduced our emissions by 85% compared with the base year of 2002. Based on emissions in 2017, the Folksam Group developed a plan towards the net-zero target that involves a 9% reduction in emissions every year. The roadmap is based on Carbon Law and is in line with the Paris Agreement. Since we began working on the goal of net-zero emissions by 2030 in our own operations, the results have been in line with the annual targets. In 2022, emissions from our own operations increased by 45 (-17) per cent compared with 2021. As can be seen in the table below, emissions from Folksam's own operations continue to be in line with an annual 9% reduction compared with the base year, despite the increase in 2022. The increase is largely due to more travel after the pandemic. The Folksam Group offsets all of its estimated emissions from its own operations each year through Vi-skogen's project, which is certified according to the globally recognised Verified Carbon Standard.

A sustainable insurance offering

Eco-labelled insurance Since 2011, Folksam's home, holiday home and car insurance policies have been certified with the Good Environmental Choice label. In 2022, 1.5 million home insurance policies received the Good Environmental Choice label. In order for our insurance to receive the label, we must meet a number of requirements set by the Swedish Society for Nature Conservation. A few examples:

- Asset management applies both negative and positive investment criteria and conducts advocacy work for science-based climate targets, for example.
- We ensure environmentally friendly purchases and use eco-labelled electricity in our offices.
- We inform our customers about how they can contribute to a sustainable lifestyle and provide access to energy savings advice.
- Our claims settlement works with environmentally friendly material choices and repairs in e.g. home and car insurance

At the end of 2022, around 880,000 (890,000) cars, 440,000 (435,000) homes and 117,000 (120,000) holiday homes were insured under our Good Environmental Choice-labelled insurance policies. These insurance policies achieved a turnover of around SEK 8.7 billion.

The requirements for something to be called a good environmental choice is based on the realisation that we must conserve natural resources, biodiversity and that human health may not be threatened.

Sustainable claims settlement

Folksam's cost for repairs of damaged houses amounted to more than SEK 1 billion in 2022. The cost of car repairs was roughly twice as high. The scope enables us to set tough requirements on our suppliers. We train our suppliers to ensure that claim settlement is long-term, sustainable and effective, which is having a significant impact. There is an established second-hand market for car parts and we require that car mechanics repair and use reused parts wherever possible and appropriate. During the year, this helped a mountain of waste of around 1,710 (1,880) tonnes to be avoided and we saved approximately SEK 306 (290) million in the repair of damaged cars. In total, reuse in connection with car repairs has brought a saving of just over SEK 3 (2.8) billion since the beginning of the millennium. In addition to influencing the industry, we are also hoping to be able to influence our customers' attitude towards repairs and the circular economy.

Circular claim settlement is central to reducing our customers' consumption of energy and materials. Since 2015, we have been working together with Godsinlösen (GIAB) to create a circular flow for damaged objects such as sofas, glasses, bicycles, mobile phones, computers and other electronics. A special "mobile circle" has been developed for mobile phones, where customers hand in their damaged phones and, in most cases, receive an equivalent remanufactured or repaired phone in return. Through our cooperation with GIAB, the majority of our customers' mobile phones are reused. All usable parts are reused as a resource for other customers' mobiles, rather than becoming electronic waste. The burden on the environment is reduced, in the form of reduced waste volumes and lower carbon dioxide emissions. According to GIAB's calculations, in 2022 our circular claims handling together with GIAB helped to avoid 1,627 (1,634) tonnes of carbon dioxide emissions and 1,406 (1,903) tonnes of waste. The reported saving of carbon dioxide and waste is a comparison of whether the claims have been replaced by new units instead of repairing or replacing them.

Source: Sophie Hemne de Robien, Folksam

17.5 The evolution of sustainability: navigating ESG in contemporary marketing practices

In this section, sustainability and governance guru, Sallie Pilot, explains how ESG has moved the CSR debate on from an essentially optional aspiration for the more enlightened companies within the corporate world, to assume the role of a more muscular and mandatory regimen that is gaining far more traction.

In recent years, the landscape of marketing has undergone a profound shift as businesses increasingly recognise the importance of sustainability. Here we delve further into the concept of sustainability, focusing on the key aspects of Environmental, Social, and Governance (ESG) principles. We will explore the meaning of ESG, its relationship with Corporate Social Responsibility (CSR), the driving forces behind its adoption, influential organisations in promoting the ESG message, the global reach of ESG and practical implications for businesses today.

Where we've come from – CSR

In many ways CSR marked the starting point for businesses taking ownership of their impact on society and was a way of identifying companies looking to do good, and consumers and investors seeking socially conscious organisations to do business with. George Serafeim, a Professor of Business Administration at Harvard Business School, refers to CSR is a broad concept that encompasses a company's overall commitment to ethical business practices, sustainability and social responsibility. CSR traditionally includes philanthropy, community engagement, and ethical behaviour beyond the financial bottom line. CSR activities are very broad and can vary massively between businesses, sectors and geographics and the lack of comparable metrics available. Over the last few years, the term CSR has experienced a shift in usage and interpretation, driven by an increasing demand for greater accountability and measurement. The traditional notion of companies simply "giving back" is evolving. Rather than solely focusing on the outward appearance of charitable activities, businesses are now scrutinised for possessing a more profound purpose and a comprehensive vision that extends beyond philanthropy. This transition reflects the growing recognition of the need for a structured framework that aligns with the contemporary demand for transparency, accountability, and a more comprehensive assessment of a company's impact on various fronts.

Where we are going to – ESG

ESG, which stands for environmental, social, and governance, is emerging as a prominent concept. This shift is explained by Serafeim (2019), who describes ESG as:

> A more focused and systematic framework for evaluating a company's performance in specific areas.[7]

In essence, ESG provides a structured framework that enhances transparency, drawing increased attention from investors, regulators, standards setters, and other discerning stakeholders. Environmental criteria may include a company's carbon footprint, energy efficiency, and waste management. Social criteria involve the company's relationships with employees, communities and suppliers, as well as aspects like diversity and labour practices. Governance criteria assess the quality of a company's leadership, internal controls, and shareholder rights.

Investors are drawn to ESG as a lens through which they can assess a company's resilience in the face of emerging risks, such as climate change and social inequality, while also identifying potential opportunities tied to sustainable and responsible business practices. The prominence of ESG reflects a broader shift in investor attitudes, acknowledging the interconnectedness of financial success and responsible corporate behaviour. As a result, ESG has become a key element in investment strategies, reflecting a growing understanding that sustainable practices contribute not only to societal and environmental well-being but also to long-term financial success.

This focus on tangible metrics significantly enhances the attractiveness of ESG as a comprehensive and robust evaluative tool, crucial for investors and broader stakeholders in assessing a company's sustainability and overall performance. Key dimensions of ESG are presented in Figure 17.2.

Social
- Diversity & Inclusion
- Human capital
- Health & Safety
- Product liability
- Security (inc. cyber/data)
- Stakeholder opposition
- Opportunity access to finance / health etc.

Environmental
- GHG emissions
- Natural capital
- Waste and pollution
- Biodiversity
- Circularity
- Energy Efficiency

Governance
- Corporate governance
- Board independence
- Ownership and control
- Renumeration (executives & employees)
- Corporate behaviour / ethics
- Accounting & audit
- Board diversity and structure

Figure 17.2 Key dimensions of ESG[8]

17.6 The relationship between CSR and ESG and key drivers for ESG adoption

So, while CSR aims to make a business accountable, ESG criteria make its efforts measurable. Alex Edman[9], professor of finance at London Business School underscores the interconnectedness of ESG and CSR in his work. Both involve a commitment to ethical business practices, but ESG provides a more structured and measurable framework. CSR activities, according to Edman, contribute to a company's social capital, which can positively influence long-term financial performance. ESG metrics offer a quantitative way to assess and communicate a company's CSR efforts, reinforcing the financial relevance of responsible business practices.

In Serafeim's work (Serafeim, 2019), he highlights the financial materiality of ESG factors. His research suggests that ESG performance is not just a matter of social responsibility but has a direct impact on a company's financial performance, underscoring the integration of ESG factors into the core business strategy and decision-making processes as can be seen in Table 17.1.

Table 17.1 Integrating CSR, ESG and sustainability[10]

CSR	ESG	Sustainability
Qualitative	Quantitative	Qualitative and quantitative
Self regulated	Externally regulated	Both self and externally regulated
Not directly related to business valuation	Directly related to business valuation	Often related to business valuation
Implemented through corporate culture, values and brand management	Implemented through measurable goals, actions and audits	Implemented through a combination of ESG and CSR

Shifting stakeholder expectations

Stakeholders, including investors, customers and employees, now expect companies to be accountable for their impact on the world. Companies are feeling increased pressure to improve their performance and disclosure on environmental, social, governance (ESG) and climate related issues to demonstrate commitment and leadership. ESG has become a crucial tool for companies to build and maintain trust with stakeholders by demonstrating their commitment to responsible business practices.

Increasing importance to investors

These factors are becoming not only core business matters for all leading companies but are also increasingly fundamental to the way investors are considering how and where they invest. Investors believe that ESG is important in understanding a company's full risk profile. It's about the risks and opportunities which could impact a company's ability to create long-term sustainable value. It's therefore essential that companies are integrating forward-looking ESG considerations into their strategy, implementing relevant governance controls that will lead to long-term corporate resilience and better allocation of capital. This coupled with the shift towards sustainable investing and recent growth in sustainable finance instruments is gaining traction, as part of the effort to achieve national commitments under the Paris Agreement on climate change.

The basic principles remain the same. From a marketing perspective, the contribution of marketing professionals can play an important role in strategic planning as well as carrying out marketing-related tasks which support the sustainability strategy. A solid understanding of the environmental social and governance risks, issues and concerns of both existing and potential investors, customers, employees, and wider stakeholders can provide the basis for developing a sustainability strategy that increases trust between the firm and its customers, enhance cross-selling potential and strengthen customer retention levels. These effects also consequently reduce acquisition costs. What is different is the speed of change, increasing regulation, the extent of issues that need to be addressed and rising stakeholder expectations.

Regulatory pressures

Governments and financial regulators are increasingly mandating ESG reporting, reflecting a move towards more standardised, comparable, and financially relevant metrics that can be used by investors and other stakeholders to assess a company's sustainability performance.

The UK regulatory landscape

At present, the UK has no single ESG law or regulation although ESG disclosure regulations primarily rely on the Companies Act, applying to larger listed companies with over 500 employees or exceeding £500 million in annual turnover. The Act was extended in 2022 to mandate sustainability details, including energy usage and carbon emissions reporting. Section 172 of the Companies Act and the UK Corporate Governance Code reflect the broader trend of encouraging companies to adopt responsible and sustainable business

570 Managing customer relationships and the future of marketing

practices. They underline the significance of considering environmental, social, and governance factors in decision-making and in the pursuit of the company's success over the long term. Companies are encouraged to integrate these considerations into their strategies and operations, aligning with the principles of ESG.

Further, Sustainability Disclosure Requirements (SDRs) from 2023 will establish a framework for handling sustainability aspects, with full mandatory disclosure expected by 2025. Starting from April 6, 2022, over 1,300 major UK companies and financial institutions were mandated for TCFD-based reporting (Task Force on Climate-related Financial Disclosures) extending to significant private companies in the future. This legislation not only impacts large entities but also reverberates through their supply chains, emphasising the imperative for comprehensive ESG reporting across businesses.

The European landscape

The European Union's Corporate Sustainability Reporting Directive (CSRD) came into force in January 2023, creating new environmental, social and governance (ESG) reporting standards for some 50,000 companies starting in 2025. The EU has introduced the Sustainable Finance Disclosure Regulation (SFDR), requiring financial market participants to disclose the ESG impact of their investments. Such regulations make ESG a legal requirement for both investors and corporates and encourage widespread adoption.

The USA landscape

The U.S. Securities and Exchange Commission (SEC) is continuing to work to finalise its proposed climate disclosure rules, the timing of final action remains as yet unclear. This will result in new ESG reporting and compliance requirements for publicly traded companies. There are already some states like California enacting their own climate disclosure laws.

17.6.1 Influential organisations in promoting ESG

United Nations Principles for Responsible Investment (UN PRI)

The UN PRI is a global network of investors working together to implement ESG principles. By signing the PRI, investors commit to incorporating ESG factors into their investment decisions and ownership practices. This initiative has significantly influenced the integration of sustainable practices into investment strategies worldwide.

Sustainability Accounting Standards Board (SASB)

SASB provides industry-specific standards for ESG disclosure, ensuring that companies report on the factors most relevant to their industry. This approach enhances the comparability of ESG information, making it easier for investors to evaluate and compare companies within the same sector.

Stop and think?

Which inspirational people from the past have been champions of what we now call ESG, and do any individuals from your own country come to mind?

How would you describe the differences between CSR and ESG?

Are there insurers in your country who have sustainability policies similar to those of Folksam?

17.7 Global reach of ESG

ESG has achieved global recognition, with various countries adopting its principles. The Task Force on Climate-related Financial Disclosures (TCFD), for example, has gained international support, emphasising the importance of climate-related financial risk disclosures for companies across borders.

In 2021, IFRS Foundation Trustees announced the formation of the International Sustainability Standards Board (ISSB), consolidation with Value Reporting Foundations (VRF), (which is made up of recent merger of SASB (Sustainability Accounting Standards Board) and IIRC (International Integrated Reporting Council) and the Task Force for Climate-related Financial Disclosures (TCFD) and CDSB). Building on the work of existing investor-focused reporting initiatives, the ISSB is the global standard-setter for sustainability disclosures for the financial markets. IFRS Sustainability Standards are developed to enhance investor-company dialogue so that investors receive decision-useful, globally comparable sustainability-related disclosures that meet their information needs. Two standards were published in 2023, general requirements for sustainability and climate related disclosure requirements.

Clarity, accountability, and greater comparability should result from the standardisation of the similar concepts, that are expressed in different language across the existing frameworks. This convergence will give us a welcome baseline to build on and a consistency in language.

Universal adoption

A recent report about ESG disclosures and assurance practices[11] around the world by the International Federation of Accountants (IFAC) and the Association of International Certified Professional Accountants, found that nearly all big global companies disclose environmental, social and governance (ESG) information, with 95% having done so in 2021.

Reporting enables transparency which allows for stakeholders, employees, customers, investors, policymakers to match with the companies that fit their ESG criteria. As more stakeholders make choices based on ESG criteria the stronger are the incentives for companies to change behaviour and improve their ESG outcomes. Edman's research argues that companies voluntarily adopting ESG measures before regulations are imposed not only mitigate risks but also gain a competitive advantage by being ahead of the curve, aligning with the principles of responsible business.

Figure 17.3 The reporting landscape[12]

Progress check

- As far as internal sustainability is concerned, marketing plays a vital role in maintaining the strategic triangle referred to at various points in this book. Of note is the importance of marketing's role in environmental scanning.
- Brands should build up a stock of goodwill and trust to maintain their reputation in the challenging and uncertain times ahead.
- CSR activities contribute to a company's social capital, which can positively influence long-term financial performance. ESG metrics offer a quantitative way to assess and communicate a company's CSR efforts, reinforcing the financial relevance of responsible business practices.
- ESG has achieved global recognition, with various countries adopting its principles, and nearly all big global companies disclose ESG information, with 95% having done so in 2021.

Marketing in practice 17.2: international sustainability initiatives in the insurance market from ICMIF

The International Co-operative and Mutual Insurance Federation (ICMIF) champions sustainability and ESG within the insurance industry globally, collaborating with the key players and members to focus on individual protection through insurance and community and planetary resilience. ICMIF emphasises risk prevention, mitigation, and education, offering unique value aligned with co-operative/mutual insurance sector principles.

In 2023, ICMIF hosted the first Sustainability Summit, uniting global members to discuss sustainable investments, resilience and underwriting strategies. Scheduled as a hybrid event in London, this summit aimed to address industry challenges, share solutions, and integrate sustainability into business strategies. Topics included building sustainable strategies, greening investment portfolios, and embedding the Sustainable Development Goals (SDGs) into underwriting.

Another initiative ICMIF runs for their members is the ICMIF-calibrated Insurance SDG Calculator, launched during the Centenary Conference (2022 in Rome), which measures the impact of insurance sustainability against SDGs. Developed by the ICMIF members and the Swiss Re Institute, it assesses impact within insurance portfolios, aligning with mutual values like risk prevention and inclusive insurance. This tool aids members in gauging their SDG efforts, identifying improvement areas, and fostering collaboration to achieve a sustainable future. As a milestone of the programme, ICMIF launched the ICMIF Insurance SDG Benchmark for their members to showcase the impact the mutual and co-operative insurance industry has as a global force for change.

In 2019, ICMIF and the United Nations Office for Disaster Risk Reduction (UNDRR) joined forces to deliver on three main priorities:

1. Create a framework to show how mutual and co-operatives can reduce disaster risks; this relationship culminated in a joint report highlighting seven mechanisms for the co-operative/mutual insurance sector to shift focus from risk transfer to prevention. The joint report inspires the broader insurance industry, showcasing possibilities for preventing and reducing disaster risks.
2. Produce a hub of case studies showcasing resilience practice in insurance, available to the public.
3. Formulate a benchmark for insurance resilience, which any insurer can use to score themselves and further improve, develop, and create their resilience and sustainability strategies.

The partnership between ICMIF and UNDRR aims to transition the insurance industry's focus from risk transfer to prevention, leveraging the co-operative/mutual sector's member-driven model.

For additional details, refer to ICMIF's Resilience Hub and Resiliency Benchmark, reinforcing the commitment to reducing disaster risks and promoting prevention within the insurance sector.

One ICMIF member who truly accepts the challenge of ESG, Sustainability and Resilience issues by putting them at the heart of their business strategy is the Co-operators in Canada. The Co-operators demonstrate this commitment by being instrumental in delivering both the iSDG Calculator and the Resilience Benchmark.

In the latest annual Corporate Knights Best 50 Corporate Citizens ranking, Co-operators is ranked as the top insurer globally, the top financial institution in Canada and sixth overall. This marks the 14th consecutive year Co-operators has been in the Best 50 ranking and continues to underscore the organisation's leadership across environmental, social, and governance-related sustainability performance indicators.

"This recognition amongst our peers reflects our ongoing work to embed sustainability into our business and to catalyse sustainability in society through our partnerships, products, services and investments," said Chad Park, Vice-President of Sustainability & Citizenship at Cooperators. "This work is fundamental to our co-operative identity and critical to our long-term success as we bring our purpose of financial security for Canadians and our communities to life".

Some key highlights of sustainability achievements by Co-operators:

*   23.6% of investments are invested for impact. That's CAD 2.69 billion directed to improve the well-being of the environment and society.
*   Co-operators is carbon neutral, and on a journey to achieve net zero in its operations and investments.
*   The organisation designs products with sustainability in mind, with 28.2% of total revenue coming from sustainable products or services.

Source: Liam Carter, Senior VP Sustainability, ICMIF

17.8 Practical implications for companies

Strategic marketing alignment

Aligning marketing strategies with ESG values involves communicating sustainability efforts transparently. This can include showcasing eco-friendly product development, ethical supply chain practices, and community engagement initiatives. Successful communication requires authenticity and a genuine commitment to ESG principles.

Risk management and opportunity identification

Companies that integrate ESG factors into their risk management processes can identify potential risks related to environmental and social issues. Simultaneously, they uncover opportunities for innovation and market differentiation, ultimately leading to a more resilient and competitive position in the market.

As sustainability pressures continue in an upward trend, a company's sustainability policies, practices and performance will increasingly impact on the company's value. Its ability to communicate its sustainability performance more effectively – and investors' ability to track this better – is increasingly impacting access to capital.

Focus on key issues and authenticity

It is impossible for companies to respond to every single demand that is out there or to be leading the way on every single issue. The challenge for the future will be for companies to step back and determine what their unique positioning is in the marketplace and understand what they can do to make a difference. Too many companies have a programme of activities or initiatives to address ESG rather than it being embedded into the way they think and do business. Corporate purpose and ESG can serve as effective tools to reframe. Leading organisations are those that understand that purpose, culture, values and strategy are inextricably linked. They have a purpose that sets a clear direction on why they exist and the positive impact they seek to have. They are strategic about their core capabilities and connect strategy and a differentiated proposition to drive performance. Communicating this consistently across all communications, reports, websites, new releases, regulatory filings, video, and social media to key stakeholders will be central to building trust in businesses as we move forward in a new and increasingly complex world.

Meaningful transition

The past few years has been marked by a step forward in global efforts to drive climate change, and a plethora of "net zero" and other climate signalling initiatives upon which companies intend to take action. The United Nations Climate Change Conference (COP28) in December 2023, closed with an agreement that signals the "beginning of the end" of the fossil fuel era by laying the ground for a swift, just, and equitable transition, underpinned by deep emissions cuts and scaled-up finance. So, good intentions will no longer be enough. Many a company's plans have not been matched by crucial details on how they will reshape business strategies, capital allocation, governance mechanisms and plans for long-term value creation.

Investors and other key stakeholders are demanding meaningful disclosure on plans with specific impacts on businesses to give them confidence that a company is set up for success in a transitioning world and so they can fulfil their stewardship role. This extends to financial statements reflecting risks and opportunities and valuations to reflect assumptions with credible, science-based targets. TCFD (Taskforce for Climate Related Disclosures) is now a must for premium listed companies in the UK from April 2022. There is also increasing focus on other issues such as nature related risks and biodiversity, particularly with the momentum around TNFD (Taskforce on Nature Related Financial Disclosures)

Future of digital communications and technology

Embracing digital communications and technology has become pivotal, driven significantly by the transformative impact of the Covid-19 pandemic. One of the areas most affected is the way we communicate with one another. This is no different in the corporate world, where companies have had to adapt and innovate to reach their stakeholders. We've seen acceleration in use of digital sources as investors eagerly explore alternative sources of information.

Corporate websites have emerged as not only extensively used but also highly trusted sources of information. With a general expectation for leadership presence on digital and social media, e-mail newsletters, LinkedIn and YouTube; thus social media sources are becoming even more central to marketing strategies. In addition, technological advancements, including AI, blockchain, and big data, are reshaping the production, distribution and consumption of information.

The traditional reliance on regular results, year-end announcements and one way communication is a thing of the past. Companies need to develop marketing from static communications to active, engaging strategies to meet the perpetual demand for data. Digital channels offer companies an ever-increasing choice about how, what and when they communicate to their stakeholders. While technologies and communication methods will continue to evolve rapidly, the current challenge lies not in producing more information but in delivering content that is more accessible, accurate, relevant and timely. Amid the perceived challenges, these trends also present many opportunities. Companies and investors with a forward-thinking approach recognise the advantages of effective engagement, innovative communications, and staying at the forefront of technological advancements. Ultimately, leveraging these themes contributes not only to meeting evolving expectations but also to creating substantial value in the dynamic marketing landscape.

17.9 ESG in practice: examples from financial services and consumer goods

Edmans' research underscores the financial relevance of ESG in the financial services sector. Firms like BlackRock, embracing ESG principles, align with Edmans' argument that responsible investment positively correlates with financial performance. By actively engaging in shareholder activism and incorporating ESG metrics into decision-making, financial institutions can contribute to both societal well-being and financial success.

Edmans' perspective on corporate social responsibility also aligns with consumer goods companies like Unilever, which emphasise sustainability in their business models. Edmans argues that companies with a commitment to social responsibility can build strong relationships with consumers, leading to enhanced financial performance. Unilever's Sustainable Living Plan exemplifies how ESG practices can drive positive brand perception and, ultimately, financial success.

Patagonia, the outdoor apparel company is another firm well-known for its strong commitment to environmental sustainability, fair labour practices, and social responsibility. Patagonia's ESG initiatives include using recycled materials, fair trade sourcing, and actively addressing climate change.

Danone, multinational food-products corporation exemplifies ESG practices in the consumer goods sector. Danone focuses on environmental sustainability, social inclusivity, and transparent labelling. Edmans' argument about the financial benefits of responsible business aligns with Danone's emphasis on the dual objective of business success and societal well-being.

17.9.1 The benefits of embracing ESG

Embracing ESG practices not only aligns with societal and environmental goals but also delivers many benefits for various stakeholders, including investors, employees, customers, and society at large. The role of marketing in conveying these ESG initiatives is crucial in ensuring widespread awareness and positive perception.

- *Customers – Building trust through responsibility*
  Customers are increasingly drawn to companies that prioritise ESG principles, and marketing plays a central role in conveying these efforts. By aligning with sustainable practices, companies demonstrate a commitment to ethical and responsible business conduct. Marketing campaigns effectively communicate these values, resonating positively with consumers who are becoming more conscious of the environmental and social impact of their purchasing decisions.
- *Employees – Fostering purposeful workplaces*
  For employees too, a company's commitment to ESG signifies a deeper purpose and responsibility. Marketing initiatives internally communicate the significance of ESG efforts, creating an environment that is not only values-driven but also fosters a sense of contributing to a greater good. This helps to enhance employee morale, engagement and overall job satisfaction. External marketing campaigns can also highlight the company's ESG initiatives, attracting talent that values socially responsible employers.
- *Investors – Sustainable returns*
  Investors also stand to gain from ESG engagement, and marketing is playing an increasing role in conveying these efforts to the investment community. A recent PRI report highlights that when approached thoughtfully, ESG engagement creates value by fostering the exchange of crucial information. This, in turn, enhances communication channels, enabling investors to make more informed decisions. Furthermore, such engagement drives the acquisition of fresh ESG knowledge, thereby increasing awareness and understanding. Investors engaging with companies on ESG matters are better equipped to navigate the evolving landscape of sustainable investment, and marketing materials can play a key role in disseminating this information.
- *Society – Beyond profit*
  On a broader societal level, embracing ESG contributes to positive social and environmental outcomes, and marketing serves as a powerful tool in amplifying this impact. By prioritising purpose over profit, companies actively participate in addressing pressing global challenges. This shift blurs traditional boundaries between corporate, investor, and regulatory roles. Companies are urged to prioritise a broader purpose, investors are encouraged to act as "universal owners" and stewards of long-term value, while regulators are prompted to focus on issues such as corporate purpose and culture.

- *Leveraging ESG marketing for genuine brand narratives*

  Overall, marketing is critical in conveying the benefits of embracing ESG throughout various stakeholder groups. It ensures that the positive impact of ESG initiatives is effectively communicated, contributing to improved communication, heightened awareness, strengthened relationships, increased consumer trust, enhanced employee satisfaction, and a positive impact on society and the environment. Embracing change, engaging stakeholders, effective communication through marketing, and innovation in ESG practices today are imperative steps to meet the evolving expectations of tomorrow.

17.10 The pursuit of barrier-free brand experience

An important aspect of ESG in the context of financial services is that of inclusion. At various stages in this book we have discussed issues concerning financial exclusion and inclusion. Usually this is in the context of exclusion based upon socio-economic factors and we will look at this again shortly when we consider the role and work of the Financial Inclusion Commission. However, in this section we will consider exclusion that arises from a person's disability as this can be a major source of consumer detriment Although governments have many powers to legislate for change and introduce new regulations, actual change itself is far more likely to be driven by the business community. Often it is companies that act as the catalyst for change and marketing should be in the vanguard of championing inclusive product and service design. In January 2022 Interbrand established an inclusive design practice aimed at helping organisations to design products and services that are fully inclusive and thus allow people of all abilities to enjoy the utility they have to offer. In the following marketing in practice, Marianne Waite, the Director of Interbrand Inclusive Design, explains the importance of inclusive design as an engine of business growth as well as the discharging of ESG responsibilities.

 Marketing in practice 17.3: the pursuit of barrier-free brand experience

Interbrand

Most of us negotiate the world on autopilot. We get dressed, we grab a coffee, we travel to work, we go for dinner etc., etc. No trouble at all. All part of a subconscious process we take for granted throughout our daily lives. It is not like that if you have a disability. Imagine inhabiting a world that simply isn't designed for you. Each day being confronted with environments, interactions, and experiences, that all present physical or attitudinal barriers. These barriers aren't always related to explicit accessibility issues like whether there's a lift or not. They're often smaller, more discrete exchanges that knock confidence and hinder participation.

And it's this lack of consideration and provision that makes an experience exclusive. So, unless brands actively consider how to remove these barriers, they disable by default.

Accessibility is the bedrock of improved experiences not only for this market, but for nondisabled people too, as our collective desire for innovation, utility and simplification grows. Because the reality is that we will all experience disability at some point in our lives – some sooner than others. This could be because of long-term illness or health challenges, temporary disabilities (poor mental health or short-term injury), or situational disability (exclusion experienced through lockdown restrictions). Consider the Coronavirus pandemic; the brands that worked quickly to meet the needs of employees and customers confined to their homes did rather well (Hello, Besos…). Whereas businesses that hadn't invested in accessibility and user experience to the same extent struggled. (Primark's profit's plunged by 60% in 2020[1]).

Increasingly brands have become drivers for change, harnessing this generation's willingness to invest in those they believe will help fight for the causes they care about. Brands have become vehicles through which consumers can make their voices heard. This accelerated rate of change over just a few years has helped break down barriers that have been holding people back for centuries. But significant challenges remain. Challenges that go deeper than representation and recruitment. It's now crucial to focus on how we address disability in all aspects of business, including the customer journey. This is how brands can create truly enhancing experiences: from retail access and product development to cultural engagement.

The global spending power of disabled people, their carers and families has been calculated at $13trillion. 73% of consumers are touched by disability, yet 75-80% of consumer experiences are deemed to be a failure by disabled people.[2] Catering to the needs of disabled people is not just about doing the right thing as decent human beings. Although providing human rights through consumer rights seems like a pretty strong reason in itself. Inclusivity is becoming an increasingly important business driver, and therefore, imperative to brands.

So far, most efforts to tackle disability have been superficial and at times, tokenistic. A few however, have become shining beacons of hope; demonstrating how brands can create impactful change. Their success demonstrates any efforts must go beyond regulatory box-ticking and trend following. Rather than one-off projects, or quick-fix "firework" efforts, brands need to invest in longer- term efforts to remove barriers. This is about embarking on a journey, not to reach the end, but to make a continued commitment to learning and evolution. Brands such as Amazon, Apple, Microsoft and P&G are proving that inclusivity provides sustainable growth opportunities as they demonstrate the vast number of benefits including stronger brand loyalty; greater distinction; enhanced credibility; innovation opportunities; improved talent retention and higher brand engagement.

We are also seeing exciting examples within the financial services sectors too. For instance, Barclays' audio cash machines (also known as audio ATMs or talking cash machines) can help customers safely and independently withdraw cash and use other services, such as getting a balance. They're also useful if you have dyslexia or learning difficulties, or if the sun is compromising readability. Halifax's stripped back visual and verbal identity was purposefully designed to make personal finances more accessible. Built on the insight that the reading age of the UK population is 9 years old, Halifax stripped back unnecessary jargon, wording, and imagery to make managing money super simple to understand. This empowered people with learning disabilities and age-related illnesses as well as the wider public, many of whom are overwhelmed by the amount of information provided by banks. Mastercard extended its commitment to inclusivity by introducing an accessible card standard for blind and partially sighted people, called the Touch Card. There are few effective ways for the visually impaired to quickly determine whether they're holding a credit, debit or prepaid card, particularly as more cards move to flat designs without embossed name and numbers. Mastercard is addressing this challenge with a simple yet effective innovation, making life easier for disabled and nondisabled people. The new standard includes a system of notches on the side of the card to help consumers use the right card, the right way, by touch alone. The new Touch Card credit cards have a squarish notch, debit cards have a rounded notch, and prepaid cards have a triangular notch.

Over recent years, Interbrand has observed a correlation between accessibility and its Best Global Brand rankings[3]. It's becoming clear that by putting accessibility at the heart of their business strategies, brands can positively impact their brand strength and improve their value. Becoming a purpose-driven inclusive brand involves a process of awakening which requires having new and different conversations with disabled and older consumers on an ongoing basis. By having these conversations and by using key insights from this audience to understand what needs to change as well as a creative starting point, brands can ensure that no-one is left behind.

Consider how environmentalism is now firmly in our individual and community conscience, business objectives, and international political agendas. Brands need to approach disability inclusivity in much the same way. This means strong strategies, board-level investment, and ongoing measurement. It takes time and perseverance. But the time is now, and the only real risk is being left behind. On behalf of the 73% (and your future selves), consider hardwiring inclusive design at the heart of your strategy to help create a world that works for everybody.

Marianne Waite, Director of Inclusive Design, Interbrand

1. http://www.retailgazette.co.uk/blog/2020/11/primark-profits-plunge-60-after-a-di covid/
2. https://www.rod-group.com/insights/rod-research
3. https://interbrand.com/best-brands/

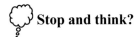

Stop and think?

To what extent do you believe that CSR considerations are a distraction from the primary corporate goal of making profits?

In what ways do you think that Marketing can further the goals of ESG?

What examples of ESG practices in your country do you find inspiring?

17.11 ESG and inclusive growth

In this final section former UK Member of Parliament Chris Pond provides us with a policymaker's view of the relationship between ESG and the aims of financial inclusion. As Chair of the Financial Inclusion Commission Chris is uniquely placed to address this issue that is of global significance.

The growth of inequality, both between and within nations, together with somewhat anaemic growth in many Western economies, has stimulated increased interest in the concept of inclusive growth. Diversity and inclusion, traditionally associated with the "S" in ESG also has an economic dimension. Mastercard, which has invested globally in projects to promote financial inclusion, provided start-up funds to establish an independent Financial Inclusion Commission in the UK 10 years ago. Made up of parliamentarians from the main political parties, together with policy experts and representatives of both consumers and business, the Commission has argued the need for a National Strategy for Financial Inclusion. The Commission has been working with the Aspen Institute in Washington who are promoting the idea of a similar national strategy in the United States.

The Commission has made some, albeit limited, progress in the UK. One of it's earliest proposals was for the appointment of a Minister within government with responsibility for promoting inclusion. Two such ministers were subsequently appointed and the current incumbent of that role, Treasury minister Bim Afolami, MP, was formerly a member of the Commission itself. Other members of the Commission include the Chair of a House of Lords Select Committee on Financial Exclusion (Baroness Tyler) and the former head of the financial services regulator, the FCA.

Yet despite this limited progress financial exclusion remains a major challenge in the UK, despite the historic strength of its financial services sector. More than a million adults

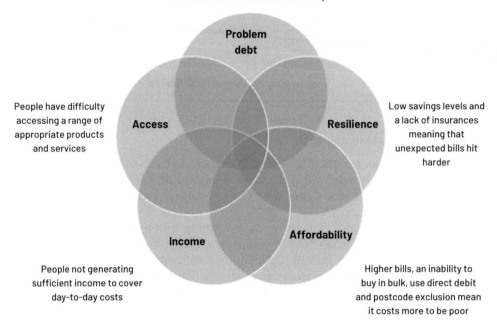

Figure 17.4 The drivers of financial exclusion

Source: The Financial Inclusion Plan, developed by Fair4All Finance (2023)[13]

in the UK don't even have a bank account, while 1 in 4 have less than £100 in savings and a similar proportion have no home contents insurance. Many have no access to affordable credit, needing to turn to high-cost, short term credit when needed. As a result, those households without access to financial services face a "poverty premium" which, according to research commissioned by Fair by Design, can amount to £430 a year – a significant sum for those on an already low income. There are 6 core drivers of financial exclusion as shown in Figure 17.4.

The Financial Conduct Authority estimates the numbers facing financial vulnerability to be of the order of 17.5 million. In consumer driven economies, this vulnerability extends beyond households to the economy as a whole. With such a large proportion of the population in a precarious financial position, the impact of economic shocks can be magnified.

Thus, the Commission has argued that there is a strong economic and business case for inclusive action by firms and governments alike. In a speech delivered to a roundtable of business leaders hosted by the Lord Mayor for London in 2023, John Godfrey of Legal and General, a former Head of the Prime Minister's Policy Unit and a member of the Commission, argued that:

> Government can't do it all. Business needs to step up (which) requires it to move financial inclusion from CSR to the mainstream and this in turn requires businesses to operate out of enlightened self-interest. ….. Making provision for financial inclusion is also an expected and attractive part of the package for hiring and retention. From a customer perspective, the financially excluded constitute an under-served market. One good example is provision of contents insurance for social housing tenants with premiums collected with rent. It would significantly expand insurers' customer base while adding financial resilience.
>
> A second effect of greater financial inclusion is that it closes markets to illegal or egregious operators and opens them to mainstream providers. As was pointed out in the CSJ's "On the Money" Report, financial inclusion underpins long-term financial stability. This in turn reduces reliance on illegal or unauthorised lenders, on predatory pricing in the "buy now, pay later" sector.

The exclusion from access to financial services represents a significant lost opportunity for business and acts as a drag-anchor on economic growth. But so too does a lack of diversity in the workforce. The Money and Mental Health Institute, established to highlight the link between over-indebtedness and mental health challenges, has a highly successful employment access programme, helping those facing mental health difficulties into employment with financial services firms. The organisation, Ambitious about Autism, is helping young adults on the autistic spectrum into employment in a range of businesses and public sector bodies. Silicon Valley has long recognised the value of neurodiversity as a driver of technological innovation.

And so programmes to promote inclusion and diversity are no longer the preserve of CSR policies. They are now firmly part of the ESG agenda, with an emphasis on the "S" but with an important contribution to make in promoting growth and productivity.

17.12 Summary and conclusion

The reputational damage suffered by the financial sector in recent years points to a new business narrative that is rooted not simply in maximising short-term shareholder value but in an engagement with the interests of a wider group of stakeholders and with society in general. As we have seen, the requirements of corporate social responsibility and sustainability imply that marketing managers must be aware of and responsive to the broader social consequences of the products and services they provide and the ways in which they are marketed. Whereas CSR may hitherto have been considered a nice-to-have aspect of corporate life, its more muscular bedfellow ESG is fast becoming mandatory across financial services. It is essential that those engaged in marketing financial products and services appreciate the role they must play in this new world of ESG.

This is an exciting time to be engaged in the marketing of financial services, and the advent of ESG makes it even more so. Finally, focus must never be lost of the simple fact that marketing is about getting and keeping customers. Ultimately, its success can only be judged on that basis.

Learning outcomes

Having completed this chapter, you should now be able to:

1. **Appreciate that financial services companies inhabit a wide social, economic, and environmental ecology in which good corporate citizenship is vital for sustainable success in the ever-changing marketplace.**
   Governments worldwide are now looking to create greater transparency, openness, and responsiveness in the business sector by introducing both "hard" and "soft" legislation to improve standards of corporate governance in the boardroom and social responsibility towards internal and external stakeholders. It should fall to marketing to appreciate the interrelationships between the organisation and variables at play in the external environment beyond the micro-environment referred to earlier in Part I. There is a growing appreciation of how marketing can contribute to broader issues concerning the social and physical environment. The avoidance of practices that involve polluting the atmosphere, and the efficient use of natural resources, for example, have a role to play in contributing to environmental sustainability.

2. **Understand what is meant by the terms CSR and ESG and how they relate to each other.**
   Both CSR and ESG involve a commitment to ethical business practices, but ESG provides a more structured and measurable framework. Arguably, CSR activities contribute to a company's social capital, which can positively influence long-term financial performance. ESG metrics, on the other hand, offer a quantitative way to assess and communicate a company's CSR efforts, reinforcing the financial relevance of responsible business practices. Research suggests that ESG performance is not just a matter of social responsibility but has a direct impact on a company's financial performance, underscoring the integration of ESG factors into the core business strategy and decision-making processes.

3. **Understand marketing's wider contribution within the contexts of corporate social responsibility and ESG.**
   We have seen how marketing at both the strategic and tactical levels has a major role to play in enabling an organisation to fulfil its ESG aspirations, requirements, and obligations. Through its environmental scanning activities marketing can give direction to business strategy by identifying opportunities and threats in the sphere of ESG. By reviewing the positioning of its brand, marketing is best placed to identify opportunities for repositioning in the light of ESG developments. The marketing mix comprises many of the elements that will need to be deployed and managed in order to respond to ESG.

4. **Appreciate some of the ways on which FSCs are fulfilling their ESG responsibilities.**
   Marketing in practice and other cases referred to in this chapter and elsewhere provide solid and compelling evidence of the ways in which FSCs around the world are rising to the challenges posed by ESG. From Folksam's sustainability policies

and practices in Sweden; to Starling being a first-of-its-kind digital bank, with no branches, intuitive in-app features and other innovations it sets out to have less impact on the planet; and on to Cooperators in Canada which is already carbon neutral, and on a journey to achieve net zero in its operations and investments, we see how successful FSPs can be in fulfilling their ESG responsibilities.

Review questions

1. Discuss how you feel that CSR impacts upon the interests of various stakeholder groups.
2. Discuss the role that marketing can play in furthering the goal of environmental sustainability. Do you believe that it is a legitimate use of marketing resources?
3. Identify which banks and insurance companies operating in your country you believe are the best exemplars of ESG. What impresses you most about their CSR policies and practices?
4. Some people would argue that the resources devoted to ESG represent theft from the shareholder, to what extent do you think they have a point?
5. Thinking of the future, in what ways do you believe that the business models of financial services companies in your country may evolve to reflect drivers of change such as the rise of so-called populism and desire expressed by organisations such as the World Economic Forum to share wealth amongst all communities?

Notes

1 Wealth, Andrew Carnegie, North American Review, No. CCCXCI, June, 1889.
2 United Nations Framework Convention on Climate Change, United Nations 1992, FCCC/INFORMAL/84 GE.05-62220 (E) 200705 (accessed January 2024)
3 Kyoto Protocol to the United Nations Framework Convention on Climate Change, United Nations, 1998
4 World Economic Forum Annual Meeting 2017 Overview Davos-Klosters, Switzerland 17-20 January 2017, Responsive and Responsible Leadership
5 Citizen Brands: Putting Society at the Heart of your Business, 2003, by Michael Willmott
6 Social Media in Financial Services: Benefits, Tips, Examples, https://blog.hootsuite.com/social-media-financial-services/ (ccessed January 2024)
7 Serafeim, G. (2019). ESG Metrics: Reshaping Capitalism? *Harvard Business School Working Paper*, 20-056.
8 *IRSociety ESG Essentials Course: Agendi*
9 Alex Edmans, A. (2023). Applying Economics-Not Gut Feel-To ESG. *Financial Analysts Journal*, 79(4), pp.16-29.
10 www.hbs.edu/ris/Publication%20Files/23-069c3b42539-b1f3-4acf-a7d7-60e85806f96d, Adapted from DavidCarlin via Linkedin
11 www.unpri.org/research/how-esg-engagement-creates-value-for-investors-and-companies/3054. article (accessed January 2024)
12 *Source: IRSociety ESG Essentials Course: Agendi*
13 https://fair4allfinance.org.uk/resources/financial-inclusion-plan/ (accessed January 2024)

References

Bhattacharya, C. B. and Sen, S. (2004). Doing better: When, why, and how consumers respond to corporate social initiatives. *California Management Review*, 47(1), pp. 9–24.

Bidhan L. Parmar, R. Edward Freeman, Jeffrey S. Harrison, Andrew C. Wicks, Simone de Colle, Lauren Purnell: (2010) *Stakeholder Theory: The State of the Art*. The Academy of Management Annals, doi:10.1080/19416520.2010.495581,

Freeman, R E (1984, 2010) *Strategic Management: A Stakeholder Approach,* Cambridge: CUP.

Jackson, I. and Nelson, J. (2004). *Values-Based Performance: Seven Strategies for Delivering Profits With Principles*. Cambridge, MA: John F. Kennedy School of Government, Harvard University. (Corporate Social Responsibility Initiative, Working Paper No. 7).

Serafeim, G. (2019). *ESG Metrics: Reshaping Capitalism?* Harvard Business School Working Paper, 20–056.

Waheed, A., Zhang, Q., Zafar, A.U., Zameer, H., Ashfaq, M. and Nusrat, A. (2021). Impact of internal and external CSR on organizational performance with moderating role of culture: Empirical evidence from Chinese banking sector. *International Journal of Bank Marketing*,39(40, pp. 499–515. https://doi.org/10.1108/IJBM-04-2020-0215

Willmott, M. (2003). *Citizen Brands: Putting Society at the Heart of Your Business*, Chichester: Wiley.

Zainuldin, M.H. and Lui, T.K. (2022) A bibliometric analysis of CSR in the banking industry: A decade study based on Scopus scientific mapping. *International Journal of Bank Marketing*, 40(1), pp. 1–26. https://doi.org/10.1108/IJBM-04-2020-0178

18 Marketing culture, challenges and evaluation

Learning objectives

At the end of this chapter, you should be able to

1. Develop an understanding of how culture is defined, and its relationship to competitive advantage,
2. Appreciate the importance of integrating functional marketing activities holistically within the overall corporate culture,
3. Understand the challenges that a more customer-centric approach presents to marketers of financial services now and in the future,
4. Have an appreciation of how to evaluate the contribution made by marketing to an organisation.

18.1 Introduction

By now it should have become clear to readers that the financial services sector is frequently a source of controversy, mistrust, and scepticism. Indeed, in 2015 the US Federal Reserve imposed fines totalling more than $1.8 billion against six major banking organisations for their unsafe and unsound practices in the foreign exchange (FX) markets. The fines, among the largest ever assessed by the Federal Reserve, include: $342 million each for UBS AG, Barclays Bank PLC, Citigroup Inc. and JPMorgan Chase & Co.; $274 million for Royal Bank of Scotland PLC (RBS); and $205 million for Bank of America Corporation. In January 2017 Germany's Deutsche Bank has agreed a $7.2bn (£5.9bn) payment to US authorities over an investigation into mortgage-backed securities. In 2022 American banking giant Wells Fargo incurred the highest ever charges imposed on a US bank by its Consumer Financial Protection Bureau (CFPB), some $US3.7bn in respect of poor treatment of customers (see Marketing in practice 17.1). And Switzerland's Credit Suisse has a history of financial misdemeanours the most recent of which in 2022 involved a massive data leak on thousands of customer accounts. According to RiskScreen reporting on 8 November 2022:

> Credit Suisse recently announced that it would lay off 9,000 employees: 2,700 by the end of 2022 and a further 6,300 by the end of 2025. To stabilise itself, it is seeking $4

DOI: 10.4324/9781003398615-32

billion in a fundraising round, from the Saudi National Bank and others. As a result, in 2022 Credit Suisse's stock price has fallen by almost 60%.[1]

Many critics of banks have blamed their misdeeds on cultures that put greed and personal ambition above the interests of customers and shareholders. Coming on top of the various other mis-selling scandals in the UK, it is only too easy to argue that financial services in general, and banking in particular, is in crisis. The antecedents of what would appear to be an endemic reputational challenge are complex and many of them have been discussed at various points in this book. Arguably, much of the malaise can indeed be traced back to cultural issues through which the individual greed of a relatively small, yet highly influential, cadre has served to disadvantage customers and undermine the morale of the vast majority of employees who are decent, honest and trustworthy individuals. Historically such organisations placed undue emphasis on the acquisition of new customers to the detriment of properly serving the interests of their existing ones, and to the detriment of their organisation's long-term viability and success. They have also been far too product-focused as opposed to being customer-oriented. The fundamental principle of a marketing-led approach to business is that the interests of customers must lie at the very core of any commercial organisation and that profit will be an outcome of the successful delivery of good customer experiences at a fair price. The challenge for marketers is to strive to create corporate cultures that are true to this philosophy and engage all staff in appreciating their personal role in best serving the interests of their customers. It is only by so doing that commercial success may be achieved on a sustainable basis.

Looking to the future, marketing must be seen as an overarching principle for running a business and not as a functional departmental specialism, i.e., "we are all part of the marketing process". That said, the appreciation of marketing's role in managing continuing customer relationships requires a qualitatively different approach than applies in situations where customer acquisition is the primary purpose of marketing. It is interesting to note how much of the language used in connection with acquiring customers appears somewhat militaristic. Terms such as strategies, campaigns, targets, tactics, and marketing armoury all seem to somehow resonate with a notion that marketing is concerned with a heroic battle to *win* customers. Hopefully, it has been firmly established that to see marketing just in terms of the single-minded pursuit of new customers is a view that deserves to be consigned to history.

By way of contrast, the discourse regarding marketing's role in customer development has attached itself to the language of social science and anthropology. Words such as relationships, communities, dialogue, intimacy and advocate are commonly encountered in the context of the use of marketing to retain and develop customers following the point of acquisition. This change of emphasis has implications for the ways in which individual components of the marketing mix are used. Importantly, it has implications for the cultural context within which marketing activities reside. The coercive customer acquisition-based model of marketing often seemed to coincide with organisational cultures that were typified as being macho, male-oriented, and somewhat cynical. In such cultures, the rewards and recognition systems were overly biased in favour of new business KPIs such as: number of new policies (not customers) issued, value of new premiums, new loan cases proposed, and value of loans approved.

Such a cultural backdrop has resulted in practices that over-rewarded elements within the distribution channels, under-rewarded staff involved in serving the day-to-day needs of customers and delivered poor value to customers. Sales organisation often wielded undue power and influence, and this rendered organisations vulnerable to a range of risks and dangers. Poor quality business, bad debts, mis-sold products, and a number of often unforeseen risks have resulted from organisations where cultures were too acquisition based.

When the emphasis is firmly placed upon long-term customer relationships, culture and the marketing mix must interact to reinforce each other. In this chapter we will consider the implications for marketing practice of a truly customer-centric approach to managing financial services organisations. Additionally, we will devote some attention to matters concerning the implementation of marketing principles and practices and how their success might be evaluated.

The chapter will begin by reflecting on key elements of the marketing mix which were originally outlined in Chapter 9. In addition to the core mix elements of customer benefits, charges, communication and channels, there will also be specific consideration given to issues regarding people and process including further reflections on how marketing of financial services is likely to be affected by AI.

18.2 Some observations on culture

At various points throughout this book, reference has been made to the word culture – a term that is notoriously difficult to define. It is a concept that has its roots in the study of anthropology: the American anthropologists, Kroeber and Kluckhohn (1952), critically reviewed the concept of culture and compiled a list of 164 different definitions. This simply serves to emphasise what a complex concept culture is. However, this text is not an anthropological treatise, and the authors view the concept through a more prosaic lens. At the outset of this book its authors set out to present marketing as an interconnected set of disciplines that is outcome-oriented, pragmatic and, as such, is viewed through an instrumental lens. Culture is indeed difficult to define, but in the commercial context is perhaps best appreciated as a set of norms and attitudes that help to shape and define an organisation's mores. We contend that culture is inextricably linked to competitive advantage and, as such, is a means to an end and not an end in itself. And so, culture is an enabler or, indeed, a disabler as a means of achieving sustainable competitive advantage and longevity of success.

In the 1980s, Michael Porter (1980, 1985) was arguably the first authoritative voice to articulate the centrality of culture to the pursuit of competitive advantage. Porter highlighted the need to align culture, competitive advantage and strategy. Amongst other examples, Porter referred to a low-cost strategy which needed a commitment to and a culture of cost control, and that this should be reflected in the way staff behaved throughout the entire business. In 2013 Amah and Daminabo-Weje identified how corporate culture is used as a means of control to facilitate organisational effectiveness. Based upon their review of the literature they concluded that corporate effectiveness is determined to a very large extent by corporate culture. In particular, they recommended that businesses pay more attention to corporate mission, and how well it is understood by employees and guides their attitudes and behaviours.

The notion of corporate culture as an important independent variable affecting employee attitudes and behaviours gained traction during the 1980s, including the work of Michael Porter, and this continued into the next decade. In 1998 Davenport commented that culture should be seen as an organisations' DNA "invisible to the naked eye yet a powerful template that shapes what happens in the workplace". But perhaps the best definition of culture is provided by Hofstede and Minkov (2010) who observed that:

> Culture is the software of the mind.

This memorable phrase encapsulates the instrumental and operational role that culture plays in organisational behaviour and is reflected in a study by Graham et al (2017). This study was based upon a survey and interviews with 1,348 North American companies and aimed to answer the question "Does Corporate Culture Matter?". In the event, more than 50% of senior executives rated culture as a top three driver of a firm's value. Indeed, some 92% of participants believed that improving a company's culture would increase a firm's value. Interestingly, only 16% believed that their own company's culture was where it should be, to quote from the study:

> Executives link culture to ethical choices (compliance, short-termism), innovation (creativity, taking appropriate risk), and value creation (productivity, acquisition premium). We assess these links within a framework that implies cultural effectiveness depends on interactions between cultural values, norms, and formal institutions. Our evidence suggests that cultural norms are as important as stated values in achieving success.

The present author can attest to the disconnect between theory and practice when it comes to culture and the extent to which concepts such as Mission, Vision, and Values as embedded within financial services organisations. In an exercise involving some twenty main board directors of insurance companies in a developed country, none of them was able to identify their own company's mission statement when presented to them. Clearly there is much work to be done.

18.3 People and culture

When marketing becomes oriented more toward the retention and development of customer relationships, the culture must adapt accordingly. For example, there must be a recognition that responsibility for determining the experience of customers belongs to almost the entire organisation. It is no longer appropriate for sales organisations to wield undue power. In the past this has led to abuses which have caused detriment to those involved in administering customer services. However, in the customer-oriented culture of the present and future, administration staff see themselves as shouldering major responsibility for delivering customer satisfaction. Through their interactions with customers they can provide valuable feedback to improve elements of service procedures and systems and even product design. Those involved in the IT function must perceive that they are empowered to use their knowledge, skills, and resources to improve customer satisfaction. Similarly, people involved, say, in procurement can play a valuable role in improving the quality of bought-in products and services such that the organisation operates more efficiently for the benefit of customers. Such benefits may arise because of improved functionality for customers or, possibly, by reducing costs and thereby making price reductions possible. The costs to the organisation of such cultural shortcomings can be huge.

Marketing in practice 18.1: Wells Fargo, USA

Wells Fargo is an example of a financial services organisation whose culture has resulted in material costs – direct as well as reputational. Adverse media coverage has been considerable and has had a decidedly negative impact upon the company's reputation as can be appreciated from the following coverage in the Guardian newspaper:

> In December 2022 US banking giant Wells Fargo agreed to pay $3.7bn in respect of practices that caused detriment to consumers including: charging illegal fees and interest on car loans and mortgages, as well as incorrectly applying overdraft fees against savings and checking accounts. The US Consumer Financial Protection Bureau (CFPB) ordered the bank to repay $2bn to consumers and charged it an additional $1.7bn as a penalty for its behaviour. Ito quote the Guardian newspaper:
> It's the largest fine to date against any bank by the CFPB and the largest fine against Wells which has spent years trying to rehabilitate itself after a series of scandals tied to its sales practices. The bureau says the bad behaviour by the bank affected more than 16 million customers.
> That came on top of other scandals that have bedevilled the bank in recent times such as the falsifying and accessing 2.1 million deposit and credit card accounts without authorisation reported in 2017. The previous year it agreed to pay $US 185 million to regulators to settle charges of manipulating and creating false accounts in its Community Banking division. And in July of that same year, the bank admitted that it took out auto insurance on behalf of 570,000 car loan customers without telling them, resulting in higher payments and some vehicle repossessions. That resulted in some 5,300 members of staff being fired as well as the CEO and other executives.

Source: www.theguardian.com/business/2022/dec/20/wells-fargo-settlement-banking-illegal-fees-interest

Source: knowledge.wharton.upenn.edu/article/wells-fargo-scandals-will-take-clean-mess/

Those wishing to study this case in more detail are encouraged to read Brian Tayan's paper *The Wells Fargo Cross-Selling Scandal²*, in the Stanford Closer Look series of January 2019. Tayan examines the tensions between corporate culture, financial incentives, and individual behaviour and how a lack of alignment between the three can result in endemic customer detriment and, in the long term, shareholder detriment.

What is indicated is the necessity for all staff to appreciate the ways in which what they do, and how they do it, impacts upon customer perceptions. In the ideal world, all members of staff will see themselves as being, to some extent, customer-facing. Businesses that are based upon the maintenance of long-term customer relationships, as opposed to essentially the one-off sale, see the *people* element of the mix as representing a primary, if not *the* primary, determinant of customer satisfaction and advocacy. It is interesting to note evidence that the Yorkshire Building Society has identified regarding the importance of experienced staff in enhancing levels of customer satisfaction. The Society has conducted extensive research into the factors that appear to be causally and independently associated with high levels of customer satisfaction and hard-nosed commercial performance. The analysis suggests that such a causal relationship is in evidence in branches that have relatively low staff turnover and high average length of services. Staff in such branches display relatively high levels of commitment to the organisation, and this is reflected in relatively superior business results across a balanced scorecard of KPI's. Although not independently verified, such a finding is indicative of the importance of continuity of staff/customer interaction in the maintenance of mutually beneficial long-term relationships and is consistent with the concept of a service-profit chain as discussed in Chapter 15.

18.4 Product considerations

Of paramount importance is that a product should be fit-for-purpose. This means that care should be taken to ensure that the features it comprises, and functionality that applies, should be clearly identified at the point of purchase and should be appropriate for the customer's needs given her or his circumstances at that time.

Owing to the characteristics of financial services as outlined in Chapter 3, care must be taken to ensure that products are presented in as transparent way as possible. In the absence of sufficient transparency, a customer may have, unwittingly, bought a product that was not suitable to her needs or personal circumstances. Regulators often lay down quite prescriptive requirements about the disclosure of product features at the point-of-sale. However, responsible marketing should not depend solely on the regulator; it is up to the individual product provider to ensure that products are presented in a suitably transparent manner. It is relatively straightforward to carry out a study to establish the degree to which consumers understand the product features as presented in promotional and point-of-sale material. Such basic research could obviate costly administration queries, complaints handling and, potentially, compensation for mis-sold or mis-represented products.

Leading on from transparency at the point-of- sale, is the requirement to ensure that the provider can deliver the features and functionality that it promises. In the past, it was commonplace for new products to be launched even though the systems and administrative infrastructure to deal with a range of customer requirements during the lifetime of the product had not been put in place. The euphemism for these unresolved processes is deferred features, and their prevalence was the price that had to be paid for launching new products within an unrealistically short timescale. Examples have been encountered in which around 50% of total IT development resource has been devoted to resolving deferred features. An example of such a deferred feature could be the ability to handle, say, a switch from one fund into another fund in the case of a unit-linked whole-of-life policy or a personal pension. Deferred features create a range of difficulties for an organisation and can be a major contributory factor to the lessening of respect and credibility of a marketing department. The IT systems development staff find involvement in deferred features a source of frustration. Administration staff find themselves having to devise various manual workarounds while they wait for the outstanding systems support to be made available. Such a scenario can typically occur in organisations that are overly oriented in favour of new business to the detriment of the long-term interest of customers. But in the longer term this approach to product development is costly and will tend to reduce satisfaction. For the organisation that is serious about building long-term customer relationships, product development should be organised such that what is promised at the time of initial purchase can be fully supported from the launch date of the product.

A further consideration regarding *product* is that product design should seek to provide sufficient flexibility to cope with reasonable changes in a customer's circumstances during the anticipated lifetime of the product. There are certain changes which might reasonably be expected to occur regarding most financial services. Therefore, the ability to respond appropriately to changing circumstances is an important aspect of most financial products, certainly those of more than 12 months' duration. The lack of sufficient product flexibility results in poor persistency and poor product profitability. It can act greatly against the customer's interests where penalty charges are applied to products that lapse in their early stages. Clearly, a judgement must be made regarding the costs associated with providing flexibility for the duration of a long-term product. However, the failure to do so, within reason, may result in much higher costs to the organisation.

Progress check

- Many critics of banks have blamed their misdeeds on cultures that put greed and personal ambition above the interests of its customers and shareholders.
- Culture and the marketing mix must interact to reinforce each other to deliver against strategic goals.
- Product and service features and functionality should be clearly identified at the point of purchase and should be appropriate for the customer's needs given her or his circumstances at that time and over the anticipated timescale of the enjoyment of the product.

18.5 Pricing, value and a single-customer view

Care must be taken to ensure that *price* is managed in such a way as to safeguard long-term, mutually beneficial relationships. There is little point in attracting new customers with a price that is so low as to be commercially unsustainable. Equally, the practice of acquiring customers with an attractive price tag only subsequently to introduce a substantial price rise is a cynical practice that can endanger long-term relationships.

A pricing policy that is geared towards customer retention and development must address the respective merits of long-term customer value over short-term product profitability. This emphasises the need to model long-term customer value and evolve a pricing policy that achieves a balance between such value and the short-term profit requirements of the company. This makes it even more important that a company's systems architecture is able to provide a holistic view of an individual customer's relationship with the company. By joining up all of the customer's product holdings the company can identify opportunities to add value to the customer through special pricing arrangements. This is consistent with the economics of customer retention discussed in Chapter 15.

A single-customer view forms an essential part of any strategy aimed at delivering a truly personalised service. And so, it is perhaps surprising that many banks lack a single-365 degrees view of their customers. Research published by data analytics company Fico in 2023[2] identified shortcomings in firms' ability to manage customer relationships in a suitable holistic manner. The report included a survey of 52 providers of financial services worldwide research carried out by Forrester Consulting and highlighted that:

- 65% of respondents prioritise single view of customer through accurate, accessible data
- 81% are expanding automation of customer services
- 69% of UK respondents process KPIs with real-time, customizable data visualisation across decision ecosystem, only 49% do so globally
- 83% are or are planning to enhance customer engagement through real-time decision making
- Yet only 50% have governance capabilities for their change-management ecosystems

The context to the study was the introduction of new regulations by the FCA regarding firms' Customer Duty. Introduced in July 2023, greater onus will be placed on the providers of financial services to take account of all customer information when it makes a decision that will impact on the customer. Commenting on the report, Matt Cox, Managing Director, EMEA, FIC observed:

"Many banks are taking a narrow approach to personalization," concluded Cox. "Digitally empowered customers are now seeking and expecting better, more relevant experiences, but product-oriented strategies handicap most banks.

> As banks strategically advance towards hyper-personalization at hyper-scale, adopting a single platform that enables the expansion of data, insights, actions, and outcomes capabilities for personalization will help firms drive more profitable customer relationships, better manage risk and fraud, optimize operations, and drive differentiation. It will also improve performance across performance indicators and counteract top challenges by lowering costs, increasing customer satisfaction scores (CSATs), and strengthening customer retention.

18.6 Advertising and promotion

A particular feature of marketing in the context of existing customer development has been the usage of promotional campaigns and programmes aimed specifically at such individuals. At a very basic level it is obviously important that consistency is achieved between what is said and presented during the acquisition process and that which is said and presented over the customer life cycle. This is, at least in part, to do with the issue of expectations as discussed in Chapter 15. Advertising and promotional devices have a major role to play in activities such as customer retention, upselling, cross-selling and advocacy development. Much of what was presented in Chapter 11 regarding communication and promotion applies in the context of marketing to existing customers. However, once an individual becomes a customer there is a presumption that the provider company really does have in-depth, detailed knowledge about the customer and that her needs can be addressed on a highly personalised basis. To refer to the concept of zones of tolerance (see Chapter 15), customers exhibit a relatively narrow zone of tolerance regarding the communications they receive. They expect a high degree of relevance, customer knowledge and accuracy. Crucially, there is a presumption that their customer is valued, and that the relationship is appreciated and respected.

In contrast to the acquisition of new customers, direct response-type forms of communication are significantly more important when marketing to existing customers. Largely this is because of the availability of detailed customer data that allows messages and propositions to be targeted on an individual basis with great precision. Therefore, competencies in digital, direct mail and telemarketing are especially important when using the marketing mix for existing customers.

A well-established aspect of marketing is the use of loyalty programmes. Unlike one-off *ad hoc* mail-shots and campaigns, the loyalty programme focuses on long-term goals for the customer base through the use of the marketing mix. Such goals are typically based upon providing long-term benefits to the organisation by providing long-term value-for-money to the customer. Amongst the goals that apply to such programmes are:

- Increasing customer retention,
- Promoting customer advocacy,
- Increased share of customer wallet,
- Reinforcing competitive advantage.

In the context of current customers, communication has an important role to play in providing reassurance that the relationship is in the customer's best interests. This relates to the concept of cognitive dissonance – the feelings of anxiety that are frequently associated with important decisions. Well-chosen and carefully executed messages can aim to reassure customers that they are exercising sound judgement in maintaining a relationship with the provider company. This has become especially significant in the field of financial services in marketplaces that are close to, or at, saturation point. Such marketplaces result in customer acquisition strategies that blatantly seek to achieve defections from competitors. Clear evidence of this is to be seen in sectors such as the gas and electricity market and telecommunication arenas where defection-based strategies are commonplace. The use of marketing communications programmes to reassure customers of the wisdom of declining the overtures of competitors and maintaining an existing relationship can work effectively in conjunction with the customer retention model of Bitner and Zeithaml discussed in Chapter 14. Again, the availability of a great deal of information about individual customers lends itself to highly focused, well-targeted customer communication.

18.7 Distribution and access

In the context of customer development, there are many linkages between people and channels of distribution. Take the case of the bank branch; its role is far more significant as a distribution point for existing customers than as a means of securing new customers. The branch is the most visible and potent manifestation of the bank for most of its personal customers. Thus, the way in which it transacts the requirements of customers has a profound influence upon customer perceptions. Indeed, the branch is, arguably, the most powerful means a bank or building society has for increasing customer value by soliciting for product cross-sell and upsell. In this way, branch-based distribution is a powerful selling resource that is not available to its non-branch-based remote rivals. Of course, this capability comes at a cost and such organisations are continually having to evaluate the value-added of individual branches and adjusting their portfolios of branch outlets. That said, the fact that product cross-sales by banks to date have been heavily dependent upon face-to-face interactions in the branch does not mean that this will always be the case. Digital natives can be expected to display behaviours regarding remote transactions that are greatly at variance to older age cohorts. They may well display a greater propensity to be open to remote cross-buying as technology becomes ever more sophisticated. For example, thus far in their development chatbots have been somewhat clunky and incapable of effective personalised interaction with the customer. However, that is all changing as better AI capability means that a genuine inter-personal dialogue will soon become routine. Thus, the combination of greater IT functionality and the associated consumer acceptance can be expected to strengthen banking business models that do not require branches.

It is understandable that some question the very existence of the bank branch in the not-too-distant future as from Australia through to Europe and on to the USA and Canada, fewer and fewer customers are visiting bank branches for normal service requirements. However, it is just possible that the death of the bank branch may be less certain to predict. There are significant variations in the relative importance of the bank branch between countries and recent evidence from the USA suggests that the decline in the number of visits to branches may be slowing. According to Raddon Research[3], in 2022 77% of Americans visited branches at least monthly, up eight points from 2019. Figure 18.1 would appear to show that while mobile banking activity grew rapidly between 2010 and 2020, branch traffic declined relatively modestly in comparison. This could suggest that both forms of banking behaviour can co-exist in a somewhat complementary manner.

In January 2023 Standard & Poors[4] noted that while branch closures in the USA continued during 2022 the pace has slackened and that new branches openings have continued, albeit at a slower rate than closures. In effect net closures on a 12 month moving average basis fell from 172 to 76 by the end of 2022, and comment:

> Many banks have reduced their branch footprints since 2020, but recently, banks have been balancing branch reductions and increased digital adoptions for several reasons, including maintaining a physical presence to compete.

It must be appreciated that a high degree of granularity is required when interpreting such findings. Most of the branch closures are by large firms such as JPMorgan Chase & Co and Bank of America, whilst openings tended to be by smaller rivals such as Fifth Third Bankcorp. It should be noted that as well as closing branches, JPMorgan Chase has also been opening new branches as it re-aligns its outlets to better fit the changing needs of the market. Significant variations are also in evidence geographically that reflect local factors and the history of the banks concerned.

Another piece of data of note in the Raddon Research report concerns the demographics of branch usage. Surprisingly, it identified millennials as the age cohort most likely to visit their branch as at June 2021, moreover, branch usage by that group grew substantially compared with the previous. There may be a post-Covid pandemic effect in evidence, but it adds to a view that it is far too soon to write off the branch-based model of retail banking.

 Stop and think?

What is the trend in bank branch numbers in your country and what explains that trend?

What role do you foresee bank branches performing in, say, ten years' time?

Is a hybrid "bricks and clicks" business model likely to be the dominant force in future?

In its 2023 report on banking, Accenture[5] reinforces the view that while mobile banking represents a tremendous opportunity for reducing the cost of serving bank customers, it also comes at the price of weaker customer relationships. The report notes that whilst digitisation has delivered convenience in a range of aspects of banking and has been empowering, it has served to erode differentiation, facilitate higher rates of switching and made banking less personal.

Marketing in practice 18.2: the future of banking, Accenture 2023

The renaissance of the bank branch is one of Accenture's top ten trends for 2023 and beyond based upon its assessment of banking models and the importance it attaches to the role of the branch in engendering mutually beneficial relationships. It contends that: Many banks will follow the lead of JPMorgan Chase, which 18 months ago reported it was more than halfway through its 2018 plan to open 400 branches in new markets across the US by the end of 2025. Banks will be inviting customers back and welcoming them home. More importantly, they will be shifting their emphasis from meeting specific needs and selling individual products to talking about improving customers' general financial wellbeing. Banks will use their branches to learn more about their customers, show interest and empathy, offer advice and build loyalty. This won't be a pivot away from digitalisation; rather, a horses-for-courses approach that recognises the strengths of each channel. Customers today do most of their banking on their mobile devices, with only 3% of interactions happening face-to-face. However, an in-person meeting remains the preferred option when opening new products— 27% of consumers said it was their first choice, ahead of mobile apps (22%) and websites (21%).The opportunity is to move beyond a marketplace where the value of a customer is equal to the sum of the products they use, to one where a multiplier effect is at work. This is where the branch comes into its own, but it will take a retrained and re-oriented workforce that is motivated, engaged and feels appreciated. It will also take a more tailored and purposeful customer journey than we saw before the pandemic.

To compete in the future, it is vital that the branches that do remain offer outstanding levels of service. Increasingly, banks are trying to make branches more welcoming – contemporary design, speciality coffee and informal environments in which bank staff can explore consumers' financial needs. The challenge is not just a human one that concerns the interpersonal and selling skills of branch staff but is also a technological one. As mentioned in Section 18.4, what is also required is an IT system that is truly customer-centric whereby all a customer's product holdings and service interactions can be displayed holistically on a single customer dashboard. In this way branch staff can engage in meaningful and mutually worthwhile customer dialogue. Thus, the role played by branch staff is crucial in satisfying the needs of customers whilst reconciling this with the needs of the bank itself. This calls for skill and diplomacy in striking the right balance between providing services associated with a product currently held and endeavouring to introduce the possibility of the customer buying an additional product. For example, a customer may call in at her branch to pay a bill and the cashier notices that the customer maintains a significant credit balance. This might indicate an opportunity to sell, say, an investment product of some kind. Skill and sensitivity are needed to introduce this possible cross-sell opportunity such that the customer does not feel she is somehow being taken advantage of. To a considerable extent, the answer lies in adopting an approach that is customer-centric and will demonstrably offer value. It is also important to ensure that such branch staff are skilled and trained in interpersonal skills of a high order. We saw earlier the lengths to which Metrobank goes to ensure it recruits staff who have the interpersonal skills required to create effective customer rapport. It is fair to say that few things are more likely to cause customer irritation, dissatisfaction, and defection than the perception of being coercively sold to every time he or she enters a branch.

The use of the branch as a means of distributing additional products to current customers relies squarely upon the *people* element of the marketing mix. Other scenarios that also facilitate the role of people are those involving direct face-to-face sales and service, such as an insurance company's direct sales force, or the call agent in a telephone call centre. Direct sales forces are of immense importance as a means of reinforcing customer relationships. Insurance agents of all forms, brokers, direct sales advisers and independent financial advisers can all be instrumental in reinforcing the relationship between product provider and customer. One sometimes encounters the use of the expression *hunters* and *farmers* in the context of direct sales forces. *Hunters* are advisers that perform the role of acquiring new customers whereas *farmers*, as the name implies, are responsible for looking after the servicing needs and new product requirements of existing customers. Sometimes one encounters companies that have a *hunting* sales team that is distinct from a separate *farming* sales team. Such a division of responsibilities, so it is argued, permits a high degree of focus on the respective goals of acquiring, and developing customer relationships. There is much to commend such an argument; however, in practice, customers often build a positive, trusting relationship with the adviser who initially sold the product to them and resent being handed off to the *farming* adviser. For this reason, companies that experiment with the hunting/farming focused approach tend to revert to the hybrid model whereby all advisers are responsible for both hunting and farming. This latter approach is more in keeping with the relationship marketing philosophy in that, by having the responsibility for an ongoing customer relationship, the adviser is more likely to provide only what she knows can be delivered. A well-trained, properly resourced, conscientious direct sales force is a powerful vehicle for generating both shareholder value and customer benefits.

The clear separation of hunting and farming roles are more prevalent in the business-to-business environment where the need for complex, costly and time-consuming new business pitching can make such an arrangement practically and economically viable. For example, a finance company selling leasing facilities to used car dealers may involve considerable effort to prospect for business and secure such a sale. However, the setting-up of the new processes and procedures and their continuing review can be even more complex and time consuming and call for a different skill set requiring a dedicated organisational structure. Thus, the complexity of many aspects of large-scale B2B product-service provision frequently calls for a degree of specialisation that makes a separation of sales and client management roles a necessity.

It must be borne in mind that issues relating to access vary widely, and in rural parts of Africa, particular problems are encountered. In Case Study CS10 we see how London-based Five Talents has sought to make micro-finance available to people who would otherwise be denied access.

18.8 Processes

As an aspect of the financial services marketing mix for customer development, *process* plays a role in facilitating both the delivery of service and administrative routines as well as the purchasing of additional products. Although, the *people* element of the mix has a role to play in providing both the sales administrative functions associated with customer development, processes are closely allied. For example, the telephone call centre and internet have made an enormous contribution to the development of customer development in view of their capacity to perform selling, buying and administrative roles.

The internet has empowered customers to satisfy their needs in respect of data availability and the performance of a range of administrative functions on a 24:7 basis, at minimal cost. As such, it complements the much more costly branch-based resources of banks and building societies. Whereas ten years ago the internet performed a complementary rather than a substitutional role, it has since evolved to a point where it has become a fully stand-alone business model, it has been a true disrupter creating wholly new business models. The telephone call centre has been particularly important as part of the marketing mix for customer development. It is a relatively low-cost means of providing a range of purchasing and administrative routines. In recent years, the offshore outsourcing of call centres, most notably to India, has played an increasing role for companies such as Fidelity, Aviva, Barclays and Mastercard. They offer a low-cost means of transacting inbound customer administration and buying requests. However, more controversial is their role in proactive outbound selling to the existing customer bases of a range of industries, not just financial services. The mobile phone and telecomms sector has been especially active in using offshore call centres to make outbound sales calls and there is evidence of growing hostility to this form of selling. It is suspected that this hostility has more to do with its intrusiveness than necessarily with the origin of the actual call itself. Nevertheless, the cost-effectiveness of the use of unsolicited outbound sales calling must be balanced against its negative impact upon overall customer satisfaction levels. As commented upon earlier, several companies have repatriated their formerly offshore customer service centres owing to a reduction in the cost advantage and in response to adverse customer feedback.

In the case of the use of the internet and call centre, aspects of design and process often serve to frustrate and reduce customer satisfaction rather than heighten it. Websites can be difficult to navigate and make presumptions about the nature of enquiries that may not best reflect the needs of customer or indeed prospective customers. For example, it is commonplace for such sites to be product-based, rendering it impossible to make enquiries of a general nature. Complaints handling is often poorly dealt with, and a number simply ask for written requests for service and resolution. The absence of appropriate telephone numbers to assist the customer or a failure to respond to calls is a frequent source of frustration and this has not changed materially since the first edition of this book was published in 2007. Again, it is reasonable to expect IT to resolve many of these frustrations through the use of AI, but providers have not yet consistently harnessed and maximised the opportunities AI offers. Many are using it to power chatbots to service both customers and internal operations, however its reach is exponential, particularly with the emergence of generative AI (GAI) in recent years. Where traditional AI uses machine learning algorithms and data to solve specific problems, GAI analyses vast quantities of data to produce new and original content and is able to apply a human-like lens to problem solving. GAI can fulfil tasks that usually need human intelligence which has huge potential to support complex processes and workflows.

Right across FS, GAI could radically shift consumer expectations and internal business operations, driving efficiency and accessibility. McKinsey posit "To compete successfully and thrive, incumbent banks must become 'AI-first' institutions, adopting AI technologies as the foundation for new value propositions and distinctive customer experiences."[6] (AI is covered more in chapters 10 & 13).

Progress check

- To compete in the future, it is vital that the bank branches that do remain offer outstanding levels of service.
- A single-customer view forms an essential part of any strategy aimed at delivering a truly personalised service.
- it is just possible that the death of the bank branch may be less certain to predict.

Call centres can result in similar frustrations as automatic call-handling procedures (IVR) fail to deliver the required degree of service responsiveness. What is indicated is far greater use of what is termed the *customer journey*. By this term we mean that executives should thoroughly test the responsiveness, functionality and effectiveness of both internet and telephone-based processes first hand. This is somewhat analogous to the practice of super-market CEOs devoting considerable personal time to their customers' experiences as users of their stores. Such an approach has yielded enormous benefits not only to shoppers but to the shareholders of those retail companies. Rising seniority is no excuse for becoming remote from the real needs and concerns that affect customers.

No matter what elements of the marketing mix are used to develop customer relationships over the long-term, it is vital that effort be expended to assessing their impact. It is relatively straightforward to measure the impact of the customer acquisition process. A prospect either buys, and becomes a customer, or declines the invitation. Both types of individuals can be invited to take part in some form of feedback aimed at informing future policies and practices. However, once a prospect has become a customer, there is a wide variety of ways in which the customer interacts with and is exposed to the provider company. All the customer's interactions with the marketing mix have an impact, at both the subconscious as well as the conscious level, in forming perceptions: negative and positive.

18.9 Evaluating marketing performance

In this section we will consider issues concerning the implementation of marketing concepts and practices and how their contributions might be evaluated. Hopefully, by now it has been firmly established that marketing is less about the practical activities engaged in by departments bearing that name but, rather, constitutes a business philosophy or orientation. Central to this orientation is being able to understand customer problems, needs and wants, and then providing the means by which these may be satisfied. Quite simply, marketing is about getting and keeping customers and success in this endeavour demands that the customers' interests are given paramount significance. Thus, the truly marketing-oriented organisation believes from top to bottom that delivering competitively superior customer satisfaction leads to the long-term optimisation of all stakeholder interests. Arguably, the CEO of an organisation should view themselves as the de facto marketing director given that responsibility for the organisation's customer centricity rests with them. Similarly, the Board of Directors share collective responsibility with the CEO for ensuring that the company is appropriately customer focused and possesses a culture that underpins that orientation.

Thus, marketing is not simply about the tasks carried out by the marketing team; rather it is the sum of all the organisation's activities that impact upon customer experience. Any audit of marketing performance should therefore take a thorough, holistic approach by evaluating the outcomes of all functions that impact upon customer satisfaction. In 2016 the consultancy 3R Insights commissioned market research agency Opinium to carry out a study into consumer attitudes towards and beliefs about CEOs and other board directors of financial services companies. The research findings and their implications are addressed in detail in the Support Material, however, suffice it to say that significant potential exists for boards of directors to achieve a greater degree of synergy with their marketing teams in creating organisations that are truly customer focused. Three particular issues of note that were surveyed concerned the degree to which consumers believed that CEOs and board directors:

a)   Care about service quality,
b)   Put customer interests first,
c)   Treat customers fairly.

In Table 18.1 we see the response to the question "To what extent do you believe CEOs and directors care about the quality of customer service they provide?". Here we see that for boards of insurance companies, banks, and investment firms, the overwhelming majority of consumers do not believe they care about service quality.

When it comes to putting customers first, the great majority of consumers have little or no confidence that CEOs and directors intend to put the interest of customers first as can be seen in Table 18.2.

Table 18.1 Care about quality of service

	All		Aged 18-34 years		Aged >55 years	
	Reasonable/ great extent %	Little/ poor extent %	Reasonable/ great extent %	Little/ poor extent %	Reasonable/ Poor extent	Little/ poor extent %
Insurers	26	62	29	51	25	68
Banks	30	59	37	44	26	67
Investment firms	28	57	34	45	28	61

Table 18.2 Confidence that CEOs and directors intend to put customer interests first

	All		Aged 18-34 years		Aged >55 years	
	Some/ complete confidence %	Little/no confidence %	Some/ complete confidence %	Little/no confidence %	Some/ complete confidence %	Little/no confidence %
Insurers	21	69	23	60	22	72
Banks	22	68	29	54	21	74
Investment firms	21	68	24	57	20	70

Table 18.3 Confidence that CEOs and directors intend to treat customers fairly

	All		Aged 1v4 years		Aged >55 years	
	Some/ complete confidence %	Little/no confidence %	Some/ complete confidence %	Little/no confidence %	Some/ complete confidence %	Little/no confidence %
Insurers	24	66	28	57	24	70
Banks	28	63	34	52	27	67
Investment firms	25	29	29	53	24	66

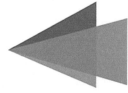

3R Insights

Q10: What do you like **least** about your experience as a customer of financial services companies?

Online Experience
Unprofessional **Communication**
Wrong Values Bad Attitude
Arrogance
Poor Products **Impersonal** Unfair Practices
Don't Listen **Hard Sell**
Lack of Access **Don't care** Charges
Bad Advice
Automation PPI   Jargon
Poor Customer Service
Complexity Everything Poor Value
Admin
Call Centres   Incompetence
Branch Closures Bonuses and Pay
Poor Quality Staff
Telesales Calls Untrustworthy
Staff Turnover

Figure 18.1 What do you like least?

Finally, we see in Table 18.3 how little confidence consumers have that CEOs and directors intend to treat customers fairly.

The research also examined what aspects of the sample consumers' experience and attitudes might explain their beliefs about CEOs and directors' intentions towards their customers. In figures 18.1 And 18.2 we get a sense of what appears to drive consumer perceptions. The word cloud in Figure 18.1 summarises what consumers said about what they like least about their own customer experience. In Figure 18.2 we see what advice consumers would like to give to CEOs and directors.

3R Insights

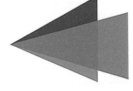

Q12: What simple piece of advice would you give to CEOs and Directors of financial services companies, to improve the reputation of their companies?

More face to face contact
Communicate better
Simplify products and services
Care more about your customers
Be more human **Improve customer service**
Resign   Respect your customers
Be more open
Show humility **Behave ethically** Be honest
Get real Train staff

Address Bonuses and Pay
Up your game Act Fairly   **Put customers first**
Improve VFM Walk the Talk
Improve culture Listen to customers
Build trustworthiness
Maintain branches **Increase transparency**
Be more socially responsible
More UK Call centres

Figure 18.2   What advice would consumers give

☁ Stop and think?

In tables 18.1, 18.2 and 18.3 it is interesting to note that the older of the two age cohorts reported upon rated CEOs and directors' intentions significantly more harshly than the younger cohort:

1. What factors do you think might explain those differences in perceptions?

2. If you were the CEO of a bank how might you respond to the findings?

3. From your personal experience, would you expect there to be differences in ratings in those three issues between the customers of traditional branch-based firms and those which operate a digital-only business model?

4. Can you think of companies in the non-financial services market space that would evoke more positive ratings by consumers, and what factors do you think could explain the difference?

The efficient use of marketing resources

In addition to assessing the extent of an organisation's overall marketing orientation, as well as the impact of all departments that have an influence upon customer perceptions, there remains the need to assess the contribution of the marketing department itself. It falls to the marketing team to ensure that the activities of marketing strategy, customer acquisition and customer development are conducted in an appropriate, effective, efficient and professional manner. Marketing teams can easily become responsible for undermining credibility in marketing as a concept as well as that of its adherents by failing to operate to the required standard of effectiveness, efficiency and professionalism. This can arise because of the prevalence of several gaps that are somewhat analogous to those that occur in the SERVQUAL model (see Chapter 15). Of note are the following gaps:

Marketing performance gap analysis

*   **Gap 1 – The External Role Gap:** The expectations that senior management have of what marketing's role should be. The expectations of other functional staff regarding the role of marketing.
*   **Gap 2 – The Internal Role Gap:** The expectations that marketing management and staff have regarding their roles.
*   **Gap 3 – The External Delivery Gap:** The difference between what external management and staff expect marketing to deliver and what they perceive it to deliver.
*   **Gap 4 – The Internal Delivery Gap:** The difference between what the marketing team set out to deliver and what they believe they actually do deliver.

It may be readily appreciated that all four of the above gaps involve a combination of what is perceived and what can be objectively evidenced. The two constructs may well not be in alignment if senior marketing management fail to devote sufficient attention to the management of perception. There are many examples of hardworking, productive marketing teams that do a great job influencing customer perceptions of their company whilst failing to manage their department's internal perception. Too often the assessment of performance by senior marketing management is biased in favour of Gap 4, followed by Gap 2. Scant attention is devoted to addressing Gap 1 and 3 and this oversight serves to undermine marketing's credibility. Therefore, senior marketing staff must ensure that they identify the dangers inherent in all four gaps and formulate strategies to close them.

Marketing executives need to be acutely aware of the risks that may be associated with any given activity or course of action. Indeed, it is probably fair to say that there are more risks facing the unwary in the field of financial services than most other commercial sectors. Financial and regulatory risks present particular challenges, and failure to exercise due prudence and diligence can in extreme cases lead to the collapse of an enterprise. The credit crunch has shown all too vividly how failures in the financial services sector have the potential to afflict the whole global financial system and economy.

Chief executives and marketing directors frequently struggle to evaluate the value they gain from their marketing resources. The Canford Centre for Customer Development has set out to assess marketing's contribution to corporate goals by means of the Marketing Mentor. Using Marketing Mentorâ, CEOs and marketing directors have the means to identify which marketing activities they should:

*   **Maintain:** as they make a valid and worthwhile contribution to corporate goals and should be continued.
*   **Improve:** as they are performing at a level below what should be expected of them and should be the focus for an improvement programme.
*   **Initiate:** as they are not currently in evidence and should be introduced to marketing's programme of activities.
*   **Delete:** as they add little value to the organisation's goals and should be abandoned.

Central to its methodology is the assertion that marketing performance rests upon seven core moments of truth:

- Marketing strategy,
- Customer acquisition,
- Customer development,
- Product and service management,
- Communication and perception management,
- Planning and implementation,
- People and development.

Finally, rigour, flair and judgement will come to nought unless the individual marketing executive is able to make things happen. Despite the commonplace mantra of "empowerment", an array of forces serves to prevent marketing-related change taking place. Numbered among such inhibiting forces are:

- Risk aversion,
- Fear of failure,
- Individual and group cynicism,
- Inertia and lack of corporate ambition,
- Senior management control freakery,
- Blame-oriented cultures.

The above list is neither comprehensive nor fully mutually exclusive, however, each captures the essence of the kind of organisational backdrop that makes it difficult to become a truly marketing-oriented organisation.

 Stop and think?

How would you describe the reputation of the financial services industry in your country for treating its customers fairly?

Are there sector differences regarding the fair treatment of customers?

What do you consider to be key moments of truth in the evaluation of marketing's contribution to a company?

Assessing the impact of the company's activities on customers

Many financial services companies have mission and vision statements that embody their good intentions towards consumers. Often, they are supported by customer research programmes which provide evidence of high levels of customer satisfaction. Additionally, companies frequently point to their expansive, and sometimes expensive, corporate social responsibilities activities which benefit a wide array of communities and interests. A plethora of training programmes have been spawned, aimed at ensuring compliance with the current regulatory requirements. And yet, as we have seen at various stages in this book, the mis-selling has continued, the fines keep piling up and survey after survey point to the low regard in which the industry is held. It is true to say that company Chairs and their colleagues on the Board are often

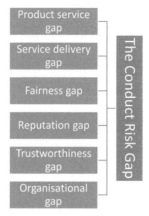

Figure 18.3 The components of the Conduct Risk Gap

surprised and dismayed by the inappropriate behaviours displayed by members of staff who bring their companies into disrepute. Clearly, some kind of disconnect is at work and Boards would gain confidence from having the means to bridge the gaps between expectations and delivery that is so much in evidence with regard to what is termed *the conduct of business*. One such approach has been pioneered by London-based 3R Insights; it's called Conduct Risk Gap Analysis (CRGA). The CRGA comprises the following set of six gaps that define the degree to which an organisation is likely to operate in ways that result in customer detriment. This is a practical tool as it allows boards to measure Conduct Risk Gaps and is shown in Figure 18.3

Progress check

- Responsive and responsible leadership therefore entails a deeper commitment to inclusive development and equitable growth, both nationally and globally.
- As far as internal sustainability is concerned, marketing plays a vital role in maintaining the strategic triangle referred to at various points in the book. Of note is the importance of marketing's role in environmental scanning.
- Brands should build up a stock of goodwill and trust to maintain their reputation in the challenging and uncertain times ahead.

The first three gaps can be viewed as representing the customer viewpoint, taken in the round they are referred to as The Expectations Gap. These allow a company's board to measure, in an objective and honest manner, the gap between the firm's expectations and perceptions of its own performance, customer expectations, and customers' actual experience of the firm's products, quality of services and fair treatment. The latter three represent the organisational viewpoint. Outline descriptions of the six CCRGA components are as follows:

1. **The product performance gap**
   What expectations should the organisation's customers have of the benefits they receive in return for giving it their business and how this compares with perceived experience?

This focuses on product performance and the extent to which product features are fit for purpose.

2. **The service delivery gap**

   What represents good customer outcomes in the context of the sector in which the firm operates and what are the evidenced outcomes experienced by customers? This focuses on the quality of the service experienced by the firm's customers which should enhance and complement the product delivery experience identified in number 1 above.

3. **The fairness gap**

   What does fairness mean to the organisation? What is the firm's desired position in terms of fair treatment of customers and other key stakeholders and how does it compare with actual perceptions?

4. **The reputation gap**

   What characteristics, policies, behaviours and perceptions define the organisation's desired reputational status and position amongst significant stakeholder groups and how is the firm perceived in practice?

5. **The trustworthiness gap**

   What does trustworthiness mean to the organisation? What is the firm's desired position in terms of trustworthiness and how does it compare with actual perceptions?

6. **The organisational gap**

   To what degree are the above expectations and outcomes universally known and understood throughout the organisation's entire workforce and its third-party associates? How does the customer proposition align with corporate strategy and the business model? Where are the gaps between the board's expectations and aspirations for the firm's performance and actual impact of strategy and business models on customer outcomes and, ultimately, the success of the firm?

18.10 Summary and conclusions

The world over, the financial services industry has faced reputational challenges. This is although it plays a fundamental role in furthering a range of social goods such as economic development, poverty reduction and the mitigation of a wide range of hazards associated with the pursuit of economic and personal well-being. In part, this is a legacy of decades of lax regulation and, as we have seen, regulation is developing continually to outlaw poor practice and ensure the delivery of good outcomes for customers. All of this will take time, and progress will vary from country to country, but the trajectory is clear, a paradigm shift is well underway whereby the imperative of the unqualified acquisition of new customers is shifting in favour of managing the customer base in a holistic manner. New business models devoted to new customer acquisition to the detriment of long-term customer value are dying out rapidly.

Strategies to initiate, maintain and develop customer relationships must be supported by appropriate marketing practices and, particularly, through the careful use of the marketing mix to develop mutually beneficial relationships with customers. This in turn requires a market or customer-oriented organisational culture which ensures commitment to meet customer needs at all levels of the organisation. Thus, the core of this chapter has been the imperative of aligning marketing activities across the entire organisation to manage customer relationships effectively throughout the customer journey..

It is also to be hoped that those engaged in marketing display a heightened appreciation of the fact that success in this ever-changing world calls for a combination of skills, aptitudes and inclinations, notably:

1   The rigorous application of relevant concepts and tools.
2   A genuine concern to advance the cause of consumer financial well-being.
3   Creative insight and flair.
4   Sound commercial judgement and risk awareness.
5   Drive and can-do attitude.
6   A strong sense of social responsibility.

It is to be hoped that this book has made a contribution to the above six factors. Important as the first factor is, of itself it is insufficient to ensure the successful application of marketing to the commercial needs of a financial services enterprise. The rigorous application of good marketing processes must be complemented by creative flair that resonates with the expectations of staff, distributors and customers. Given two very similar options, as humans we will typically make a choice in favour of that which is the more interesting, attractive and appealing. Again, rigour and flair will fail to guarantee success unless the proposals and outputs of marketing executives display sound commercial judgement. There is no place for naivety for those involved in marketing, and credibility is earned by the demonstration of well-justified and argued cases that can convince even the most sceptical of colleagues of marketing's value. Of crucial importance is a genuine desire to further the financial well-being of one's customers through their purchase and consumption of the company's products and services. Commercial success must be a consequence of satisfying consumer needs fairly and equitably. And yet, notwithstanding the commercial imperative, marketing must be conditioned by and responsive to its social context.

Learning outcomes

Having completed this chapter, you should now be able to:

1. **Understand how culture is defined, and its relationship to competitive advantage.**
    With its roots in the field of anthropology, culture concerns the norms that give direction to attitude formation and behaviours. Arguably, the best shorthand for understanding culture is that it is *software for the mind*. It facilitates consistency and should galvanise the efforts of all employees towards delivering customer outcomes that are in accordance with the company's positioning and competitive advantage.
2. **Appreciate the importance of integrating functional marketing activities holistically within the overall corporate culture.**
    A theme throughout this book has been the tensions between corporate culture, financial incentives, and individual behaviour and how a lack of alignment between the three can result in endemic customer detriment and, in the long term, shareholder detriment. And we have seen that what is indicated is the necessity for all staff to appreciate the ways in which what they do, and how they do it, impacts upon customer perceptions. In the ideal world, all members of staff will see themselves as being, to some extent, customer-facing. Businesses that are based upon the maintenance of long-term customer relationships, as opposed to essentially the

one-off sale, see the *people* element of the mix as representing a primary, if not *the* primary, determinant of customer satisfaction and advocacy.

3. **Appreciate the challenges that a more customer-centric approach presents to marketers of financial services now and in the future.**
   We saw how important it is that corporate culture acts as the glue which cements all of the functions within a company together in pursuit of customer centricity. To achieve this it is vital that direction and leadership comes from the top and that CEOs and directors lead by example. Marketing can only do its job properly if the whole company is united by a culture that is truly customer facing. Thus, at the strategic level, dysfunctional cultures represent the greatest challenge to customer centricity. We explored a number of other challenges such as the lack of a single customer view, something that is all too commonly encountered in financial services, especially among some of the long-established companies.

4. **Understand how to evaluate the contribution made by marketing to an organisation.**
   We identified that CEOs and marketing directors frequently struggle to evaluate the value they gain from their marketing resources. There is a relative lack of well-established methodologies and tools available with which to conduct a forensic appraisal of the cost-effectiveness of marketing activities. In this chapter we identified a number of approaches that can be used as the basis for appraising marketing's effectiveness. One pragmatic approach known as the Marketing Mentor examines the performance of marketing in the following seven key areas of activity:
   - Marketing strategy,
   - Customer acquisition,
   - Customer development,
   - Product and service management,
   - Communication and perception management,
   - Planning and implementation,
   - People and development.

Review questions

1. What are the characteristics of the cultures of companies that seem to be dominated by customer acquisition? Compare and contrast these with those that seem to be advocates for a relationship-based approach to marketing.
2. Refer to tables 18.1, 18.2, 18.3 and discuss the extent to which you believe that the views of consumers expressed in this study are particular to financial services or do you believe they might apply equally to other commercial sectors?
3. Imagine you are the Marketing Director of an insurance company and you have just read this study. What actions might you take in response to its findings?
4. Refer to figures 18.1, and 18.2, how do you think chairmen, CEOs and directors of financial services companies should respond to the study's findings regarding consumer perceptions of them being greedy, fat cats? Do you believe the study's findings would apply to financial services companies in your country?
5. In what ways do you see AI and other aspects of digital impacting on the marketing of financial services in your country 5 years from now?

Notes

1   Riskscreen.com/blog/the-credit-suisse-scandal-2022-what-went-wrong-this-time (ccessed January 2024)
2   www.fico.com/en/forrester-report-unlocking-hyper-personalization-hyper-scale   (accessed January 2024)
3   www.raddon.com/en/insights/raddon_report/strategic-issues-for-financial-institutions-in-2022. html (accessed January 2024)
4   www.spglobal.com/marketintelligence/en/news-insights/latest-news-headlines/us-banks-close-159-branches-open-83-in-december-2022-73920168 (accessed January 2024)
5   Accenture Banking: Top 10 Trends for 2023
6   www.mckinsey.com/industries/financial-services/our-insights/ai-bank-of-the-future-can-banks-meet-the-ai-challenge (accessed January 2024)

References

Amah, E., Daminabo-Weje, M. (2013) Corporate Culture: A Tool or Control and Effectiveness in Organisations. *Research Humanities and Social Sciences*, 3(15). pp.42–49. https://core.ac.uk/downl oad/pdf/234673642.pdf

Davenport, T. O. (1998). The Integration Challenge: Managing Corporate Mergers. *Management Review,* 87 (Jan) pp. 25–28.

Graham, J.R, Harvey, C.R, Popadak, J., Rajgopal, S. (2017). Corporate Culture: Evidence from the Field, Working Paper 23255, National Bureau of Economic Research, March.

Hofstede, G.J, Minkov, M. (2010). *Cultures and Organisations: Software for the Mind,* 3rd Edition. New York: McGraw Hill.

Kroeber, A. L. and Kluckhohn, C. (1952). Culture: A Critical Review of Concepts and Definitions, Pp. 247. Cambridge, Massachusetts: Peabody Museum Press.

Porter, M. E. (1980). *Competitive Strategy*. New York: Free Press.

Porter, M. E. (1985). *Competitive Advantage*. New York: Free Press.

Part III
Case studies

The following case studies are provided in relation to Part III of this book and they focus particularly on customer relationship and broader corporate responsibility. They serve to complement the examples provided in each chapter through "marketing in practice" and can also be used for more extensive discussion of a range of marketing issues. Each case is provided with an indicative set of questions which may be useful for individual self-study or for group work and assessments.

The cases are:

- Case 9: American Express
- Case 10: Five Talents UK – Savings-led Microfinance
- Case 11: Safeguarding the Financial Fortress:
- Case 12: Starling Bank

DOI: 10.4324/9781003398615-33

Case study CS9

The American Express international loyalty programme

American Express (Amex) is one of the best known and most respected brand names in the world. In 2023 it was the second highest ranked financial services brand in Interbrand's global rankings. The company started in the middle of the 19thcentury in the US freight forwarding market. It rapidly established a reputation as a trusted transport provider for people's most valuable possessions. Building on its reputation and its US network, the end of the 19th and early 20th century saw American Express diversifying into travel services and financial services (see Figure CS9.1) – both areas in which it could build on the idea of helping to support the everyday lives of its customers. In 1891, the Travellers Cheque was launched; in 1915, Amex started selling rail and steamship tickets and in addition to its established offices in the US and Europe, it also opened in Buenos Aires, Manila and Hong Kong. Three years later Amex left the rail transport side of its business and focused instead on the travel and financial markets.

Figure CS9.1 American Express moves into travel services
"American Express Tours and Cruises 1922" by Nesster licensed under CC BY 2.0.
"American Express: Mauretania Winter Cruise to the Mediterranean, 1922" by Nesster licensed under CC BY 2.0.

DOI: 10.4324/9781003398615-34

In 1958, Amex introduced its iconic charge card, offering customers a new and convenient way to pay. Ever since, the company has innovated with its card products, its services and its other offerings. Today, American Express is one of the largest global payments network and it continues to pride itself on being forward-looking and customer-focused.

In the 1960s and '70s it enjoyed a dominant role in the global credit card market. However, from the 1980s onwards it has had to respond to an unprecedented growth in competition in all of the territories it served. In the face of such competition the company has had to work hard to earn the loyalty of customers and build lasting relationships. American Express has invested heavily in new products, expanded its rewards and loyalty programmes, and strengthened its servicing capabilities to better meet the needs of its customers. Its brand is strong, and the company is delivering a strong market and financial performance. Currently, Amex has:

- 140m cards in circulation (slightly more than half of these are global) although spending in the US is higher.
- Around 60% of Amex cards are proprietary (issued directly by Amex) and around 40% are co-branded with partners.
- The exclusive Amex Black Card (the Centurion Card) is available by invitation only, has a $10,000 initiation fee and a $5,000 annual fee.
- In 2022, Amex customers spent around $23,000 on their cards annually, up from around $20,000 in 2021.
- Only Mastercard and Visa handle more transactions that Amex.
- Both Mastercard and Visa are significantly larger than Amex in terms of card holders, but Amex consistently records higher revenue.

In sharp contrast to many of its rivals, American Express has generated most of its growth organically, rather than by mergers and acquisitions. Through this approach the company has grown its card-in-force base to over 140 million card members (with a little under half in the US and more than half internationally).

American Express first introduced a customer loyalty programme in its home USA market in 1991. During the course of the next few years the model proved its worth and was rolled out to many other markets around the world. By 2016 the international Membership Rewards Programme (MRP) had expanded significantly and was operating in 60 separate countries. American Express Membership Rewards is considered to be particularly flexible because they are transferable meaning card holders can use them for a wide range of purchases. In outline the scheme is as follows:

- High-value customers are invited to become card members of American Express. Value is based upon characteristics such as household income and credit scores.
- In the majority of cases Membership Rewards is part of the lending or charge card product benefits and features and as such the fee for the programme is mostly included in the product fee.
- Once enrolled in the programme, the member earns points on the basis of the monetary value of each transaction registered on their card.
- Regular bonus opportunities encourage rapid points bank growth.
- The points accumulate in the member's personal "bank account" and they can be redeemed for a wide range of goods and services via an online rewards catalogue, a smartphone app or telephone call centres located locally.

- The breadth of premium partners and brands included in the programme differentiates it from many other programmes. Redemption options cover a broad range of interests including: gift cards/certificates, merchandise, charities, experiences, car hire and transfer into other frequent flyer and hotel programmes.
- In recent years broad-based innovation has been utilised to deliver growth through new capabilities: pay with points online at merchant sites (e.g. Amazon in UK) and on bookings through Amex Travel; redemption of points for statement credits, or against a merchant's charge on a consumer's bill; pay with points at point of sale in real time.

The local American Express management is responsible for promoting the programme to card holders in their respective countries. Additionally, they are responsible for negotiating local partnership arrangements with providers of goods and services listed in their member catalogue and for organising the fulfilment service.

Overall business management of the programme takes place in London to ensure that it is achieving its goals and that the brand is being managed in a consistent fashion. The central function is also responsible for driving new reward innovations that keep the programme evolving, negotiating supplier relationships with major strategic partners such as major airlines and international hotel groups and for ensuring that the common systems platform and infrastructure provides the necessary functionality and access to the programmes being operated across the territories that comprise the MRP.

Partnerships

More than 1200 partners provide the goods and services that MRP members enjoy in exchange for the points they have accumulated. This includes brands such as Hertz, AVIS, Sony and Hugo Boss, Apple, Tiffany & Co, as well as companies such as Starwood, Hilton, Amazon and GAP. Airlines represent particularly important partners, and American Express has partnership arrangements with over 30 of them, many of which are national carriers in their market. This includes Virgin Atlantic, Cathay Pacific, British Airways and Singapore Airlines.

Through becoming a partner with American Express, the company benefits in a number of ways. First, it receives the value of the goods that the member receives in exchange for his or her points from American Express. Second, it provides the partner with access to highly desirable customers.

A third benefit that partners gain is access to information about the spending behaviour of the MRP members. American Express has access to unique consumer data from its closed loop network, through their relationships with both card members and merchants. By knowing their card members and their spending habits, they can provide merchants with insights to help them understand and target their customers better.

Results

At the close of 2023 Amex announced that annual revenue had increased by 14% to over $60 billion. Earnings per share had increased by14% and dividends were expected to rise by 17%. The company reported that demand for premium cards remained strong and some 12 million new proprietary card holders were added during the year, bringing the total number of active cards to 140 million globally. Since announcing a growth strategy at the start of 2022, Amex has seen revenue growth of around 40% and a 37% increase in card member spending.

MRP has received numerous awards across the globe for its dedication and innovation in the loyalty programme sector and the current value of the programme (in terms of the ability of members to spend) stands at around $14 billion, according to the company's accounts.

Case study source: Mindy Davidowksi, Vice President American Express with additional information sourced from https://www.wallstreetzen.com/stocks/us/nyse/axp/statistics and https://ir.americanexpress.com/financials/earnings-and-sec-filings/default.aspx and https://www.americanexpress.com/en-us/company/who-we-are/ (all accessed 30 January2024)

Case study questions

1. This case is a good example of a company seeking to influence consumer behaviour. Which particular aspects of consumer behaviour does Amex aim to influence, and which models and concepts of how consumer behaviour works do you think it draws upon? (Clue: start by examining behavioural economics.)
2. Suggest ways in which Amex could use the range of digital marketing tools presented in Part II to enhance the effectiveness of its affinity programme.
3. Drawing on your understanding of the approach used by Amex, propose ways in which the 2P2C marketing mix introduced in Chapter 9 could be applied in the case of a general insurance company to create a customer affinity programme.

Case study CS10

Five Talents UK – savings-led microfinance

Introduction

Five Talents was established 25 years ago to help the rural poor in low-income countries to start and grow the businesses they depend on. Working through local partner organisations, Five Talents has reached 270,000 families worldwide through savings and loan groups.

Five Talents (www.fivetalents.org.uk) helps the poorest communities, with a specific focus on eastern and central Africa. Rates of financial inclusion have increased significantly in many countries in the region in the past decade. However, the poorest, those in rural areas and young people are the most likely to remain financially excluded (FinAccess, 2021). There are many reasons for this: for some the distance to a bank, and therefore cost, outweigh the benefit of the small amounts they could deposit, others can't read or write so understanding the paperwork is impossible, and some feel unwelcome in banks which they see as being for the wealthy. The banks often view the demographics Five Talents works with as a credit risk and see little scope for profit on small transactions in remote places.

The programmes that Five Talents supports operate a savings-led model based on an asset-based approach. An asset-based development approach focuses on what communities have, rather than what they do not have. Marginalised communities may have been told that they are poor, lack education and have little hope. Instead, in an asset-based approach, communities are supported to identify assets they have whether financial assets, physical assets, experiences, knowledge, relationships, etc.

The savings groups (known as "Trust Groups") build on this approach as groups identify and then use the financial resources they do have and existing relationships with each other to begin to save – often starting with relatively small amounts. The groups are entirely self-managed and the groups themselves make lending decisions.

Five Talents was founded by the Anglican Church and continues to work alongside the local Church (although of course people of all faiths and no faith can join the Trust Groups freely and there is no proselytising or discrimination). In the areas where Five Talents works, there is a church in even the most remote or conflict-affected locations meaning there is a ready-made, trusted outreach network helping us to reach every community.

Through Five Talents' local partners, Trust Groups begin with a process of "resource mobilisation"– supporting communities to identify resources they do have and build their confidence. After this, the training focuses on financial literacy and business skills

DOI: 10.4324/9781003398615-35

Figure CS10.1 Trust Group meeting in Burundi

Photo credit: Taking Pictures, Changing Lives Foundation

Participants Reporting a Significant Improvement in Incomes, Welfare and Resilience as a Result of the Programme

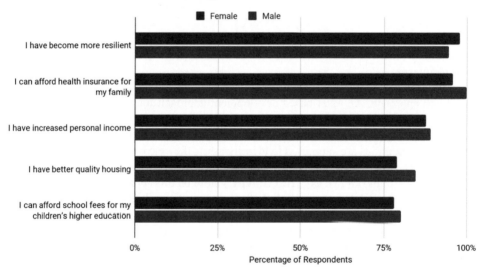

Figure CS10.2 The impact of Five Talents

training. The curriculum includes basic principles such as how and why to save, record-keeping, profit and loss, business planning, marketing, diversification, and customer service. These skills enable members to make the most of the financial services which our model provides.

Whilst receiving the training, members also begin saving what they can, normally around £1 to £2 a month initially. These savings are kept in a communal bank account or lockbox depending on how practical it is for the group to access a bank account. Unlike traditional credit-led microfinance, the loan capital comes from the Group's accumulated savings, a model not dissimilar to a credit union.

Loans are then invested in businesses and repaid at an interest rate agreed by the group; normally around 1% per month. The interest goes back into the communal pot and is distributed amongst members as dividends at the end of the year. This enables members to effectively earn an interest on their savings, providing some protection from high levels of inflation and meaning that everyone benefits, even if they chose to save only and not to take a loan. The groups normally receive training support from Five Talents partner organisations for two to three years. After this, the groups continue to operate, saving and loaning, without ongoing support from Five Talents partners.

Impact

In 2022, an independent evaluation was conducted looking at the longitudinal impact of a programme run by Mothers' Union Burundi which Five Talents supports. The evaluation found that:

Sustainability: The evaluation included re-visiting groups that were first supported by the programme ten years ago and which have, therefore, been operating without support for eight years. Overall, the evaluation found that 84% of the Trust Groups formed under the programme are still actively saving and loaning.

The evaluator found that the groups were sustainable because they formed strong relationships as a result of meeting together regularly, they were self-selected and self-governing and built social cohesion through non-financial activities.

Business growth: Prior to joining a group, the majority of group members in Burundi were involved in subsistence farming; farming for their own domestic consumption rather than for sale to market.

Through the loans borrowed from groups and increased self-confidence, members often invested in growing their agricultural businesses – for example, through investments in livestock or more significantly, land.

The evaluation found that members moved from subsistence farming to becoming employers; 35% of women and 48% of men have businesses with more than two employees. This speaks to the growth of businesses and employment opportunities for those beyond direct programme participants.

Outcomes for households: The evaluation found that there had been a significant improvement in household outcomes. As a result of increased incomes, 80% of families reported benefiting from improved housing, 97% reported improved access to healthcare, and 78% of their children benefit from access to higher education.

97% of members reported feeling more able to cope with unexpected events. Through loans from the Trust Groups, participants purchased assets which, if needed, they could sell in times of crisis. This, in combination with better preparedness as a result of the financial education they received, gave them a greater sense of resilience.

In Kenya, rates of financial inclusion are significantly higher than in Burundi. And yet in Kenya, informal financial services and specifically informal savings groups, are still used by nearly 28.7% of the population (FinAccess, 2021). Organisations like Five Talents provide important services to the financially excluded enabling them to save, invest and grow their incomes.

Case study source: Hannah Wichmann, Five Talents

Case study questions

1. How important do you think micro-finance is as a way of tackling poverty in developing countries?
2. What do you think are the factors that might limit the growth of micro-finance and which organisations and agencies could help to overcome those limiting factors?
3. Do you believe that micro-finance has a role to play in your country? If so, should commercial financial services companies devote resources to the development of the micro-finance market?
4. What resources might commercial companies devote to micro-finance, and in what ways might such activities be of benefit to those companies?

Case study CS11

Safeguarding the financial fortress: cyber detection and prevention in financial services marketing – One Brightly Cyber

Context

There are many factors that underpin consumer trust but in a digital environment it is becoming increasingly important to reassure customers about digital security and transparent practice.

Banking customers must be able trust that their money is safe with their bank, even where that bank has no obvious physical presence. It is difficult, if not impossible for consumers to evaluate actual security levels and protocols and often what matters is perceptions of security.

In the fast-evolving landscape of the financial services industry, technological advancements have brought both unparalleled opportunities and unprecedented risks. As financial institutions strive to meet the ever-growing demands of their clients in an increasingly digital world, the need for robust cyber detection and prevention measures has become paramount. Financial services have been revolutionised by technology. With online banking, mobile payment apps, and investment platforms at our fingertips, consumers expect easy access to their financial assets anytime, anywhere. This digital transformation has given rise to a new marketing and customer engagement era, where financial institutions leverage data and technology to understand better and serve their clients. However, this digital dependence also opens a Pandora's box of vulnerabilities.

The very convenience and accessibility that customers appreciate also serve as entry points for cybercriminals. From data breaches and identity theft to ransomware attacks and phishing schemes, financial institutions are prime targets for malicious actors seeking to exploit vulnerabilities in their digital infrastructure.

The scale of the problem

The stats (below) show that money spent on cyber prevention needs to catch up with cyber losses across businesses, especially financial services. Furthermore, many cybercrimes go unreported in sensitive industries like financial services because of reputational concerns.

The weakest links are often employees and external service providers, and once infected, it's a short step to a financial services organisation becoming infected with malware. Polymorphic malware (which changes shape and form) is often undetectable with virus-scanning software and can lie dormant for months before an attack. For this reason, it's necessary for financial services organisations to deploy a second security layer to detect externally breached data and "at risk" service providers and marketers, who often hold sensitive customer information.

DOI: 10.4324/9781003398615-36

THE PROBLEM

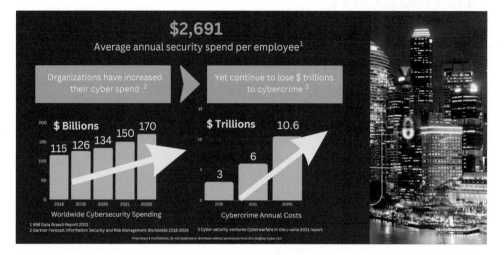

Figure CS11.1   The Importance of Cyber detection and prevention

To safeguard the financial fortress and maintain trust with customers, proactive cyber detection and prevention measures are non-negotiable. Such measures are of paramount importance to:

1. **Protect Customer Data**
2. **Safeguard Regulatory Compliance**
3. **Preserve Corporate Reputation**
4. **Maintain Financial Stability**
5. **Protect Intellectual Property**
6. **Preserve Competitive Advantage**

Mitigating cyber threats

Technology alone will not prevent cyber-attacks and consequential financial losses. It's also necessary to take pre-emptive action by identifying and eliminating external threats from breached employee or supplier data and malware that indicate the likelihood of an imminent attack and to take immediate remedial action. Speed is of the essence. As can be seen in the fuller paper in the Support Material, it takes a business an average of 207 days to realise a breach has occurred, often with fatal consequences.

In one company, through our external threat scan of the company URL we uncovered extensive, serious breaches, indicating an imminent cyber-attack requiring immediate remediation assistance. The company and its IT department had no idea of the breaches. The malware breach was caused by an employee logging onto a travel site outside of work hours. This single breach had the potential to cause a multi-million-dollar loss.

MARKET STATS (BUSINESS)

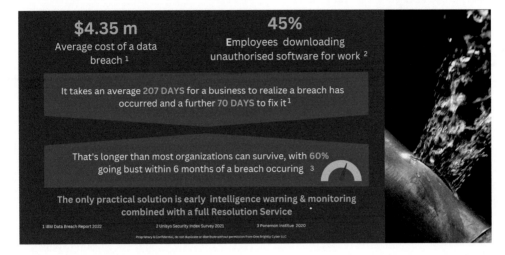

Figure CS11.2   Market statistics

Conclusions

Cyber awareness in financial services marketing is not just a "nice to have" but a non-negotiable imperative. It's critical for marketers, and the organisations employing them, and their suppliers, to implement 24/7 vulnerability scanning to detect external data breaches and threats that may not be detectible within the organisations themselves. Early detection and remediation is the single most important factors to reduce losses from cybercrime. This case study is a summary of a more detailed paper that can be accessed via the Support Material.

Case study questions

1. To what extent do you believe that consumer concerns regarding data security are undermining trust in the financial services industry?
2. Do you believe that it is possible for a company to claim competitive advantage because of its capabilities regarding data security? What arguments support your opinion?
3. Imagine you are the Chief Marketing Officer of a fintech bank, how would you use the marketing mix to reassure customers that their data is safe?

Case study CS12

Starling Bank, UK changing – banking for good, and the planet

> Climate change is one of the biggest challenges that we face globally, and Starling is 100% committed to playing its part in the fight against it, not just in the lead up to 2030, but starting right away. This is urgent and we know that our customers expect no less from us.
>
> – Anne Boden, founder of Starling Bank

Starling Bank was founded in 2014 by industry veteran Anne Boden. After a distinguished career working in senior leadership at some of the world's best-known financial heavyweights, she spotted earlier than most the opportunity to transform retail banking using digital technology. In the wake of the financial crisis, she felt ashamed to be a banker and wanted to do something about the state of the industry. She remains the only woman in the UK to start a bank, and her vision for Starling was unlike any bank that had come before it.

Starling would be a first-of-its-kind digital bank, with no branches, and intuitive in-app features that help customers better manage their money. It would offer a better customer experience and would have less impact on the planet.

The bank launched to the public in 2017. It has raised £685 million in investment, acquired more than four million customer accounts across its retail and SME services and gained industry-wide recognition from the consumer champion Which? and the British Bank Awards. It consistently sits at or near the top of the independent banking performance tables compiled by the UK government's Competition and Markets Authority (CMA).

Starling reported its first full year of profitability in 2022, a first in the UK digital banking world, balancing its low-cost base with its best-in-class customer service, intensive product development and innovation, as well as an approach that puts the environment first.

Starling recognises that banks play a critical role in addressing climate change. It does not invest in the fossil fuel industry and has set itself some tough carbon emission reduction targets, having applied to the Science Based Targets initiative (SBTi). Starling is also a member of the Partnership for Carbon Accounting Financials (PCAF).

Preventing emissions when servicing customers

- Branchless and paperless, Starling puts sustainability at the heart of its operations.
- Customer interactions take place on Starling's digital infrastructure, held on the AWS Cloud which runs on 92% renewable energy as of 2022.

DOI: 10.4324/9781003398615-37

Figure CS12.1 Startling Bank – changing banking for good

Source: provided by Starling Bank Image to illustrate the importance of Cyber detection and protection

- The only physical asset customers receive is a bank card made from recycled plastic, which arrives in fully recycled and recyclable packaging. The bank also champions the use of mobile wallets and virtual cards that use no materials at all.
- Starling's four offices in London, Southampton, Cardiff and Manchester all run on renewable energy. Employees benefit from tax-free EV leases, bikes and season ticket loans to reduce their carbon footprint when commuting….…..As well as reaching new customers.
- Starling puts sustainability first when carrying out advertising and marketing campaigns and consciously chooses to work with partners that are pioneering more sustainable changes in the advertising industry. The bank sponsored a documentary series with environmental activist Jack Harries that explored the impact of climate change in the lead up to COP26.
- All of Starling's brand partnerships have purpose, and the bank has partnered with influential organisations that champion sustainability. Starling's work with Trillion Trees saw a tree planted for every customer referral; 100,000 trees have and will be planted as part of this work. The bank now offers free day passes to National Trust properties and grounds for each customer referral to encourage access to and restoration of nature using customer deposits sustainably.

- Starling does not bank or invest in fossil fuel companies and is not exposed to polluting commodities such as oil, gas, coal or wood.
- Starling offers green mortgages through its specialist Buy to Let mortgage lender, Fleet Mortgages, that encourage owners to improve the energy efficiency of their properties.

Towards Carbon Net Zero

Starling recognises that its carbon footprint, while already low, could be reduced further and has committed to reducing its carbon emissions (relating to its operations and supply chain) by a third by 2030 and to become Carbon Net Zero by 2050. To meet these goals, the bank is assessing its scope one, two and three emissions annually in line with the Greenhouse Gas Protocol. In addition, it determines emissions associated with its lending and investment activity using the Partnership for Carbon Accounting methodology. It also assesses the environmental impact of new partners and suppliers before it embarks on new projects and relationships, which encourages its customers and staff to make more mindful choices. Finally, the bank has submitted near and medium-term reduction targets to the Science Based Targets initiative to go through the rigorous approval process, thereby ensuring that its ambitious targets are robust and realistic.

To offset its carbon emissions, Starling invests in avoidance and carbon capture environmental community projects. Projects invested into date include deforestation and tree planting projects in Tanzania, Uganda and the Congo basin; renewable energy projects in Bulgaria, Kenya and India; and the distribution and installation of clean and efficient cookstoves in Tanzania. The bank has also signed a three-year partnership with the National Trust that involves the restoration of peatland and an education programme for children on why the preservation of nature is so important.

Its sustainability reporting, including details of climate-related risks, is rapidly evolving with growing regulatory reporting requirements. In its annual report for 2021 to 2022, and 2022 to 2023, Starling published its Streamlined Energy and Carbon Reporting (SECR) report. For the 2023 to 2024 financial year, Climate Related Financial Disclosures, in line with the requirements of Section 414CB of the Companies Act 2006, will be disclosed in its annual report. It will also submit its first Energy Savings Opportunity Scheme (ESOS) audit in 2024.

Customer impact

Starling's sustainable positioning resonates with customers in the retail and SME space as well as the wider industry; it was the most switched to bank via the Current Account Switch Service (CASS) in 2021 overall and was named ESG Bank of the Year at the 2023 Impact AM Awards. Its online sustainability content is some of the bank's best read, from case studies of sustainable businesses powered by Starling, to its sustainability jargon buster and guidance on calculating carbon emissions.

The bank's path to Carbon Net Zero will remain a priority for all stakeholders and employees. Starling is on a mission to change banking for good – for customers, and the planet.

Case study source: Grace Wilson, Starling Bank

Case study questions

1. Carry out some research into Starling Bank to help you to gain a better understanding of its business model and strategy. Would you say that the company has based its competitive advantage on its sustainability credentials?
2. To what extent do you believe that Starling is right to use ESG as a means of cementing relationships with its customers? How important do you think it is as a means of achieving customer retention?
3. Which fintech companies in your country promote their adoption of ESG principles and what traction do you think it has in cementing customer relationships?
4. To what extent does the role and use of social media for fintechs such as Starling differ to its use by traditional banks?

Index

Abrdn 419
Accenture 213, 297, 417, 597
Access to insurance initiative 266
Acorn 205
active fund management 52
advertising (*see also* communications;
      promotion)
   above-the-line advertising 357–8
   advertising and promotion 357–9, 594, 595
   below-the-line advertising 358
Advertising Standards Authority (UK) 347
ageing populations 132
Aggregators 300, 388–2, 396
Agricultural Bank of China 268
AIA 145
AIDA 353, 358, 359, 363
AIG 110
Aktif Bank (*see also* N Kolay Kredi) 441–4
algorithms 417, 418
Alipay 322
Alliance and Leicester 110
Allianz 353, 361
Ally Bank 364
Amazon 110, 119, 145, 466, 475, 579
   Amazon Echo/Alexa 140, 321
American Express 110, 117, 175, 243, 254, 288,
      326, 361, 470, 489, 490, 613–16
ANZ Bank 99
Ansoff's product and market matrix 108–10
Annuities 59, 60
Apple 579
   Apple Pay 40, 45, 138, 214, 322, 476
artificial intelligence (AI) 80, 93, 139, 284, 291,
      299, 333–5, 369, 391, 419, 477, 481, 560,
      596, 599, 600
ASB Bank 303
Asda 39
Aseguradora Tajy 150, 151
Aspen Institute 581
Association of Financial Mutuals 23, 24, 25
AT Kearney Global Retail Development Index
      49
ATMs 83, 98, 136, 412

Atom Bank 20, 39, 109, 300, 415
Australian Seniors 199
automated voice recognition 137
avatars 359–60
Aviva 172, 174, 399
Axa 102, 258

Bain & Co 459
bancassurance 110, 145, 276, 410, 427–9
Baillie Gifford 176
Bankinter 79
Bankislami 102
Bank Islam 113, 220
Bank Negara 64
Bank of America 76, 392, 587
Bank of China 268
Bank of England 29, 127, 129
banking and money transmission 42–7
bank switching 40, 165
Barakan Islamic Bank 220
Barclays 40, 64, 75, 166, 173, 198, 235, 246,
      322, 332, 341, 342, 343, 360, 362, 405, 414,
      466, 544, 580, 587
BBVA 346–7
behavioural economics (finance)167–71
Betterment 417
binance 63
biometrics 321, 413, 476
birthrates 132–3
Bitcoin 62, 63, 64, 332
Blackrock 247, 305, 332, 360, 576
blockchain 62, 330–2, 425
BNP Paribas 346, 410, 544
bonds (relationship) *see* customer relationships
Boston Consulting Group Matrix (BCG) 111–12
BPER 228–31
BNY Mellon 485
Bradesco 136
branch closures 19, 20, 298, 343, 410–11
branch networks 176, 271, 343, 409–11
brand/branding 124, 227, 254, 324–6
   awareness 357, 360, 366–7, 464
   building 292, 452

equity 147, 184
inclusivity 578
name 316, 324
research 184–6
saliency 421
stretch 39
Brexit impact 32, 126, 247–9
bucket theory of marketing 467
Building societies 19
bundling 470
Burger King 221
business-to-business 5, 210, 211, 218, 251, 383, 489
buying behaviour (*see* consumer, customer)
buy now, pay later (BNPL) 48, 84

call-centres 79, 292, 333, 430, 599
Canford Centre for Customer Development 604
capacity management 79
Capital One 147, 246, 321
capabilities (*see* competences/capabilities)
cash usage 40
Caixa 40
Centre for Risk, Banking and Financial Services (CRBFS) 537, 538, 541, 546, 549
channels of distribution (*see* distribution, channels)
Chase Bank (*see also* JPMorgan Chase) 297, 392
Chatbots 79–81, 83, 297, 358, 414, 596
ChatGPT 284, 334, 419, 451
cheque usage trends 43, 44
Child Trust Fund 116
China Construction Bank 268
Chime 138
China Merchants Bank 112, 148, 268–72
Citibank 109, 117, 235, 253, 257, 332, 362, 410
Citi Index 298
CIC Group 101, 103
CIC Insurance 292–4
Cirrus 243
Clerical Medical 177
climate change 30, 33, 62, 391, 267, 559, 623
Clinc 302
Cline 334
cognitive dissonance 165, 595
Coinbase 39
commission-based selling 163, 177, 425–6, 488
Commonwealth Bank 80, 304
communications (*see also* promotion) 288, 342–8, 480, 484, 512
digital 366–8
mix, 355
planning 351–6
process 342
research 182–3
Comparethemarket.com 349–51, 353
competences/capabilities 147–8

competitive advantage 104, 116–18, 201, 221, 224, 226, 288, 589
competitive bidding (*see also* competitive tendering) 383
competitive environment (*see also* market environment) 462
competitive parity 250, 354
competitive position 97, 111, 144, 222, 247, 254, 282, 288, 308, 332, 376, 401, 575
competitive strategy (*see also* strategic marketing) 116–17, 150
cost leadership 116–17
differentiation leadership 117
focus/niche strategies 117
stuck in the middle 117
competitive strength 104, 111, 112, 242
competitive threats 95
conduct risk gap analysis 606
consumers (*see also* customers)
consumer choice 156, 157, 159, 168, 182, 193, 202, 347, 361, 473
consumer credit 48, 144, 147, 442
consumer decision-making 129, 155–8, 168, 194, 555
consumer expectations 501–2, 509, 527–9
consumer needs, 159, 313–14, 320, 321–2
consumer perceptions 224, 501, 537, 602
consumer protection 13, 127, 129
consumer 'pull' 161
consumer vulnerability 20, 21, 551
Consumers Federation 463
Consumer Finance Protection Bureau 591
Consumer Intelligence 389–92, 552
Consumers Union 462
contingent consumption (*see* financial service characteristics)
conversion 110, 150, 358, 367, 368, 414, 431
cookies 215, 358, 485–7
CO-OP Financial Services 353
Co-operative Bank 64, 176, 203, 208, 222, 415
Cooperators 574
Co-operative Insurance 22
COP28 575
core competencies 148, 152, 247
corporate culture 588, 589
Corporate Governance Code 569
corporate identity 361, 410
corporate image 326, 352, 360–1
corporate reputation 270, 326, 361, 407, 536, 561, 622
corporate social responsibility (CSR) (*see also* ESG) 558–66
evolution of 559–62
origins 558, 559
sustainability 563–8
corporate markets 110, 137, 144, 197, 198, 235, 236, 254, 270, 313, 359, 363

corporate mission 102, 589
corporate objectives 100, 104, 120, 507
corporate reputation 270, 326, 361, 407, 536,
    561, 622
corporate strategy 96, 105, 607
cost drivers 246
cost leadership 116, 117, 453
coupons 344, 362
covert pricing (*see* implicit pricing*)*
Covestor 300
Covid 19, 53, 79, 82, 93, 123, 234, 411, 413,
    450, 452, 576, 579
CRM 459–93
    drivers 460–6
    impact of digital 475–87
    international 488–90
    role of intermediaries 487, 489
    systems 484–5
creative insight 202, 203, 232, 583
creative intuition 230
Credit Agricole 102
Credit Suisse 587
credit unions 20
critical illness insurance 57
customer relationship marketing (CRM) 543
cross-sell and cross-selling 86, 215, 404, 427,
    494, 515, 591
cryptocurrency 62–4
culture 133–4, 587–2
cultural differences 238, 244, 426, 563
cultural proximity 238, 255, 489
current accounts 19, 42, 295
customers (*see also* consumers)
    customer acquisition 292–6, 306–8, 462, 465,
        472, 588
    customer advocacy 303, 473, 504, 595
    customer analytics 446, 447, 451, 469, 476,
        477, 478
    customer/consumer dissatisfaction 405, 411,
        430
    customer/consumer duty 31, 548–53, 547, 594
    customer/consumer satisfaction 201, 425, 495,
        496, 515, 524, 526–7, 530–3
    customer convenience and distribution 403–37
customer data management 478–9
    customer expectations 501–2, 509, 527–9
    customer experience (CX) 365, 369
    customer lifetime value 473–5
    customer management strategies 47
customer perceptions 224, 501, 537, 602
customer persistency 467, 468
    customer relationships and bonds 470, 471
    customer relationship chain 472, 473
    customer retention 468–70
    customer retention strategies 470–2
    customer satisfaction surveys 479, 530–3
    customer value 479, 473–5

customisation 70, 88, 210, 258, 260, 290, 471,
    489
customisation bonds 471
customised targeting 221, 222
cybersecurity 39 (*see also* One Brightly Cyber)

Danone 577
data privacy 486–7
DBS (Singapore) 241
debt 47, 48
decision making unit (DMU) 156–7
defensive strategies 112–13
deferred features 592
Deloitte 304, 414
demographics 113, 205, 389, 394
dependency ratio 16, 17
deposit accounts 49, 51, 53, 398
Deutsche Bank 76, 147, 241, 242, 258
DeVere 253
differential advantage 217
differential pricing (*see* price, pricing)
differentiated marketing 216, 217
differentiated product 116
differentiated segmentation 216
differentiation 40, 116, 117, 192, 201, 202, 208,
    215, 221, 226, 232, 255, 288, 318, 319, 324,
    349, 383, 392, 393, 394, 398, 445, 466, 470,
    471, 575, 594, 597
digital devices 45
digital banks 40, 45 (*see also* fintech, neobanks)
digital marketing
    CRM 463, 475, 478–81, 484
    CRM systems 484, 485
    customer acquisition 296–306
    data privacy and cookies 485–7
    data security 297, 299, 621–3
    digital tools 366–8, 484, 485
    pricing 399
    social crm 481–4
    strategy 198, 282, 207, 283, 447
    usability 300
digital migrants 302
digital natives 302
direct distribution (*see* distribution channels,
    channels of distribution)
Direct Line 345
direct mail 335, 357, 358, 363, 371, 406, 409,
    430–4, 446, 484, 543, 595
direct marketing 107, 342, 344, 348, 355, 362
direct sales 3, 404, 409, 423–7, 433, 434, 598
direct-response advertising 357, 358, 362, 363,
    371, 406, 409, 432
disconfirmation 527
disruptive technology 2
distribution (*see also* customer convenience and
    distribution)
    channel features 404–6

channels 409–33
  bancassurance 427–9
  branch-based 409–11
  direct mail 431, 432
  distribution and access 595–9
  face-to-face 423–7
  internet-based 411–16
  methods and models 406–8
  multi-channel 433
  non-FS retailers 421, 422
  others 432
  quasi-FS outlets 422, 423
  robo-advice 416–20
  telephone-based 429, 430
distribution strategies 433, 434
Dutch-Bangla Bank 138

Ecclesiastical Insurance 217
Ecology Building Society 116
economic development 10
economic environment 129–32
Edelman Trust Barometer 464, 542, 545, 563
Education Mutual 25
Egg 238
EMC Insurance 211, 212
emotional appeals (*see also* functional appeals) 326–7
employee satisfaction 495–6, 530, 533
employment participation rate 14, 15
empower 78, 82, 363, 511, 518, 605
Endsleigh Insurance 217
Ensure 406
entry mode, choice of 257, 260
environment, analysis and scanning 123–9, 148–50
environmental sustainability (*see* ESG)
environmental, social and governance (ESG)
    (*see also* CSR) 42, 93, 135, 560, 566–78
  benefits 577–8
  ESG and CSR 568–70
  ESG and inclusion 578–83
  ESG in practice 576–81
  sustainability 563–6
Equifax 389
Equitable Life 26
Equity Bank 75
equity release 42, 346, 432, 528
Ernst & Young 418
essential evidence (*see* evidence)
Ethereum 62, 332
ethics and customer acquisition 306–8
European Court of Justice 27
European Systemic Risk Board 31, 32
evaluating marketing activities 600–7
Everyman Insurance 386
evidence
essential 172, 291

  peripheral 172, 291
  physical 75, 172, 282–3, 288, 290, 291–2
Experian 48, 205–7
external environment (*see* marketing environment)

Facebook 283, 303, 464, 465, 449
family, the role of 12
fairness
  Fairness Index 549
  Treating customers fairly (TCF) (*see also* customer duty) 35, 543, 546
fiduciary responsibility 74, 83–5, 165, 176, 177, 236, 345, 404
financial advice 40, 41
financial capability/literacy 160–1
Financial Conduct Authority (FCA) 20, 21, 25, 30, 35, 62, 127, 173, 398, 464, 543, 546, 582
financial inclusion 57–9
financial exclusion 18, 19
Financial Inclusion Commission 581
Financial Inclusion Centre 27
Financial Ombudsman Service 548, 550
Financial Policy Committee 29, 127
financial service characteristics (*see also* services characteristics)
  contingent consumption 85
  credence qualities 74, 75, 162, 164
  duration of consumption 86, 177
  experience qualities 74, 75, 162
  fiduciary responsibility 83–5, 165, 176–7
  heterogeneity 72, 81–3, 176, 289
  intangibility 71, 74–7, 172–5, 289
  inseparability 72, 77–8, 175–6, 289
  perishability 72, 78–81, 175–6, 289
  search qualities 162
Financial Services Compensation Scheme 63
fintech (*see also* digital, insuretech, neobanks) 20, 33, 38, 39, 67, 145, 273, 274, 544, 545
FinGoPay, 322
financial product variants 41, 42
financial services providers 37–67
Fidelty 138, 470
Finder.com 464
First Direct 176
First National Bank 136, 137
First Reliance bank 75
Five Talents 617–20
five-force analysis 103, 143–5
Folksam 222, 223, 564–6
Forbes 392
Foresight Factory 124–5
foresight investment 181–2
Friendly societies 19, 23
Frost Bank 325–6, 361
FTX 62, 63

Fujitsu 299
Fundsmith Equity 75
functional quality (*see also* service quality, process quality) 324, 501
functional appeals (*see also* emotional appeals) 326–7

gap model of service quality (*see* service quality)
gateway product 484
GDP 460, 461
General China 324
General Electric (GE) Business Screen 112–13
General Motors 144
geography of supply 38
Giffen effect 392
global customers bank account penetration 43
global distribution channels 243
globalization 10, 122, 242, 243, 248, 252–4
globalisation, drivers of 243–50
Golf Savings Bank 117
Google Pay 40, 45, 214
Goldman Sachs 110, 334–5
Grameen Bank 18
Great Eastern 359
growth strategies 108, 112
Guinness 226

Halifax Bank 580
Hallmark Insurance 385
Handlesbanken 78, 410
Hargreaves Lansdown 138
Haven Knox-Johnston 199, 200
HDFC Bank 97, 173, 176, 328, 393, 410, 412, 445–9
Hello 346, 353
heterogeneity (*see* service characteristics)
Hiscox 217
Home Equity Bank 346
household savings 131
household structure 133
HSBC 40, 64, 80, 101, 117, 149, 177, 222, 223, 235, 241, 244–5, 246, 253, 298, 342, 343, 359, 411, 465, 466
HUK 24, 450
hybrid strategy 221

ICBC (Industrial and Commercial Bank of China) 166, 268
ICICI Bank 241, 254, 412
ICMIF 22, 573, 574
iDGate 39
IFuree, 322
IMF 12
income smoothing 14, 18, 47
indebtedness 47, 84, 208, 583
Independent Financial Advisers (IFAs) 295, 300, 419, 420, 487, 488

index tracker funds 52
indirect channels (*see* distribution channels, channels of distribution)
information asymmetry 381
ING Direct 140, 298
inseparability (*see* service characteristics)
Insights, 3R Insights 422, 606
Instagram 464, 465, 482
Institute of Business Ethics 306–8
insurance
    critical illness 57
    general 60
    health 57
    inclusive 265, 267
    life 55
    long term care 57
    PHI 57
    term 55
InsuranceBASE 75
insuretech (*see also* fintech) 39, 364–5, 399, 451
intangibility (*see* service characteristics)
Integrated Marketing communications (IMC) 356
integrated marketing theory 480
Interactive Brokers Group 300
Interbrand 227–31, 273, 274, 326, 578–80
interest rates 131–2
Internationalisation
    firm specific drivers 239–42
    global strategies 253–4
    international strategies 252–3
    macro drivers 243–50
    market entry 256–8
    multidomestic strategies 254
    transnational strategies 254–5
Internet of Things (IoT) 140–1, 142, 391, 399, 415
internet banking 94, 134, 137, 303, 410, 411, 415
intermediaries 313, 332, 407, 409, 415, 422, 434, 487, 488, 490, 511, 512, 532
Integrated marketing communications (IMC) 356
Investec 297
Investengine 419
investing 49, 50
2iQ Research 39
Isbank 334
Islamic Bank of Britain 66, 220
Islamic financial services 64–6, 110, 134, 220, 238, 246
IVR (automatic call-handling procedure) 600

Japan Seven 136
Joseph Rowntree Foundation 52
JP Morgan Chase 241, 326, 332, 335, 361, 596, 597
Justice theory 549

KB Financial Group 273, 274
KB Kookmin Bank 318
key performance indicators 184
Kickstarter 39
KPMG 547
Kuwait Finance House 242
Kyoto agreement 560, 564

Leakbot 399
LEBC 419
legacy systems 20, 40, 300, 304, 329, 451, 462, 477
Legal and General 253, 405
Lemonade 81, 331, 335
lending and credit 47
Lexus 226
life insurance products 5659
Liiv 273, 274
Linkedin 297, 465–6
Lloyds Banking Group 40, 64, 176, 247, 298, 332, 415
loyalty (*see also* retention) 86, 117, 495–6, 497, 504–5, 512–15
    attitudinal 514
    behavioural 168, 514
    programmes, 166, 295, 362, 490, 595, 613–15
LV= 24, 419

MagiClick Digital 45
Maif 201, 224
M & G Investments 482, 483
market attractiveness 49, 112, 255
market development strategy 110
market environment 3, 96, 99, 123–6, 389
market penetration strategy 109, 113, 410
market planning 104
market orientation 122–3
market research 103, 178–93, 266, 336, 356, 510, 537, 601
market research ethics 193–2
market segmentation (*see* segmentation)
market selection decision 256
market targeting 84, 197–233
marketing
    campaign 112, 115, 201, 246, 346, 361
    internal (*see also* internal marketing) 83, 87, 89, 109, 175, 341, 361
    management 104, 281, 604
    objectives 100, 101, 104, 105, 285, 286, 354
    plan, planning 93–120, 563
marketing environment 123–5
macro 125–6
market 143–5
internal 146–8
marketing strategy/strategies 143, 145, 150, 179, 225, 275–7, 281, 283, 287, 323, 384, 386, 398, 460, 475, 488, 551, 558, 561, 603, 604

Marketing Mentor 608
marketing mix
    challenges for financial services 292–6
    introduction 281–5
    four Cs 282
    four Ps 282
    impact of digital 296–306
    management of 288–92
    migrants, natives and social media 302, 303
    role of 287–8
    seven Ps 282
    two Ps two Cs 283
Marks and Spencer 39
Mars 319–20
marriage and finance 12
Maslow's hierarchy 213
mass customization 471
mass market 117, 199, 210, 283, 289, 395, 432, 433, 446, 460
Mastercard 580, 581
mature market 109
maturity phase 320
Maybank 75, 288, 318, 326, 343
McDonald's 221
McKinsey 298
Medical Professional 118
Metrobank 92, 360, 598
micro-finance 11, 18, 42, 617–20
micro-insurance 11, 16, 57, 265–76
Microsave 543
Microsoft 64, 579
Mintel 388
mis-selling 55. 85, 161, 164, 405, 463, 588
mission statement 102, 103, 305, 590
mobile banking 43, 45, 138
mobile internet 138
mobile payments 45–7
Moda 419
Money Advice Service 160
Moneybox 321, 415
Moneyfarm 360, 419
Moneysupermarket 362
Money Helper 160–1
Monzo 109, 110, 139, 328, 364–5, 415, 466
Mortgages 112, 130, 138, 159, 238, 295–8, 314, 321, 328, 387, 396, 408, 409, 414, 416, 422, 423, 432, 591, 625
Morgan Stanley 110, 222, 335
MOSAIC 206, 207
Motim Manufacturing 474. 475
Motif Investing 39
Motley Foo 52l
Moven 321, 420
M-Pesa 19, 117, 138–40, 476
MPOWER Financing, 315
multi-channel distribution strategies (*see* distribution channels, channels of distribution)

multivariate testing (MVT) 300
Munich Reinsurance 400
Mutuality 21, 22, 23, 26

N26 138
NACFB Mutual 25
National Saudi Bank 588
Nationwide Building Society 23, 173, 175, 343
National Savings and Investments 18, 423
Nat West, 322, 324, 369
Navigators and General 38
neobanks 297, 414
Net Zero Asset Owner Alliance 223
new entrants 39, 40, 113, 143, 144, 145, 215,
    300, 322, 329, 410, 419, 462, 553
new market entry 112, 113
NFSRs (Non–Financial Services Retailers) 421,
    422
NFU Mutual 220
niche markets 210
N Kolay Kredi (*see also* Aktif Bank) n441–4
Northern Trust 75
Nottingham University Business School 537,
    546
Novofina 418
NPD (new product development) 125, 184, 188,
    312, 313, 319, 328–30, 336–8
Nubank 137
Nutmeg 360, 419

objectives, marketing 100, 101, 104, 105, 285,
    286, 354
Octopus 300
OFCOM 476
Office of National Statistics 51
Officialdata.org 53
offensive strategies 112–13
offshore outsourcing 429
Omnicom 227
One Brightly Cyber 621–3
Open banking 136
Opinium 180–6, 335, 422, 601
organisational capabilities 97, 147–8
outcome quality (*see* service quality, technical
    quality)
outsourcing business processes 246–7
overseas market 235, 239, 257

P&G 579
Parish National Bank 106
Parmenion Capital Partners 419
Partnership for Carbon Accounting 626
Passive fund management 52
Patagonia 576
Payment Systems Regulator 30
Paypal 300, 301, 361
pay per click 364–5

peer-to-peer lending 48
pensions
    defined benefit pensions 54
    defined contribution pensions 54
    general 54, 55
    mis-selling 85
    occupational 54
    retirement ages 15
    retirement income 15
    personal 55, 378
    stakeholder 387, 388
perceived justice 518–19
perceptual mapping 224, 225
peripheral evidence (*see* evidence)
perishability (*see* service characteristics)
personal selling 359–60
Personetics 80
PEST (political, economic, social, technological)
    103
PESTLE (political, economic, social,
    technological, legal, environment) 126
phone banking 94, 97, 137
Phygital 417
physical evidence (*see* evidence)
Pingit 415
place (*see* distribution, channels)
planning, annual 285–7
PLC (*see* product)
Plum 302, 334
podcasts 298, 367
Police Mutual 201, 224
political environment 126–9, 241
population structure 133
Porter's Five Forces (*see* five-force analysis)
positioning (*see also* brand/branding) 221–5
Postgrid 432
post-purchase evaluation 157, 163, 165
poverty 10, 11, 18, 19
preferred lives approach 393–5
premium price position 392
price, pricing
    price and cost to consumer 374–402
    challenges of price 374, 375, 376–9
    comparison sites 389, 390
    competition-based pricing 383
    cost-based approach 381–3
    determination process 395–7
    differentiation and discrimination 393–5
    full-cost approach 381, 382
    impact of digital 399, 400
    marginal-cost approach 381, 382
    marketing-oriented pricing 383–91
    methods for setting price 380–93
    positioning 384–7
    preferred lives 393–5
    pricing terminology 376, 377
    product line pricing 387

role and characteristics 375, 376
strategies 379, 380, 397, 398
value to consumer 393
processes, reflections on 599, 600
process quality (*see* service quality, functional
quality)
Prodigy, 315
Prudential 235, 246, 275–7, 323
product
attributes 324
development (*see also* product line stretching),
327–8
elimination 329
major innovations 330–4
modification of 327–9
nature of the service product 313, 316–17
new product development (NPD), 329–33,
336–8
product elimination 329
Product Life Cycle (PLC) 319–20
product/service lines 318–19, 324, 335
product line stretching 328–9
product management 317–24
product range 318–19
product strategies 126
promotion (*see also* communication)
advertising 344, 357–9
budget 354–5
campaign (*see also* planning) 344, 348–9
direct marketing 344, 362–3
effectiveness 355–6
message framing 347–8
planning 351–6
personal selling 359–60
promotional mix 344, 355
publicity 344, 360–1
public relations 344, 360–1
sale promotion 344
sponsorship 361
social media 356
proprietary supply 21, 26
prospect 213, 305, 417, 424, 434, 472, 488,
498, 600
prospect theory 169
Protectourfamily 75
Prudential plc 323
Prudential Regulation Authority 29, 30, 127
public relations 305
psychographic variables 208
publicity 344, 360–1
public relations 344, 360–1

Qatar National Bank 136
Quicken 138
Quidco 362

Raisin 66, 110, 117, 136, 175, 236–7
RBS 80, 138, 365, 368–9

RBS NatWest 40, 64, 217, 454, 587
RIAS 201
rapid market penetration 338
RATER (reliability, assurance, tangibles,
empathy and responsiveness) 499, 502, 505
Regulation 127
Financial regulation 27–33
Edinburgh reforms 32
European 31
impact of Brexit 32
role of financial markets 27
major regulatory challenges 27, 28
UK regulatory architecture 28–31
philosophy 31
reinsurance 60–2
relationship chain 472, 473, 475, 490
relationship marketing 459, 460, 463, 487,
488–90, 554, 598
relationship strategy 489
RenRen 270
repeat customer 472
repositioning 225–9
Resources 146–7
Retail Insight Network 300
retention (*see also* loyalty) 95, 166, 178, 266,
276, 281, 287, 330, 367, 393, 413, 446,
459–62, 457–71, 480–7, 490, 495–9, 514,
515, 524, 530, 533, 554, 569, 590–5
Retirement 13–6, 27, 42, 54, 55, 131, 133, 170,
173, 209, 313, 346, 347, 408, 417, 419, 424
Revolut 39, 64, 138, 238, 364, 415
risk management 18, 29
robo-advice 135, 360, 400, 416–20
Royal London Insurance 23

Saas systems 481
Saga 199, 394
Sainsbury 39, 144–5
sales promotion 288, 292, 342, 344, 348, 355,
361–3, 370, 468
Sales push 161, 170
Samsung Pay 45
Santander 46, 140, 258, 325, 332, 341, 413, 415
saving and investing 49–53
saving endowments 55
SCM Direct 419
Schwartz Centre for economic Policy Analysis
54
Scottish Widows 145
search engine optimisation (SEO) 364, 366, 368,
544)
secured loans 42, 48, 50, 409, 432
segment of one 198, 212–15, 229, 478, 490
segmentation 84
benefits 198–201
criteria for success 201–4
digital 212–15, 299
lifestage 276

methods 204–12
strategy 208, 217, 473, 479
variables 203
segmenting business-to-business markets 210–12
service characteristics (*see also* financial services characteristics)
    credence qualities 74, 75, 162, 164
    experience qualities 74, 75, 162
    heterogeneity 72, 81–3, 176, 289
    intangibility 71, 74–7, 172–5, 289
    inseparability 72, 77–8, 175–6, 289
    perishability 72, 78–81, 175–6, 289
    search qualities 162
service definitions 70
service delivery 77–8, 495, 527, 607
    failures, 516
    gap model of 509–12
    management of 77, 87, 176, 237, 290, 291, 509, 511
    process 81–2
Service Dominant Logic 71, 72, 97
Service classifications 87–8
service failure and recovery 515–19
Service profit chain (SPC) 95, 495–8
service quality
    Expectations 499, 500, 501, 502–3, 504, 505–6
    functional (process) quality 324, 500, 501
    gap model 509–12
    Measurement 502–3, 506–7
    Nordic model 500–1
    North American model 501–7
    Perceptions 499, 500, 501, 502–3
    outcomes of 512–15
    SERVQUAL (*see also* RATER dimensions) 499, 502–3, 506, 509, 604
    technical (outcome) quality 324, 500, 01
    zones of tolerance 503–6, 594
service recovery 494, 495, 516–19, 524
shadow banking system 28
shareholder value 95, 119, 253, 287, 583, 598
Sheila's Wheels 84, 199
Simple 223, 321, 415
Single customer view 481, 484, 593
situation review 104
Skandia 303
social media and CRM 302, 464–6, 481–4
social environment 132–5
social media 245, 274, 276, 282, 284, 288, 302, 341, 342, 358, 366–9, 413, 447, 449, 460, 464–6, 475–7, 479, 481, 483, 490, 513, 527, 543, 563, 577, 576
social networking 173, 284, 302
SoFi 465
Solvency II 382, 383
Stakeholder theory 559, 562
Standard and Poors 298, 411, 596
Standard Bank 353

Standard Chartered 362
sponsorship 117, 325, 344, 353, 360, 361, 471
Square 476
Standard Chartered Bank 410
Starling Bank 20, 40, 139, 415, 624
State Bank of India 412, 544
Statista 50, 268
strategic marketing 95–100
    Boston Consulting Group Matrix (BCG) 111–12
    defensive strategies 113–14
    General Electric (GE) Business Screen 112–13
    growth strategies 108–10
    implementation 107–8
    market specific strategy 107
    mission and vision 101–3
    objectives 104–5
    offensive strategies 112–13
    product-market matrices 111–13
    product portfolio 111–16
    Product Life Cycle (PLC) 114–16, 319–20
    segmentation, targeting and positioning (STP) 105–7
    situation analysis (*see also* marketing environment) 103–4
    strategic marketing plan, planning 93, 100–1
subprime/payday loans 20, 84, 142
sustainability (*see also* Environmental, Social and Governance (ESG)) 223, 394, 563–70
Sustainability Accounting Standards Board 570
Swiss Reinsurance 57–9, 573
SWOT analysis (strengths, weaknesses, opportunities, threats) 103–4, 148–50

takaful 276
targeting strategies 215–21
technological environment 136–42
telemarketing 429, 430, 595
telematics 400, 451
telephone-based distribution 429–30
Tesco 39, 144
Tether 62
The Bankcorp Bank 301
The Global Economy.com 43
The Investment Association 50
The Money Charity 47
ThreeR (3R) Insights 422
TikTok 444, 464
Trajectory 228, 229
transparency 3, 4, 41, 102, 151, 160–3, 302, 303, 330, 331, 367, 374, 375, 379, 388, 400, 404, 435, 443, 464, 482, 543, 553, 560, 567, 592
Treating Customers Fairly 546–54
Triodos Bank 208
Trust 76, 535
    affective 536, 536
    definitions 535–7

Cognitive 536, 537
digital implications 543–6
drivers 539–43
Interpersonal 545
measurement 537–9
trust index 537
trust and data security 542, 544, 545
trustworthiness 537, 539 41
Twitter (now X) 173, 176, 284, 303, 350,
  464, 465

UBS 238, 332
UK Finance 43, 45, 299
undifferentiated strategy 216, 287
Unicredit 173
Unilever 576
Unimutual 217–19
UNEP Statement of Environmental Commitment
  564
UN Principles for Responsible Investment
  570
unsecured loans 42, 48, 50, 296, 409, 421

valence 508, 509
value (*see also* Service Dominant Logic) 97–8,
  524–6
values-driven strategy 560
variable-rate mortgages 238
video banking, 360
Virgin 39, 145, 327, 330, 335

vision and mission 101, 441
Visa 254, 361
Vitality 327, 328, 400

Wealthfront 39
Wealthify 419
Wealth Wizards 419
wearables 140, 141, 309, 363, 400
welfare, role of government 12, 13
Wells Fargo 587, 591
Western Union 138
Westpac 369
Which? 55, 462
World Bank 10, 16, 42, 413, 461
World Economic Forum (Davos) 560
World Trade Organisation 235, 269, 323
wholesale market 41
word of mouth 304, 469, 475

X, formerly Twitter (*see* Twitter)
Xoom 39

Yorkshire Building Society 592
YouGov 45, 297, 388, 537, 541
YouTube 298, 464–5, 576

Zest 142
zone of tolerance 503–6, 594
Zopa 48
Zurich Financial Services 38, 246